SILENCER

HISTORY AND PERFORMANCE

SPORTING AND TACTICAL SILENCERS

VOLUME ONE

SILENCER

HISTORY AND PERFORMANCE

SPORTING AND TACTICAL SILENCERS

VOLUME ONE

ALAN C. PAULSON

PALADIN PRESS • BOULDER, COLORADO

Silencer History and Performance: Volume 1
Sporting and Tactical Silencers
by Alan C. Paulson

ISBN 0-87364-909-5
Printed in the United States of America

Published by Paladin Press, a division of
Paladin Enterprises, Inc., P.O. Box 1307,
Boulder, Colorado 80306, USA.
(303) 443-7250

Direct inquiries and/or orders to the above address.

Visit our Web site at www.paladin-press.com

CONTENTS

ACKNOWLEDGMENTS

ore than a decade ago, I began a quest to develop a scientific understanding of silencer performance. That quest has proved to be both exhilarating and humbling. As my research began to amass a great deal of scientific data and unique historical information, my goal became clear. I would assemble the results into a series of books that represent both good science and good history. While this first volume of *Silencer History and Performance* is based on many years of my own research, I also owe a considerable debt to a lot of folks who have provided substantial help with the project. I especially thank the following people.

John Anderson

Steve Baughman

Bill Beatty

Tim Bixler of SCRC

Dr. John W. Brunner

Steve Colboch of SLC Enterprises

Dr. Philip H. Dater of Gemtech

The late Dr. Edward C. Ezell of the Smithsonian Institution

Jean Pierre Gragnolati

Roger Hale of Parker Hale Limited
Juha Hartikka of Asesepänliike BR-Tuote Ky
C. Reed Knight of Knight's Armament Company
Peter Kokalis of *Soldier of Fortune* and *Fighting Firearms* magazines
Ron Kovalik
Dr. William L. Kramer of Ball State University
Illka Kyttälä of the Finland Ministry of Labor
Greg Latka of L&L Engineering
Lynn McWilliams of AWC Systems Technology
Capt. Monty Mendenhall
Noel Napolilli
John Norrell of John Norrell Arms
Dr. Rauno Pääkkönen of the Tampere Regional Institute of Occupational Health
Janne Pohjoispää of *Fighting Firearms* magazine
N. Robert Parker of *Fighting Firearms* magazine
John Ross of BI Manufacturing
Jim Ryan of Gemtech
Ralph Seifert of RASE
Mike Smith of Leighton Technologies
Tommy Walls
Polly Walter
Mark White of Sound Technology
John White
Bill Woodin of Woodin Laboratory

CHAPTER ONE

SILENCERS, SOCIETY, AND SOUND

ilencers, which have been more properly called *sound suppressors* since the 1960s, are the most maligned and misunderstood aspect of small-arms development in the twentieth century. Most Americans view silencers with suspicion or outright contempt. Even an appalling number of law enforcement personnel and members of the National Rifle Association believe that silencers have no place in a civilized society and are properly illegal. Not only are these folks wrong on both counts, they are buying into the bankrupt philosophy that objects can be intrinsically evil—as if the objects were sentient incarnations of evil spirits visited upon the mortal world by the gods of darkness.

One might expect such superstitious animism from a primitive Stone Age culture, which might display an institutionalized fear of a particular mountain, forest, or lake. But institutionalized fear of *objects*—whether they are a natural object like a sacred mountain in New Guinea or man-made objects like a silencer, handgun, rifle with folding stock, or an open closet at the foot of the bed—is hard to swallow in the midst of the Information Revolution, when truth and enlightenment should be democratically available for all to worship at the altar of the Information Superhighway. Unfortunately, information access does not translate into accessed information. Nor does information access guarantee the quality of information. Now more than ever, there is a desperate need for straight talk, not faulty mumbo jumbo.

While the entire subject of small arms is polluted with politically correct, animistic, knee-jerk nonsense, the fields of silencer history, technology, and employment have particularly suffered from prejudice, inadvertent misinformation, and intentional disinformation. Even so-called gun writers and proponents of silencer technology have sometimes muddied the waters. So separating the proverbial wheat from the chaff can be a challenge, whether the subject is the legitimate application of silencer technology, the history of that technology, or the quality of a particular technology's performance.

Furthermore, the silencer industry has seen an explosion of technological advances in the years since J. David Truby wrote *Silencers, Snipers, and Assassins* and *Silencers in the 1980s*, Siegfried Huebner wrote his somewhat inaccurate *Silencers for Hand Firearms*, and Jean Marino wrote *Le grand livre des Silencieux*. The intervening years really represent the Golden Age of Silencers, which means there is a lot of history to report and a lot of technology to evaluate. In addition, newly declassified documents obtained under the Freedom of Information Act, the cultivation of new information sources in the United States and overseas, and the application of scientific methodology to the testing of suppressor performance together enable a reevaluation of the subject—from the early Maxim models to some of the latest technologies used by civilians for so-called "legitimate sporting purposes," as well as to technologies used by Uncle for special and black operations.

Thus, *Silencer History and Performance* has several objectives that should complement rather than duplicate the aforementioned books. Scientific testing procedures will be used to compare silencer performance from all periods of technological development. Sporting and tactical applications of silencer technology will be discussed in detail. New sources of information will be used to flesh out the historical record, and new technological developments will be explored. The scope of this project requires three volumes.

This first volume of *Silencer History and Performance* begins by documenting the legitimate uses of silencers for civilians. It is important to realize that more than 61,000 Americans presently use legally owned silencers. Four years after the debut of the first commercially successful silencer (the Maxim Model 1910), Robert Frost wrote that "good fences make good neighbors." He could have just as easily written, "Good silencers make good neighbors," for that has proved to be the reality, from the lawns of Victorian homes in Connecticut, to arctic villages in Finland, to cramped gardens in Cannes, and throughout the Scottish countryside. The French and Scots have long recognized the value of silencers for making sport shooters better neighbors. And the Finns participate in an active collaboration among military and academic researchers; the ministries of health, labor, education, and defense; sporting clubs; civilian shooters; and silencer and ammunition manufacturers, to promote the widespread use of silencers to improve the health and well-being of its citizens. Most fellow passengers on the spaceship Earth have a lot to learn from the Finns.

After examining the sporting uses of silencers and the legalities of ownership in the United States, *Silencer History and Performance* turns to the use of silencers for reducing hearing loss during training. This discussion is relevant not only for sport, law enforcement, and military trainees, but especially for trainers and for young civilian shooters, who are particularly at risk.

The first volume goes on to discuss the tactical uses of suppressors. Tactical doctrine has matured considerably in recent years, both driving the field of suppressor design and responding to the evolution of suppressor technology. A biologist would refer to the process as *coevolution*. The discussion then turns to the process of scientifically measuring suppressor performance, not only describing how the data reported in this treatise were obtained, but enabling the reader to debunk

Good silencers make good neighbors. An AWC Nexus suppressor enables this person to discretely and safely shoot a .45 caliber H&K Model P9S pistol into a safe backstop in his yard without disturbing the neighbors. Photo by Polly Walter.

outrageous claims by some manufacturers and writers, as well as to understand the flawed procedures used by some law enforcement agencies.

This preliminary material sets the stage for the remaining discussions. This volume goes on to examine the evolution and performance of .22 rimfire suppressors, submachine gun suppressors, and centerfire pistol suppressors.

The second volume discusses suppressor technologies designed for close-quarter battle, suppressed carbines of pistol caliber, and the evolution of centerfire rifle suppressors, especially as the technology applies to sniper rifles. The discussion of suppressed sniping systems is divided into two categories, depending on whether the systems are designed to employ long-range supersonic ammunition or the more stealthy, short-range subsonic ammunition.

The final volume in this series will discuss major silencer manufacturers and their product lines, from the Maxim Silent Firearms Company, to modern manufacturers targeting the market of qualified civilians, to the latest low-profile manufacturers who provide Uncle and Uncle's selected offshore friends with exotica designed to meet the MENS (Mission Essential Needs Statements) of elite organizations working in the realms of special and black operations. Throughout these discussions, hard scientific data will provide reliable benchmarks for comparing these technologies. Whenever possible, personal interviews, archives of personal papers, and other suitable sources will help develop a glimpse of the designers themselves to provide a human perspective to this interesting history.

But before diving into the meat of *Silencer History and Performance*, it would be useful to briefly examine the nature of sound and the human response to sound. Taking the time to peruse this material should enable the reader to learn more from the technical discussions that follow.

THE NATURE OF SOUND

For the purposes of this discussion, the simplest definition of sound is *any pressure variation* (in air, water, or other elastic medium) *that the human ear can detect.* For some tactical operations involving firearm suppressors, the phrase "human ear" is too restrictive, since the perception of guard dogs, guard geese (they have better hearing than dogs), or even livestock may be relevant. But for the sake of simplicity, this discussion will focus on human perception of pressure variations in air.

Not all pressure variations in air are detectable by the human ear. The pressure variations caused by changing weather patterns, for example, occur too slowly for direct sensory perception, so we measure these changes with a barometer. Therefore, by definition, these pressure changes are not sounds.

Sound has several characteristics relevant to the study of suppressor performance. Sound travels through an elastic medium like air as a wave (see Figure 1.1). The height of the wave provides a measure of sound *pressure*, which relates to the perceived intensity of a sound. The sound pressure level is commonly measured in decibels (dB), which will be explained later. The distance between wave crests is called the *wavelength*. The wavelength is commonly measured in meters or fractions of a meter. And the number of wave crests that pass a given point in one second is called the *frequency*, which is perceived as the tone of a sound. Measured in hertz (Hz), a frequency of 2,000 Hz is the equivalent of 2,000 wave crests per second, or 2 kilohertz, which can also be abbreviated 2 k Hz or 2 kHz. The rumble of distant thunder is an example of a low-frequency sound, while the sharp whistle of a tea kettle is an example of a high-frequency sound. As we'll see throughout this treatise, suppressors that reduce certain frequencies appear to be quieter than their measured sound pressure levels might otherwise suggest.

This is because gunshots, like most sounds encountered in the real world, are not composed of a single frequency (known as a *pure tone*). Rather, gunshots produce a wide band of frequencies commonly known as *broadband noise*. Unsuppressed gunshots produce a characteristic mix of frequencies that the brain soon learns to register as the discharge of a firearm. A suppressor can fool the brain. Consider two suppressors that eliminate different frequencies and yet produce the same sound pressure level. For people with normal hearing, the suppressor that is especially good at eliminating the higher frequencies of a suppressed gunshot will seem quieter than the suppressor that eliminates predominantly lower frequencies.

This phenomenon occurs for several reasons. As Figure 1.2 shows, the human ear does not respond uniformly to all frequencies encountered in broad band noise. Therefore, the perceived loudness of a gunshot, whether suppressed or unsuppressed, relates primarily to several variables: the frequency content of the sound signature and the intensity (wave height) of each frequency. The duration of the event can also affect the perceived loudness. For example, McMillan M89 sniper rifles fitted with M89 suppressors from AWC Systems Technology produce the same sound pressure levels whether in .308 Winchester or .300 Winchester Magnum.

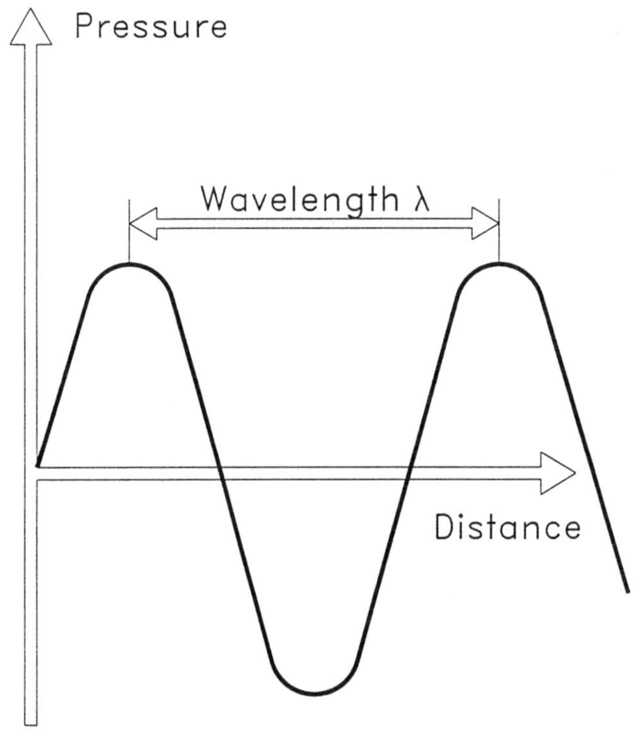

Figure 1.1. Sound travels through air like a wave. The height of the wave is called the sound pressure, while the distance between crests is called the wavelength. Drawing by Mike Smith.

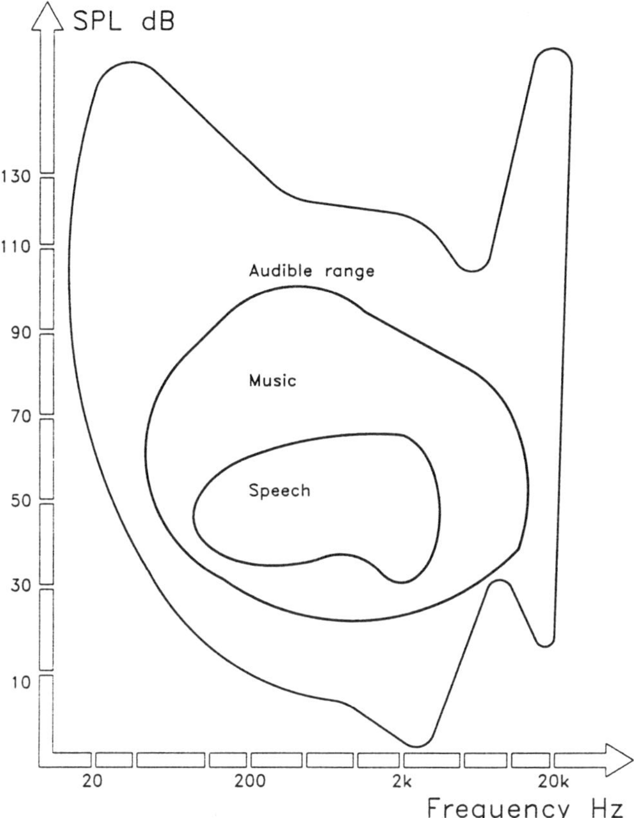

Figure 1.2. The human ear does not respond uniformly to all frequencies encountered in broadband noise. Drawing by Mike Smith.

But the magnum seems a decibel or so louder because the duration of the peak pressure level of the suppressed sound signature is longer.

Another potential complication relates to the ability of the individual to perceive different frequencies. People who have lost their ability to hear high-frequency sounds, such as an old gunnery sergeant exposed to years of intense impulse noise, might evaluate suppressors quite differently than someone with a normal frequency response. Using the previous example of the two suppressors eliminating a different range of frequencies, the gunny would prefer the suppressor that was better at eliminating low-frequency sound (since he can't hear the higher frequencies anyway), while folks with normal hearing would prefer the suppressor eliminating the higher frequencies.

A predominantly low-frequency sound signature may seem quieter because the ear does not respond as efficiently to that range of frequencies. Furthermore, low-frequency sounds are likely to seem more like naturally occurring environmental sounds (sometimes referred to as earth sounds) rather than a suppressed gunshot. Suppressor performance is in the ear of the beholder.

Yet in spite of such potential complications, the most practical way to compare suppressed and unsuppressed gunshots is to measure the height of the highest sound pressure wave, the *peak sound pressure level*, since suppressors commonly reduce the various frequencies in a similar fashion. Therefore, little if any bias is normally introduced by using the vastly more practical (and inexpensive) equipment that only measures the peak sound pressure level and ignores the frequency content of a sound signature.

Nevertheless, it is useful to keep in the back of one's mind that some suppressors, whether by accident or design (we'll see examples of both), do dramatically change the frequency content of a sound signature. Some eliminate higher frequencies. Some eliminate lower frequencies. And some actually change a portion of a sound signature's energy to frequencies outside the range of human perception. Yet these are the exceptions, which will be duly noted where they occur. The internationally accepted methodology for comparing the performance of suppressors, which will be discussed in detail later in this volume, simply measures the sound pressure level of a gunshot and ignores its frequency content. For now, simply bear in mind that this methodology, rather like Newtonian physics, is merely a convenient simplification of the real cosmic verities.

Simply measuring the sound pressure produced by a gunshot is not as simple as it might seem. Procedural difficulties will be discussed in the chapter on sound testing. But the central conceptual difficulty for the average reader will be the strange units of measure that are required: the decibel scale. The subject is not difficult. But few people have an intuitive grasp of decibels, so a few comments will help put this measure of suppressor performance into perspective. Comprehending the decibel is essential to understand the technical discussions that follow.

THE DECIBEL AND THE HUMAN EAR

Physicists normally measure the intensity or amplitude of pressure differences using a unit of measure called the pascal. The pascal, like the decibel, is an eponym—which means that the word was coined, as Dr. Philip Dater puts it, "to honor some dead scientist." The minimum pressure that the human ear can detect is 20 millionths of a pascal, which is typically reported as 20 micropascals (abbreviated 20 µPa). This is equivalent to a pressure of 0.0002 dyne per square centimeter.

It's hard to imagine that the human ear can respond to such a small pressure variation, which is about five billion times less than normal atmospheric pressure. It's even more amazing when one considers that this threshold pressure only displaces the tympanic membrane (ear drum) a distance that is less than the diameter of a hydrogen molecule! One of the difficulties in providing a handy measure of sound intensity is that the human ear can respond to a sound pressure that is more than a billion times greater than the threshold level. The ear is a remarkable bit of engineering.

Measuring sound pressure using a linear scale like the pascal or micropascal can provide some rather large and awkward numbers. The threshold of hearing is 20 µPa. A conversation might be about 18,000 µPa. And an unsuppressed .22 rimfire rifle might produce a sound signature of 200,000,000 µPa. Since the human ear responds to sound pressure in a logarithmic rather than a linear fashion, using a logarithmic scale like the decibel to measure sound pressure has several advantages. The log scale more closely approximates the response of the human ear, and it provides smaller, more manageable numbers.

For the technically oriented reader, the point should be made that the term *sound pressure* refers to measurements made in pascals, kilopascals, and micropascals, while the term *sound pressure level* (SPL) refers to measurements made in decibels. Furthermore, it may be useful to point out that the decibel is not an absolute unit of measure like the meter and gram. The decibel is actually a ratio between the measured sound pressure and a standard reference level. The decibel scale uses the hearing threshold of 20 µPa as the reference level for the bottom of the scale. The actual formula used to calculate the SPL is

$$SPL = 20 \log_{10}(P_1/P_2)$$

where SPL is the sound pressure level in dB,
P_1 is the measured sound pressure in µPa,
and P_2 is the threshold of human hearing, 20 µPa.

Since the decibel scale is logarithmic, multiplying a sound pressure in micropascals by 10 adds 20 dB to the sound pressure level to the decibel scale. Therefore, 20 µPa is the same as 0 dB, 200 µPa is the same as 20 dB, 2,000 µPa equals 40 dB, 2,000,000 µPa equals 100 db, and 2,000,000,000,000 µPa equals 220 dB. Thus, the decibel scale displays the first of its advantages: it compresses a range of a 2 trillion to a mere 220. This makes the scale far more comprehensible.

The threshold of human hearing is 0 decibels. A quiet conversation is about 56 dB, an IBM Selectric II typewriter is 84 dB, a Daisy Red Ryder BB Gun is 101 dB, an integrally suppressed Marlin 780 rifle from Jonathan Arthur Ciener is about 124 dB, a .22 CB is about 131 dB, and a standard-velocity Long Rifle is about 137 dB when shot from a bolt-action rifle. Hearing damage begins at about 140 dB, the pain threshold is about 141 dB, a Heckler & Koch MP5 is about 157 dB, a .45 pistol is about 162 dB, an M16 is about 165 dB, a 122mm howitzer is about 183 dB, and death of the observer can occur in the neighborhood of 220 dB. Purists will note that a conversation is continuous (steady-state) sound, while the other values are impulse sound. And the body does respond differently to those two types of sound. For example, the pain threshold is commonly 140 dB or less for continuous sound and 141 dB for impulse sound. But including continuous sounds in this series of benchmarks is still appropriate, since there are few impulse sounds in our common experience quieter than a BB gun. Most adults can distinguish a 3 dB difference if listening to a continuous sound. Remarkably, research by Dr. Bill Kramer at Ball State University has demonstrated that adults can distinguish a 1 dB difference if listening to an impulse sound such as a gunshot.

Another benefit of the decibel scale is that it much better approximates the response of the human ear to perceived loudness of a sound. Furthermore, a change of 1 dB anywhere on the scale corresponds to the same amount of change as perceived by the human ear. With the exception of some early literature on silencer performance that reported sound signatures in kilopascals, the decibel has become the standard unit of measure for what should now be obvious reasons. For the reader with access to such early literature, Figure 1.3 provides a handy nomogram for converting data in micropascals to the more useful decibel scale.

Finally, it would be useful at this time to point out some conventions used throughout *Silencer History and Performance*. Although test data on silencer performance reported as decibels should, strictly speaking, be referred to as *sound pressure levels*, it is usually more convenient to refer to these data simply as *sound signatures*.

It is also useful to note that both unsuppressed and suppressed sound signatures differ from test to test. This is because different atmospheric conditions (such as temperature, humidity, and altitude) affect the burning characteristics of gunpowder. Even the speed of sound changes with the temperature. Therefore, the unsuppressed weapon signatures reported in this treatise were remeasured each day of testing as a control or benchmark. It is also important to remember that each reported sound signature is the mean (average) of at least 10 replicate samples (i.e., suppressed or unsuppressed gunshots).

The best way to compare suppressors tested under different conditions is to subtract the suppressed sound signature from the unsuppressed sound signature to get the *amount* of suppression. This difference is much less susceptible to change in response to environmental conditions than the actual sound pressure levels, so it makes a better benchmark for comparing suppressor performance. This more useful number is called the *net sound reduction*.

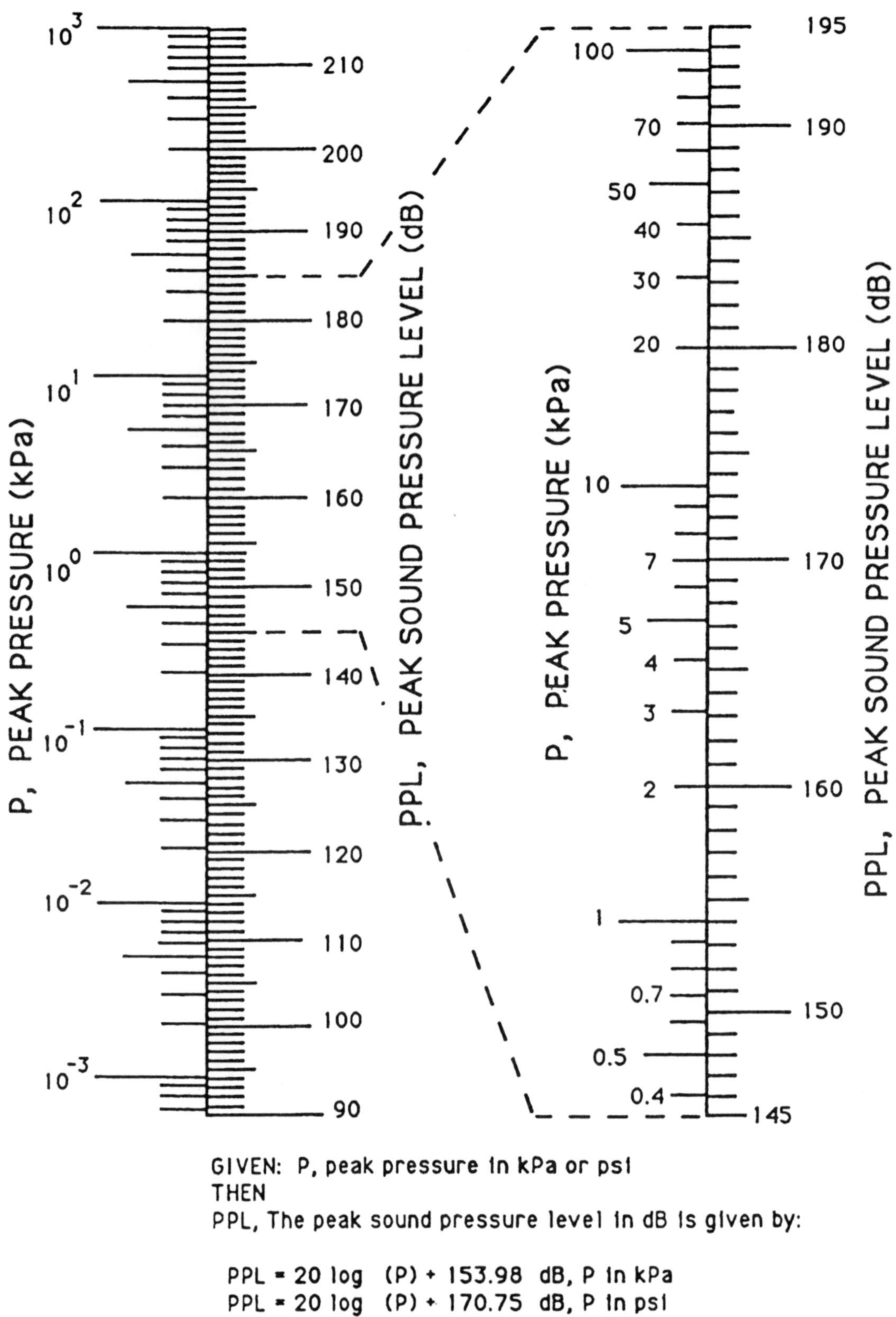

Figure 1.3. A nomogram for converting sound data in micropascals to the more useful decibel scale (from U.S. Army Missile Command, 1993).

CHAPTER TWO

SPORTING USE OF SUPPRESSORS

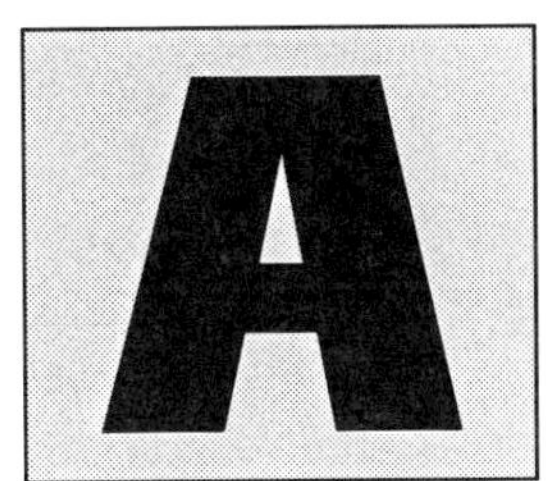

s population density increases in the United States, it is becoming increasingly difficult to find a place to shoot where the sound of gunfire will not offend someone. Gunshots seem to be among the most offensive category of noise pollution for the public at large. The response to this problem in several European countries has been to equip rifles and pistols with silencers. Sweden, for example, allows the use of silencers for hunting. In France, employing silencers is simply a matter of good manners. In Finland, encouraging the use of silencers is government policy.

Contrary to popular belief, silencers provide a viable, fun, and *legal* solution to the problem of noise pollution in the United States. More than 61,000 Americans use legal silencers for discreet target practice, plinking, and animal control.

The first successful silencer was marketed in 1909 by Hiram P. Maxim. He dramatically improved his design in 1910, and silencers gradually became relatively common among sport shooters, especially in the northeastern United States. Silencers provided an innocent and inexpensive source of family fun. Over the years, I have seen photographs of people quietly target practicing in the yards of beautiful Victorian homes.

Although the movies show silencers being used by villains of the period, I have found only a single documented case of a crime committed with a silencer prior to the Gun Control Act of 1934. Two men used silenced rifles to kill six horses on a New Jersey farm, and then they attempted to extort $800 from the farmer as the price for sparing the rest of his livestock. The scoundrels were caught, but the salient point is that one misuse of a technology does not constitute a crime wave.

Apparently, silencers were subjected to the same controls as machine guns in 1934, because the Great Depression created a lot of hungry people. Few of us today understand the depth and breadth of hunger in America during the Depression. William Manchester writes in his memoir about combat during World War II, *Goodbye, Darkness*, that "in 1940 two out of every five draftees had been rejected, most of them victims of malnutrition." That suggests that at least 40 percent of the adult population was not getting enough food during the Depression.

Thus, it is at least understandable that the pandemic hunger in the United States of the early 1930s led game managers to fear that silencers might be used by poachers and that this fear led to the heavy restrictions that were placed on silencers in 1934.

Even though legal silencers are once again becoming commonplace in the United States, according to federal government records not one registered silencer in the hands of a civilian has ever been used for poaching or any other illegal act since 1934. The only two illegal acts involving registered silencers or machine guns since 1934 involved *law enforcement officers* who ran amok, not civilians. *Thus, civilian owners of registered silencers and machine guns have a better track record as law-abiding citizens than the law-enforcement community, the United States Congress, and even the Presidency itself.* Hoplophobes take note. ("Hoplophobe" is a word Jeff Cooper coined for a person with an unreasoning fear of firearms.)

The Gun Control Act of 1934 forced people in the Unites States

A suppressed pistol makes a popular addition to a picnic or family gathering. The Precision Arms Stealth shown here features light weight, low sound signature, and accuracy, making it ideal for casual shooters and as the first experience for nonshooters. Unfortunately, this suppressed pistol proved to be substantially less durable than a suppressed Ruger pistol. Photo by Polly Walter.

to destroy their silencers or register them. The original owner had a brief amnesty period in which to register the silencer without cost. If not registered within that period, the silencer became unregisterable contraband, which could subject the owner to a big fine and jail sentence. Most owners never got the word in time. Others decided it was too much trouble since each time a registered silencer was sold, the new owner had to pay a $200 transfer tax. That was an incredible amount of money in the depths of the Great Depression. Therefore, few Maxim silencers survive to this day, and these tend to be expensive. Some models perform well by modern standards. Others do not. After the Gun Control Act of 1934, the use of silencers in the United States virtually ceased.

Silencers slipped into obscurity until World War II, when silenced weapons were used with remarkable success for clandestine and commando operations. Prior to this time, silencers were fitted to the end of a barrel. This design is now commonly referred to as a *muzzle silencer* or *muzzle can*. World War II silencers were commonly built around a highly modified barrel drilled with ports to vent combustion gases into the silencer as near as possible to the chamber. This sort of design is called an *integral silencer*.

One of the most effective integral designs of the period was a silenced High Standard HD-MS .22 pistol used by Office of Strategic Services (OSS) operatives on clandestine missions from Berlin to Burma during the World War II. The pistol was remarkably quiet, even by modern standards. Former OSS personnel formed the nucleus of the Central Intelligence Agency when it was created in 1947, and the silenced HD-MS pistols formed the nucleus of the CIA's clandestine armory. Francis Gary Powers had one when his U2 spy plane was shot down over the Soviet Union on May 1, 1960. The pistol was subsequently used by CIA personnel, Navy SEALs in the Mekong Delta of Vietnam, and Delta Force soldiers during the failed attempt to rescue hostages in Iran during the Carter administration. This aging pistol is arguably a dozen generations behind current suppressor technology, yet the HD-MS remains in Uncle's inventory, and the blueprints for the suppressor remain classified.

Silencers finally began to reach their military potential during the Vietnam conflict. New silencer designs abounded, and silencers became known by a new and more accurate name: *suppressors*. By then, inflation had rendered the $200 transfer tax much less painful than in 1934. So suppressors once again began to appear in the civilian marketplace, largely through the efforts of Mitchell WerBell III and the Military Armament Corporation (MAC).

The company folded in the early 1970s due to management problems and a decline in government sales, and its assets were auctioned off. While original MAC suppressors can still be found in the modern marketplace, they are expensive because of their appeal to collectors. They tend to provide minimum acceptable sound suppression by modern standards, and many designs tend to have a limited lifespan (about 200 rounds). Although limited lifespan is not a liability to military and clandestine users, it is naturally a major concern for the sport shooter.

For several years, a few post-auction MAC suppressors remained in the marketplace, and that was it. Then in 1976, Jonathan Arthur Ciener and Dr. Philip H. Dater began manufacturing a new generation of suppressors that began to attract a large number of sport shooters. Other manufacturers appeared to tap into this growing market with innovative suppressors, and the modern era of silencer design really began in earnest. This interest in developing better suppressor technology for sport shooters began to generate spinoffs for military and law enforcement applications. This point cannot be overemphasized!

The inverse is also true. Arbitrary legislation aimed at civilians can profoundly inhibit the development of useful and even essential technology for the military and law-enforcement communities.

THE EFFECTS OF ARBITRARY LEGISLATION

Legislators who rush to restrict civilian ownership of technology related to the field of small arms invariably fail to recognize that the technical innovation developed for the civilian drives the development of small-arms technology for the military and law-enforcement communities in important ways.

1. Designers of military and law enforcement technologies do not suddenly appear out of some mysterious primordial ooze. They evolve from tinkers, gunsmiths, and sport shooters who gradually develop and hone their skills designing products for the civilian marketplace. There is no university that confers a degree in small-arms design. Eliminating a category of technology within that marketplace eliminates the school of hard knocks that would otherwise have educated a potential designer of technology that would serve the national interest in terms of military and law enforcement applications. Without the background and experience of sport shooting, and developing innovative technologies to solve problems for civilian shooters, it is most unlikely that true geniuses like Eugene Stoner, Gale McMillan, and C. Reed Knight would ever have made their important contributions of innovative technology for the national defense.
2. Technology developed for civilian shooters is frequently superior to technology developed expressly for the military by traditional defense contractors or military design teams. While a separate book could be written about examples of this phenomenon, several examples will suffice.

One of the best designers and builders of ultra-accurate civilian match rifles in history, Gale McMillan, took the lessons he learned as a tournament shooter and builder of sporting rifles and applied them to the development of the outstanding M40A1 sniper rifle for the U.S. Marine Corps. The culmination of McMillan's skills was expressed as the McMillan M89 sniper rifle, which groups under 1/2 MOA at 1,000 meters when the shooter does his part. McMillan directly applied the designs and skills developed for the civilian marketplace to the military requirement for a rifle producing the maximum possible hit probability at long range. He had also developed the interesting habit of listening to the needs and complaints of civilian marksmen, so he naturally sought out the needs and complaints of military snipers during the final design process for these two fine sniper rifles. Thus the attitudes, design skills, and even the technology that McMillan used to develop these outstanding examples of military technology all came from the civilian sector. If Congress had outlawed pre-1964 Winchester Model 70s with telescopic sights as having no legitimate sporting purpose (after all, they look too much like real sniper rifles, and besides, grandpa only needed a lever action rifle with buckhorn sight to get a deer!), then the U.S. Navy and a number of hostage rescue and counterterrorist units would now be working with inferior equipment.

Similar examples can be produced in the realm of silencer technology. Back in the 1960s, the U.S. government funded extensive research to develop better silencer technology. One of the weapons Uncle particularly wanted to silence was the Uzi submachine gun. After throwing cubic dollars at the problem, these researchers concluded that it was theoretically impossible to effectively silence the Uzi. Several years later, stimulated by the small but growing civilian market for silencers, Jonathan Arthur Ciener designed an effective silencer for the Uzi on his own, without the big bucks and high-powered scientists the government had thrown at the problem.

More recently, federal legislation in 1986 (Public Law 99-308) that prohibited the subsequent manufacture of machine guns for civilian ownership also redefined what constituted a silencer under the law. Before this legislation, only the suppressor tube was considered to be the restricted component (like a firearm receiver) that had to be registered. The new legislation—as interpreted by the Bureau of Alcohol, Tobacco, and Firearms (BATF)—determined that any single component within a suppressor was legally the equivalent of a complete silencer. This effectively killed an entire area of suppressor technology that used flexible disks called *wipes* to restrict the flow of

The most popular civilian use of suppressor technology is to permit an individual to find a convenient place to shoot without disturbing the neighbors. Brian Beatty and his father, Bill, are able to discretely target practice in their own backyard thanks to a Ciener SBER suppressor on a Beretta Minx pistol.

combustion gases after the bullet passed through the wipes. Since polyurethane, polyester, and neoprene wipes commonly last from only 2 to 30 rounds, depending on their design, they must generally be replaced after every magazine or two. Under the new legislation, the legal owner of a suppressor using wipes could not purchase wipes from the manufacturer to service the suppressor. The only option under the law was to return the entire suppressor to the manufacturer via a BATF-approved Form 5 so the manufacturer could replace the wipes. Since the required paperwork can take several months in each direction, it clearly became impractical to go through this cumbersome process every 30 rounds or so.

Without the economic incentive of a civilian market, the development of suppressors using wipes to solve unique military and law enforcement problems virtually ceased overnight. Once again, the arbitrary denial of reasonable technology to civilians has denied a useful technology to the military and law-enforcement communities as well. Furthermore, the preceding discussion ignores the larger issue that restricting technology to law-abiding citizens does not work in terms of reducing the incidence of violent crime, but that discussion is beyond the scope of this book.

While the 1986 legislation has largely halted the development of machine guns in the United States, the development of increasingly more sophisticated suppressor technology (with the exception of technology using wipes) has prospered with the rapidly growing civilian market. As the technology has become more widely used within the civilian community, many appropriate sporting uses for suppressor technology are becoming apparent.

SPORTING USES FOR SUPPRESSOR TECHNOLOGY

Many uses for suppressor technology are of a personal nature to the sport shooter, although we will discuss broader benefits to society that become available through the civilian use of this technology.

Perhaps the most popular civilian use of suppressor technology is to permit an individual to find a convenient place to shoot without disturbing nearby individuals or livestock. My own shooting enjoyment vastly increased once I could target practice in my backyard without disturbing the neighbors. I knew I had a safe backstop. But neighboring hoplophobes remained unconvinced. Using suppressed firearms with subsonic ammunition (to avoid the loud sonic boom, more properly called the *ballistic crack*, of a supersonic projectile), the neighbors simply do not hear the activity. In this case, both literally and figuratively, what the neighbors don't know won't hurt them.

As an NRA instructor, I've frequently used silenced .22s to help troublesome students get over their fear of shooting a firearm. The technique even helps such experienced shooters as military and law enforcement personnel improve their shooting fundamentals, since the exotic qualities of a silenced firearm increase their concentration on what they are doing as well as on the instructor's comments. Another consideration is that small kids—who are the future of sport shooting—can find shooting muffs uncomfortable. In fact, the muffs may not effectively seal on their heads, so they may experience discomfort and even hearing loss as a result. Suppressors provide a practical alternative to hearing protectors for young shooters. Finally, using suppressors instead of hearing protectors makes it easier for the instructor to communicate with the students, which not only facilitates instruction but also enhances the instructor's ability to maintain safe and effective control over shooters on the firing line. This is an especially critical consideration with beginning students, who are more likely to exhibit unsafe behaviors.

Using suppressors instead of hearing protectors makes it easier for instructors to communicate with their students. Since Josh Beatty is using an AWC Archangel I suppressor on a Ruger 77/22 rifle, he can easily hear coaching tips.

Julie Dater, daughter of suppressor designer Dr. Philip H. Dater, uses a Vortex suppressor on her personal rifle so that she doesn't need to wear a Hearing Protection Device (HPD). Photo by Polly Walter.

Another valuable application for some individuals is discreet animal control. Whether raising horses, llamas, ostriches, or other valuable animals, feral dogs and other predators can maim or kill animals worth many thousands of dollars. Using a silenced firearm to neutralize such predators enables the livestock owner to solve the problem without disturbing his animals or neighbors with a loud gunshot. Suppressed firearms confer the same advantages to the professional animal control officer, who might also have to contend with outraged animal rights activists if a problem animal is not put down discreetly.

Silencers also have a legitimate and useful place in the collective sporting use of firearms. This relates to the growing pressure to prohibit the establishment of new shooting ranges and to close existing shooting ranges as the suburbs sprawl into once rural areas where most open-air shooting ranges are located. The noise pollution generated by active shooting ranges disturbs the quality of suburban life.

Since 5 million Finns own 4 million personal firearms, this is an issue that affects nearly everyone in that country. The Finnish government has led the world in addressing the various problems generated by the noise of gunshots. Initially, the government responded to complaints from homeowners reacting to the noise generated by military shooting ranges. But government interest has since expanded to include the noise generated by civilian shooting ranges and even hunters while training for or taking the annual marksmanship test that is obligatory for anyone wanting to hunt elk. Initial interest focused on the use of bullet noise embankments and barriers to reduce the amount of noise leaving the shooting range. The results of that research (Pääkkonen, Anttonen, and Niskanen, 1991; Kyttälä and Pääkkönen, 1996) suggest that the arrangement shown in Figure 2.1 is effective enough, attenuating bullet flight noise by 10 to 20 dB. The optimal configuration features barriers less than 1 meter (3.3 feet) from the bullet flight path. The barrier should extend 2 meters (6.6 feet) above the bullet flight path. The barriers can be tied together for mutual support using overhead safety wings.

While these Finnish researchers demonstrate that surrounding each shooter with an enclosure does reduce the amount of noise pollution leaving the shooting range, this practice effectively doubles the duration of the sound signature produced by the firearm. This increased length of exposure significantly increases the risk of hearing damage to the shooter. Furthermore, placing each shooter in an enclosure inhibits the control of the instructor or rangemaster over the firing line, which can adversely affect range safety.

The use of suppressors reduces the amount of noise pollution leaving the range far more effectively than using enclosures, provides substantially less (rather than more) risk to the hearing of both shooters and instructors, and permits rangemasters to effectively maintain safety on the firing line. No earthen ridges or manufactured sound-abatement structures are necessary when only suppressed firearms are used at a shooting range. If a shed is desirable at the firing line of an outdoor range to provide shelter from rain or intense sun, Kyttälä and Pääkkönen (1996) suggest different shed designs depending on whether suppressed or unsuppressed firearms will be used (see Figure 2.2).

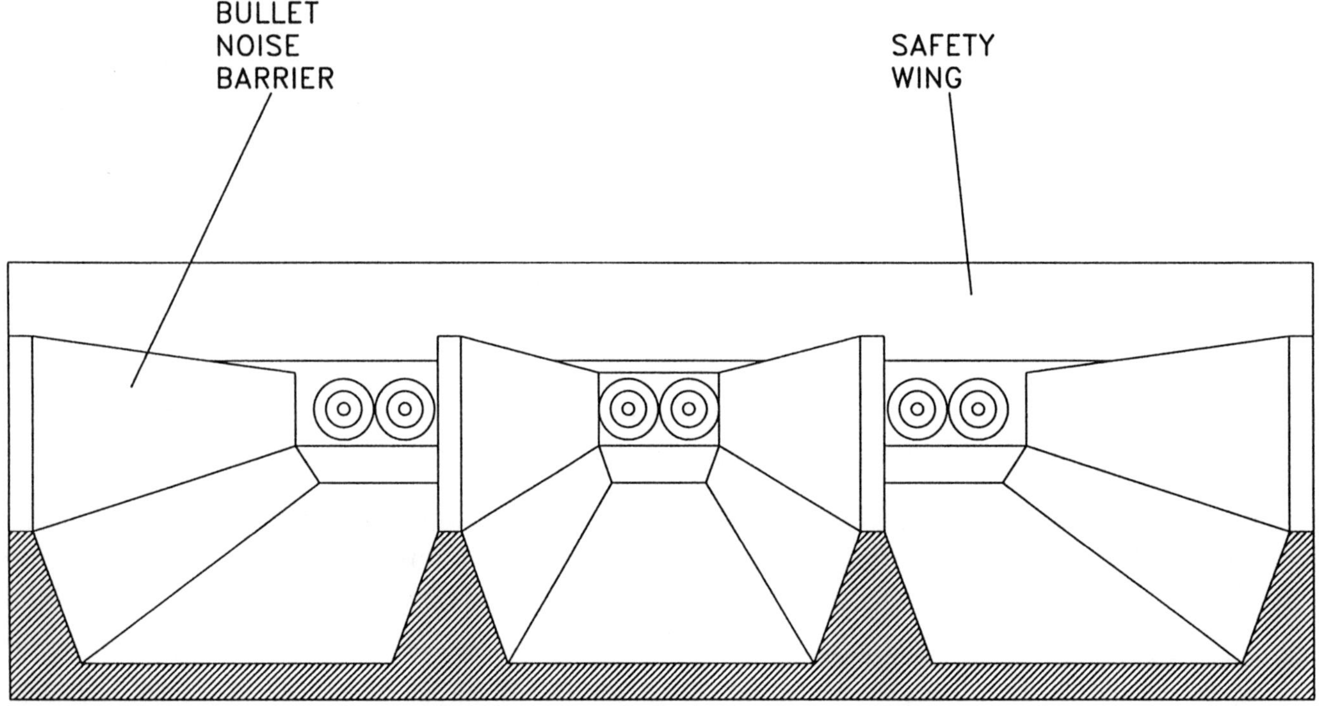

Figure 2.1. Optimal use of noise embankments and barriers to reduce the noise pollution generated by shooting ranges (adapted by Mike Smith from Kyttälä and Pääkkönen, 1996).

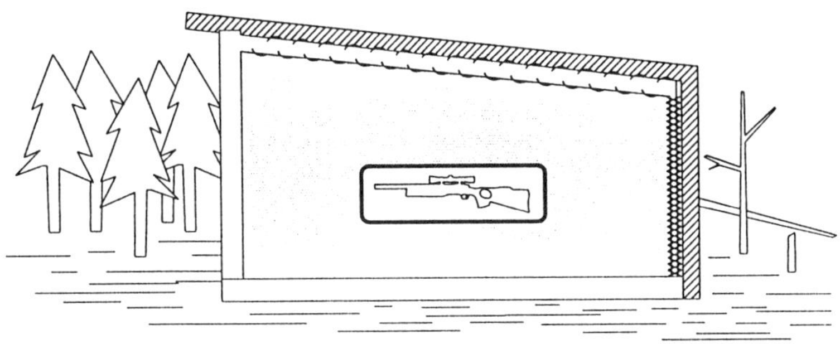

Figure 2.2. Finnish research suggests the use of thick, absorptive material in shed walls to minimize noise pollution from the firing line when unsuppressed firearms are the norm, while an open shed roof is all that's required (if protection from sun and rain is desired) when suppressed firearms are used (adapted by Mike Smith from Kyttälä and Pääkkönen, 1996).

When suppressors are used, no special engineering is required to minimize disturbing any neighbors. Simple open construction with no walls minimizes the duration of exposure to impulse sound on the firing line, maximizes ventilation, and facilitates communication on the firing line. The underside of the roof should, however, be lined with fiberglass or mineral wool to absorb sound that might otherwise be reflected back by the roof. If suppressors are always used at an indoor range, then only a modest layer of fiberglass or mineral wool is needed over the walls and ceiling.

The use of unsuppressed firearms, however, requires the use of a shed enclosed on three sides to minimize the noise pollution leaving the range. A heavy layer of insulation is necessary on all walls and ceilings of such an enclosed shed or an indoor range.

Another benefit of always using suppressed firearms at an outdoor range is that considerably less land is needed to keep the noise pollution acceptable to encroaching neighborhood development. The distance to the nearest neighbor can be cut in half for every 6 dB of suppressor performance. The research team looked at using suppressors on shotguns at a sporting clay range. Finnish neighbors apparently find that 65 dB is the maximum amount of sound that they will tolerate from a shooting range. Assuming the use of subsonic loads and shotgun suppressors delivering a modest 12 dB net sound reduction, the amount of land necessary for adequate sound abatement was reduced to 1/16 of the requirement when using unsuppressed shotguns (see Figure 2.3).

With the common problems of urban sprawl into the countryside, reducing the land requirement in the face of increasing land prices and taxes can represent a huge monetary savings. As civilization encroaches on long-established shooting ranges, the use of suppressed firearms can not only extend the useful life of those ranges, it can also mean the difference between the survival and demise of shooting clubs and shooting schools. The only caveat is that the use of supersonic loads—whether on ranges intended for shotguns, handguns, or rifles—will require bullet crack barriers and/or embankments to achieve a dramatic reduction in the amount of land required for sound abatement if natural sound barriers do not already exist.

Another potential benefit of using silencers at shooting ranges is the reduction of airborne lead pollution, which constitutes a particular health hazard at indoor shooting ranges. It is widely understood that unjacketed bullets such as .22 rimfire projectiles produce far more lead vapor than jacketed bullets and thus constitute a serious health risk. Kyttälä and Pääkkönen (1996) suggest that suppressors

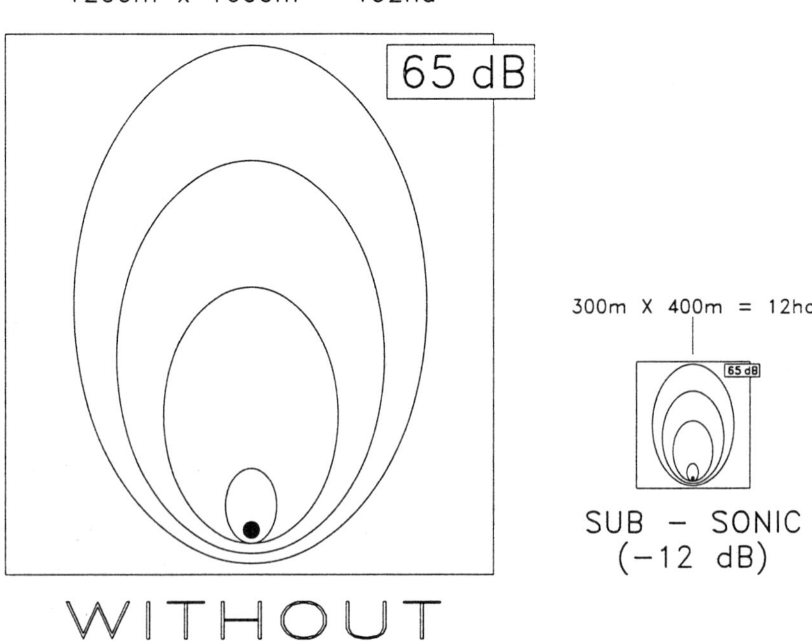

Figure 2.3. Assuming the use of subsonic loads and shotgun suppressors delivering a modest 12 dB net sound reduction, the amount of land necessary for adequate sound abatement (as perceived by neighboring residences) was reduced to 1/16 of the requirement when using unsuppressed shotguns (adapted by Mike Smith from Kyttälä and Pääkkönen, 1996).

stimulate the precipitation of lead-bearing gases inside the suppressor. The lead deposits can then be removed chemically at very low cost, thereby reducing the expensive ventilation requirements mandated for indoor ranges. Unfortunately, the Finnish researcher who discovered evidence of this phenomenon has not yet secured government funding to fully explore the ability of suppressors to reduce atmospheric lead pollution.

A more unusual hazard with indoor ranges became apparent in 1993, when the accumulation of unburned powder residue in an indoor range exploded in Argenbühl, Germany, killing five people. Recent research in Finland demonstrated that suppressors reduce the release of unburned powder residue into indoor ranges, significantly lowering the likelihood of fire or explosion.

Finally, the use of silencers is immensely desirable for improving occupational and public health resulting from the biological effects of exposure to loud impulse noise. This is a major issue that will be covered in the following chapter on using suppressors to reduce hearing loss. But before we turn to that issue, it would be useful to wind up this discussion on the sporting use of silencers with a look at the legal issues involving the civilian ownership of silencers in the United States.

LEGALITIES OF OWNING A SILENCER

Silencers and machine guns are tightly controlled but legal under federal law, as long as state or local laws do not prohibit them. The net result is that silencers and machine guns are legal in about two-thirds of the states.

There are three ways to legally obtain a silencer in the United States. FFL (federal firearm license) holders can pay $500 per year for a Class 3 special license, which allows an unlimited number of tax-free transfers. Police departments and other government agencies are exempt from federal licenses and transfer taxes. Individuals who are 21 and older, are either U.S. citizens or resident aliens, and have never been convicted of a felony can obtain a transfer by paying a one-time $200 tax and surviving an intense background check.

The paperwork required to transfer a silencer or machine gun for individual ownership is somewhat intimidating the first time through. But, in reality, the paperwork requires the individual to invest about as much time as it usually took to buy 3 pounds of sausages in Poland during the final days of the communist regime there. The simplest way to proceed is to have the manufacturer recommend a Class 3 dealer in your area. The dealer orders the suppressor on the buyer's behalf. Once the feds have approved transfer of the suppressor to the dealer and he has logged it into his bound book, you can begin the paperwork to transfer the suppressor to you.

The process requires two passport photos, which are attached to two Form 4s provided by the dealer. He'll fill out part, and you'll fill out part. He'll also give you two fingerprint cards. Take these documents to the top law enforcement officer in your community or county. After fingerprinting, this department head must sign both Form 4s, certifying that you are not a bad person as far as he knows. Give the Form 4s and fingerprint cards back to the dealer along with $200 for the one-time-only transfer tax. The dealer submits everything to BATF, which submits the fingerprint cards to the FBI for a background check that has historically required two to three months. Once the FBI clears you, BATF approves the paperwork and returns it to the dealer. You can then take possession.

The FBI has recently computerized its fingerprint database so it can provide an almost instantaneous background check. The entire process still takes two to three months, however, because BATF has developed bottlenecks of its own.

A photocopy of the approved Form 4 should accompany the suppressor at all times. The original Form 4 should be kept in a safety deposit box or other safe place. The suppressor can be written into your will and passed on as a family heirloom to another generation without incurring an additional transfer tax, but the same paperwork and background checks will be required. Selling or even giving someone the suppressor would require a repeat performance of the paperwork and transfer tax.

If there is no Class 3 dealer in your area and you hold a conventional FFL, you can fill out the same paperwork through the manufacturer and take delivery directly. But this will be a tax-paid transfer via a Form 4. This is a recent BATF concession. Qualified individuals can also transfer silencers among themselves using the Form 4 tax-paid transfer.

CHAPTER THREE

USING SUPPRESSORS AND OTHER HPDs TO REDUCE HEARING LOSS

"SHIFT happens!"

—Dr. William L. Kramer

Back in the 1980s, I ran across an epidemiological study that evaluated the danger posed by participating in the 50 most popular active sports in the United States. Mountain climbing headed the list, skydiving made the top 10, riding a bicycle made the top 20, and shooting was right at the bottom of the list—46th or 47th as I recall. Thus, shooting was just about the safest sport in America in terms of the incidence of major injury per thousand hours. But there is one nonlethal health hazard that places all shooters at considerable risk: hearing loss. In fact, this health hazard could be termed *pandemic* among people who began shooting before the early 1970s, when hearing protection devices such as muffs and plugs began to become popular.

Thus, almost all shooters older than 40 at the time of this writing have experienced some hearing loss due to their participation in shooting sports or working as armed professionals. Shooting instructors are particularly vulnerable due to their daily exposure to loud impulse sound. Even though younger shooters have probably used hearing protection devices for most of their lives, chances are that hearing protection devices (HPDs) were not used 100 percent of the time or the HPDs did not always fit properly, so some hearing degradation has still been sustained. This problem is undoubtedly worse than it might be because some gunshots seem a lot less unpleasant than others. In fact, a .50/70 Sharps carbine sounds downright musical to my ear. But such perceptions can be both flawed and dangerous.

Experienced shooters readily distinguish a wide range of loudness generated by rifles, shotguns, pistols, and automatic weapons. Everyone understands that a centerfire rifle is louder than a rimfire rifle, a .22 pistol is louder than a .22 rifle, and shooting a black powder muzzleloading rifle is less traumatic than shooting a belted magnum rifle. And anyone who has fired the .50 caliber BMG cartridge, whether in a sniper rifle or the M2 Browning machine gun, remembers the experience as a bracing exposure to an elemental force of nature. Unfortunately, many shooters equate a lack of pain when shooting the more friendly combinations of cartridge and firearm with a lack of danger to their hearing.

Suppressors make very effective hearing protection devices. Shooters with small hands may find the Volquartsen's forestock on this Gemtech Quantum-2000 suppressed Ruger 10/22 a bit wide for ideal use offhand, but this eventually becomes less distracting. Photo by Polly Walter.

Such intuition is complicated because our subjective impression of the sound generated by a firearm is really based on three variables: 1) *intensity*, which is the loudness of the sound, and is more properly termed the sound pressure level or SPL; 2) *duration*, which is how long the sound lasts; and 3) *frequency*, which is what most of us think of as pitch. A shooter may perceive less of a threat to his or her hearing if a gunshot has a shorter duration, lower frequency (the gunshot sounds more like a *boom* than a *crack*), or less intensity.

Yet such intuition is faulty because hearing can be damaged at SPLs below the pain threshold. Furthermore, loud impulse sounds such as gunshots have a cumulative effect analogous to heavy-metal poisoning, even when exposure is at infrequent intervals. The frequency content of an impulse sound also affects the amount of damage that can be inflicted. For example, the relatively high-frequency 141 dB *crack* of a .22 rimfire rifle coincides closely with the frequency range of human hearing, while much of the energy in the low-frequency 183 dB *boom* of a 122mm howitzer is below the most sensitive range of human hearing. Thus, repeated exposure to a .22 rimfire rifle can be harder on an individual's hearing than an occasional exposure to the awesome report of a 122mm howitzer.

The bottom line is that all gunshots are loud enough to cause hearing damage, although some can create more damage than others. As Table 3.1 shows, gunshots are among the loudest sounds likely to be encountered in everyday life. And as Table 3.2 shows, even the relatively friendly combination of .22 standard-velocity ammunition in a Ruger 10/22 rifle—which produces a sound signature of 139 dB—can only be tolerated for a tenth of a second per day without risking some hearing damage. Most combinations of ammunition and firearms produce significantly higher decibel readings and therefore produce substantially more risk to human hearing.

While beyond the immediate focus of this discussion, a few words about blast effects would also be appropriate. Blast effects refer to high-intensity wave effects created by peak SPLs over 170 dB. Most blast effects are generated by the muzzle blast of a heavy weapon or the impact of a high-explosive round, passive or command-detonated mine, demolition charges, or even artillery simulators used for training. Blast overpressure damages lungs and other internal organs, and even influences the circulatory system. Medical effects of impulse blasts have received a great deal of study since World War II. For example, Kokinakis and Rudolph (1982) report that an impulse measuring 199 dB will induce lung damage, and one individual died when subjected to a 208 dB impulse that lasted for 3 milliseconds. A human can tolerate intense impulse noise better if the duration of the impulse is less than 1 millisecond. Some military impulse noise can last significantly longer. Various studies report somewhat different thresholds for producing mechanical damage of internal organs, varying by as much as 15 dB. But the bottom line based on NATO data is that death is likely at 220 dB. As Appendix 1 shows, that corresponds to a pressure impulse of more than 200 pounds per square inch!

Table 3.1. Typical SPLs of a diverse spectrum of events. Gunshot and typewriter data are measurements of peak impulse SPLs, while the other data are measurements of continuous SPLs.

SOUND SOURCE	SPL, dB	EFFECTS
Silence	0	Threshold of hearing
Mechanical wristwatch (held near ear)	25[c]	
Rice Krispies	30[c]	Threshold of sleep disruption
Soft whisper	40[c]	
Average residence	45[c]	
Average office	55[c]	
Quiet conversation	56[b]	
Midsize automobile	70[c]	
Manual typewriter	75[c]	
Vacuum cleaner	80[c]	Maximum safe continuous exposure (24 hours per day)
IBM Selectric II typewriter	84[b]	
Gas-powered lawn mower	85[c]	Regular exposure (8 hours per day) endangers hearing
Dry-firing Ruger 77/22 rifle on virgin rim of once-fired case	94[b]	

Table 3.1 (continued).

SOUND SOURCE	SPL, dB	EFFECTS
Nightclub music	100[c]	Communication difficult even at close range; hearing damage can actually begin after a 15 minute exposure to continuous sound
Daisy Red Ryder BB Gun	101[b]	
Operating bolt of Marlin 780 rifle	103[b]	
Chain saw	105[c]	Dual hearing protection (plugs and muffs) may be necessary for continuous sound; safe exposure limit without hearing protection is about 5 minutes
Hammer fall when dry-firing Winchester Model 06 rifle with empty chamber	106[b]	This seems much quieter than a chain saw[e]
Dry-firing Marlin 780 rifle with empty chamber	107[b]	
Chambering a round in a Ruger Mark II pistol	108[b]	
Riveting machine	110[c]	
Dry-firing Ruger 77/22 rifle with empty chamber	112[b]	
Dry-firing Sterling Mark 5 submachine gun (i.e., bolt falling on empty chamber)	118[b]	
Crossman Model 1377 .177 caliber air pistol, 5 pumps	120[a]	
Crossman Model 1377 .177 air pistol, 10 pumps	123[a]	
Pneumatic chipper	125[c]	
Jet takeoff (from 100 feet or 30 meters)	130[c]	Unaided voice communication is impossible
.22 CB in Winchester Model 06 rifle	131[b]	
.22 standard velocity LR in Ruger 10/22 rifle	139[b]	Safe exposure limit is only 0.11 second per day, so hearing protection should be worn for impulse sound
50 HP siren (from 100 feet or 30 meters)	140[c]	
.22 standard-velocity LR in Marlin 780 rifle	140[b]	Danger threshold for impulse sound, hearing protection is mandatory
.22 high-velocity LR in Ruger 77/22 rifle	141[b]	Pain threshold for impulse sound
.410 bore shotgun	150[a]	Well above danger threshold for impulse sound
20 gauge shotgun	153[a]	
12 gauge shotgun	156[a]	
.44 Special revolver	156[a]	

Table 3.1 (continued).

SOUND SOURCE	SPL, dB	EFFECTS
.22 high-velocity LR in Walther TPH pistol	157[b]	
9x19mm MP5 submachine gun	157[b]	
.38 Special revolver	158[a]	
9x19mm Beretta 92SB pistol	160[b]	
.45 ACP pistol	162[b]	
5.56x41mm M16A1 rifle	165[b]	
.357 Magnum revolver	165[a]	
.44 Magnum revolver	165[a]	
5.56x41mm CAR-15	167[b]	
7.62x39mm AKM rifle	167[b]	
7.62x51mm Macmillan M89 sniper rifle	168[b]	
122mm howitzer	183[d]	
High explosive	220[f]	Death of the observer can occur from mechanical damage by pressure wave

[a] data measured in dB(L) at the shooter's ear using a B&K 2218 sound meter (with a 35 microsecond rise time) set on peak hold and linear (no weighting), using a B&K 4135 mike 32 to 36 inches behind the muzzle, by Dr. William L. Kramer.
[b] data measured in dB(A) at 1.00 meter to right of muzzle using a B&K 2209 sound meter with a 20 microsecond rise time by Alan C. Paulson
[c] data from Cabot Safety Corporation
[d] data from Dr. Rauno Pääkkönen
[e] this is true because human perception of brief impulse events is very different from long steady-state events
[f] data from NATO

Table 3.2. New human exposure limits to noise developed by the American Conference of Government Industrial Hygienists and published in the Summer 1993 issue of *Spectrum*, which is published by the National Hearing Conservation Association. Note that the allowed exposure for 139 dB, which is quieter than the sound signature of .22 high-velocity LR ammunition fired from some bolt-action rifles, is only a tenth of a second per day. Sound pressure levels (SPLs) use "A" weighting.

DURATION PER DAY	SPL, dB(A)	DURATION PER DAY	SPL, dB(A)	DURATION PER DAY	SPL, dB(A)
24 hours	80	15.00 minutes	100	7.03 seconds	121
16 hours	82	7.50 minutes	103	3.52 seconds	124
8 hours	85	3.75 minutes	106	1.76 seconds	127
4 hours	88	1.88 minutes	109	0.88 second	130
2 hours	91	0.94 minute	112	0.44 second	133
1 hour	94	28.12 seconds	115	0.22 second	136
30.00 minutes	97	14.06 seconds	118	0.11 second	139

Technology provides several solutions to mitigate the risk of hearing loss from gunshots. After a brief discussion of the biology behind this health problem, this chapter will go on to look at the relative advantages and disadvantages of the various technologies available for mitigating hearing loss. The resultant conclusions may be surprising.

THE BIOLOGY OF HEARING AND HEARING LOSS

Impulse noise constitutes the single most destructive type of sound that can threaten human hearing. Impulse sounds such as gunshots, firecrackers, and explosions introduce energy so quickly deep into the structure of the ear that the body's natural defense mechanisms cannot react fast enough to dampen the sound and thus limit the amount of energy reaching the most sensitive structural components of the ear.

Figure 3.1 shows a cross section of the human ear, which contains (as an engineer might describe it) three subassemblies: the outer ear, middle ear, and inner ear.

The outer ear consists of the pinna and lobe (the visible portion of the system), plus the auditory canal and the eardrum. The pinna collects sound waves from the air (or from the water if

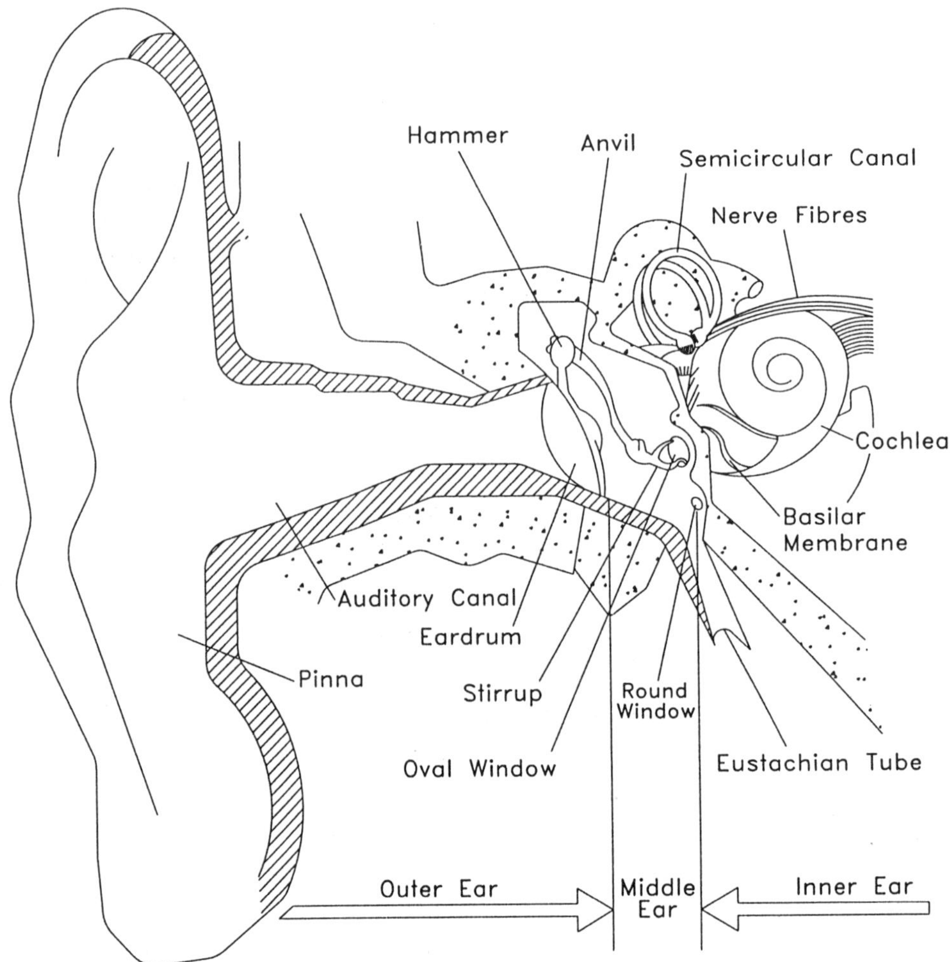

Figure 3.1. Cross section of the human ear, which contains three subassemblies: the outer ear, middle ear, and inner ear. Drawing by Mike Smith.

the individual is submerged) and directs the sound energy via the rather long auditory canal (commonly longer than 1.0 inch or 2.5 cm) to the eardrum, which vibrates with an amplitude and frequency determined by the properties of the incident sound waves.

The air-filled middle ear contains three small bones (called the hammer, anvil, and stirrup) that form articulating levers which transfer the vibrations from the eardrum of the outer ear to the membrane forming the oval window of the inner ear. From an engineering point of view, the three bones of the middle ear function as an impedance-matching device between the outside world and the inner ear.

Filled with two liquids called endolymph and perilymph, the inner ear consists of two separate subsystems. The semicircular canals consist of several loops of ducts filled with perilymph (a thin, watery fluid). These ducts control balance. The other subsystem, the cochlea, which is a snail-shaped tube that makes 2-3/4 spiral turns, is the actual sound-sensing structure of the ear. The tube is divided longitudinally into two parts by the basilar membrane, with a smaller tubular enclosure resting atop this membrane. The membrane is covered with thousands of sensory hairlike cilia that move when the stirrup bone of the middle ear vibrates against the oval window to create sympathetic movement of the liquid inside the cochlea. The base of each hair cell connects to the cochlear branch of the auditory nerve (also called the cranial nerve VIII). Movement of the liquid disturbs the hairs, causing them to send electrical signals via the auditory nerve to the brain. Different patches of hair cells respond to different frequencies. Hair cells at the base of the basilar membrane, for example, seem to respond to high frequencies, while hair cells at the apex of the membrane respond to low frequencies.

As alluded to earlier, the ear does have several natural defense mechanisms for reducing the potential damage from very loud continuous sounds.

One mechanism involves the tensor tympani and stapedius muscles. Together they can produce what is called the *acoustic reflex*, which occurs when both muscles contract upon exposure to loud sounds in a protective reflex action. Specifically, the contracted stapedius muscle provides tension that reduces the force applied to the oval window of the cochlea by the stirrup bone. The reaction time for this mechanism is 65 milliseconds. The other half of this reflex is created by the contraction of the tensor tympani muscle, which has a reaction time of 150 milliseconds. Contraction of the tensor tympani dampens the movement of tympanic membrane (more commonly known as the eardrum). I should mention, however, that some people no longer believe that contraction of the tensor tympani is an important part of the acoustic reflex.

Audiologist Dr. William L. Kramer shoots a .44-40 Winchester Model 1873 while wearing SoundScopes custom-molded ear plugs made by Starkey Labs, which incorporate electronic circuitry similar to the Dillon/Peltor Tactical 7S electronic muffs. The old rifle still groups all shots offhand into a 3 inch circle at 50 yards, which Kramer describes as "one minute-of-deer accuracy from an iron-sighted old gun."

A more curious defense mechanism involves the

movement pattern of the stirrup bone. When exposed to loud sound, the stirrup begins to rock back and forth in a new vibration mode which dramatically reduces the amount of energy transferred to the cochlea.

Unfortunately, impulse sounds occur too quickly to initiate either of these defense mechanisms. Muscles just can't contract quickly enough for the first mechanism, and there just isn't enough time to induce a new vibration pattern of the stirrup bone for the second mechanism to work.

Assuming that the incident sound is continuous rather than impulse noise, either defense mechanism reduces the amount of sound energy available in the inner ear. That energy is manifested as vibratory motion of the liquid in the cochlea. Excessive motion can bend or break the hairlike cilia.

The acoustic trauma that results from overexposure to either continuous or impulse sound takes the form of bent or broken sensory hairs. Since damaged hairs no longer respond to vibration, either temporary or permanent loss of hearing over the frequency range of the damaged hair cells will occur as more and more cells are affected. This is the actual mechanism that causes hearing loss.

At first, damage to a few hair cells is not noticeable. But as more hair cells are damaged, the brain can no longer compensate for the missing information. Music becomes muffled, words run together, and conversation becomes hard to distinguish from background noise. By the time an individual notices a problem, chances are that considerable and even permanent damage has been sustained.

If not excessively damaged, bent hairs can eventually heal if they are not subjected to further trauma. Bent but healable hairs cause a short-term loss of hearing called a *temporary threshold shift* (TTS), which can clear up after a day or so. Broken and severely bent hairs will not heal, causing a *permanent threshold shift* (PTS).

Dr. William L. Kramer, who is an associate professor in the Speech Pathology and Audiology Department at Ball State University, has conducted a great deal of research since 1980 into the problem of hearing loss related to sport shooting. In an article entitled, "Black Powder Noise and Hearing Conservation," Kramer (1995) observed that "anything over 140 dB SPL is very hard on the ears. When you can't hear very well for a day or so and then the sound comes back, that short-term loss of hearing is called a temporary threshold shift. Too many of those TTSs cause a permanent threshold shift, which means you lost that hearing forever. In a manner of speaking, if you don't wear hearing protection, then "SHIFT happens!"

In order for the shooter to avoid serious shift, it is useful to learn something about how to evaluate hearing protection devices. Traditional published evaluation methods, including the rating numbers that appear on the packaging of HPDs, may not serve the shooter well.

EVALUATING HEARING PROTECTION DEVICES

Each hearing protection device sold in the United States is packaged with a number called a Noise Reduction Rating (NRR) that provides a measure of the device's efficiency. Unfortunately, the U.S. government testing standard created for this purpose leaves a great deal to be desired for shooters, since the standard was really designed for continuous sounds such as produced by machinery, chain saws, heavy equipment, and other common work-related hazards. In fact, the NRR is almost meaningless when related to gunshots, since the testing procedure employs a person wearing earphones who is subjected to continuous pure-tone sounds while seated in a small test chamber. The person isn't subjected to an impulse sound with a broad frequency spectrum similar to a gunshot while the person is in a typical shooting environment. Why is testing HPDs using continuous sound vastly inferior to using impulse sound?

Dr. Kramer has developed an interesting analogy. "Imagine you have a metal disk about a yard (or meter) wide and about 2 inches (5 cm) thick," Kramer begins. "The disk has several hundred

1/8 inch (3 mm) holes drilled through it. With the disk standing on edge, stand off to one side and throw a big bucket of water at it. Does all the water go through? No way! There is a lot of back pressure, so only a small amount of water comes out the other side. Now, if you take that same disk, lay it inside a barrel, and slowly pour a bucket of water into the barrel, then most of the water will seep to the bottom. Slowly pouring the water is analogous to using pure tones for determining NRRs, while throwing the water at the vertical plate is analogous to the blast pressure generated by a gunshot. Since the vertical plate is more efficient at keeping out an impulse (splash) of water, it should come as no surprise that research conducted by the U.S. Army at Alamogordo, New Mexico, has shown that HPDs provide *more* protection from impulse sound than indicated by the NRRs determined by using continuous pure tones."

That's the good news. The bad news is that hearing protection devices don't always fulfill their potential when used in the real world. Earmuffs, for example, may not properly fit children and people of small stature. A more common problem with adults is that few people install ear plugs properly.

Therefore, a certain amount of yin and yang clouds the issue of the NRR used to evaluate hearing protection devices. Dr. Kramer correctly reports that HPDs work better with impulse sounds like gunshots than their published NRRs suggest. Research in Finland by Dr. Rauno Pääkkönen, Ilkka Kyttälä, and others suggests that circumstances sometimes reduce the actual performance of HPDs when employed by real people in the real world. Keep these considerations in mind throughout the following discussions on the advantages and liabilities of the various HPDs.

Discussions of hearing protection devices within the international community have been traditionally limited to ear plugs and earmuffs. Recent research has developed an entirely new class of HPD for people exposed to the substantial sound pressure generated by tank guns, artillery, explosions, jet engines, turbine generators, and other unusually intense sounds. Called the *noise helmet*, the most advanced device of this type was developed by a Finnish team led by Rauno Pääkkönen. The noise helmet totally encloses the head and seals around the neck to provide better direct protection of the ears as well as better indirect hearing protection by dramatically reducing bone conduction of sound energy impacting the skull. The broad spectrum of recent Finnish research also supports my long-held contention that silencers should be considered as legitimate and even uniquely useful HPDs for sport shooters and shooting instructors as well as members of the military and law-enforcement communities. Therefore, the following discussion of HPDs will include four, rather than the traditional two, categories of hearing protection devices.

Ear Plugs

Modern ear plugs can be classified into three categories: closed-cell foam plugs, rubber plugs with flanges, and custom-made plugs. All plugs share the considerable advantage that, unlike muffs, they do not interfere with obtaining a proper cheek weld with a rifle, shotgun, or submachine gun. Many people also find plugs more comfortable than muffs, since plugs do not pinch the ears and head. Nor do plugs induce sweating in hot weather or serve as a painful heat sink in very cold weather.

Closed-cell foam plugs can be made from PVC (typically yellow) or polyurethane (typically colors other than yellow). They have a number of advantages for shooters. They're cheap enough to be disposable but durable enough to be reusable. When properly installed in the ear canal, they provide better noise reduction ratings than muffs. (The original E-A-R Classics, which are made from PVC and retail for about $1 per pair, are among the most effective foam plugs.) They can also be washed easily by putting them in a sock when doing the laundry (Kramer, 1995).

The principal disadvantage of foam plugs is that few people install them properly. The plugs must be rolled between the fingers to compress them, and then they must be inserted deeply into the ear canal. Few people insert them far enough. Although polyurethane plugs feel softer between the fingers than those made from PVC, urethane may be less comfortable than PVC because urethane plugs actually exert more pressure in the ear canal. Some people find this increased pressure objectionable. Others do not.

The second category of plugs are made from rubber or silicone and typically feature two or three sets of flanges that provide a seal with the ear canal. Their principal advantage over foam plugs is that some people find them easier to insert and remove. Relatively trivial advantages are that they don't get dirty as fast as foam plugs and they're easier to clean. Their main disadvantage is that they come in three sizes, so it might be necessary to purchase several sets to determine the optimal fit.

Custom-made plugs are actually cast to conform exactly to an individual's ear canals, which are similar to fingerprints in that no two are alike. Normally made from acrylic, custom plugs are relatively expensive (about $75 at the time of this writing), but they generally provide better performance than foam plugs, which are rarely inserted correctly. The performance of custom plugs is about the same as cheap foam plugs when the latter are installed properly. Another advantage of custom plugs is that proper installation is so easy that it is almost foolproof. About the only disadvantage of custom-made plugs (other than cost) is that the configuration of the ear canal can change when the individual's physiological state changes due to events such as a cold or ear infection. Then the custom plugs can either create uncomfortable pressure or fail to seal the ear, and alternative ear protection will be required. Since the shooter may only notice the problem after a painful gunshot or two, some hearing damage may already have occurred.

Nevertheless, custom plugs are my HPD of choice when I can't use a suppressed firearm. Dr. Kramer introduced me to the best of the custom plugs, which incorporates electronic circuitry similar to a hearing aid that both blocks out sound above a certain level and amplifies continuous sound of normal intensity. Made by Starkey Labs (6700 Washington Avenue South, Eden Prairie, MN 55344), the SoundScopes cost about $350 per pair at the time of this writing. They have all of the advantages of other ear plugs. Their only liability is the same as any other custom-molded plug: they may not provide effective protection when the dimensions of the ear canals change during colds and ear infections. SoundScopes enable students to hear range commands and instruction, instructors can easily understand student questions, shooters on the firing line can readily conduct conversations, hunters can hear the movement of game, and armed professionals have the opportunity to hear the movement of potential hostiles. When a gunshot or other loud event occurs, the electronic circuitry temporarily shuts off all sounds that exceed a predetermined level, thus protecting the operator's hearing. Considering the cost of hearing

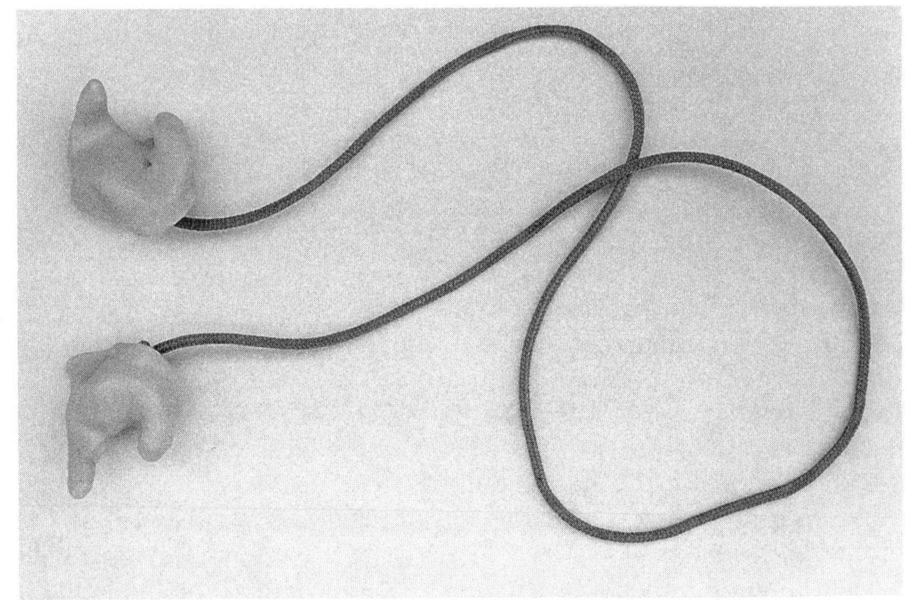

Custom-made ear plugs are actually cast to conform exactly to an individual's ear canals.

aids, not to mention the continual irritation of constantly asking people to repeat what they've just said, the cost of the custom-made SoundScopes is trivial compared to the monetary, social, aesthetic, and psychological costs of hearing loss.

Earmuffs

The principal advantages of earmuffs are that they cannot be installed improperly and their effectiveness cannot be negated by a cold or ear infection. The principal disadvantage of muffs is that they tend to interfere with obtaining a good sight picture when shooting firearms other than handguns and tripod-mounted machine guns. Muffs also tend to be less comfortable than plugs, as discussed in the previous section of this chapter. Muffs are more expensive than foam plugs, bulkier to carry, and incompatible with many hat styles. A disadvantage for youngsters, whose hearing is particularly vulnerable to impulse noise, is that earmuffs may not seal effectively when worn on small heads. Muffs may also be uncomfortable for people wearing glasses.

The traditional earmuff might be termed a linear, passive (nonamplified) hearing protection device. A high-tech earmuff incorporating microphones and electronic peak-clipping circuitry might be termed a nonlinear, active (amplified) HPD. These electronic muffs function like the SoundScope electronic plugs and have similar advantages. Even though electronic muffs may interfere with obtaining a good sight picture when shooting long arms, they are not affected by changes in the ear canals like electronic plugs. It is important to note that when turned off, or if the batteries die, electronic muffs still provide good passive hearing protection. Some electronic muffs are monaural while other are stereo. The stereo units provide the ability to locate the source of a sound, making them much more useful to hunters and tactical users. Since there is little price difference, I strongly suggest the purchase of stereo rather than monaural muffs. The best stereo muffs are the T&T Impulse Pro-Tek Model M2, Dillon/Peltor Stereo Tactical 7-S, and the Gentex Wolf Ears 1030A.

The circuitry of the Gentex Wolf Ears 1030A provides similar amplification to the Dillon/Peltor and T&T muffs and superior performance to other competitors in the marketplace. Weighing in at 16.9 ounces (478 grams), the Wolf Ears are noticeably heavier than the Dillon/Peltor muffs. The Wolf Ears have several other eccentricities that provide a constant source of irritation. The muffs tend to snag strands of hair from all but short-haired shooters, with painful consequences. And the headpiece exerts considerable tension, which forces the ear cups against the head with more pressure than competing designs. This pressure gives Wolf Ears the best seal, but it also makes them so uncomfortable that I develop a headache after several hours of continuous wear. Individuals with a smaller hat size or less susceptibility to pressure may find Wolf Ears more comfortable than I did.

One P675 battery powers the system and provides about 60 hours of service. A three-position toggle switch can be set to AMP (which provides 6 dB of amplification but cuts off sounds above 90 dB), ON (which transfers external sounds but cuts off anything above 84 dB), or OFF (which simply provides passive protection). While Wolf Ears do not provide a volume control, the system does feature two controls for adjusting gain. Gentex Wolf Ears (which can be obtained from Armorer of New Hampshire, P.O. Box 122, Concord, NH 03302-0122) retail for about $200 at the time of this writing.

I find that the Dillon/Peltor Stereo Tactical 7-S earmuffs are much more comfortable than the Wolf Ears. Weighing in at 12.8 ounces (362 grams), the Dillon/Peltor uses a single 9 volt battery to provide about 110 hours of service. The circuitry transmits normal sounds and cuts off sounds louder than 85 dB, providing a maximum NRR of 21 dB.

One knob on the Dillon/Peltor muffs serves as both an on/off switch and volume control, while internal balance is provided by a control in the right ear cup. The Dillon/Peltor Stereo Tactical 7-S

Dillon/Peltor Stereo Tactical 7-S hearing protection devices are one of the two best active muffs in the marketplace.

(which is available from Dillon Precision Products, Inc., 8009 East Dillon Way, Scottsdale, AZ 85260, phone 800-223-4570) retails for about $170 at the time of this writing.

It is important to note that most electronic earmuffs cut off all sound for a fraction of a second when subjected to a loud sound, since the circuitry actually shuts off briefly to protect the wearer. The muffs made by T&T Technologies (P.O. Box 44, Clodine, Texas 77469) work on a different principal. The amplifier in the T&T circuitry can only be driven to a certain level, where the output becomes saturated regardless of the input energy. In essence, the circuitry clips off intense noise while simultaneously transmitting normal sound, so conversations and environmental sounds below the cutoff level can be heard without interruption. This feature means no lost words from conversations at the range or while working in loud environments.

T&T makes two different active muffs using its own patent-pending circuitry, which the company installs in modified Swiss muffs. The standard Model M2 cuts off all sound above 85 dB, while the Hunter Model cuts off all sound above 90 dB. The former is ideal for sport and training purposes. The Hunter Model enables the wearer to hear more environmental sound, but it also provides 5 dB less sound protection, so it is intended for hunters who will only shoot occasionally, shooters with considerable hearing loss, or tactical users who will turn up the gain to magnify environmental sounds. Some SWAT teams, for example, use active muffs while stalking desperados not only to preserve operator hearing but also because the electronic circuitry can be used to amplify sounds that might not be detectable to the unaided, naked ear.

T&T has been manufacturing active muffs since 1984, and its current Model M2 is the best stereo muff in the marketplace, in my opinion. Not only do T&T muffs provide uninterrupted hearing during gunfire, the microphone is placed in the middle rather than the front of each ear cup, which provides optimal sound reception from all directions. The single power switch is protected by a shield, and each ear cup has its own volume and balance control. This is especially useful for older shooters who have more serious hearing loss in their downrange ear.

T&T muffs weigh about 14 ounces (400 grams), making them lighter than Wolf Ears but slightly heavier than Dillon/Peltor muffs. The T&T system uses a standard 9 volt battery to provide about 300 hours of service, making the T&T muffs unusually energy efficient. Changing the battery involves pulling off the inner ring of the ear cup and lifting out the foam cup liner to access the battery. Although this is more inconvenient than competing designs, the T&T uses a standard battery (unlike the Wolf Ears). Furthermore, the T&T provides two to three times longer battery life than the Dillon/Peltor muffs and five times the battery life of Wolf Ears.

I have only two complaints with the T&T electronic muffs: the felt covering for the microphones is not as durable as I'd like, and service can be slow—delivery took five weeks after placing my order.

That said, the T&T standard Model M2 is my favorite active muff at this time. Numerous government agencies, private training facilities, and competitive shooters agree. The T&T M2 sells for $145 at the time of this writing, proving that it is not always necessary to pay more to obtain the best possible performance.

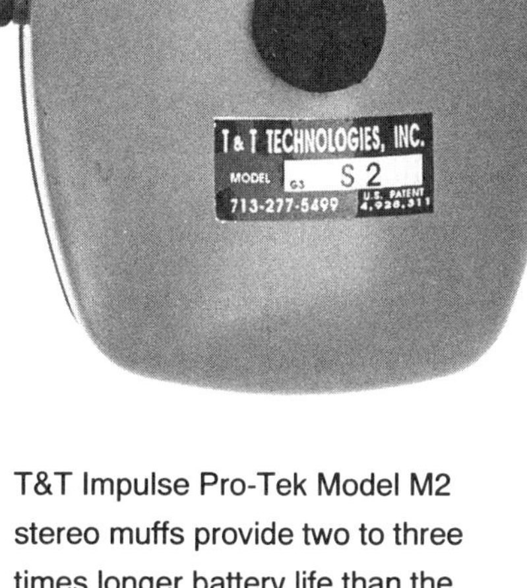

T&T Impulse Pro-Tek Model M2 stereo muffs provide two to three times longer battery life than the Dillon/Peltor muffs.

Noise Helmets

Traditional hearing protection devices such as plugs and muffs do not provide enough hearing protection when the sound pressure levels are very high or when the frequencies of the sounds are low. Heavy weapons such as .50 caliber sniper rifles and machine guns, mortars, rocket launchers, 20mm and 30mm antiaircraft guns, tank guns, artillery, naval guns, and command-detonated mines are commonly encountered by military personnel, who will not be well protected by traditional HPDs. Some noise helmets have been introduced into the marketplace to provide some protection from very loud industrial noise, but these devices do not provide a suitable level of protection from the intense impulse sounds generated by heavy weapons. In fact, they do not provide any better protection than earmuffs alone!

Neither muffs nor plugs attenuate low-frequency impulse sounds as efficiently as the higher frequencies normally associated with a gunshot. For example, while earmuffs reduce the peak impulse sound of a rifle by 20 to 30 dB, the efficiency of muffs drops to less than a 10 dB reduction due to the predominantly low-frequency content of the sound signature generated by a heavy weapon. Ear plugs perform somewhat better, producing a 17 dB reduction of the SPL generated by a 105mm cannon. The best solution using traditional HPDs is to wear both plugs and muffs together. This provides a 23-26 dB reduction of the SPL produced by a 105mm cannon.

While bone conduction of impulse sound impacting the skull may or may not present a significant risk to an individual's hearing when shooting most firearms (the jury is still out on this issue), it becomes a significant liability when operating heavy weapons. Obviously, plugs or muffs cannot mitigate bone conduction.

First-generation Finnish noise helmet prototypes. Photo courtesy Dr. Rauno Pääkkönen.

The Finnish Defense Forces recognized this problem and funded research to develop better hearing protection for personnel operating heavy weapons, particularly during training and testing and evaluation. Therefore, Dr. Rauno Pääkkönen at the Tampere University of Technology in Finland, together with colleagues Teppo Vienamo, Jyrki Järvinen, and Eero Hämäläinen, set out to meet this requirement. They concluded that the only viable solution was to develop a noise helmet that would provide a reasonable level of protection to operators of the most unfriendly heavy weapons. They were fairly successful (Pääkkönen, Vienamo, Järvinen, and Hämäläinen, 1991).

The final prototype, constructed of modern plastics and laminates, provided an 8-13 dB improvement over traditional HPDs at a frequency range of 63 to 500 Hz. It beat traditional HPDs by 18 to 29 dB over the most sensitive range of human hearing: 1,000 to 8,000 Hz. The helmet actually provided a net sound reduction of 55 dB at frequencies above 2,000 Hz, but the system provided disappointing performance for very low-frequency impulse sound common to heavy weapons. This proved to be a very tough nut to crack because the throat seal and the joints within the helmet proved relatively transparent to very low-frequency sound.

Nevertheless, the Finnish noise helmet represents a valuable step forward in the quest for protecting the operators of heavy weapons. Besides improved hearing protection, the noise helmet includes some interesting features, such as a comfortable throat seal, room inside the helmet to permit the wearing of earmuffs, and fan-aided ventilation. Kemira, the maker of Silenta earmuffs, originally planned to produce an improved model of the Finnish noise helmet, but the company is now under new ownership, and the future of commercially produced helmets is unclear at the time of this writing. If it is produced, the Finnish design will undoubtedly be more expensive than previously discussed HPDs due to the helmet's complexity and limited production (anticipated at several hundred units per year). Nevertheless, the noise helmet does fill a unique niche among hearing protection devices.

As must be apparent from the preceding discussions, earmuffs, ear plugs, and noise helmets are very useful tools, but each has some significant liabilities. Many of these problems can be solved by using a sound suppressor as the hearing protection device of choice.

Silencers

Even though Finnish army officers use traditional hearing protection devices during training,

Second-generation Finnish noise helmet. Photo courtesy Dr. Rauno Pääkkönen.

research published in 1986 revealed that they suffer hearing injuries at a level that is approximately 13 times greater than the population at large. Civilian shooters are also at greater risk for many of the same reasons: earmuffs may not fit small individuals well, few people install ear plugs properly, and HPDs may not always work when individuals are exposed to intense sound pressure levels from .50 caliber and larger weapons.

Children have particular problems getting traditional HPDs to fit properly, and yet their especially sensitive hearing is much more vulnerable to damage from intense sound than adults. NRA instructor Bill Beatty, for example, has found that youngsters may find the muzzle blast of firearms painful when wearing either muffs or plugs. In such cases, he has the kids wear *both* plugs and muffs. That makes instruction and the maintenance of safe gun handling more difficult, however. Using silenced rifles and pistols for beginning instruction provides some significant benefits over having the children wear multiple layers of HPDs to avoid a literally painful shooting experience.

Besides children, another segment of the shooting community faces a greater risk of hearing damage: those who use firearms fitted with recoil-reduction devices such as muzzle brakes and EDM porting. These folks are at greater risk because recoil-reduction devices generally direct high-pressure gas back toward the shooter. While such porting can increase shooter comfort by reducing felt recoil, eliminate flinching caused by the anticipation of painful recoil, and increase the speed of follow-up shots, these technologies can dramatically increase the overpressure striking the skull and ear drums. Handguns fitted with recoil compensators, belted magnum rifles with Mag-Na-Porting, and .50 caliber sniper rifles with muzzle brakes are examples that come immediately to mind.

Finally, muffs and plugs are not always effective because they are not always worn by sporting and tactical shooters. Unfortunately, muffs and plugs can be uncomfortable, get in the way, or interfere with hearing game, conversations, or hostile opponents.

Suppressors can address all of these issues. Furthermore, state-of-the-art suppressors commonly provide a greater level of hearing protection than muffs or plugs, even when the muffs fit properly and the plugs are inserted correctly.

Unfortunately, most folks view silencers as sinister devices that have no legitimate role in civilized society. Dr. Kramer was such an individual until he stumbled across one of my articles on .22 rimfire suppressors, and we began to correspond. Now he believes so strongly in the desirability of using suppressors as hearing protection devices that he advocates the total deregulation of suppressors that reduce a firearm's sound signature by up to 13 dB. The use of such simple suppressors would in no way make the firearms anything close to silent (a concession to hoplophobes) but would dramatically reduce the incidence of hearing loss in the United States.

Finnish soldier with M62 assault rifle and Russian PSO-1 scope uses BR-Tuote TX4 suppressor as a hearing protection device. Photo by Juha Hartikka.

Dr. Kramer makes a very compelling argument. Implementation of his proposal at the federal level would dramatically improve the public health while significantly decreasing the financial and social costs of widespread hearing loss. Such simple suppressors could probably be mass-marketed at a cost of $15 for .22 rimfire units and $100 for centerfire rifle units, making them quite affordable to the average shooter. Simple suppressors could even be offered as optional equipment directly by the firearms manufacturers. Ilkka Kyttälä and I both agree that Kramer's proposal would be significantly more effective from a medical perspective if deregulated suppressors produced a 20 dB sound reduction.

Nevertheless, consider both the medical and political implications for deregulating 13 dB suppressors. From a medical perspective, a 13 dB suppressor reduces the amount of sound pressure to 5 percent of what it was. From a contemporary U.S. political perspective, a firearm with a 13 dB suppressor still generates a considerable amount of noise, so it would be unsuitable for all the nefarious deeds that political paranoia is heir to. Dr. Kramer uses the following analogy to illustrate this point. Say you win $10 million and spend all but 5 percent of that money. Having $500,000 in the bank is a far cry from being broke. Similarly, cutting the noise of a centerfire rifle from 163 to 150 dB or a rimfire rifle from 141 to 128 dB is a far cry from creating a silent gunshot.

An interesting spinoff of Dr. Kramer's proposal from my perspective is that the deregulation of 13 dB suppressors would improve the public's image of silencer technology. Perhaps we could eventually make the wholly reasonable argument that more efficient suppressors would further improve the public health, just as the introduction of air bags made automobiles safer than using seat belts alone.

Who knows, maybe a presidential candidate could then campaign for a flat tax rate, a chicken in every pot, and a silencer in every closet. If such a candidate won, then we might even see government programs sponsored by the Environmental Protection Agency (EPA) and the National Institutes of Health (NIH) to encourage the widespread use of silencers in the United States.

Has this discussion degenerated into demented rambling? Not really. I do admit that the probability of EPA and NIH funding programs to encourage the proliferation of silencers is vanishingly small, given the current political climate in the United States. The reality is very different, however, elsewhere in the world. Consider, for example, that bastion of enlightenment, Finland.

A broad spectrum of government agencies, academic researchers, civilian organizations, and industries in Finland came together in the 1990s to solve the noise pollution and public health problems created by gunshot noise. This diverse team, which is summarized in Table 3.3 (pages 47-48), focussed on using suppressors and shooting-range structures to solve these problems.

SUPPRESSOR RESEARCH IN FINLAND

Finnish researchers began their cooperative study by looking at the sound signatures of firearms with and without suppressors (Kyttälä and Pääkkönen, 1996). Most of the effort focussed on the 7.62x39mm Valmet M62 assault rifle (a product-improved Kalashnikov), common 7.62x51mm (.308 Winchester) hunting rifles, and 12 gauge semiautomatic shotguns. All rifle suppressors reduced the operator's exposure to less than the European risk limit of 140 dB for impulse sound. Shotgun suppressors were not as effective, so sound reductions only approached the 140 dB risk limit when using subsonic rounds. Suppressors attenuate environmental noise particularly well to the back and sides of the firearm (see Figures 3.2 and 3.3). Therefore, suppressors proved quite effective at reducing the exposure risk for instructors and trainers located 10 meters (33 feet) behind and to the side of the shooter, respectively (see Figure 3.4).

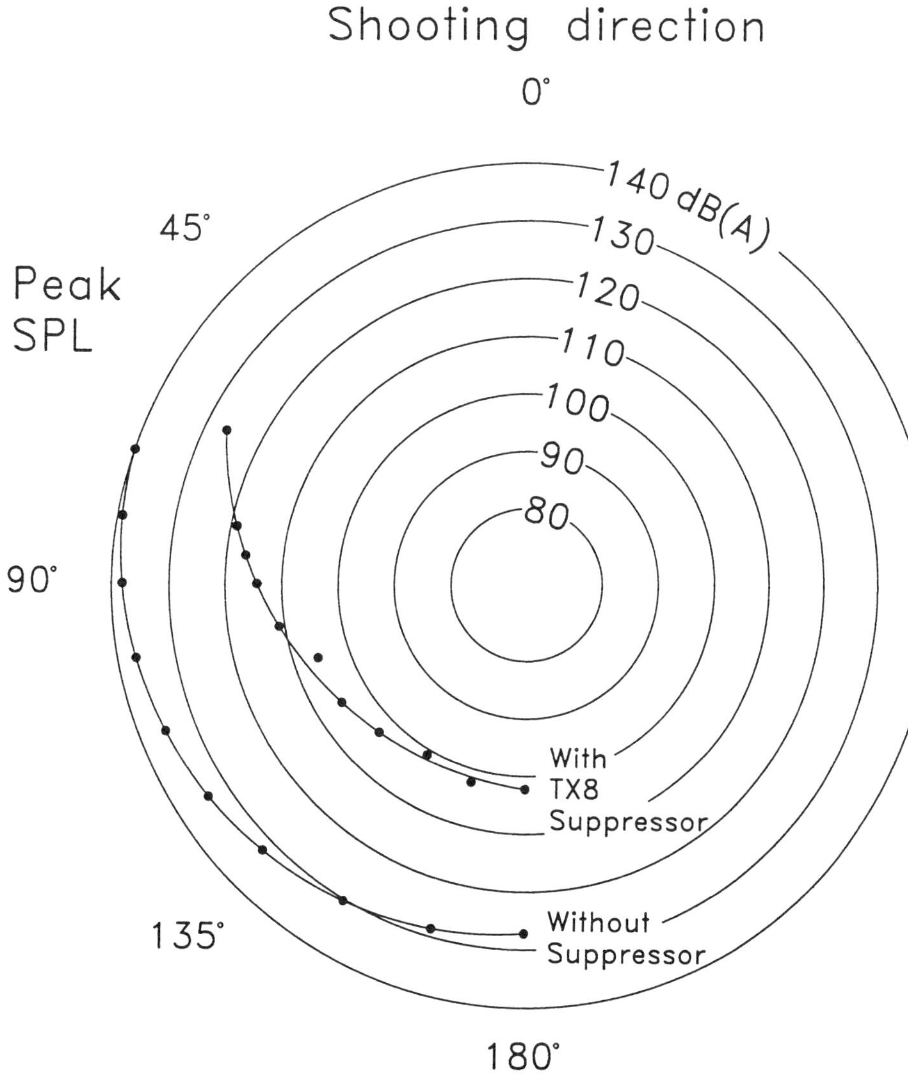

Figure 3.2. Peak sound pressure levels behind and to the side of a 7.62x39mm assault rifle fired with and without a suppressor (redrawn by Mike Smith from data by Kari Pesonen Oy published in Kyttälä, Pääkkönen, and Pesonen, 1993).

The scientists then went on to compare the sound and recoil generated by firearms with and without muzzle brakes and suppressors. All muzzle brakes increased the sound pressure level at the shooter's ear by 5 to 10 dB (see Figure 3.5). Unpublished research by Dr. William L. Kramer shows that KDF muzzle brakes produce an additional 11 decibels of impulse noise at the shooter's ear.

Kyttälä and Pääkkönen demonstrated that the actual amount of SPL increase experienced by the shooter proved to be directly proportional to the amount of recoil reduction. In other words, more recoil reduction means more intense sound at the shooter's ear and more risk to the shooter's hearing. Thus, replacing a muzzle brake with even a modest silencer that only produces a 15 dB net sound reduction, compared to a firearm with no muzzle brake, will effectively reduce the shooter's exposure by 20 dB.

This principal proved valid for every type of firearm equipped with a muzzle brake. Furthermore, sound suppressors reduced recoil energy by 20 to 30 percent, making them about as effective as muzzle brakes for reducing felt recoil. To quote J.D. Jones of SSK Industries, "The best muzzle brake is a sound suppressor or silencer." Suppressors also eliminated muzzle climb during rapid semiautomatic fire and during full-auto bursts when shooting assault rifles.

I found one aspect of the Finnish research rather surprising. Blank cartridges can pose more of a threat to a shooter's hearing than bulleted cartridges (see Figure 3.6). In fact, scientists studying the hearing loss

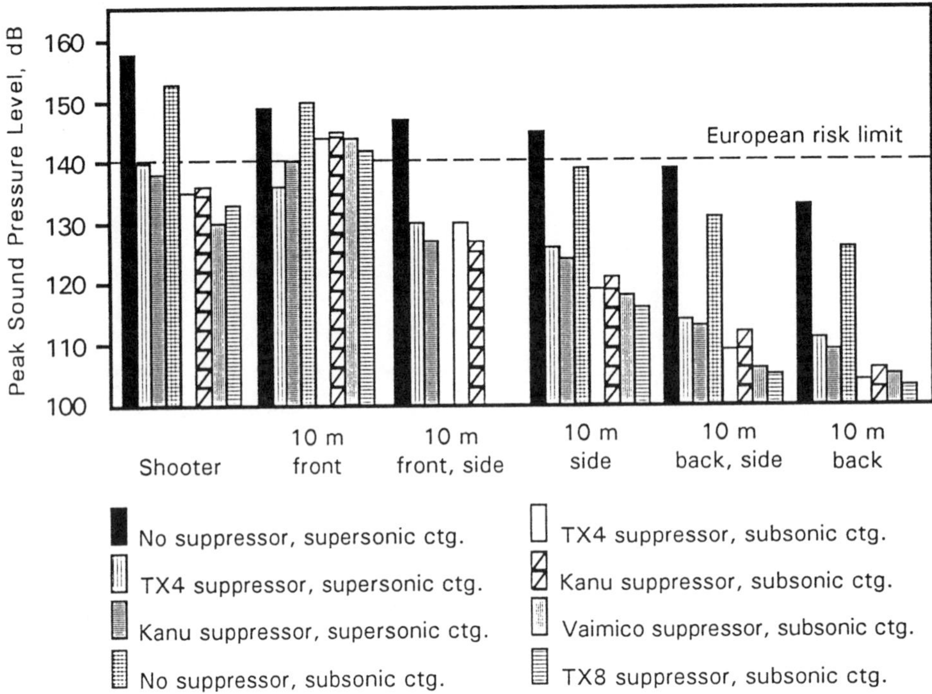

Figure 3.3. Peak sound pressure levels at a variety of positions around the shooter when a 7.62x39mm assault rifle is fired with and without suppressors, using supersonic and subsonic ammunition (adapted by Polly Walter from Kyttälä, Pääkkönen, and Pesonen, 1993).

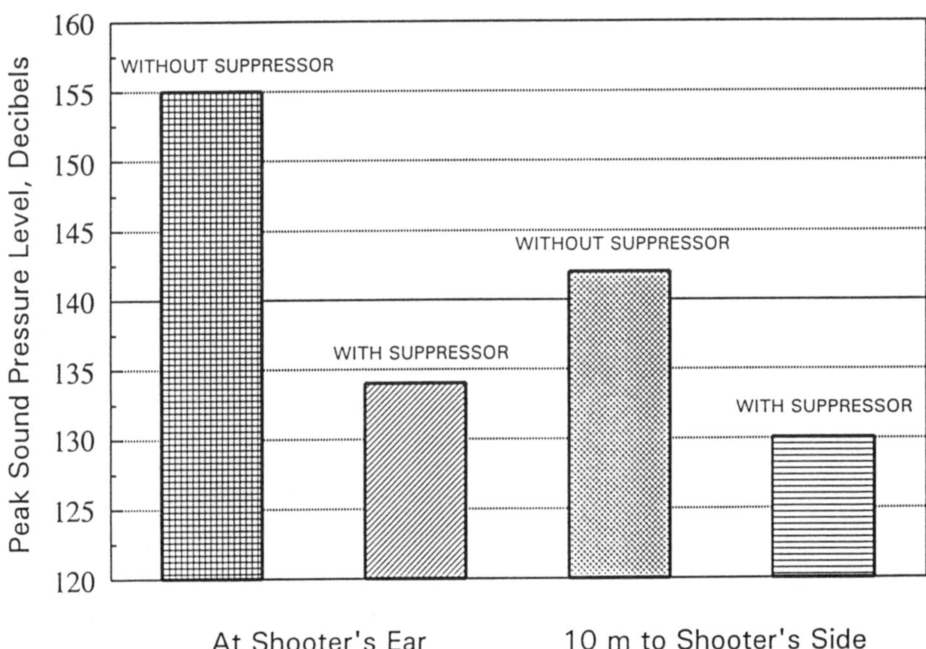

Figure 3.4. Finnish research showed that all rifle suppressors reduced the shooter's exposure to below the European risk limit for hearing loss of 140 dB (shown as a dark horizontal line). Suppressors were also effective at reducing risk to the hearing of bystanders and instructors behind and to the side of the shooter (adapted from Kyttälä and Pääkkönen, 1996).

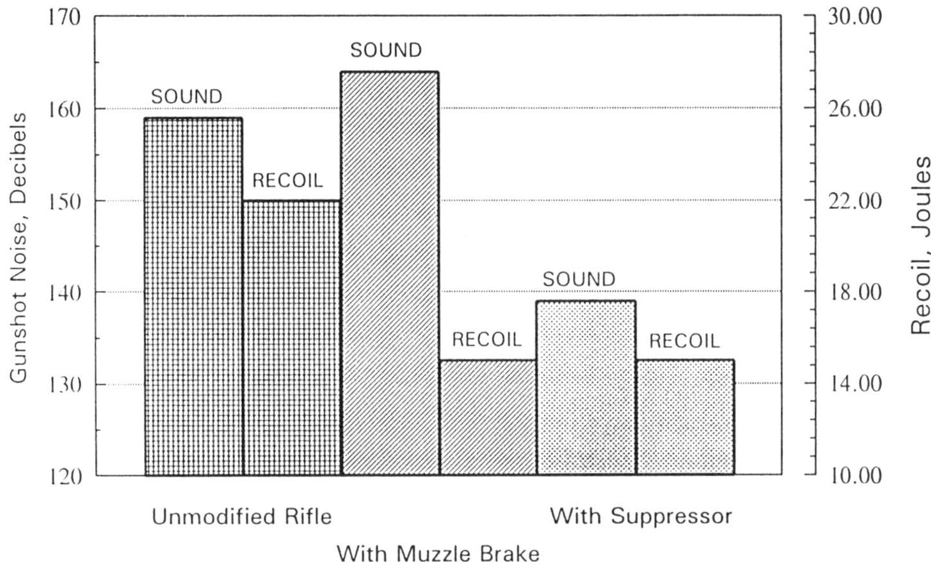

Figure 3.5. Suppressors reduce recoil about as much as muzzle brakes while exposing the shooter to much less noise exposure. This has profound implications regarding the risk of hearing loss (adapted from Kyttälä and Pääkkönen, 1996).

Machine rest used for Finnish accuracy experiments. Photo courtesy Dr. Rauno Pääkkönen.

experienced by conscripts in the Finnish army found that tactical exercises involving the use of blanks created most of the acute hearing damage among infantrymen. Ilkka Kyttälä attributes much of this acute acoustic trauma when using blanks to several factors: 1) wearing helmets is required during military tactical exercises, which precludes wearing earmuffs; 2) engagement distances are frequently very close; and 3) opponents are typically directly in front of the muzzle. While suppressors can't be used with Finnish military blank cartridges using wooden bullets, they can be used when shooting traditional blank cartridges with a crimped head. This research is also relevant to theatrical and movie productions, since the blanks used in props pose an immediate threat of hearing damage. Figure 3.7 shows the schematic of a sound suppressor designed by Juha Hartikka expressly for use with blank ammunition during theatrical productions.

Military exercises can mitigate the health risk from blank ammunition with silencers or traditional HPDs (passive plugs or muffs).

Ballistic pendulum used by Finnish researchers to test gun recoil. Photo courtesy Dr. Rauno Pääkkönen.

Since the use of a suppressor does not reduce a soldier's normal hearing, he can still hear telltale sounds of opponents and whispered commands. Therefore, in my opinion, suppressors represent a much more appropriate technology for this problem. Since theatrical and movie productions need to simulate real gunshots for an audience, flesh-colored active (not passive) ear plugs for everyone on stage represent the most viable solution when using blank-firing props.

When actually firing bulleted ammunition rather than blanks, most folks view reducing a weapon's sound signatures as the most important aspect of stealthy shooting. Other important aspects include bullet flight noise, the additional length and weight added by a suppressor, and muzzle flash.

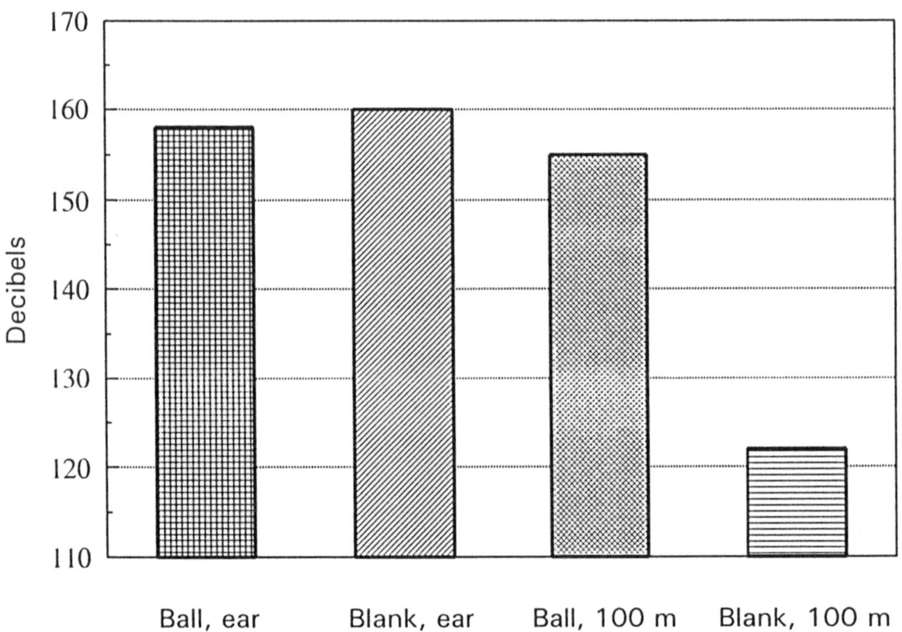

Figure 3.6. Blank cartridges can pose more of a threat to a shooter's hearing than bulleted cartridges (adapted from Kyttälä and Pääkkönen, 1996).

The muzzle flash issue is primarily relevant to tactical personnel. Finnish research demonstrated that most suppressors hide a muzzle flash better than a flash hider (see Figure 3.8). In my experience, some U.S. suppressors totally eliminate muzzle flash. Completely eliminating flash does require a conscious and insightful effort by the suppressor designer, however. Suppressors provide the additional benefit of preventing the movement of

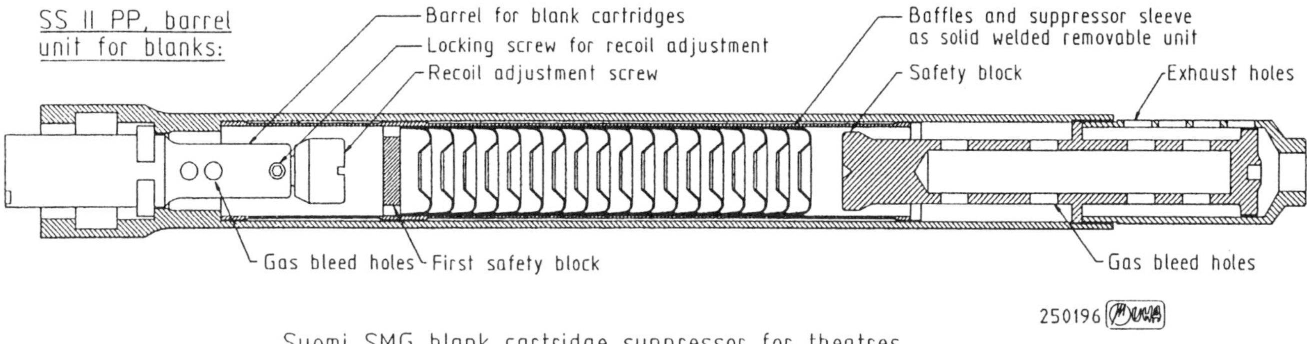

Blank cartridge version of "Suhina-Suomi II" (Sighing Suomi II) integral suppressor barrel unit was designed and built for City of Turku Theatre by Juha Hartikka. The user asked for a means to drop the noise of burst fired blank cartridges to safe and comfortable level for the actors and the audience in an indoor theatre. The SS II PP barrel unit was made to resemble closely an original Suomi SMG barrel jacket, with the exception of missing barrel jacket perforations. Bolt blowback may be adjusted from barrel valve screw to eject fired shells to desired distance from the gun. Built-in multiple safety blocks stop any ball cartridge mixed by accident between blanks.

Figure 3.7. Schematic of a sound suppressor designed by Juha Hartikka expressly for use with blank ammunition during theatrical productions. This suppressor is manufactured by Asesepänliike BR-Tuote Ky in Finland.

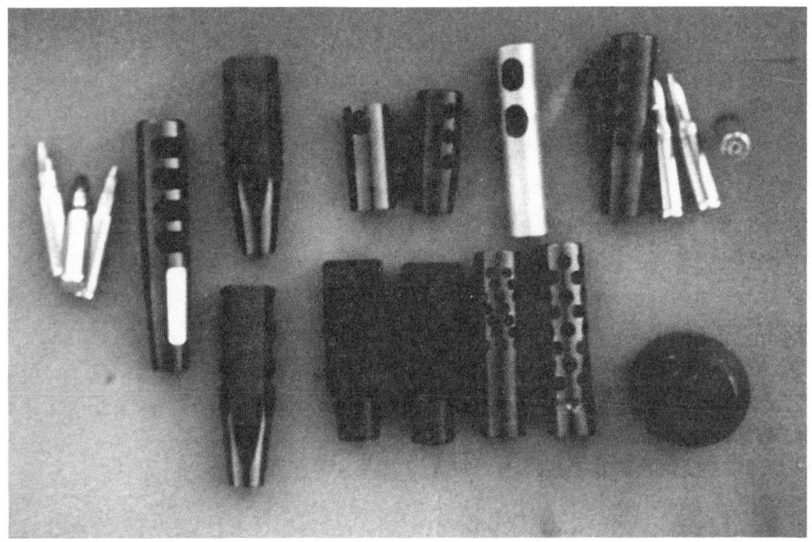

Muzzle brakes used by Finnish researchers to test the effects of these devices on sound signature and recoil. Photo courtesy Dr. Rauno Pääkkönen.

grass, leaves, twigs, and dust. For the armed professional, especially the sniper, this latter function may often be the single most important advantage of using a suppressor—even more important than the reduced sound signature. The combined reduction of visual and sound stimuli explains the wonderful Finnish proverb that introduces the next chapter.

Length and weight of a suppressor can be a significant factor in the performance equation, especially when used on rifle-caliber firearms. In my experience, the size and weight of .22 rimfire suppressors are generally inconsequential. Length and weight of centerfire pistol suppressors are critical in that these factors affect whether or not a pistol will cycle reliably when fitted with a can. The diameter of any pistol suppressor is also highly relevant. A suppressor must have a diameter small enough to avoid occluding the pistol's iron sights if the operator actually wishes to place his or her shots precisely. An excellent, but rarely used, alternative is to incorporate sights on the pistol suppressor. Suppressor diameter then becomes irrelevant unless the weight of a large-diameter suppressor prevents reliable cycling. Rifle suppressors for the 5.56x45mm cartridge are light enough for shooting the weapon offhand, while most suppressors for the 7.62x51mm cartridge are too heavy for practical offhand shooting. Thirty caliber and larger suppressors also tend to be too long for optimal practicality.

Finnish suppressor designer Juha Hartikka has developed a particularly innovative suppressor design that simultaneously eliminates the length and weight problems, is relatively inexpensive to produce in quantity, and solves pretty much all of the health and many of the tactical issues involved with using suppressors on rifles and automatic weapons. Hartikka calls his design the *reflex suppressor* (see Figure 3.9).

Manufactured by Asesepänliike BR-Tuote Ky, a steel reflex suppressor only increases the weight of an assault rifle by about 10 percent (for example, from 3.6 to 3.9 kg). If used to replace a state-of-the-art muzzle brake or flash hider, then the reflex suppressor only increases an assault rifle's weight by about 5 percent. Since the reflex suppressor only extends beyond the end of a barrel by 4 to 5 cm (1.6-2.0 inches), these muzzle cans add about the same length as a good flash hider or muzzle brake.

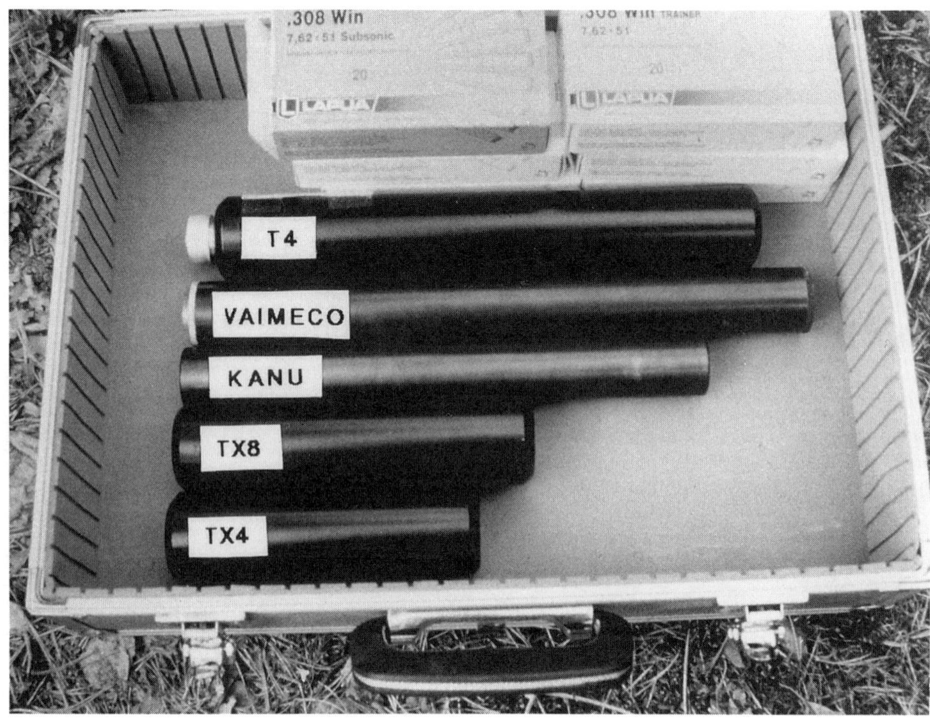

Sound suppressors used by Finnish researchers to test the effects of these devices on sound signatures and recoil of .30 caliber firearms. Photo courtesy Dr. Rauno Pääkkönen.

Figure 3.8. Finnish research has demonstrated that most suppressors hide a muzzle flash better than a flash hider (redrawn by Mike Smith from Kyttälä and Pääkkönen, 1996).

The current crop of U.S. suppressors produce dramatically more sound reduction than the reflex suppressor, but I believe that Hartikka's design represents one of the most important achievements since the Maxim Model 1910 suppressor. My logic is that the compact envelope and light weight afforded by the reflex suppressor makes it practical for widespread use on firearms of rifle caliber for virtually all applications not requiring the maximum possible sound reduction. Since most hearing loss among soldiers occurs during training, reflex suppressors could be used by everyone at all times during training. And they are light enough to be widely used for tactical

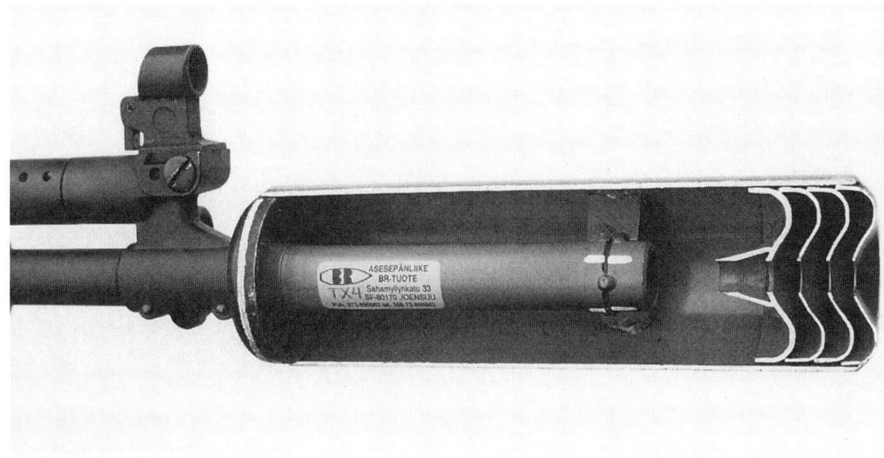

An inside look at a cutaway of the TX4 reflex suppressor manufactured by Asesepänliike BR-Tuote Ky of Finland. This suppressor is mounted on the M62 assault rifle, which is a product-improved clone of the Kalashnikov. Photo by Juha Hartikka.

BR-Tuote XRS shotgun suppressor disassembled, showing gas ports in the barrel extension, which keeps the shot cup and pellets from expanding inside the reflex suppressor. Photo by Juha Hartikka.

applications, hunting, and other sporting activities.

Furthermore, the reflex design generates almost no back pressure and, therefore, almost no additional heat build-up in a weapon's barrel, even during full-auto fire. Quickly dumping a battle pack of ammunition through an M16 set on AUTO with a traditional suppressor causes so much heating of the barrel that the rifling suddenly goes away after 180 to 200 rounds. A reflex suppressor can be used on a belt-fed machine gun without destroying the weapon's rifling. Juha Hartikka's brainchild is apparently the first suppressor design that is truly compatible with full-auto fire in weapons of rifle caliber.

Although reflex suppressors, more traditional muzzle cans, and integral suppressors all reduce the muzzle signature of a firearm, there is one aspect of a weapon's overall sound signature that remains completely unaffected: bullet flight noise. Since the phenomenon of bullet flight noise is discussed at length in Chapter 4 on the tactical use of suppressors, only a few points from recent Finnish research need be addressed here. Figure 3.10 shows a generalized synthesis of Finnish research on bullet flight noise measured from a distance of 0.65 meter (2.1 feet) from the bullet flight path. The graph, which is adapted from Kyttälä and Pääkkönen (1996), suggests several things. Subsonic projectiles produce flight noise well below the European risk limit of 140 dB. Bullet flight noise increases dramatically with velocity in the transonic range. And supersonic projectiles generate bullet flight noise that exceeds the 140 dB risk limit by a considerable margin.

The only place where I part company with the conclusions from the broad spectrum of interdisciplinary research conducted on suppressors in Finland in the 1990s involves the health implications of bullet flight noise.

Kyttälä and Pääkkönen (1996) assert that "ballistic noise [i.e., bullet flight noise] does not affect

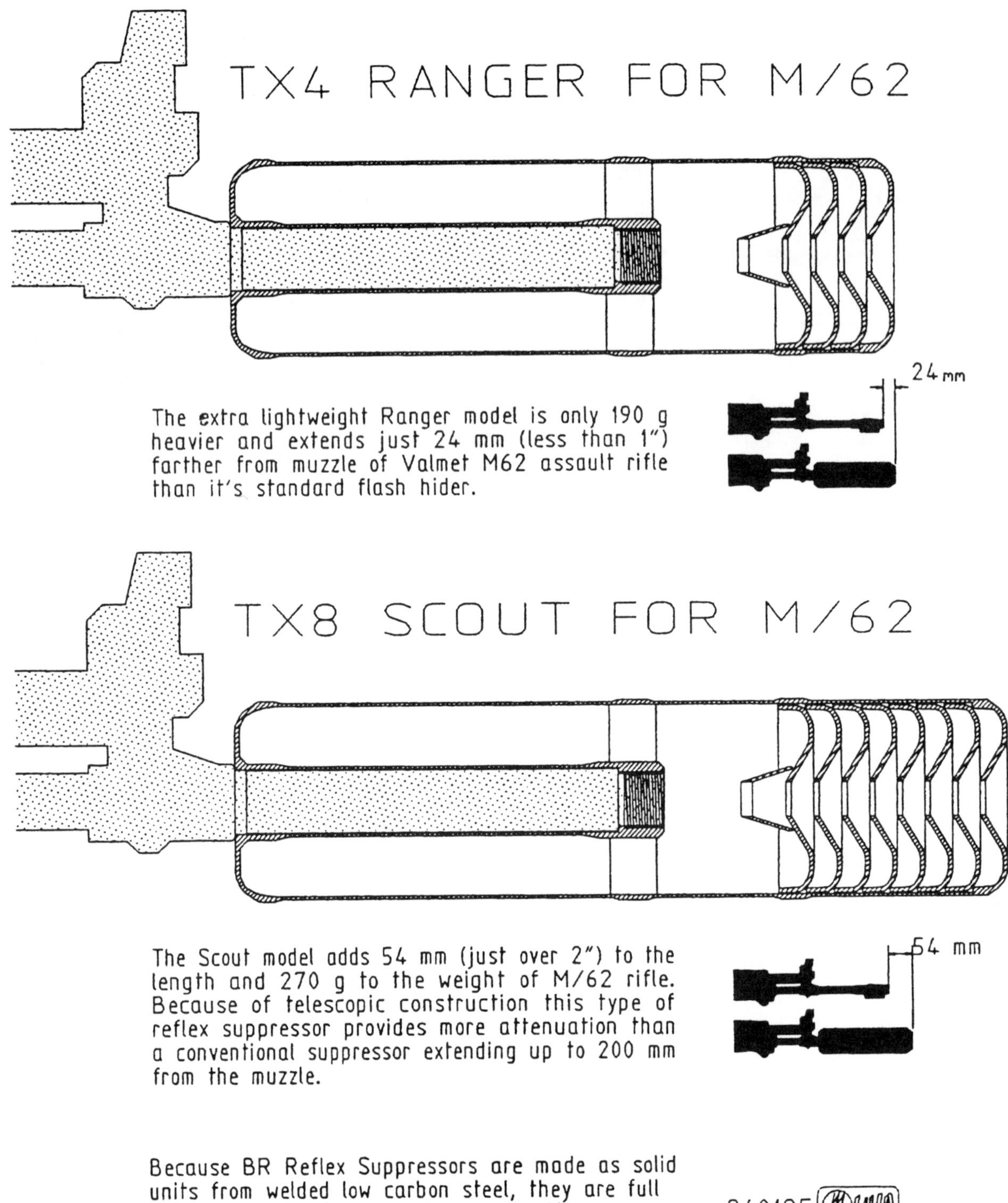

Figure 3.9. If used to replace a state-of-the art flash hider, the steel reflex suppressor designed by Juha Hartikka and manufactured by Asesepänliike BR-Tuote Ky only increases the weight of an assault rifle by about 5 percent. These muzzle cans add about the same length as a good flash hider or muzzle brake.

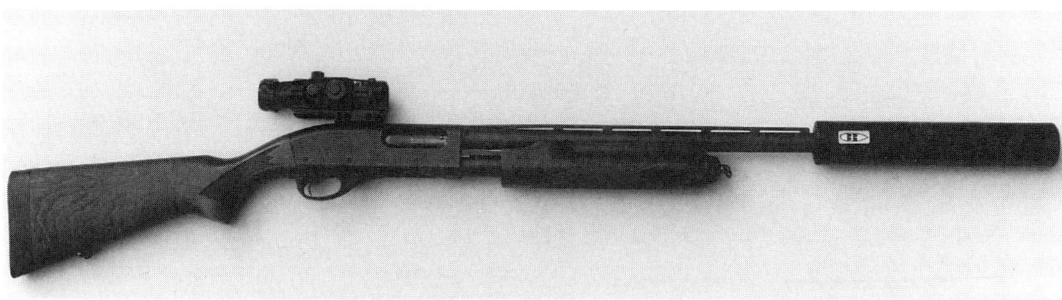

BR-Tuote XRS shotgun suppressor on 12 gauge semiautomatic shotgun used during the course of Finnish research. Photo by Juha Hartikka.

Figure 3.10. Bullet flight noise as a function of projectile velocity.

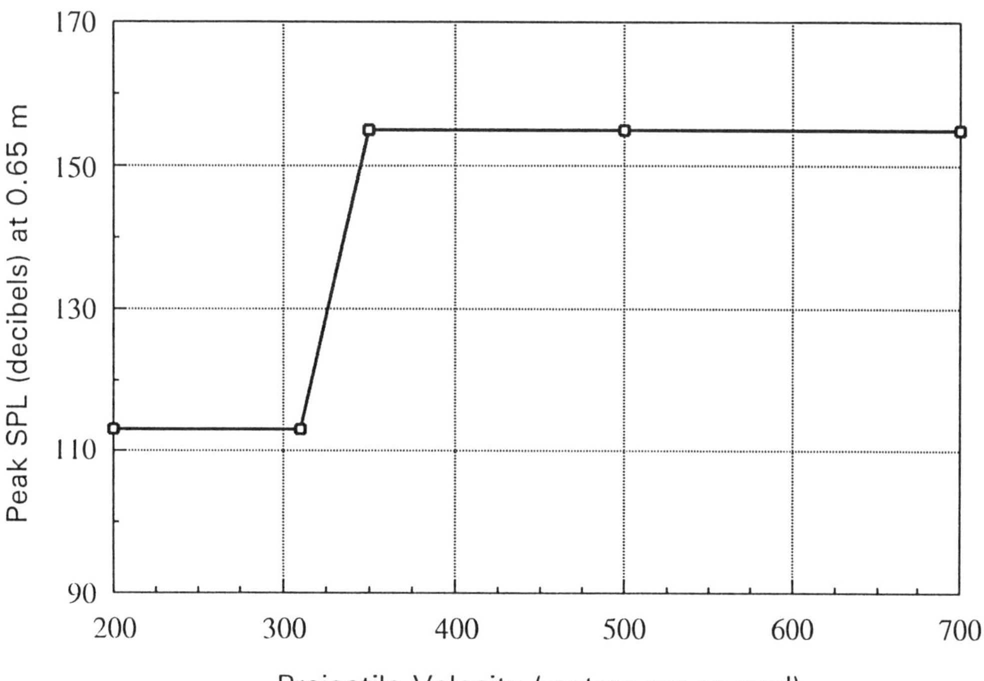

Figure 3.10. A generalized synthesis of Finnish research shows that subsonic projectiles produce flight noise well below the European risk limit for hearing loss of 140 dB. Bullet flight noise increases dramatically with velocity in the transonic range, and supersonic projectiles generate bullet flight noise that exceeds the 140 dB risk limit by a considerable margin.

the shooter's exposure [to dangerous sound pressure levels] *in open range* [the italics are mine]. Ballistic noise concentrates in the higher frequencies and thus attenuates, when propagating, faster than the muzzle blast." Yet in my experience using suppressed firearms, the bullet flight noise generated by supersonic projectiles can sometimes be painful to the shooter. While environmental surfaces such as trees or walls can reflect painful shock waves from the wakes of supersonic projectiles, I've also experienced this effect when shooting in the open. Since the pain threshold of 141 dB exceeds the European risk limit of 140 dB, plugs or muffs should ideally be worn when shooting supersonic projectiles from suppressed firearms for optimal hearing protection, in my opinion.

CONCLUSIONS

Silencers provide a number of advantages over such traditional hearing protection devices as ear plugs, earmuffs, and noise helmets.

Early research by Dr. Rauno Pääkkönen and Ilkka Kyttälä focused on suppressed military rifles, sporting shotguns, and sporting rifles such as this Sako 7.62x51mm rifle with BR-Tuote T8 suppressor. Photo by Juha Hartikka.

1. Suppressors do not interfere with normal hearing as do passive HPDs.
2. Unlike active HPDs, such as electronic muffs and plugs, suppressors have no batteries or electronics to fail. A corollary to Murphy's Law states that electronic technology fails at the worse possible moment, especially in the tactical environment.
3. Suppressors cannot fail because of the physical size or physiological state of the operator.
4. Suppressors can provide a higher level of hearing protection than muffs or plugs, even when the traditional HPDs are fitted properly.
5. Suppressors do not interfere with obtaining a fast and repeatable sight picture, while muffs can.
6. Besides protecting the hearing of shooters and nearby observers, suppressors can also provide additional benefits simultaneously, including but not limited to recoil reduction, flash reduction, better accuracy, hiding the location of the shooter, hiding the fact that a shot has been fired (when using subsonic ammunition), improved command and control, less public relations (PR) problems following tactical shootings, less PR problems from neighbors of shooting ranges, less PR problems for animal control officers, less atmospheric lead pollution, and reduced risk of explosion from the accumulation of unburned powder residue at indoor shooting ranges.

In my opinion, one can make a very strong case that suppressors should be deregulated by the U.S. Congress. Then both the EPA and NIH should encourage the widespread use of silencers to reduce noise and lead pollution as well as to more effectively safeguard the public health from hearing damage. Mufflers are *required* on lawn mowers, motorcycles, and automobiles. Surely mounting mufflers on firearms should at least be *encouraged*, since firearms not only provide the most aesthetically offensive category of noise pollution, but they also offer a greater risk of hearing loss to a vast segment of the American population. Since approximately 60 million households in the United States contain at least one firearm, a significant portion of the population runs the risk of hearing damage due to gunshot noise. Sound suppressors provide the most efficacious solution to that pandemic medical problem.

Table 3.3. Summary of the diverse team of government agencies, academic researchers, civilian organizations, and industries in Finland that came together in the 1990s to solve the noise pollution and public health problems created by gunshot noise. Their research focused on using suppressors and shooting-range structures to solve these problems.

FINANCING	
Ministry of Education	
Ministry of Environment	
Ministry of Labor	
Lapua Oy	
SUPERVISORS AND THEIR AFFILIATIONS	
Yrjö Tolonen	Ministry of Education
Pertti Kärpänen	Ministry of Education
Risto Järvelä	Ministry of Education
Antero Honkasalo	Ministry of Environment
Seppo Palmu	Ministry of Defense
Ilkka Heikkilä	Defense Materiel Establishment
Esa Puurtinen	Technical Inspection Center
Juha Tikkanen	Finnish Shooting Association
Ilkka Kiianlinna	Finnish Shooting Association
Juha Kairikko	Finnish Hunters' Association
Erkki Kiukas	Hunters' Central Organization
SCIENTISTS AND THEIR AFFILIATIONS	
Illka Kyttälä	Ministry of Labor
Rauno Pääkkönen	Tampere Regional Institute of Occupational Health
Kari Pesonen	Kari Pesonen Consulting Engineering Ltd.
Juha Eväsoja	Cartridge Factory, Lapua Ltd.
Matti Vähäpassi	Cartridge Factory, Lapua Ltd.
Juha Hartikka	Asesepänliike BR-Tuote Ky
Kalevi Nurmentaus	n/a
Juhani Salo	Asetiimi Ltd.
Rauli Lonka	n/a
Jorma Santala	n/a
P.T. Kekkonen	n/a
Seppo Martiskainen	Kuopio Arms Depot
Tarmo Romppanen	Kuopio Arms Depot
Jaakko Seppänen	Kuopio Arms Depot

Table 3.3 (continued).

SCIENTISTS AND THEIR AFFILIATIONS	
Veli Oravainen	Kuopio Arms Depot
Seppo Roininen	Soil and Water Ltd.
Lauri Heikkinen	PI-Consulting Ltd.
Lauri Suomalainen	PI-Consulting Ltd.
Heikki Tuominen	Finnish Acoustics Centre Ltd.
Juhani Nuotio	Finnish Acoustics Centre Ltd.
Juhani Ollila	Institute of Occupational Health

CHAPTER FOUR

TACTICAL USE OF SUPPRESSORS

A silencer does not make a soldier silent, but it does make him invisible.

—Old Finnish Proverb

ound suppressors make effective tactical tools when employed for any of several reasons. Suppressors are typically used to 1) hide the fact that a shot has been fired; 2) hide the location of the shooter; 3) reduce muzzle blast and recoil; 4) enhance command and control; 5) preserve operator hearing, especially in confined spaces; or 6) reduce the likelihood of detonation when operating in a potentially explosive atmosphere. While a suppressed weapon may provide several of these functions simultaneously, the tactical user will commonly view one of these functions as the primary task of the suppressed system for a given mission. Some of the complexities involved with each of these applications are worth exploring in detail.

HIDING THE EVENT

The uninitiated commonly believe that a silencer always hides the fact that a shot has been fired. While this effect can be achieved with the proper combination of weapon, cartridge, and environmental circumstances, attaining this level of performance can be difficult. A suppressed firearm is generally used to hide the fact that a shot has been fired for one of three reasons: 1) to quietly eliminate a sentry, pointman, or other hostile without alerting nearby individuals; 2) to quietly

A suppressed .22 rimfire rifle like this Ruger 77/22 fitted with a Gemtech Vortex-2 muzzle can is very useful for the selective destruction of objects—such as vehicle tires and yard lights—prior to an entry or tactical operation.

DP27 machine gun firing the 7.62x54R cartridge with BR-Tuote T8D telescopic reflex suppressor. Photo by Juha Hartikka.

Professional operators have a long tradition of using suppressed .22 rimfire pistols to hide the event when engaged in discreet up-close and personal diplomacy. Shown is a Walther TPH pistol with Gemtech LDES-2 suppressor.

eliminate a guard dog; or 3) to quietly destroy selected objects (such as vehicle tires or yard lights) prior to an assault.

Unless there is considerable environmental noise (such as a helicopter overhead or a nearby firefight), hiding the fact that a shot has been fired generally requires the use of subsonic ammunition to avoid the loud ballistic crack that would be generated by a supersonic projectile. The use of subsonic ammunition limits the effective range of a weapon. If the suppressed firearm employs subsonic ammunition with a poor ballistic coefficient (such as the 9x19mm and .45 ACP pistol cartridges), then the system could have a maximum effective range on the order of 100 yards (91 m). If the subsonic weapon employs ammunition with a good ballistic coefficient (such as the 7.62x39mm and 7.62x51mm NATO subsonic rifle cartridges), then the system could have a maximum effective range on the order of 200 yards (183 m).

In practice, placing accurate hits out to 200 yards with a subsonic rifle cartridge is very difficult. Two factors create most of the problems: the rifling's rate of twist and range estimation. Current laser range-finding binoculars solve the latter problem, but finding a source for barrels of the proper twist rate can be a challenge.

A fast rate of twist is typically needed to stabilize a subsonic projectile of conventional weight, although ongoing (unpublished) research by suppressor authority Janne Pohjoispää as well as R&D by Lapua Oy may revolutionize traditional wisdom on this subject. Using conventional 7.62x39mm ammunition, Pohjoispää found that a tired Hungarian Kalashnikov delivered 6 MOA groups at 100 yards. That's typical performance for a Kalashnikov. Yet with a new Lapua subsonic round, his groups shrank to 3 or 4 MOA. Using the Finnish version of the Kalashnikov with the Lapua subsonic round gave Pohjoispää groups under 1 MOA! That's unprecedented accuracy with an assault rifle based on the Kalashnikov design. I await future publications by Janne Pohjoispää with a great deal of anticipation.

Many subsonic cartridges employ a heavier than normal bullet to improve both external and terminal ballistics (which translate into improved shot placement and better stopping power). Using a heavier bullet may require such a fast rate of twist that appropriate barrels are extremely difficult to obtain, even from custom barrel makers. A further complication is that such a fast-twist barrel probably won't provide acceptable performance with conventional supersonic ammunition, so it is generally necessary to dedicate a rifle to a subsonic cartridge. The Vaime Mk2 Silent Sniper Rifle represents one of the few suppressed rifles designed for a subsonic cartridge that will deliver good accuracy with both subsonic and supersonic rounds out to 200 yards.

Range estimation is critical when using a suppressed rifle with subsonic cartridge at long range, even if the projectile has a good ballistic coefficient. The 7.62x51 NATO subsonic round, for example, produces a bullet drop of about 3 feet (0.9 meter) between 100 and 200 yards.

Assuming that a suppressed firearm and its cartridge deliver sufficient accuracy and adequate terminal ballistics, it is also important to realize that the muzzle signature is only part of the story when evaluating a system for tactical employment. Two other events are involved with a suppressed gunshot that can influence the stealthiness of that shot: bullet flight noise and bullet impact.

For example, when using a .22 rimfire rifle with a muzzle suppressor for the selective destruction of objects, it is important to realize that the muzzle can will not eliminate the ballistic crack produced by high-velocity loads and or even sometimes by standard-velocity loads. The subjective impression is that the ballistic crack is as loud as an unsuppressed .22 rifle, so subsonic Long Rifles or CB Longs should normally be used for the selective destruction of objects to keep the event from sounding like a gunshot. With the resultant dramatic reduction of the weapon signature and bullet flight noise, bullet impact becomes the dominant sound of the gunshot.

When employing a suppressed *centerfire* rifle with conventional ammunition, for example, the bullet impact in flesh is a loud and distinctive "pukk!" If the target is engaged over an open area with little ambient (environmental) noise, bullet impact can be heard clearly for hundreds of meters. When using a suppressed rimfire rifle or when using a suppressed centerfire rifle with subsonic cartridge, the sound of bullet impact in flesh is considerably less, but it's still distinctive. When using a subsonic rimfire round on a tire, the muzzle signature might be undetectable to an observer 33 yards (30 meters) away around the corner of a house, while the bullet impact may or may not be heard as a hollow thump. When using a CB Long to break a light bulb outside a house, the only thing a close observer might notice is the sound of breaking glass, while occupants of the house might hear nothing. The metallic ring of a hit from a CB Long on a tire rim, however, might be quite noticeable to the house occupants.

Merely using a quality suppressed firearm does not provide carte blanche to the operator. Some other variables that will also affect the stealthiness of a suppressed gunshot include such things as ammunition, ambient noise, location of potential hostiles relative to the target, composition of target, composition of material behind the target, presence or absence of reflective materials (such as pavement or brick walls), presence or absence of absorptive materials (such as grass, bushes, and trees), and shot placement.

A final footnote to hiding the event relates to the employment of suppressors with supersonic projectiles at very close range. Entry teams are increasingly using suppressed carbines of rifle caliber (commonly the Colt M4 with an AWC HRT suppressor) because of the weapon's superior terminal ballistics compared to those of a submachine gun and because the 5.56x41mm cartridge will defeat most body armor. Armed confrontations in this environment tend to be up close and personal, and a suppressed weapon may be fired at a target who is so close that the supersonic projectile does not travel far enough to generate a ballistic crack. In such cases, the dominant sounds become the suppressed muzzle blast and the sound of bullet impact. Given ideal environmental conditions and a *very* short engagement distance, plus an excellent muzzle can, suppressed weapons with supersonic ammunition can be very stealthy. This phenomenon has been largely ignored by professional operators, but it might provide an interesting option given the right tactical scenario.

It is much easier to hide the location of the shooter than to hide the fact that a shot has been fired. This is a particularly valuable phenomenon for military (as opposed to law enforcement and clandestine) applications.

HIDING THE SHOOTER

Using a suppressor to hide the location of the shooter is most commonly used by military snipers employing conventional (i.e., supersonic) ammunition. The suppressor thus enables the sniper to shoot more times (i.e., engage more targets) than might otherwise be prudent. An old sniper instructor questioned this premise, however, saying, "It's not how many you kill, but *who* you kill that matters." After a moment of thought, he added, "Of course, killing them all is good, too." Using a suppressor also dramatically reduces the risk from effective countersniper fire and improves the odds of a successful withdrawal from the enemy contact if circumstances warrant. Ideally, of course, the sniper should have planned three alternative routes for withdrawal.

The suppressor hides the location of the shooter for three reasons.

1. At typical engagement distances, most suppressors will lower the muzzle signature to less than the action noise of a self-loading rifle and less than the bullet flight noise. Thus, an individual who is downrange will attempt to locate the source of the sound not from the muzzle blast but rather from the bullet flight noise. It is not uncommon for an individual downrange to turn his attention 45 to 180 degrees away from the shooter under such circumstances. I've experienced this phenomenon myself, both from the shooter's position and from an observer's position as bullets fired from a silenced rifle passed close to my body while I stood in the open. Both were dramatic experiences.

A suppressed machine gun is very effective on the short leg of an L-shaped ambush since enemy fleeing from the noisy long leg of the ambush do not realize they're running into another field of fire. This photo shows an MG34 fitted with an early variant of the R8MG suppressor. Photo courtesy Juha Hartikka.

Generating this level of confusion by the use of a suppressor only works when the observer is within an arc of about 150 degrees in front of the shooter. Suppressors are less effective when observers are to either side of the shooter. Observers behind the shooter can locate the source of a suppressed shot from the direction of the sound as readily as if the shooter was using an unsuppressed rifle, as long as they can hear the ballistic crack. (Of course, if an observer can hear the muzzle blast or action noise from behind the shooter, then locating the source of the shot is easy.)

Using a suppressor with supersonic ammunition confuses downrange observers because the brain interprets the location of the sound as perpendicular to the shock wave generated by the bullet. The amount of confusion is actually determined by three variables: bullet speed, distance between the observer and the shooter, and distance between the observer and the bullet flight path. Equations can be used to precisely calculate the amount of anticipated observer bias (the angle between the real and apparent location of the shooter) at a given temperature.

Ironically, when subsonic ammunition is used, an observer near the bullet flight path can frequently follow the "swishing" flight noise of the bullet back to the source of the shot. If a target is missed, he or she may have a pretty good idea where to shoot back, depending on such factors as environmental conditions and observer alertness.

2. Using a suppressor dramatically reduces the amount of energy available to disturb grass, leaves, twigs, and dust. This mitigates one of the greatest risks to a sniper's survival.

3. Although flash hiders can be quite effective at eliminating flash, which can be the most dramatic giveaway of a shooter's position, they do nothing to tame recoil. And recoil compensators do not eliminate flash. All suppressors provide a substantial reduction of recoil, and properly designed suppressors dampen muzzle flash more effectively than flash hiders.

Thus a suppressor, combined with good fieldcraft, can maximize the effectiveness and survivability of a sniper. One aspect of good fieldcraft that is rarely discussed, yet could easily negate the advantages of using a suppressor, relates to the ejection of brass.

The ejection of a spent cartridge case can catch sunlight and blaze for an instant, like a camera flash. In Vietnam, U.S. snipers found that the flash of expended brass was one of the best tools for locating enemy shooters. This phenomenon is the main reason why most military snipers prefer manually operated, rather than semiautomatic, rifles. Admittedly, at least in theory, manually operated rifles should also be capable of better accuracy and reliability. When ejecting a case from a bolt-action rifle, the operator should operate the bolt slowly and quietly until he can palm the empty case. Never leaving behind the spent cases (or food wrappers or other artifacts) has become a common operational theme so that the enemy cannot readily detect where the sniper's hide was located. This makes tracking the sniper and anticipating future hide locations much more difficult. Getting back to the stealthy ejection of a spent case, it is desirable, if circumstances permit, to actually move the rifle under the operator's body to help muffle the sound and to shield any possible glint from the brass case.

Even as suppressor technology has matured dramatically in recent years, one aspect of stealthy shooting remains virtually ignored: the bright reflective finish of the brass cartridge case. Surely a manufacturer could develop a practical coating process that would give the case a nonreflective black finish. That would greatly facilitate the speed of follow-up shots and might also make semiautomatic rifles more practical for military sniping. Nonreflective black cases would certainly complement the use of a suppressor.

As previously mentioned, sound suppressors are useful for reducing recoil as well as muzzle blast. The definitive work on this subject was conducted in Finland, and is worth examining.

REDUCING MUZZLE BLAST AND RECOIL

Dr. Rauno Pääkkönen of the Tampere Regional Institute of Occupational Health and Illka Kyttälä of the Ministry of Labor in Finland have conducted the most interesting research to date on the effects of rifle-caliber muzzle brakes and sound suppressors on such important performance

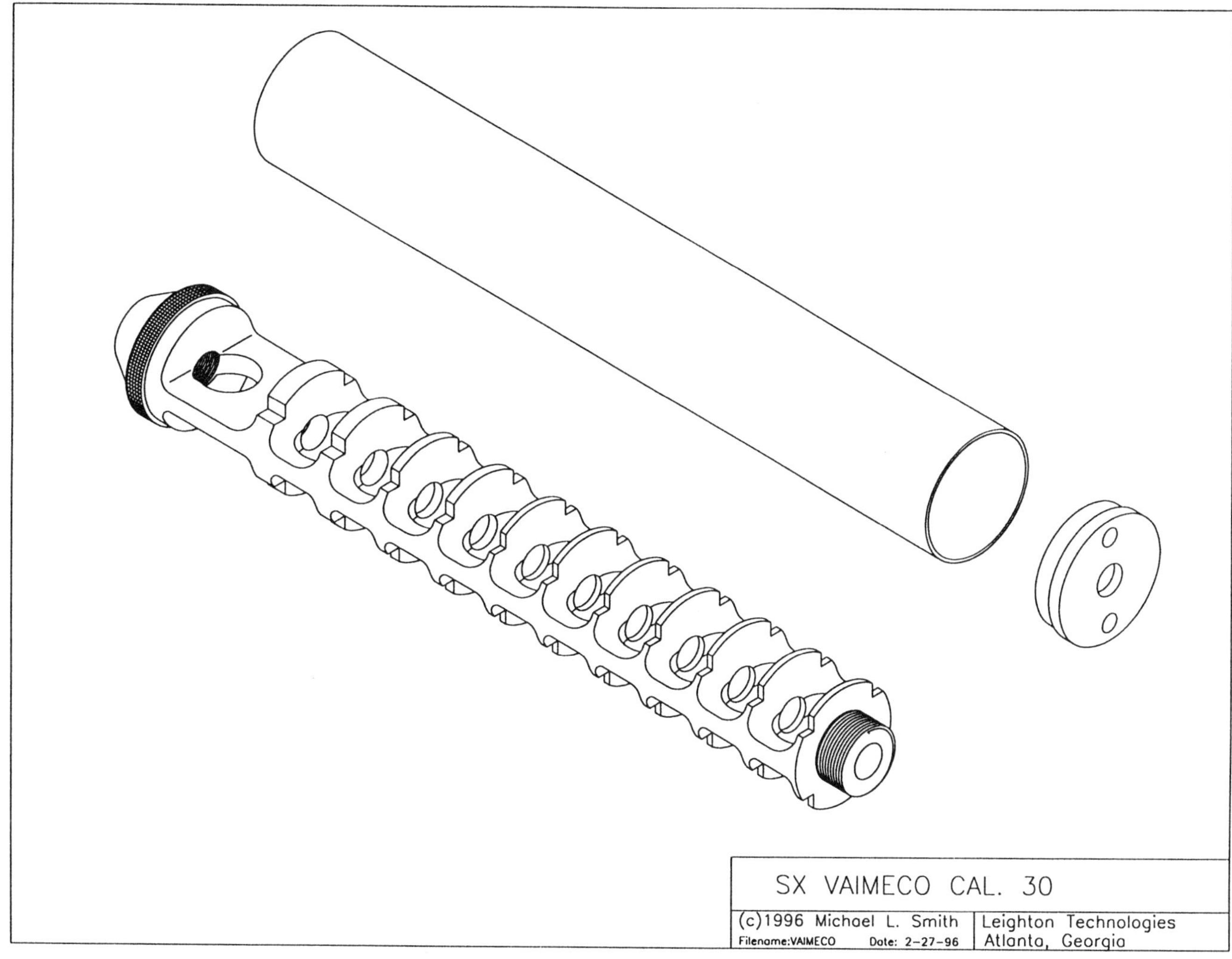

Figure 4.1. Vaimeco suppressor design. Drawing by Mike Smith.

criteria as muzzle blast, recoil, and accuracy. The following discussion is distilled from their paper published in the April 1994 issue of the science journal *Acta Acoustica (*Pääkkönen and Kyttälä, 1994b). This work was part of the large interdisciplinary study cited in the previous chapter on hearing protection.

For this particular study, Pääkkönen and Kyttälä used 7.62x51mm (.308 Winchester) hunting rifles that were threaded for muzzle brakes and sound suppressors. Both a conventional muzzle can made by Vaimeco and a reflex suppressor made by BR-Tuote were tested (see Figures 4.1 and 4.2), along with 12 muzzle brakes sharing the general features shown in Figure 4.3. They conducted sound tests with Lapua supersonic and subsonic ammunition, measuring sound signatures at both the shooter's left ear and 10.9 yards (10 m) to the right of the shooter at a height of 63 inches (1.6 m). They measured recoil using a ballistic pendulum, which held the firearm at the end of a 39.37 inch (1.00 m) arm to which a weight was added to reduce the angle of rotation during recoil. Accuracy tests were conducted at the Lapua Oy range using a machine rest that incorporated a spring mechanism to absorb recoil. Here's what they learned.

Muzzle brakes significantly increased the sound pressure level at the shooter's ear, from an average peak SPL of 159 db without the muzzle brake to an average of 167 dB with muzzle brake (see Table 4.1 on page 60, and Figures 4.4 and 4.5). That 8 dB difference represents a significant

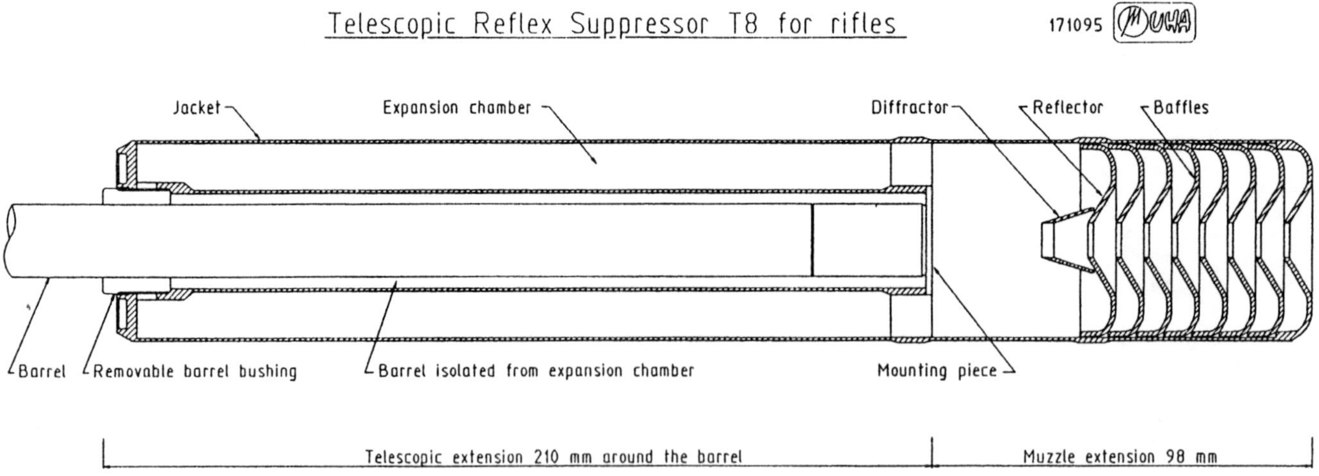

Figure 4.2. Reflex suppressor designed by Juha Hartikka and manufactured by Asesepänliike BR-Tuote Ky.

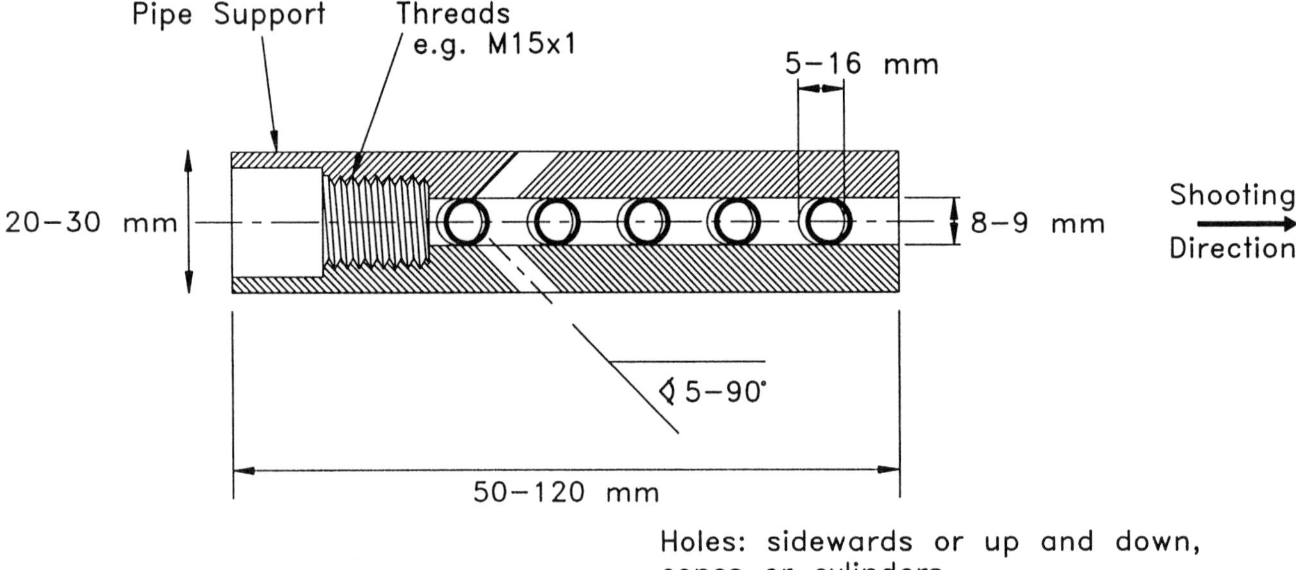

Figure 4.3. General features of the 12 muzzle brakes studied by Pääkkönen and Kyttälä. Redrawn by Mike Smith.

increase in both discomfort and health risk. The muzzle brakes were effective, however, at reducing recoil momentum from 10.9 to 6.2 kg m/s, which represents a 43 percent reduction. Converting the SPLs shown in Table 4.1 to *sound exposure levels* (which include a time factoring to quantify health risk), then the data display a linear correlation between the sound exposure level and recoil momentum. As Figure 4.6 shows, those muzzle brakes most effective at reducing recoil also produced the greatest risk to the shooter's hearing.

Tables 4.2 and 4.3 (page 61) show the results of testing with and without suppressors at the shooter's left ear and 10 meters to the right of the shooter, respectively. The BR-Tuote reflex suppressor, which only extends a few centimeters beyond the muzzle of the rifle, produced a modest net sound reduction of 18 dB at the shooter's ear. The reflex suppressor did, however,

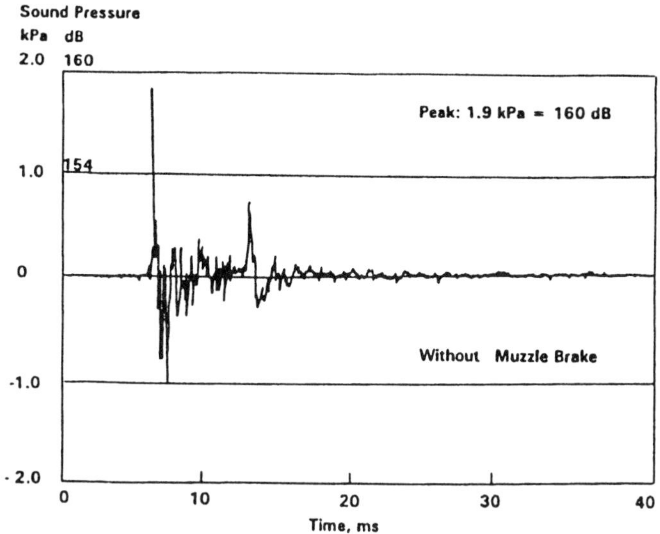

Figure 4.4. Time analysis of sound pressure level produced by 7.62x51mm hunting rifle without muzzle brake, measured at the left ear of the shooter (used with permission from Pääkkönen and Kyttälä, 1994b).

Sound Pressure
kPa dB
5.0 168
2.5 162
0
-2.5
-5.0
Peak: 4.6 kPa = 167 dB
With Muzzle Brake
0 10 20 30 40
Time, ms

Figure 4.5. Time analysis of sound pressure level produced by 7.62x51mm hunting rifle with muzzle brake, measured at the left ear of the shooter (used with permission from Pääkkönen and Kyttälä, 1994b).

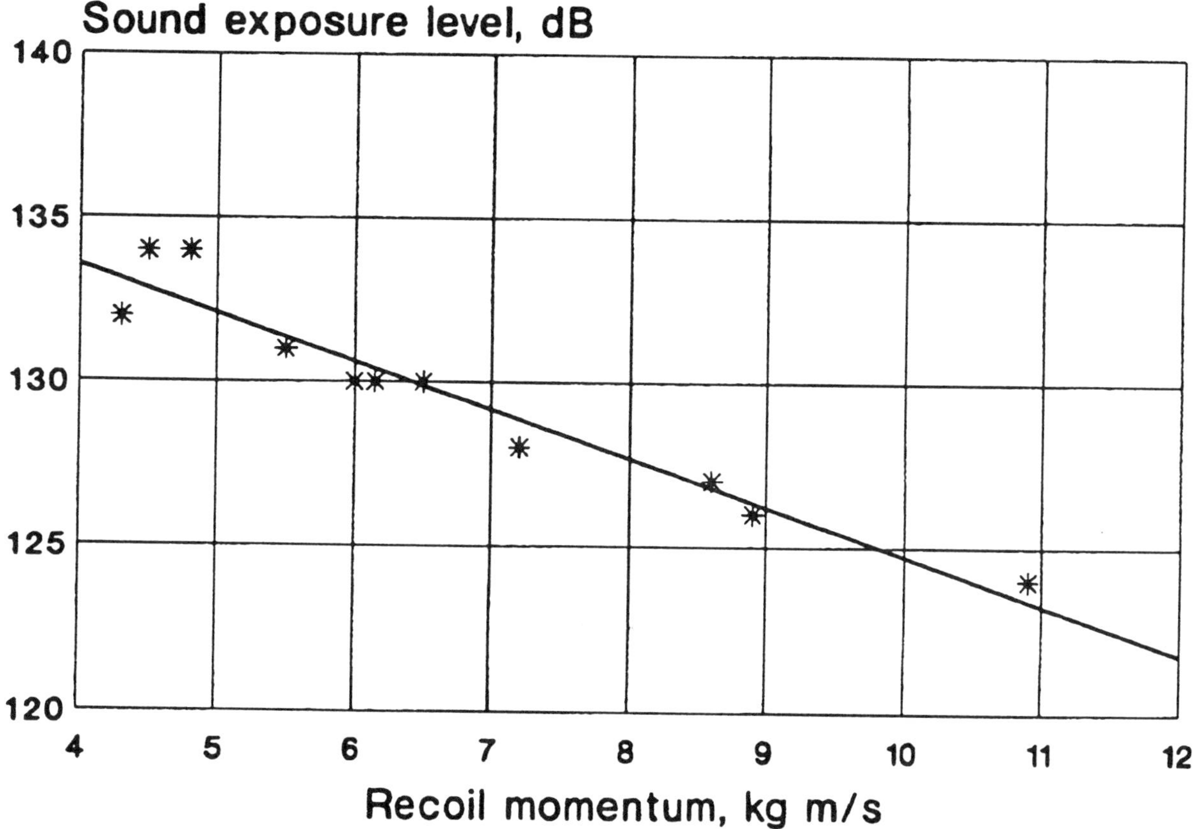

Figure 4.6. The linear correlation between sound exposure level and recoil momentum shows that those muzzle brakes which are most effective at reducing recoil also produce the greatest risk to the shooter's hearing (used with permission from Pääkkönen and Kyttälä, 1994b).

reduce the recoil energy from 23 to 15 joules, which represents a reduction of 35 percent. The more traditional Vaimeco muzzle can extends well beyond the muzzle and provides an impressive 35 dB sound reduction. Using Lapua subsonic ammunition, the Vaimeco suppressor delivers an amazing 41 dB reduction at the shooter's ear.

When Pääkkönen and Kyttälä looked at how these suppressors affected accuracy, they found no difference in group size with or without either suppressor. The average point of impact did, however, move downward 60 to 70 millimeters (2.4 to 2.8 inches) at 100 meters (109 yards). Simply adjusting a rifle's sights corrected for this phenomenon.

A suppressor, like the BR-Tuote T4AR on this M16, reduces both muzzle flash and recoil even when the weapon is fired on full auto. Note the lack of muzzle climb even though three empty cases are clearly visible. Photo by Juha Hartikka.

This research is relevant to tactical users, since recoil reduction is particularly desirable in weapons using a cartridge larger than the 7.62x51mm round. Using a suppressor with .300 Winchester Magnum rifles, for example, permits extended training without shooter fatigue. The suppressor also reduces the risk of both short-term and long-term hearing loss by the sniper, spotter, and training cadre. Using a suppressor to mitigate recoil with the increasingly popular .50 BMG sniper rifles is especially valuable in both the training and tactical environments. Not only is fatigue a more serious problem with this big boomer, the recoil impulse of unsilenced .50 caliber rifles has separated more than one shoulder, thus rendering the shooters *hors de combat* for a period of months. Mounting a suppressor on a .50 caliber rifle reduces the recoil impulse and thus reduces the risk of shoulder injury, while reducing overpressure that pounds the face and eardrums of the shooter. Of course, the other benefits of suppressor use are even more valuable with a .50 caliber BMG rifle, especially the reduction of muzzle flash and environmental disturbances that can disclose the position of the shooter.

There are two main liabilities of .50 caliber suppressors: they are large and heavy. Since a .50 caliber sniper rifle is essentially viewed as a crew-served weapon because of its size and weight, the additional burden of a massive suppressor is mitigated somewhat. Nevertheless, the impedimenta carried by the modern soldier is already burdensome, to say the least, and the additional bulk added by a .50 caliber suppressor must be considered.

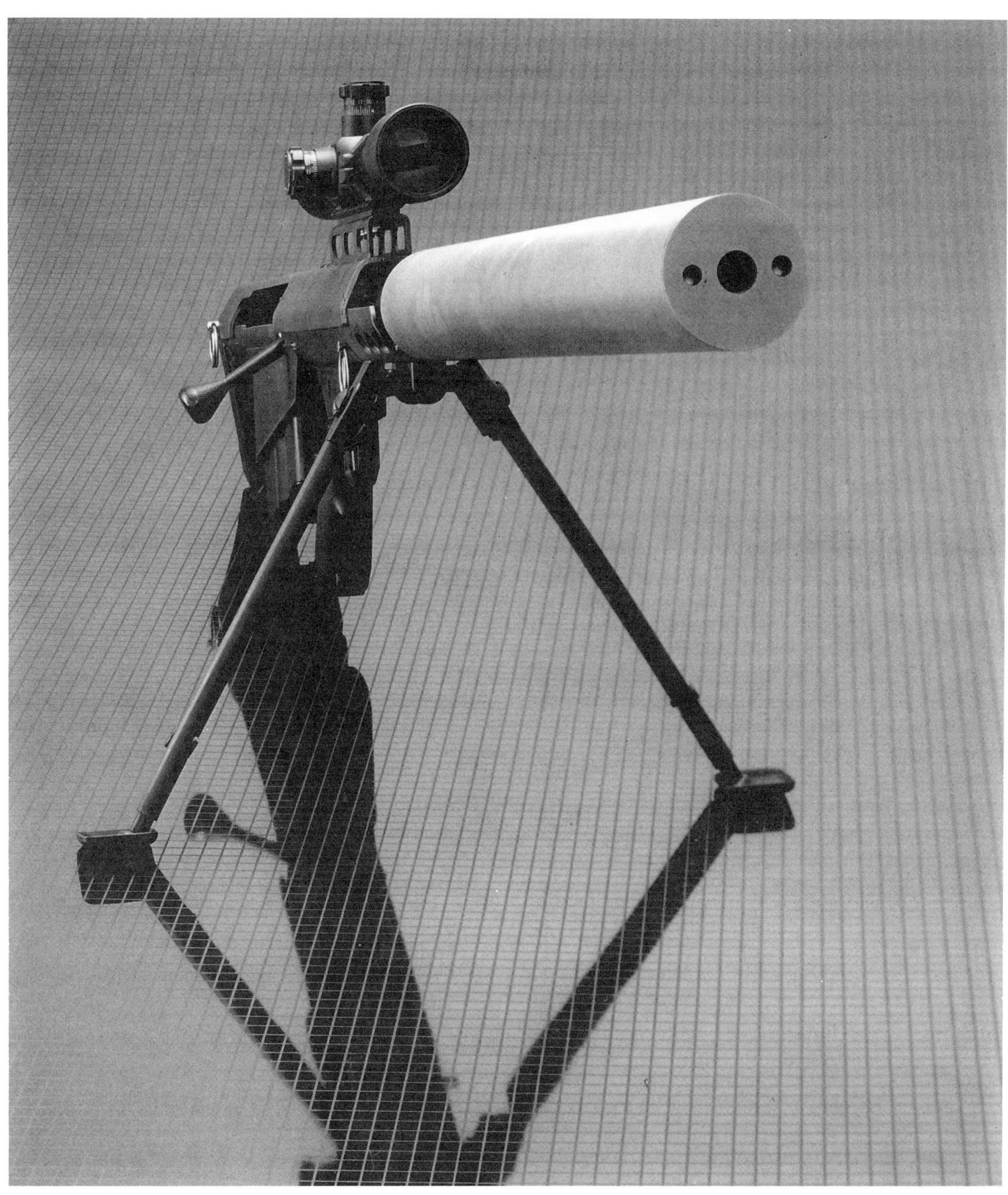

A suppressor is particularly useful for reducing muzzle flash and recoil when shooting big boomers like this Barrett Model 50 bolt-action sniper rifle. The .50 caliber titanium SIOPTS Model SO-50 suppressor measures 2x20 inches (5.1x50.8 cm) and weighs 4.5 pounds (2.5 kg).

Table 4.1. Peak sound pressure levels at the left ear of a shooter using a 7.62x51mm hunting rifle with and without a muzzle brake and the resulting recoil momentum. All data in this table were generated using Lapua supersonic ammunition and were originally published by Pääkkönen and Kyttälä (1994b).

MUZZLE BRAKE	PEAK SPL, dB	INCREASE AT EAR, dB	RECOIL MOMENTUM, kg m/s
None	159[a]	n/a	10.9
Löppönen	168	9	6.2
Pirkan ase	169	10	4.7
Laxmit	168	9	5.5
Vaimeco	169	10	5.5
Arctic Arms	169	10	4.3
Asesepät 1	167	8	6.5
Asesepät 2	167	8	6.3
BR-Tuote	165	6	7.3
MH-Työkalu	164	5	8.7
Konkola 1	169	10	4.5
Konkola 2	161	2	8.9
Kanu	167	8	—
Mean	167	8	6.2
Standard deviation	2.5	2.5	1.6

[a] Lapua subsonic 7.62x51mm ammunition produced a peak SPL of 147 dB

Table 4.2. Peak sound pressure levels measured at shooter's left ear using a 7.62x51mm hunting rifle with and without a sound suppressor and the resulting recoil momentum. Data were originally published by Pääkkönen and Kyttälä (1994b).

MUZZLE BRAKE	AMMUNITION	PEAK SPL, dB	NET SOUND REDUCTION, dB	KINETIC ENERGY OF RECOIL, JOULES
None	Lapua supersonic	163	n/a	23
None	Lapua subsonic	163	n/a	—
BR-Tuote T8L1	Lapua supersonic	145	18	15
Vaimeco	Lapua supersonic	128	35	—
Vaimeco	Lapua subsonic	122	41	—

Table 4.3. Peak sound pressure levels measured 10 meters to the right of a shooter using a 7.62x51mm hunting rifle with and without a sound suppressor. Data were originally published by Pääkkönen and Kyttälä (1994b).

MUZZLE BRAKE	AMMUNITION	PEAK SPL, dB	NET SOUND REDUCTION, dB
None	Lapua supersonic	147	n/a
None	Lapua subsonic	145	n/a
BR-Tuote T8L1	Lapua supersonic	127	20
Vaimeco	Lapua supersonic	122	25
Vaimeco	Lapua subsonic	109	36

ENHANCING COMMAND AND CONTROL

Using suppressed weapons during an unconventional operation enhances command and control for several reasons.

Suppressors facilitate verbal communications both directly (by lowering weapon noise) and indirectly (by eliminating temporary threshold shift of the operator and nearby personnel). Gunshot-induced TTS can last for a day or more. Furthermore, severe TTS is a particular problem if unsuppressed weapons are used in a confined space such as a building, ship, or aircraft. Temporary threshold shift not only impedes communication among the good guys, it also impedes the ability of the good guys to hear the movement and verbal communications of the bad guys.

The use of passive hearing protection devices (such as muffs or plugs) is incompatible with the maintenance of effective command and control. Active HPDs will permit effective command and control, but these electronic devices have liabilities discussed in the previous chapter and are subject to failure at inopportune moments. Suppressors are not subject to battery failure or a broken wire.

PRESERVING OPERATOR HEARING

As already discussed, the use of suppressed weapons dramatically reduces the risk of both temporary threshold shift and permanent threshold shift. This is an important consideration during training as well as during actual tactical operations. It's hard to overstate the value of using suppressors to reduce TTS and PTS.

OPERATING IN POTENTIALLY EXPLOSIVE ATMOSPHERES

Both military and law enforcement operations are sometimes conducted in environments with potentially explosive atmospheric conditions. Muzzle flash might cause ignition in such environments as chemical plants, oil refineries, and illegal drug labs. Using a suppressor,

Using suppressed weapons, such as this BR-Tuote T4AUG suppressor on a Steyr AUG, can dramatically enhance command and control in the CQB (Close Quarter Battle) envelope. Photo by Juha Hartikka.

Using a suppressor on a rifle, whether during training or a tactical operation in an enclosed space, can reduce the operator's risk of both short- and long-term hearing loss. Photo by Juha Hartikka.

The SCRC MK-26 suppressor is designed to eliminate muzzle flash as an ignition source when operating in potentially explosive atmospheres.

preferably with special low-flash ammunition, can reduce the risk of muzzle flash causing an explosion. Two approaches show promise: using a suppressor with wipes to contain the flash, and using a wet suppressor to prevent the flash.

The SCRC Model MK-26 suppressor, which will be evaluated in the third volume of *Silencer History and Performance*, is an example of the former. When mated to an MP5 submachine gun, this suppressor (unlike many designs) seems to eliminate ejection port flash, which can also provide a source of atmospheric ignition. The safest route, however, is to use a manually operated, locked-breech weapon so that ejection port flash is no longer a potential issue.

Arms Tech, Inc. manufactures a matched artificial-environment suppressor and low-flash ammunition specifically designed to minimize the risk of detonation when operating in explosive atmospheres, although each weapon must be individually tested to ensure the absence of ejection port flash even with this system. The Russians use captive-piston ammunition, which contains the by-products of ignition within the cartridge case, in special silenced weapons that provide the safest solution to this operational requirement.

Arms Tech has also developed a captive-piston round for use in potentially explosive atmospheres. Called the 6mm Hazmat, this round and weapons for it are available for sale only to government clients in the United States.

The last word in this chapter on the tactical use of suppressors belongs to Clint Smith, the director and head trainer at Thunder Ranch. “Don’t forget,” he admonishes, “incoming fire has the right of way.”

CHAPTER FIVE

MEASURING SUPPRESSOR PERFORMANCE

ilencers work by reducing the energy content of a gun's muzzle blast. Some suppressors also change the frequency content of the muzzle blast away from the range of greatest human sensitivity. But the most important mechanism in suppressor performance is reducing the energy content of combustion gases. Muzzle blast is actually a pressure wave, which can be measured accurately with appropriate equipment. There are several ways to visualize a muzzle blast.

In simplistic terms, the spatial aspects of muzzle blast can be visualized as a three-dimensional version of the two-dimensional wave created when a stone is cast into calm water. More energy input, such as using a bigger stone or throwing an identical stone harder, will make a bigger wave on the water. The spatial aspects of muzzle blast can be measured using a number of sound meters appropriately spaced around a firearm to provide a rigorous view of impulse propagation around the gun.

The temporal aspects of muzzle blast can be visualized by the changes in sound pressure level that occur at one place during a gunshot using appropriate sound-test equipment. The amount of pressure generated by a muzzle blast is measured over time, yielding a plot that would look like Figure 5.1 under theoretically ideal circumstances. A short burst of acoustic energy characterized by a rapid rise to peak pressure, followed by a somewhat slower decay to ambient pressure, is called *impulse noise.*

The muzzle blast begins with an instantaneous increase in pressure to a peak level. This peak pressure then decays at a fairly brisk rate until the pressure falls to the ambient pressure that existed before the impulse began. The time between the beginning of the instantaneous pressure increase until the pressure returns to the ambient level is called the *A-duration* (not to be confused with "A" weighting, which is discussed later in this chapter and relates to frequency filtering). The A-duration is the duration of the primary pressure wave generated by the impulse. A precision impulse sound meter measures the height of the peak that occurs during the A-duration. The impulse event does not end here, however.

Pressure continues to fall below the ambient level for a while and then returns to the ambient level. At least that's the way things work in theory. The reality is a bit muddier, thanks in large measure to various surfaces and materials in the experimental area, some of which tend to reflect sound waves back at the microphone, some of which tend to absorb or attenuate the sound waves, and some of which do both. In the real world, an actual impulse noise looks like Figure 5.2.

Actual pressure versus time plots of suppressed and unsuppressed gunshots appear in Figures 5.3 and 5.4 and are adapted from an article in *Acta*

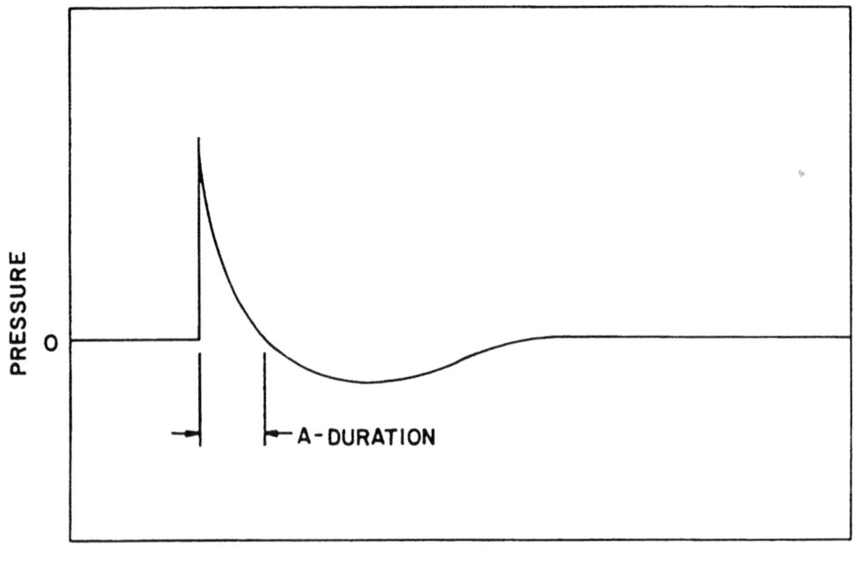

Figure 5.1. The amount of pressure generated by a muzzle blast is measured over time, yielding a plot that would look like this under theoretically ideal circumstances. The time between the beginning of the instantaneous pressure increase until the pressure returns to the ambient level is called the A-duration (from U.S. Army Missile Command, 1993).

A firearm's sound signature is only one part of a system's overall performance equation. Projectile velocity is another. Mounting a muzzle can on a pistol provides substantially more velocity than most integrally suppressed pistols with comparable barrel length. This translates into a flatter trajectory and noticeably more energy delivered to the target.

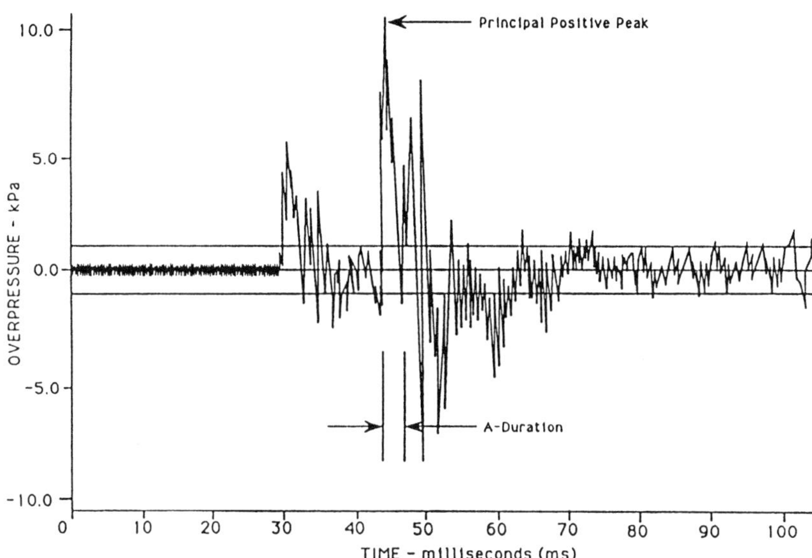

Figure 5.2. In the real world, an actual impulse noise looks more complicated thanks in large measure to various surfaces and materials in the experimental area, some of which tend to reflect sound waves back at the microphone, some of which tend to absorb or attenuate the sound waves, and some of which do both (from U.S. Army Missile Command, 1993).

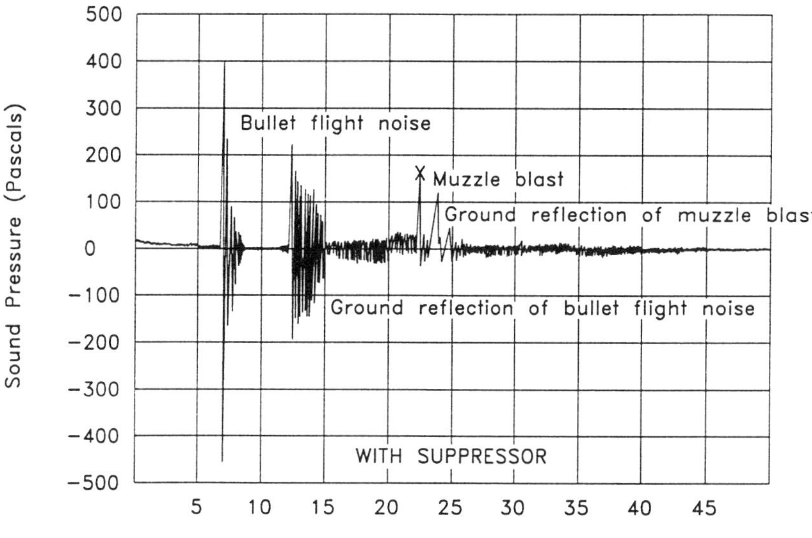

Figure 5.3. Actual pressure versus time plot of a suppressed gunshot (redrawn by Mike Smith from Pääkkönen and Kyttälä, 1994a).

Acoustica by Rauno Pääkkönen and Ilkka Kyttälä (1994a). While these figures convey a great deal of useful information, several conclusions are particularly important for understanding suppressor performance as viewed by the shooter as well as by observers downrange and behind the shooter.

The first thing to notice is that the scales on the Y-axis of each graph are different, so each plot can convey the maximum amount of information.

One of the most important things to learn is that the A-duration of a suppressed gunshot is significantly shorter than the A-duration of an unsuppressed gunshot. Even if the suppressor did not reduce the peak sound pressure level of a gunshot, the shorter A-duration would make it seem slightly quieter. Zwislocki (1966) and others have shown that, for sounds shorter than 200 milliseconds, loudness is proportional to both sound pressure and duration. Therefore, decreasing the duration of an impulse by one-half would have about the same effect as decreasing the sound pressure level by 3 dB.

A much more important implication relates to the selection of suitable sound-test equipment. A meter capable of responding fast enough to accurately record an unsuppressed muzzle blast may not respond fast enough to accurately record the shorter duration suppressed blast. This is the single most important cause of misinformation in the public domain.

Also notice that bullet flight noise is louder than the muzzle blast when a suppressor is used. This has important tactical implications, and should also be taken into account when considering the use of suppressors to reduce the temporary and permanent threshold shift that can be experienced by shooters.

Finally, notice the importance of reflected sound to the overall impulse event. This has implications when trying to understand the propagation of sound around a weapon. Impulse propagation is an important phenomenon, whether an individual is using a suppressor for sporting purposes, hearing protection, or tactical applications.

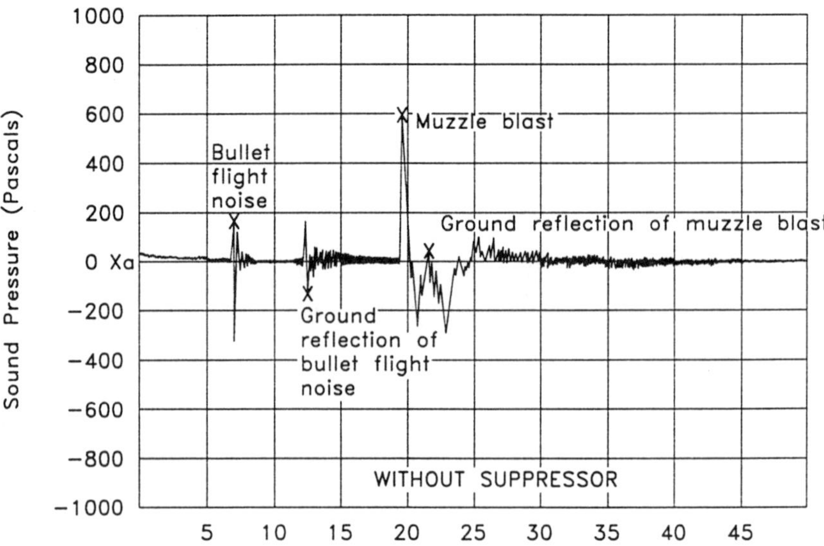

Figure 5.4. Actual pressure versus time plot of an unsuppressed gunshot (redrawn by Mike Smith from Pääkkönen and Kyttälä, 1994a).

IMPULSE PROPAGATION AROUND A WEAPON

The Inverse Square Law is frequently used to describe the theoretical attenuation of sound pressure level over distance.

$$S = 1/r^2$$

where S is the sound pressure level in decibels, and r is the distance from the sound source.

A workable rule of thumb is that muzzle blast of a firearm attenuates by 6 dB with every doubling of the distance (in meters) from the muzzle.

The reality is a bit more complex, however. Juha Tikkanen and Rauno Pääkkönen (1990) have conducted some of the most interesting research to date on the propagation of impulse noise around a wide range of personal and crew-served weapons. Figure 5.5 compares their results for a rifle and a bazooka. Notice that

Dr. Rauno Pääkkönen (left) and Illka Kyttälä measuring the sound signature of a BR-Tuote TX4 suppressor on M62 rifle fired by Kari Haantio at the Pyhäselkä shooting range in Finland. Photo by Juha Hartikka.

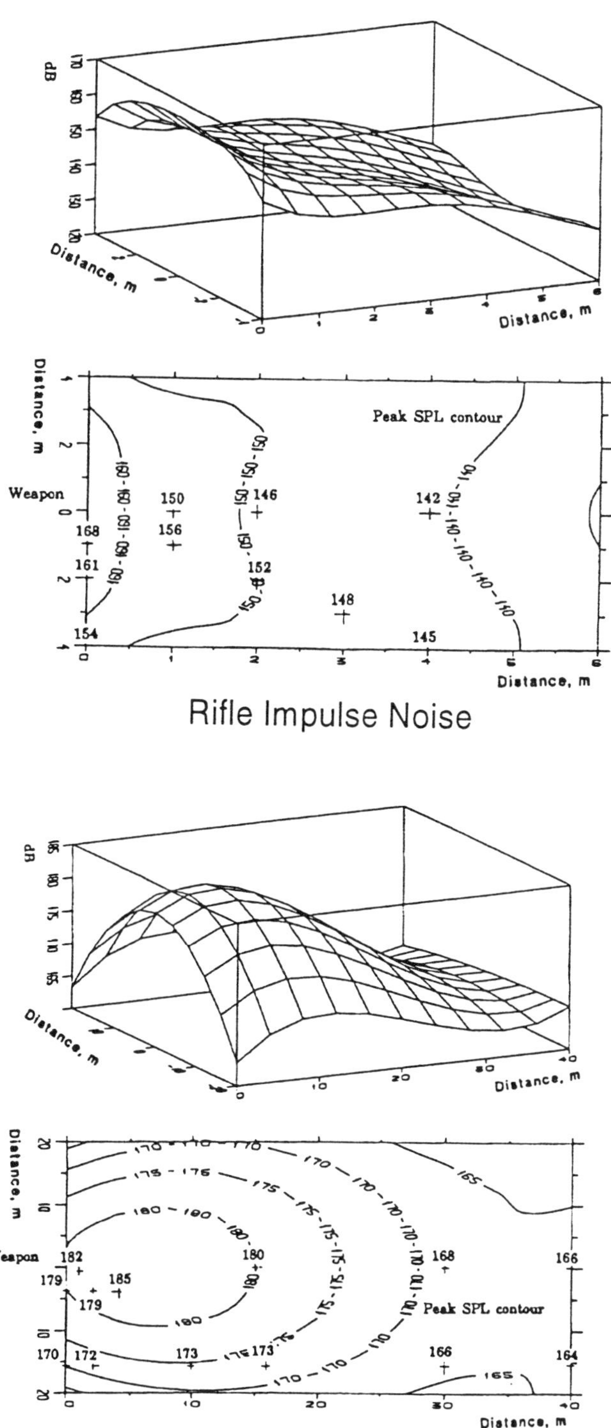

Figure 5.5. Propagation of impulse noise around a rifle (top two illustrations) and a bazooka (bottom two illustrations). Notice that the sound pressure levels drop quickly behind the rifle but increase behind the bazooka because of rocket exhaust (used with permission from Tikkanen and Pääkkönen, 1990).

the sound pressure levels drop quickly behind the rifle but increase behind the bazooka because of rocket exhaust.

Generally speaking, their results showed that a diverse array of weapons acted as elliptically radiating noise sources. The only exceptions were cannons fired at a high angle, howitzers, and mortars; these weapons acted as spherically radiating noise sources. Tikkanen and Pääkkönen always found that the shooter had a significant shielding effect with all weapons of rifle caliber, so measured sound pressure levels were always less directly behind the shooter. Suppressors magnified this effect. Recoilless rocket launchers (such as bazookas and LAWs) produced two sound impulses (one behind the shooter and one in front), so these weapons show an atypical pressure profile.

Figure 5.5 shows the results behind the shooters in part because projectile flight noise adds an additional level of complexity in front of a weapon. Bullet flight noise becomes an especially important phenomenon when using small arms in the tactical environment.

BULLET FLIGHT NOISE

Bullet flight noise is an important component of a firearm's overall sound signature, especially when a suppressor is employed. The projectile essentially creates a three-dimensional, cone-shaped wake in air not unlike the two-dimensional wake created by a boat in water. The cone-shaped pressure wave generated by a supersonic projectile is sometimes called a Mach wave. Actually, the projectile forms two cone-shaped waves, one emanating from the point of the projectile and one emanating from the base.

Since the wake travels at a speed of Mach 1, while most rifle projectiles travel around Mach 2 or so at typical engagement distances, individuals downrange commonly experience a noticeable time delay between hearing the ballistic crack from the bullet and the muzzle blast from the rifle. This enables the downrange observer to accurately estimate the

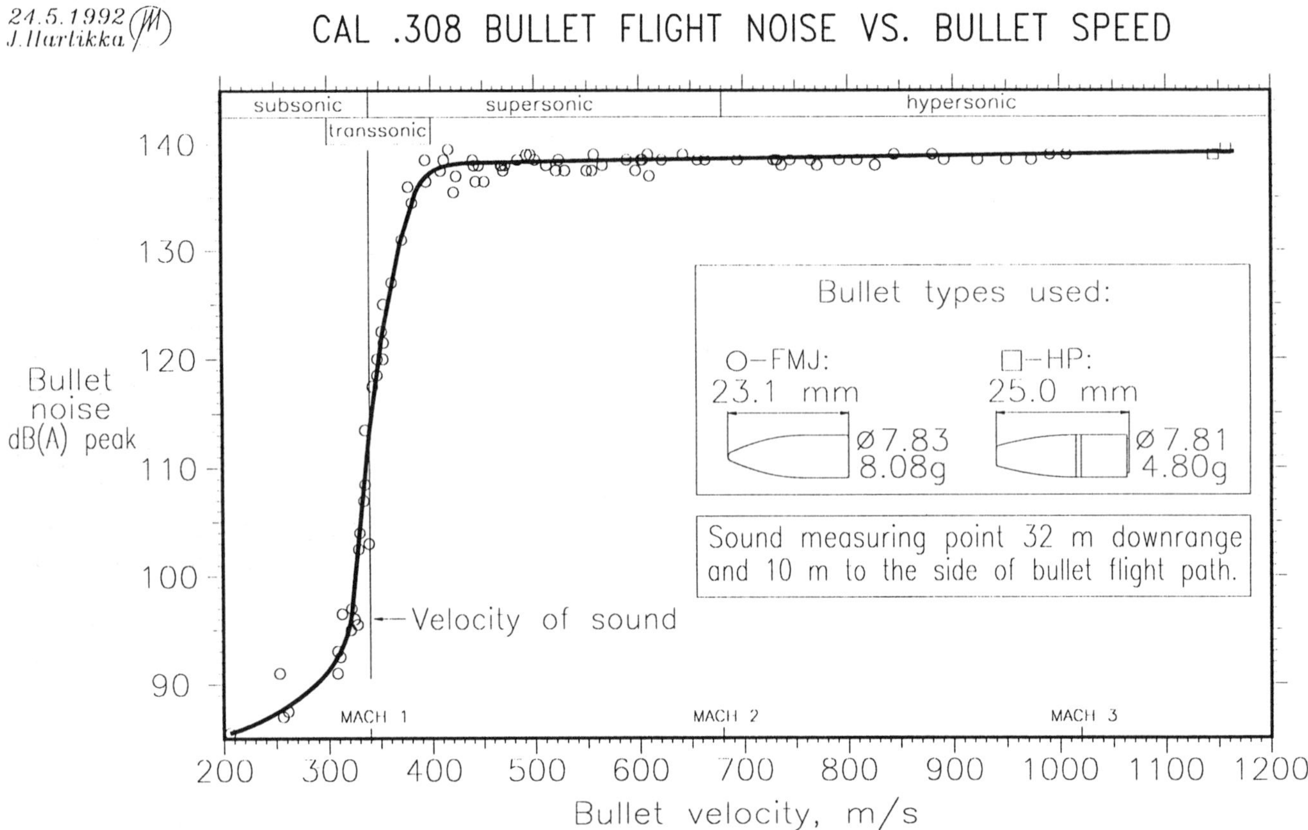

Figure 5.6. Bullet flight noise generated by 7.62x51mm cartridges as a function of velocity (English captions added by Mike Smith to AutoCad file provided by Juha Hartikka).

location of the shooter because of three interrelated factors: 1) the human brain concludes that the source of a sound is perpendicular to the wave front of the sound; 2) the muzzle blast is distinctly separated in time from the bullet flight noise; and 3) the muzzle blast is the last element of the weapon's sound signature perceived by the downrange observer. This makes it easy to estimate the location of the shooter. Obviously, any supersonic projectile will generate a perceived delay that is inversely proportional to bullet speed and directly proportional to distance between the shooter and the observer. Thus, slower bullets and longer distances increase the time between the perception of these events.

When a suppressor is used, however, the downrange observer is likely to notice only the ballistic crack of the bullet. This will cause the observer to misinterpret the location of the shooter, as discussed in the previous chapter.

The reactions of the shooter and an observer behind the shooter are more difficult to understand. At first glance, it is tempting to infer that the muzzle blast and onset of the ballistic crack originate within several meters of each other relative to the shooter or observer behind the shooter. It would then follow logically that both pressure waves reach the shooter and observer behind the shooter at the same time, as far as the brain is concerned. Of course, appropriate sound equipment responds faster than human hearing and recognizes that the bullet flight noise reaches the microphone before the muzzle blast, as shown in Figures 5.3 and 5.4. But there is a proverbial fly in the ointment.

The wake of the bullet (i.e., the bullet flight noise) has been traditionally thought to propagate

P.T. Kekkonen conducting research on the effect of bullet velocity on bullet flight noise using a Tikka M65 rifle featuring a 7.62x51mm heavy barrel, "coat-hanger" stock designed by Juha Hartikka, and BR-Tuote T8 suppressor. Every single cartridge used to generate Figure 5.6 was handloaded just prior to firing it. Photo by Juha Hartikka.

downrange and expand outward away from the line of flight. Thus, the bullet flight noise propagates away from the shooter and away from any observer behind the shooter. This explains why Hiram Maxim could shoot his Model J silencer on a Springfield M1903 rifle straight up into the air and perceive no ballistic crack from the .30-06 bullet. Then how can a shooter possibly hear a ballistic crack if the wave is propagating downrange and away from the muzzle of a suppressed firearm? Even more curious—how can an observer behind the suppressed firearm hear the ballistic crack?

I originally suspected that ground reflection of the bullet wake provides most of the flight noise perceived by the shooter. I assumed that a reflection from a diverse array of environmental surfaces (e.g., trees, bushes, surface relief of the ground) enables an observer behind the shooter to hear bullet flight noise. Since shooters rarely operate in an environment totally devoid of reflective surfaces, an observer behind the shooter can usually hear the ballistic crack of a supersonic projectile. This seems to explain why Maxim was able to shoot his silenced Springfield down a line of telegraph poles and hear a machine gun-like burst of ballistic cracks as the wake of the supersonic projectile reflected off the succession of poles.

Very recent work by Augustine Lee at the Defense Science and Technology Organization in Australia has shown this view of the bullet flight noise to be a bit simplistic, however. Lee has developed a relatively low-cost, LED-based schlieren imaging system for photographing bullets and gas pressure waves coming out of barrels and suppressors. He is generating some revolutionary images. It turns out that reflection is not the only mechanism that directs energy from the bullet wake back at the shooter. Lee's images show that the shock wave generated by the projectile actually bends around the muzzle of a barrel or the front of a suppressor and travels backward as a half-spherical pressure wave. Although the intensity of this backward-moving wave is considerably less than the conical Mach wave traveling downrange, the energy content can still be significant.

Another surprise from Lee's images is that the pressure waves emanating from the point and from the base of a bullet are not always parallel, especially within 4 inches (10 cm) of the projectile. Furthermore, he's used this technique to actually show how the behavior of combustion gases differs when using four-baffle versus eight-baffle suppressors. Anyone with reasonably intact hearing can tell that the eight-baffle suppressor is quieter than the four-baffle design. Anyone with appropriate sound-test equipment can measure how much quieter the eight-baffle design is. But

Lee's imagery allows one to actually *see how* the eight-baffle design works better. One can only hope that Lee's brilliant work will be published in the open literature some day.

Supersonic projectiles generate conspicuous flight noise, but the shooter rarely hears the flight noise of *subsonic* bullets when shooting centerfire cartridges of rifle or pistol caliber from a suppressed firearm. The remaining muzzle blast tends to be 5 to 15 dB louder than the bullet flight noise. The only time I've personally heard the flight noise of a subsonic bullet while firing a suppressed centerfire rifle involved shooting Sako subsonic tracer 7.62x51mm ammunition from a McMillan M89 sniper rifle with AWC M89 suppressor. The M89 suppressor was so effective that I could actually hear the sizzle of the burning tracer material as the bullet traveled downrange. That was a savory experience.

Even with suppressed rimfires, muzzle blast or action noise tends to mask the bullet flight noise as far as the shooter is concerned. If, however, the firearm is manually operated and the suppressor is exceptionally effective, then a soft hissing can sometimes be heard traveling downrange as the sound is reflected back.

There is one notable exception, however, to the limited perception of subsonic flight noise as experienced by the shooter. If the bullet grazes a baffle or end cap inside the suppressor, then the bullet will be deformed to some degree. Deformation increases turbulence, which can increase the amount of sound generated by the projectile in flight. If substantial deformation has occurred, then the resultant flight noise is much louder and is perceived as a hard and pronounced arrow-like sound. Once heard, this product of baffle contact can never be mistaken for another sound. This unique sound is most pronounced when shooting lead—as opposed to jacketed—bullets, since the former are more easily deformed. I should note, however, that a bullet can graze a baffle just enough to ruin accuracy without creating this distinctive flight noise.

Scientists have conducted research to determine factors of bullet design and environmental conditions that affect the production and propagation of bullet flight noise. The results are particularly relevant when suppressors are used for sport shooting, training, and tactical operations. A brief look at these issues should prove insightful to the serious suppressor user who is concerned about the stealthiness of a suppressed gunshot.

STEALTHINESS OF A SUPPRESSED GUNSHOT

The stealthiness of a suppressed gunshot depends upon such obvious factors as muzzle blast, muzzle flash, action noise, ambient (background) noise, and bullet flight noise. Less obvious factors that might affect stealthiness include the human threshold for detecting different kinds of impulse noise, projectile shape and velocity, atmospheric and geographic factors, skill and attentiveness of the observer, and human detection limits for impulse noise.

Back in 1966, the U.S. Army Human Engineering Laboratory (HEL) published a fascinating report entitled, *Acoustical Considerations for a Silent Weapons System: A Feasibility Study*. The report describes the acoustical requirements that would make a Silent Weapons System (SWS) truly undetectable by enemy personnel in or near the target area. They ignored the easier design goal of providing a silenced weapon system that merely hides the location of the shooter but does not hide the fact that a shot has been fired.

The researchers looked at the information received by a downrange observer when he hears the firing of weapons using supersonic and subsonic projectiles. The scientists measured both actual flight noise and detection distances. They studied factors such as projectile shape on flight noise. And they tested several silenced weapons to determine actual detection distances. Some of the results remain extremely valuable to tactical users of suppressed firearms, while other results do not translate well to suppressed arms of rifle and pistol caliber. Finnish research plugged those gaps.

The stealthiness of a suppressed gunshot depends on a number of variables, including muzzle signature, projectile velocity, atmospheric conditions, ambient noise, and alertness of the observer. Here Marko Ruotsalainen is shooting a custom integrally suppressed Mosin-Nagant M1891 rifle rebarreled to 7.62x39mm and fitted with a Russian PSO-1 scope commonly seen on the SVD Dragunov sniper rifle. This rifle is particularly stealthy when subsonic ammunition is used. Photo by Juha Hartikka.

The quest for designing a truly silent weapon depends on the minimum impulse-sound level that a person can barely detect. While this quest has never attained its goal, what has been learned along the way has certainly influenced the evolution of tactical doctrine.

Human Detection Limits

HEL scientists used several sources to determine how close an observer needed to be to just barely detect several different types of impulse noise: 1) hammer fall produced by an M14 rifle, which produced an SPL of 108 dB at a distance of 2 meters; 2) the muzzle blast of an air rifle, which produced an SPL of 131 dB at 2 meters; and 3) the second "click" produced by a toy cricket, which produced an SPL of 110 dB at 2 meters. HEL scientists conducted a well-designed and executed series of experiments that quantified such variables as ambient noise level and factors that affect the attentiveness of the subjects.

Before designing the field studies, researchers used laboratory studies to determine the detection limits (in decibels) for observers of several different sources of impulse sound, since each source produced sounds with characteristic impulse frequencies and durations. The lab studies revealed an average detection threshold of 36 dB when two 2x4 inch boards were slapped together, 38 dB for the muzzle blast of an air rifle, and 42 dB for a toy cricket. The field tests attempted to control for both attentiveness of the test subject and ambient noise level by exposing the subjects to the conditions shown in Table 5.1. A well-established fact is that a listener's response to an auditory stimulus depends on the individual's mental and physical activity, since these factors influence concentration on the activities at hand and attentiveness to other stimuli.

The actual measurements varied considerably from day to day due to atmospheric conditions. In fact, meteorological conditions generated more variation in the data than the inherent capabilities of individual test subjects. For example, detection distances measured on a cold, windy morning were 121, 298, and 126 meters for the M14 hammer, air rifle, and cricket, respectively. Testing the following day while light drizzle was falling, the detection distances increased to 392, 512, and 341 meters respectively for these three sound sources.

Table 5.1. Detection distances (expressed in meters) for different impulse noises under different test conditions. Data from U.S. Army Human Engineering Laboratory.

TEST CONDITIONS	M14 HAMMER, AVERAGE (RANGE)	AIR RIFLE, AVERAGE (RANGE)	TOY CRICKET, AVERAGE (RANGE)
Expecting noise (in quiet)	200 (121-392)	394 (298-512)	180 (98-341)
Concentrating on matters other than noise, such as working a puzzle, writing a letter, or reading (in quiet)	91 (69-134)	213 (155-305)	117 (91-160)
Listening to speech (in quiet)	103 (75-137)	203 (137-283)	106 (80-124)
Walking through grass, as if on guard duty (in quiet)	117 (80-160)	227 (163-341)	112 (75-200)
Expecting the noise (standing 15 meters from a generator)	65 (50-89)	112 (75-200)	60 (45-101)

These results have important implications for modern tactical doctrine regarding the use of suppressors. Note that the M14 hammer and the cricket produce SPLs well below the flight noise produced by subsonic projectiles of rifle and pistol caliber. Also note that the air rifle produces SPLs that are about the same as the muzzle signature of a reasonably good submachine gun suppressor with subsonic ammunition. Finally, the air rifle is much quieter than the flight noise from a supersonic projectile of rifle or pistol caliber. Regrettably, I do not have any data at the time of this writing on the SPLs produced by bullet impact in flesh, for that would also make for a useful comparison.

Suffice it to say that these results demonstrate that relatively quiet impulse sounds can be detected at remarkable distances in open areas.

Bear in mind, however, that an increase in ambient noise, observer concentration on other matters such as a conversation or television, and the presence of intervening absorptive materials such as shrubbery or building walls can all have a profound effect on the detection distance of suppressed gunshots. Specific examples from my own experience in the real world are discussed in subsequent chapters where the muzzle blast and sometimes even bullet impact from suppressed gunshots were not detected by individuals 2 to 10 armspans away from the muzzle of the suppressors. Since environmental effects can have such a strong influence on the detectability of impulse sound, a few results from the HEL study are worth discussing.

Environmental Effects on Detectability

Both environmental conditions and boundary conditions profoundly affect the propagation and detectability of sound, especially over substantial distances. Under ideal circumstances, sound intensity decreases in a pattern of spherical divergence according to the Inverse Square Law, but Finnish research has demonstrated a more elliptical propagation from small arms, as already discussed (Tikkanen and Pääkkönen, 1990). Some factors that affect the attenuation of small-arms noise include 1) molecular absorption in air; 2) wind; 3) temperature gradients; 4) rain, snow, or fog; 5) absorptivity versus reflectivity of the ground; 6) absorption by trees and other vegetation; and 7) surface topography.

Although the HEL study did not address all of these factors, the final report does provide some interesting observations. Impulse sound, for example, carries farther when there is fog or a slight drizzle. Sound also carries farther when the ground is covered with snow. These phenomena occur in part because wind and temperature gradients are usually small during these conditions. Except during rain, sound also carries farther because background noise levels are usually lower during these conditions.

The effects of vegetation on sound propagation depend on the density of the vegetation and the frequency of the sound. Dense stands of evergreens, for example, attenuate sound in a linear fashion at a rate of 5 to 45 dB per 1,000 feet (305 meters) for frequencies from 40 to 3,300 Hz.

Boundaries that occlude the line of sight between the sound source and the observer inhibit the propagation of sound past those boundaries. Boundaries that do not occlude the line, however, tend to produce reflections that reach the observer and lengthen the duration of transient sounds, making the sound seem louder.

What about the U.S. Army's quest for a truly undetectable Silent Weapons System? It proved to be the impossible dream. Assuming that the SWS produced a sound signature with a frequency spectrum similar to an air rifle, the HEL research suggested that the SWS could only produce a muzzle blast of 92 dB and mechanical noise of 94 dB (measured at 10 meters) to remain undetectable to an *alert* sentry located 200 meters from the weapon. If the sentry was only 50 meters away, then the weapon noise could not exceed 60 dB at 10 meters.

If the sentry was not alert or was walking guard duty, however, then the shooter could move 40 percent closer to the target before the SWS could be heard. If ambient noise was similar to the sound produced by a 1/2 kilowatt gas-powered generator located 15 meters from the sentry, then the shooter could move more than 70 percent closer with the aforementioned SWS. Low humidity or wind coming from the shooter toward the target could significantly reduce the detection distance. Even though building an SWS with a 94 dB signature is not likely based on any foreseeable nonlaser technology, these results provide a useful frame of reference when operating with actual suppressed weapons in the real world.

One of the most important aspects regarding the stealthiness of a real-world suppressed weapon system is a phenomenon no silencer can affect: bullet flight noise. The scientists at HEL undertook an intense study into the two variables they felt would affect bullet flight noise: projectile shape and velocity.

Projectile Shape and Velocity

HEL scientists conducted research on how projectile shape and velocity affect bullet flight noise (and, therefore, the detectability of a silenced weapon). The most interesting portion of the study sought to determine how projectile shape and velocity affect the behavior of subsonic projectiles.

They used an imaginative array of projectile sizes and shapes. The Type 1 variant was a 20mm projectile with a pre-engraved, body-length rotating band, a secant ogive nose, and a flat base. It looked very similar in profile to a FMJ projectile from standard 7.62x51mm military ball ammunition. The Type 2 variant was the same as the Type 1 projectile, without the rotating band. The Type 3 projectile was like the Type 1 variant, except that is was one caliber longer. The Type 4 was like the Type 1, except that it had a 9 degree boat-tail. The Type 5 was like the Type 1, except that the nose was replaced with a hemisphere. And the Type 6 was shaped like a tear drop with the blunt end pointed downrange. They also tested several projectiles of smaller diameter, but a lot of their equations and conclusions were based on the 20mm data.

Preliminary Finnish research that followed suggested that not all of the conclusions based on 20mm data scale down well when applied to typical projectiles of rifle and pistol caliber. This apparent problem surfaced when Finnish researchers turned their attention to projectile flight noise in the early 1990s.

Only several of the most important conclusions in the HEL study need to be reported here: 1) flight noise (i.e., peak SPL) is directly proportional to the cross-sectional area of the projectile; 2) subsonic flight noise increases by 6 dB with every 150 fps increase in velocity; 3) peak SPLs increase very rapidly with increasing velocity within the transonic range; 4) velocity has very little effect on projectile flight noise at supersonic velocities; and 5) projectile shapes producing the least drag (such as a boat-tail projectile) also produce the least flight noise.

Remarkably, Finnish research generally confirms all but the last conclusion. The work by Kyttälä, Pääkkönen, and Pesonen (1993) does not support the HEL assertion that bullet shape affects flight noise, even at subsonic velocities. Even shooting the bullet backward (i.e., base forward) had no measurable effect on bullet flight noise. Subsequent Finnish work does demonstrate, however, that projectile shape has a significant effect on the frequency spectrum of the bullet flight noise, according to unpublished data gathered by Juha Hartikka.

Hartikka collaborated with Kyttälä, Pääkkönen, and Pesonen and assembled their .30 caliber data into Figure 10.6, which was adapted for an English-speaking audience by Mike Smith. Hartikka also confirms that "bullet flight noise seems to depend on projectile caliber. Smaller bullets generate a few decibels less noise. While I have not measured the flight noise of other calibers," Hartikka said, "the difference is clear enough to be heard. I would estimate about a 3-6 decibel difference in the flight noise produced by .308 and .223 caliber projectiles."

The preceding discussion has covered a lot of ground. How does all of this information relate to the detectability of real suppressed weapons? The last phase of HEL research addressed this issue directly.

Detectability of Silenced Weapons

Unfortunately, this phase of the research at HEL was simplistic, sloppy, and incomplete. The photos accompanying the report reveal, for example, that several suppressors labeled as Maxim silencers in the study were not really Maxims. Therefore, I did not repeat the insult when transcribing the data into Table 5.2. The Sten suppressor, as one example, was labeled a Maxim but was, in fact, standard British issue, probably a Type II design.

Some of the SPLs in Table 5.2 agree with testing conducted in Europe and the United States in recent years, while other SPLs are off by a considerable margin (much too low). It's hard to determine why, since the equipment used for this phase of the study is not described. Interpreting these data is especially exasperating because some numbers are quasi-believable, while others are not. All that is mentioned in the HEL report regarding testing procedures and equipment for this phase of the research is that the microphone was placed 3.8 meters in front of the muzzle at a point 0.3 meter below bullet trajectory.

A more interesting aspect of this work involved placing observers in an open field a few meters from the bullet path while suppressed M16 rifles were fired. When fitted with the HEL 14-inch suppressor, the muzzle blast of the M16 could not be heard by an observer beyond 150 meters. When fired with the HEL M-2 suppressor, the muzzle blast was inaudible beyond 50 meters. In my own experience standing directly in front of an operator using an SCRC Model 24D suppressor on an M16A1 rifle, the muzzle blast could not be heard at 35 meters.

Inherent suppressor efficiency is only part of the story explaining why the muzzle blast remains undetected by an observer at such a close range. Two other factors also contribute to this reality. First, the ballistic crack stimulates the acoustic reflex in the observer's ear, as described in Chapter 3, "Using Suppressors and Other HPDs to Reduce Hearing Loss." This natural defense mechanism responds fully about 100 milliseconds after the arrival of wake generated by the supersonic projectile and thus lowers the effect of the muzzle blast on the inner ear by about 15 dB. Another factor is also at work. When the time between the arrival of the projectile wake and the muzzle blast is less than 50 milliseconds, then the brain cannot separate the two events, so all of the sound will seem to come from the loudest source. The loudest impulse from a suppressed firearm tends to be bullet flight noise.

All of the aforementioned work on impulse noise at HEL resulted in three ultimate conclusions: 1) it's impossible to design a supersonic projectile that would be undetectable at distances less than 200 meters; 2) a suppressor that produces a net sound reduction of 38 dB with a subsonic projectile will not be inaudible at 200 meters; and 3) the only way to make a truly silent weapon is to use a pressure-sustaining cartridge in conjunction with a silencer. That's pretty interesting stuff.

It is also interesting to note that recent research by Kyttälä, Pääkkönen, and Pesonen (1993) shows that a subsonic projectile from a 7.62x51mm cartridge traveling at 984 feet per second (300 mps) produces flight noise of 92 dB at 10 meters. Recall that the better, early phase of research at HEL suggested that a Silent Weapons System could only produce a muzzle blast of 92 dB and mechanical noise of 94 dB (measured at 10 meters) to remain undetectable to an *alert* sentry located 200 meters from the weapon. Although designing a SWS may be the impossible dream when using supersonic projectiles, it just might be possible with subsonic projectiles of .30 caliber or less.

Table 5.2. Performance of silenced firearms tested at Aberdeen Proving Ground in 1966.

GUN	SILENCER	CARTRIDGE	PROJECTILE VELOCITY	SOUND SIGNATURE, dB	NET SOUND REDUCTION, dB
Welrod pistol	integral	9x19mm	subsonic	137	9
M3 submachine gun	1-stage integral	.45 ACP	subsonic	135	10
M3 submachine gun	2-stage integral	.45 ACP	subsonic	131	13
ArmaLite AR-7 rifle	HEL 14-inch	.22 LR	subsonic	127	16
High Standard pistol	French	.22 LR	subsonic	129	17
Sten MK II smg	British integral	9x19mm	subsonic	133	18
M16 rifle	HEL 14-inch	5.56x45mm	supersonic	139	19
M16 rifle	HEL M-2	5.56x45mm	supersonic	120	37.5
Springfield M1903 rifle	Maxim Model J	.30-06	subsonic (special reduced load)	129	20

EQUIPMENT AND PROCEDURES FOR TESTING SILENCER PERFORMANCE

Dr. Philip H. Dater and I have for many years maintained an intense dialogue on testing equipment and procedures. Although we use different equipment at different altitudes, temperatures, and other environmental variables beyond our control, we achieve remarkably comparable data. To refine our procedures, we've gone so far as to swap testing equipment, firearms, suppressors, and even lots of ammunition so that we could: 1) minimize extraneous variability; 2) assess the compatibility of our equipment, procedures, and results; and 3) generally improve the level of our enlightenment.

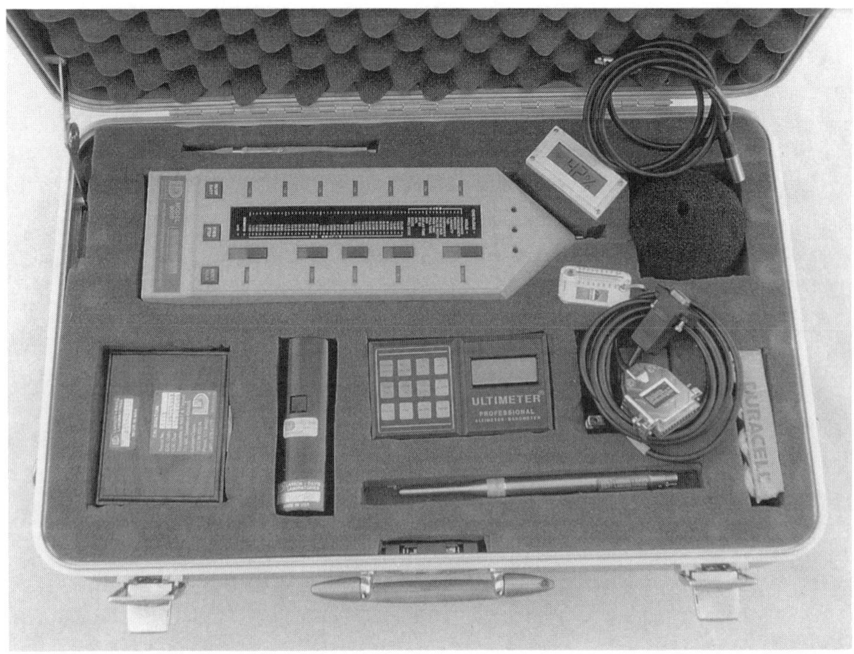

Since the Brüel and Kjaer Model 2209 meter has not been manufactured in some time, the only practical, off-the-shelf portable impulse sound meter suitable for measuring suppressed gunshots, at the time of this writing, is this Larson Davis Model 800-B meter. Photo by Dr. Philip H. Dater.

While I conduct a great deal of sound testing for technical articles, I also conduct proprietary and confidential sound testing for the R&D programs of numerous suppressor manufacturers. I sometimes share sound data with Dr. Dater when I have the specific permission of his competitors to share a particular data set, and Dater has access to the same model suppressor for sound testing. That has enabled Dater and me to learn a great deal about the science and the art of evaluating the performance of sound suppressors. Each of us has learned, and continues to learn, a great deal from the other. Each of us has modified testing procedures and conceptual models as a result of this interchange.

Dater has assembled what he's learned into the single most useful publication on the subject of suppressor testing. Published in 1995, his manual is entitled *Firearm Sound Level Measurements: Techniques and Equipment*. It can be purchased for $4 plus $1 shipping and handling from ATI Star Press, P.O. Box 3538, Boise, ID 83703. Anyone who is serious about suppressor testing needs this manual. Suppressor cognoscenti take note.

Those who are merely interested in being able to critically evaluate the tangle of information, misinformation, disinformation, and outright foolishness to be found in articles, books, product literature, and even the courtroom can learn the basics (plus some important things not in Dater's manual) by reading the rest of this chapter.

Other scientists and designers who have provided me with a great deal of enlightenment on equipment, procedures, and data interpretation include Dr. William L. Kramer of Ball State University, Dr. Rauno Pääkkönen of the Tampere Regional Institute of Occupational Health, Illka Kyttälä of the Finland Ministry of Labor, and Juha Hartikka of Asesepänliike BR-Tuote Ky. Their help, plus postgraduate work at the Polytechnic School of Hard Knocks, has inspired the following thoughts on sound testing.

Testing Equipment

Several suppressor manufacturers, and many armchair experts, so-called gunwriters, and U.S.

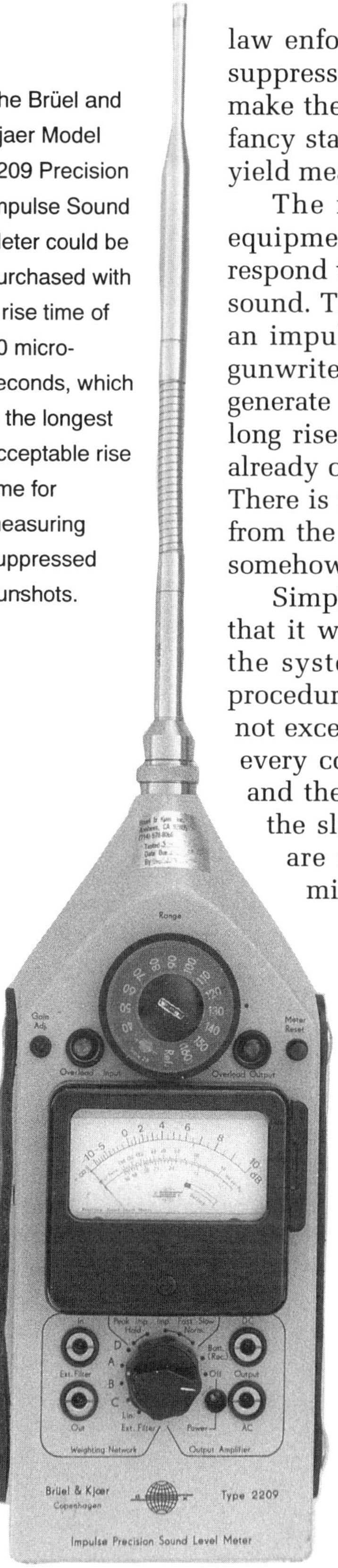

The Brüel and Kjaer Model 2209 Precision Impulse Sound Meter could be purchased with a rise time of 20 microseconds, which is the longest acceptable rise time for measuring suppressed gunshots.

law enforcement agencies use inappropriate sound equipment for measuring suppressed gunshots. Using the wrong equipment introduces major biases that make the data meaningless. There is no way to massage such biased data with fancy statistical procedures or scientific fudge factors to make the flawed data yield meaningful information. Here's what works, what doesn't—and why.

The most important "why" behind the requirement for appropriate equipment relates to how fast the microphone and sound-meter system can respond to the rapidly rising A-duration pressure wave generated by an impulse sound. The time that the system requires to measure the peak SPL generated by an impulse sound is called the *rise time*. The reason that armchair experts, gunwriters, law enforcement agencies, and several suppressor manufacturers generate meaningless data is because they use sound meters that have such a long rise time that the most powerful crest of the impulse pressure wave has already come, *and gone past the microphone*, by the time the system responds. There is no way to take a reading from the back slope of that primary wave—or from the crests of the much smaller waves that follow the primary wave—and somehow determine just how high the crest of that primary wave had been.

Simply using a sound meter costing thousands of dollars does not ensure that it will produce meaningful data, even if the manufacturer promises that the system is ideal for the job. One must dig deeper. U.S. Army testing procedures specified in MIL-STD-1474C require that a system's rise time must not exceed 20 microseconds. This level of performance must be achievable by every component in the system, including the meter itself, the preamplifier, and the microphone. The complete system (see Figure 5.7) is only as fast as the slowest component of the system. That said, the two components that are most commonly inappropriate for the testing of gunshots are the microphone and the meter.

Whether one is generating sound data or simply evaluating someone else's data, it is important to understand some basic facts about these components.

The microphone is really a transducer that converts sound pressure waves into an electrical signal. The mike must not only respond quickly, it needs to perform at (and survive) much higher pressure levels than normally encountered to measure unsuppressed gunshots. For all practical purposes, this requires a condenser microphone no larger than 1/4 inch (6 mm). The Brüel and Kjaer Type 4136 1/4-inch pressure-type microphone and the Larson Davis 2530-1133 random incidence microphone provide a fast enough response and yet can tolerate the muzzle blast from unsuppressed small arms at a distance of 1 meter. These two particular microphones are the most appropriate mikes in the industry for measuring gunshot noise. Several other 1/4- and 1/8-inch microphones can also be used. Larger microphones simply cannot respond fast enough to the very brief impulse generated by a gunshot because of their size or because the diaphragm actually bottoms out inside the mike before the peak pressure can be recorded.

Finding an appropriate sound meter is much harder than finding an appropriate microphone. Part of the problem is that very brief

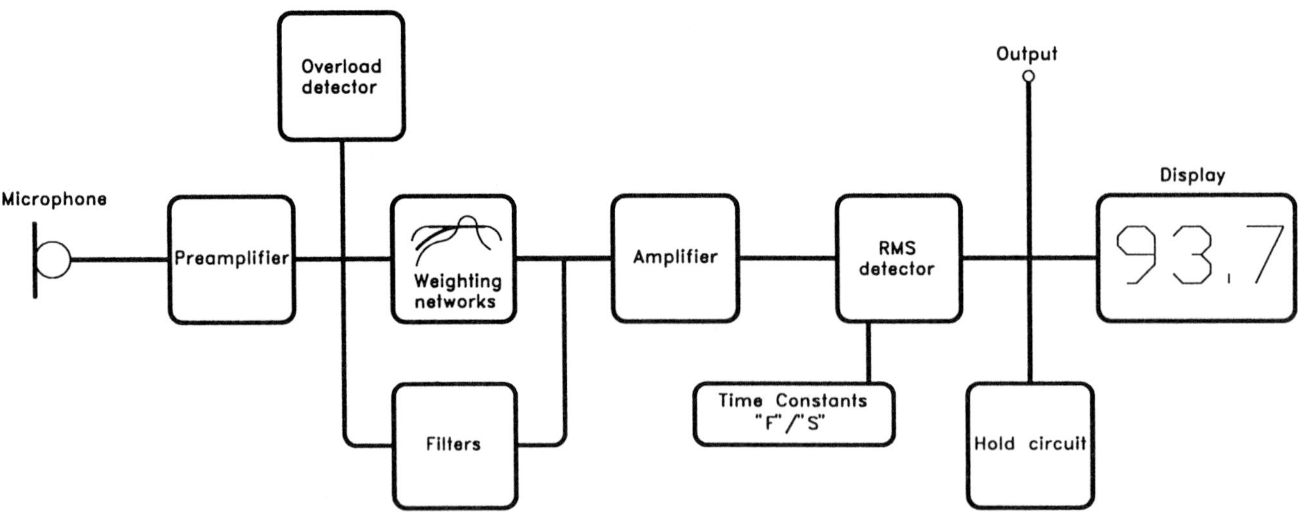

Figure 5.7. The components of a precision impulse sound meter. Drawing by Mike Smith.

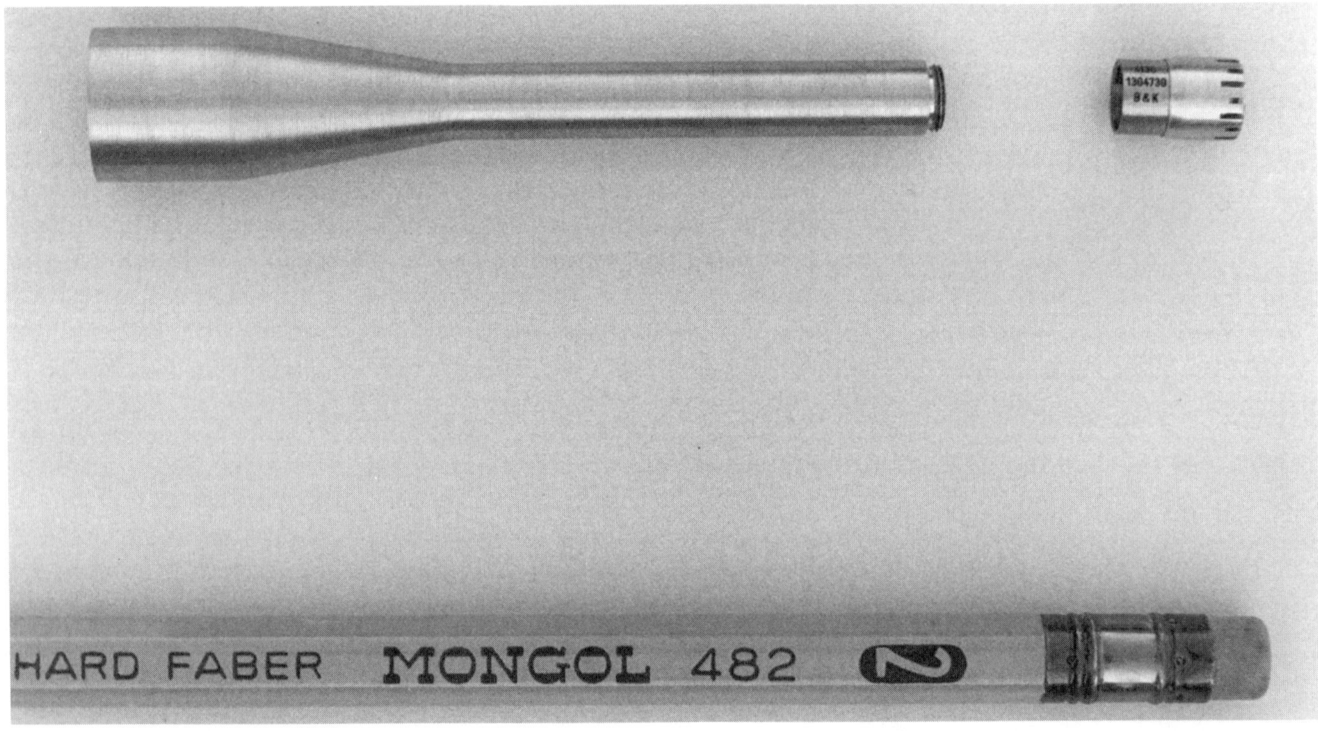

The Brüel and Kjaer Type 4136 1/4-inch pressure-type microphone, which is about the size of a pencil eraser, provides a fast enough response and yet can tolerate the muzzle blast from unsuppressed small arms at a distance of 1 meter.

impulse events are not common in the workplace, so occupational health and safety organizations (outside of Finland, anyway) tend to ignore such events. These public health organizations, and to a much lesser extent the industries they regulate, purchase the vast majority of the precision sound meters manufactured on the planet. Naturally, there is little financial incentive to design meters beyond the needs of virtually every client.

Brüel and Kjaer, which is based in Denmark but has offices worldwide, pioneered the concept of a commercially manufactured precision sound meter. This company has maintained its lead in the industry over the decades by technical innovation, excellent engineering, and superb quality control. Unfortunately for those interested in measuring the sound of gunshots, especially suppressed gunshots, progress in terms of technical innovation has been inversely proportional to the rise time engineered into each new model. Thus the old Model 2209 Impulse Precision Sound Meter could be purchased with a rise time of 20 microseconds. It was replaced by the Model 2218, which is a much better meter but only has a rise time of 35 μsec. The 2218 was subsequently replaced by the very impressive Model 2231, which regrettably has a rise time of only 50 μsec.

Technical representatives at Brüel and Kjaer Instruments, Inc. (185 Forest Street, Marlborough, MA 01752) have complete confidence in recommending the Model 2218 and 2231 meters for measuring gunshot noise. After all, their precision impulse meters with rise times of 35 to 50 μsec give virtually the same peak SPL readings as a B&K Model 2209 with its 20 μsec response. The problem, as illustrated by Figures 5.3 and 5.4, is that the A-duration of a suppressed muzzle blast is a lot shorter than the A-duration of an unsuppressed gunshot. Therefore, the currently produced Model 2231 misses the peak SPL generated by a suppressed firearm and provides a suppressed SPL that is on the order of 10 dB less than the reading generated by a Model 2209 meter.

This means that the net sound reduction of a suppressor will be on the order of 10 dB higher (i.e., better) using the currently produced Model 2231! (My thanks to John Leasure for providing comparative data.)

This phenomenon has profound implications for comparing published data. It also has some interesting implications for the courtroom, since the FBI and BATF currently use the Model 2231 meter for testing silencers (and devices they would like to believe are silencers for the purposes of prosecution).

Unfortunately, the Model 2209 meter has not been built for decades. The only systems now being made by Brüel and Kjaer that are suitable for measuring suppressed gunshots are digital measurement amplifiers, which are prohibitively expensive (circa $30,000) and require AC power. Given tenacity and luck, one might be able to locate a used Model 2209. The process took me more than a year and cost me $5,000 back when that was still real money.

Therefore, the only practical, off-the-shelf, portable impulse meter suitable to the task, at the time of this writing, is the Larson Davis Model 800-B meter (Larson Davis Laboratories, 1681 West 820 North, Provo, UT 84601). The Larson Davis requires some trivial tweaking that Dater describes in his aforementioned manual, but the 800-B is immediately available and affordable. The meter, 1/4-inch pressure microphone, microphone extension cable, and calibrator (which is essential for providing a reliable reference standard) will cost about $5,000 at the time of this writing. I'd strongly recommend spending an additional $850 to have Larson Davis install an RS-232 computer port in the meter so data can be dumped directly into a laptop computer.

Dr. Dater, who has no relationship to Larson Davis, has written a nifty program to drive the Larson Davis 800B from a DOS-based laptop computer. Dater's software sets and resets the meter, records data on the hard drive, and automatically performs statistical analyses on the data. This computer-controlled system speeds both testing and analysis to a remarkable degree. Anyone interested in obtaining a copy of this program should contact Dater at Antares Technologies Inc. (Box 3538, Boise, ID 83703).

I should emphasize that the only suitable, battery-powered, precision impulse meters are the currently produced Larson Davis 800B and the out-of-production Brüel and Kjaer Model 2209. Other meters in the marketplace, such as the B&K 2231 and the Quest 2700, will not provide meaningful data when measuring suppressed gunshots; both are excellent sound meters, but they are simply the wrong tools for the job.

Simply using the appropriate hardware does not ensure meaningful data. Appropriate and standardized testing procedures are also mandatory.

Testing Procedures

Testing procedures used for measuring the sound signatures of gunshots include such things as sound-meter settings, weighting scales, microphone placement, firearm placement, number of replicate samples, and the recording of supplementary but important data. The nature of the testing environment is also important. Testing over grass is most desirable, since testing over a hard surface (such as asphalt or concrete) or near a reflective surface (such as a wall, tree, or embankment) will increase the sound readings by 2 dB or more. This suggests that the actual peak of a gunshot is slightly less than 20 microseconds. The presence of a hard surface under the experiment reflects the pressure wave, and the reflected wave takes just enough time to travel the extra several meters so more of the event can be recorded. Both NATO and U.S. Army testing procedures specify that testing shall be conducted over grass.

BATF and FBI testing procedures (Crum and Owen, 1987) do not prohibit testing over hard surfaces and even permit sound testing indoors. This oversight will increase sound readings by several dB. Contrary to recently published tripe, however, testing near a reflective surface *does not* increase the sound level. That would violate the law of physics regarding the conservation of energy. The resultant sound seems louder to an observer because the reflections make the sound last longer. The sound seems louder to a sound meter because the extra time delay caused by the reflection enables the meter to measure more of the main pressure pulse.

Another potential problem is that some people habitually set the sound meter on the incorrect setting. Since Type 1 sound meters have an "impulse" setting and gunshots are impulses, misguided individuals incorrectly select the impulse setting. This results in a rise time measured in milliseconds rather than microseconds. Use the "peak hold" setting to ensure the fastest rise time. Likewise, adding a module to measure sound in octave or third-octave bands also slows the rise time unacceptably.

P.T. Kekkonen and Kari Haantio conducting suppressor research at the Pyhäselkä shooting range in Finland with M62 assault rifle and BR-Tuote TX4 suppressor. Photo by Juha Hartikka.

The weighting selection

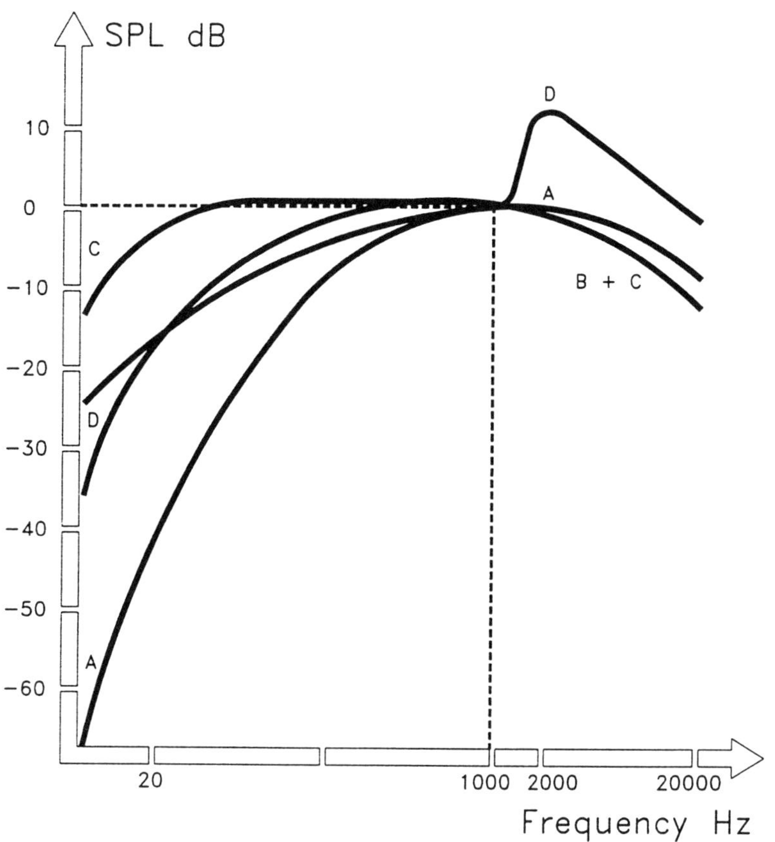

Figure 5.8. Four different filtering schemes are commonly used to remove different frequencies at different sound pressures levels for different analytic purposes. Drawing by Mike Smith.

on the meter is also important. Since most sound meters are used to study sound in relation to occupational health and safety, the meters have several settings that filter out a portion of the frequency spectrum not relevant to some aspect of hearing loss in humans. Four different filtering schemes are commonly used to remove different frequencies at different sound pressures levels for different analytic purposes (Figure 5.8).

"A" weighting correlates best with hearing loss in humans, since it reduces the amount of irrelevant low-frequency sound that is recorded (up to 55 dB at 20 Hz). "C" weighting doesn't cut out nearly as much low-frequency sound as "A" weighting. "B" weighting more or less splits the difference. "D" weighting is only used for specialized measurement of aircraft noise and so is irrelevant to this discussion. Most sound meters provide three filter settings: "A" weighting, "C" weighting, and "linear." The latter provides no frequency filtration at all. While "A" weighting is firmly established as the international standard for measuring gunshots, Dr. C. Richard Price at the U.S. Army Human Research and Engineering Directorate (formerly known as the Human Engineering Laboratory) at the Aberdeen Proving Ground in Maryland makes an interesting case for using the "linear" setting.

Price asserts that the unweighted "linear" setting most approximates a person's subjective opinion of the intensity of a gunshot, since that "linear" weighting measures more of the low-frequency sounds that slap the face and upper body of the shooter. "A" weighting was developed to most accurately predict the effect of sound on hearing loss rather than to best model how a person actually responds to the sound.

The problem, which Price acknowledges, is that the sheer mass of data using "A" weighting now precludes changing the weighting standard for evaluating suppressors on the basis of perception rather than health risks. The issue is further muddied because of the increasing interest, at least in northern Europe, of promoting the use of suppressors as hearing protection devices, and that requires an "A" weighting.

Nevertheless, using "A" versus "linear" weighting generates suppressor data that vary by only 1 or 2 dB, for the most part. Even using "A" versus "C" weighting provides fairly comparable data (see Tables 5.3 and 5.4). A few designs (such as the Sterling Mk5 submachine gun and recent muzzle cans of the slanted-sidewall type) may exhibit significantly different peak SPLs with different weightings, because these suppressors tend to be especially good at eliminating the lower frequencies.

Other procedural variables include microphone placement, firearm placement, and the number of replicate samples. The subtleties of the first two subjects are discussed at length in Dater's manual, and any textbook on statistics will provide a good background on sample size. The procedures I use are summarized in the following section on "Specific Testing Protocol."

Some experimental variables are outside of the experimenter's control but may affect the results of sound testing directly or may affect subsequent interpretation of the data. Variables that have generated a fair amount of concern include ambient temperature, wind velocity, altitude, humidity, and barometric pressure.

Temperature influences the microphone and sound meter, as well as the speed of sound, atmospheric absorption of sound, and the burning characteristics of gunpowder. The meter may give reliable data at temperatures below its design specs (microphones are commonly rated for operation between -10 and +50 °C), especially if the batteries are kept warm at very low temperatures. Temperature can also affect microphone sensitivity.

All condenser microphones seem to work well up to 90 percent relative humidity, when moisture can begin to condense on the mike's diaphragm. This significantly reduces microphone sensitivity, so no sound testing should be conducted when relative humidity exceeds 90 percent.

Wind is the remaining environmental variable that can significantly affect the sound readings. The porous foam wind shield that comes with each microphone should be used to minimize the direct effect of wind on the microphone, which actually affects the movement of the diaphragm, especially at higher frequencies. Free-field microphones like the B&K 4135 and LDL 2520 are particularly vulnerable to this effect. The shield also protects the mike from the by-products of gunpowder combustion.

Wind also affects the results indirectly by attenuating sound upwind and reinforcing the sound downwind. The combined effects of wind become significant at velocities above 12 miles per hour (5 meters per second). This explains why both NATO and U.S. Army testing standards require that sound testing only be conducted when wind speed is less than 5 meters per second.

Table 5.3. Sound signatures using "A" weighting versus "C" weighting.

GUN	CALIBER	SUPPRESSOR	AMMUNITION	dB(A)	dB(C)	TEMPERATURE °F(°C)
McMillan M89	7.62x51mm	none	NATO M80 ball	168.4	168.0	56(13)
McMillan M89	7.62x51mm	none	Federal 308M	168.1	168.0	56(13)
McMillan M89	7.62x51mm	none	Sako subsonic	157.4	156.4	56(13)
McMillan M89	7.62x51mm	AWC M89	NATO M80 ball	136.6	136.8	56(13)
McMillan M89	7.62x51mm	AWC M89	Federal 308M	136.7	135.4	56(13)
McMillan M89	7.62x51mm	AWC M89	Sako subsonic	123.4	122.2	56(13)
Sterling Mk4	9x19mm	none	Winchester USA	159.2	158.5	74(23)
Sterling Mk5	9x19mm	integral	Winchester USA	133.8	129.5	74(23)
Colt 1911-A1	.45 ACP	none	CCI Blazer JHP	164.1	163.5	56(13)

Table 5.4. Net sound reductions using "A" weighting versus "C" weighting.

GUN	CALIBER	SUPPRESSOR	AMMUNITION	dB(A)	dB(C)	TEMP., °F(°C)
McMillan M89	7.62x51mm	AWC M89	NATO M80 ball	31.8	31.8	56(13)
McMillan M89	7.62x51mm	AWC M89	Federal 308M	31.4	32.4	56(13)
McMillan M89	7.62x51mm	AWC M89	Sako subsonic	34.0	34.2	56(13)
Sterling Mk5	9x19mm	integral	Winchester USA	25.4	29.0	74(23)

Specific Testing Protocol

I used the following testing protocol to generate the data reported in this three-volume treatise. Sound signatures were measured using a Brüel and Kjaer Type 2209 Impulse Precision Sound Pressure Meter (set on "A" weighting and peak hold) with a B&K Type 4136 1/4-inch condenser microphone. The microphone was placed 1.00 meter away from the front of the suppressor or muzzle, using a calibrated length of dental floss attached by a rubber band to the muzzle or suppressor to maintain the proper distance from the mike.

The pressure microphone was oriented at a 90 degree angle from the bullet flight path, with the mike pointed straight up toward the sky so the plane of the diaphragm intersected the suppressor or muzzle. (A free-field microphone such as the B&K 4135 is oriented 0 degrees to the sound source, so it points directly at the suppressor or muzzle. A random incidence microphone such as the Larson Davis 2530-1133 is oriented 80 degrees to the sound source.) The weapons were fired at a height of 1.6 meters over grass (or snow at temperatures below 0°F or -18°C). The meter was calibrated just before and just after the tests with a B&K 4230 calibrator. No instrument drift was ever observed except at temperatures below -5°F (-21°C), and then the worst drift was about 1.2 dB over several hours at -16°F (-27°C).

These procedures, including the use of "A" weighting and firing the guns at a height of 1.6 meters above the ground, generally follow NATO testing procedures specified in Document AC/243(Panel 8/RSG.6)D/9, the International Standards Organization (ISO) 1994 draft international standard for testing of silencers in situ, U.S. Army testing procedures specified in MIL-STD-1474C, and procedures used by the Finnish army and academic researchers as specified by Tampere University of Technology Publication 117.

The microphone in these experiments was placed to the right rather than left of the weapon, since some suppressor designs significantly increase the back pressure of combustion gases, with the result that the ejection port noise can exceed the muzzle signature. Extensive testing suggests that unsuppressed sound signatures and the suppressed signatures of manually operated weapons remain unaffected by right- or left-hand mike placement, whereas the signatures of suppressed self-loading weapons (other than top-ejecting or bottom-ejecting models) will commonly run 0.5 to 2 dB louder with right-hand mike placement. A few suppressor designs will, however, produce signatures that are up to 7 dB louder when measured from the same side as the ejection port.

Therefore, right-hand microphone orientation provides a worst-case measure or *net system performance*, while left-hand mike orientation provides a best-case measure of suppressor performance. Whether a suppressor is used for tactical requirements, to reduce the risk of hearing damage during training, or for sporting purposes, right-hand mike placement provides a more conservative measure of suppressor performance.

The ambient temperature during each test is always given. Velocities were measured using a P.A.C.T. MKIII or MKIV timer/chronograph with MKV skyscreens set 24 inches apart and the start screen 8 feet from the muzzle (P.A.C.T., P.O. Box 531525, Grand Prairie, TX 75053). At least 10 rounds were fired to obtain an average sound signature or muzzle velocity.

The preceding discussion provides the necessary technical background for critically evaluating the data found throughout this treatise and elsewhere. Furthermore, the reader is ready to debunk the tangle of misinformation, disinformation, and outright foolishness found in articles, books, product literature, and even the courtroom. The following very short chapter provides some good rules of thumb for evaluating data and bunk, and offers some hints about evaluating courtroom exhibits and testimony. It goes on to provide recently published examples of misinformation that never should have seen the light of day.

CHAPTER SIX

DEBUNKING MYTHS, ARTICLES, AND CLAIMS

he preceding chapters have already debunked several common myths about silencers. Contrary to popular belief, silencers are not silent. They are not illegal in the United States. Registered silencers are not used by criminals. And silencers do, indeed, have a legitimate role to play in civilized society. Subsequent chapters will demonstrate that no silencer is as quiet as a BB gun, contrary to the reports of some authors. This chapter will debunk several other myths, shoot down the scientific validity of sound testing conducted by some law-enforcement agencies, and show how to assess some of the outrageous claims and unintentional misinformation published by armchair experts and some manufacturers.

Here are some red flags that should make the reader wary when confronted with sound data on suppressed or unsuppressed gunshots:

- Equipment and procedures are not specified.
- Equipment and procedures do not conform to accepted standards discussed in the previous chapters.
- Unsuppressed SPLs of centerfire rifles and pistols are less than 150 dB.
- Rimfire pistol SPLs are less than 150 dB.
- Rimfire rifle SPLs are less than 130 dB.

Do remember, however, that placing the microphone at the ear, which is common practice for occupational health purposes, will produce lower SPLs than placing the mike a meter to the side of the muzzle. That's why the red-flag benchmarks I just mentioned are lower than the data found throughout *Silencer History and Performance*.

A properly designed suppressed firearm will be at least as accurate as the same gun before it was suppressed, as demonstrated by Marko Ruotsalainen with his integrally suppressed, 7.62x39mm Mosin-Nagant M1891 rifle. Photo by Juha Hartikka.

Another warning sign is a manufacturer's claim of net sound reductions exceeding 40 dB. The most likely explanation for such claims is using a meter with too slow a rise time (like the Brüel and Kjaer Model 2231 or any meter made at the time of this writing by Quest). The B&K 2231, for example, will yield a credible unsuppressed sound signature. But it will miss the actual peak SPL of the suppressed gunshot, so the meter's measurement of the suppressed SPL can be as much as 10 dB too low. When using a Quest meter, even the unsuppressed SPLs are meaningless. This is not an indictment of the B&K 2231 and Quest meters. They are good instruments, but they are simply the wrong tools for the job of measuring very brief impulse events.

Sometimes, however, a manufacturer obtains sound reductions in the high 30s or 40s by willful manipulation of the experiment. One manufacturer, who will remain nameless, intentionally uses an inappropriate sound meter and sprays the inside of each suppressor with oil to further enhance its performance, even when the suppressor is advertised as a dry design.

Bear in mind, however, that the state of art in suppressor design is evolving at an unprecedented pace, and a few suppressors for .22 rimfire pistols have broken the 40 dB "barrier." Thus, when a manufacturer claims a sound reduction in the 40s or high 30s, be wary but don't reject the claim out of hand. Be especially wary of sound-reduction claims in the high 30s and 40s for centerfire suppressors. By the time you have read all three volumes of *Silencer History and Performance*, you'll have an excellent ability to separate the proverbial wheat from the chaff.

Serious suppressor users realize that the stealthiness of a gunshot is only part of the issue when evaluating suppressor performance. They also wonder whether suppressors hurt or help accuracy. The answer is: "Yes!"

SUPPRESSORS AND ACCURACY

A French colleague and I have discovered that many muzzle cans out there in the real world align so poorly with the bores of their firearms that bullets graze the baffles. It also appears that some (but not all) baffle designs that force jets of gas across the bullet path may increase bullet yaw inside the suppressor. That can lead to bullets grazing the baffle, according to the theory. A careful examination of the gas velocities and distances involved seems to undermine this theory, however.

A more plausible explanation is that bore diameter or alignment with the barrel may be the real underlying problems.

The two most common causes of alignment problems are: 1) the threads are not concentric with the bore, and 2) the threaded barrel lacks a shoulder perpendicular to the bore that acts as a stop to force the suppressor into proper alignment. The very coarse Ingram/SIONICS threads, for example, feature such a shoulder that provides good alignment of the suppressor as long as the can remains screwed tightly against the barrel shoulder. If the suppressor loosens and backs off the threads several degrees, however, the shoulder no longer has any effect and the suppressor can become dangerously misaligned. This has caused more than one operator to shoot through the side of the suppressor.

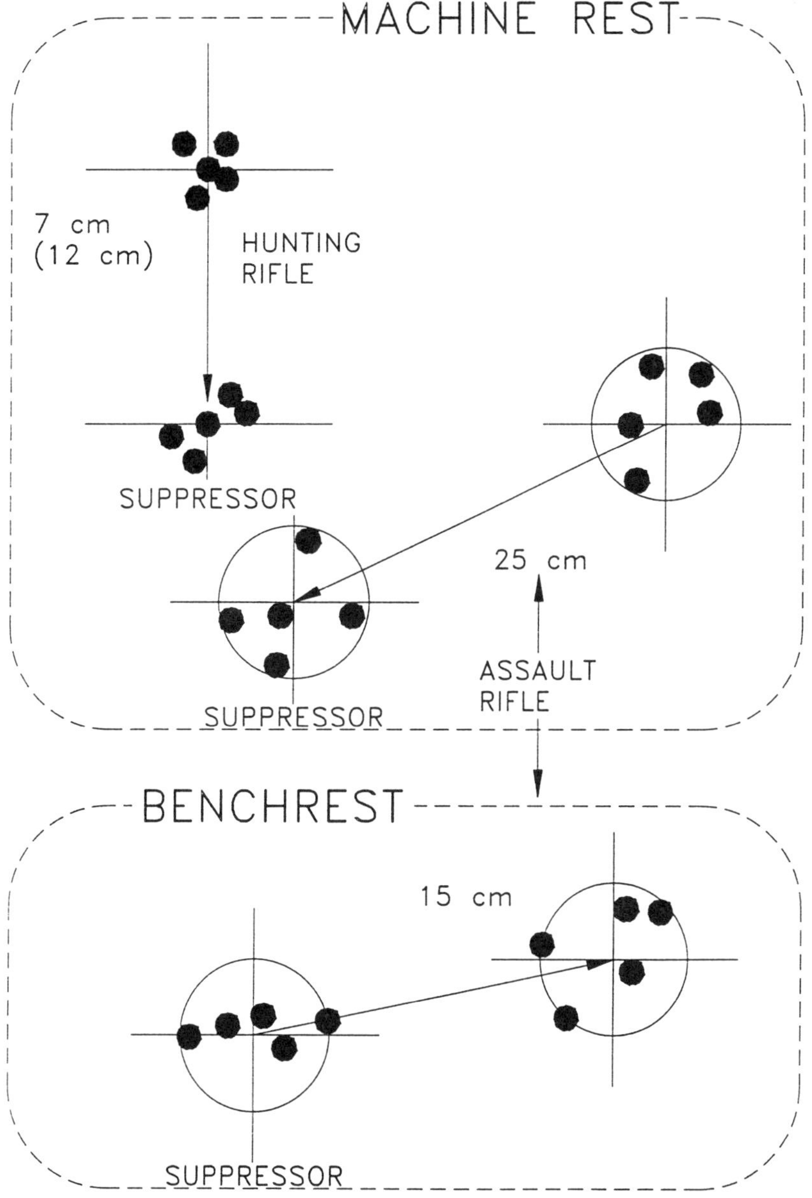

Figure 6.1. A suppressor (or equal weight) changes the geometric center of a five-round group in a characteristic and reproducible fashion (redrawn by Mike Smith from Kyttälä and Pääkkönen, 1996).

Some suppressors unquestionably have such tight bores through their baffles that bullet grazing is likely.

Properly designed and installed suppressors do not exhibit these problems, however. Recent Finnish research (Kyttälä and Pääkkönen, 1996) looking into the effect of silencers on accuracy demonstrated that silencers did not have an adverse effect on accuracy. In fact, rifles tended to deliver their tightest groups when fitted with a silencer. Recent research conducted by Peter Kokalis agrees with the Finnish findings. The Finns report that long suppressors required skilled installation (i.e., precision threading and indexing) to avoid misalignment, which can cause bullets to graze baffles and deliver unacceptable accuracy. Short muzzle cans are more forgiving in this regard, and the very short reflex suppressors made by BR-Tuote Oy are the most forgiving of all.

A suppressor will, however, significantly shift the point of impact because the suppressor's weight significantly changes barrel harmonics. Kyttälä and Pääkkönen demonstrated that a suppressor (or equal weight) changes the geometric center of a five-round group in a characteristic and reproducible fashion (see Figure 6.1).

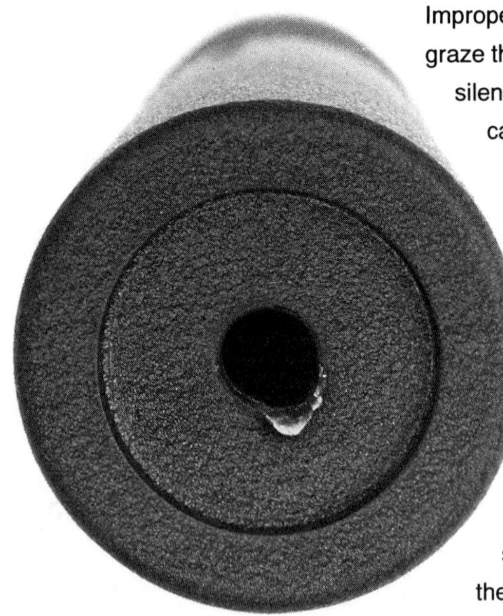

Improper alignment can cause bullets to graze the baffles or end cap of a silencer, ruining accuracy. In mild cases, no visible damage is sustained; in moderate cases, the some structural damage can be seen; and in extreme cases, the suppressor might self-destruct, placing both the weapon and its operator at serious risk. This suppressor loosened after firing about 10 rounds through an M16A1 and sustained moderate damage to the end cap as a result.

When fired from a machine rest at a target 100 meters (109 yards) downrange, mounting a suppressor on a hunting rifle generally shifted the group downward by about 10 cm (4 inches). Mounting a suppressor on a Valmet assault rifle generally shifted the group about 25 cm (10 inches) down and to the left.

This effect depended on whether the gun was fired from a bench rest or machine rest. When shooting from a bench rest, mounting a suppressor on an assault rifle generally shifted the groups up and to the right about 15 cm (6 inches) rather than down and to the left when firing from a machine rest. The most important point here is that a rifle must be rezeroed whenever a suppressor is mounted or removed.

Juha Hartikka participated in Finnish research conducted by Army Arsenal 1 staff on the effect of suppressors and flash hiders on group shift and group size, and he provides some additional insight. Using a Valmet M62 7.62x39mm assault rifle (a Kalashnikov clone) and standard issue military ball (lot VPT 78), accuracy tests were performed using a machine rest, while tests on group shift used sandbags and a bench rest. Shooting at 98 yards (90 meters) with a machine rest, five-shot groups averaged 2.94 inches (74.8 mm). Using five different suppressors, the groups were an average of 10 percent smaller (see Figure 6.2). The Br-Tuote TX8 suppressor provided the best improvement of accuracy, yielding an average group size of 2.05 inches (52.0 mm). Thus, the TX8 suppressor improved accuracy by 37 percent.

Finnish researchers suspected that these suppressors (which did not use wipes) improved accuracy and shifted bullet impact because suppressor weight dampened barrel harmonics rather than because the suppressors were somehow affecting the flight of the bullet directly. Their research demonstrated that any mass attached to the muzzle, including flash hiders and empty tubes built specifically for this research, all shifted bullet impact. The amount of shift, Hartikka reports, was roughly proportional to the mass and the center of gravity of the muzzle device.

Clearly, barrel harmonics are a significant factor in the accuracy delivered by Kalashnikov-type weapons. Hartikka points out that "the barrel tends to vibrate diagonally up and to the right, and down and to the left. The muzzle is already moving diagonally as the bullet emerges, so any mass attached to the muzzle (including a flash hider, muzzle brake, or suppressor) affects the phase and amplitude of muzzle vibration."

In my own experience, several other factors also affect group shift and group size. An important variable, especially with precision rifles, is the amount of torque applied while attaching a suppressor to a barrel. Each system will provide the best accuracy with a particular amount of torque. If circumstances prevent the use of a torque wrench when mounting a thread-mount suppressor, then care should be taken to install the can precisely the same way every time. Another factor affecting group shift is whether a muzzle suppressor uses a one- or two-point mount. A two-point mount may be better at reducing barrel harmonics, especially if the two-point mount

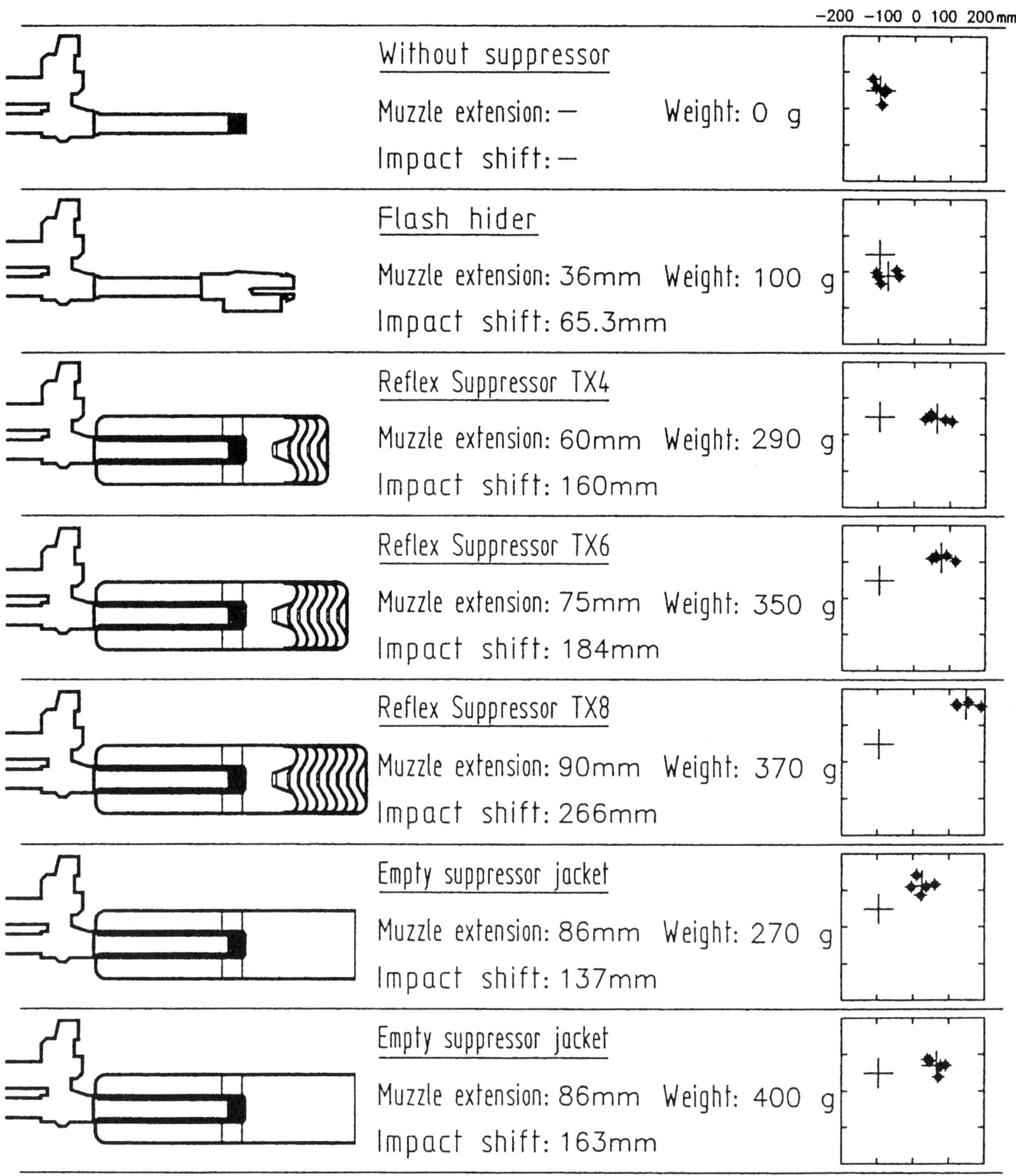

Figure 6.2. Tests conducted by Finland Army Arsenal 1 staff on how suppressors and flash hiders affect group shift and group size using a Valmet M62 7.62x39mm assault rifle. Drawing by Juha Hartikka.

stretches the barrel. A two-point mount is also less likely to loosen (i.e., unscrew) during rapid or full-auto fire, in my experience.

I've found that another factor affecting both group shift and group size is the orientation of asymmetric internal components of some suppressors as viewed from the front. Shot placement is most reproducible if the same part of the suppressor always points to 12 o'clock, as an arbitrary standard. If the silencer has an unusually tight bullet passage, like the Knight's Armament SOCOM .45 pistol suppressor, and the can is not aligned precisely, bullets may graze baffles, which will either shift the group, degrade accuracy, or both. Knight's suppressor can be indexed at 10 different radial positions "around the clock" until the suppressed pistol aligns properly and delivers acceptable accuracy. That's an ingenious solution.

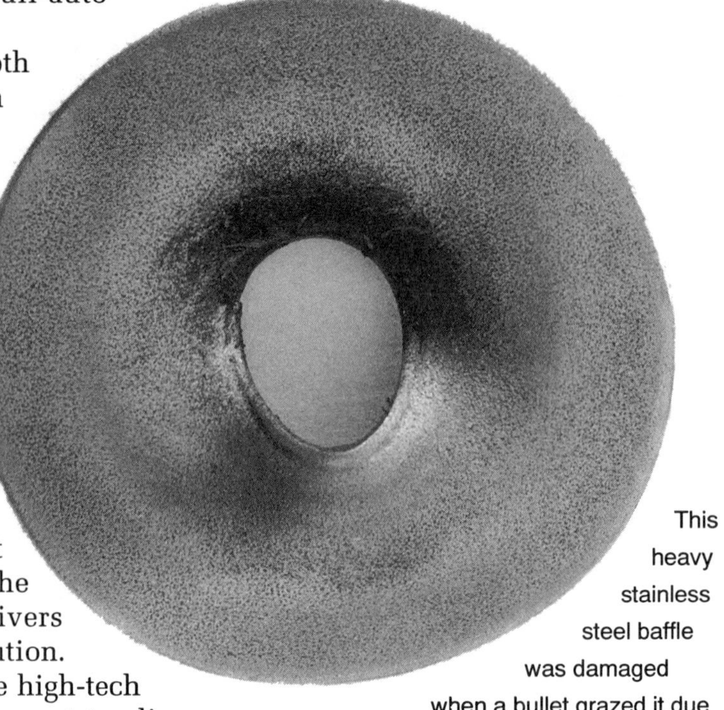

This heavy stainless steel baffle was damaged when a bullet grazed it due to improper alignment with the bore.

This phenomenon is also seen with some high-tech MP5 suppressors using Tim Bixler's otherwise outstanding quick mount for the three-lug barrel. Suppressor cognoscenti place a temporary mark on the tube of their MP5 suppressors using the Bixler mount and check for this phenomenon. If present, the operator then determines the optimal orientation and places a dab of paint or a small scratch as an index mark to ensure repeatable alignment with a particular barrel lug. The reason some suppressors exhibit a sweet spot in terms of orientation with the weapon is that the main component of the Bixler mount is a casting. Small variations from one mount to another can sometimes cause subtle variations in alignment. This is not a design flaw per se, since a mount that is machined (not cast) to the same specs will not exhibit a sweet spot. This occasional problem with the Bixler mount is the design's only liability, in my experience.

Everyone on the planet who uses a suppressor must at least consider the accuracy issue, but residents of the United States must face some potential legal issues not faced by folks in more enlightened jurisdictions. These problems can arise when law enforcement officials decide that a flash hider, muzzle brake, or other accessory is an unregistered silencer under the law.

SOUND TESTING AND THE COURTS

Scientifically valid sound testing provides a legitimate and useful tool for prosecuting individuals who manufacture or smuggle unregistered suppressors for the underworld. Sometimes, however, law-enforcement personnel make arbitrary or frivolous assessments as to what constitutes a silencer. There are two established legal precedents for determining whether or not a particular device is a silencer: 1) any device that claims to be a silencer is a silencer under the law, whether it decreases or even increases the SPL produced by a firearm; and 2) any device that lowers the SPL by 3 dB is a silencer.

If an honest individual finds that a muzzle brake or other device has been erroneously determined to be a silencer, and the government's sound testing actually reveals a small sound reduction, then an independent authority needs to address the following points in court. Does the sound meter have a maximum rise time of 20 microseconds? If the meter is a Brüel and Kjaer Model 2231, for example, then the net sound reduction may have been overestimated by as much as 10 dB. If the testing was conducted over a hard surface, then the sound readings may be biased by 2+ dB. Was the device cleaned prior to testing, leaving water or oil inside the device? The presence of liquid inside the device could lower the resultant SPL by several decibels. What frequency weighting was used? The device might give significantly different SPLs (up to 3-4 dB) depending on the weighting regime. If any of these points seems relevant to the case at hand, then an independent expert should also conduct sound tests using established procedures and either a Brüel and Kjaer Model 2209 or a Larson Davis 800-B sound meter with the appropriate 1/4-inch mike to provide scientifically valid data.

Courtrooms and product literature are not the only places where misinformation may be encountered. Magazine articles can provide another source of flawed information.

RECENTLY PUBLISHED MISINFORMATION

Popular nontechnical magazines seem to abound with misinformation about the measurement of gunshot noise, as well as the effects of muzzle blast on human health and human performance in tactical situations. Without embarrassing specific authors and publications, it would be useful to discuss several examples of flawed information that have appeared in the mid-1990s. The following discussion will illustrate a number of common misconceptions from recent publications that aspiring suppressor cognoscenti will want to avoid.

A recent article on the effects of muzzle blast on hearing, for example, provides a table purporting to give the "decibel level by caliber" of common handgun rounds from .22 rimfire to .45 ACP. The published values range from 106 dB for .22 LR Stingers to 116 to 125 dB for 9x19mm and 121 to 130 dB for .45 ACP pistols. Anytime someone claims that unsuppressed rimfire and centerfire pistol SPLs are less than 150 dB (with barrels of typical length and the microphone located within a meter or two of the firearm), it is safe to conclude that the data are probably meaningless. Since the subsequent discussion on hearing loss is based on the author's faulty handgun data, specific assertions relating to his own SPLs must be dismissed. Other warning signs appearing throughout the article should alert the reader.

A photograph, for example, shows the author holding pistol in his left hand and a meter in his right. The meter sports what appears to be a large (circa 1 inch) microphone. Recall that a 1/4-inch mike is the maximum acceptable diameter. The author is holding the meter out at arm's length with his weak hand, with the microphone located about 3 feet behind and 3 feet to the right of the muzzle. Furthermore, the microphone is pointed at an angle of 90 degrees away from the rear of the shooting arm. This arrangement corresponds to no commonly accepted microphone placement or orientation. That's another reason to question the validity of the data.

One author used a Radio Shack meter for measuring gunshot noise. While the Radio Shack meter is fine for balancing a set of stereo speakers, it is not a precision sound meter, much less a precision *impulse* meter. Another author used a Quest Model 215 sound meter set on "impulse" to obtain his own data. Using the Quest is a double whammy. As previously discussed, the Quest does not have a rise time fast enough for measuring gunshots. And even if it did, the use of an "impulse" rather than "peak hold" setting would have negated the fast rise time.

Weighting is another issue that causes confusion among gun writers. In an article on shooting muffs and hearing loss, an author turned his back on "A" weighting, which is expressly designed for occupational health studies (the point of his article). Instead, he used the "linear" setting on the weighting scale, which theoretically makes more sense when describing one's subjective impression of suppressor performance but makes poor sense when talking about TTS and PTS in humans.

A more embarrassing conceptual problem is revealed when an author asserted, "The rise time response was set on the IEC impulse mode. This is very different from the A-scale with a slow response specified by OSHA to measure steady state industrial noise." Note that he is confusing *response time* and *frequency weighting.*

One of the most curious examples of misinformation appeared when an author asserted that "gunfire inside a room may be 25 times *more intense* than on the open range" [the italics are mine]. The author goes on to provide a table which alleges that decibel measurements of the muzzle blast from a .38 Special revolver increase as room size gets smaller. He claims the .38 Special produces 117 dB on open range, 129 dB in a three-car garage, 131 dB in a bedroom, and 137 dB inside a car. All of this is utter nonsense. As discussed in the previous chapter, the Quest Model 215 sound meter is simply able to measure more of the event because reflected sound waves take longer to reach the microphone than the original blast wave. His results for different rooms vary by so much because his meter is so slow. If the author had gone back to his high school science, he might have realized that genuinely higher decibel readings in smaller spaces would have violated the First Law of Thermodynamics. The event seems louder to the observer because reflections make the overall impulse event last longer.

Thus, when critically reading anything related to the measurement of suppressed and unsuppressed gunshots, pay particular attention to the equipment that was used. Not all quality sound meters are suited to measuring unsuppressed gunshots accurately. Even fewer are suited to measuring *suppressed* gunshots properly. Make sure the unsuppressed sound pressure levels are believable or all other data and conclusions will be flawed. And make sure the author does not make fundamentally flawed conclusions, such as louder SPLs in smaller rooms.

CHAPTER SEVEN

SILENCED .22 RIFLES

he dawn of the twentieth century was also the dawn of the silencer. A noted firearms authority of the period, W.W. Greener, claimed to have developed a silencer long before the turn of the century, but he didn't seek patent protection since there was "no clear need [for silencers] at that time." Unfortunately, no Greener silencer or even sketch of his design survives. The first patent to clearly lay out the principle of baffles and expansion chambers was issued to J. Borrensen and S. Sigbjornsen in 1899. While a number of silencer patents were issued in the following decade, the first commercially successful silencer was designed by Hiram Percey Maxim. The most successful Maxim silencers were designed for the .22 caliber rimfire cartridge.

In fact, the evolution of silencers for the .22 rimfire rifle provides an interesting perspective on the development of silencer technology in general throughout the twentieth century. That story really begins with Maxim.

Born on September 2, 1869, Hiram P. Maxim was the son of Sir Hiram Stevens Maxim (the inventor of the first practical machine gun) and the nephew of Hudson Maxim (the inventor of smokeless powder and the self-propelled torpedo). A mechanical engineer by training and a prolific writer by inclination, Hiram P. wrote a weekly column on "Science for the Layman" for the King newspaper syndicate, an eclectic array of magazine articles, a book published in 1915 entitled *Defenseless America*, and two books published in 1936 entitled *A Genius in the Family* and *Horseless Carriage Days*. While his writings are largely forgotten, Maxim is well remembered by ham radio operators as the founder of the American Radio Relay League and the creator of a code of ethics for amateur radio operators. (Many decades later, another silencer designer—Dr. Philip H. Dater—would make his own contributions to ham radio technology.)

Amateur radio operators still remember Maxim's work in that field, but historians generally remember him for his genius as an inventor. Even though he was a pioneer in the technology of such diverse fields as electrically powered vehicles, aviation and motion pictures, it was Maxim's engineering in the realm of sound suppression that seems to attract the most interest today.

Maxim began his engineering career in 1886 when he graduated from MIT (the Massachusetts Institute of Technology) at the remarkable age of 17. Not surprisingly, this *Wunderkind* was the youngest graduate in his class. After working a total of 20 years for several pioneering companies in the electrical industry and several companies in the electric motorcar industry, his interest in the internal combustion engine eventually convinced him that he had a limited future as the designer of electrically powered vehicles. Maxim concluded that he needed to take control of his destiny by forming his own company. He founded the Maxim Silent Firearms Company and received his first silencer patent in 1908.

EARLY MAXIM SILENCERS

The Maxim Model 1908 silencer, from a distance, looked something like a soup can stuck perpendicular to the underside of a rifle barrel. Closer inspection revealed a wide piston valve system

The Maxim Model 1910 was the first commercially successful silencer and provided a lot of innocent fun to sport shooters and their families. Photo by Polly Walter.

extending from the right of the can and a smaller escape valve with vent ports extending from the left side. The design was intended to briefly trap high-pressure combustion gases near the muzzle of the firearm and then gradually vent low-pressure gas from the silencer. (Study of early patents suggests that attempting to mechanically trap combustion gases using spring-powered valves was a common theme in early silencer design.) The design was complicated, expensive, and not particularly effective. Maxim developed a simplified variant of this design, but it also provided disappointing performance. Maxim quickly abandoned this approach in favor of a different principle.

The following year, Maxim received a patent (see Figure 7.1) for a silencer designed to swirl the gases entering the rear of the silencer, causing the gases to expand and lose energy before exiting the front of the silencer. This Model 1909 silencer apparently sold in limited numbers, but its concentric design (relative to the bore of the firearm) occluded the gun's front sight. This aspect of the can's design required either mounting a front sight on the silencer itself or using a telescopic sight. Furthermore, Maxim believed that the Model 1909 allowed a pencil-shaped gas jet to exit the front of the silencer, thus significantly reducing its performance. Solving these two problems led to Maxim's most successful silencer, the Model 1910 (see Figures 7.2 and 7.3).

MAXIM MODEL 1910 SILENCER

The Maxim Model 1910 was not only quieter than the Model 1909, its eccentric design permitted employing a firearm's regular front sight. According to a long-since retired Colt employee, the Colt plant in Hartford, Connecticut, actually manufactured the Model 1910 silencer for the Maxim

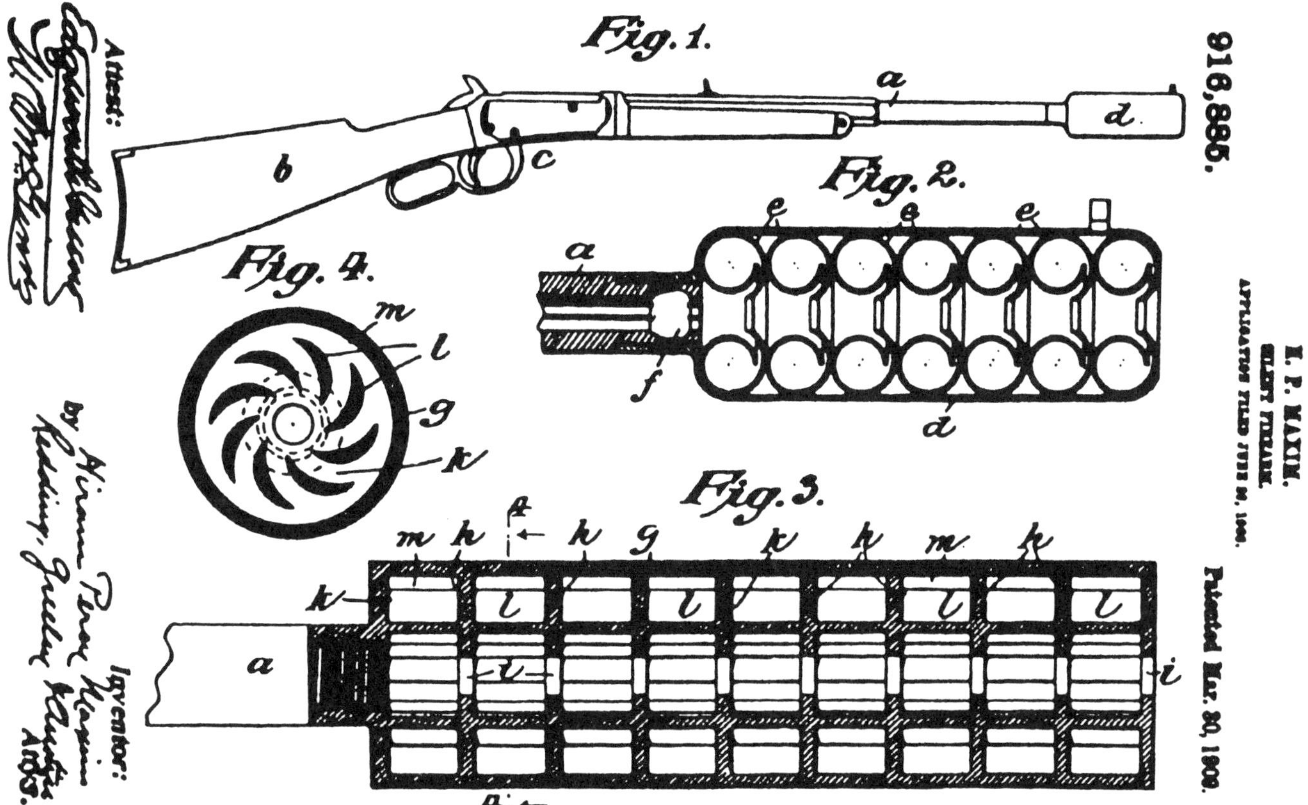

Figure 7.1. Patent drawings of Maxim Model 1909 silencer.

Silent Firearms Company, which was initially based in New York but then moved to Hartford.

Another interesting feature of the Model 1910 was the use of interrupted threads, which permitted mounting the silencer by slipping it over a barrel with interrupted threads and then simply twisting the silencer clockwise 90 degrees. This permitted almost instantaneous mounting and dismounting, which greatly facilitated reloading rifles with tubular magazines.

Made of soft, malleable steel, the silencer tube is press-fit into a rear end cap that features interrupted threads for mounting on a barrel. A primary expansion chamber forward of the rear end cap is separated from the stamped baffles by a ring-shaped ridge pressed into the tube (seen as a circular groove around the outside of the tube). In variants designed for centerfire cartridges, the rearmost baffles are stamped from thicker material than the forward baffles to withstand the higher pressures generated by the muzzle blast in the primary expansion chamber. While the thicker baffles function as blast baffles, they retain the sculptured design of all the baffles in the baffle stack. When the thicker

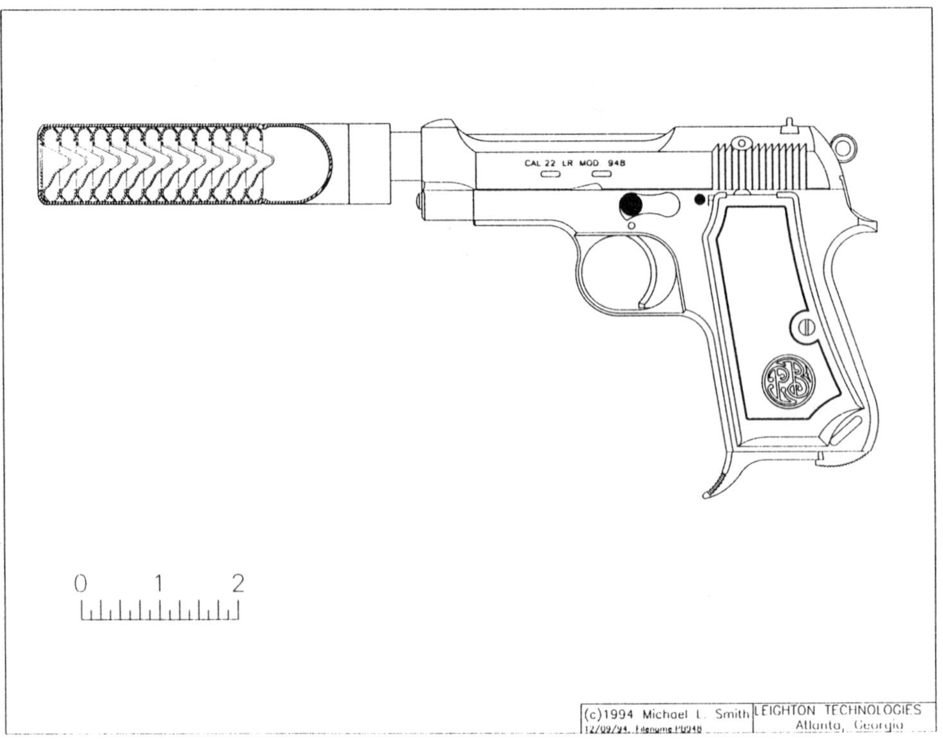

Figure 7.2. Maxim Model 1910 .22 caliber rimfire silencer on Beretta Model 948 pistol. Drawing by Mike Smith.

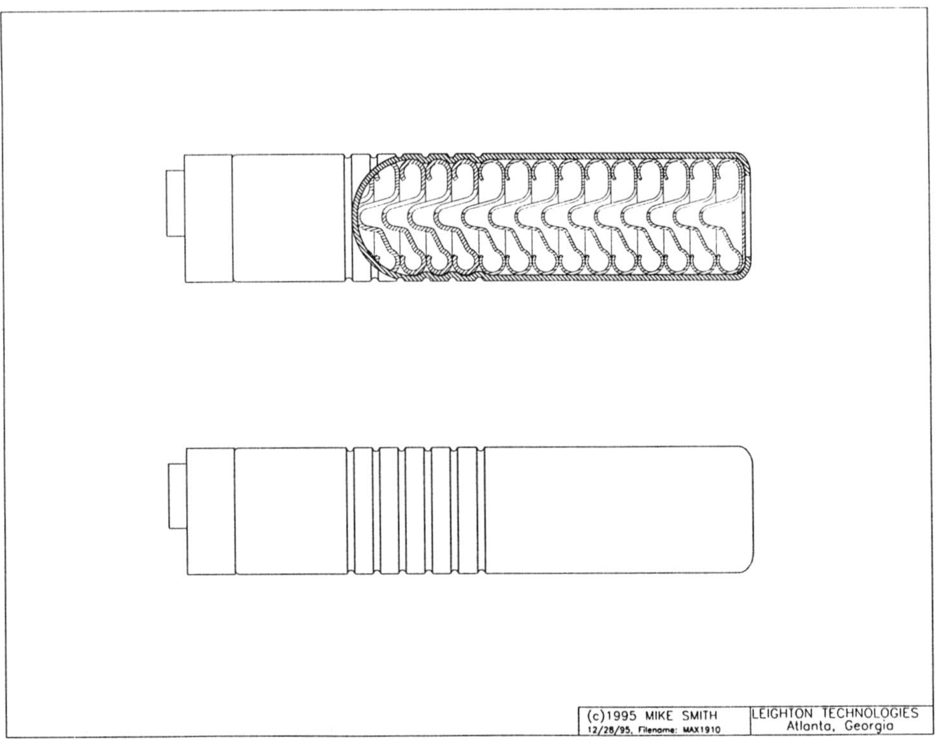

Figure 7.3. Maxim Model 1910 .44 caliber centerfire silencer. Drawing by Mike Smith.

The Maxim Model 1910 silencer mounted on a Winchester Model 06 pump rifle. Photo by Polly Walter.

baffles are present in the Model 1910, they are individually held in place by a series of ring-shaped ridges pressed into the tube. A single pressed ridge (seen as a straight groove running lengthwise along the bottom of the can) keeps the eccentric baffles properly aligned with the bore.

The .22 rimfire variant of the Maxim Model 1910 tested in this study features 13 baffles (not counting the front end cap) in a tube measuring 4.5 inches (113.6 mm) long and 1.0 inch (25.4 mm) in diameter. The eccentric mount extending from the rear end cap is 0.4 inch (11 mm) long and 0.6 inch (16 mm) in diameter.

It's an ingenious design even by modern standards, and the eccentric Model 1910 quickly became relatively common among sport shooters, especially in the northeastern United States. Silencers provided an innocent and inexpensive source of family fun. The Model 1910 cost an affordable $5 for the .22 rimfire version and $7 for the centerfire version. A subsequent variant called the Model 15, which was designed for the Springfield rifle, sold for $8.50, including a quick-couple device that wrapped around the Springfield's front sight.

The Maxim Model 1910 silencer achieved greater commercial success in the United States than any design until Jonathan Arthur Ciener, Dr. Philip Dater, and others began to build silencers for the civilian marketplace nearly three-quarters of a century later. While the fascinating design and historical importance of the Maxim Model 1910 has been cited frequently in relevant articles and books, it is hard to find even anecdotal information on its actual performance. Since the .22 rimfire version of this silencer was particularly popular, it is appropriate to scientifically test the performance of the .22 caliber Model 1910.

The first step was to find a suitable firearm of the period for use as a test weapon. A Winchester Model 06 pump .22 rifle was acquired and the suppressor was transferred via Form 5 to master craftsman and Class 3 manufacturer John Norrell. John installed interrupted threads on the rifle that precisely locked the silencer in place with a quarter turn. His workmanship was nothing short of flawless.

Upon return of the silencer and rifle from

Norrell Arms, the formal T&E could begin. The Winchester Model 06 rifle was tested with and without a Maxim Model 1910 silencer attached using Federal high-velocity, Hansen standard-velocity target, and Baikal Junior Brass subsonic Long Rifle ammunition. Federal CB Longs, CCI high-velocity Shorts, and CCI standard-velocity Shorts were also used.

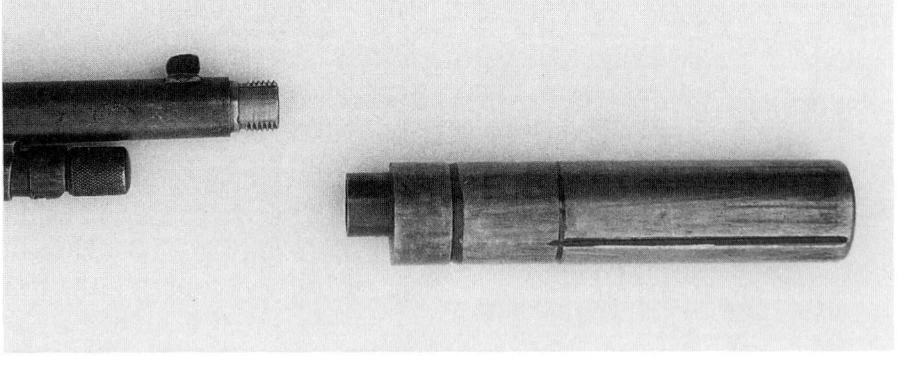

Details of the interrupted threads installed on the rifle by John Norrell. Note also the circular groove that separates the baffle stack from the primary expansion chamber and the straight groove along the bottom of the tube that keeps the eccentric baffles properly aligned with the bore.

Performance

From a historical point of view, the most appropriate rounds to use with the Maxim Model 1910 silencer are standard-velocity Long Rifles and standard-velocity Shorts, for these are essentially the rounds that were available when H.P. Maxim designed the Model 1910.

The .22 Short was the first metallic cartridge to be produced commercially in the United States. As hard as it is to imagine today, the .22 Short was originally developed for self-defense. The earliest firearm chambered for the round was the First Model revolver produced by Smith & Wesson in 1857. Many wealthy officers carried this pistol during the Civil War. The original load was 4 grains of black powder driving a 29 grain bullet. Remington introduced the first noncorrosive .22 Shorts in 1927 and the first high-velocity Shorts in 1930, about the time that H.P. Maxim turned his attention from firearm to industrial silencers.

The .22 Long Rifle was originally developed in 1887 by the J. Stevens Arms & Tool Company. The Long Rifle featured a 40 grain bullet and 5 grains of black powder. The cartridge proved much more accurate than the Longs and Extra Longs of the day, as well as being more effective against game, so the popularity of the Long Rifle spread like wildfire. Soon available with semi-smokeless and then smokeless powder, ammunition manufacturers started crimping the case in 1900. But the high-velocity Long Rifle cartridge was not introduced until 1930 (by Remington).

Using standard-velocity Short and Long Rifle rounds is appropriate to test what the Maxim silencer sounded like when it appeared in the marketplace. Testing the Maxim with the more modern high-velocity and new subsonic ammunition provides a useful benchmark for comparing its performance against modern muzzle suppressors and integrally suppressed firearms.

The performance of the Maxim Model 1910 silencer was compared to Vaime A8 and AWC Archangel I muzzle cans mounted on a Ruger 77/22, as well as a Ciener integral suppressor on a Marlin Model 780 rifle. The suppressed and unsuppressed sound signatures appear in Table 7.1, net sound reductions appear in Table 7.2, and muzzle velocities appear in Table 7.3. Note that the peak SPL created by cycling the pump action of the Winchester Model 06 is 105 dB, while the external hammer creates a 106 dB sound signature when the trigger is pulled on an empty chamber.

It quickly becomes obvious from the data in Tables 7.1 and 7.2 that the Maxim Model 10 performs very well even by modern standards. Using high-velocity ammunition, the Maxim delivers more sound reduction than either muzzle can and even the integral suppressor. A loud ballistic crack does occur, however, with every system using a muzzle can. There is no ballistic crack with the integral system since its ported barrel drops high-velocity projectiles to subsonic speeds.

Table 7.1. Sound signatures in decibels of Maxim suppressor tests.

GUN	SUPPRESSOR	FEDERAL HV	HANSEN SV LR	BAIKAL JB SS LR	CCI HV SHORTS	CCI SV SHORTS	FEDERAL CB LONGS	TEMP., °F (°C)
Winchester 06	None	142	138	138	136[b]	130	129	78(26)
Winchester 06	Maxim 1910	119	115	114	122[b]	112	107	78(26)
Ruger 77/22	None	141	139	137[a]	—	—	131	64(18)
Ruger 77/22	AWC Archangel I	123	121	115[a]	—	—	106	64(18)
Ruger 77/22	None	141	138	138[a]	—	—	132	50(10)
Ruger 77/22	Vaime A8	121	118	117[a]	—	—	106	50(10)
Marlin 780	None	143	140	140[a]	—	—	134	83(28)
Marlin 780	Ciener integral	124	121	115[a]	—	—	111	83(28)

[a] RWS subsonic LR
[b] ambient temperature = 77°F (25°C)

Table 7.2. Net sound reductions of Maxim tests.

GUN	SUPPRESSOR	FEDERAL HV LR	HANSEN SV LR	BAIKAL JB SS LR	CCI HV SHORTS	CCI SV SHORTS	FEDERAL CB LONGS	TEMP., °F (°C)
Winchester 06	Maxim 1910	23	23	24	14[b]	18	22	78(26)
Ruger 77/22	AWC Archangel I	18	18	22[a]	—	—	25	64(18)
Ruger 77/22	Vaime A8	20	20	21[a]	—	—	26	50(10)
Marlin 780	Ciener integral	19	19	25[a]	—	—	23	83(28)

[a] RWS subsonic LR
[b] ambient temperature = 77°F (25°C)

Table 7.3. Muzzle velocities of suppressed and unsuppressed rifles used in Maxim tests, expressed in feet per second (and meters per second).

GUN	SUPPRESSOR	FEDERAL HV LR	HANSEN SV LR	BAIKAL JB SS LR	CCI HV SHORTS	CCI SV SHORTS	FEDERAL CB LONGS	TEMP., °F (°C)	SPEED OF SOUND fps (mps)
Winchester 06	Maxim 1910	1,236(377)	1,120(341)	1,018(310)	1,162 (354)[b]	872(266)	668(204)	78(26)	1,137(347)
Ruger 77/22	AWC Archangel I	1,272(388)	1,133(345)	982(299)[a]	—	—	644(196)	64(18)	1,122(342)
Marlin 780	Ciener integral	1,065(325)	986(301)	851(259)[a]	—	—	568(173)	83(28)	1,142(348)

[a] RWS subsonic LR
[b] ambient temperature = 77°F (25°C)

Using standard-velocity target ammunition, the Maxim also outperforms all of the other suppressed systems tested in this study. Note from Table 7.3 that the standard-velocity ammunition remained subsonic in the Winchester 06. But the same lot of ammunition produced supersonic velocities in the Ruger 77/22, so there was a loud ballistic crack that no suppressor can mask.

The Maxim was much more effective than all of the other muzzle cans with subsonic ammunition. The Ciener integrally suppressed rifle was barely quieter with subsonic ammunition, but the integral system only produced 84 percent of the velocity delivered by the Winchester/Maxim system.

The Maxim delivered disappointing performance with high-velocity Shorts. Not only was the net sound reduction the poorest in this study, but the high-velocity Shorts produced a ballistic crack since they exceeded the speed of sound on this day by 25 fps (8 mps).

The Maxim did, however, produce a significantly better net sound reduction with standard-velocity Shorts. The actual suppressed sound signature using standard-velocity Shorts was a mere 112 dB, which is within 6 decibels of the sound generated by the rifle's hammer fall. Most observers are astonished by this level of performance. They typically think a suppressed gunshot using the Maxim with standard-velocity Shorts sounds like a BB gun, although the Daisy Red Ryder actually produces a sound signature of 101 dB. The Maxim's report with standard-velocity Shorts does not sound like a gunshot, and the dominant event is the sound of the bullet striking the target. The old rifle is quite accurate with these standard-velocity Shorts, and they have become my favorite load for the Winchester/Maxim system.

For short-range target shooting or potting squirrels pilfering the insulation from my attic, I use CB Longs. The muzzle signature with the Winchester/Maxim system is just 1 dB louder than the rifle's hammer fall. Since the hammer is closer to the shooter's ear than the front of the Maxim silencer, the shooter only hears the hammer fall and bullet impact. The shooter hears no muzzle signature at all with the Winchester/Maxim system and CB Longs. That's a heady and rather addictive experience. The CB Longs are not as accurate as the standard-velocity Shorts in this rifle, but the CB Longs do provide enough accuracy for reliable head shots on meddlesome squirrels at typical engagement distances.

The data in Table 7.3 demonstrate that a muzzle can like the Maxim provides significantly more velocity than an integrally suppressed rifle (which vents combustion cases into the suppressor through ports drilled in the rifle barrel). This increased velocity translates into both a flatter trajectory (i.e., superior shot placement) and more velocity for penetration in live targets (i.e., superior terminal ballistics). Figures 7.4

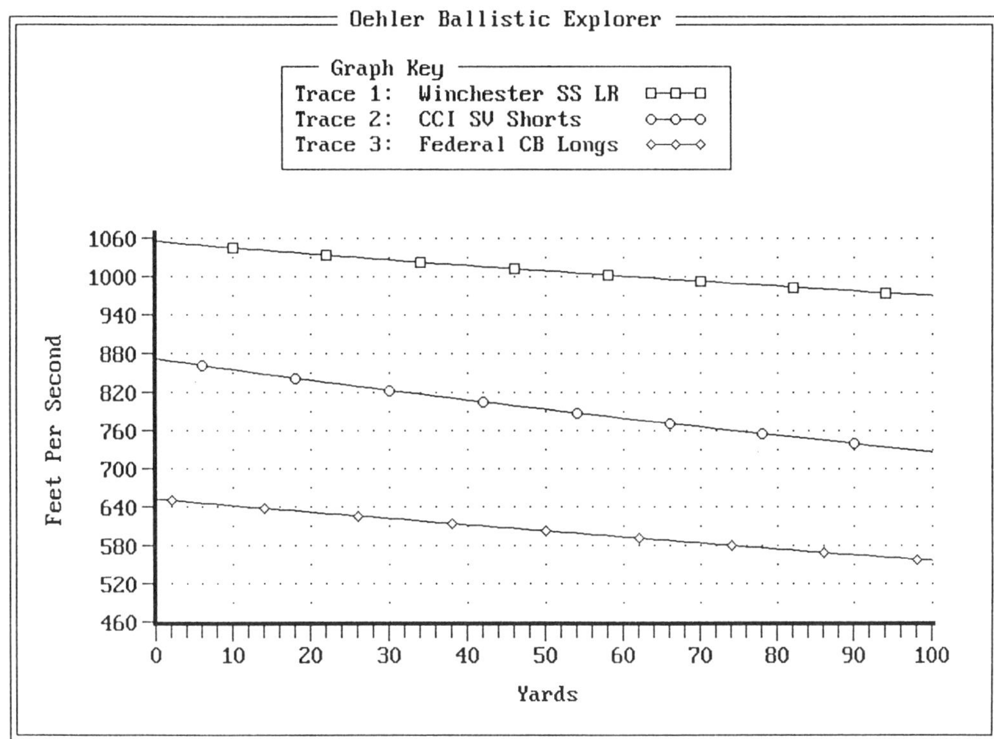

Figure 7.4. Bullet velocities produced by several kinds of ammunition fired in the Winchester Model 06 rifle with Maxim Model 1910 silencer.

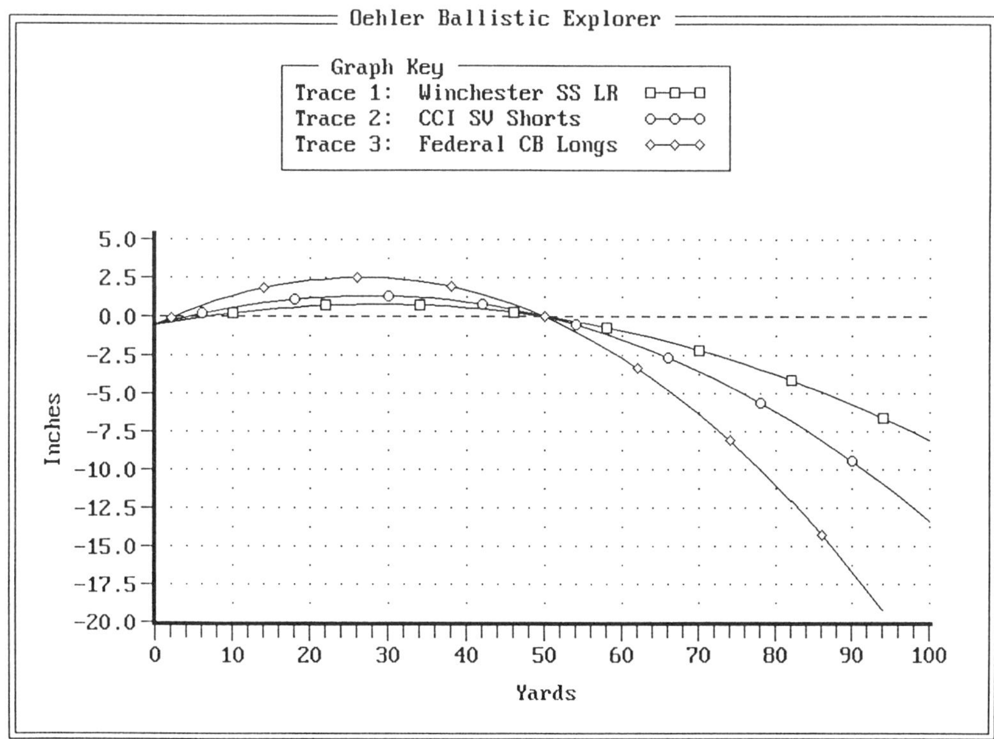

Figure 7.5. Bullet trajectories produced by several kinds of ammunition fired in the Winchester Model 06 rifle with Maxim Model 1910 silencer.

and 7.5 compare the velocities and trajectories produced by several kinds of ammunition fired in the Winchester 06 rifle with the Maxim Model 1910 silencer. Subsonic Long Rifle ammunition clearly offers the flattest trajectory and the most velocity for penetration of the three rounds compared in Figures 7.4 and 7.5, making subsonic ammunition the preferred round of these three for hunting small game. Figures 7.6 and 7.7 compare the performance of the Winchester/Maxim system with a Ruger 77/22 and AWC Archangel I suppressor, and the Marlin 780 rifle with integral Ciener suppressor (all using Hansen standard-velocity ammunition).

Just as Hiram Percey Maxim certainly showed great promise when he graduated from MIT in 1886 at the age of 17, the excellent performance of his Model 1910 silencer demonstrates that his engineering prowess fulfilled that expectation. Like his contemporary, John Moses Browning, Hiram P.

Maxim's technology is still quite relevant today.

Maxim did not, however, rest on his laurels after developing the Model 1910. He continued to design and market new suppressors for nearly two more decades. We'll continue the Maxim story when we examine the design and performance of the Maxim Model 1921 silencer in the chapter on the Maxim Silent Firearms Company in the third volume of *Silencer History and Performance*. Maxim dominated silencer design until the Gun Control Act of 1934 signaled an abrupt end to silencer development in the United States. Decades of doldrums in silencer development followed.

DECADES OF DOLDRUMS

After the Gun Control Act virtually destroyed the civilian market for silencers, serious silencer development virtually ceased in the United States until the outbreak of World War II. As the

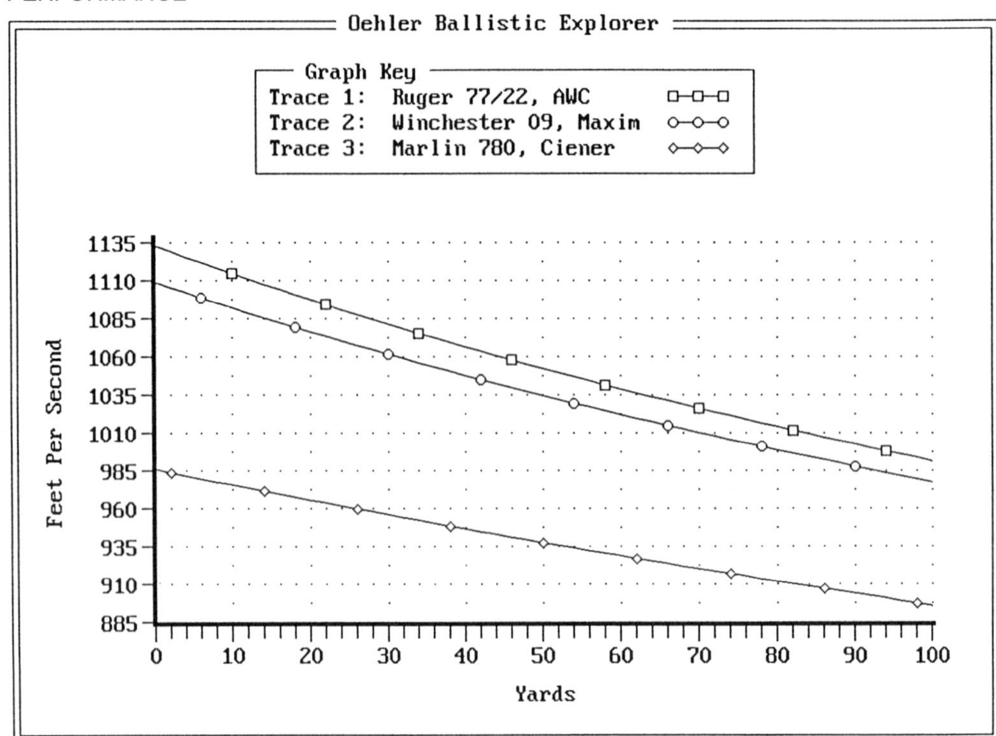

Figure 7.6. Bullet velocities produced by the Winchester/Maxim system, a Ruger 77/22 and AWC Archangel I suppressor, and the Marlin 780 rifle with integral Ciener suppressor (all using Hansen standard-velocity ammunition).

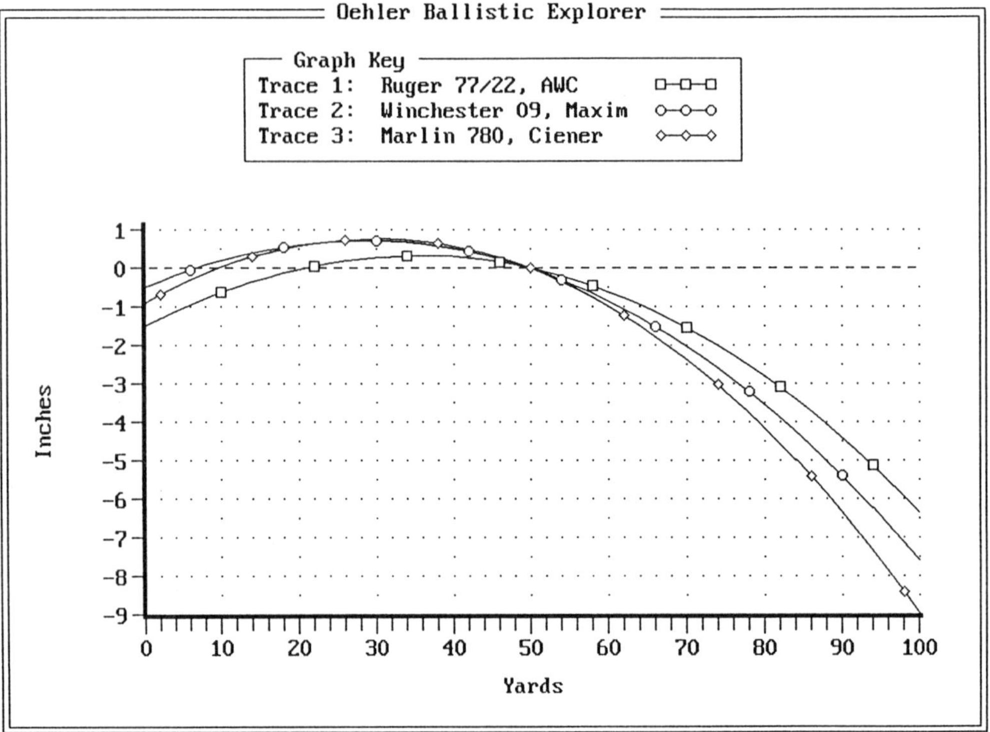

Figure 7.7. Bullet trajectories produced by the Winchester/Maxim system, a Ruger 77/22 and AWC Archangel I suppressor, and the Marlin 780 rifle with integral Ciener suppressor (all using Hansen standard-velocity ammunition).

Allies deployed clandestine and commando operations, the usefulness of silent weapons quickly became apparent. Early operations used knives and crossbows for silent killing. Even though everyone understood that silenced firearms would be far more appropriate and effective, the demise of the civilian marketplace meant that neither design expertise nor production facilities were immediately available to fill the military requirements for silenced firearms. (Subsequent legislation in the 1986 and 1994 aimed at civilians would have a similar effect on restricting the technology available for military and law enforcement applications.)

While the U.S. government considered a proposal to resume the manufacture of Maxim silencers, research and development in Britain rejected the use of muzzle cans in favor of a new trend in silencer development: the integral silencer. The new type of design featured a shortened, ported barrel designed to vent combustion cases into the rear of the silencer. The venting had several functions: 1) reduce the projectile velocity to below the speed of sound so there would be no ballistic crack; 2) reduce the overall length of the silenced firearm, which was important in both clandestine and commando operations; and 3) improve the amount of sound reduction. Furthermore, an integrally suppressed firearm tends to be more robust than a similar system with a muzzle can. The U.S. government imported samples of new British silenced weapons, and the subsequent development of U.S. technology followed the British interest in integrally suppressed weapons.

While none of the new technology made it into civilian hands (except for a fortunate handful of collectors), the development of silencers during World War II is relevant to a discussion of civilian silencers in general, and silenced .22s in particular, for several reasons. World War II marked a change in focus from muzzle cans to integral suppressors, a trend that would dominate the subsequent development of .22 rimfire silencers (as well as submachine gun suppressors) until the 1980s, when the availability of subsonic ammunition made muzzle cans interesting once again.

After World War II, silencer development dried up once again until the American involvement in Vietnam heated up and Mitchell WerBell III developed a new and diverse line of silenced weapons for SIONICS and then for the Military Armament Corporation (MAC). While WerBell developed effective muzzle cans for the new Ingram family of submachine guns and the Colt Huntsman .22 pistol, many of his products continued to employ integral designs. Although he developed the first silenced Ruger 10/22 rifle, the design was intended for covert and special operations. Many of WerBell's designs—such as his suppressed Ruger rifles and pistols—had finite lifespans that were incompatible with the civilian marketplace, since it was impractical to purchase a new silenced firearm with its $200 transfer tax after a few hundred or a few thousand rounds.

Nevertheless, some SIONICS and MAC suppressors did make it into the civilian marketplace, where inflation had rendered the $200 transfer tax much less oppressive than in 1934. This influx of silencers stimulated an increasing interest in the civilian marketplace just about the time MAC died due to a combination of mismanagement and declining military sales. Soon other manufacturers appeared to fill the void left by the demise of MAC.

After the demise of MAC, the first new silencer manufacturer to appear was Jonathan Arthur Ciener. Since MAC had always focused on the military marketplace as its bread and butter, it is probably safe to assert that Jonathan Arthur Ciener became the first successful manufacturer of silencers for the American public since Hiram P. Maxim a half century before.

CIENER SUPPRESSED MARLIN 780 RIFLE

Jonathan Arthur Ciener is the oldest active suppressor manufacturer in the United States. When he began manufacturing suppressors in 1976, a few post-auction MAC suppressors were kicking around, and that was it. Since that time, his muzzle cans and integrally suppressed firearms have become known for their solid performance and handsome appearance. Ciener's economy offering is

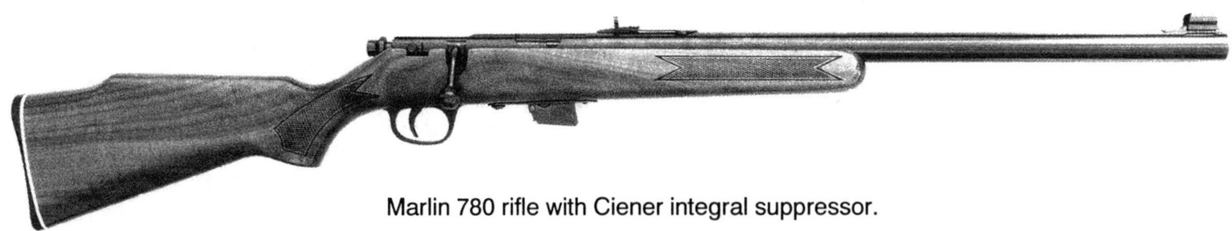

Marlin 780 rifle with Ciener integral suppressor.

the integrally suppressed Marlin Model 780 bolt-action .22 rifle. The Marlin uses the same suppressor technology that is found in Ciener's top-of-the-line Ruger 10/22 and 77/22 rifles as well as his Browning take-down semiautomatic rifle.

The Model 780 was Marlin's top-of-the-line rifle, which employed a seven-round detachable magazine featuring a built-in catch. It was replaced by the Model 880, which is basically the same rifle with a different detachable magazine, a new safety that fires in the forward position (the 780 fires from the dangerously unconventional rear position), and other minor improvements. The 780 rifle weighs 5.5 pounds (2.5 kg) unsuppressed with its black walnut stock. The suppressed version weighs 6.06 pounds (2.75 kg). Ciener's Model 780 is one of the few suppressed bolt-action rifles that comes with iron sights, which is why I bought the gun. Ciener bought a quantity of these rifles when they were discontinued, so the rifle continued to be available into the 1990s. This was one of the very first suppressed rifles that I personally acquired.

Unbeknown to me, after firing only three rounds through the new rifle, the encapsulator slipped off the barrel, allowing brass eyelets to occlude the bullet path. The fourth round fired through the rifle was extremely quiet compared to the preceding rounds, partly because the bullet never emerged from the suppressor! Although this most unusual problem (I've never heard of another occurrence) would have been covered under Ciener's warranty, I decided to solve this problem myself and seize the opportunity to examine the internal construction of Ciener's system.

The suppressor is not designed to be disassembled. In fact, the gun comes with a written statement that disassembly voids the warranty. Nevertheless, disassembly of a virgin rifle is straightforward and intuitive. After a few hundred rounds, however, accumulated powder residue and corrosion make disassembly impossible.

To begin disassembly, unscrew the large bolt at the rear of the magazine well, which ties the action to the stock. A light tap upward with the heel of the hand at the front of the suppressor tube will unseat the barreled action. Unscrew the front end cap of the suppressor. Note that the barrel terminates several inches before the front end of the suppressor tube. A terminal expansion chamber of this sort commonly reduces the sound signature of an integral suppressor quite noticeably over the same design without this feature.

Remove the set screw on the underside of the suppressor tube near the receiver. Now twist off the tube, which is friction-fit onto a shoulder at the rear of the turned-down barrel. Pulling the tube forward allows several ounces of very small brass eyelets to fall out. The tube then slips off the barrel easily. A thick aluminum washer at the end of the barrel serves as a friction-fit encapsulator to keep the eyelets in place. Ciener uses a sheet of Kleenex as packing between the washer and eyelets to ensure that the eyelets don't rattle.

To facilitate reassembly, pop off the front sight hood and remove the two screws holding the front sight to the tube. Using a large wooden dowel, drive the aluminum washer out of the tube. That completes disassembly.

As the photos show, the barrel is turned down to minimum thickness and is ported with four alternating rows of small holes. I was surprised by heavy corrosion and pitting at the rear of the barrel, since I had purchased this gun new in the box from Ciener. It appears that this rifle was not stored

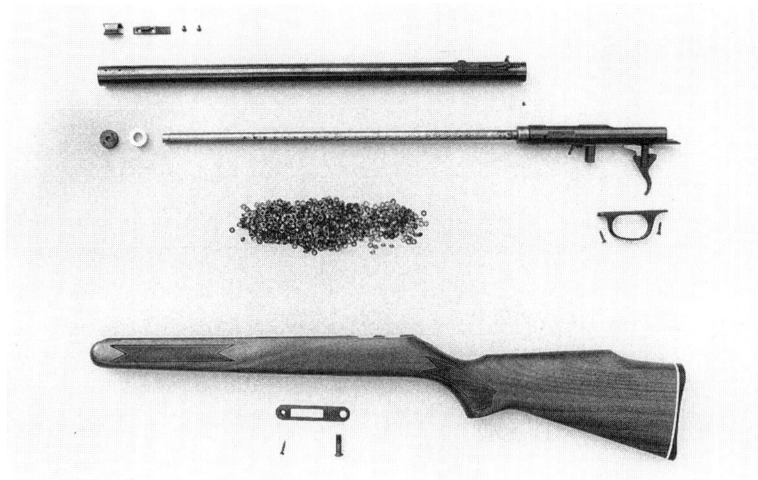

Disassembled Marlin 780 rifle with Ciener integral suppressor.

The turned-down barrel of the Marlin 780 exhibited corrosion even though the new rifle had just arrived from Ciener.

in a dehumidified environment after production.

The barrel retains dense tooling marks with fine, sharp ridges that gripped and tore patches I used to wipe oil on the barrel, trapping scores of cloth fibers on the barrel, which were removed with difficulty using a bronze brush. I've subsequently learned that spraying the internal components with unflavored Pam cooking spray or Kroil (an inexpensive penetrating oil that makes a good powder solvent) would have been a better solution. The rough finish on the barrel cannot be criticized for several reasons: the suppressor is not meant to be disassembled, this is an economy offering, the rough exterior of the barrel is not visible, and it does not adversely affect performance. I mention the rough machining of the barrel only for sake of completeness. This contrasts with Ciener taking the time to crown the barrel, which does enhance performance (accuracy).

In the form letter that comes with the gun, Ciener stresses that no attempt should be made to disassemble the suppressor. He says that the design is self-cleaning without periodic rebuilding. Here I must part company with Ciener. The design is not self-cleaning. An acquaintance once cut one of Ciener's integrally suppressed .22 rifles apart, since it no longer provided acceptable sound reduction. The eyelets were filled tightly with powder residue, and all the barrel ports were clogged. Well over 10,000 rounds had been fired through the system, although the owner didn't know precisely how many rounds had been fired. The system has a finite lifespan before it becomes clogged with fouling.

One can maximize this lifespan by only using clean ammunition. Avoid ammo that has a thick wax coating like RWS and Baikal Junior Brass subsonic ammunition. Avoid rounds that produce a lot of powder residue. Follow Ciener's recommendation that the bore should only be cleaned with a *dry* brush and *dry* patch. Ciener stresses that every effort should be made to keep the inside of the suppressor dry. Considering the deep corrosion I observed on the turned-down barrel hours after the gun arrived, that seems like very good advice. The corrosion problem can be minimized by always storing the rifle with the bolt open to encourage the evaporation of any moisture in the suppressor, which would otherwise combine with the powder residue to form nitric and sulfuric acids. The receiver can be cleaned like any firearm.

To reassemble the suppressor, first coat the shoulder of the barrel and the threads on the front end cap with a colloidal molybdenum or copper high-temperature antiseize compound to facilitate future disassembly of the suppressor if necessary. Without this treatment, disassembly will become impossible after a few hundred rounds. Next, slide the suppressor tube back on the shoulder at the rear of the barrel and replace the set screw.

The next task is replacing the brass eyelets, which barely squeeze between the barrel and tube. This requires slow and patient refilling, which is aggravated by the fact that the crown cut into the barrel is a perfect match to the flange of the eyelet Ciener uses. To facilitate introducing eyelets, insert a cleaning rod into the barrel from the back end to keep the eyelets out of the barrel crown, and guide them into the space between the barrel and tube. Tap the butt of the rifle on a padded carpet or rubber bench pad throughout this process to settle the eyelets in the tube.

Unlike Ciener, you may wish to use a thin sheet of neoprene or other closed-cell foam (which won't absorb moisture like Kleenex) to fill in the remaining space between the eyelets and the aluminum washer. Tap the washer in place with a large wooden dowel. I made a spacer from plastic tubing that precisely fit between the encapsulator and the suppressor's front end cap. This simple expedient will prevent another mishap like the one I experienced. I've made this modification on every integrally suppressed Ciener .22 rifle that I've owned as a dose of preventive medicine, even though the procedure voids my warranty. Continue reassembly by screwing the end cap in place, making sure its threads are coated with antiseize compound. Finally, reinstall the front sight and replace the barreled action in the stock.

Once this simple repair was completed, I was able to put the suppressed Marlin through its paces. Here's what I learned.

Performance

In terms of sound suppression, Ciener's suppressed Marlin performs about as well as AWC's Archangel I muzzle can on a Ruger 77/22. While the muzzle can actually produced lower sound signatures than the suppressed Marlin with high-velocity Long Rifles and CB Longs, this is only part of the story since the signatures of the unsuppressed Marlin and Ruger rifles differ. Since the two systems were tested on different days with different environmental conditions, a better sense of system performance is afforded by the net sound reductions in Table 7.2 rather than by the sound signatures listed in Table 7.1. Using net sound reductions as the yardstick, Ciener's suppressed Marlin slightly outperforms the Ruger 77/22 with AWC Archangel I suppressor. While these differences can be perceived when the systems are shot side by side, the mind perceives (i.e., remembers) no difference if they are fired hours apart.

When fired with RWS subsonic LR ammunition and Federal Hi-Power CB Longs, the subjective opinion of the observer is that Ciener's Marlin is very quiet indeed. Unfortunately, the heavy wax coating on RWS subsonic ammo will dramatically reduce the lifespan of the Ciener suppressor and should not be used. Eley and Remington subsonic ammunition do not have a heavy wax coating and would be better choices for Ciener's integrally suppressed .22 rifles.

What is the lifespan of this Ciener suppressor using clean ammo (like Federal high-velocity and Hansen standard-velocity target) if the suppressor is not disassembled for cleaning? One Ruger 77/22 with a Ciener integral suppressor I've shot is still quiet after slightly more than 10,000 rounds. That's several lifetimes—the owner and kids and grandkids and maybe even great grandkids—for most folks. Those serious sport shooters, however, who run through a lot of ammunition

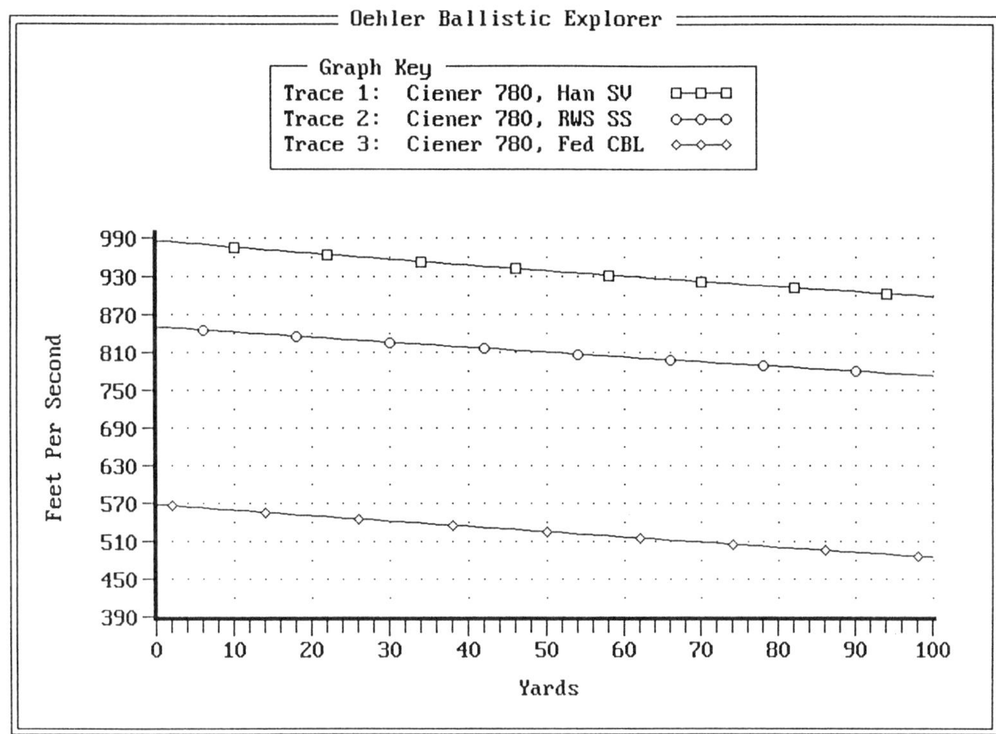

Figure 7.8. Bullet velocities of the three rounds tested in the Ciener-suppressed Marlin when sighted in at 25 yards.

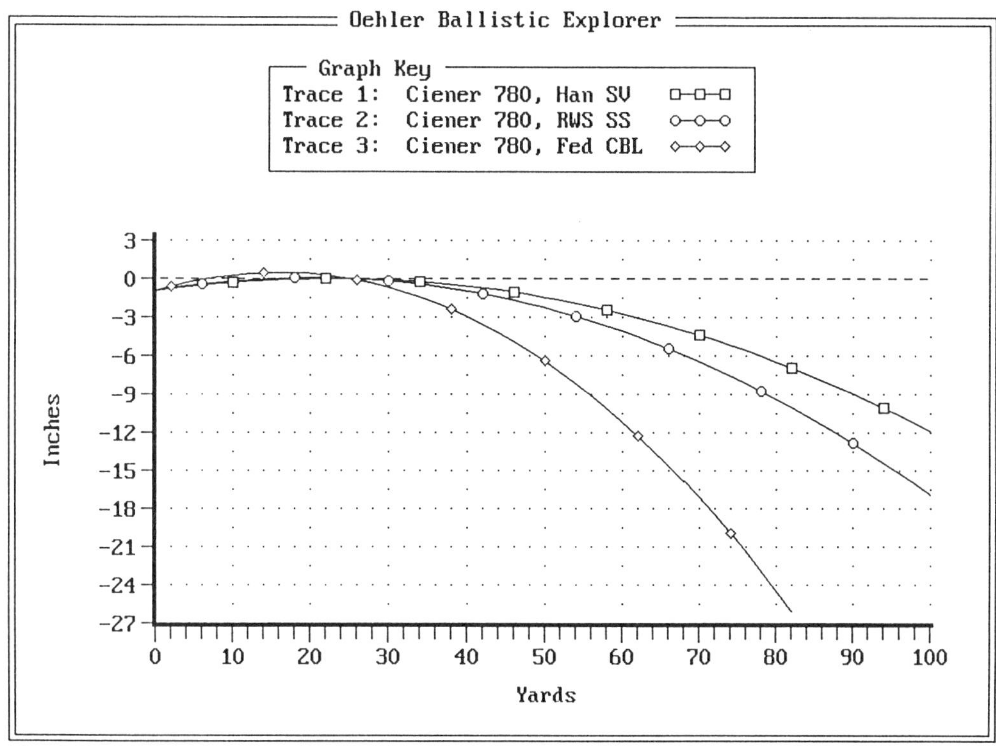

Figure 7.9. Bullet trajectories of three rounds tested in Ciener-suppressed Marlin 780 when sighted in at 25 yards.

may be better served by an alternative design. Such folks tend to buy ten, twenty, or even thirty thousand rounds of .22 ammunition at a time.

As Table 7.6 shows, the Ciener integral suppressor kept all loads subsonic, dropping a cartridge's velocity an average of 18 percent. Note, however, that both the high-velocity and standard-velocity LR ammo produced supersonic velocities (and, therefore, ballistic cracks) when fired in an unsuppressed Marlin rifle. Figure 7.8 shows the bullet trajectories of three rounds tested in the suppressed Marlin. While all three cartridges shot close to the same point of aim for close-range plinking, bullet paths of the Long Rifle rounds began to diverge at 85 feet. The CB Longs generally hit within a half inch or so of the other loads out to 25 yards when sighted in at 25 yards. Figure 7.9 shows bullet velocities to the same distance.

Table 7.4. Bullet velocities in feet per second (and meters per second) through suppressed and unsuppressed Marlin 780.

GUN	SUPPRESSOR	FEDERAL HV LR	HANSEN SV LR	RWS SUBSONIC LR	FEDERAL CB LONGS	TEMP., °F (°C)	SPEED OF SOUND fps (mps)
Marlin 780	None	1,297(395)	1,172(357)	1,044(318)	707(215)	83(28)	1,142 (348)
Marlin 780	Ciener	1,065(325)	986(301)	851(259)	568(173)	83(28)	1,142 (348)
Percent Reduction		18	16	18	20	83(28)	1,142 (348)

As we evaluate other suppressed .22 rifles and pistols throughout the three volumes of *Silencer History and Performance*, these graphs will provide a valuable benchmark in addition to the sound test data. Some suppressed firearms achieve a low sound signature by excessive porting of the barrel, producing such low velocities that performance downrange is impaired severely. Even some integrally suppressed submachine guns exhibit this problem. Ciener's suppressed Marlin 780, however, delivers fine performance downrange in terms of external ballistics. But the Marlin's mediocre trigger is another matter.

The poor trigger on the Marlin dramatically degrades the effectiveness of one's marksmanship. The Marlin is no Ruger 77/22. But then the Ruger is no Anschutz. I was trained to shoot target rifles at the point between heartbeats when blood pressure is at a minimum. This significantly improves my accuracy. But such discipline is meaningless with the Marlin's trigger. If you've ever shot a .22 target rifle, you'll want to invest in a good trigger job, which is easier said than done. Due to liability concerns, it's hard to find a competent gunsmith who will do a trigger job on a .22 anymore. The Marlin will be a disappointment without one. In fairness, every Ruger 77/22 I've shot needed one too—just not as badly as the Marlin.

So what's the bottom line on Ciener's suppressed Marlin 780? The rear of the barrel was corroded. That was irritating. But Ciener could minimize this problem with improved storage. He could even coat the barrels with a molybdenum resin like the one the military uses to refinish M16s at a cost of a dollar or two per gun. I'd gladly pay extra. The design is dated, but the system delivers good sound suppression for at least 10,000 rounds without sacrificing velocity downrange. Its cosmetic appearance is outstanding. And it comes at a budget price. Ciener's suppressed Marlin 780 is a solid value.

Ciener has been manufacturing suppressors since 1976 and can claim to be the oldest continuously operating suppressor manufacturer in the United States. A former medical officer in the Air Force and doctor with a medical subcontractor (Lovelace Clinic) for the U.S. space program, Dr. Philip H. Dater also started making suppressors that same year. But Dater actually started designing and building suppressors under the license of Sid Garrett's S&S Arms Company before he founded the Automatic Weapons Company, so he is two years shy of Ciener's record of operating continuously under his own license. Dater's suppressed Ruger pistol (eventually known as the RST) and his suppressed Ruger 10/22 and 77/22 rifles (eventually designated the R10) were destined to become classics in the history of suppressor development.

AWC R10 SUPPRESSED 10/22

Dr. Phil Dater founded the Automatic Weapons Company in 1976 while he was a practicing

AWC R10 rifle designed by Dr. Philip H. Dater.

The AWC R10 rifle provides comparable accuracy to an unsuppressed Ruger 10/22 rifle.

radiologist in Albuquerque, New Mexico. Initially, the company held a Class 6 license and remanufactured ammunition for local machine gunners on a little Star machine. AWC actually existed before Dater bought his first machine gun or silencer. Dater got into the suppressor business when he tried to redesign a Ruger Mark I pistol that had been suppressed by the original Military Armament Corporation but was no longer functioning. His improvements made the rebuilt pistol significantly quieter than the MAC.

Dater began to build suppressed Ruger pistols using his new design, which could be fully serviced by the owner to restore it to original factory specifications—unlike the MAC design, which only had a service life of about 500 rounds. He produced these first suppressed pistols under the license of the S&S Arms Company in Albuquerque as the Model AWC. Dater then developed a suppressed Ruger 10/22 using the design principles he developed for the suppressed pistol and adding them to the very simple design of the suppressed 10/22 that was built by MAC.

AWC R10 rifle with extra suppressed barrel assembly showing internal construction, made when AWC was in Albuquerque, New Mexico. Photo by Dr. Philip H. Dater.

The suppressor that MAC built on the Ruger 10/22 featured an 11 inch (28 cm) barrel and a tube diameter of 1-3/8 inches (3.5 cm). The MAC suppressor was absolutely empty, save for a sort of encapsulator that supported the barrel inside the tube. A screw-in end cap featured a thick neoprene wipe that had a service life of about 500 rounds. Dater improved upon the MAC suppressor by adding diffusion materials to the inside of the can and by designing the system for full disassembly for cleaning and maintenance. He gave his suppressed Ruger 10/22 rifle the same designation as his Ruger pistol: Model AWC. One wag called Dater's suppressed rifle a glorified glass-pack muffler. That wag was Phil Dater himself.

Dr. Dater built about 40 Model AWC suppressed Ruger pistols and 20 suppressed Ruger 10/22 rifles under Garrett's license. When Dater obtained a Class 2 manufacturing license for the Automatic Weapons Company in 1978, he began building suppressors under the trade name of Automatic Weapons Company, which was still located in Albuquerque. The same suppressed pistol was manufactured as the Model RST. The same basic rifle suppressor was manufactured as the Model R10 for the Ruger 10/22, the Model AR7 for the ArmaLite AR-7 Explorer rifle, and the Model R11 when the suppressor was built on any other .22 rifle.

The AWC R10 system provided one of the first sporting rifles with a user-maintainable suppressor designed to be shot a lot and to last the life of the barrel. Beginning in 1979, Dater introduced another useful innovation to the suppressor industry: the technical manual. Superficially resembling an Army Technical Manual, TM-R10 provides detailed information on the design, construction, and maintenance procedures for the R10 suppressed rifle. While several manufacturers have picked up on Dater's lead and provide manuals with their own suppressors, regrettably the practice of including a manual with every suppressor is by no means universal.

The R10 system consists of standard Ruger 10/22 rifle with an integral suppressor built around the original barrel, which is highly modified and shortened to 16.25 inches (41.3 cm). The design of the R10 suppressor and its modified Ruger barrel are shown in Figure 7.10. The barrel is turned down and threaded to accept a rear end cap, center support, front end cap, and suppressor tube, which are constructed of 6061-T6 aluminum alloy finished in a black hard-coat anodizing. The suppressor tube is 14.0 inches (35.6 cm) long and 1.25 inches (3.2 cm) in diameter. The suppressed Ruger 10/22 with R10 suppressor is 1.0 inch (2.5 cm) shorter than an unmod-

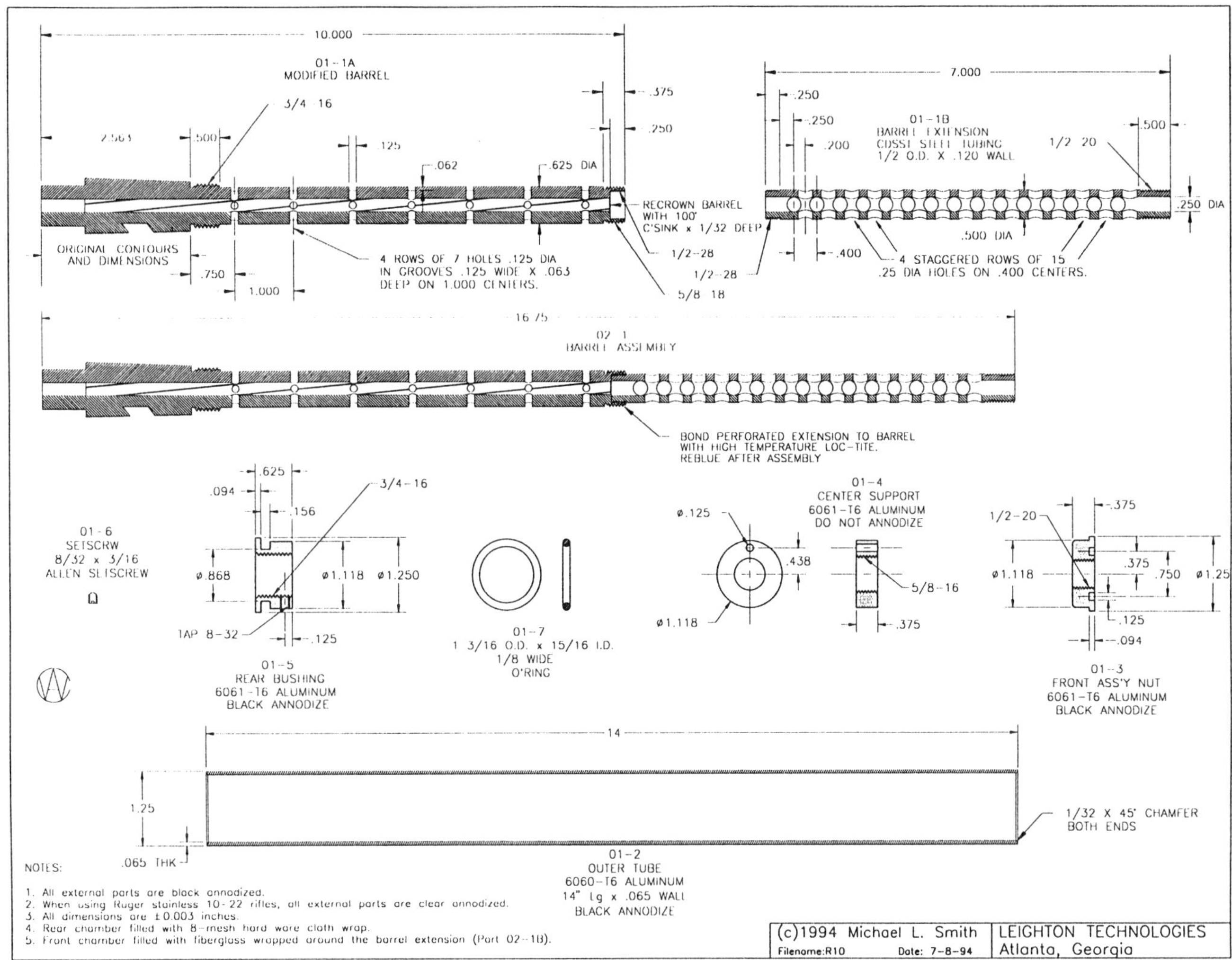

Figure 7.10. Design of Dr. Dater's R10 suppressed Ruger 10/22 rifle. Drawing by Mike Smith.

ified rifle and the system weighs about 6.5 pounds (2.9 kg), depending on the density of the stock. A neoprene O-ring prevents high-pressure combustion gases from leaking out via the threading in the rear end cap, while the lower pressure remaining in the front of the suppressor does not require this extra engineering.

The primary expansion chamber between the rear end cap and the center support features four rows of six holes each, which have a diameter of 1/8 inch (3.3 mm). A grooved ring is cut to help locate each set of four adjacent holes and to minimize the buildup of leading. This rear chamber is filled with a roll of 8 mesh (1/8 inch, 3.3 mm) galvanized steel mesh (called hardware cloth in the United States). The roll of mesh is prepared by cutting a 6.25 inch (15.9 cm) by 18.0 inch (45.7 cm) sheet of hardware cloth and rolling it tightly around a 5/8 inch (1.6 cm) dowel. The roll is bound with four loops of nylon filament strapping tape, and then slid over the barrel from the dowel. The center support is then screwed in place to secure the mesh roll in position.

The front portion of the barrel is turned to a smaller diameter for the secondary expansion chamber, and the barrel is ported with four rows of 13 holes each, which have a diameter of 0.25 inch (6.4 mm). This front portion of the barrel is wrapped with a 6x7 inch (15.2x17.8 cm) piece of 0.5 inch (1.3 cm) fiberglass.

Dater's design goals when he developed the R10 were twofold: 1) make a quiet suppressor, and 2) make a user-maintainable rifle that will last the life of the barrel. Before analyzing the R10's performance in terms of sound suppression, it would be useful to make a few comments on maintaining the R10 system. Many of the following suggestions do not appear in TM-R10.

Maintenance

The R10 suppressor should be disassembled for cleaning and maintenance every 2,000 rounds. Begin disassembly by removing the barreled action from the stock. Unscrew the front end cap with the spanner that comes with the suppressor. While the suppressor tube is simply held in compression by the system's two end caps, a screwing or twisting motion is useful for removing the tube. But other components are screwed in place, so the tube must always be twisted or screwed clockwise when attempting to remove it from the rest of the system. Cut the strapping tape around the fiberglass and remove it from the barrel. Those who own R10s should note that mineral wool is more durable than fiberglass for this application. Unscrew the center support and slide the roll of hardware cloth off the barrel. Clean the barrel and other components with a suitable solvent such as Varsol or Kroil. Use drill bits of suitable diameter twisted between the fingers to thoroughly clean the barrel ports, and clean the grooves around the rear portion of the barrel with a bronze brush.

A few words about Kroil are useful. Kroil is actually a penetrating oil that makes a good powder solvent. Class 3 dealer John Ross told me about the product, which has the advantage of leaving behind a thin layer of lubricant on all surfaces, facilitating future cleaning and disassembly. When cleaning suppressors by immersion, John discovered that Kroil can be recycled by straining out particulates with a coffee filter. Kroil is available directly from the factory (Kano Laboratories, 1000 Thompson Lane, Nashville, TN 37211). Perhaps the best way to try the product is to order the Kroil Smart Deal, which includes a gallon of Kroil plus a pump sprayer and a small aerosol can—all for only $20.30 at the time of this writing, which includes shipping by UPS.

I used to think that Kroil's only disadvantage is that suppressors and firearms cleaned in it retain a rather strong pungent odor, which delicate noses find objectionable. But Kroil also gives many people severe headaches, and I've become increasingly sensitive to its physiological effects myself. I now reserve the use of Kroil for problem disassemblies and have adopted Varsol as my general-purpose cleaner since it evaporates without a trace. Both are undoubtedly carcinogenic, so take every precaution to avoid skin contact and breathing the fumes.

Prior to reassembly after cleaning and maintenance, be sure to also coat all threaded surfaces as well as the outside shoulders of the end caps and central support with colloidal molybdenum or copper high-temperature antiseize compound to facilitate future disassembly. The barrel and inner surface of the suppressor tube should be sprayed with Kroil or unflavored Pam cooking spray to ensure future disassembly and to facilitate cleaning. Replace the roll of hardware cloth and the fiberglass wrap with new material and reassemble. Following this maintenance regimen, plus cleaning the Ruger action as appropriate, will give the system a very long life. I know of one properly maintained suppressed Ruger that has digested more that 100,000 rounds and is still functioning reliably.

So Dater's R10 system lives up to expectations in terms of maintenance and longevity, but how does it stack up in terms of sound suppression?

Performance

The principal competition facing Dr. Dater when he introduced the R10 was Jonathan Arthur Ciener's suppressed Ruger 10/22, so it is particularly interesting to compare the performance of these two systems. The measured sound signatures and net sound reductions produced by the AWC R10 and Ciener 10/22 appear in Tables 7.12 and 7.13, respectively. Velocity data appear in Table 7.14. In terms of net sound reduction, the AWC R10 noticeably outperforms the Ciener rifle with high-velocity ammunition and significantly outperforms the Ciener with standard-velocity ammunition. This superior suppression comes at a slight cost to velocity, as Table 7.14 shows. The R10 produces projectile velocities that average 66 fps (20 mps) slower with high-velocity ammunition and 57 fps (17 mps) slower with standard-velocity ammunition. Figures 7.11 and 7.12 compare several aspects of exterior ballistics produced by the AWC R10 and the Ciener suppressed 10/22. While the lower velocity means a slight performance loss in terms of exterior and terminal ballistics, the R10 still delivers one-shot kills on small game such as cottontails and squirrels. The R10 remained the state of the art in suppressed .22 rifles well into the 1980s.

Dater's suppressor business increased dramatically after several magazine articles appeared on his designs. The most influential was written by Peter Kokalis and appeared in the November 1981 issue of *Soldier of Fortune*. It was called "Doc Dater's Deadly Devices." By 1983, Dater was offering 12 different silencers. But he was still working as a diagnostic radiologist. The increasing demands of the suppressor business soon had him working two full-time jobs, and Dr. Dater no longer had any time for fun.

So in 1983, Dater began to look for someone to take over much of the manufacturing so he could devote more attention to R&D as well as his personal life. Lynn McWilliams (and his partner in Armament Systems & Technology, Inc., Charles Hair) approached Dater with an offer to build and market Dater's designs on a royalty basis. McWilliams started to produce suppressors in Houston, Texas, using the trade name Automatic Weapons Company, since AWC already had developed a fair amount of name recognition in the industry.

By 1985, AWC was offering a variety of silencers for .22 rimfire rifles and pistols, 9mm pistols and submachine guns, and centerfire rifles. Most of the products designs were based primarily on Dater's work. During this period, Tim Bixler (of SCRC in Houston) was the primary machinist and made improvements on some of the designs to enhance ease of manufacturing.

In 1986, Lynn McWilliams withdrew the Houston Automatic Weapons Company from Armament Systems and Technology, forming AWC Systems Technology in Friendswood, Texas. McWilliams and Dater continued their licensing arrangement. McWilliams began to use additional machine shops in Houston for production, although the most intricate machining was still performed by Tim Bixler at SCRC.

Dater relocated his Automatic Weapons Company to Taos County in northern New Mexico in 1987. Two years later, McWilliams relocated AWC Systems Technology to Phoenix, Arizona, under the corporate name of Special Technologies Group, Inc. He began producing silencers designed by Charles A. "Mickey" Finn of Qualatec. He also hired Finn's chief designer, Doug Olsen, who stayed for two years before joining Knight's Armament Company in Florida.

By this time, McWilliams had discontinued the R10 suppressed rifle in favor of a more modern design employing exotic baffles, no mesh or other materials that needed replacing, and a permanently sealed tube designed for cleaning by immersion in a suitable solvent. Called the Ultra, the new suppressed Ruger from AWC Systems Technology was significantly quieter than the aging R10. Tim Bixler of SCRC introduced several improvements to the R10 design and continues to manufacture this improved variant as the MK-21. This descendent of Dater's original 1976 design remains quite popular two decades after its first appearance.

The 1980s also saw a proliferation of very small Class 2 manufacturers. One of the smallest, Ward Machine, produced what has to be the one of the most unusual suppressed firearms of the modern era: the Red Ryder Stealth Rifle.

RED RYDER STEALTH RIFLE

Ward Machine's Red Ryder rifle is the stealthiest, zaniest suppressed .22 I've ever seen. Bill

Ward takes the classic Daisy Red Ryder BB gun (which was first introduced in 1938) and builds a single-shot suppressed rifle into the BB gun's mechanism, so you can't tell from the outside that this is anything other than what it appears to be . . . a BB gun.

Even the weights are so similar that the rifle still appears to be a BB gun. The empty air rifle weighs 38.2 ounces (1.083 kg), while the .22 suppressed rifle weighs 50.7 ounces (1.437 kg) with its 20 inch (50.8 cm) suppressor/barrel assembly. That may seem like a lot more weight for the suppressed rifle on paper, but the Ward's Stealth Rifle only weighs 3.2 pounds, which seems way too light to be anything but an air rifle when you heft it. You can even hear BBs rattling around inside it. That's a really nice touch. The original safety works too.

To load the rifle, push the safety button (just behind the trigger) from left to right so the red band

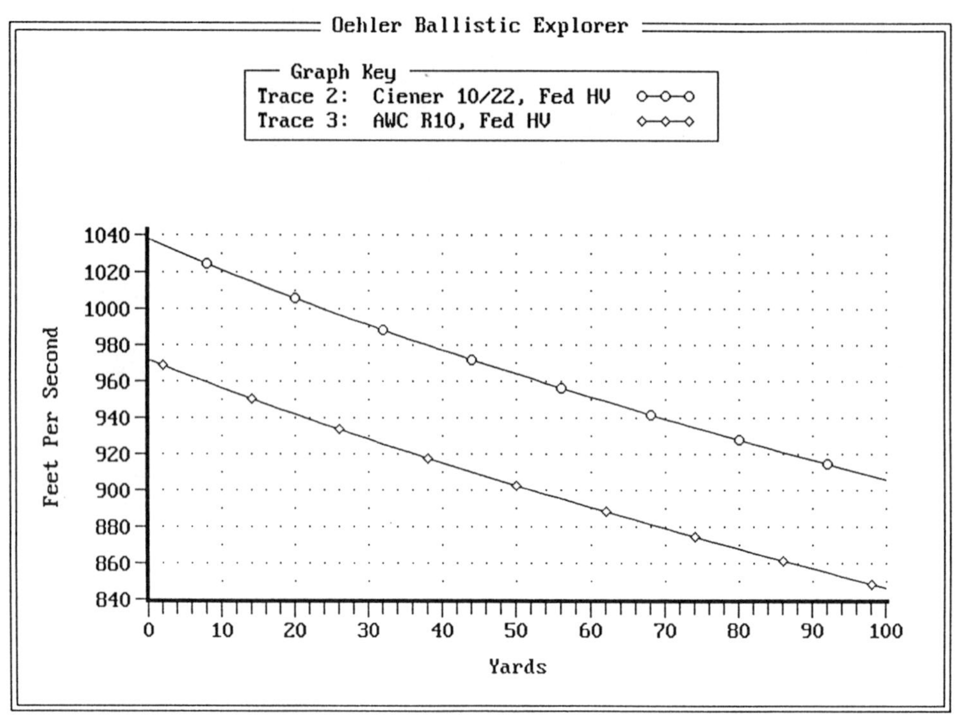

Figure 7.11. Bullet velocities produced by the AWC R10 and Ciener suppressed Ruger 10/22 rifles using Federal high-velocity LR ammunition.

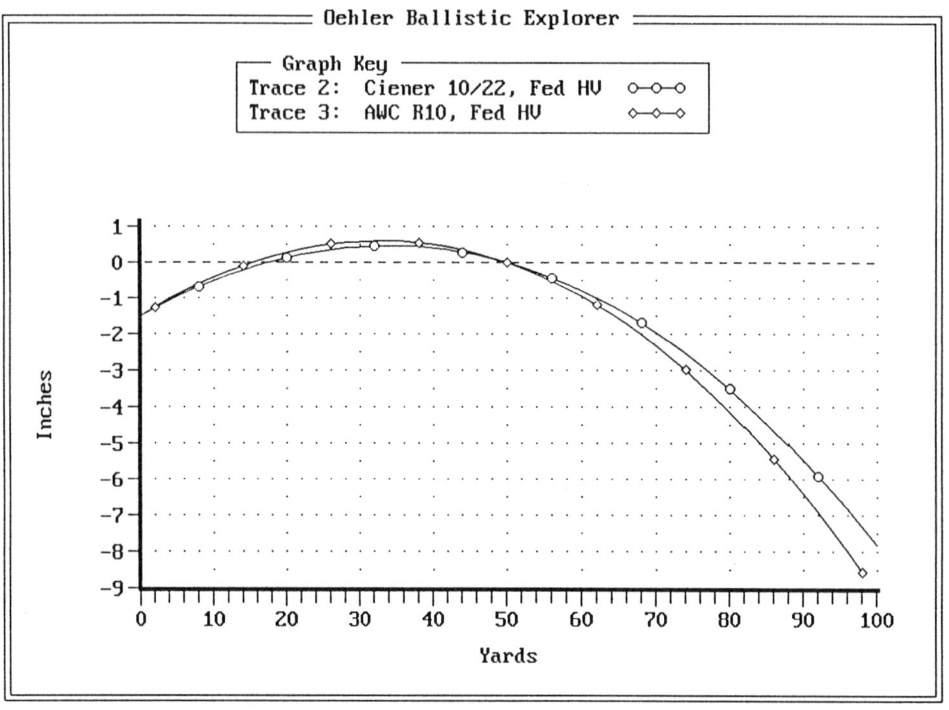

Figure 7.12. Bullet trajectories produced by the AWC R10 and Ciener suppressed Ruger 10/22 rifles using Federal high-velocity LR ammunition.

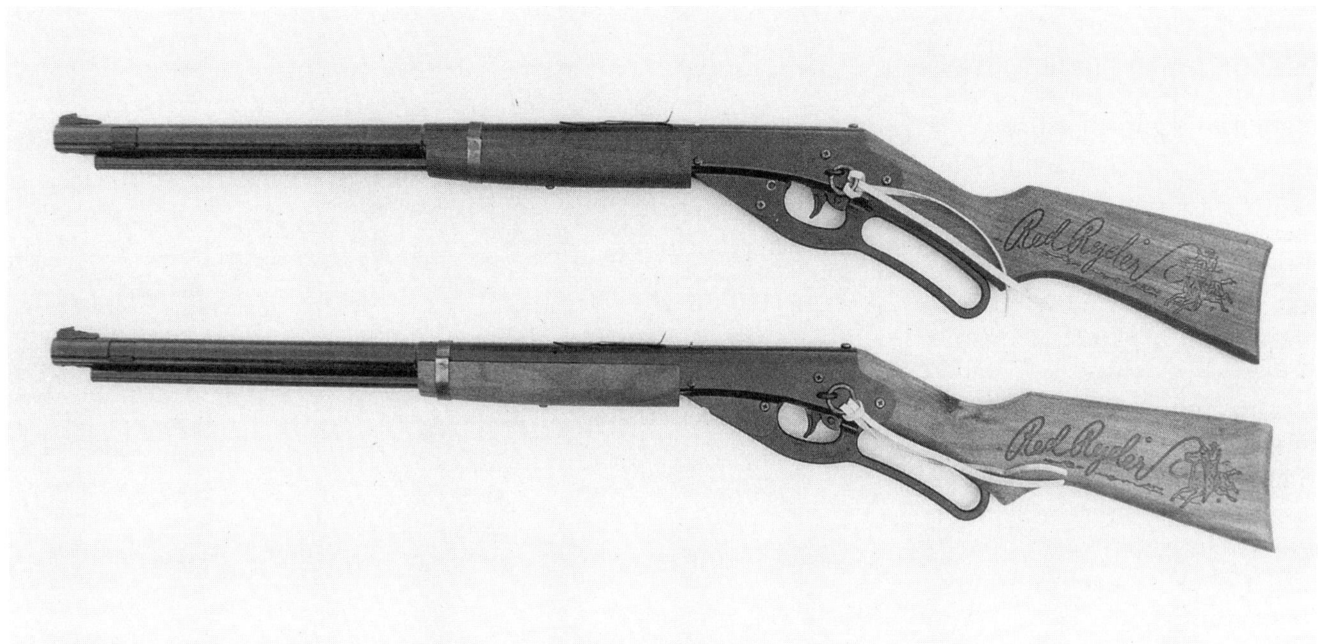

Left side of Red Ryder silenced .22 rifle (top) and unmodified BB gun (bottom). The most conspicuous difference is the darkness of the walnut stocks, which exhibit normal production variation from Daisy.

disappears. Open the lever as if cocking the gun. Turn the rifle upside down, with the muzzle pointed down about 15 degrees, and drop in a cartridge between the front of the lever and the barrel. Shorts and Longs normally plop partially into the chamber and then they can be fully chambered with the lever. Sometimes Long Rifle cartridges will hang up and require a bit of jiggling, but that's no big deal. Occasionally, the cartridge may end up backward. Just turn the rifle rightside up, catch the cartridge in your free hand, and try again.

An idiosyncrasy of the Red Ryder suppressed rifle is that the lever must be held tightly against the stock when firing, since this is necessary to lock the bolt closed during ignition. My natural hold placed the knuckle of my middle finger too close to the trigger guard portion of the handle, which painfully stung the knuckle. I soon learned to modify my grip to place plenty of space between my middle finger and the trigger guard. Only the CB Longs did not produce this problem. The rifle shot pretty close to the point of aim with the BB gun's original sights.

The only real liability with the rifle's design is that you can't get at the chamber with a cleaning brush from the rear. But then, the Red Ryder suppressed rifle was designed to be a nifty toy, not a serious shootin' iron digesting hundreds of rounds in an afternoon. And this rifle is indeed nifty. It's too bad Ward has only built six of these wonderful toys.

Bill Ward has been building Title 2 weapons and suppressors for several decades. He designed and built a drum-fed, full-auto shotgun in 1974, and he is now making a suppressed .22 rifle based on a patent to his friend, Gary Richardson, that uses a hidden suppressor in the stock. The original barrel, barrel contour, and markings are kept. The system uses a single port to vent combustion gases into the suppressor. His submachine gun cans are used by police departments in Huntsville, Alabama, and Corpus Christi, Texas, among others. But Ward builds suppressors as a hobby, not as a business. He actually makes his living building flow-measurement equipment for the oil industry, with clients in the Middle East and Far East. (He owns Richardson Machine.) Like many small manufacturers, Ward builds suppressors at his home's 1,400 square foot machine shop just for grins.

The Red Ryder BB gun produced a sound signature of 101 dB and a projectile velocity of 246 feet per second. The OSS silenced HD-MS pistol used by spooks during World War II has been frequently reported to sound like a BB gun. It has a sound signature of 132 dB with Federal high-velocity ammunition. That OSS pistol produces a thousand times the sound pressure of a BB gun! (If you ever doubted that the ear functions in a logarithmic rather than linear fashion—there's the proof. That's why measuring a weapon's sound signature makes more sense using the decibel scale rather than reporting the data as pascals.)

I mention this thousand-fold discrepancy as a frame of reference when you read anecdotal descriptions of suppressed firearms. Many suppressed firearms have been described as sounding like a BB gun. While they may have been excellent suppressors, chances are they were a lot louder than a BB gun. One's recollection

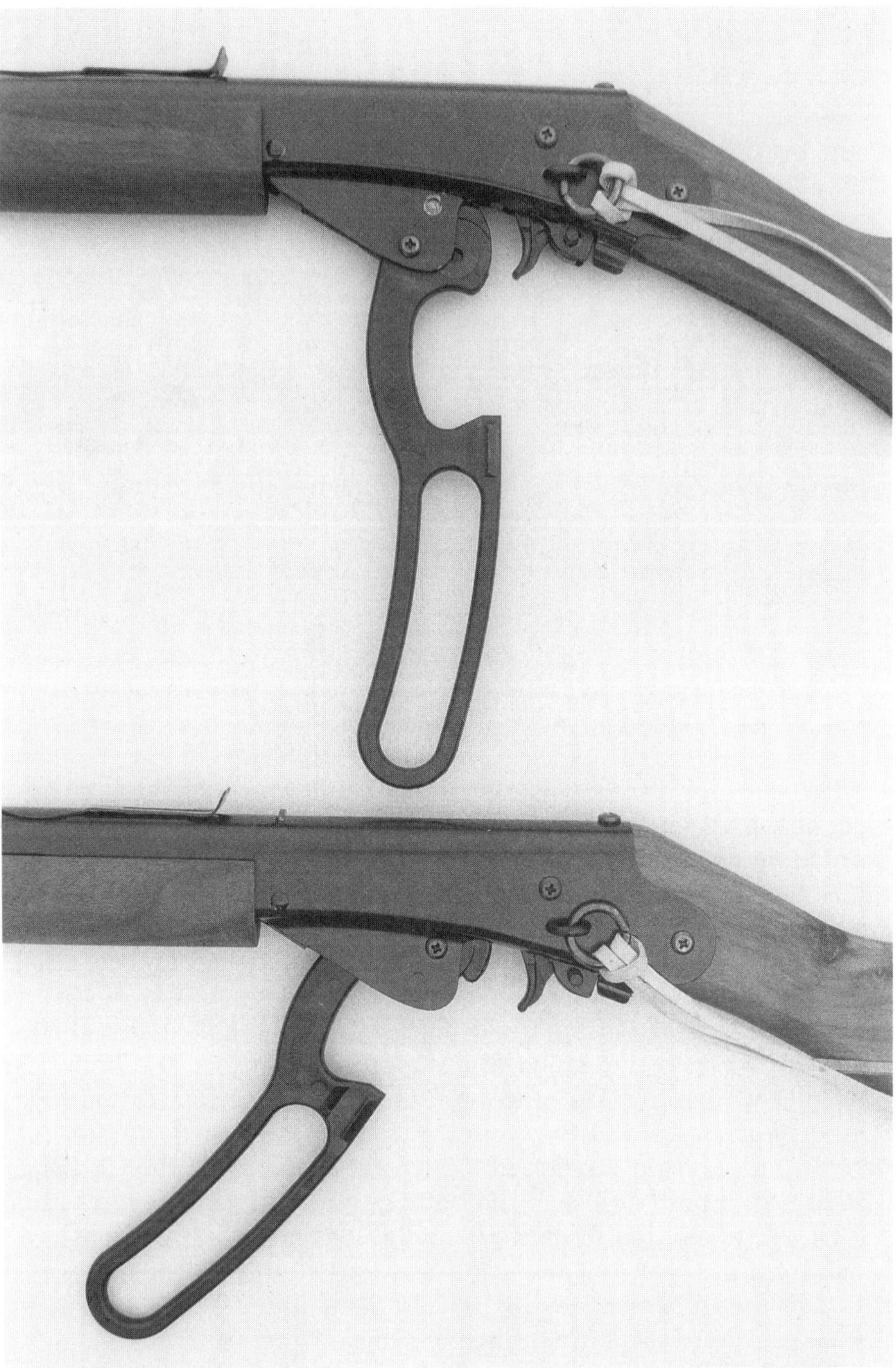

Both the pivot point of the cocking lever and its length of throw are different on the Ward Red Ryder suppressed rifle (top) than the original Daisy BB gun (bottom).

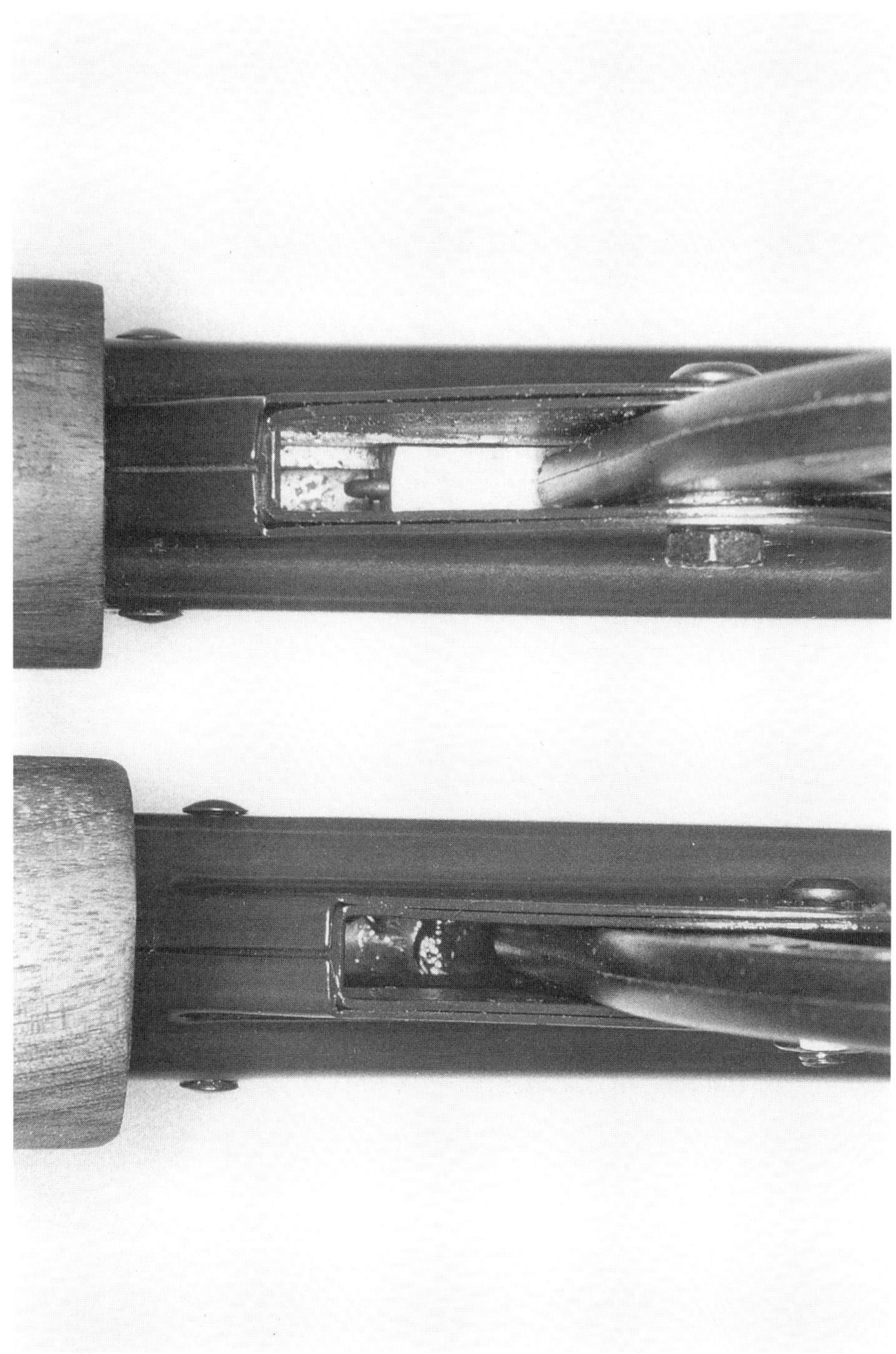

of sound levels tends to be less than perfect. Who of us has not turned on a car's ignition to discover that the radio was left on at an impossibly high volume? Clearly, measuring sound signatures with appropriate equipment provides the most reliable comparisons.

Tables 7.5 and 7.6 compare the sound data from tests of the Red Ryder suppressed rifle with an earlier test of the Marlin 780 bolt-action rifle with Ciener integral suppressor. Tables 7.7 and 7.8 compare velocity data. The Ward suppressor in the Red Ryder is significantly louder than the Marlin 780 with Ciener suppressor. The Red Ryder does not deliver good sound reduction according to modern standards. Thus, the performance of the Red Ryder's suppressor could be called "barely adequate" in terms of cold, hard facts. One's subjective opinion with RWS subsonic LR and Federal CB Longs, however, is kinder than the numbers might suggest.

The action of the Ward Red Ryder suppressed rifle (top) is widened and reinforced. Note the bolt and powder residue in the modified action. The unmodified action is shown for comparison.

Table 7.5. Sound signatures in decibels of Red Ryder Stealth Rifle tests.

GUN	SUPPRESSOR	FEDERAL HV	HANSEN SV	RWS SS	FEDERAL CB LONGS	CCI SHORTS	TEMP., °F (°C)
Ruger 77/22	None	141	137	136	130	135	60(16)
Red Ryder	Ward	130	126	125	118	126	60(16)
Marlin 780	None	143	140	140	134	—	83(28)
Marlin 780	Ciener	124	121	115	111	—	83(28)

Table 7.6. Net sound reductions in decibels of Red Ryder Stealth Rifle tests.

GUN	SUPPRESSOR	FEDERAL HV	HANSEN SV	RWS SS	FEDERAL CB LONGS	CCI SHORTS	TEMP., °F (°C)
Red Ryder	Ward	11	11	11	12	9	60(16)
Marlin 780	Ciener	19	19	25	23	-	83(28)

Table 7.7. Velocities of suppressed and unsuppressed rifles used in Red Ryder Stealth Rifle tests, in fps (mps).

GUN	SUPPRESSOR	FEDERAL HV	HANSEN SV	RWS SS	FEDERAL CB LONGS	CCI SHORTS	TEMP., °F (°C)	SPEED OF SOUND, fps (mps)
Ruger 77/22	None	1,256(383)	1,129(344)	988(301)	643(196)	1,192(363)	60(16)	1,118(341)
Red Ryder	Ward	1,082(330)	982(299)	823(251)	542(165)	1,052(321)	60(16)	1,118(341)
Marlin 780	None	1,297(395)	1,172(357)	1,044(318)	707(215)	—	83(28)	1,142(348)
Marlin 780	Ciener	1,065(325)	986(301)	851(259)	568(173)	—	83(28)	1,142(348)

Table 7.8. Percent reductions of bullet velocities.

GUN	SUPPRESSOR	FEDERAL HV	HANSEN SV	RWS SS	FEDERAL CB LONGS	CCI SHORTS	TEMP., °F (°C)
Red Ryder	Ward	14	13	17	16	12	60(16)
Marlin 780	Ciener	18	16	18	20	—	83(28)

The velocities produced by the Red Ryder rifle are higher than the suppressed Marlin. If the Ward integral suppressor had dropped the velocities as much as the Ciener suppressor, chances are the Red Ryder rifle would have been quieter.

Nevertheless, shooting the Red Ryder rifle was a pleasant experience with CB Longs and RWS subsonic LR ammunition. Shooting the other ammunition was not nearly as impressive. Furthermore, the thin but reinforced sheet-metal receiver and somewhat delicate two-stage collapsible firing pin suggest that high-velocity ammo should be avoided. Ward agrees.

Another reason to stick with the milder ammo is that I experienced about a 20 percent failure to eject spent cases with the Federal high-velocity ammunition. I only experienced one other failure to eject with lower-velocity ammunition. These failures were easily cleared with a cleaning rod.

I'd recommend using only CB Longs and subsonic Long Rifles when you want to impress your friends and neighbors. Personally, I'd stick with CB Longs.

The Daisy Red Ryder suppressed rifle is not a robust rifle for serious field use. It's a rifle inside a BB gun. It's the perfect grown-up toy for someone who cherished a Red Ryder BB gun as a child. Certainly, the best Christmas I ever had as a youngster was the year I got a Red Ryder BB gun, which was the most glamorous, adventurous toy I could imagine. More than that, the responsibility of receiving the first gun that shot something other than water meant that I had reached the second major benchmark in growing up. (The first major achievement was the day I got my first pocket knife.) I remember both days as if they were yesterday.

I hadn't thought about those momentous occasions until the Red Ryder suppressed rifle arrived from Bill Ward. Playing with it brought a flood of rich and wonderful memories that I had lost. Ward had built the rifle for a friend in another part of the country, who had Bill transfer the gun to me for testing. After waiting nearly a year, with all the building anticipation of boyhood, that friend let me play with the new Red Ryder before he even saw it. If that's not friendship, I don't know what is.

Bill Ward can be reached at Ward Machine. While the Red Ryder Stealth Rifle is not meant to be shot extensively, the products manufactured by Sound Technology are designed for serious shooters who demand maximum suppression and accuracy.

SOUND TECHNOLOGY SUPPRESSED 15/22 AND BLACK OPS

The Ruger 15/22 is a particularly handsome variant of the 10/22 that features stainless steel barrel, brushed aluminum receiver, and an attractive laminated stock. Apparently, the 15/22 is only available from Wal-Mart retail stores. This unusual rifle appeals to Mark White of Sound Technology, who is a small but innovative suppressor manufacturer making a number of somewhat unusual suppressed rimfire rifles. All of his suppressed rifles feature a steel coaxial suppressor and barrel-tensioning system that squeeze the maximum accuracy potential from a rifle's barrel. They also feature a hole in the rear of the receiver so the barrel can be cleaned from the rear, as a rifle should be.

White's rifles feature a ported barrel, which is encapsulated by a steel inner coaxial tube that forms part of the tensioning system. The tension stretches the barrel, which dampens barrel harmonics that are produced by firing a round. Even though Ruger makes notoriously mediocre barrels for the 10/22, this tensioning system typically produces rifles that will print dime-sized 10-round groups at 50 meters (55 yards) with a factory barrel. This performance was achieved with a rather wide variety of ammunition, while custom ultra-accurate 10/22s made by companies such as Clark and Volquartsen are quite ammunition sensitive.

An outer coaxial tube of 1 inch (2.5 cm) diameter encapsulates a series of baffles as well as the inner suppressor tube. The suppressor components are made from 4130 steel, with the exception of

Mark White and his suppressed Ruger 15/22 Silent Stalker with 16 inch tube.

woven steel mesh located between the baffles. The suppressed 15/22, however, features a 321-series stainless steel tube and end caps. The chrome moly steel tubes are 0.058 inch (1.47 mm) thick and are finished with a baked-on milspec molybdenum resin finish. The stainless tubes are 0.058 inch (1.47 mm) thick and are polished to a bright finish.

Most folks seem to like suppressed 10/22s with tubes from 16 to 18 inches (41 to 46 cm) in length, but White initially preferred a suppressor length of 22 inches (56 cm) for several reasons. The system provides superior sound suppression but does not require shortening the factory barrel, so the suppressed rifle transfers on a single tax stamp. White's variants with 12 and 16 inch (31 and 41 cm) tubes use barrels shorter than 16 inches, so they had to be registered as short-barreled rifles, and that requires an additional tax stamp. Now that White has perfected his baffle design and spacing, however, he prefers a suppressor length from 18 to 19 inches (46 to 48 cm). Furthermore, his compact designs with short barrels now have the suppressor tubes spot-welded in place so they transfer on a single tax stamp.

One of the most unusual options from Sound Technology is that the rifles can be ordered with custom match-grade bull barrels that exactly match the size and contours of the crowned suppressor. Since Ruger barrels are very easy to swap, unsuppressed and suppressed barrels can be exchanged with impunity. With a scout scope mounted on each barrel (or a cantilevered mount on each barrel with a conventional scope), the rifle need not be rezeroed when the barrels are swapped.

Until federal legislation outlawed folding stocks in 1994 in the so-called Crime Bill, White

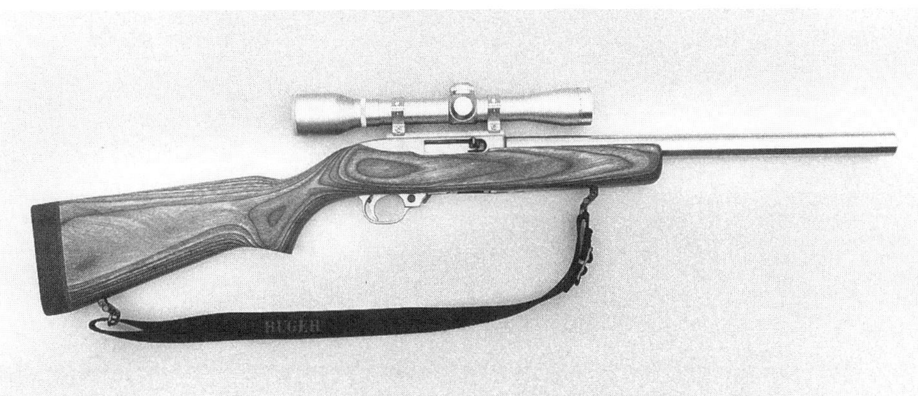

Above: Mark White and his suppressed Ruger 10/22 Black Ops with 22 inch tube.

Left: The suppressed Ruger 15/22 is available with a 16 inch stainless tube (shown) or a 22 inch stainless tube.

offered 10/22s with 10 or 12 inch (25 or 31 cm) unsuppressed match barrels and folding stocks, which stow in a remarkably small space such as a kayak, cockpit, or day pack. Now, these short-barreled rifles are only available with nonfolding stocks unless the receiver of the rifle in question was made before passage of the 1994 legislation. White also builds suppressed 10/22s in similar lengths. These make outstanding survival tools. White also builds suppressors on takedown rifles such as the Marlin Papoose, AR-7 Explorer and Browning Takedown, which are well-suited for bush and survival applications.

Here's a quick survey of the various models of integral .22 suppressors available from Sound Technology.

Suppressor Models

The Silent Stalker is an integral suppressor that is available on the Ruger 10/22, 15/22, or 77/22. Since the 15/22 is only available only through the Wal-Mart chain of stores, clients must purchase the 15/22 themselves and forward the gun to Sound Technology for installation of the integral suppressor. With a 16 or 22 inch (41 or 56 cm) stainless suppressor, this is the best looking system available from Sound Technology. The crowned suppressor looks for all the world like a custom match barrel.

Observers on the firing line of typical club ranges rarely suspect that the Silent Stalker is a suppressed rifle. They will briefly inspect the gun in an effort to learn why it is so quiet, and then lay it back down on the shooting bench. They'll examine the ammunition, thinking some sort of exotic fodder is the secret to the firearm's lack of report. Even when told they are looking at a suppressed firearm, some folks will refuse to believe that explanation. The suppressor looks like a match barrel—not a silencer—since the endcap seam is so tight that it is virtually invisible. Therefore, Sound Technology 10/22s, 15/22s, and 77/22s do not appear in any way covert, thanks to White's "reverse camouflage."

The Black Ops is a Ruger 10/22 that features a black folding stock and a black 22 inch (56 cm) suppressor tube. It is less than 30 inches (76 cm) long with the stock folded. A compact variant called the Black Ops Scout features a 10 or 12 inch (25 or 31 cm) unsuppressed barrel (one stamp) or a 6 inch (15 cm) barrel with a 12 inch suppressor tube (two stamps).

White will build suppressors with a larger tube than 1 inch (2.5 cm) diameter on a custom basis, which he calls the Hi-Volume option. Most Hi-Volume suppressors are mounted on takedown rifles such as the Marlin Papoose, AR-7 Explorer, and the Browning Takedown. Extra barrels can be purchased for shooting these two rifles in either suppressed or unsuppressed mode.

Options

Responding to the considerable interest in falling plate competition with a small bore, self-loading rifle, White offers stainless match barrels of 1 inch (2.5 cm) diameter. The most popular length is 16.1 inches (40.9 cm). Changing the barrel on a Ruger 10/22, 15/22, or 77/22 simply involves the removal of two Allen screws. Since the stainless barrel appears identical to the stainless suppressor, it can be inserted and used in competitive target shooting on the same firearm.

A conventional scope base can be installed directly on the barrel and fitted with a Burris Scout scope. Or a cantilevered scope base can be used to mount a conventional scope. With either approach, the suppressed and unsuppressed barrels can be swapped at will without the need to rezero a sight. Leaving a scope on the receiver would require a rezero every time a barrel was changed.

The Black Ops Scout with 12 inch tube and folding stock requires little space in a cockpit, kayak, or day pack, and the Scout Scope provides extremely rapid target acquisition.

The Hi-Volume Option suppressor on a Daisy Legacy takedown rifle.

The Burris Scout scope is interesting because it allows extremely rapid target acquisition. The system is so fast that it allows a skilled shooter to hit clay targets in flight and to place effective snap shots on game such as running rabbits.

The best-looking suppressed rifles built by Sound Technology are the stainless suppressors built on the stainless Wal-Mart Ruger 15/22 or the standard stainless 77/22 bolt action. A silver Simmons scope provides aesthetically pleasing and cost-effective sighting, with optics that provide a very bright field of view. These rifles will turn heads and capture the most jaded eye on the shooting range.

Maintenance

While Sound Technology suppressors cannot be disassembled for cleaning, White has designed them for cleaning by immersion in a suitable solvent such as Varsol, which is used in machine shops since it removes all hydrocarbons and evaporates without leaving any residue behind. Hoppe's No. 9 and Sweet's bore cleaner should never be used in a suppressor manufactured by Sound Technology since they can damage some of the construction materials. These solvents should never be used with any suppressors containing aluminum. White recommends the following regimen for maintaining his suppressors.

He periodically treats the bore with GI gun oil, which he inserts into the bore ahead of the chamber. As shots are fired, the gas drives the oil deep into the suppressor components and mixes with any moisture in the system to slow corrosion. Every 5,000 rounds, he plugs the muzzle of the suppressor and fills it with Varsol, allowing it to soak for several days.

Drain the muzzle downward while rotating the suppressor to facilitate drainage. All integral suppressors from Sound Technology incorporate drain holes to facilitate draining with the muzzle down. After draining, use compressed air to blow out and dry the suppressor. Finally, add a few drops of GI oil and fire a few oiling shots. Some oil may drain from the suppressor during storage, so when using this maintenance regimen, always hang the suppressed rifle muzzle down, and use a rag or wad of paper towels to catch any further drainage.

Since the Sound Technology suppressors are designed for cleaning, they should provide a substantially longer service life than sealed, so-called self-cleaning systems like the Ciener suppressed rifles. I've shot one Sound Technology suppressed 10/22 with more than 18,000 rounds through it, and the rifle is still accurate, reliable, and quiet.

Performance

The following Long Rifle ammunition was used for the testing: Federal high-velocity, Hansen standard-velocity, Baikal Junior Steel subsonic, Baikal Junior Brass subsonic, Baikal Sniper subsonic, and Winchester subsonic hollowpoint.

The sound signatures of various suppressed and unsuppressed rifles appear in Table 7.9, and the net sound reductions are shown in Table 7.10. The ST Black Ops with 22 inch suppressor provides outstanding sound suppression. The ST Silent Stalker with 16 inch suppressor provides slightly less suppression than Ciener's integral suppressor. Since the tests on the 16 inch ST Silent Stalker, White has reduced the size of the hole in his baffles from 0.390 inch (0.99 cm) to 0.275 inch (0.70 cm), and the rifle is now a bit quieter.

Tables 7.9 and 7.10 show that the ST Black Ops Scout provides the same amount of sound suppression as John Norrell's shorty. Both White's and Norrell's 12 inch integral suppressors produce net sound reduction of 12 dB with high-velocity ammunition (compared to a full-length unsuppressed factory barrel). They both slow projectiles to subsonic velocities. Compared to almost any full-length integral suppressor or modern muzzle can, a 12 dB reduction is not very impressive. Nevertheless, these compact systems can be used for many applications. Consider that their sound signature of 129 dB is quieter than using subsonic ammunition with many 9mm submachine gun muzzle cans.

Table 7.11 shows that Mark White does not achieve sound suppression at the expense of velocity. Many other suppressed Ruger rifles produce projectile velocities that run 60 to 100 fps less than the ST suppressors. More velocity produces both better terminal ballistics and flatter trajectory (which translates into better shot placement). The rifles with ST Black Ops and Silent Stalker suppressors produce similar velocities to Ciener integral suppressors, which are among the best integral suppressors in the marketplace for maintaining projectile velocities.

Figure 7.13 shows projectile velocities produced by the ST Black Ops using high-velocity, standard-velocity, and subsonic ammunition. Figure 7.14 shows bullet trajectories downrange. Figures 7.15 and 7.16 compare the performance (in terms of velocity and trajectory) of three rifles with Federal high-velocity ammunition: an ST Silent Stalker Ruger 15/22 with 16 inch suppressor, an ST Black Ops Ruger 10/22 with 22 inch suppressor, and a Ciener suppressed Ruger 10/22. The Silent Stalker and Black Ops outperform the Ciener suppressed 10/22 in terms of minimizing the sound signature and maximizing projectile velocity.

Conclusions

Mark White's Black Ops rifle with 22 inch suppressor is the quietest and most accurate suppressed Ruger 10/22 I've ever shot. The technology is by no means state of the art, yet the performance is outstanding. The Ruger 15/22 with 22 inch stainless suppressor provides the same accuracy and suppression as the Black Ops in a remarkably handsome package. It's definitely the pick of the litter in my opinion. The stainless 15/22 barrels are not as accurate as blued 10/22 barrels in my experience. Therefore, I recommend having White install a blued factory barrel inside the stainless suppressor when mounted on the 15/22.

The Black Ops Scout with folding stock and Burris Scout Scope makes an outstanding survival rifle, which requires little storage space when I'm flying in the bush or kayaking through the wilderness. It's a valuable companion in wild places.

Mark White may be best known for making the quietest .45 caliber suppressed Marlin Camp Carbines on the market. White has used what he's learned with the Camp Carbines to produce the quietest Ruger 10/22s in my experience. The technology may be simple in concept, but it works.

Table 7.9. Sound signatures in decibels of Sound Technology suppressor tests.

GUN	SUPPRESSOR	FEDERAL HV	HANSEN SV	BAIKAL JS SUBSONIC	BAIKAL JB SUBSONIC	BAIKAL SNIPER SUBSONIC	RWS SUBSONIC HP	TEMP., °F (°C)
Ruger 15/22	None	142	139	139	139	138	—	82(28)
Ruger 15/22	ST Silent Stalker[a]	121	120	120	121	120	—	82(28)
Ruger 10/22	ST Black Ops[b]	116	113	112	113	113	—	82(28)
Ruger 15/22	None	141	138	—	—	—	136	33(1)
Ruger 15/22	ST Silent Stalker[a]	122	121	—	—	—	121	33(1)
Ruger 10/22	ST Black Ops[b]	116	114	—	—	—	112	33(1)
Ruger 10/22	ST Black Ops Scout[c]	129	—	—	—	—	—	33(1)
Ruger 10/22	None	141	139	—	—	—	—	72(22)
Ruger 10/22	Norrell Shorty[c]	129	126	—	—	—	—	72(22)
Daisy Legend	None	141	—	—	—	—	—	33(1)
Daisy Legend	ST HV Option	121	—	—	—	—	—	33(1)
Marlin 780	None	143	140	—	—	—	140	83(28)
Marlin 780	Ciener	124	121	—	—	—	115	83(28)
Ruger 10/22	None	141	139	—	—	—	139[e]	75(24)
Ruger 10/22	Ciener[d]	120	120	—	—	—	117[e]	75(24)

[a]Suppressor is 16 inches long
[b]Suppressor is 22 inches long
[c]Suppressor is 12 inches long
[d]Suppressor is 18 inches long
[e]Action will not cycle with this round

Table 7.10. Net sound reductions in decibels of Sound Technology suppressor tests.

GUN	SUPPRESSOR	FEDERAL HV	HANSEN SV	BAIKAL JS SUBSONIC	BAIKAL JB SUBSONIC	BAIKAL SNIPER SUBSONIC	RWS SUBSONIC HP	TEMP., °F (°C)
Ruger 15/22	ST Silent Stalker[a]	21	19	19	18	18	—	82(28)
Ruger 10/22	ST Black Ops[b]	26	26	27	26	25	—	82(28)
Ruger 15/22	ST Silent Stalker[a]	19	17	—	—	—	15	33(1)
Ruger 10/22	ST Black Ops[b]	25	24	—	—	—	24	33(1)
Ruger 10/22	ST Black Ops Scout[c]	12	—	—	—	—	—	33(1)
Ruger 10/22	Norrell Shorty[c]	12	13	—	—	—	—	72(22)
Daisy Legend	ST HV Option	20	—	—	—	—	—	33(1)
Marlin 780	Ciener	19	19	—	—	—	25	83(28)
Ruger 10/22	Ciener[d]	21	19	—	—	—	22[e]	75(24)

[a]Suppressor is 16 inches long
[b]Suppressor is 22 inches long
[c]Suppressor is 12 inches long
[d]Suppressor is 18 inches long
[e]Action will not cycle with this round

Table 7.11. Projectile velocities and speed of Sound Technology suppressor tests, expressed in feet per second (and meters per second).

GUN	SUPPRESSOR	FEDERAL HV	HANSEN SV	BAIKAL JS SUBSONIC	BAIKAL JB SUBSONIC	BAIKAL SNIPER SUBSONIC	RWS SUBSONIC HP	TEMP., °F (°C)	SPEED OF SOUND fps (mps)
Ruger 15/22	None	1,250(381)	1,118(341)	1,037(316)	1,020(311)	1,058(322)	—	82(28)	1,141(348)
Ruger 15/22	ST Silent Stalker[a]	1,102(336)	988(301)	915(279)	883(269)	937(286)	—	82(28)	1,141(348)
Ruger 10/22	ST Black Ops[b]	1,083(330)	988(301)	914(279)	887(270)	928(283)	—	82(28)	1,141(348)
Ruger 10/22	Ciener[c]	1,038(316)	992(302)	—	—	—	780(238)[d]	75(24)	1,134(346)

[a]Suppressor is 16 inches long
[b]Suppressor is 22 inches long
[c]Suppressor is 18 inches long
[d]Action will not cycle with this round

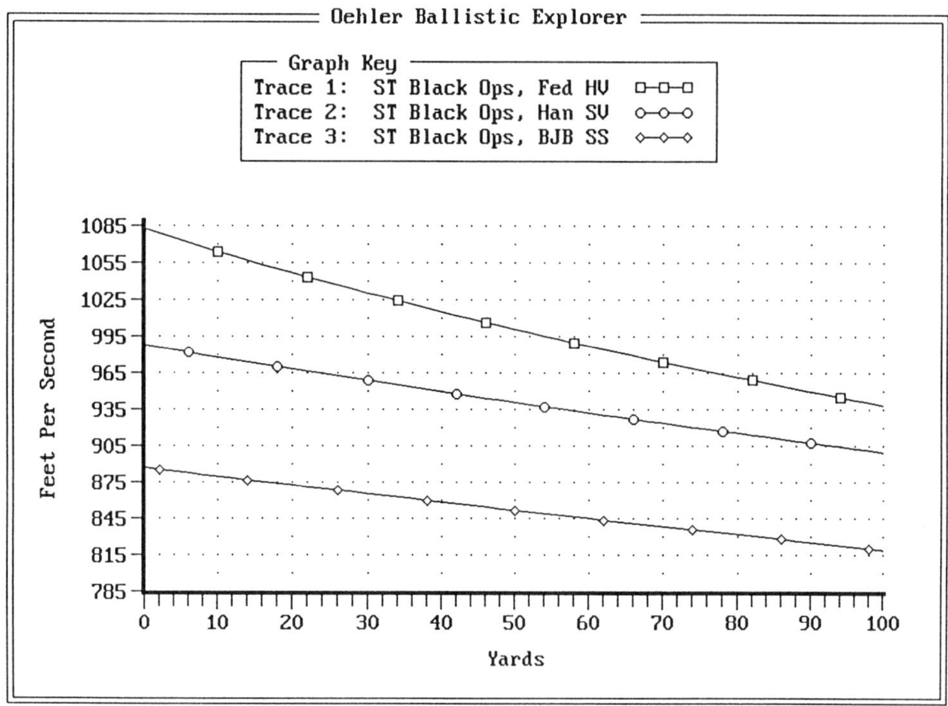

Figure 7.13. Bullet velocities produced by the Sound Technology Black Ops using high-velocity, standard-velocity, and subsonic ammunition.

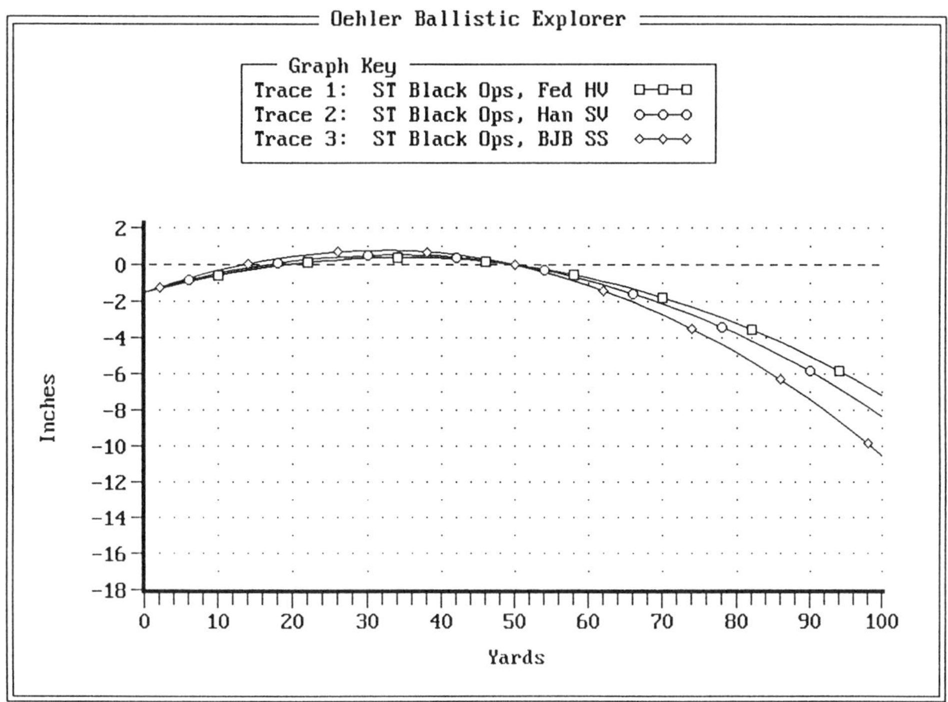

Figure 7.14. Projectile trajectories produced by the Sound Technology Black Ops using high-velocity, standard-velocity, and subsonic ammunition.

There will always be room in the marketplace for eccentric, innovative, small shops like Sound Technology and Ward Machine. They can afford to produce specialized and even zany products in limited numbers. Technical innovations or custom touches are more likely to be available from small shops, although not all small shops can compete with the exotic materials and manufacturing processes that require a larger economy of scale or a large metropolitan area with aerospace subcontractors. Some small shops produce excellent products and have developed small but fiercely loyal clienteles. Others produce junk. *Caveat emptor.*

The most advanced technology now being used in suppressed .22 rifles involves the use of sophisticated baffles that work the combustion gases harder than suppressors that derive their performance largely through volume, diffusion through materials such as eyelets or mesh, or the use of simple, symmetrical baffles. The Gemtech Quantum suppressed rifle is a good example of this trend.

GEMTECH QUANTUM

Gemtech's Quantum rifles are actually a family of integrally suppressed Ruger 10/22 and 77/22 rifles representing the different design philosophies of Jim Ryan and Dr. Phil Dater. They provide very solid performance in a top-of-the-line system.

All variants of the Quantum are based on the baffle design originally developed by Ryan and Dater for the outstanding Operator pistol, although the rifles use two more baffles than the pistol. All variants also feature a tensioned barrel for optimal accuracy and only incorporate two gas ports in the barrel. Furthermore, Gemtech is apparently the first manufacturer beside Sound Technology to incorporate Mark White's suggestion for adding a hole in the rear of the receiver of the

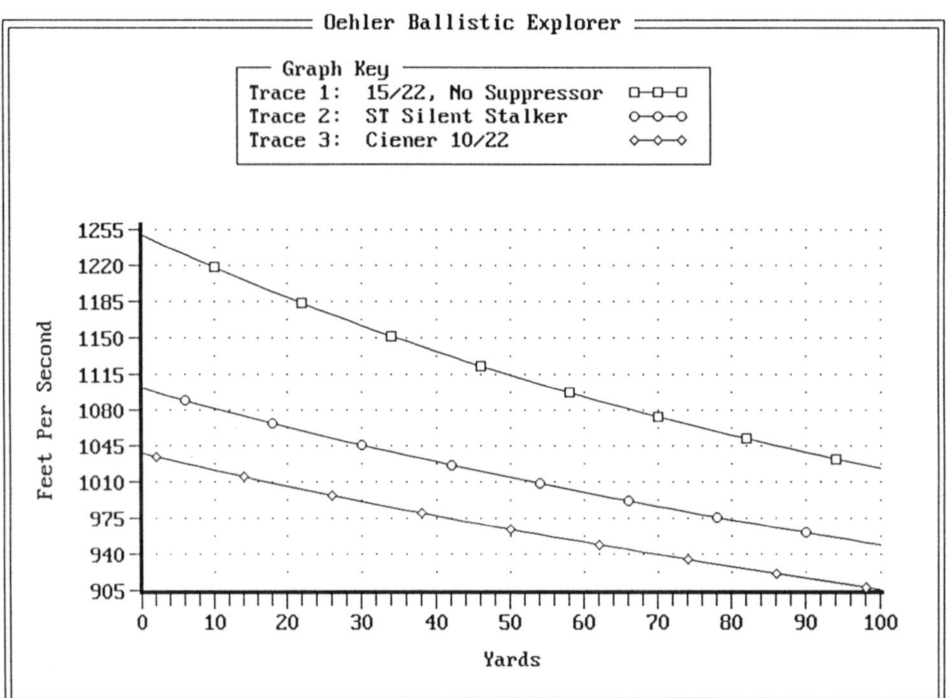

Figure 7.15. Bullet velocities produced by three rifles with Federal high-velocity ammunition: an unsuppressed Ruger 15/22, an ST Silent Stalker Ruger 15/22 with 16 inch suppressor, and a Ciener suppressed Ruger 10/22.

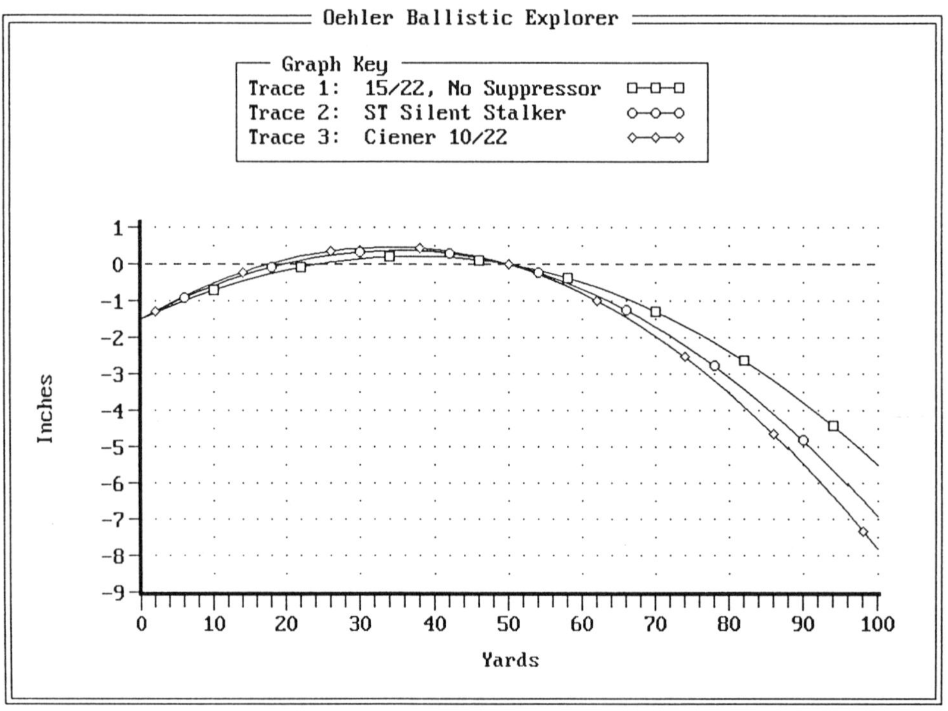

Figure 7.16. Bullet trajectories produced by three rifles with Federal high-velocity ammunition: an unsuppressed Ruger 15/22, an ST Silent Stalker Ruger 15/22 with 16 inch suppressor, and a Ciener suppressed Ruger 10/22.

Ruger 10/22. This hole (which is normally hidden by the stock) allows the operator to run a cleaning rod through the barrel from the rear to avoid damaging the barrel crown. The internal design of Dater's and Ryan's suppressors are identical; they use the same baffle design in front of the barrel, the same porting, and the same tube mounting system.

Every Quantum contains seven 2024 aluminum baffles, and standard models feature a 304 stainless steel suppressor tube that is 1.0 inch (2.5 cm) in diameter. For clients with blued receivers who demand a matching suppressor tube, a blued 4130 carbon steel suppressor tube is available as a custom option. For all practical purposes, only the length of the barrel and suppressor tube vary. While the different variants provide essentially the same performance in terms of sound suppression and accuracy, they also offer the user some interesting choices.

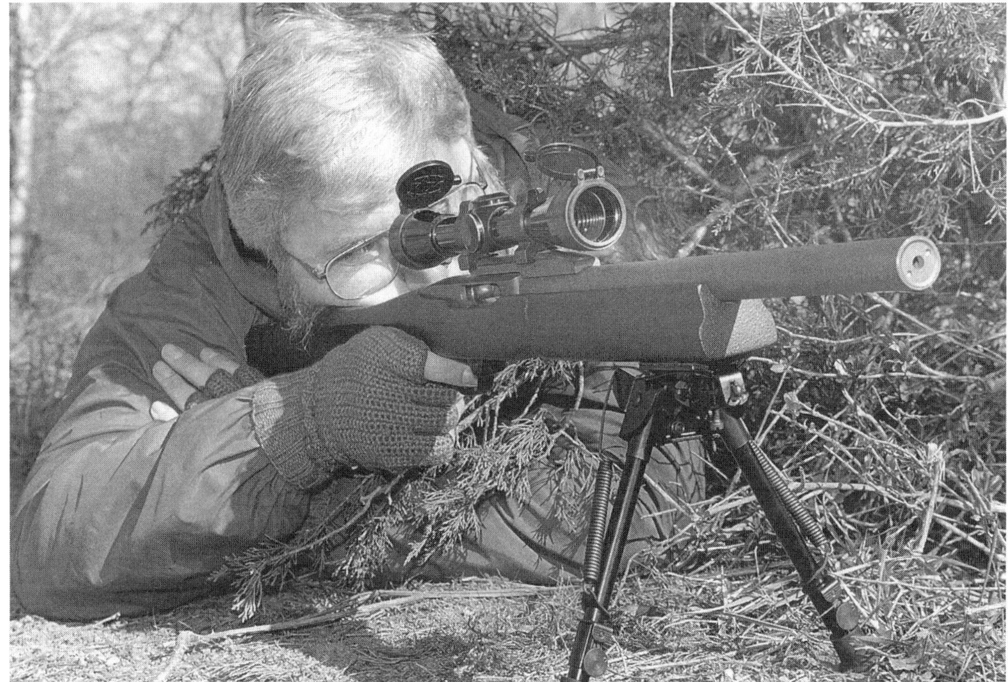

Firing the Gemtech Quantum-2000 prone using a Harris bipod attached to the front sling swivel stud is a solid and comfortable support option. Photo by Polly Walter.

The custom Gemtech Quantum-2000 suppressed rifle evaluated in this study features a Volquartsen thumbhole stock and a Weigand cantilever scope mount.

Long-Barreled Quantum

Dater was one of the earliest proponents that suppressors should be designed so they can be disassembled for cleaning. It should not be surprising that his design features a 16.5 inch (41.9 cm) barrel, so the suppressor tube can be removed to facilitate cleaning while the barrel is long enough to make this a one-stamp gun. The 5 inch (12.7 cm) baffle stack is permanently retained in the front of the suppressor tube and increases the overall suppressor/barrel length to 21.5 inches. The removable tube provides direct access to the barrel ports and the expansion chamber that surrounds the barrel. This model will henceforth be referred to as the long-barreled Quantum.

Cleaning the long-barreled system is somewhat easier than the short-barreled system thanks to the removable suppressor tube, which gives direct access to the primary expansion chamber, barrel, and ports. The captive baffle stack is easily cleaned by removing the suppressor tube and immersing the tube in a suitable solvent. For clients who absolutely, positively demand the ability to disassemble the baffle stack for cleaning, Gemtech will provide that ability as a custom option.

Short-Barreled Quantum

Ryan's design for the 10/22 and 77/22 features a short (10 inch, 25.4 cm) barrel and short (16 inch, 40.6 cm) suppressor tube, which provides a compact package similar in length to Dater's old R10 suppressed rifle of the early 1980s. This model will henceforth be referred to as the short-barreled Quantum. To avoid two tax stamps (for the suppressor and as a short-barreled rifle), Ryan permanently attaches the suppressor tube to the barrel. A hex screw in the bottom rear of the suppressor tube, which is normally hidden by the stock, permits access to the barrel ports for removing accumulated fouling and to assist draining the suppressor after cleaning by immersion in a suitable solvent such as Varsol or Kroil. Use in a well-ventilated area and wear rubber gloves since good organic solvents are carcinogenic. To facilitate cleaning with the tube permanently attached to the receiver, the baffles can be removed from the front of the tube on the short-barreled model.

To facilitate future disassembly, I recommend a brief bit of preparation when the Quantum is first purchased. Remove the front end cap and encapsulator from the suppressor tube with the provided takedown tool. Tap the front of the tube against a nylon (or similar) bench pad to drive the baffle stack forward for removal. Spray the baffles and spacers with Kroil or unflavored Pam kitchen spray and reinstall. Treat all threaded surfaces with a colloidal molybdenum or copper high-temperature antiseize compound, and replace the encapsulator and front end cap. This procedure will greatly facilitate removing these components after they have become encrusted with powder residue and lead dust.

Custom Quantum

I tested a custom short-barreled Quantum 10/22 for this study. This particular gun was built for an advanced marksman who wanted a rifle *system* rather than merely a factory Ruger with a good suppressor. The design goals for this project were to provide an optimal mix of sound suppression, ergonomics, and accuracy in a compact envelope that would appeal to a serious rifle shooter rather than a casual plinker. Ryan polished the bolt and hammer spring and removed a spiral or two from the hammer spring to ensure reliable functioning with subsonic ammunition. The proprietary porting in the Quantum also contributes to the rifle's reliability with subsonic fodder.

My thanks to the owner of the Quantum, who wishes to remain anonymous, for transferring the gun to me for several months so I could evaluate the system for publication. We've never even met face to face, so this gentleman was very gracious, indeed, to send his favorite rifle to someone he'd never looked in the eye.

This particular rifle features a nonreflective, black, molybdenum resin finish over its stainless steel suppressor tube and anodized receiver, giving the package a rather milspec ambience, which I like.

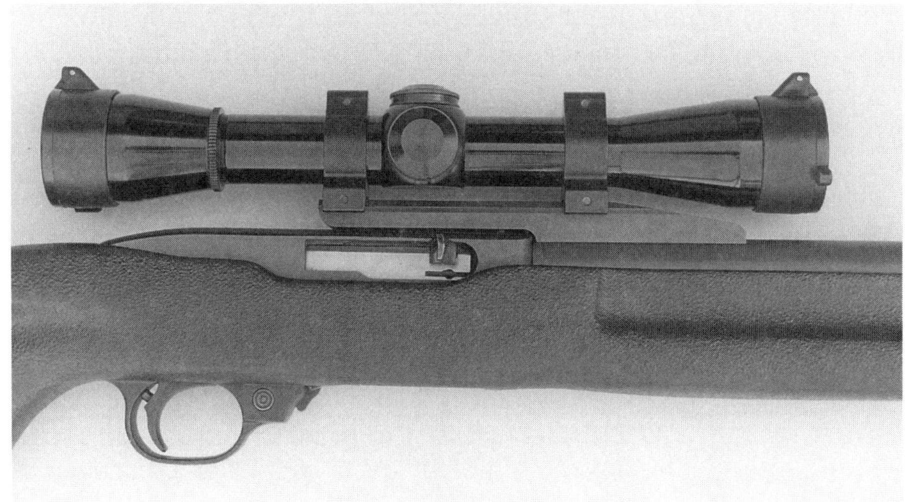

The Weigand cantilever scope mount attached to the suppressor tube permits the use of a standard eye relief scope without resorting to excessively high scope rings that destroy the shooter's ability to form a proper and repeatable check weld.

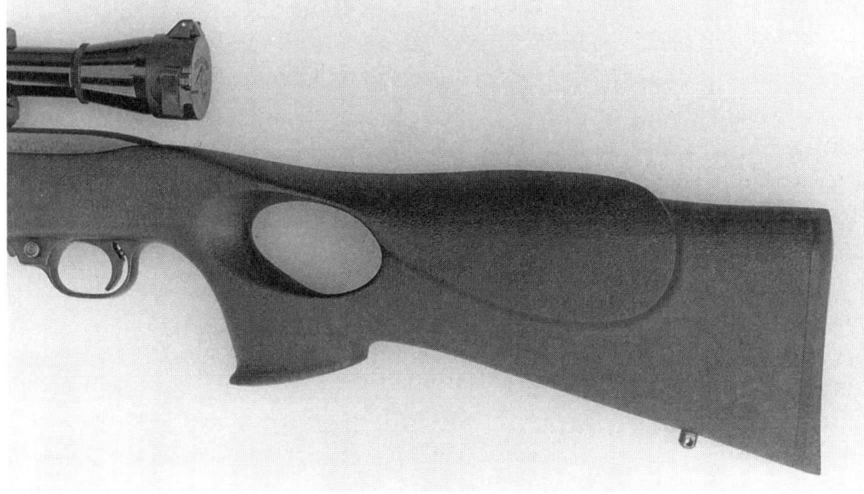

The Volquartsen thumbhole stock with Monte Carlo cheekpiece is made from reinforced, high-density, ultrastable fiberglass.

The rifle measures 35.5 inches (90.1 cm) in overall length. The rifle weighs 6.98 pounds (3.17 kg) with a 4 power Leupold scope and a Weigand cantilever scope mount.

A cantilever scope mount attached to the suppressor tube permits the use of a standard eye relief scope without resorting to excessively high scope rings that destroy the shooter's ability to form a proper and repeatable check weld. I've developed a dislike of cantilever scope mounts over the years because they've generally not been robust enough to suit me. The Weigand mount is a notable exception. Well-engineered and therefore sufficiently rigid, the Weigand aluminum mount complements the Quantum very well.

Unfortunately, the cantilever mount is only practical on a suppressor tube that is permanently attached to the barrel, for proper indexing after disassembly would otherwise be a problem. Granted, an indexing screw could be used to properly align a suppressor tube with cantilever mount for reassembly, and the screw could be hidden by the stock. But the very presence of an indexing screw would preclude tensioning the barrel properly, and this would adversely affect accuracy.

The custom Quantum features a Volquartsen thumbhole stock. I've disliked every rifle I've ever handled with a thumbhole stock—until now. The ergonomics of the Volquartsen thumbhole grip are reminiscent of a good pistol grip, so the Volquartsen will feel very natural to anyone who's spent a lot of time with an M16 or MP5. The very positive grip afforded by this particular thumbhole arrangement, while carrying the rifle at Rhodesian ready during a rabbit hunt, permitted rapid and positive target acquisition that was unprecedented in my hunting experience. The broad, flat forestock is well-suited to benchrest shooting off a sandbag or prone shooting off a backpack. Firing this rifle prone using a Harris bipod attached to the front sling swivel stud is also a solid support option. Shooters with small hands may find the forestock a bit wide for ideal use offhand, but this eventually becomes less distracting.

The Volquartsen thumbhole stock with Monte Carlo cheekpiece is made from reinforced, high-density, ultrastable fiberglass. The stock features a textured finish for a positive grip, front and rear sling swivel studs, an oversized bedding screw, and a 1 inch (2.5 cm) rubber recoil pad. The stock is 28.5 inches (72.4 cm) long, has a 0.5 inch (1.3 cm) drop at the heel, and has a length of pull that is 1 inch (2.5 cm) longer than the factory stock. The stock weighs 1.8 pounds (822 g) and is available in four colors: black, blue, red, and hunter green.

The Volquartsen's multiple-pressure-point pillar bedding system holds the suppressed rifle more rigidly than a factory stock, which should enhance the accuracy potential of the system. The only liability of the pillar system becomes apparent when shooting a suppressed rifle in the stock. The expanding combustion gases ring the suppressor tube against the pillars, causing a hollow *knock!* with each shot that is apparent to the shooter but not to nearby observers. Once I discovered that no one besides the shooter experienced this phenomenon, that extra knock in the sound signature no longer bothered me. Besides the pillars, the stock also features a notch at the rear of the action that expands slightly when the action is installed and holds it rigidly in place under tension. Finally, a pad of fiberglass at the takedown screw holds the action in downward compression.

The features of the custom Quantum have now become a standard item in the Gemtech product line. Called the Quantum-2000, Gemtech's top-of-the-line system includes the standard Quantum suppressor with stainless steel tube on a brushed stainless steel finished Ruger 10/22, black Volquartsen thumbhole stock, modified trigger with Volquartsen hammer, Weigand Combat 10/22 cantilever scope mount, and Burris Weaver-style "Zee" scope rings. Black finish is available for a small extra charge.

While even the unusually long suppressed rifles from Sound Technology are still practical in the field, I've developed a fondness over the years for compact, high-performance rifles. I discovered over the several months I had this rifle on loan that I had become particularly fond of the short-barreled Quantum. By the time the transfer cleared back to the kind subscriber to *Machine Gun News* who loaned me the rifle, I was shooting the Quantum in preference to every other .22 rifle in the safe. It fit my body and my personality to perfection.

But how does the Quantum-2000 perform from an objective, rather than a subjective, point of view?

To answer this question, I tested the custom Quantum against several other suppressed 10/22s as well as an unsuppressed 10/22 using Federal Hi-Power high-velocity, Hansen standard-velocity, and Baikal Junior Brass subsonic ammunition.

Performance

The custom short-barreled Quantum was test fired against a vintage AWC R10 suppressed rifle and a factory original unsuppressed 10/22 at 38°F (3°C). The sound signatures are shown in Table 7.12, and the net sound reductions are shown in Table 7.13. Muzzle velocities are shown in Table 7.14. (All of the tables are on page 137.)

Note that the sound generated by chambering a loaded round was 112 dB. This experiment was accomplished by drawing the bolt fully to the rear and then releasing it smartly. The process was repeated 10 times and the mean (average) was calculated. Allowing the main operating (recoil) spring to close the bolt on an empty chamber generated a sound signature of 115 dB. Thus, the process of chambering a round buffers the bolt closing. Some suppressed sound signatures recorded in this study were less than 112 dB, so the action noise should have masked the muzzle signature. It therefore appears that the chambering data are somewhat biased. The most logical explanation is that the bolt does not recoil fully rearward during semiautomatic cycling, so the bolt has less for-

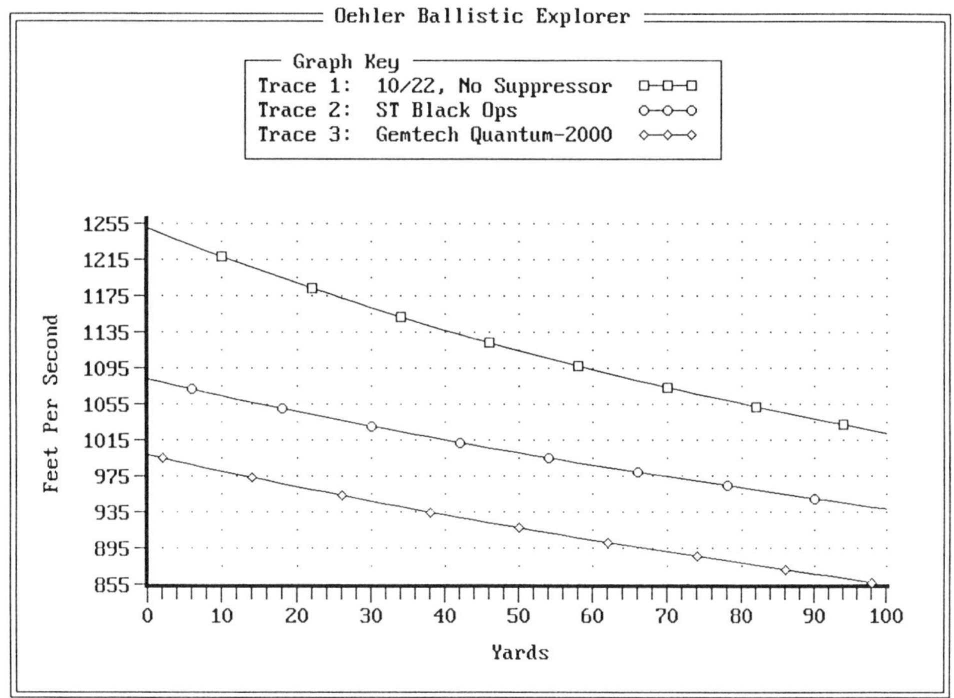

Figure 7.17. Bullet velocities produced by the Gemtech short-barreled Quantum-2000, ST Black Ops, and an unsuppressed 10/22.

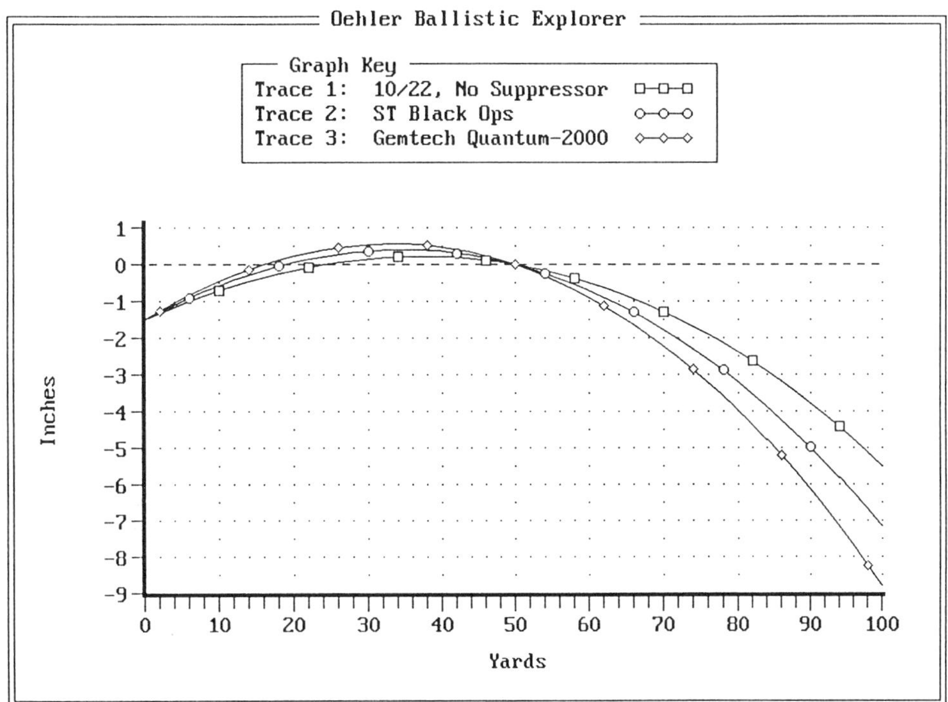

Figure 7.18. Bullet trajectories produced by the Gemtech short-barreled Quantum-2000, ST Black Ops, and an unsuppressed 10/22.

ward velocity than when it is retracted fully by hand and released. Less velocity means less sound when the bolt closes. Therefore, these chambering data are too high.

Although the custom Quantum cycled reliably with the Baikal subsonic ammunition, the AWC R10 never once cycled with subsonic fodder. Comparative data are also included for the Sound Technology Black Ops (which did cycle reliably with subsonic ammunition) and a Ciener suppressed 10/22 (which did not cycle with subsonic fodder). Projectile velocities and trajectories of selected rifles are compared in Figures 7.17 and 7.18.

The Gemtech short-barreled Quantum produces the same amount of sound reduction as Dater's earlier R10 rifle with high-velocity ammunition, whereas the Quantum provides better performance using standard-velocity and subsonic fodder. The Quantum provides slightly higher muzzle velocity than the R10 with high-velocity ammo and slightly lower velocity with standard-velocity and subsonic ammunition.

Unfortunately, the sound data tell nothing about the quality (frequency content) of the sound signatures. The R10 produced a much higher frequency sound than the Quantum. So in terms of frequency content, the Quantum dramatically outperformed the R10. The Quantum's lower frequency signature sounds less like a gunshot than the R10. Furthermore, the lower frequency Quantum signature is more rapidly absorbed by vegetation, so the sound does not carry as far afield.

In terms of sound reduction, the Sound Technology Black Ops outperforms the Quantum with high-velocity ammunition, but the Quantum beats the Black Ops with standard-velocity and subsonic fodder. The Quantum is noticeably quieter than the Ciener suppressed 10/22 with high-velocity ammo, and this performance gap widens considerably with standard-velocity ammunition. It is fair to say that the Quantum provides spectacularly better performance than the Ciener system with standard-velocity ammunition in terms of sound suppression.

For applications against live targets, however, note that both the Ciener and Sound Technology systems provide significantly higher velocities than either the Gemtech Quantum or AWC R10. Even though the Quantum provided clean kills on cottontails and squirrels, I suspect that the velocity differences would enable the Sound Technology rifle to noticeably outperform the Quantum against larger animals such as snowshoe hares and feral dogs. I did not have the opportunity to test this hypothesis, however.

It is interesting that the Sound Technology rifle provides the highest velocities of all suppressed rifles in this study, and yet its performance—in terms of both measured sound signatures and subjective opinion of frequency content—is profoundly better than the Ciener system and AWC R10, and is similar to the Quantum in terms of overall performance.

While the projectile velocities produced by the Quantum are lower than two of the best performers in the industry in terms of muzzle velocity (the Sound Technology and Ciener rifles), its performance is dramatically better than some other suppressed rifles in the marketplace that achieve quiet sound signatures by excessive porting of the barrel.

Conclusions

Gemtech's short-barreled custom Quantum provided outstanding performance in terms of both the amount of sound reduction and the frequency content of the sound signature. The ergonomics provided by the system's Volquartsen thumbhole stock and Weigand cantilever scope mount, combined with the short suppressed action, made this an addictive rifle to shoot. Projectile velocity was good but not outstanding, yet the Quantum provided one-shot kills on rabbits and squirrels. Thanks to minimal porting and a tensioned barrel, accuracy equals the factory barrel from which a given rifle is made. Avoid using a stainless steel factory barrel, for it provides disappointing accuracy. If you are lucky enough to get a good carbon steel barrel from Ruger, the Quantum will deliver dime-sized groups at 50 yards (1.8 cm at 46 m) with the right ammunition, a tuned trigger, and good optics.

This brings up my only substantive criticism of the custom Quantum tested in this study: the owner did not spend a few extra shekels for a trigger job. At the time of this writing, Jim Ryan charges $125 for a trigger job that includes a precision Volquartsen hammer. For a top-of-the-line system like a custom Quantum, a good trigger job is mandatory in my opinion. This trigger job now comes standard on the Quantum-2000.

For those who demand the ultimate accuracy, Ryan will line bore the action and screw in a match barrel. That would certainly make an extraordinary suppressed rifle. Whether you want a simple, off-the-shelf suppressed rimfire rifle or a custom system built to your particular requirements, the Gemtech Quantum family of rifles offers the discriminating user a wealth of interesting choices.

Table 7.12. Sound signatures in decibels of Gemtech Quantum-2000 suppressor tests.

GUN	SUPPRESSOR	FEDERAL HV LR	HANSEN SV LR	BAIKAL JB LR	TEMP., °F (°C)
Ruger 10/22	None	141	140	138	38(3)
Ruger 10/22	Gemtech Short Quantum	117	112	109	38(3)
Ruger 10/22	AWC R10	117	114	110	38(3)
Ruger 10/22	None	142	139	139	82(28)
Ruger 10/22	Sound Technology Black Ops	116	113	112	82(28)
Ruger 10/22	None	141	137	—	28(-2)
Ruger 10/22	Ciener	119	119	—	28(-2)

Table 7.13. Net sound reductions in decibels of Gemtech Quantum-2000 suppressor tests.

GUN	SUPPRESSOR	FEDERAL HV LR	HANSEN SV LR	BAIKAL JB LR	TEMP., °F (°C)
Ruger 10/22	Gemtech Short Quantum	24	28	29	38(3)
Ruger 10/22	AWC R10	24	26	28	38(3)
Ruger 10/22	Sound Technology Black Ops	26	26	27	82(28)
Ruger 10/22	Ciener	22	18	—	28(-2)

Table 7.14. Muzzle velocities of Gemtech Quantum-2000 suppressor tests, expressed in feet per second (and meters per second).

GUN	SUPPRESSOR	FEDERAL HV LR	HANSEN SV LR	BAIKAL JB LR	TEMP., °F (°C)	SPEED OF SOUND fps (mps)
Ruger 10/22	None	1,228(374)	1,085(331)	961(293)	38(3)	1,094(333)
Ruger 10/22	Gemtech Short Quantum	999(304)	911(278)	779(237)	38(3)	1,094(333)
Ruger 10/22	AWC R10	972(296)	935(285)	791(241)	38(3)	1,094(333)
Ruger 10/22	None	1,249(381)	1,118(341)	1,020(311)	82(28)	1,141(348)
Ruger 10/22	Sound Technology Black Ops	1,083(330)	987(301)	887(270)	82(28)	1,141(348)
Ruger 10/22	Ciener	1,038(316)	992(302)	—	75(24)	1,134(346)

While the suppressed Ruger 10/22 in all its guises is by far the most popular suppressed rimfire rifle in the U.S. marketplace, the Ruger 77/22 certainly occupies second place. Some shooters feel that the 77/22 affords more accuracy potential than the 10/22. Other advocates of stealthy shooting believe that a bolt-action rifle helps concentrate the marksman's mind on making that first shot count. And those who desire the absolute best in sound suppression eschew the action noise generated by a self-loading rifle. But perhaps the 77/22's greatest advantage over the 10/22 for suppressed applications is that the 77/22 has significantly tighter chamber dimensions than the 10/22 (which requires a bit more slop, if you will, to facilitate extraction and reliable semiautomatic function).

Tighter chamber dimensions have two definite advantages: 1) greater accuracy potential and 2) more complete powder combustion, which translates into less secondary combustion of powder residue and partially oxidized combustion gases when they leave the barrel. This secondary combustion takes place with explosive rapidity, generating a significant "pop" when it occurs. Thus, more complete powder combustion means that the suppressor has less work to do, so most suppressor designs (whether integral or muzzle devices) seem to produce a lower sound signature when installed on a Ruger 77/22 than on a 10/22. To test this hypothesis, I studied the performance of the mid-sized integral suppressor made by Sound Technology for the Ruger 77/22 and compared its performance to essentially the same suppressor mounted on the Ruger 10/22.

SOUND TECHNOLOGY SILENT STALKER 77/22

Until 1994, Sound Technology focused primarily on producing integrally suppressed rimfire rifles like the Black Ops with 22 inch (55.9 cm) suppressors to afford the maximum practical projectile velocity coupled with maximum sound reduction. While these long systems handle well, even in the field, some people find the aesthetics of such a long suppressor tube objectionable. Others simply prefer a more compact envelope for a rifle. To satisfy the needs of these folks, Sound Technology developed a line of mid-sized suppressors that feature a can with more modest length. The Silent Stalker 77/22, for example, has a suppressor length of 17.6 inches (44.6 cm). With a factory injection-molded, fiberglass-reinforced Du Pont Zytel stock, this gives the Silent Stalker 77/22 a modest overall length of 37.8 inches (96.0 cm). All ST integral suppressors have a diameter of 1.0 inch (2.5 cm). With no scope attached, the Silent Stalker 77/22 has a weight of 5.7 pounds (2.6 kg). This is slightly shorter and lighter than an unmodified Ruger 77/22.

The suppressor tube and its end caps are constructed of 300 series stainless steels. The barrel has only six ports, which vent into a coaxial chamber that is also used to stretch the barrel under more than 800 pounds of pressure. This tensioning enhances the accuracy of the barrel by greatly

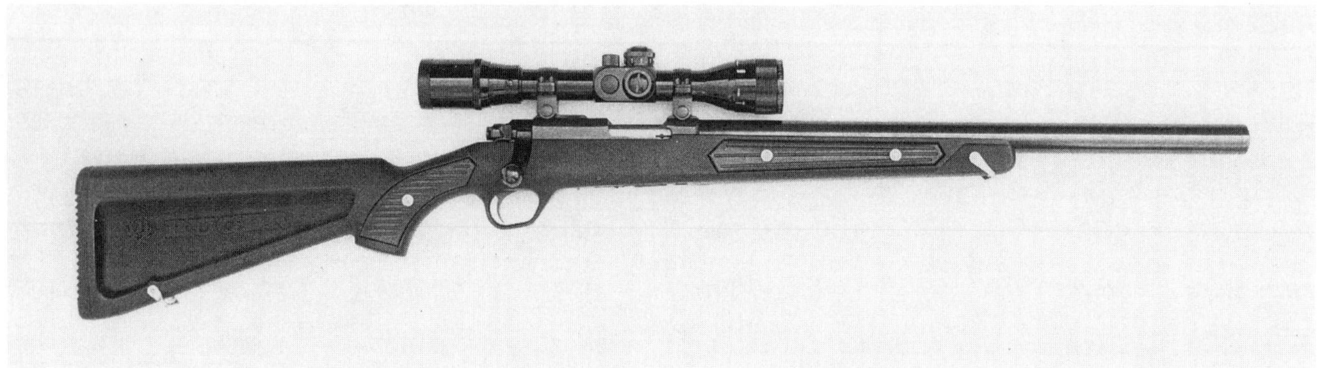

Suppressed Ruger 77/22 from Sound Technology.

Mark White fires one of his suppressed Ruger 77/22s.

reducing barrel harmonics and increases the efficiency of the suppressor by slowing down the release of combustion gases. This inner coaxial chamber extends part of the way into the outer tube. The remaining length of the outer tube is filled with a series of chambers consisting of woven coarse steel mesh between steel baffles, in a manner analogous to but different from the system developed by Lynn McWilliams for the Archangel I suppressor. Even though the Sound Technology system predates the Archangel I system, it is important to note that both designs were developed independently.

The performance of the Silent Stalker 77/22 was compared to a similar system on the Ruger 10/22. The suppressor on the Silent Stalker 10/22 was, however, slightly longer, with a can length of 19.7 inches (47.6 cm). Mounted in a Fajen laminated stock, this gave the Silent Stalker 10/22 an overall length of 37.8 inches (96.0 cm) and a weight of 6.7 pounds (3.0 kg) without a scope. Thus the 10/22 system has the same overall length as the 77/22 system but is 1 pound (0.45 kg) heavier thanks to the Fajen stock. In an effort to make the best possible system rather than to maximize profits, Sound Technology provides an excellent trigger job with each Silent Stalker rifle at no additional charge.

I also compared the performance of the Sound Technology stretched (unsuppressed) barrel with integral recoil compensator that has the same dimensions as the Silent Stalker suppressor. This barrel enables the owner of a Sound Technology system to freely switch an integrally suppressed rifle to unsuppressed mode for those applications where using a suppressed rifle would be illegal (such as for hunting in many, but not all, states) or would otherwise be undesirable.

Suppressed and unsuppressed Ruger 77/22s were compared to suppressed and unsuppressed 10/22s using Federal Hi-Power high-velocity LR, Hansen standard-velocity target LR, and Baikal Junior Brass subsonic LR ammunition. The bolt-action guns were also tested with Federal CB Longs. The tests were conducted on two adjacent days and the temperatures were recorded.

Performance

Sound signatures are shown in Table 7.15, and the net sound reductions appear in Table 7.16. Muzzle velocities are shown in Table 7.17. (All of these tables appear on page 141.)

It is obvious from Table 7.15 that the suppressed 77/22 is much quieter than the suppressed

10/22 with high-velocity and standard-velocity ammo, in spite of the fact that the 10/22 produced higher velocities (presumably due to the higher ambient temperature during the second day of testing). It is also interesting that the stretched barrel with integral compensator produced the same sound signature as an unmodified factory barrel. Since the stretched barrel has a size and appearance similar to those of the suppressed barrel, this is useful information if an overzealous law enforcement officer tries to call the stretched barrel a silencer.

Since the unsuppressed sound signatures differ between the 77/22 and 10/22, one must look at the net sound reductions shown in Table 7.16 to test the hypothesis I posed in the introduction to this discussion: does a suppressor produce a lower sound signature when installed on a Ruger 77/22 than on a 10/22? Based on net sound reductions, the hypothesis is vindicated when using high-velocity and standard-velocity LR ammunition. But the hypothesis does not hold using subsonic ammunition.

As far as I can recall, the Silent Stalker 77/22 is the only suppressed rifle I've ever studied that was quieter with standard-velocity ammunition than with subsonic ammo. I suspect the reason for this phenomenon is the same reason that this experiment failed to validate my hypothesis using subsonic fodder. The real world of scientific experimentation frequently provides challenging surprises. At the time of this writing, I'm at a loss to explain the behavior of the Silent Stalker 77/22 with subsonic fodder. This will disappoint the serious student of suppressor technology. For the serious shooter, however, such subtleties are not terribly important. Overall performance is.

Conclusions

While Sound Technology's Silent Stalker 77/22 does not provide as much sound suppression as the company's Black Ops with its much longer suppressor, the Silent Stalker still provides plenty of sound suppression for discreet target shooting, hunting, and animal control. Since the barrel of each Silent Stalker is carefully lapped and polished, and the suppressor design stretches the barrel under considerable tension, this system delivers surprising accuracy, which is enhanced by the trigger job provided with each Silent Stalker system. Intelligent porting provides significantly more velocity than many competing designs. This suppressed 77/22 would be a good choice for SWAT and other tactical teams for taking out exterior light bulbs or the tires of potential getaway vehicles prior to an assault. CB Longs provide the quietest and safest method for neutralizing lights, but a more powerful round will be necessary to flatten tires.

The Silent Stalker 77/22 was significantly quieter than the Silent Stalker 10/22 with high-velocity and standard-velocity ammo, but the 10/22 outperformed the 77/22 with subsonic ammunition. Both systems delivered excellent velocities, although temperature variations between testing of the 77/22 and 10/22 systems preclude a more detailed analysis of this subject.

The Silent Stalker 10/22 with Fajen laminated stock is a particularly handsome rifle. Sound Technology also can provide a stretched, unsuppressed barrel with built-in recoil compensator that quickly replaces the suppressed barrel and provides similar handling characteristics and appearance. After investing in expensive accessories like the Shepherd Autoranging Rimfire scope and the Fajen laminated stock, this additional option of a matched unsuppressed barrel is quite compelling. The Silent Stalker family of suppressed rifles from Sound Technology provides some interesting and useful possibilities.

Table 7.15. Sound signatures in decibels of suppressor tests.

GUN	SUPPRESSOR	FEDERAL HV LR	HANSEN SV LR	BAIKAL JB LR	FEDERAL CB LONGS	TEMP., °F (°C)
Ruger 77/22	None	140	137	137	131	58(14)
Ruger 77/22	Silent Stalker 77/22	114	112	114	106	58(14)
Ruger 10/22	None (factory barrel)	142	139	139	—	66(19)
Ruger 10/22	None (ST stretched w/comp)	142	—	—	—	66(19)
Ruger 10/22	Silent Stalker 10/22	123	119	113	—	66(19)

Table 7.16. Net sound reductions in decibels.

GUN	SUPPRESSOR	FEDERAL HV LR	HANSEN SV LR	BAIKAL JB LR	FEDERAL CB LONGS	TEMP., °F (°C)
Ruger 77/22	Silent Stalker 77/22	26	25	23	25	58(14)
Ruger 10/22	None (ST stretched w/comp)	0	—	—	—	66(19)
Ruger 10/22	Silent Stalker 10/22	19	20	26	—	66(19)

Table 7.17. Muzzle velocities of suppressed and unsuppressed rifles, expressed as fps (and mps).

GUN	SUPPRESSOR	FEDERAL HV LR	HANSEN SV LR	BAIKAL JB LR	FEDERAL CB LONGS	TEMP., °F (°C)	SPEED OF SOUND fps (mps)
Ruger 77/22	None	1,257(383)	1,136(346)	1,045(319)	649(198)	58(14)	1,116(340)
Ruger 77/22	Silent Stalker 77/22	1,033(315)	978(298)	868(265)	536(163)	58(14)	1,116(340)
Ruger 10/22	None (factory barrel)	1,222(372)	1,065(325)	1,010(308)	—	66(19)	1,124(343)
Ruger 10/22	None (ST stretched w/comp)	1,228(374)	1,110(338)	1,025(312)	—	66(19)	1,124(343)
Ruger 10/22	Silent Stalker 10/22	1,096(334)	1,016(310)	892(272)	—	66(19)	1,124(343)

CHAPTER EIGHT

SILENCED .22 PISTOLS

Most .22 pistols suppressed since the heyday of the Maxim silencer employ integral suppressors rather than muzzle cans, since it is much easier to design a system that is effective in terms of sound suppression, easily permits the employment of iron sights, and yet remains aesthetically attractive. The use of an integral suppressor also permits tailoring the pistol for particular kinds of ammunition by the use of properly designed porting, and it permits the design of a suppressed pistol that is practical for holster carry. Finally, an integrally suppressed pistol is inherently more robust than a pistol with a muzzle can.

The most popular pistol to suppress for sporting or clandestine purposes has been the Ruger Mark I and its successor, the Mark II. The Ruger has dominated this market because it is accurate, robust, capable of quiet performance, and relatively easy to silence with an integral suppressor from an engineering point of view. Although the Military Armament Corporation (MAC) manufactured silenced Ruger pistols in the 1970s, the first successful integrally suppressed .22 pistol dates back to 1943: the High Standard HD-MS.

Featuring a relatively short ported barrel and a suppressor filled with tinned bronze screen washers to diffuse, cool, and slow expanding combustion gases, the HD-MS was used by the OSS in Europe and the Far East during World War II, including a successful liquidation on the busy streets of Berlin. According to OSS veteran

Dr. John Brunner, author of the outstanding book *OSS Weapons*, the HD-MS was the most popular and most frequently used special weapon in the OSS inventory. The pistol was subsequently used by CIA personnel, Navy SEALs in the Mekong Delta of Vietnam, and Delta Force during the attempt to rescue hostages in Iran.

This aging pistol is arguably a dozen generations behind the state of current suppressor technology, yet the HD-MS remains in the U.S. government's inventory, and the blueprints for the suppressor remain classified. The HD-MS will be discussed thoroughly in the second volume of *Silencer History and Performance* along with other silenced weapons intended for tactical applications in the CQB (Close Quarter Battle) environment.

Highly skilled operators have used suppressed .22 caliber pistols for a half century to complete missions where quiet was more important than terminal ballistics. This operator is using an AWC Amphibian II.

When American involvement in Southeast Asia heated up a decade after the silenced HD-MS went out of production, MAC introduced suppressed Ruger pistols for spooks and special forces. It was this pistol that inadvertently got Dr. Philip H. Dater interested in suppressor design. "One of my first [Class 3] toys," Dater recalls, "was a new suppressed Ruger Mark I pistol from the Military Armament Corporation, which was still in business at the time. They eventually had two models; this was the original MAC with a 6 inch tube on it. The gun had a ported barrel that was surrounded by stacked bronze screen washers."

But after putting 500 to 600 rounds through MAC's suppressed Ruger, the pistol became so loud that its sound signature was indistinguishable from an unsuppressed Ruger pistol. So Dater called MAC and spoke to Charles Pitts about his problem with the suppressed Ruger. (Later, Pitts would become one of the principals at RPB after MAC went under.)

"Gee," Pitts said, "I don't know what can be done about it. That system is not designed to be taken apart and rebuilt."

So Dater asked him, "What about the tax-stamper?"

"That's not our market," Pitts replied. "Our market is spooks. They qualify with the weapon using 40-50 rounds per year and, within about two years, the weapon is commonly used on a mission and then deep-sixed."

"I'm not about to deep-six my weapon," Dater said. He went on to ask whether the MAC system could be rebuilt if he returned the pistol to MAC.

"Yes," Pitts replied, "but there's no way to transfer it back and forth without two more tax stamps." He was wrong—the pistol could have been returned for repair using an ATF Form 5 without incurring any additional tax liability. But Dater didn't know any better at the time.

Dater concluded that he had nothing to lose, so he disassembled the MAC-suppressed Ruger. Or he tried to. After a great deal of tribulation, Dater eventually managed to unscrew the suppressor tube, but only after inflicting some substantial pipe-wrench gouges on the tube. That was the price of enlightenment. He discovered why the suppressor stopped working. The mesh packing inside the suppressor had filled up with shaved lead, since none of the holes were deburred.

"I started," Dater recalled, "to look for something like the bronze screen that MAC used. One day I spotted a likely product in the grocery store: Chore Girl [now called Chore Boy] scouring pads, which were a coarse-weave copper mesh. I cleaned up the MAC pistol, deburred the holes, and repacked the can with yarn made by twisting strands of Chore Boy mesh. I replaced the old wipe in the front of the MAC can with a reflective end cap of my own design. The old MAC worked like new. I later would use the same packing and front end cap in my RST suppressor." While MAC's suppressed Ruger Mark I became Dater's first Class 3 toy, Dater's RST on a Ruger Mark II became my first Class 3 toy.

AWC RST

I purchased my RST pistol from Armament Systems & Technology, Inc., which was producing Dater-designed suppressors in Houston, Texas, using the trade name Automatic Weapons Company (AWC). My suppressed Ruger Mark II was actually built by Tim Bixler soon after he joined AWC as vice president in charge of manufacturing. The quality of Bixler's work was impressive. Lynn McWilliams named this variant of the RST the Model MK-2.

Two AWC RST suppressed Ruger Mark I pistols with the takedown tools provided with each system, made when AWC was in Albuquerque, New Mexico. Photo by Dr. Philip H. Dater.

I remember the day I brought that pistol home as if it were last weekend. My wife was washing dishes. I loaded a magazine with nine rounds, snuck up to just outside the kitchen window until I was two arm spans away, and carefully emptied the gun into a rotted stump. I then went inside and asked if she had heard anything unusual. No, not a thing. I was impressed—and thoroughly hooked on stealthy shooting.

The Dater pistol also provided uncanny accuracy. I

could routinely hit pop cans at 70 yards (64 m) from a sitting position. The RST proved to be more accurate in my hands than my venerable old S&W Model 41 target pistol with bull barrel. My affection for the RST pistol became an outright love affair when I got to shoot it side by side with a new Ciener-suppressed Ruger 10/22 rifle. Dater's pistol was substantially quieter than Ciener's rifle.

The RST pistol is about 3 inches (7.6 cm) longer and 5 ounces (142 grams) heavier than the factory Ruger pistol from which it is fabricated. The blued-steel suppressor tube is 6.0 inches (15.2 cm) long and 1.0 inch (2.5 cm) in diameter. The RST suppressed pistol weighs 42 ounces (1.2 kg) and has an overall length of 11.6 inches (29.5 cm), making this a practical pistol for extended holster carry.

As Figure 8.1 shows, the RST features a turned-down barrel with four rows of seven 1/8 inch (3.3 mm) ports and an aluminum barrel extension with four rows of five 0.25 inch (6.4 mm) ports. The barrel ports vent hot combustion gases into the rear chamber of the suppressor, which is filled with densely packed copper mesh. The copper diffusion material in the rear chamber cools and slows the combustion gases, a process that is enhanced by the expansion of the gases. Allowing a gas to expand always reduces its pressure (which is perceived as sound), and some simple suppressors depend upon their large volumes for much of their performance.

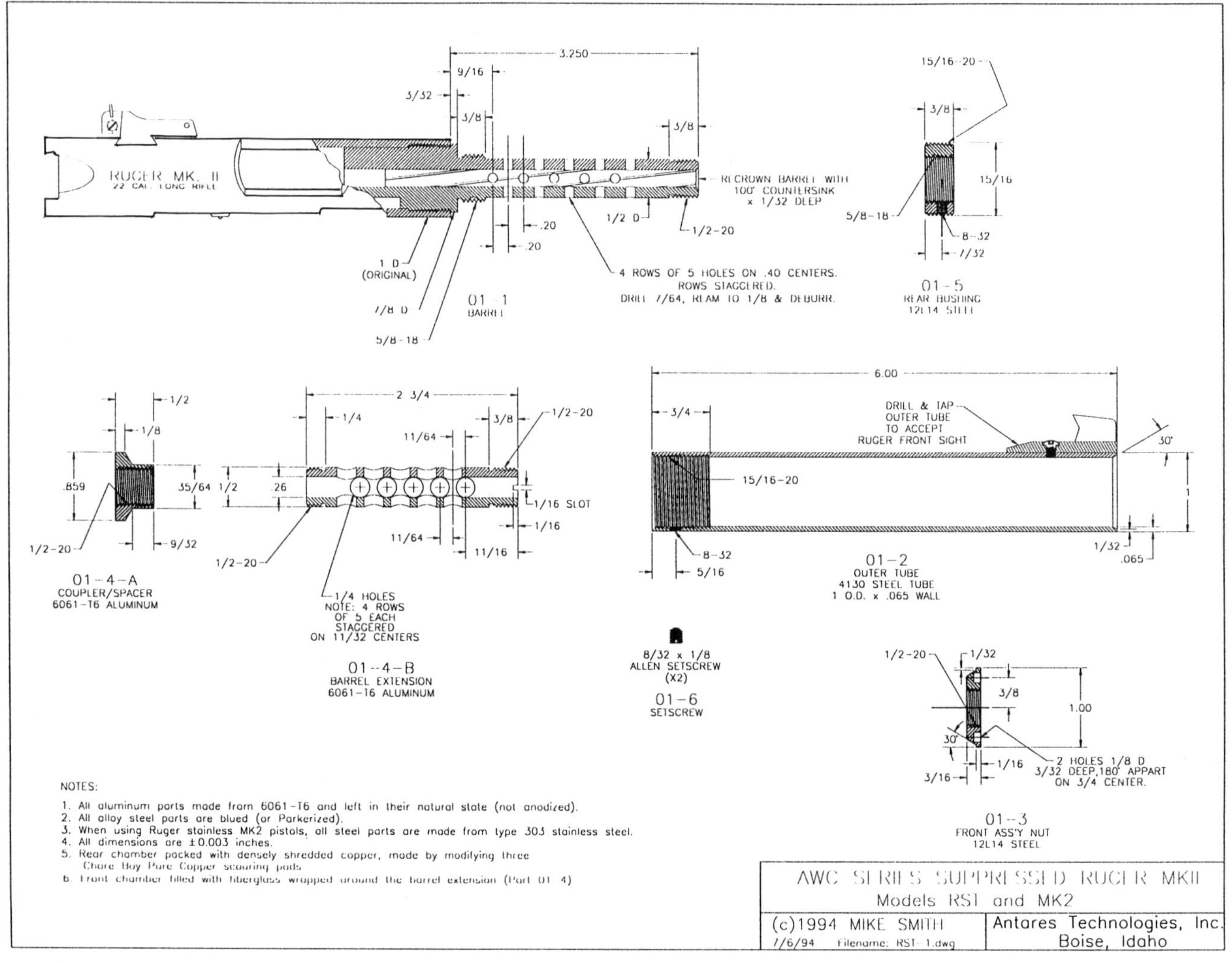

Figure 8.1. Design of AWC RST suppressed Ruger pistol. Drawing by Mike Smith.

The front chamber is filled with fiberglass, which further slows down the expanding combustion gases. The early and extensive porting of the barrel reduces the rearward energy (recoil impulse) delivered to the bolt face, so Dater shortened the recoil spring by four turns. He found that the modified pistol functioned reliably with all .22 Long Rifle ammunition of the day except CCI standard velocity. A greater diversity of .22 LR ammunition is currently available. If the owner of an RST system finds that the pistol does not cycle reliably, it is possible to remove an additional one or two coils of the recoil spring, working in half-coil increments. A better alternative is to remove one turn of the hammer spring or to chamfer the rear of the bolt as described in Chapter 10, "Optimizing the Performance of Suppressed .22s."

When building the RST, the pistol's original fixed rear sight is replaced with the adjustable rear sight Ruger used on its target pistol. A new front sight is fitted to the front of the suppressor tube, giving the RST a sight radius of about 10 inches (25.4 cm).

Since assembly of the suppressor stretches the barrel with at least some tension, I've often wondered whether that aspect of the design gave the RST its remarkable accuracy. When I asked Dater about this possibility, he replied, "I'm not sure if barrel tensioning is the answer, because there's not that much tension on the barrel."

Dater went on to explain that there was nothing fancy about the barrel crown, which can have a dramatic affect on accuracy. "The funny thing is," Dater said, "that the crown on the RST was just done with a 100 degree countersink. It's recessed just slightly. I think a lot of the accuracy has to do with the porting of the barrel, where it was ported, and the velocity control. The reality is that, when you get within 10 percent of the speed of sound, you start to get some instability of the bullet—some buffeting. I think the RST produced velocities with CCI Mini Mags somewhere around 850 fps, well within the subsonic range. Furthermore, I always deburred the port holes, which a lot of people don't do."

Dater also made a small number of low-maintenance RST pistols, which dispensed with the bronze mesh and fiberglass packing. This variant featured a 7.0 inch (17.8 cm) tube, which Lynn McWilliams named the Model MK-2-LM. Two rear expansion chambers were machined into the surface of the barrel and wrapped with aluminum window screen. In place of the front chamber with fiberglass wrapped around a ported barrel extension, the MK-2-LM featured four funnel-shaped aluminum baffles that nested together. The low-maintenance variant never developed a niche in the marketplace, and only three were manufactured.

Since the RST and its variants pioneered the concept of user maintainability and employed a rather novel, even zany, approach to maintenance, it is appropriate to look at the maintenance procedures in some detail. Some of the following suggestions represent improved procedures over those outlined in the original technical manual.

Disassembly

Separate the barreled receiver from the trigger assembly according to the Ruger manual and remove the bolt. Use a hex (Allen) wrench to remove the 8-32 set screw from the bottom rear of the suppressor tube. Use the spanner provided with the RST to unscrew the suppressor's front end cap. Use a U.S. quarter or similar-sized coin to unscrew the barrel extension about 0.25 inch (6 mm). Since the extension is soft aluminum, use your fingers rather than a pliers or other tool to withdraw the extension from the suppressor.

Clamp the rear of the suppressor tube in a vise using a contoured plastic liner. I prefer the Flexbar Model 14001 Vise Liner, because the liners have magnets that hold them against the face of the vise and because the V-shaped channels in the face of the inserts are well suited to the Ruger receiver. If possible, wrap the suppressor tube with a layer of thin neoprene (such as 1/8 inch or 3 mm wetsuit material) to increase friction and use a strap wrench to help prevent the suppressor from twisting during the next step. A Rigid No. 2 strap wrench works as well as any.

Now insert a large Phillips screwdriver through the holes in the receiver that normally accommodate the bolt stop pin while maintaining pressure on the receiver tube with the strap wrench. Unless you disassembled the suppressor when new and treated the suppressor and receiver threads with high-temperature antiseize compound (colloidal molybdenum or copper compounds work best), then considerable force will probably be required to unscrew the receiver. If, however, the suppressed pistol was built personally by Dr. Dater, then all threaded surfaces were properly treated with antiseize compound, and this initial treatment is not required. The downside of this conservative approach with a new suppressor is that removal of the suppressor tube will necessitate completely repacking the RST system.

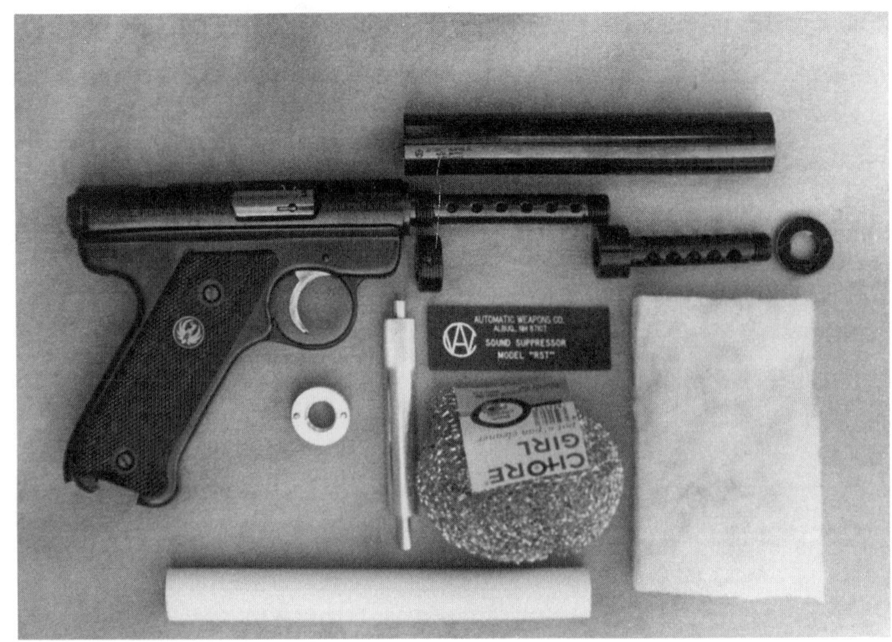

AWC RST pistol disassembled to show internal construction. Photo by Dr. Philip H. Dater.

It is imperative with the RST system that the suppressor be disassembled for maintenance every 500 rounds. It is also imperative that antiseize compound always be applied to all threaded surfaces as soon as the pistol is purchased and every time the suppressor is maintained.

Clean the disassembled components with a suitable solvent such as Varsol, Kroil, or carburetor cleaner. Avoid Hoppe's No. 9 since it will attack the aluminum components. If the ports are clogged with lead or carbon residue, try removing the fouling with an ice pick. If that fails, try using a small twist drill secured in a handle used for taps. One must be very careful when cleaning ports by hand with a drill bit to avoid damaging the ports.

Maintenance and Reassembly

The packing material for the rear of the suppressor is fabricated from three Chore Boy copper scouring pads, which are available in most grocery stores. The mesh is welded together where the manufacturer's label is attached; pull this weld apart and unfold the mesh, which will form tubular sheet measuring about 5x12 inches (13x30 cm). Cut each sheet across the tube (the short dimension) into four tubular pieces measuring about 5x3 inches (13x8 cm). Twist each piece of mesh tightly into a rope, which should turn out about 8 inches (20 cm) long and about 1/4 inch (6 mm) in diameter. Although this operation can be accomplished with the fingers alone, it is much easier to chuck a screw hook into a variable speed drill, loop one end of the mesh over the hook, and then twist the mesh at the drill's lowest speed. The three pads will yield 12 copper ropes, but it is quite difficult to install more than 11 of them.

Next, treat the threads on the receiver and inside the suppressor tube with antiseize compound, and screw the receiver back into the suppressor tube. Align the tube using the index marks on the

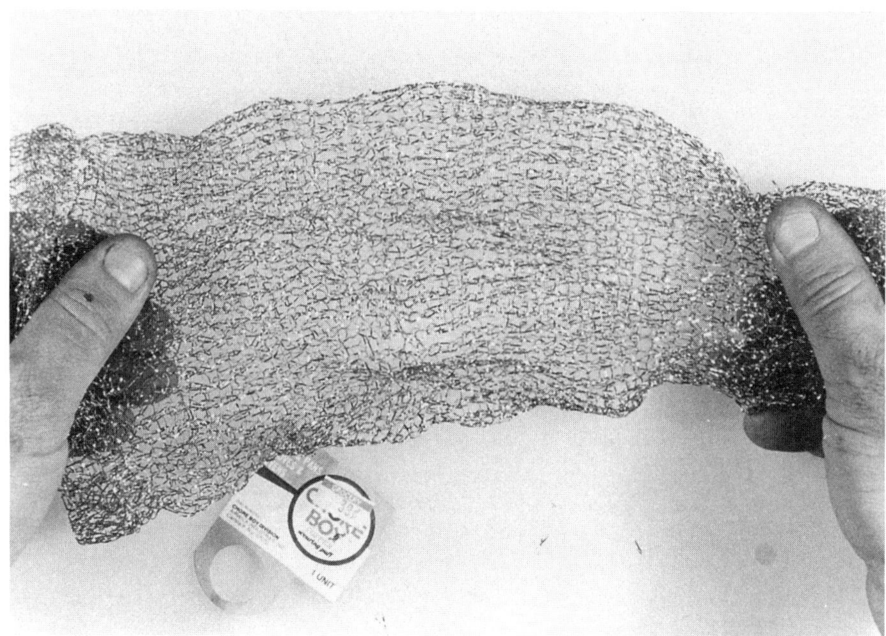

Packing the RST suppressor with copper mesh begins by unfolding a Chore Boy scouring pad into a tubular sheet. Photo by Dr. Philip H. Dater.

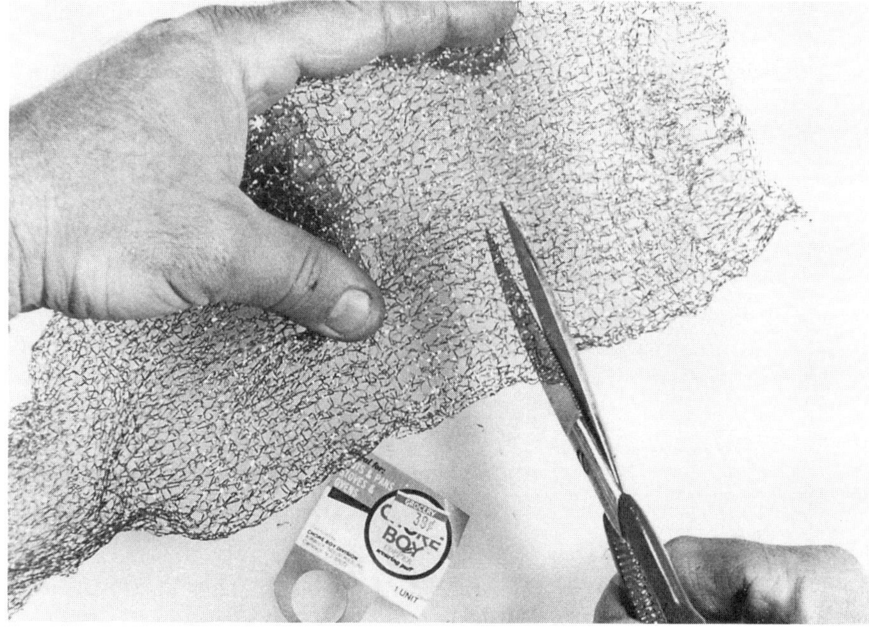

Next, cut across the tube to form four tubular pieces measuring about 5x3 inches (13x8 cm). Photo by Dr. Philip H. Dater.

bottom of the suppressor tube and receiver. Place the set screw on a hex wrench, treat the threads with antiseize compound, and screw through the tube into the receiver, taking care not to smear any antiseize compound onto the outside of the suppressor tube.

Place a hard rubber bench pad or similar surface on the work bench. Stand the pistol on the rear surface of the receiver so the suppressor tube is vertical. Insert the narrow end of the aluminum packing guide into the barrel. Wrap one of the mesh ropes (fabricated earlier) around the packing guide, and use the length of 1/2 inch (13 cm) Schedule 40 PVC water pipe that came with the RST to push the mesh as far as possible into the suppressor. Hand pressure will not compress the mesh sufficiently. Inset an identical length of 3/8 inch (10 mm) Schedule 40 PVC pipe inside the 1/2 inch pipe and drive them downward with a mallet. Note that using Schedule 80 PVC pipe eliminates the need to use a length of 3/8 inch pipe, but this type of pipe is harder to find.

It is virtually impossible to overcompact the mesh, so be sure to use enough force to thoroughly compress it or the suppressor will be relatively loud. Keep repeating this process until at least 11 ropes have been installed and 1/4 to 3/8 inch (6 to 10 mm) of threaded barrel remains exposed above the compacted mesh ropes. If more threading is exposed, add more mesh rope. If less threading is exposed, the mesh requires further compaction. Some folks have managed to install 12 ropes, but I've only been able to install 11. Remove the packing guide.

At this point, check to see whether any strands of copper have protruded through the porting into the bore. A few strands won't do any harm and will be removed by the first few shots, but you should remove as many strands as possible at this time, using an oiled bronze bore brush. Never, under any circumstances, use a stainless brush in the bore of a firearm.

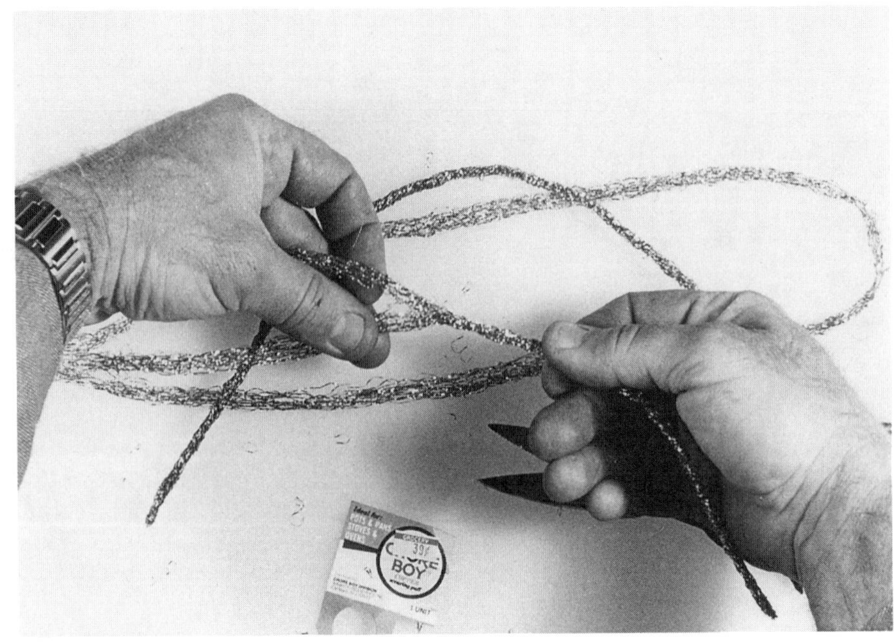

Twist each piece of mesh tightly into a rope, and then use the provided tools to pack the suppressor tube with 11 or 12 of these mesh ropes. Photo by Dr. Philip H. Dater.

Cut a piece of 1/2 inch (1.3 cm) thick mineral wool that measures 3x4 inches (8x10 cm). While fiberglass can be used instead, mineral wool is more durable. Treat the barrel threads and the threads in the rear and on the front of the barrel extension with anti-seize compound. Wrap the mineral wool around the barrel extension, securing it with several strips of masking tape. Insert this assembly into the suppressor tube and screw the extension onto the barrel using a suitable coin. Be careful not to overtighten; the aluminum extension is very soft. But the barrel extension should be tightened enough so that it protrudes from the front of the suppressor tube by less than 1/16 inch (2 mm). If necessary, push the mineral wool back into the suppressor so it leaves about 1/8 inch (3 mm) of space below the front of the suppressor tube.

Reassembly is completed by using the spanner that came with the RST to screw the front end cap onto the barrel extension. Once again, be very careful not to overtighten. The cap only needs to be hand tight. Finally, carefully sight in the suppressed pistol; a small amount of sight adjustment will probably be required.

Performance

Since the RST pistol will be used as a benchmark for studying the performance of other suppressed pistols throughout this chapter, it would be redundant to discuss the pistol's performance in terms of sound reduction and projectile velocity at this time. The first discussion of these issues vis-à-vis the RST appears in the section of this chapter on the SCRC Model 22L pistol. Suffice it to say for now that the RST is conspicuously quieter than contemporary designs like the Ciener Model 512 and that it produces surprising, almost astonishing accuracy that few subsequent designs have been able to approach.

There are, however, some liabilities to the RST design:

- The suppressed pistol does not produce as much projectile velocity as those who use the pistol on medium-sized animals (such as feral dogs and coyotes) might like.
- The pistol must be disassembled, cleaned, and repacked every 500 rounds. Failure to keep to

this regimen will make future disassembly difficult or impossible long before the suppressor loses its effectiveness from the accumulation of fouling.

- Disassembly under the best of circumstances can be challenging; I once popped off the front sight while using a strap wrench on the tube. Tim Bixler is thinking about producing a video on how to make the job relatively easy, and that would be a real boon to those who own the RST and its descendents.
- The RST has too many ports in barrel—four ports near the chamber would probably have been sufficient.

Nevertheless, the RST was a significant improvement on its contemporary competitors in terms of accuracy, sound suppression, and lifespan (since it could be disassembled for cleaning and maintenance). Remarkably, in the two decades since Dater designed the RST, the Operator II pistol from Gemtech is the only suppressed .22 pistol that delivers comparable accuracy in my experience. Interestingly, the Operator was co-designed by Dr. Dater and a competitor at the time, Jim Ryan of JR Customs. Incorporating such advanced features as tritium night sights and an ingenious slide lock, it delivers maximum projectile velocity while producing excellent sound suppression. The Operator and several other tactical .22 pistols will be thoroughly evaluated in the second volume of *Silencer History and Performance.*

The original RST design under the MK-2 designation was manufactured by Armament Systems & Technology and its successor, AWC Systems Technology, until 1989. Although Dr. Dater has long since developed a high-tech replacement for the RST that produced similar (i.e., exceptional) accuracy and superior sound suppression, the RST retains a devoted following. One such diehard prevailed upon Dater to build one last RST in 1993.

A slightly improved variant of the RST continues to be manufactured under license by Tim Bixler at SCRC. Called the Mark 22, Bixler's suppressed Ruger produces virtually the same sound reduction as the original RST but has several refinements to ease disassembly and maintenance. One of the few liabilities of the RST design is that it achieves its good sound suppression at the expense of velocity. Thus some owners of valuable livestock have become convinced that the RST and pistols producing similar or lesser velocities provide disappointing performance on coyotes and feral dogs. My own experience protecting a friend's valuable horses from feral dogs using an RST is that a precisely placed head shot is effective, but a less than perfect head shot or a well-placed body shot is not.

Nevertheless, the bottom line on the RST is twofold: 1) the RST remains to this day the quietest integrally suppressed pistol with a 6 inch tube that I've ever tested, and 2) it also remains the most accurate suppressed pistol I've ever tested. There are much quieter pistols now in the marketplace, but they all have longer tubes.

Bixler decided to see if he could produce a variant of the RST design that would provide barely subsonic velocities with high-velocity LR ammunition and still achieve acceptable sound suppression. I had the privilege of testing the original prototype of Bixler's longer high-velocity design, which he calls the Mark 22L.

SCRC MARK 22L

The Mark 22L is basically the same suppressed pistol as Bixler's improved variant of the old RST design. The 22L's barrel, rear expansion chamber, and suppressor tube are 1.0 inch (2.5 cm) longer than the Mark 22, and the barrel porting starts 1.0 inch farther from the chamber to increase projectile velocity.

Table 8.1 compares the mean (average) sound signature (peak SPL) of the SCRC Mark 22L and the

AWC RST. Net sound reductions appear in Table 8.2, and the average velocities of suppressed and unsuppressed pistols appear in Table 8.3. (These tables appear on page 156.) The unsuppressed Ruger pistol used as the control throughout my research features a 5.5 inch (14.0 cm) barrel.

The velocity data show that the 22L produces 118 fps more muzzle velocity than the RST with Federal high-velocity LR ammunition. The Mark 22L produces 98 fps more muzzle velocity with Hansen standard-velocity target LR and 178 fps more velocity with RWS subsonic LR. What's more, the SCRC 22L functioned flawlessly with the RWS subsonic and Winchester subsonic ammo, since the later porting increased the amount of back pressure available to cycle the bolt. Until this moment in the evolution of integrally suppressed pistols, I'd never fired a suppressed Ruger Mark I or Mark II that functioned reliably with subsonic fodder. Of course, the 22L was expressly designed to deliver the maximum penetration with high-velocity ammunition, so reliability with subsonic ammunition is simply a happy accident.

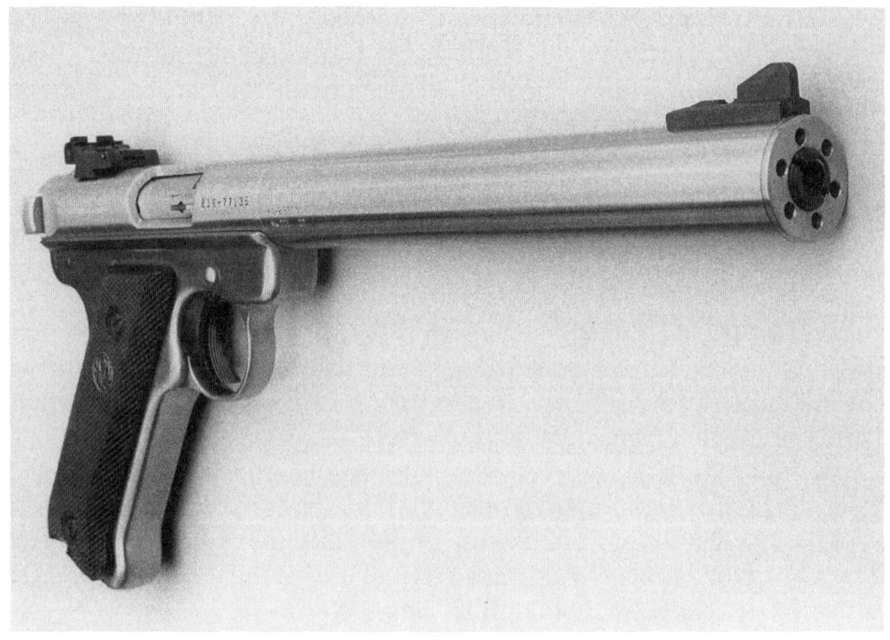

Oblique view of the SCRC Mark 22L pistol, showing the distinctive pattern of takedown holes characteristic of Tim Bixler's attention to detail.

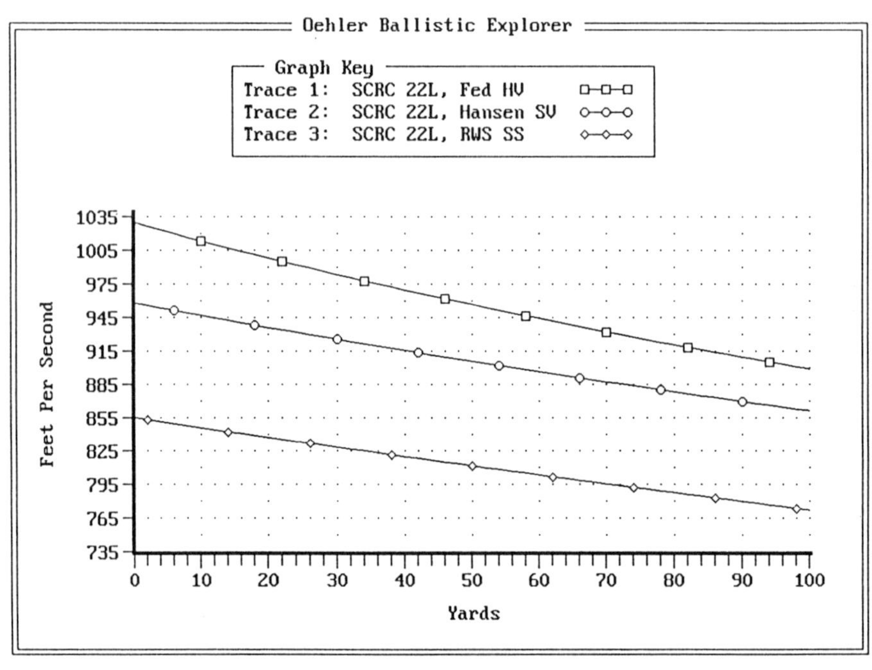

Figure 8.2. Bullet velocities produced by SCRC Mark 22L suppressed Ruger pistol.

Figures 8.2 and 8.3 show the performance of the SCRC Mark 22L in terms of projectile velocity and trajectory using Federal high-velocity LR, Hansen standard-velocity target LR, and RWS subsonic LR ammunition. Figures 8.4 and 8.5 show the same information for the AWC RST. Figures 8.6 and 8.7 compare the velocities and trajectories of an unsuppressed Ruger pistol, the SCRC 22L, and the AWC RST using high-velocity ammunition.

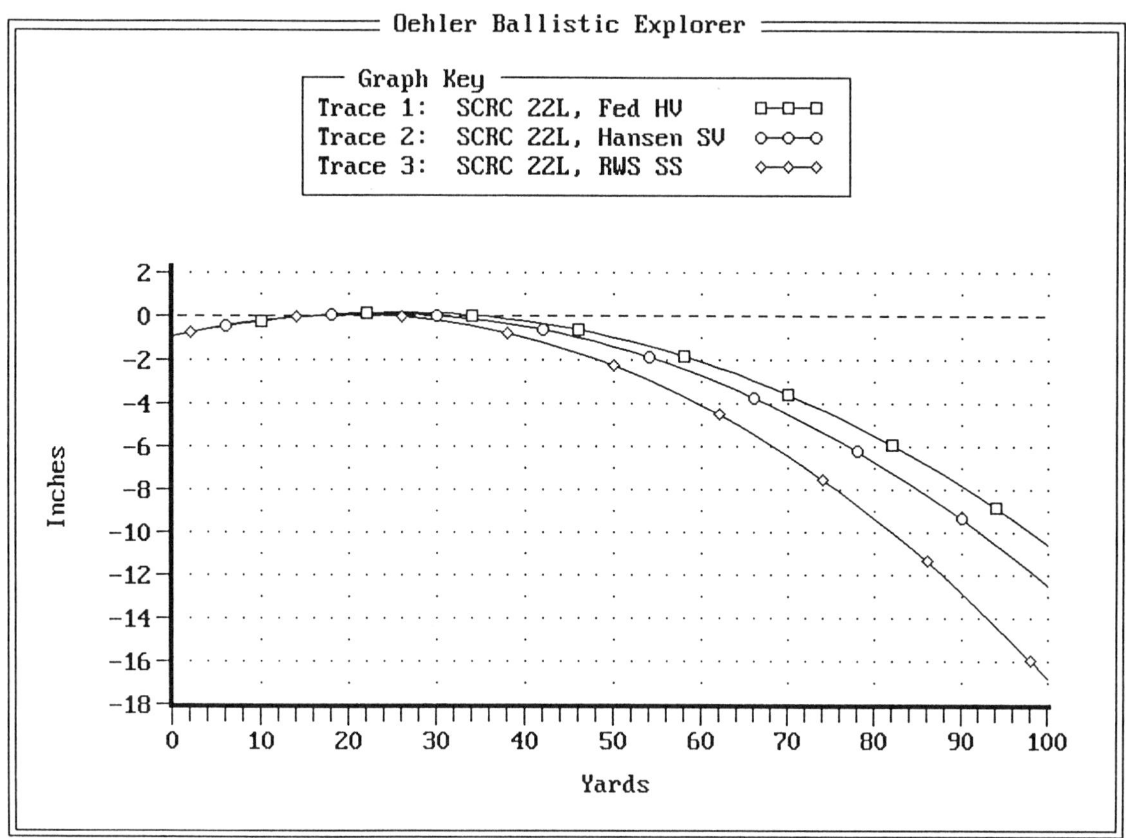

Figure 8.3. Bullet trajectories produced by SCRC Mark 22L suppressed Ruger pistol.

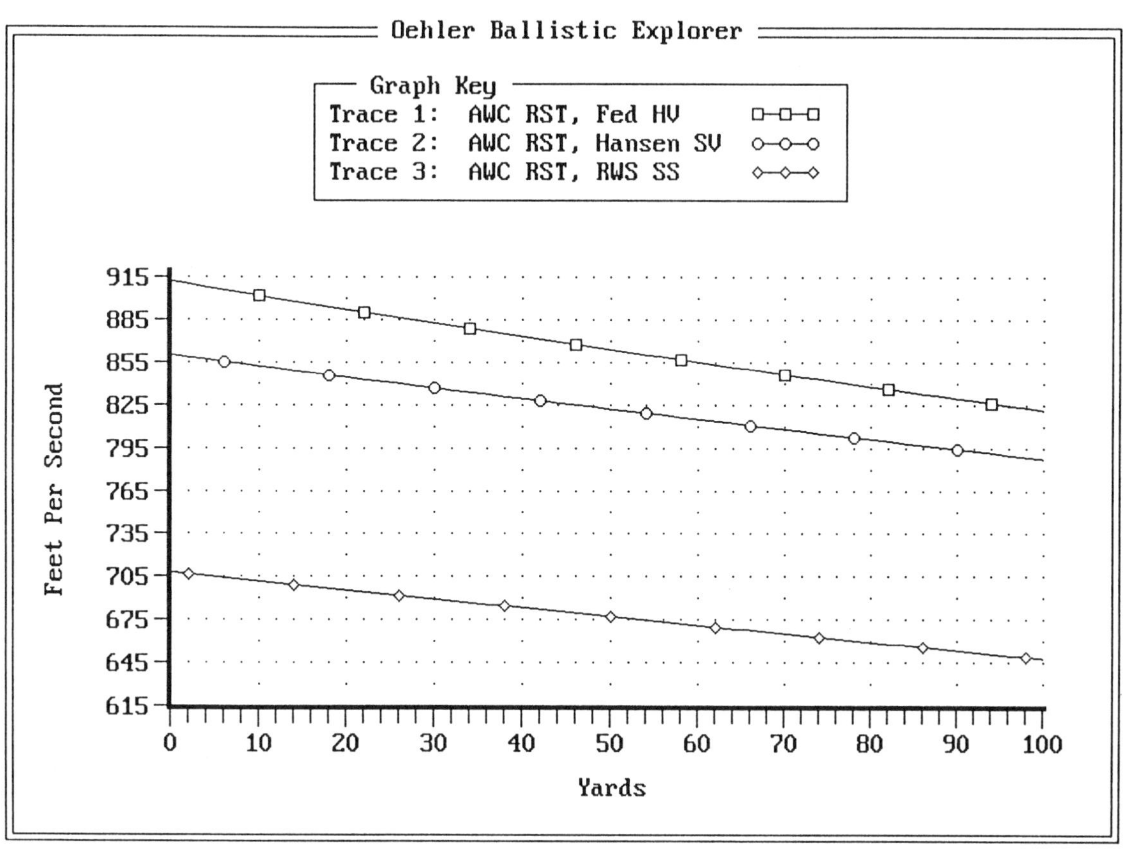

Figure 8.4. Bullet velocities produced by AWC RST suppressed Ruger pistol.

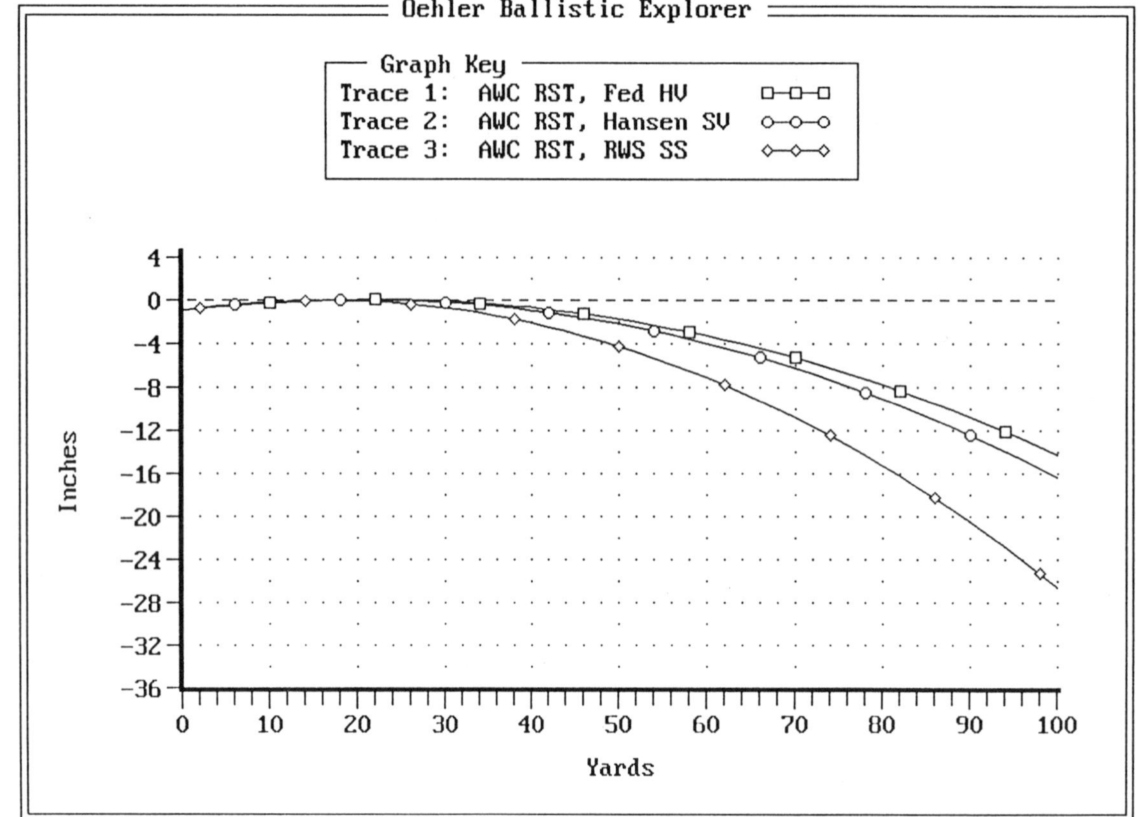

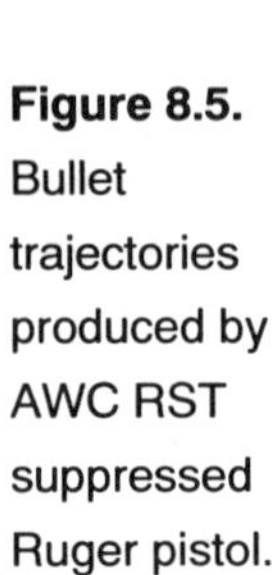

Figure 8.5. Bullet trajectories produced by AWC RST suppressed Ruger pistol.

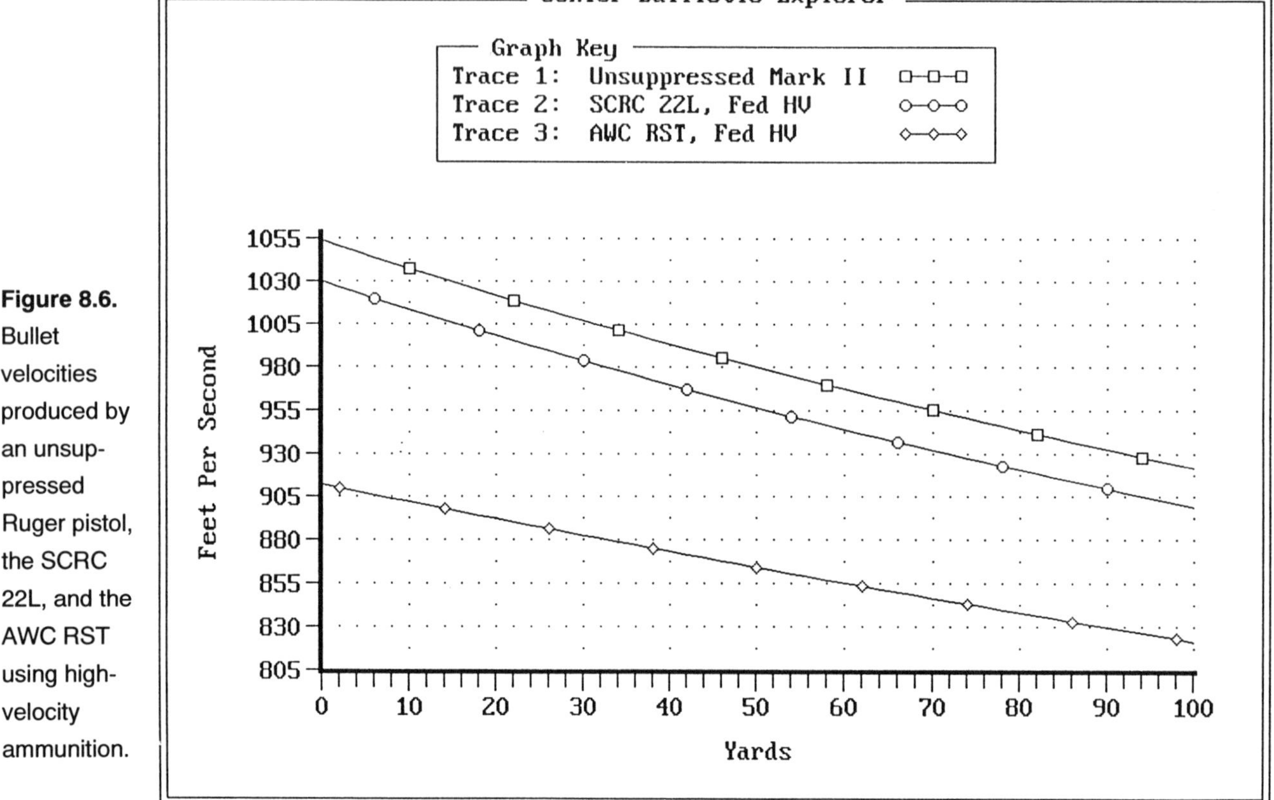

Figure 8.6. Bullet velocities produced by an unsuppressed Ruger pistol, the SCRC 22L, and the AWC RST using high-velocity ammunition.

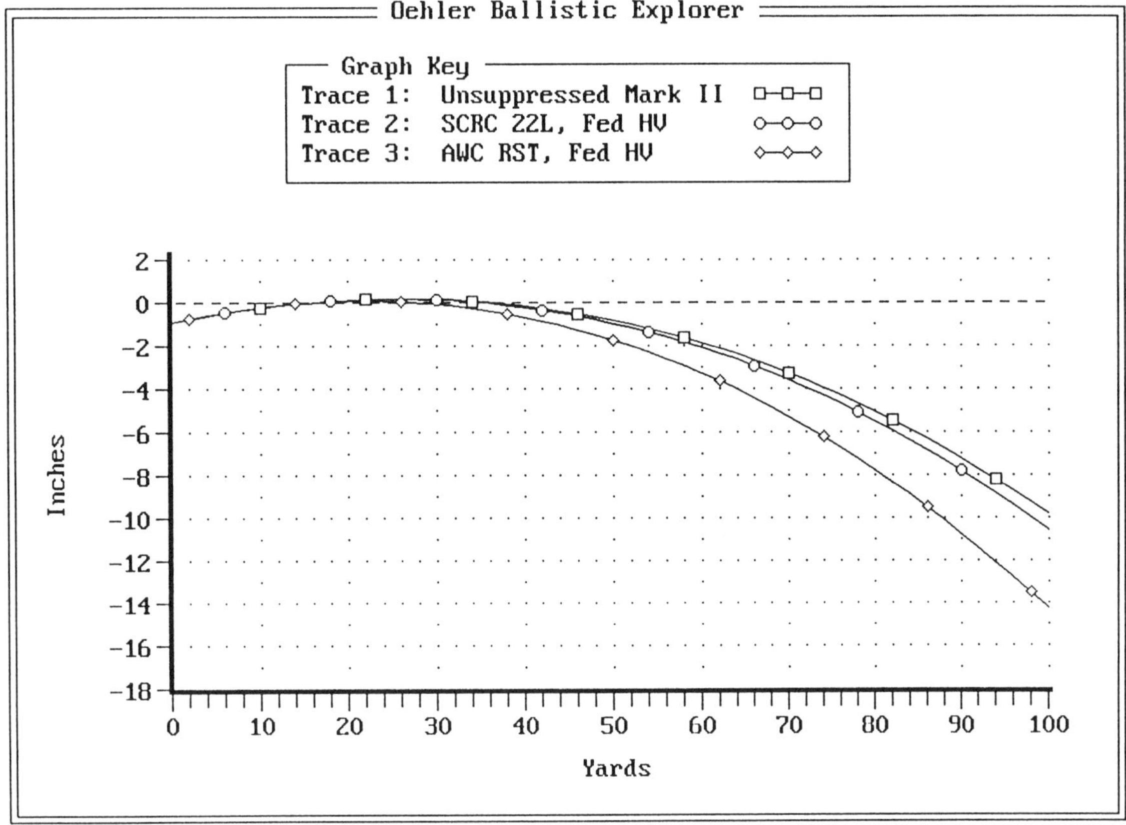

Figure 8.7. Bullet trajectories produced by an unsuppressed Ruger pistol, the SCRC 22L, and the AWC RST using high-velocity ammunition.

It is clear from these figures and the sound data that the SCRC Mark 22L allows discriminating shooters to have their cake and eat it too. Using high-velocity or standard-velocity ammo, the 22L delivers substantially better velocity (i.e., better penetration) and flatter trajectory (i.e., better shot placement) at the trivial cost of 1 dB net sound reduction. Using subsonic ammunition, the Mark 22L delivers more velocity and similar sound reduction to the AWC RST and the SCRC Mark 22 using standard-velocity ammunition. Thus, by the careful selection of ammunition, the 22L can deliver better performance than its predecessors on live targets using high-velocity ammo and duplicate the quietest performance of the RST and Mark 22 by using subsonic ammunition (which would not cycle in the 22L's shorter siblings).

Table 8.1. Sound signatures in decibels of SCRC suppressor tests.

GUN	SUPPRESSOR	FEDERAL HV	REMINGTON HV	HANSEN SV	RWS SS	WINCHESTER SS	TEMP., °F (°C)
Ruger MkII	None	156	155	154	153	153	71(22)
Ruger MkII	SCRC Mark 22L	132	134	134	129	131	71(22)
Ruger MkII	None	155	—	154	153	—	82(28)
Ruger MkII	AWC RST	132	—	132	131[a]	—	82(28)

[a] will eject most of the time, but will not chamber new round

Table 8.2. Net sound reductions of SCRC tests, expressed as decibels.

GUN	SUPPRESSOR	FEDERAL HV	REMINGTON HV	HANSEN SV	RWS SS	WINCHESTER SS	TEMP., °F (°C)
Ruger MkII	SCRC Mark 22L	24	21	20	24	22	71(22)
Ruger MkII	AWC RST	23	—	22	22[a]	—	82(28)

[a] will eject most of the time, but will not chamber new round

Table 8.3. Muzzle velocities of suppressed and unsuppressed pistols used in SCRC tests, expressed in feet per second (and meters per second).

GUN	SUPPRESSOR	FEDERAL HV	REMINGTON HV	HANSEN SV	RWS SS	WINCHESTER SS	TEMP., °F (°C)	SPEED OF SOUND fps (mps)
Ruger MkII	None	1,065(325)	1,097(334)	965(294)	939(285)	968(295)	71(22)	1,129(344)
Ruger MkII	SCRC Mark 22L	1,030(314)	1,046(319)	958(292)	886(270)	921(281)	71(22)	1,129(344)
Ruger MkII	None	1,054(321)	—	974(297)	847(258)	—	82(28)	1,141(348)
Ruger MkII	AWC RST	912(278)	—	860(262)	708(216)[a]	—	82(28)	1,141(348)

[a] will eject most of the time, but will not chamber new round

Baffles removed from Ciener KMK10 suppressor.

The Ciener KMK10 is significantly longer than the PAI Spectre.

The SCRC Model 22L was an important achievement in the evolution of serious suppressed .22 pistols. Bixler sought and achieved maximum velocity at the cost of a marginally louder sound signature with high-velocity and standard-velocity ammunition. Jonathan Arthur Ciener expanded his product line in a different direction to give target shooters and plinkers the maximum amount of sound suppression at relatively no change in velocity from his standard Model 512. There are, however, several costs for the KMK10's better sound suppression: 1) a dramatic increase in suppressor length makes the pistol less desirable for holster carry; 2) the extra weight and muzzle-heaviness slow the speed of target acquisition and increase fatigue significantly during prolonged offhand shooting, and 3) the long sight radius is hard on aging eyes like mine.

CIENER KMK10

The Ciener KMK10 suppressed Ruger pistol is a stretched variant of Ciener's Model 512. The KMK's suppressor tube and end caps are fabricated from 300 series stainless steels. The ported barrel is surrounded by a primary expansion chamber filled with brass eyelets, which are held in place with a friction-fit aluminum encapsulator. A series of conical aluminum baffles with built-in spacers fill the space between the end of the barrel and the suppressor's front end cap.

The suppressed KMK10 has a barrel length of 10.0 inches (25.4 cm), a suppressor length of 12.0 inches (30.5 cm), and a suppressor diameter of 1.0 inches (2.5 cm).

One traditional rule of thumb in suppressor design is that a longer suppressor is quieter than a shorter one, and its corollary is that increasing length is usually more effective than increasing the diameter of a suppressor using conventional internal construction. Looking at the sound signatures in Table 8.4 and the net sound reductions in Table 8.5, it should come as no surprise that Ciener's KMK10 is substantially quieter than his Model 512. A look at the velocity data in Table 8.6 shows that the suppressed KMK10 produced only slightly less muzzle velocity than the suppressed 512; the observed differences can probably be explained as day-to-day differences caused by variation of such ambient conditions as temperature, humidity, and barometric pressure.

In terms of accuracy, the suppressed KMK10 gave typical Ruger performance whether shooting offhand, from sandbags, or from a Ransom rest. It did not, however, display the superb accuracy typical of the AWC RST and SCRC Models 22 and 22L, which produced groups that generally ran about 50 to 60 percent of the dispersion produced by the suppressed KMK10. The disappointing accuracy when shooting the KMK10 offhand and from sandbags was surprising since the KMK10 has a much longer sight radius than the other suppressed Rugers. While the greater distance between the front and rear sights does not make the firearm intrinsically more accurate, it should improve the practical accuracy of the arm. The longer sight radius should enable the shooter to see and correct a smaller amount of error in the sight alignment, so the shooter should be able to shoot more precisely. That was not the case with the KMK10.

A couple of things probably contribute to the greater accuracy provided by the RST and its descendents: 1) the design's tensioned barrel, and 2) the extra hand lapping the barrel receives after porting.

Ciener's KMK10 and Model 512, as well as the now discontinued AWC RST and its currently manufactured descendents (the SCRC Model 22 and 22L), really represent 1970s technology. Although the use of diffusion materials such as mesh or eyelets and the use of simple conical baffles provide good performance, unprecedented sound reduction can be achieved by using complex, thick baffles with asymmetric surfaces to work the expanding gases much harder than conventionally designed suppressors. Based on research conducted by Charles A. "Mickey" Finn and Doug Olsen in the early 1980s, with refinements continuing into the 1990s, the following suppressed pistols represent a very different direction in the evolution of suppressor technology. The patented baffle developed by John Leasure for the Precision Arms Spectre builds upon the patented work of Mickey Finn.

PRECISION ARMS SPECTRE

John Leasure of Precision Arms International, Inc. (which was subsequently reorganized under the name Silent Options, Inc.) is a relative newcomer to the manufacturing of suppressors compared with old-timers still in the trade like Jonathan Arthur Ciener, Dr. Philip H. Dater, C. Reed Knight, Mickey Finn, and Tim Bixler. That's a tough act to follow. But Leasure has come a long way in a very short time since he filed an application for a patent on his new suppressor design in September of 1991, which builds upon the work of Mickey Finn and a foreign designer who must remain nameless. Leasure was issued U.S. Patent Number 5,164,535 on November 17, 1992. These baffle designs will be discussed in detail in the third volume of *Silencer History and Performance.*

The first thing one notices about the Precision Arms Spectre suppressor is the excellent workmanship. Except for a few "warts" illustrated in the accompanying photos, it appears to be virtually the equal of a Ciener suppressor or AWC's recently discontinued classic, the RST suppressor. The Spectre does not quite exhibit the utterly flawless cosmetics of an AWC Amphibian, nor is it manufactured to such close tolerances. But then the Spectre costs a lot less than the Amphibian.

Table 8.4. Sound signatures in decibels of Ciener pistol tests.

GUN	SUPPRESSOR	FEDERAL HV	REMINGTON HV	CCI MINI MAG HV	WINCHESTER HV	HANSEN SV	WINCHESTER T22 SV	CCI SV	RWS SS	TEMP., °F°(C)
Ruger MkII	None	154	—	—	—	152	153	—	151	51(11)
Ruger MkII (KMK-10)	Ciener KMK10	115	—	—	—	112	114	—	112	51(11)
Ruger MkII	None	—	155	156	155	153	153 1	53 1	52	45(7)
Ruger MkII (KMK-10)	Ciener KMK10	—	116	114	116	115	115	116	113[a]	45(7)
Ruger MkII	None	155	—	155	—	154	—	155	—	80(27)
Ruger MkII (512)	Ciener 512	135	—	135	—	135	—	134	—	80(27)

Table 8.5. Net sound reductions of Ciener pistol tests, expressed as decibels.

GUN	SUPPRESSOR	FEDERAL HV	REMINGTON HV	CCI MINI MAG HV	WINCHESTER HV	HANSEN SV	WINCHESTER T22 SV	CCI SV	RWS SS	TEMP., °F°(C)
Ruger MkII (KMK-10)	Ciener KMK10	39	—	—	—	40	39	—	39	51(11)
Ruger MkII (KMK-10)	Ciener KMK10	—	39	42	39	39	38	37	39[a]	45(7)
Ruger MkII (512)	Ciener 512	—	—	—	20	—	19	21	—	80(27)

Table 8.6. Muzzle velocities of suppressed and unsuppressed pistols used in Ciener pistol tests, expressed in fps (and mps).

GUN	SUPPRESSOR	FEDERAL HV	REMINGTON HV	CCI MINI MAG HV	WINCHESTER HV	HANSEN SV	WINCHESTER T22 SV	CCI SV	RWS SS	TEMP., °F°(C)	SPEED OF SOUND fps (mps)
Ruger MkII	None	1,062(324)	—	—	—	99(302)	1,034(315)	—	807(246)	51(11)	1,108(338)
Ruger MkII (KMK-10)	Ciener KMK10	882(269)	—	—	—	876(267)	885(270)	—	632(193)	51(11)	1,108(338)
Ruger MkII	None	—	1,090(332)	1,055(322)	1,033(315)	974(297)	1,029(314)	919(280)	775(236)	45(7)	1,101(336)
Ruger MkII (KMK-10)	Ciener KMK10	—	909(277)	872(266)	861(262)	820(250)	878(268)	749(228)	592(180)[a]	45(7)	1,101(336)
Ruger MkII	None	1,035(315)	—	1,053(321)	—	973(297)	—	941(287)	—	80(27)	1,139(347)
Ruger MkII (512)	Ciener 512	894(272)	—	912(278)	—	916(279)	—	866(264)	—	80(27)	1,139(347)

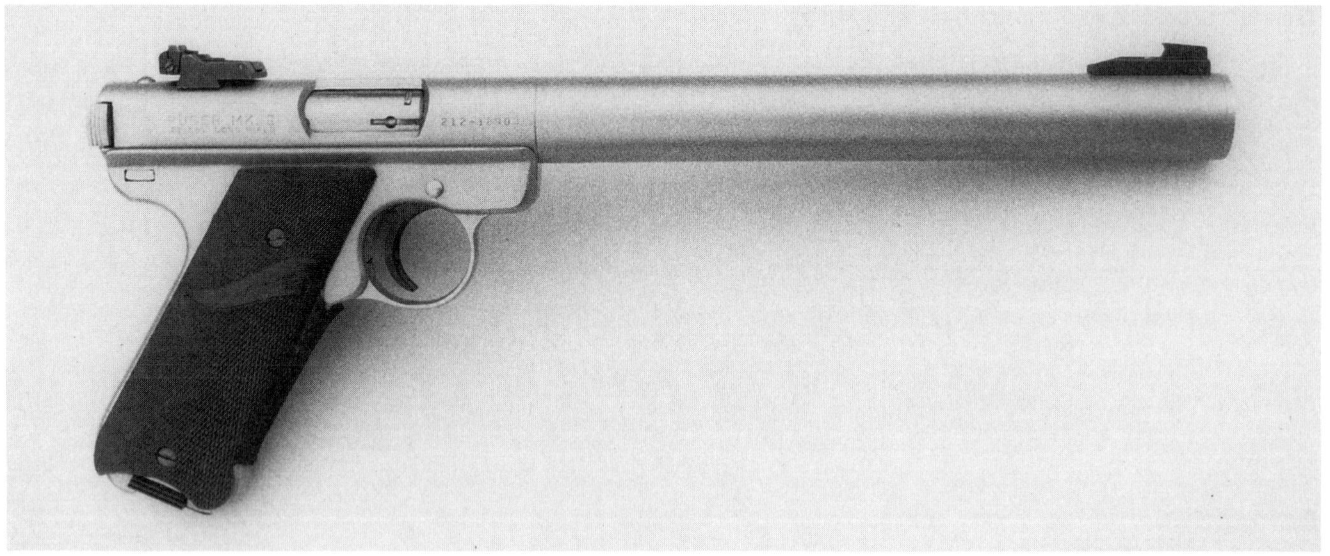

The Precision Arms Spectre has a lower sound signature than such classic designs as the venerable old AWC RST and the newer AWC Amphibian I.

The Spectre is constructed entirely out of 300 series stainless steel and features a barrel length of 5.5 inches (14.0 cm). A key feature of the design is that it employs relatively few ports installed unusually close to the chamber to provide both quieter performance and improved accuracy. It also uses relatively few baffles (four) of very sophisticated design. The Spectre's substantial length and weight lend the gun a very businesslike ambiance, although the weight tends to fatigue youngsters and shooters of small stature.

The overall length of the Precision Arms Spectre is 13.5 inches (34.2 cm), just 1 millimeter shorter than AWC's Amphibian I. That's a lot longer than the RST Ruger, which measures 11.4 inches (28.9 cm). The shorter pistol is much more comfortable in a shoulder holster than the longer pistols, especially in close quarters like an airplane cockpit or automobile.

The Precision Arms Ruger is much heavier than the other pistols, tipping the scales at 50.3 ounces (1.426 kg) unloaded. This compares to 41.5 ounces (1.176 kg) for the AWC RST with target thumb-rest walnut grips and 42.0 ounces (1.192 kg) for the AWC Amphibian I. The extra weight of the Precision Arms pistol actually improves the steadiness of my two-hand hold over the lighter long pistol, the Amphibian. I did, however, experience more fatigue after carrying the heavier pistol in a holster all day.

A more important aspect of a suppressed pistol is its sound signature. Just how quiet is it? To find out, I measured sound signatures of suppressed and unsuppressed pistols using Federal Hi-Power high-velocity, Hansen standard-velocity target, and RWS subsonic LR ammunition.

The mean sound signatures from the tests are shown in Table 8.7. The net sound reductions are shown in Table 8.8. The Precision Arms Spectre provided much better sound suppression than the RST and even beat the Amphibian I in this series of tests. The Spectre represents a quantum jump in improved sound suppression over such 1970s technology as the AWC RST and Ciener Model 512.

The Spectre's astonishing performance with subsonic ammunition is rather academic. Even though no suppressed pistol that I've ever tested has produced a 46 dB reduction with any ammunition, the Spectre would not cycle with subsonic ammunition. Therefore, one would forgo the use of subsonic fodder in the Spectre except for the very rare occasion when a single well-placed shot must be placed with utmost discretion.

As Table 8.9 shows, the Precision Arms Spectre kept all loads subsonic, dropping velocity by

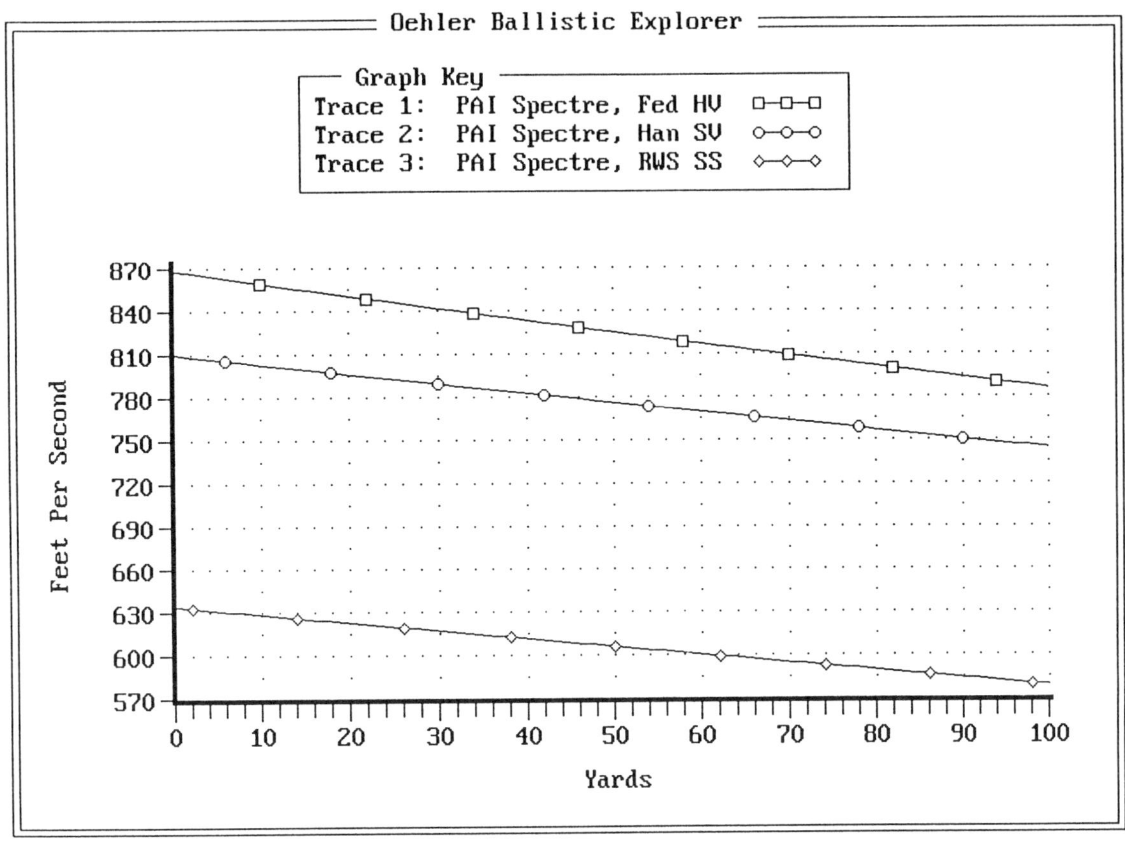

Figure 8.8. Bullet velocities produced by Precision Arms Spectre suppressed Ruger pistol.

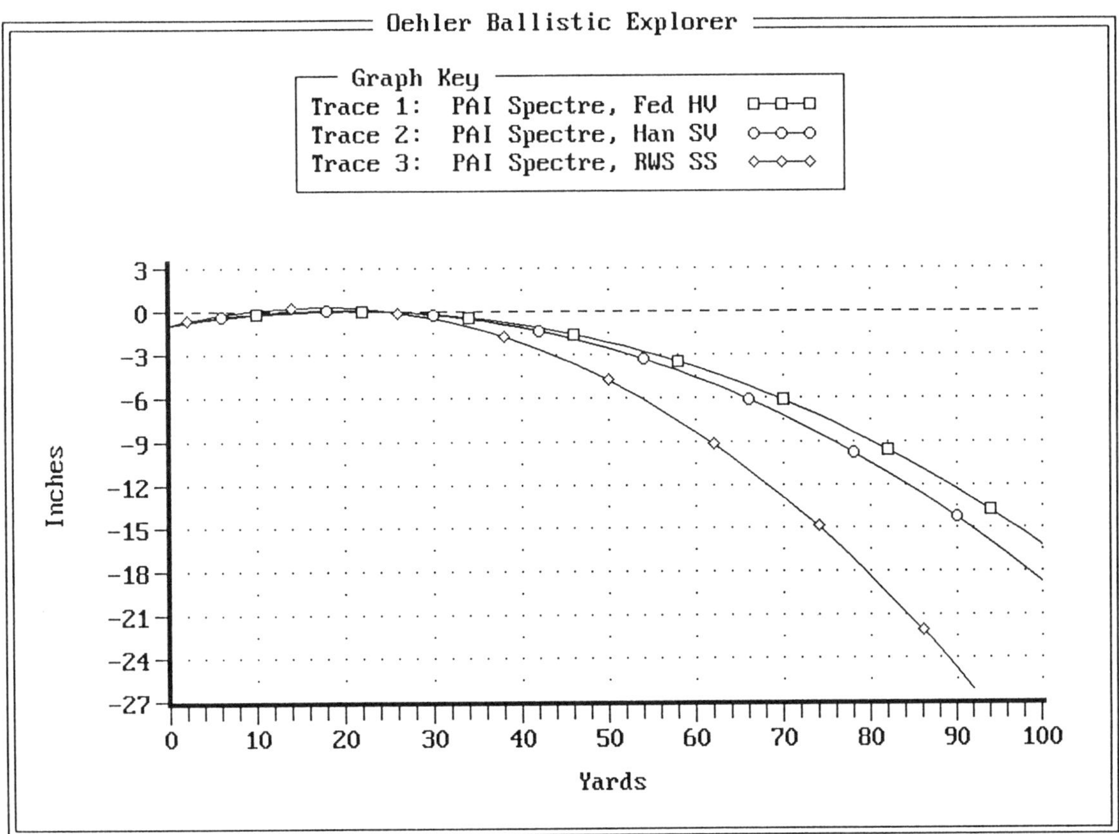

Figure 8.9. Bullet trajectories produced by Precision Arms Spectre suppressed Ruger pistol.

18 percent with high-velocity ammunition, 17 percent with standard-velocity ammo, and 25 percent with subsonic fodder. The AWC RST produced significantly higher bullet velocities (see Table 8.3), while the AWC Amphibian produced similar velocities to the Spectre.

Figures 8.8 and 8.9 compare the velocities and trajectories of the Precision Arms Spectre for each of the rounds being tested. Even though all three cartridges shoot close to the same point of aim at close range, bullet paths do diverge significantly, as one would expect. The bottom line is that the Spectre is remarkably quiet, but at the expense of velocity. The velocity issue is probably irrelevant for many sport shooters unless they use the pistol for hunting or animal control, or they otherwise like to shoot at extended ranges where the flatter trajectory afforded by higher velocities increases hit probability on reactive targets and improves shot placement on paper targets.

Table 8.7 Sound signatures in decibels of Spectre and Stealth tests.

GUN	SUPPRESSOR	FEDERAL HV	REMINGTON HV	HANSEN SV	RWS SS	WINCHESTER SS	TEMP., °F (°C)
Ruger MkII	None	156	—	154	154	—	82(28)
Ruger MkII	PA Spectre	117	—	116	108[a]	—	82(28)
Ruger MkII	None	156	—	154	153	—	74(23)
Ruger MkII	AWC Amphibian I	123	—	119	114[a]	—	74(23)
Ram-Line Exactor	None	156	155	154	153	153	88(31)
Ram-Line Exactor	PA Stealth	114	114	111	114	113	88(31)

[a] would not cycle

Table 8.8. Net sound reductions of Spectre and Stealth tests, expressed as decibels.

GUN	SUPPRESSOR	FEDERAL HV	REMINGTON HV	HANSEN SV	RWS SS	WINCHESTER SS	TEMP., °F (°C)
Ruger MkII	PA Spectre	39	—	38	46[a]	—	82(28)
Ruger MkII	AWC Amphibian I	33	—	35	39[a]	—	74(23)
Ram-Line Exactor	PA Stealth	42	41	43	39	40	88(31)

[a] would not cycle

Table 8.9. Muzzle velocities of suppressed and unsuppressed pistols used in Spectre and Stealth tests, expressed in feet per second (and meters per second).

GUN	SUPPRESSOR	FEDERAL HV	REMINGTON HV	HANSEN SV	RWS SS	WINCHESTER SS	TEMP., °F (°C)	SPEED OF SOUND fps (mps)
Ruger MkII	None	1,054(321)	—	974(297)	847(258)	—	82(28)	1,129(344)
Ruger MkII	PA Spectre	868(265)	—	810(247)	634(193)[a]	—	82(28)	1,129(344)
Ruger MkII	None	1,090(332)	—	1,043(318)	858(262)	—	74(23)	1,133(345)
Ruger MkII	AWC Amphibian I	873(266)	—	872(266)	680(207)[a]	—	74(23)	1,133(345)
Ram-Line Exactor	None	1,060(323)	1,085(331)	988(301)	858(262)	983(300)	88(31)	1,147(350)
Ram-Line Exactor	PA Stealth	929(283)	960(293)	865(264)	734(224)	849(259)	88(31)	1,147(350)

[a] would not cycle

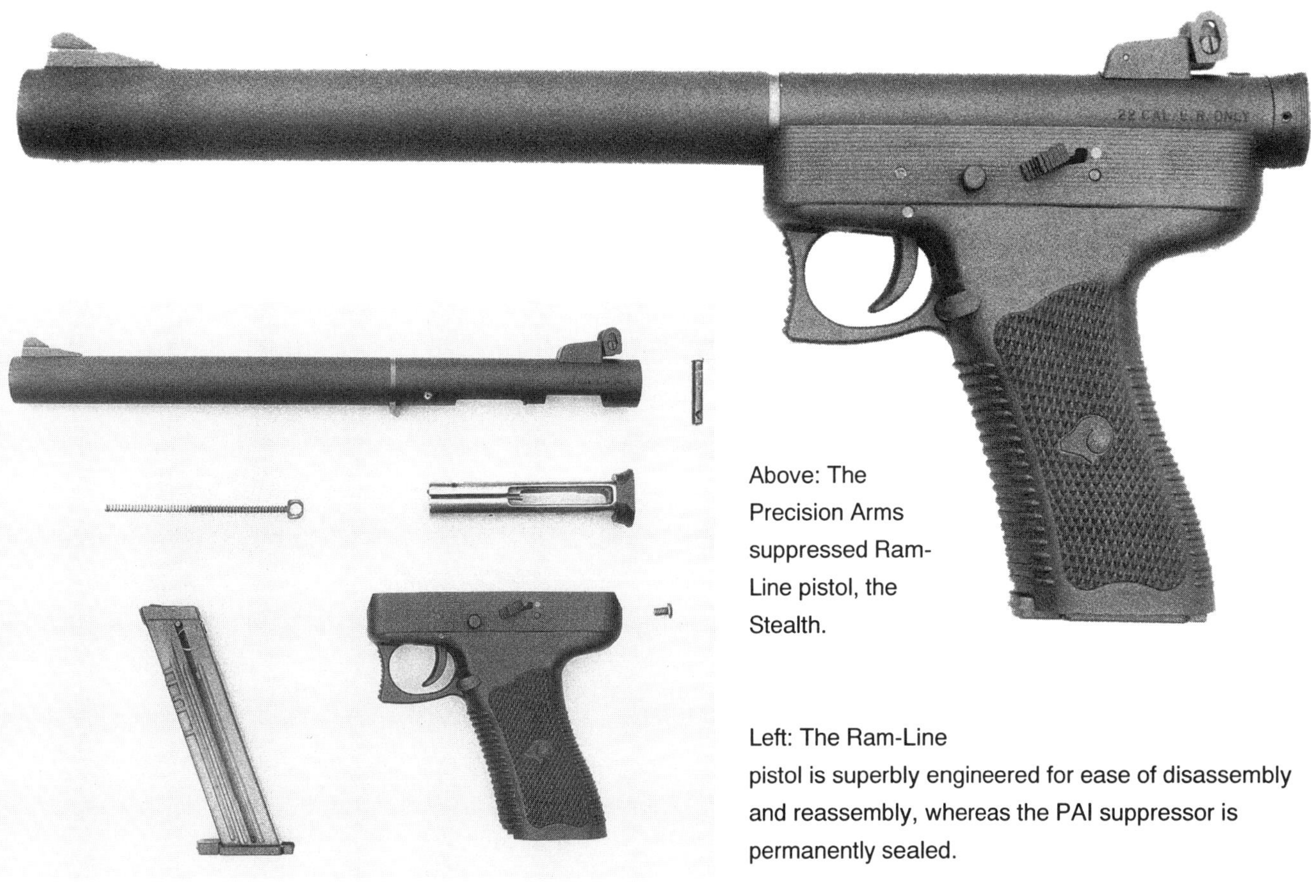

Above: The Precision Arms suppressed Ram-Line pistol, the Stealth.

Left: The Ram-Line pistol is superbly engineered for ease of disassembly and reassembly, whereas the PAI suppressor is permanently sealed.

The Precision Arms Stealth features Ram-Line's standard rear sight and Conventional target grip. Early production featured a front sight with orange insert, which has now been replaced with an all-black Ruger-like front sight.

The Spectre was an impressive first effort from Precision Arms. But the pistol is long and heavy, and it drops bullet velocity more than some shooters like. John Leasure turned to a completely different parent firearm for his second foray into the realm of integrally suppressed .22 rimfire pistols: the Ram-Line Exactor. He named the suppressed Ram-Line the Stealth, and the stealthy new system was unlike anything else in the marketplace.

PRECISION ARMS RAM-LINE

Ram-Line's "plastic" pistol turned a lot of heads when it was introduced to the shooting community in 1990. The Precision Arms suppressed Ram-Line pistol, called the Stealth, turned my head when I first shot one.

The basic concept of a largely plastic pistol is not new. The High Standard Duramatic probably began the trend, and the Heckler and Koch VP70Z accelerated the process. Interdynamic (now called Intratec) produced the KG99. Grendel developed the P-10 and P-30. And Glock pistols have taken the law enforcement market by storm. The technology is now mature. The designs are durable and sophisticated. The so-called plastic pistol is here to stay.

Gaines Chesnut designed the Ram-Line pistol with many polymer components, including the grip frame, bolt actuator (the rear end of the bolt), trigger, safety and bolt-latch levers, magazine catch, and magazine. A thin steel barrel liner is encased in a molded polymer barrel with integral front sight and ventilated rib. The receiver is made from an aluminum alloy. The bolt, springs, and other internal parts are made from steel. The 15-round magazine uses a steel constant-force ribbon-coil spring, which exerts the same amount of pressure against the magazine follower, whether there is one round left in the magazine or 15. This makes loading the magazine quite easy. More importantly, this spring enhances the reliability of feeding a round from the magazine. A 20-round magazine is also available.

Chestnut's goal was to produce a lightweight pistol at an affordable price. His 21 ounce (596 g) pistol succeeds on both counts.

Originally called the Syn-Tec, the name was soon changed to the Exactor. Ram-Line experienced some market resistance to its innovative, oddly shaped "Dynamic" grip, so a variant using a "Conventional" grip was introduced as well. It is this latter variant with 5.5 inch (14.0 cm) barrel that is being evaluated here.

Recently, Magnum Research purchased the entire production run of Ram-Line pistols, which are now made with a new molded polymer barrel that mimics the contours of the Desert Eagle .44 Magnum. The new .22 Ram-Line variant is called the Mountain Eagle. Subsequent production of suppressed Ram-Lines by Silent Options used the Mountain Eagle variant.

John Leasure designed the suppressor for the Exactor with a black-anodized 7075 T-6 aluminum tube, measuring 8.0 inches (20.3 cm) long and 1.0 inch (2.5 cm) in diameter. Overall length of the

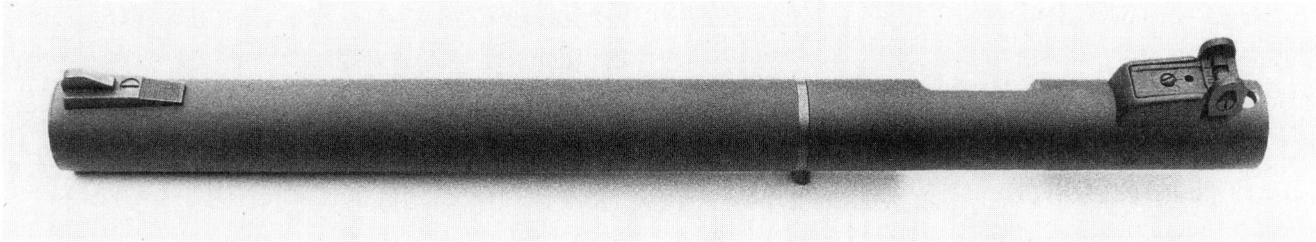

The suppressor's three patented aluminum "double diversion" baffles have serrated shapes machined into their front and rear faces, which disrupt the gas flow much more than conventionally shaped baffles.

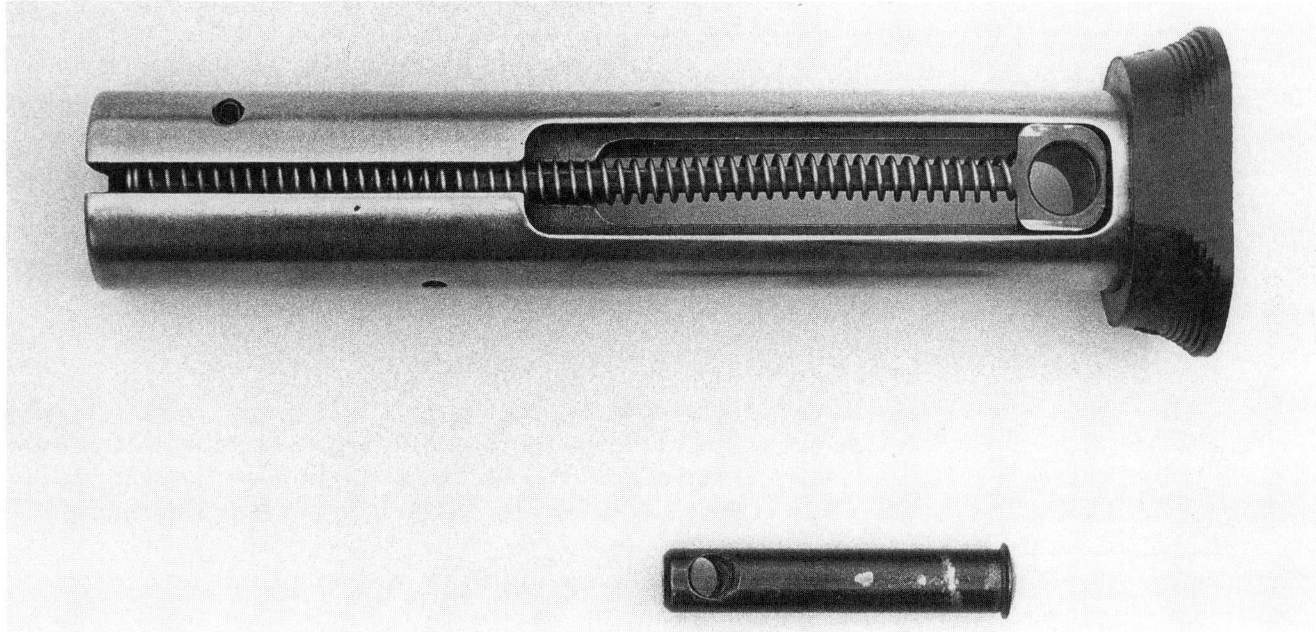

The plastic bolt actuator (the rear end of the bolt) seems to cushion the bolt when it closes, greatly reducing the pistol's action noise. The bolt stop pin is threaded to accept the pistol's takedown screw.

The grip assembly is made from a polymer; the internal parts and springs are made from steel.

Stealth pistol is 13.7 inches (34.8 cm). The suppressor incorporates three patented aluminum baffles with a turned-down barrel. The "double diversion" baffles have serrated shapes machined into the front and rear faces that disrupt the gas flow much more than conventionally shaped baffles. The spacers are threaded to increase their surface area for disrupting and cooling the combustion gases. The plastic is machined off down to the barrel liner, and EDM technology is used to port the barrel.

The design of the four ports and the process used to make the ports are critical, for the first suppressed Ram-Line I ever shot died after about 200 rounds. The barrel liner cracked on a line connecting the ports, which had been drilled too close together. Leasure went to a new design and porting process in an effort to eliminate this problem.

The Stealth pistol provides good usable accuracy. Shooting rapid-fire offhand, the Stealth consistently hit bowling pins at 30 yards. While the suppressed pistol balances well, experienced shooters who are used to relatively heavy guns will not like the Stealth's light weight (26.1 ounces, 739 grams). Experienced shooters would also prefer a solid black front sight instead of the bright orange insert used on early Stealths like mine. Leasure listened. Subsequent production sported an all-black Ruger-type sight.

Actually shooting the Stealth seems to make a convert out of most folks. This is a fun gun to shoot. And it is remarkably quiet. Not only is the suppressor itself quiet, but the Ram-Line's action noise is much less than a Ruger's. The plastic rear end of the bolt seems to dampen the sound of the bolt closing. Furthermore, the Ram-Line's aluminum receiver doesn't seem to ring like the Ruger's steel receiver.

Operation

The Ram-Line pistol features a safety on the upper left portion of the grip assembly that is easy to reach. When engaged, a conventional disconnect bar blocks the sear, disconnects the sear, blocks the trigger, and blocks the hammer. If the safety is engaged when the hammer is in the fired position, it will also lock the bolt in the closed position.

To engage the safety, push the safety lever rearward until the lever snaps upward in the L-shaped slot. The lever now covers a red dot on the grip assembly. Disengaging the safety requires two different motions. First, push the safety lever down, then push it forward, exposing the red dot. This movement is easily mastered and was designed to prevent accidental disengagement of the safety.

A fairly small bolt-latch button is located on the left side of the grip assembly just forward of the safety. The bolt latch holds the bolt open after the last shot. After inserting a loaded magazine, push the bolt-latch button downward to release the bolt and chamber a round. Alternatively, the first round can be chambered by grasping the plastic grip at the rear of the bolt, pulling the bolt slightly to the rear, and smartly releasing the bolt. As with any pistol, it is important to allow the full force of the recoil spring to drive the bolt forward. Advise beginning shooters not to continue their grasp on the bolt as it moves forward.

Another interesting feature of the Ram-Line pistol is that the bolt actuates the disconnect bar as the bolt moves backward from the face of the breach block, so the gun cannot fire out of battery.

One of the things I dislike about the Ram-Line pistol is that dry firing creates unacceptable wear on the chamber, firing pin, hammer, and sear. This reduces the pistol's value for training new shooters.

Maintenance

The Ram-Line pistol is superbly engineered for ease of disassembly and reassembly. The pistol does exhibit a few eccentricities, however, when it comes to the use of solvents and lubricants. The Ram-Line manual provides some help, but it also presents some contradictory information and numerous small errors. The manual does not measure up to the pistol. But the Ram-Line staff do measure up in terms of remarkably friendly and helpful support.

Getting back to maintenance eccentricities, general-purpose oils (like WD-40), silicone-based lubricants (such as Brownells Liquid Silicone), and Teflon-based lubricants (like Tri-Flow) tend to "gum up" the action quite quickly. While the manual does warn against this problem, it goes on to recommend Break Free, which is a Teflon-based lubricant. Sure enough, the pistol gums up after shooting as few as 30 rounds when using Break Free as a lubricant. Stick to a light, old-fashioned gun oil such as Outers Gun Oil.

Another curiosity is that Ram-Line recommends the use of Hoppes No. 9 solvent for cleaning the gun. Yet the pistol has an aluminum receiver, and Hoppes No. 9 eats aluminum. A solvent such as Kroil or Varsol will not attack the aluminum. Gun Scrubber (a halogenated solvent in an aerosol can) is the handiest way to clean the bolt, barreled receiver, and grip assembly.

The final Ram-Line eccentricity is that traditional gun-cleaning solvents should not be used with the polycarbonate magazine, especially products like Crud-Cutter and Gunk-Out that contain 1,1,1 Trichloroethane. Keep Gun Scrubber away from the magazine, too. Isopropyl alcohol is the solvent of choice for cleaning Ram-Line magazines.

These eccentricities by no means cause any aggravation once the operator knows about them. And one quickly forgets about trivial eccentricities in light of the pistol's remarkable ease of disassembly and reassembly.

Begin disassembly by removing the magazine, clearing the pistol, and placing the bolt in its closed position. Use the 1/8 inch hex wrench provided with the gun to remove the takedown screw located at the top rear of the grip assembly. Lift up on the rear of the barreled receiver to pivot this assembly from the grip assembly. Push up the bolt stop pin located behind the rear sight and remove the pin. Remove the bolt from the receiver and lift the recoil spring and its guide rod from the bolt. Pull the guide rod from the recoil spring. No further disassembly is required.

It is not necessary to remove the firing pin or extractor to clean the bolt. Wearing rubber gloves in a well-ventilated area to protect against carcinogenic chemicals, spray the bolt with short blasts of Gun Scrubber. Pay particular attention to cleaning the bolt face and the head space (the place on the front of the bolt where the rear of the cartridge is held). Use a bronze toothbrush or paper towel as necessary to remove all residue. When cleaning the receiver, pay particular attention to the corners of the receiver, the ejector, and the breech face. With the muzzle down, spray the chamber until clean, rotating the barreled receiver to facilitate cleaning of all internal suppressor surfaces as well. Clean the bore from the rear with a bronze bore brush. Clean the grip assembly with Gun Scrubber as necessary.

Use a light gun oil on all moving parts.

Repeat this procedure as necessary or every 500 rounds, whichever comes first. Every 2,000 rounds, soak the disassembled receiver and suppressor muzzle down for two or more days in Varsol or Kroil to ensure the removal of all powder residue in the suppressor. Allow to drain thoroughly. Blow out with compressed air from the rear.

Begin reassembly by inserting the guide rod into the recoil spring. Insert the spring and guide into the slot in the top of the bolt. The yoke at the rear of the guide rod must be flush with the top of the slot. Insert the bolt into the receiver. Now insert the bolt stop pin through the receiver from the top. Make sure that the threaded hole in the pin lines up with the hole at the rear of the grip assembly.

Insert the recoil lug (located between the front of the receiver and the suppressor tube) into the slot at the front of the grip assembly. Pivot the receiver down until the threaded hole in the bolt stop pin aligns with the hole in the grip assembly. Replace the takedown screw, taking care not to overtighten the screw. This completes reassembly.

Performance

The Stealth's accuracy has been discussed, but its performance in terms of sound suppression still needs to be examined. It would also be useful to know whether the Stealth's suppressor achieves its performance without excessively lowering bullet velocity.

Five kinds of Long Rifle ammunition were tested: Federal high-velocity, Remington high-

Ram-Line pistol suppressed by Sound Technology.

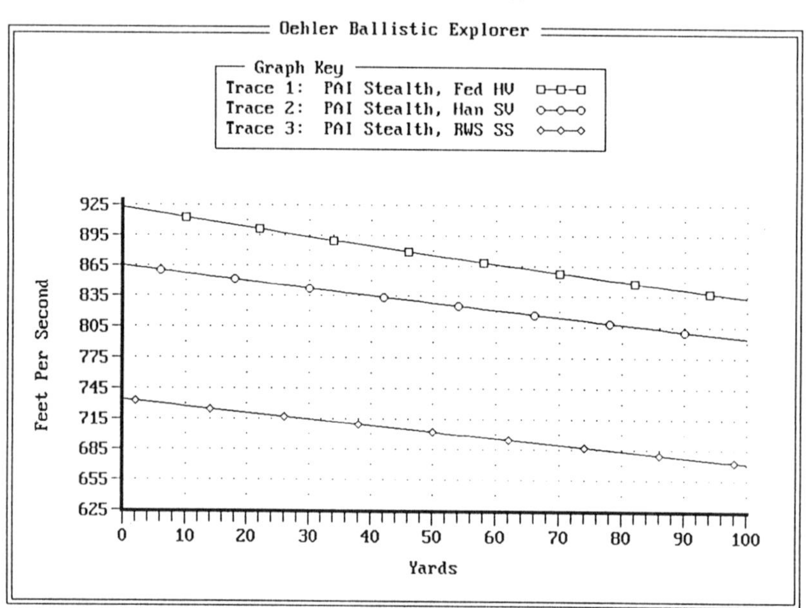

Figure 8.10. Bullet velocities produced by Precision Arms Stealth suppressed Ram-Line pistol.

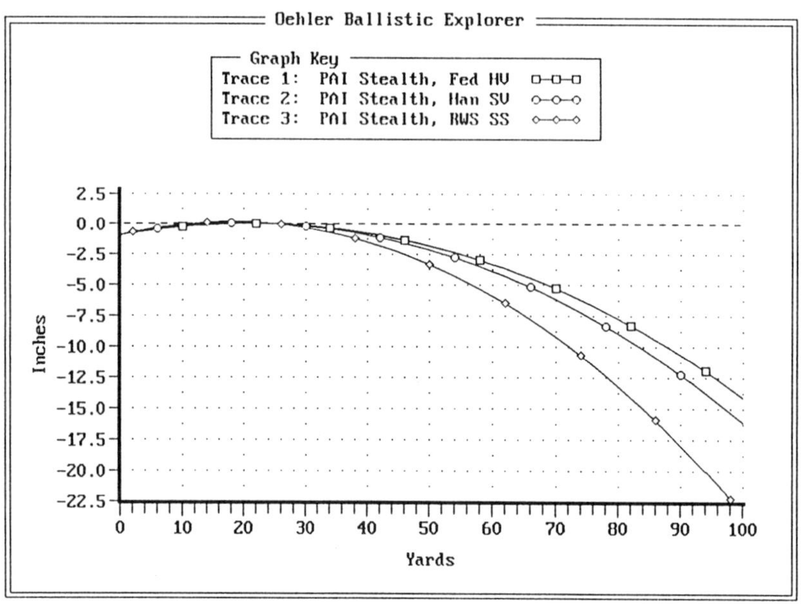

Figure 8.11. Bullet trajectories produced by Precision Arms Stealth suppressed Ram-Line pistol.

velocity, Hansen standard-velocity target, RWS subsonic, and Winchester subsonic. As Table 8.7 shows, the Precision Arms Stealth pistol was substantially quieter than the AWC Amphibian using high-velocity and standard-velocity ammunition. The sound signatures were the same with RWS subsonic ammunition. Table 8.8 shows that net sound reductions demonstrate the same pattern. To place these numbers in better perspective, chambering a round in a Ruger MK II generates 108 decibels. Using Hansen standard-velocity ammunition, the suppressed Ram-Line produced a sound signature that was only 3 dB louder that a Ruger's action noise.

Table 8.9 shows that all rounds fired through all four suppressed and unsuppressed pistols remained subsonic, including the high-velocity ammunition. Whereas the Amphibian lowers velocities by 16 to 21 percent, the Stealth only lowers velocities by 12 to 14 percent. As Figures 8.10 and 8.11 show, the Stealth shoots flatter and produces more velocity downrange. Furthermore, the suppressed Ram-Line cycles reliably with subsonic ammunition. With the exception of the highly modified Gemtech Operator, the SCRC 22L, and the massive Ciener KMK10, suppressed Ruger pistols generally do not.

Unfortunately, the barrel liner of the Stealth has a significantly shorter lifespan than the turned-down barrel of a suppressed Ruger. The Stealth does have a number of virtues, including light weight, a remarkably quiet report, and ease of cleaning. But the trade-off seems to be a typical lifespan of considerably less than 10,000 rounds.

Even though the Stealth does not provide the astonishing accuracy of my suppressed Ruger MK II, which was designed by Dr. Phil Dater and built by Tim Bixler, the suppressed Ram-Line provides plenty of usable accuracy for most applications. The Stealth does not take as big a bite out of projectile velocity as does another fine pistol, the AWC Amphibian. Finally, the Precision Arms Stealth is the quietest pistol I've ever tested (although the new Amphibian II is almost as quiet). Until its barrel liner finally split, the Stealth performed admirably for bowling-pin matches, backpacking, and sharing the fun with new shooters. While it lasted, it was the pistol I picked up most often when I wanted to have some fun myself.

Finally, I should point out the assessment of the Ram-Line Exactor by Mark White at Sound Technology, who has also suppressed a number of Ram-Lines himself at the insistence of customers who absolutely had to have a suppressed Exactor. "The Ram-Line pistol is an interesting concept," White said, "but its execution makes it a piece of junk. It doesn't hold up. Too bad Glock doesn't make a similar pistol."

Even though I enjoyed shooting and sharing the Stealth pistol, White's perspective combined with my own experience gives the following bottom line. Unless one has deep enough pockets to afford replacing the Stealth pistol periodically or unless the pistol will be fired infrequently, a suppressed system based on the Ruger Mark II pistol will prove to be a better investment. If maximum sound suppression *in a durable system* is the main performance criterion for selecting a suppressed pistol, then one would be well served by the currently produced variant of the AWC Amphibian.

AWC AMPHIBIANS

Special operations frequently involve water. The mission might involve egress from a submarine to sneak aboard a surface ship, a helicast into the ocean followed by a swim to a hostile shore, or wading upstream deep into enemy-held territory. Operators on such diverse missions are particularly vulnerable as they emerge from the water, when the ability to immediately and quietly remove a sentry or scout could mean the difference between success and failure. Weapon barrels and suppressors must be drained before they are fired. That takes time. And time may be a very precious commodity. The Amphibian pistol from AWC Systems Technology is remarkable in that it

Based on a stainless-steel Ruger Mark II pistol, both the Amphibian I (top) and the Amphibian II are remarkable in that they can be carried underwater and then fired without completely draining the system. In fact, the presence of some water in the suppressor merely makes the weapon quieter.

can be carried underwater and then fired without completely draining the system. In fact, the presence of some water in the system merely makes the weapon quieter.

The Amphibian II pistol now being marketed by AWC Systems Technology is actually the fourth generation of this amphibious pistol. The Amphibian is based on a stainless steel Ruger Mark II pistol. The barrel is shortened to less than 2 inches, and four ports are added near the chamber. Placing the ports close to the chamber has several advantages: 1) fewer ports are required, 2) the ports can be much smaller, and 3) the combustion gases are very hot and have a very high velocity when they reach the ports. Therefore, the hot gases seem to blast the ports clean with every shot. Fouling can fill more conventionally designed porting in a few thousand rounds if the design and construction are particularly uninspired.

The short (2.5 inch, 6.4 cm) barrel and special porting (1/8 inch or 3 mm porting located about 1-1/8 inches or 2.9 cm from the bolt face) that are necessary for amphibious operation reduce the back pressure available to cycle the action. Therefore, the Amphibian may require a break-in period of approximately 1,000 rounds to attain maximum reliability with high-velocity and standard-velocity ammunition, which produce subsonic projectile velocities in the Amphibian.

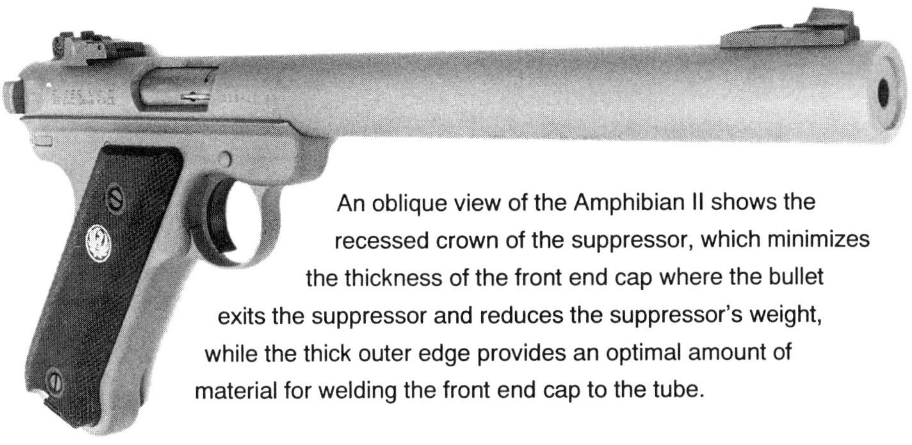

An oblique view of the Amphibian II shows the recessed crown of the suppressor, which minimizes the thickness of the front end cap where the bullet exits the suppressor and reduces the suppressor's weight, while the thick outer edge provides an optimal amount of material for welding the front end cap to the tube.

While subsonic ammunition will not function reliably in this system, this fact is by no means an indictment of the design. The Amphibian was specifically tailored to function optimally with high-velocity, military-issue ammunition. AWC never intended that the pistol be employed with standard-velocity or subsonic rounds. Even with high-velocity ammunition, however, it should be pointed out that the reduced back pressure produced by the Amphibian requires more careful attention to cleaning and lubrication than an unmodified pistol or a competing suppressed pistol like the Gemtech Operator. That's a small price to pay for the system's amphibious capability.

The Amphibian's suppressor is built entirely from 300 series stainless steels. The first variant of the Amphibian I employed ingenious baffles made from square tubing oriented perpendicular to the bore. The baffles vented combustion gas into fluted cone spacers, which acted like coaxial expansion chambers. The second variant of the Amphibian used 11 fluted cones with a slanted rear bore face. The third variant simply used the fluted cone spacers as baffles. The shorter Amphibian II uses an entirely different baffle similar to the CQB 9mm Mark II baffle described elsewhere in this volume. In all variants, the internal components are precision welded together before inserting in the suppressor tube, and then the tube is permanently sealed. This is a logical approach considering the complex internal design.

The Amphibian I (serial number 89-58) tested in this study is a first-variant design, which uses the same baffle-type AWC Systems Technology developed for its .30 caliber M89 Navy contract suppressors that were built for the McMillan M89 sniper rifle. This Amphibian I has an overall length of 13.5 inches (34.3 cm) and a weight of 42.1 ounces (1,195 grams). The suppressor tube is 8.0 inches (20.4 cm) long and 1.0 inch (2.5 cm) in diameter. The Amphibian II (serial number D-521) has an overall length of 12.75 inches (32.4 cm) and a weight of 43.8 ounces (1,243 grams). The suppressor tube is 7.6 inches (19.2 cm) long and 1.0 inch (2.5 cm) in diameter.

The Amphibians were compared to an unsuppressed Ruger pistol with 5.5 inch (14.0 cm) barrel using Federal Hi-Power high-velocity and Hansen standard-velocity target ammunition.

Performance

Sound signatures appear in Table 8.10, and net sound reductions are shown in Table 8.11. Velocity data appear in Table 8.12. The unsuppressed Ruger pistol produced a mean (average) sound signature (peak SPL) of 153 dB with high-velocity and 152 dB with standard-velocity ammunition.

The Amphibian I produced signatures of 117 and 115 dB with high-velocity and standard-velocity fodder, for net sound reductions of 36 and 37 dB, respectively. The Amphibian II produced signatures of 115 and 113 decibels with high-velocity and standard-velocity ammo, for net sound reductions of 38 and 39 dB, respectively.

Table 8.10 Sound signatures in decibels of Amphibian tests.

GUN	SUPPRESSOR	FEDERAL HV	HANSEN SV	TEMPERATURE, °F (°C)
Ruger MkII	None	153	152	43(6)
Ruger MkII	AWC Amphibian I	117	115	43(6)
Ruger MkII	AWC Amphibian II	115	113	43(6)

Table 8.11. Net sound reductions of Amphibian tests, expressed as decibels.

GUN	SUPPRESSOR	FEDERAL HV	HANSEN SV	TEMPERATURE, °F (°C)
Ruger MkII	AWC Amphibian I	36	37	43(6)
Ruger MkII	AWC Amphibian II	38	39	43(6)

Table 8.12. Muzzle velocities of suppressed and unsuppressed pistols used in Amphibian tests, expressed in feet per second (and meters per second).

GUN	SUPPRESSOR	FEDERAL HV	HANSEN SV	TEMPERATURE, °F (°C)	SPEED OF SOUND fps (mps)
Ruger MkII	None	1,048(319)	958(292)	43(6)	1,099(335)
Ruger MkII	AWC Amphibian I	834(254)	794(242)	43(6)	1,099(335)
Ruger MkII	AWC Amphibian II	835(255)	760(232)	43(6)	1,099(335)

Since the Amphibian II is shorter and has fewer baffles than its predecessor, I mistakenly assumed that it would not perform quite as well as the older Amphibian. I was wrong. The shorter Amphibian is not only friendlier in terms of holster carry and sight alignment with my aging eyes, it is also quieter. Clearly, the shorter design is working the combustion gases harder within the suppressor.

The unsuppressed Ruger pistol produced muzzle velocities of 1,048 fps and 958 fps with high-velocity and standard-velocity ammunition. The Amphibian I produced velocities of 834 fps and 794 fps, while the Amphibian II produced velocities of 835 fps and 760 fps with high-velocity and standard-velocity ammunition, respectively. Standard-velocity ammunition produced 34 fps (10 mps) less velocity in the Amphibian II. Apparently, the shorter suppressor tube in the Amphibian II provides less "freebore boost" to the projectile when using standard-velocity rounds. These data suggest that barrel length and porting are the same in the two Amphibians tested in this study.

How do these data compare to other suppressed pistols using Federal high-velocity ammunition? A Ciener Model 512 suppressed Ruger produced a net sound reduction of 20 dB and a muzzle velocity of 894 fps (272 mps) at 91 °F (33 °C). An AWC RST suppressed Ruger produced a sound reduction of 24 dB and a muzzle velocity of 882 fps (269 mps) at 72 °F (22 °C), while a first-generation Amphibian I produced a sound reduction of 33 dB and a muzzle velocity of 841 fps (256 mps) at the same temperature. A first-generation Gemtech Operator suppressed Ruger produced an average sound reduction of 26 dB and a muzzle velocity of 958 fps (292 mps) at 47 °F (8 °C). The first-generation Operator did produce a substantial first-round pop, but this problem has been corrected in the second-generation Operator. A Sound Technology suppressed Ruger produced a sound reduction of 27 dB and a muzzle velocity of 953 fps (290 mps) at 84 °F (29 °C). And an original HD-MS, which is still in the U.S. government inventory, produced a net sound reduction of 24 dB and a muzzle velocity of 904 fps (276 mps) at 72 °F. The speed of sound was 1,151 fps (351 mps) at 91 °F, 1,143 fps (348 mps) at 84 °F, 1,131 fps (345 mps) at 72 °F, and 1,104 fps (336 mps) at 47 °F. When you remember that the decibel scale is logarithmic rather than linear, it becomes apparent that the Amphibian II leaves all of the aforementioned suppressed pistols in the dust in terms of sound suppression.

Conclusions

In a sense, there is no real competition to the Amphibian, in that there is no other suppressed .22 caliber pistol expressly designed for underwater carry and amphibious operations. Furthermore, when shot in a completely dry condition, as in this study, Amphibian produced top-notch sound reduction.

The Precision Arms Spectre provides similar performance to the Amphibian II, producing 1 dB better net sound reduction with high-velocity ammunition and 1 dB less performance with standard-velocity ammunition. The Spectre also produces similar projectile velocities. The Precision Arms Stealth is 4 dB quieter than the Amphibian II with high-velocity and standard-velocity ammunition, plus the Stealth is significantly lighter and produces higher velocities. But the Stealth's finite lifespan does not make it a serious competitor to the Amphibian.

The Ciener KMK10 also produces similar sound reduction to the Amphibian II, but its long tube and muzzle heaviness do not make it a mainstream contender either, in my opinion. The Precision Arms Spectre is much heavier than the Amphibian. So the Amphibian's stiffest competition in the modern marketplace comes from the Gemtech Operator-2, which will be evaluated in the second volume of *Silencer History and Performance.*

There is a cost to the Amphibian's amphibious capabilities and impressive sound reduction, however. There is no free lunch. The Amphibian's short barrel and very small ports generate less back pressure to cycle the action and produce less projectile velocity downrange. Time constraints precluded comparing the performance of the various silenced pistols used in this study in terms of bullet penetration in ballistic gelatin. But velocity and penetration may be nonissues, according to AWC Systems Technology President Lynn McWilliams.

McWilliams points out that "this velocity issue is fully covered in the last MENS [mission-essential needs statement] we received. I have talked to the Code 20 Navy guys on numerous occasions, and we are well within the acceptable velocity range on the Amphibian I and II.

"While some folks might be concerned about projectile velocity produced by the Amphibian," McWilliams continues, "it is important to recognize that the Amphibian I is a documented mankiller. No other silenced .22 rimfire pistol in the marketplace can make that claim. A brain shot will also kill [guard] dogs. The Utah State Wildlife Commission even kills buffaloes with [the Amphibian], and 2nd Force Recon has killed numerous living things with them. The Amphibian II is an even better weapon than the Amphibian I." (Author's note: as a former biologist with the Alaska Department of Fish & Game, I am not comfortable with using *any* rimfire weapon on an animal the size of a buffalo—ACP.)

The Amphibian has proved to be so quiet and so popular that AWC Systems Technology has discontinued its more conventionally designed MK2 Ultra silenced Ruger pistol. The Amphibian has undergone a steady stream of improvements culminating in the Amphibian II, which will probably prove to be the most successful pistol ever offered by AWC Systems Technology. The impressive Amphibian has emerged from its origins as a special-purpose weapon to compete with every other suppressed .22 caliber pistol in the marketplace. Technical innovation and manufacturing excellence continue to make AWC Systems Technology a heavyweight among the world's suppressor manufacturers.

While the discussion of .22 rimfire suppressors has focused on integral suppressors thus far, and integral suppressors constitute the lion's share of the U.S. market for .22 suppressors, muzzle cans have undergone an interesting evolution since the days of Hiram P. Maxim. Furthermore, the muzzle can offers some distinct advantages over the integral suppressor.

CHAPTER NINE

.22 RIMFIRE MUZZLE CANS

onventional wisdom holds that an integrally suppressed .22 rimfire rifle or pistol will be quieter than the same firearm fitted with a muzzle can. But the muzzle suppressor does have several advantages.

The most important benefit is that the barrel with a traditional muzzle can produces higher velocities than are produced by the ported barrel of an integrally suppressed barrel. Integral suppressors are frequently optimized to drop high-velocity ammunition to subsonic velocities in order to avoid a loud ballistic crack. The higher velocities produced by an unported barrel and muzzle suppressor translate into flatter trajectory (i.e., better shot placement) and more penetration (i.e., better terminal ballistics).

The weight of the muzzle can also tends to change barrel harmonics and vibration nodes, which may enhance accuracy if the mounting system is designed properly and the can is installed correctly. In the case of the Ruger 10/22, the resulting improvement can be considerable.

The muzzle can is also more cost-effective, since the same suppressor can be fitted to a wide variety of pistols and rifles. No gun need be dedicated to the suppressor, and one does not need several suppressors for several different guns. Individuals not only save the cost of additional suppressors, but people in the United States also save the $200 transfer tax on each additional suppressor. For example, a single muzzle suppressor can be used for target practice with a rifle and pistol in a convenient location, and then the suppressor can be removed for hunting small game (most states do not allow hunting with a suppressed gun). Accuracy (i.e., group size) will probably be unaffected or slightly improved when the suppressor is installed, but sights will need to be readjusted every time the suppressor is installed or removed.

Another benefit to a muzzle suppressor is that a rifle stock need not be routed out to accept an integral suppressor. The muzzle can is frequently more benign than an integral suppressor in terms of both cosmetic appearance of the stock itself and stock strength (especially with thin stocks like the Butler Creek stock for the Ruger 10/22).

The factory 10/22 stocks with barrel band do not accept the installation of an integral suppressor gracefully either. None of the three basic options is attractive. One can remove the barrel band and simply route out the stock, leaving the front of the forestock naked, but this looks terrible. One can cut the tip off and reshape it, as was done with the old AWC R10 system. But the result is decidedly chunky, and the entire stock should be refinished with this strategy. Finally, one can cut off the top of the barrel band, forming a "U," and epoxy the band in place. John Norrell uses this strategy, which is the most attractive option. But a good hit might knock off the band. Being able to use an unmodified stock does simplify matters.

The muzzle can is also easier to clean than an integral can for several reasons: 1) powder burns cleaner when the barrel is not ported near the chamber, so there is less powder residue to accumulate with a muzzle can; 2) the muzzle can is easier to clean by immersion in a suitable solvent; and 3) the muzzle can is less likely to trap water vapor (a natural by-product of powder combustion), so there is less corrosion.

A consideration for tactical, rather than sporting, applications is that a weapon with a detachable suppressor can be broken down into a smaller package, which could be quite useful for airborne or covert operations.

Finally, the use of a muzzle can permits the operator to select the best mix of performance characteristics for a particular job by selecting the best ammunition for a particular application. Subsonic ammunition, for example, will provide the quietest sound signature (and frequently the best accuracy) for target shooting or the elimination of pests. Standard-velocity ammunition may provide the maximum subsonic projectile velocity for hunting small game with a muzzle can, although this ammunition may give a ballistic crack depending on effective barrel length and environmental conditions (such as temperature, barometric pressure, and humidity). If used against such medium-sized animals as arctic hares, coyotes, and feral dogs, where a ballistic crack is not objectionable, then high-velocity solid-point ammunition (such as CCI's .22 LR Small Game Bullet, also known as the SGB) may be the optimal load. An integral suppressor would reduce the velocities, and therefore the performance, of each type of ammunition.

PARKER HALE

Under one name or another, the Parker Hale .22 rimfire silencer has been in continuous production longer than any other silencer in the world. Soon after the introduction of the Maxim Model 1910 silencer, the British firm A.G. Parker & Co. Ltd., Rifle Experts, Birmingham, began to market .22 caliber Maxim silencers. The extensive Parker catalog produced in 1913 listed the Maxim for £21 plus an additional £5 for fitting the silencer to the rifle ($105 and $25, respectively, in 1913 U.S. dollars).

"The Silencer," according to the catalog, "consists of a Cylinder in which a number of baffle plates and chambers are arranged, the function of the last two named being respectively to intercept and delay the gases of combustion. These functions they perform so successfully that the 'muzzle blast,' responsible in the ordinary way for most of the noise when a rifle is fired, is cut out

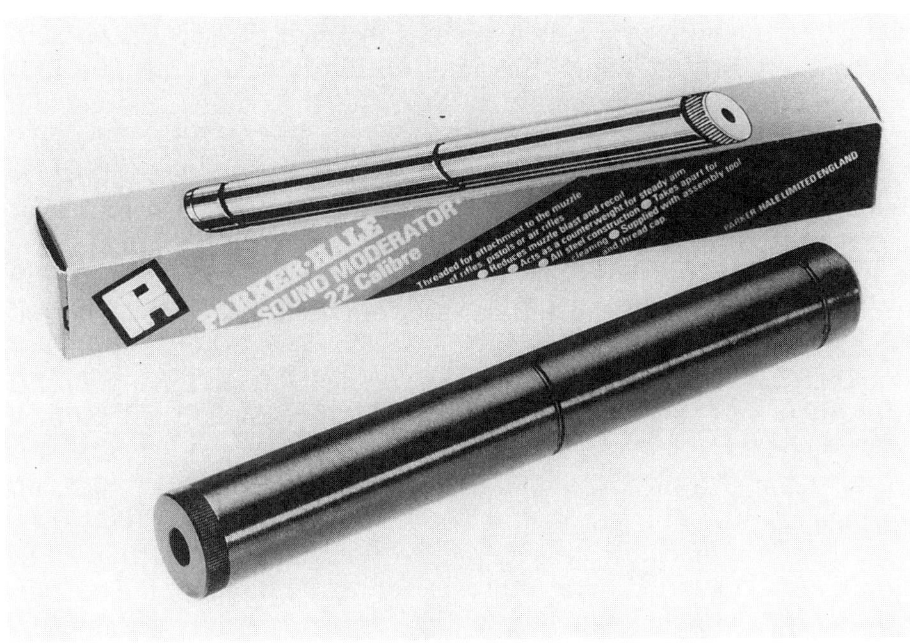

The currently produced Parker Hale MM1 silencer with factory packaging.

and the discharge thus rendered practically silent.

"To test the efficiency of the silencer," the catalog continues, "the rifle fitted with it should be fired straight into the air. Noise in this case is practically absent. When fired at an object, the passage of the bullet through the lower air, and the striking of the bullet against the object create some noise. This, of course cannot be prevented. The silencer makes the use of a rifle possible for target practice in the gardens of well populated districts, and is of course great assistance when shooting rabbits with a rifle."

This passage in the Parker Hale catalog was illustrated with the picture of a BSA No. 6 rifle (which had a Martini single-shot action) fitted with a Maxim Model 1910 silencer. The complete package sold for £68/6 ($341.50). The company also offered the BSA Model 12 fitted with a Maxim, which the catalog described as "another good Rook and Rabbit Rifle," for £56 ($280).

When Maxim replaced the Model 1910 with the Model 1921 silencer, Parker Hale marketed the new model. Catalogue 10E (circa 1926) devotes four times the space to the Maxim silencer as the 1913 catalog—clear evidence that silencers had become quite popular in Britain. Parker offered both rimfire and centerfire Maxims, and illustrations showed Maxims fitted to Colt and Reising .22 pistols as well as Winchester Automatic and Remington No. 12 rifles.

The catalog included an expanded section explaining how a silencer operates. "The silencer checks the muzzle blast. Instead of powder gases being liberated into the air instantaneously when the bullet emerges from the muzzle, they are caught by the Silencer, and allowed to escape gradually.

"This is accomplished by the SILENCING CHAMBERS, which are so constructed as to offer a very high resistance to a rapid flow of gas through them, but very little resistance to a slow flow of gas.

"The hole in the Silencer is much larger than the bullet and the latter does not touch anything in passing through, and consequently accuracy of flight and velocity are just the same with or without the Silencer."

The catalog goes on to discuss how much a silencer reduces the noise of a gunshot. "The silencer annuls almost all the noise of a gun report. On high power rifles it also reduces the recoil by over two-thirds. The reason for this is that there is a very strong tendency for the Silencer to be blown off the end of the gun. This tendency amounts to a forward pull on the gun barrel. The forward pull counter-balances part of the backward kick.

"The only noise the Silencer does not control is the noise made out in the air beyond the gun by the bullet in flight. This noise is a 'crack' like the crack of a whip and not a 'whistle' or 'shriek' as is commonly supposed. The noise is made by the same thing that causes the air to crack when a whiplash is snapped.

"This noise cannot be avoided when the bullet velocity exceeds 1,075 feet per second, no matter how quiet we make the gun. .22 Short and .22 Long Rifle ammunition is below this, and flies quietly. .22 Long and .22 W.R.F. and all high power ammunition are above the critical velocity and usually give bullet flight noise.

"Shot cartridges up to .45 calibre work perfectly in the silencer and make noiseless miniature trap shooting possible without disturbance or danger. On single shot target pistols it improves marksmanship to a surprising degree as it avoids nearly all recoil or 'flip'.

"The Maxim Silencer will not operate on revolvers. No revolver can ever be silenced. If you stop the noise at the muzzle, it makes its escape at the gap between the cylinder and the barrel. Every revolver must have this gap."

The catalog goes on to assert that the "Maxim Silencer is a practical device for use on all Repeating, Automatic, Single Shot Rifles and Single Shot Target Pistols. It is made in all calibres from .22 to .45."

A testimonial appeared in the catalogue from H.C.M. Shaw, who declared that the ".22 cal. Silencer works very well. A partridge sat and allowed me to have 4 shots at it, evidently hearing nothing. The last shot killed it." The Parker catalog offered to provide a booklet filled with American testimonials upon request, and concluded with a note declaring the intent of the company to design a suitable silencer for the .410 shotgun, which customers were apparently demanding. Parker Hale would market the shotgun silencer for many years.

When Hiram P. Maxim began to turn his attention from firearm silencers to the vastly more profitable realm of silencers for internal combustion engines in the late 1920s, A.G. Parker & Co. began to make Maxim silencers, presumably under license. Unfortunately, the records at Parker Hale Limited no longer include records of early contracts or even when each different model of silencer was manufactured. No production records survive either.

But Roger Hale, who is the managing director at Parker Hale Limited (Golden Hillock Road, Birmingham B11 2PZ, England), was able to bring the story up to date. "For the past 30 years," Hale said, "the only type of sound moderator which we have produced is the .22 rimfire model, which has undergone some minor changes in the method of manufacture, but not in the basic design. The debt to Maxim is fully acknowledged."

Regarding the legalities of silencer ownership in Britain, Hale explained that "silencer ownership in Great Britain is permitted on rimfire rifles provided that the prospective purchaser has a variation on his or her Firearms Certificate to allow this. An air rifle may be fitted with a silencer without any restriction. Full bore weapons may also be equipped with a silencer, also provided the owner has the appropriate variation on his or her Firearms Certificate. Such variations are relatively hard to come by."

Parker Hale produces three different silencers today. "We have adapted," Roger Hale said, "the basic multibaffle design to make it more appropriate for use on air rifles and now offer an aluminum body air rifle silencer, Model MM2, in addition to the all steel [.22 rimfire] Model MM1 and the .22 rimfire aluminum bodied MM1A. Between 40 and 50 percent of annual sales are made in the UK, the rest being exported to those countries, mainly in Europe, which still permit the sale and use of sound moderators."

I had the chance to test and evaluate the performance of an unauthorized French clone of the Model MM1 Parker Hale silencer. Constructed entirely out of steel and given a blued finish, the suppressor has an overall length of 7.0 inches (177 mm) and a diameter of 0.93 inch (23.6 mm). The muzzle can weighs 6.9 ounces (195 g). The silencer was tested on a Winchester 63A rifle using Federal high-velocity, Hansen standard-velocity target, and Baikal Junior Brass subsonic LR ammunition. Federal CB Longs were also used.

The sound signatures of the suppressed and unsuppressed rifles appear in Table 9.2, which also

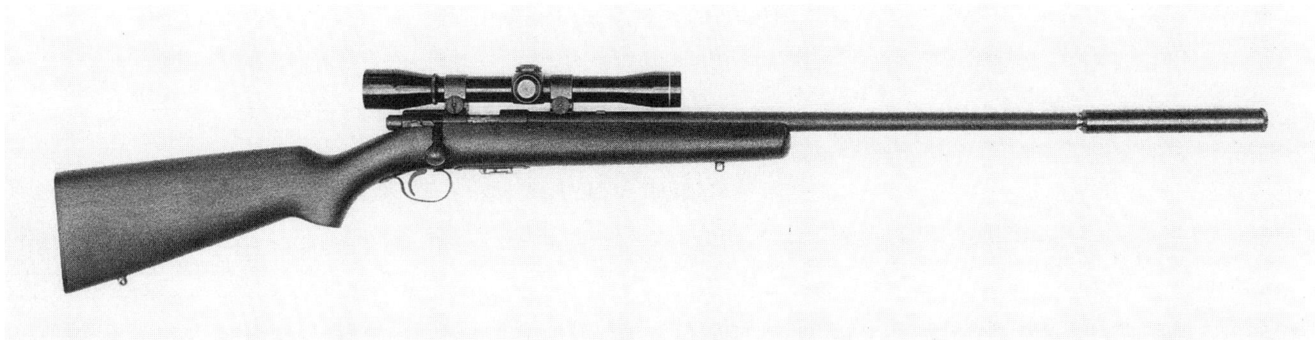

Unauthorized French clone of the Parker Hale MM1 silencer tested for this study, mounted on a Winchester 63A rifle.

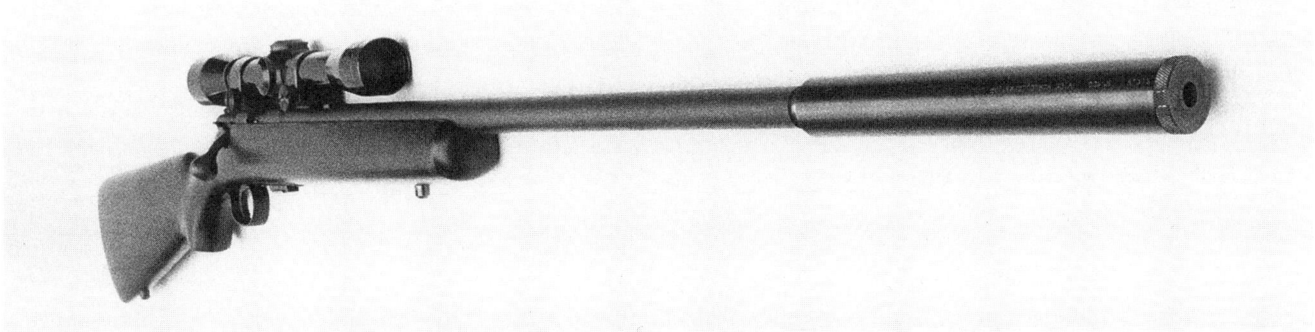

The crude French 1/2x20 TPI threading of the Parker Hale clone will not permit fully seating the suppressor on a barrel threaded for a Maxim Model 1921 silencer. This is ironic because the clone is ultimately a copy of the Maxim silencer.

includes test data on the AWC Archangel I (AWC is now building the third generation Archangel III) mounted on a Ruger 77/22, and data on a Ciener integral suppressor on the Marlin 780 rifle. Net sound reductions are shown in Table 9.3.

The Parker Hale clone performed fairly well. Looking at the net sound reductions listed in Table 9.3, the Parker Hale clone outperformed the Unique by 1 dB using high-velocity and standard-velocity LR ammunition, while these two cans produced the same level of performance with subsonic LR and CB Longs. Remarkably, a Ciener integral suppressor on the Marlin 780 rifle only provided 1 dB better performance than the Parker Hale clone with high-velocity ammo and 2 dB better performance with standard-velocity fodder. The excellent but out-of-production Archangel I provided 3 dB better sound reduction than the clone with high-velocity LR, the same performance with standard-velocity LR, 4 dB better performance with subsonic LR, and an impressive 8 dB better performance with CB Longs.

Clearly dated technology, the 70-year-old design of the Parker Hale MM1 nevertheless provides enough sound suppression to make shooters better neighbors throughout Britain and those European countries with the good sense to allow honest citizens to mitigate the noise pollution and hearing loss associated with sport shooting.

While the Parker Hale silencer takes first place for being in continuous production longer than any other silencer, the French Unique silencer takes second place, and the Australian Goldspot takes third. Like the Unique, the Goldspot .22 caliber silencer was introduced in 1949, and about 250,000 Goldspot suppressors had been manufactured by 1980. Then all Australian states banned suppressors (except by special permit in Tasmania and New South Wales). Loopholes in the wording of various Australian laws permitted the ownership of suppressors as long as the cans were not mounted on a firearm, but these loopholes were eventually closed. Since the Unique silencer is still in production at the time of this writing, it is worth taking a detailed look at this muzzle can's design and performance.

SILENCIEUX UNIQUE

Inspired by a patent issued to Walter E. Westfall in 1914, the *Silencieux Unique* (Unique silencer) is a light and inexpensive suppressor that has been in continual production in France since it was introduced in 1949. Designed for the .22 rimfire, the Unique silencer is available in two models. The *silencieux à baïonnette,* or bayonet model, secures around a firearm's front sight (Figure 9.1). The *silencieux aux embout fileté,* or screw-on model, requires a threaded barrel. The .22 caliber Unique silencer is widely encountered on French .22 rifles and pistols, but it can also be seen on .25 ACP and .32 ACP pistols thanks to the large aperture in its baffles. Several different Unique silencers were made in .380 caliber for testing and evaluation, but these variants never went into production.

One published account asserts that the Unique was used by Resistance fighters during World War II for assassinating Nazi officers. This seems unlikely, since factory literature says that the silencer did not go into production until four years after the war ended.

Other myths about French silencers abound in the literature. While neither the *Silencieux Unique* nor its use of springs was patented, Siegfried Huebner asserts in his book *Silencers for Hand Firearms* that his Figure 4f is a patent drawing. In reality, Huebner's schematic probably came from factory literature rather than a patent. The drawing that accompanies this article was also adapted from a factory flyer. Furthermore, Huebner asserts that the French Diskreet and Still silencers employ springs between baffles. Actual disassembly of Diskreet and Still silencers, however, revealed no springs in these units, contrary to Huebner's claims.

One notable French silencer using a spring did receive a patent, which was issued to Henri-Auguste-Joseph Guarniery in 1951 based on work completed two years earlier. Guarniery's silencer (Figure 9.2) used a single spring in the silencer between the second and third baffle. Expanding combustion gases pushing against the first two baffles would theoretically compress the spring, and

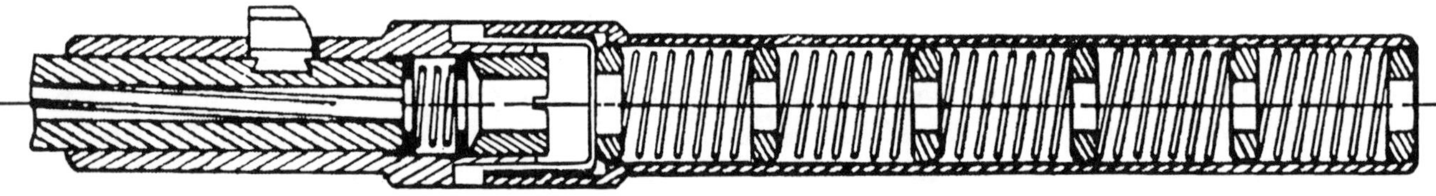

Figure 9.1. Schematic of the bayonet model Unique silencer.

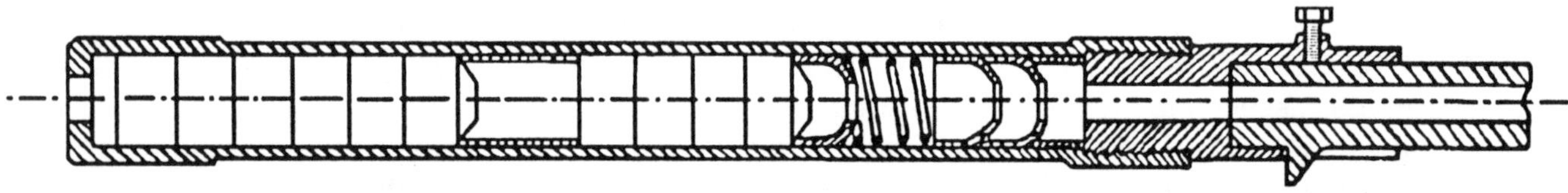

Figure 9.2. This patented design by Henri-Auguste-Joseph Guarniery used a single spring in the silencer between the second and third baffle.

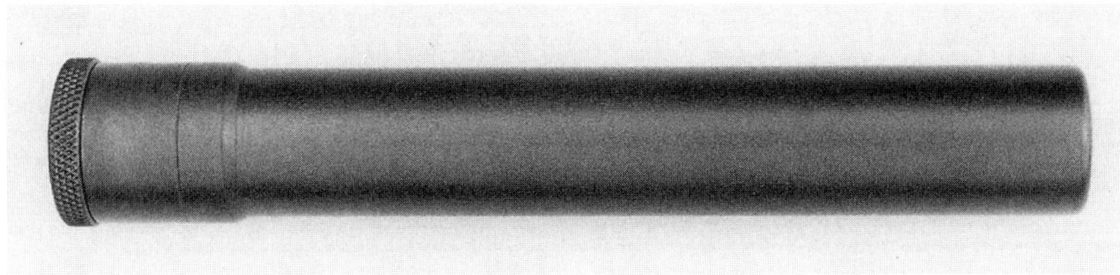
The screw-on model of the Unique silencer.

this additional work would increase the efficiency of the silencer.

In a land where barrels are licensed but receivers and silencers are not, dealer cost for the Unique runs about $10, and the can retails for about $30. The total lack of regulations governing silencers has permitted their mass production at an enviably low cost, which has helped make the *Silencieux Unique* quite attractive to French shooters.

Ubiquitous in France and virtually unknown in the United States, the Unique silencer is usually described as "inefficient" or "disappointing" in print, when it is described at all. The Unique is no Archangel III, but I was surprised to observe that this simple French suppressor performs better than English-language accounts have suggested, especially when employed with the proper ammunition.

Design

The original factory specs on the two production models of the Unique silencer are listed in Table 9.1. The screw-on Unique suppressor was tested for this work. Its specifications differ slightly from the original factory specs listed in Table 9.1 on page 184. This recently made Unique features an extruded aluminum tube 6.1 inches (155 mm) long, with a knurled rear end cap that adds an additional 0.16 inch (4 mm) to the overall length of the suppressor (6.3 inches, 159 mm). The suppressor consists of the tube, a rear end cap (mount), and a baffle stack composed of five alternating springs and baffles. The baffles are simple flat aluminum washers 0.81 inch (20.7 mm) in diameter and 0.16 inch (4 mm) thick, with an aperture of 0.39 inch (10 mm). The suppressor tube, rear end cap, and front baffle are anodized, while the remaining four baffles are left unfinished. All baffles appear black in the accompanying photographs because of carbon buildup. The front 5.2 inches (131 mm) of the tube has an external diameter of 0.91 inch (23 mm), while the remaining rear portion has a diameter of 0.98 inch (25 mm). The Unique tested for this article weighs a mere 3.0 ounces (84 grams).

The front edge of the tube is rolled over to form a small lip that captures the front baffle. The front opening in the tube is 0.68 inch (17.3 mm) across, but the front baffle reduces this aperture to 0.39 inch (10 mm), which is an unusually large opening for a .22 caliber suppressor. Incorporating such a large opening makes sense when one examines the population of rifles in the French countryside. Many .22 rifles in France feature muzzle threads. But the threading tends to be rather crude, so a suppressor will rarely line up with a rifle's bore. The 1/2x20 TPI threading in the Unique's rear end cap is also crude and will not screw more than a few turns on threading made to U.S. specs. In any event, there is no risk of a bullet striking a baffle in a Unique silencer, thanks to the very large aperture size. The trade-off is reduced efficiency to ensure accuracy and safety.

It is important to note that proper alignment is frequently a problem in the United States as well, especially when a suppressor must align itself using only threads. Much better alignment is produced by incorporating a shoulder on the barrel that is perpendicular and concentric to the bore. The suppressor must then feature a corresponding surface that properly aligns the suppressor with the bore when the suppressor is screwed tightly in place. The old Maxim silencers used such a system to achieve proper alignment.

The intent of the design in the *Silencieux Unique* is that each spring functions as more than a mere baffle spacer. The spring also absorbs some gas energy as combustion gases force the baffle forward. Compressing the spring robs the gases of energy that would be perceived as sound.

Figure 9.3. The Unique silencer was inspired by a 1914 patent on this design by Walter E. Westfall.

Disassembled Unique silencer, showing springs that both position the simple flat baffles and absorb some energy from the expanding combustion gases.

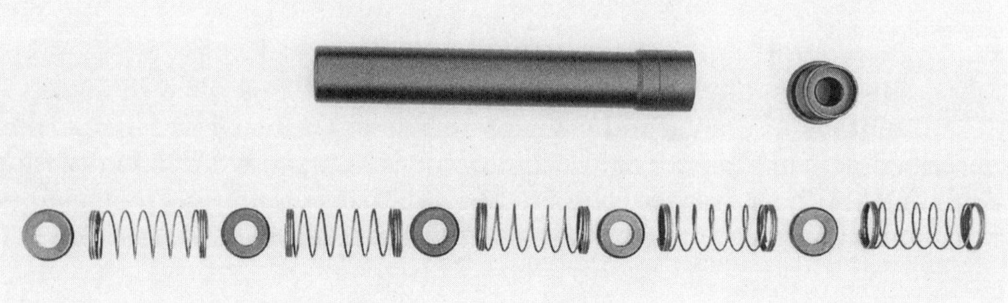

This concept was introduced in a patent issued to Walter Westfall, who lived in Maryville, Missouri. His patent incorporated several interesting features. Westfall's design (Figure 9.3) incorporated a primary expansion chamber and baffle stack in front of the muzzle. The suppressor tube also encapsulated the entire length of the unported barrel. A ported barrel bushing at the muzzle vented high-pressure gas from the primary expansion chamber into the secondary expansion chamber surrounding the barrel, much like the Vaime Mk2 Silent Sniper Rifle made in Finland in the 1980s.

The baffle stack in the Westfall silencer was encapsulated in a sleeve that was suspended between two springs. A short spring separated the baffle stack from the barrel bushing, while a long spring separated the baffle stack from the front end cap. Combustion gases would drive the entire baffle stack forward as a unit, depressing the front return spring. A simplified variant employed flat instead of conical baffles.

While the Unique silencer uses spring power to reduce the energy content of combustion gases, it employs springs for each baffle rather than one spring for the entire baffle stack. The Unique also incorporates flat washers for baffles like the simplified Westfall silencer. The outer edge of a Unique baffle is rounded to minimize friction with the inner surface of the suppressor tube. The rear spring locks the end cap (mount) in place, unless a pencil or other implement is used to push against the rearmost baffle to depress the baffle stack and release the pressure of the rearmost spring against the end cap.

The Unique might actually work in a similar fashion to the Westfall silencer. Suppressor designer Mark White speculates that the entire baffle stack may initially compress, providing a temporarily large primary expansion chamber. As combustion gases work their way through the baffles and the pressure in the rear of the suppressor subsides, the springs might push the baffles backward, expanding the distance between them as the remaining lower pressure gas traverses the baffle stack. The big question with this hypothesis is whether or not the springs can compress and then expand again within a few microseconds to effect the required movement. White also notes that this design is a good one for self-cleaning, since baffle movement would tend to scrape accumulating powder residue off the inner surface of the suppressor tube.

The relatively soft springs of 0.04 inch (1.0 mm) wire are 0.78 inch (19.7 mm) in diameter and

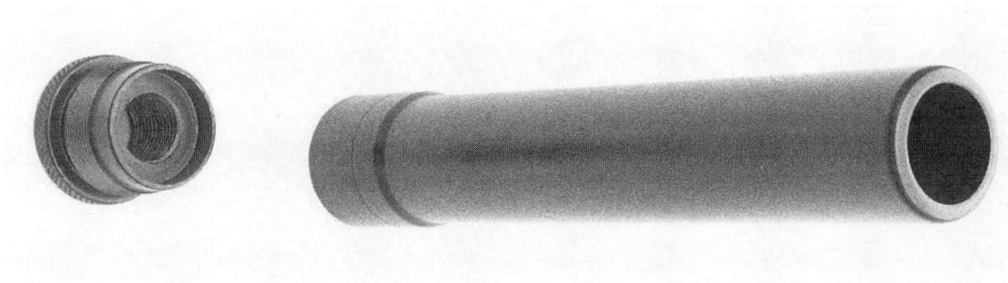

This recently made Unique silencer features an extruded aluminum tube and a knurled rear end cap.

1.9 inches (48 mm) long before assembly of the suppressor. The springs space the five baffles 0.94 inch (24 mm) apart when the suppressor is assembled. Better suppressor designers will immediately recognize that this is far from optimum spacing for a .22 rimfire suppressor. It should be possible to improve the Unique's performance significantly by using springs of different lengths to achieve optimal spacing. The Czech Skorpion suppressor uses springs of different lengths and a similar baffle design to the Unique (except for a cone-type rearmost baffle) to silence the now out-of-production 7.65x17mm Skorpion submachine gun.

The beauty of the Unique silencer is that it distills Wesfall's concepts to their minimal essence, providing a uniquely light and inexpensive product. Even though most accounts allude to the unit's poor performance, the can seemed quiet enough for discrete target practice when using subsonic ammunition. I decided to test my subjective opinion by measuring the sound signature produced by the Unique silencer using a diverse array of ammunition.

Performance

The Unique suppressor was tested on a Winchester Model 63A rifle with the following Long Rifle ammunition: Federal high-velocity, Hansen standard-velocity target, and Baikal Junior Brass subsonic. Federal CB Longs were also tested.

The sound signatures of the suppressed and unsuppressed rifles appear in Table 9.2, which also includes test data on the AWC Archangel I mounted on a Ruger 77/22 and data on a Ciener integral suppressor on the Marlin 780 rifle. Net sound reductions are shown in Table 9.3.

One widely distributed book asserts that the performance of the .22 caliber Unique silencer is "not very good." The data generated for this study suggest otherwise. The Winchester rifle with the Unique silencer produced sound signatures within 2 or 3 dB of the Marlin rifle with Ciener integral suppressor. That's not too shabby for a simple, ultralight, $30 suppressor.

Subjectively, the Unique does seem loud with high-velocity ammunition because of the ballistic crack (sonic boom) produced by supersonic projectiles. When employed with subsonic Long Rifle ammunition, however, the *Silencieux Unique* provides a pleasing sound signature that is suitable for discreet target practice in the backyard or basement. When employed with CB Longs, the sound signature is 2 dB quieter than the sound produced by pulling the trigger on a Ruger 77/22 with an empty chamber! One of the foremost foreign suppressor authorities tells me that his experiences with the *Silencieux Unique* parallel my own. He recalls that the Unique performed well on .22 caliber pistols, as well.

How many Unique silencers have been produced since their introduction nearly a half century ago? Although comprehensive production figures are not available, two runs of 5,000 units each were produced in one year for which I have information. If that year was typical, then there could be nearly a half-million Unique silencers in France. That's about 10 times the number of silencers registered in the United States since 1934!

Table 9.1. Original factory specifications for the two variants of the *Silencieux Unique*.

BAYONET-MOUNTED UNIQUE SILENCER		SCREW-MOUNTED UNIQUE SILENCER	
Length	225 mm (8.9 inches)	Length	160 mm (6.3 inches)
Maximum Diameter	25 mm (0.98 inch)	Maximum Diameter	26 mm (1.02 inches)
Weight	125 grams (4.4 ounces)	Weight	100 grams (3.5 ounces)
Number of baffles	6	Number of baffles	5

Table 9.2. Sound signatures in decibels of suppressor tests.

GUN	SUPPRESSOR	FEDERAL HV LR	HANSEN SV LR	BAIKAL SS LR	FEDERAL CB LONGS	TEMP., °F (°C)
Winchester 63A	None	141	137	137	130	81(28)
Winchester 63A	Unique	124	121	117	110	81(28)
Winchester 63A	Parker Hale	123	120	117	110	81(28)
Ruger 77/22	None	141	137	138	132	82(29)
Ruger 77/22	AWC Archangel I	120	120	114	104	82(29)
Marlin 780	None	141	138	—	—	82(29)
Marlin 780	Ciener	122	119	—	—	82(29)

Table 9.3. Net sound reductions, expressed in decibels.

GUN	SUPPRESSOR	FEDERAL HV LR	HANSEN SV LR	BAIKAL SS LR	FEDERAL CB LONGS	TEMP., °F (°C)
Winchester 63A	Unique	17	16	20	20	81(28)
Winchester 63A	Parker Hale	18	17	20	20	81(28)
Ruger 77/22	AWC Archangel I	21	17	24	28	82(29)
Marlin 780	Ciener	19	19	—	—	82(29)

Conclusions

Clearly, previously published conclusions on the importance and performance of the *Silencieux Unique* need to be revised. The Unique has arguably become as much a part of French culture as the Winchester Model 94 carbine has become part of the American. The Unique silencer provides acceptable performance on rifles and pistols, especially considering the Unique's simple design, small volume, and light weight. When employed with subsonic Long Rifle ammunition, the silencer provides enough suppression for discreet target practice almost anywhere. When employed with CB Longs in a rifle, the Unique is as discreet as dry-firing a Ruger 77/22. The sound of bullet impact becomes the dominant event when shooting CB Longs as far as spectators or neighbors are concerned. The *Silencieux Unique* enables French shooters to discreetly target practice in their garages and gardens without annoying their neighbors. There's an old saying that asserts 10,000 Frenchmen can't be wrong.

VAIME A8 VERSUS THE AWC ARCHANGEL I

Since Finnish enlightenment on encouraging the civilian use of silencers has been extolled in this book, it would be interesting to compare the design and performance of Finnish and American technology from the late 1980s: the Archangel, made by the Automatic Weapons Company, and the Finnish Vaime A8, which was briefly made in the United States by North American Sales International. Both suppressors can be used on a variety of .22 caliber firearms.

The Vaime A8 suppressor is designed for .22 rimfire ammunition only. The can is 9.6 inches (24.4 cm) long and 1.0 inch (2.5 cm) in diameter. The tube and both end caps are made from aluminum, and these components are anodized black. The original design contained 13 plastic slanted baffles with integral spacers that feature a unique tongue-and-groove system that offsets each baffle 90 degrees from the preceding one. These baffles are 21 mm in diameter and 14 mm long.

The rear of the original Vaime can contained a plastic primary expansion chamber that was 30 mm long. This system worked fine in rifles, but it could not stand up to use on pistols.

For this reason, a 13 gram aluminum primary expansion chamber was designed to replace the 4 gram plastic one and the first standard plastic baffle (which weighed 2 grams). This increased the suppressor's weight from 4.4 ounces (121 grams) to 4.5 ounces (128 grams). The aluminum chamber is 45 mm long, which adds 1 mm to the stack of internal components. Thus the front end cap no longer screws down all the way. While this is a minor cosmetic irritant, it does not adversely affect the performance of the suppressor. It would be easy to have a machinist turn off that extraneous 1 mm from the aluminum chamber.

While on the subject of minor irritants, the outside surface of the Vaime tube still shows the many scratches and scars common to aircraft tubing as it arrives from the factory. This problem is common to all Vaime muzzle cans that I have seen that were manufactured in the States. Every other modern manufacturer buffs out these scars. While such cosmetics are irrelevant to the professional user, the private collector and sportsman should be entitled to a better finish. The one

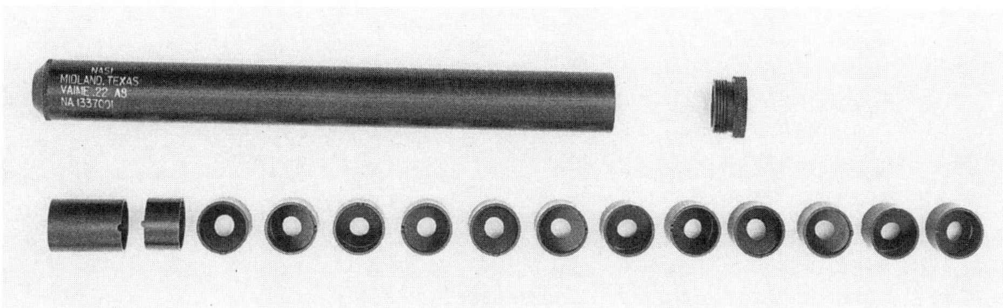

The original design of the Vaime A8 suppressor uses 13 plastic baffles and a plastic primary expansion chamber in an aluminum tube to achieve its remarkably light weight.

Vaime suppressor I've seen that was produced in Finland had a flawless finish. If only we could have obtained the Finnish finish here . . . .

The plastic baffles in the Vaime suppressor incorporate integral spacers that feature a unique tongue-and-groove system that offsets each baffle 90 degrees from the preceding one.

The Archangel suppressor (which will henceforth be referred to as the Archangel I to distinguish it from the subsequent variants, the Archangel II and the Archangel III) is 7.47 inches (19.0 cm) long and 1.0 inch (2.5 cm) in diameter. It weighs more than twice as much as the Vaime suppressor, tipping the scales at 10.1 ounces (288 grams), even though the Archangel is several inches shorter. The tube with integral barrel mount and the front end cap are made of steel, and these components have an attractive blued finish. The internal components are made of aircraft-grade aluminum (see Figure 9.4).

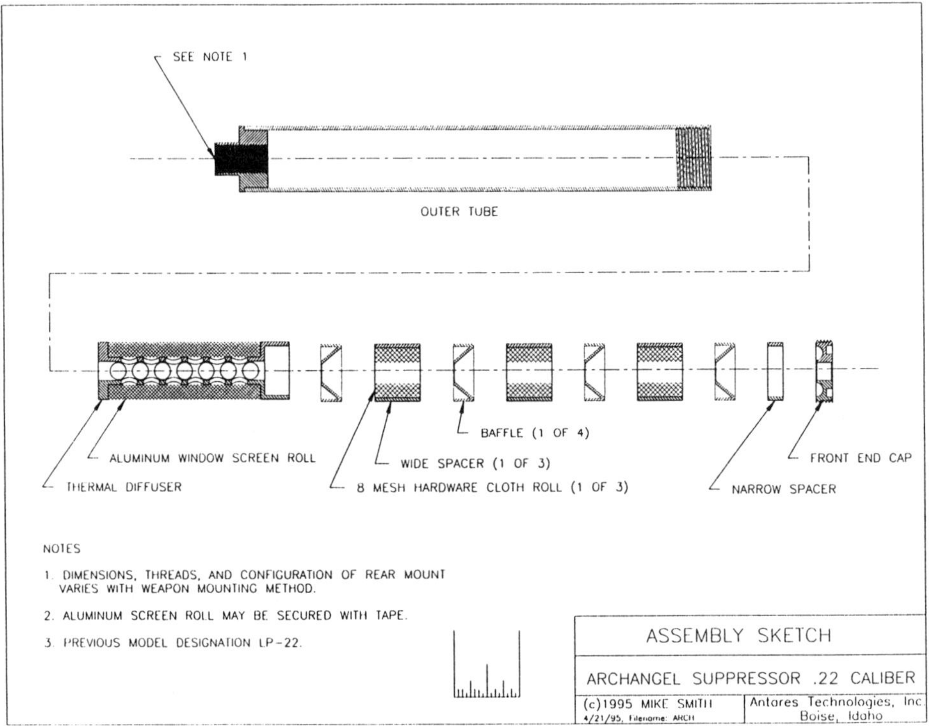

Figure 9.4. Design of the Archangel I suppressor from AWC Systems Technology. Drawing by Mike Smith.

As a bullet enters the suppressor, it enters a thermal diffuser (primary expansion chamber) that is filled with aluminum window screen (measuring 2-3/8 x 11 inches or 6.0 x 55.9 cm) wrapped around a spindle perforated with 26 holes. The bullet then passes through a series of four baffles with separate spacers. The spacers are filled with several wraps of 8 mesh hardware cloth (measur-

The Vaime plastic primary expansion chamber worked fine in rifles, but it could not stand up to the higher velocity combustion gases produced by pistols, so the first two plastic components at the rear of the suppressor were replaced by a longer expansion chamber fabricated from aluminum.

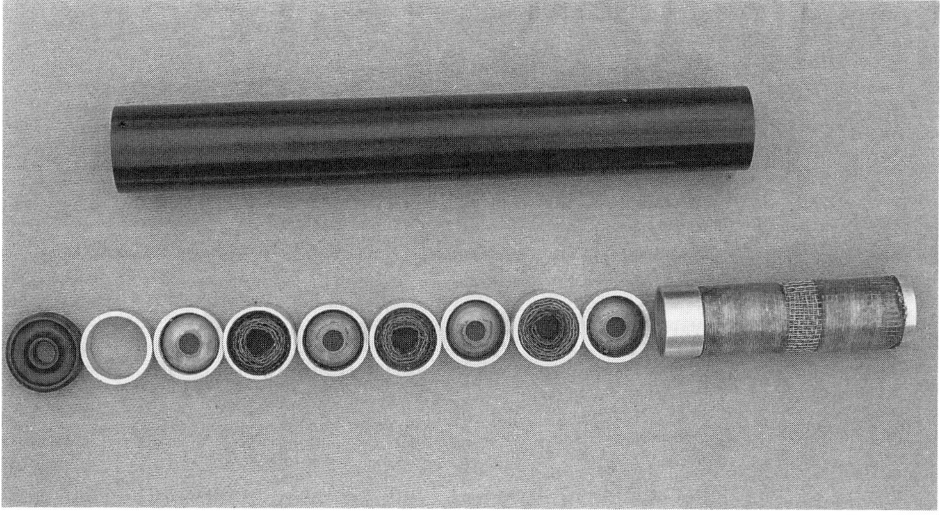

As a bullet enters the Archangel I, it enters a thermal diffuser wrapped around a perforated spindle and then passes through a series of baffles with separate spacers that are filled with several wraps of 8 mesh hardware cloth.

ing 5/8 x 12 inches or 1.6 x 30.5 cm) to further diffuse, slow, and cool the combustion gases. The Archangel I suppressor is an ingenious marriage of baffle and mesh technology. The front end cap is separated from the frontmost baffle by an aluminum spacer. The cap is designed to deflect expanding gases backward.

Maintenance

The Vaime suppressor should be disassembled and cleaned every 500 rounds. Make sure the solvent you use does not eat the plastic baffles. The Archangel suppressor should be immersed in a solvent overnight every 500 rounds with the rear of the suppressor up, but letting it drain with the rear end down. Then immerse in a lightweight oil such as Rustlick 606 or automatic transmission fluid. Do not immerse it in WD-40. If you follow this regimen, the Archangel will only require complete disassembly and cleaning every 2,000 rounds. Both the Vaime A8 and the AWC Archangel should have the threads of the front end cap coated with an antiseize compound every time the suppressor is cleaned. Colloidal molybdenum and copper compounds designed for high-temperature applications work best. Thus, the Archangel has the edge over the Vaime suppressor in terms of maintenance intervals. But what about the more important question of sound reduction?

Performance

The AWC Archangel and Vaime A8 were tested with four different kinds of ammunition. Two were supersonic: Federal Hi-Power high-velocity LR and Hansen standard-velocity LR. Two were subsonic: RWS subsonic LR and Federal CB Longs.

The mean sound signatures are shown in Table 9.4 (page 190), the net sound reductions are shown in Table 9.5 (page 190), and muzzle velocities are shown in Table 9.6 (page 191). Velocities through the Vaime suppressor were not tested because there wasn't enough light at high noon in November to operate skyscreens in subarctic Alaska. The AWC Archangel was noticeably quieter than the Vaime A8 using high-velocity and standard-velocity LR, but both suppressors delivered the same performance with subsonic LR and CB Longs. Comparing the net sound reductions in Table 9.5 with those of Table 9.3 demonstrates that both the AWC Archangel and Vaime A8 provided more sound suppression than the Ciener integral suppressor on a Marlin 780 rifle.

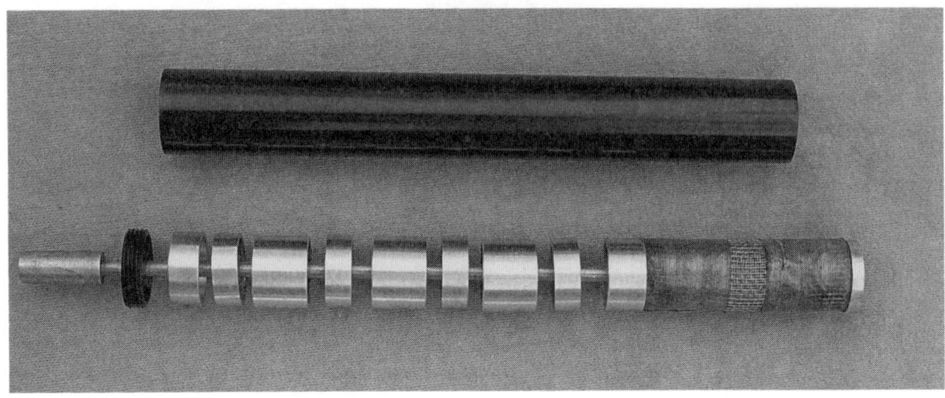

The AWC Archangel I suppressor alternates conventional baffles with spacers filled with rolled mesh. The takedown/assembly tool inserted through the baffles and spacers was issued with a Maxim Model 1921 silencer.

A close-up look at the front of the Archangel I's standard baffle/spacer, a mesh-filled spacer, the rear of a standard baffle/spacer, and the rear of the front end cap.

The velocity data in Table 9.6 suggest that the RWS subsonic load with the AWC Archangel should have produced a ballistic crack according to the calculated speed of sound. It did not! The engineering formula is based entirely on the temperature in degrees

Fahrenheit. I argued for years with suppressor designer Dr. Phil Dater, who insists that the speed of sound varies *only* with temperature, citing the formula

Speed of sound = (49.06) times the square root of (T + 459)

where T = temperature in degrees Fahrenheit,

which is widely used in engineering textbooks and physics handbooks. It is this formula that I've used to calculate the speed of sound throughout this treatise. Appendix 2 lists the speed of sound versus a wide range of temperatures for both metric and English units of measure.

The speed of sound is directly proportional to the density of the medium in which the sound waves are traveling. Thus sound travels faster in water than air. And the speed of sound is faster in steel than in water. I, therefore, argued that other factors which influence the density of the air (such as humidity, barometric pressure, and altitude) must also affect the speed of sound. Over the years, I have amassed considerable empirical evidence that seemed to support my hypothesis, because I've routinely witnessed a ballistic crack at velocities that the formula asserts should be subsonic velocities. And I've observed no ballistic crack when the formula says there should be one. It seems that the true speed of sound, as determined by the actual presence of a ballistic crack, can vary by as much as 30 fps (9 mps) from the calculated value. The formula seems to fall short most often on extremely humid or extremely dry days.

Contrary to my early thoughts on the matter, Dr. Dater has produced enough data to demonstrate to my satisfaction that only temperature significantly affects the speed of sound in the atmosphere at altitudes below 3 kilometers. Detailed research by Steve Baughman does suggest, however, that humidity can have a small effect (up to about 5 fps at 68°F or 1.5 mps at 20°C). I'm at a loss how to explain the remaining variability between the calculated and observed speeds of sound that I have experienced. Most of the time, however, the formula does provide an excellent prediction as to whether or not transonic loads will generate a ballistic crack.

This is an important issue because the ballistic crack (sonic boom) generated by a supersonic .22 projectile is quite loud. This is even noticeable when firing an unsuppressed rifle. Note in Table 9.4 that Hansen standard-velocity and RWS subsonic LR produced the same sound signatures in the unsuppressed Ruger 77/22. Yet the RWS sounded vastly quieter to the ear because its subsonic bullet did not generate a ballistic crack a few yards from the muzzle, but the Hansen's supersonic projectile did.

One final curiosity regarding velocity needs to be discussed. Note from the data in Table 9.6 that the velocities produced with the Archangel suppressor attached to the rifle were consistently higher than the velocities produced by the unsuppressed rifle when shot with Long Rifle ammunition. This curiosity relates to the behavior of combustion gases in the rearmost chamber of the suppressor. Combustion gases generated by the Long Rifle ammunition continue to push on the rear of the bullet as it passes through the primary expansion chamber in a process one might call "freebore boost." This phenomenon takes place in some muzzle suppressors but not in others, depending on their internal design. The CB Long does not produce enough gas to generate freebore boost.

Using RWS subsonic ammunition, the sound coming from the gun was only 1 dB louder than the firing pin falling on an empty chamber. The RWS is a hollowpoint round that is accurate, quiet, and expensive. It's an effective round for taking small game, but a solid-point round like the much more affordable Baikal Junior Brass LR should be used for medium-sized animals where better penetration is essential. Aside from the cost, my only other complaint is that the RWS subsonic is so heavily waxed that it's messy to handle and gums up the magazines. But the mess is a small price to pay. The dominant sound shooting this ammo with either suppressor is the bullet striking the target. The CB Longs shoot to approximately the same point of aim at 15 yards, but you'll need to hold over the target at longer ranges. A duplex reticle in your scope makes this easy out to 50 yards, where you can routinely hit the end of a pop can.

Even after shooting tens of thousands of rounds, members of my family still experience an electric thrill when shooting either of these suppressors on a Ruger Model 77/22 in the backyard with CB Longs. And if you have a landfill where it is socially and ecologically permissible to hunt glass bottles . . . well, that's about as much excitement as some folks can stand. The stifled cough from the suppressor is long gone by the time you hear the crisp and unadulterated ring of breaking glass. Whether you are punching paper, pop cans, glass bottles, or that squirrel that's been busily ruining the insulation in your attic, you will find that the ability to make things happen quietly downrange is utterly addictive. And discreet.

After a grand Thanksgiving dinner in the Alaskan taiga, several friends and I adjourned to the far end of the living room for some target shooting using RWS subsonic LR and Federal CB Longs with these two suppressors. Not wanting to wade through the deep snow, we simply opened the back door slightly and shot at a little swinging metal target about 40 yards behind the house. We had a glorious time standing in the living room and hearing the hits through the open door as the snow swirled outside. Gentle strains of a harpsichord seeped sprightly into the room from a stereo as our wives quietly chatted over dessert across the open room. The ladies were just out of our line of sight, perhaps 30 feet away on the other side of a bookcase that served as a room divider. After we had finished shooting, we sallied forth to the pumpkin pie. One of the ladies asked us when we were going to shoot. It was the perfect end to a perfect day.

Table 9.4. Sound signatures in decibels of Vaime A8 and AWC Archangel tests[1,2].

GUN	SUPPRESSOR	FEDERAL HV LR	HANSEN SV LR	RWS SS LR	FEDERAL CB LONGS	TEMP., °F (°C)
Ruger 77/22	None	141	138	138	132	50(10)
Ruger 77/22	AWC Archangel	117	114	113	106	50(10)
Ruber 77/22	Vaime A8	120	118	113	106	50(10)

[1] Firing pin on empty chamber is 112 decibels
[2] Firing pin on virgin rim of once-fired case is 94 decibels

Table 9.5. Net sound reductions in decibels of Vaime A8 and AWC Archangel tests.

GUN	SUPPRESSOR	FEDERAL HV LR	HANSEN SV LR	RWS SS LR	FEDERAL CB LONGS	TEMP., °F (°C)
Ruger 77/22	AWC Archangel	24	24	25	26	50(10)
Ruger 77/22	Vaime A8	21	20	25	26	50(10)

Table 9.6. Bullet velocities of Vaime A8 and AWC Archangel tests, expressed in feet per second (and meters per second).

GUN	SUPPRESSOR	FEDERAL HV LR	HANSEN SV LR	RWS SS LR	FEDERAL CB LONGS	TEMP., °F (°C)	SPEED OF SOUND fps (mps)
Ruger 77/22	None	1,229(375)	1,129(344)	998(304)	655(200)	50(10)	1,107(337)
Ruger 77/22	AWC Archangel	1,243(379)	1,147(350)	1,016(310)	644(196)	50(10)	1,107(337)

AWC WARP 3

Back in the 1980s, a U.S. government agency wanted a tiny suppressor that would provide acceptable sound suppression. The can was to be designed for a .22 LR pocket pistol and would maintain its efficiency for three rounds. That should have been enough for discrete, up close and personal diplomacy. The can had to be unusually small for concealed carry when under deep cover. Lynn McWilliams of AWC Systems Technology named this muzzle can the Warp 3.

The Warp 3 was initially delivered to the government agency on the Walther TPH (with special extra-length threaded barrel) along with a special Bruce Nelson ankle holster that held the pistol with detached suppressor. This system was eventually made available to qualified civilians. The can also works well on the following .22 caliber pistols: the Beretta Models 21, 70S, 71, 87W, and 950, and the Walther PP, PPK, and PPK/S. There is no reason why this suppressor couldn't be mated to other pistols as well as rifles.

The Warp 3 is 3.5 inches (89 mm) long and 0.95 inch (24 mm) in diameter. The can weighs 4.2 ounces (120 grams) without the thread protector and key ring combination that was issued with the suppressor. Constructed entirely of 304 stainless steel, the can was initially issued in a bead-blasted, optically flat finish. It was produced from mid-1990 until mid-1994, when it was replaced by the Backdraft suppressor (which will be evaluated with other tactical .22 systems in the second volume of *Silencer History and Performance*). The Warp 3 was produced in both highly polished stainless steel and black chrome sulfide finishes.

The can is sealed, so the suppressor cannot be disassembled for maintenance. This apparently is not a significant liability, however, since Break Free must be added to the rear of the suppressor every 5 to 10 shots to maintain optimal sound reduction. Maximum performance is achieved by adding coolant every three shots (see Table 9.7). Coolant can also be added to the front of the can, if necessary.

The suppressor uses baffles to force the main gas jet away from the bullet and into artificial environment cells, where some Break Free evaporates with each shot, cooling combustion gases and thus robbing them of energy that would be perceived as sound. The bonus in terms of maintenance is that Break Free also inhibits the buildup of carbon on the can's internal components.

Break Free is not the only coolant that can be used with the Warp 3 suppressor, although it is the preferred medium. Any light oil with a high flash point can be used. Water and even shaving gels work too. Professional operators have recharged these suppressors in the field with a mixture of water-soluble oil and paraffin, which is carried in little squirt bottles taped to their vests or LBE.

But perhaps the most interesting suitable coolant fluid may be urine, which has a definite advantage on a covert op when fancy lubricants or even water may not be available. Best of all, I've found that urine is readily available when the balloon goes up. How does urine affect the sound signature of the Warp 3 compared to Break Free? I know this sounds disgusting, but I just had to know.

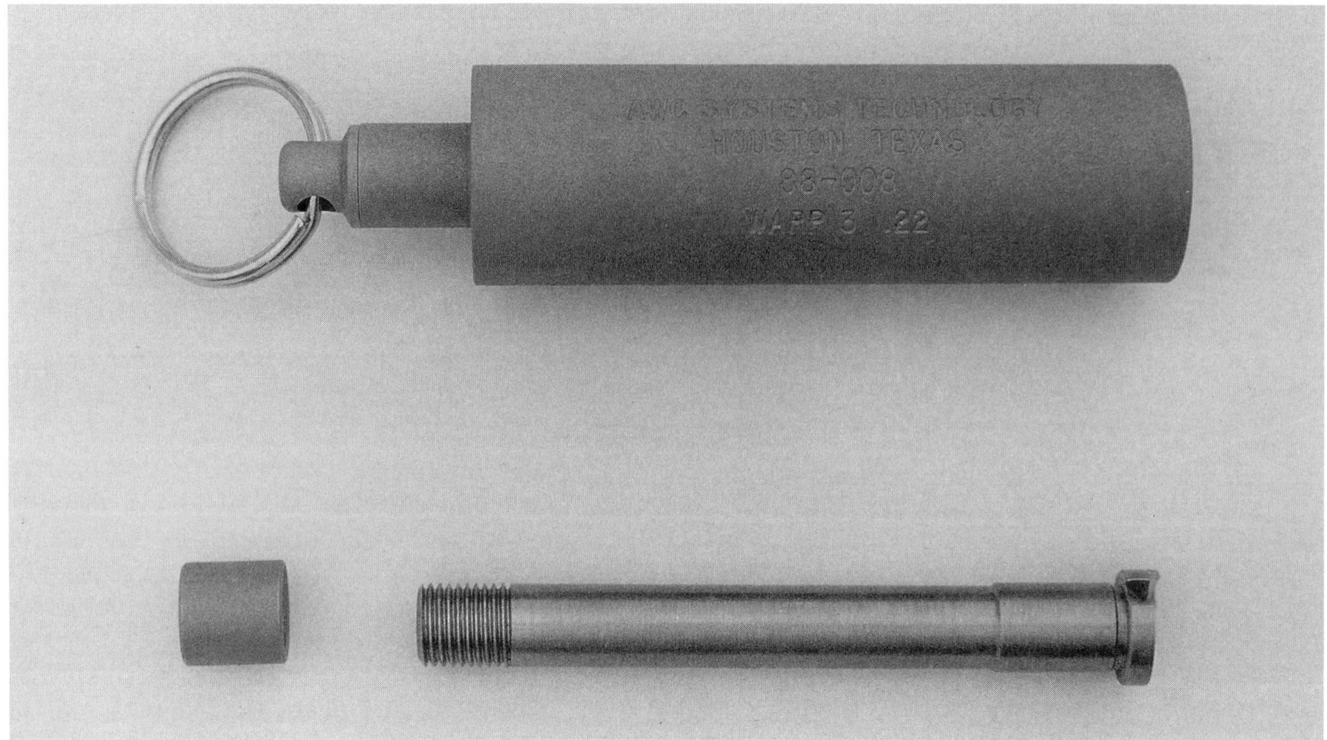

The AWC Warp 3 was originally issued to a government client with custom extra-length barrel with thread protector and a thread protector with key ring for the rear of the suppressor that enabled carrying the can as a key fob.

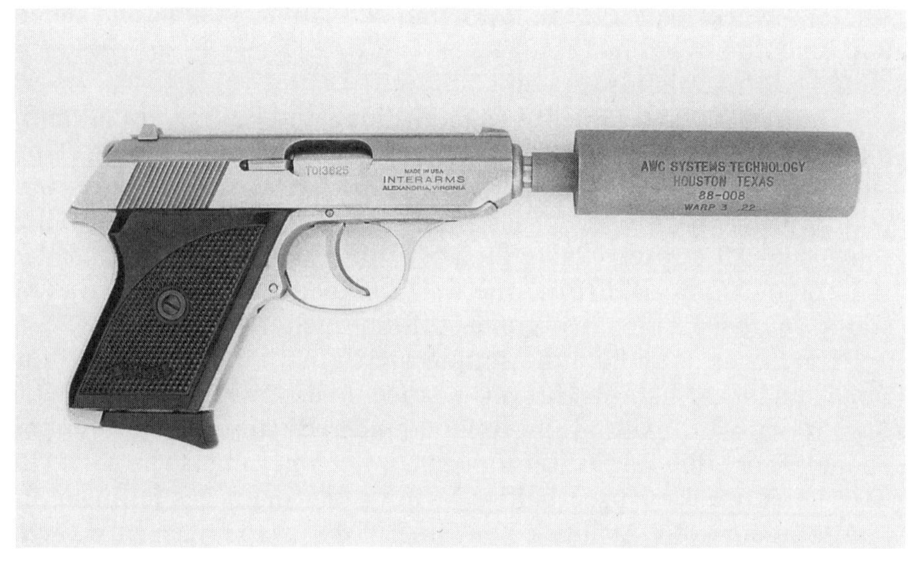

The AWC Warp 3 was the first commercially successful tiny .22 caliber suppressor that used wet technology to achieve both high performance and very small size, based on earlier work by Qualatec of Oceanside, California.

I measured sound signatures of the Warp 3 suppressor mounted on a Walther TPH pistol with RWS subsonic, Hansen standard-velocity target, and Federal Hi-Power high-velocity LR ammunition. At least 10 rounds were fired in each test to obtain a valid statistical sample. The Warp 3 was recharged with coolant after every string of three rounds, and at least four strings were shot per combination of ammo and coolant. In order to look at suppressor performance at the other end of the coolant envelope, the Warp 3 was also tested with Break Free added after each 10-shot string, which is the maximum recommended replenishment interval. The shooter and suppressor both spent a considerable time in the shower after testing the Warp 3 with urine, and the original field notes were burned after transcription. In a remarkable display of solidarity, my wife, Polly Walter, spent several hours standing in a mist of burned urine to record the test data.

Sound test data are shown Table 9.7 (page 195), and net sound reductions are shown in Table 9.8 (page 195). Bullet velocity data appear in Table 9.10 (page 196). Here's what I've learned.

Burned urine doesn't smell very good. Furthermore, a beard makes an excellent filter for removing a urine aerosol from the atmosphere. Seriously, the shooter does tend to accumulate the scent of the liquid used in the suppressor, be it Break Free, oil, or urine. A covert user should probably charge the suppressor with water rather than odoriferous alternatives if he might be closely approached (within olfactory range) after using the suppressor. Water would provide a noticeably lower sound signature than Break Free.

I've also learned through replicate tests that recharging the Warp 3 with coolant every three shots provides the best performance, after which the sound signature usually jumps 3 to 5 dB with Break Free (more with water or urine) for the rest of the magazine, which has a capacity of six. Water and urine provide a more consistent amount of sound reduction regardless of ammunition type. But Break Free lasts for more shots and probably reduces carbon buildup inside the suppressor better than water-based coolants.

It is also interesting that bullet velocities are consistently higher with the suppressor mounted on the TPH when using Federal high-velocity and Hansen standard-velocity ammo. But just the opposite is seen with RWS subsonic ammo. Gases from the faster loads continue to push on the rear of the bullet as it passes through the primary expansion chamber in a process called "freebore boost." Gases from slower loads do not.

Another surprise is that the Warp 3 packs so much performance in such a small package. The can occupies a gross volume (the volume of components plus air) of about 2.3 cubic inches. As Table 9.9 shows (page 196), this is a remarkably small volume for a .22 caliber muzzle suppressor.

Yet, almost a quarter of a century ago, Frankford Arsenal suggested that a suppressor designed for a *subsonic* projectile should be about 20 times the volume of the gun's bore. The special threaded barrel of the Walther has a volume of about 0.1 cubic inch or 1.4 cubic centimeters. This barrel volume would call for a suppressor volume of about 1.6 cubic inches or 28 cubic centimeters, about 78 percent of the can's actual volume. But Frankford Arsenal's rule of thumb involved a lower level of performance than the Warp 3 provides.

Small .22 caliber pistols exhibit notorious sensitivity to ammunition, but my TPH functioned flawlessly with all types of ammunition used in this study, whether or not the suppressor was mounted on the pistol. Tactical users, however, should fire several hundred rounds with whatever ammo they select to ensure reliable functioning with that particular ammunition. Solid-point projectiles from 37 to 40 grains are the most reliable, although my gun functioned well with RWS subsonic hollowpoints when the gun was clean. Selecting the best ammunition for your particular TPH can reduce stoppages to under 1 percent. Nevertheless, tactical users should regularly practice clearing malfunctions, as they would with any firearm.

Reliability is also strongly influenced by the shooter's grip. A loose grip can cause stoppages. And the TPH can jam if you grasp the pistol high on the grip so that the slide rubs the hand during cycling. A tight grip with large hands can cause the same problem. A high grip will also allow the slide to cut the web of the shooting hand. (This is a hard habit to break for someone with combat training in the Colt government model. I grip the Colt as high as possible to minimize recoil.) The only cure for the Walther's bite is to find a modified, somewhat lower hold that works for your hand size.

In terms of accuracy, the Walther TPH with Warp 3 suppressor can produce 1.5 inch groups when shot offhand at 15 yards. Walther sights in the pistol for this range. Group size doubles or even triples at 25 yards in my hands, unless I'm having a good day. Basic shooting fundamentals and lots of practice are especially important with this system.

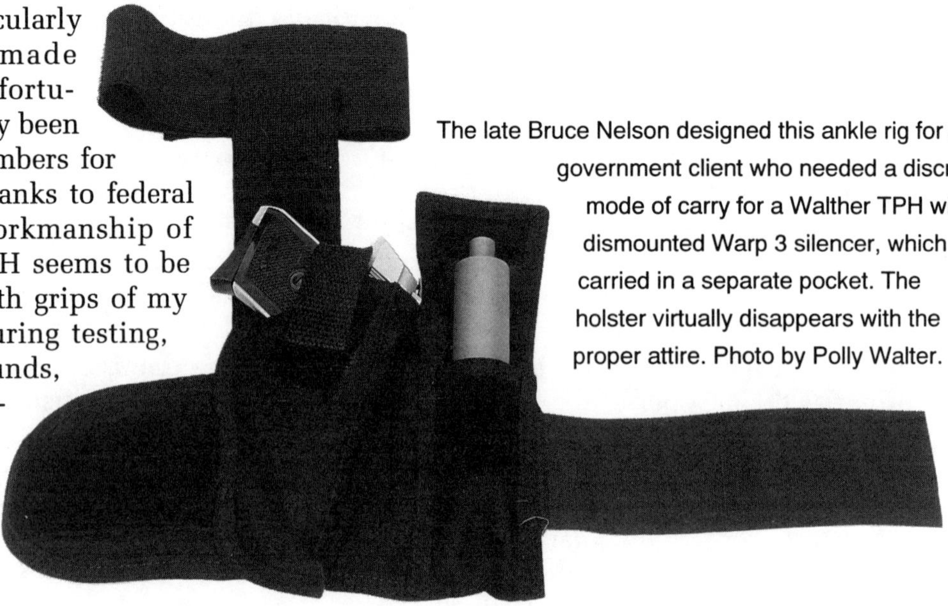

The late Bruce Nelson designed this ankle rig for a government client who needed a discrete mode of carry for a Walther TPH with dismounted Warp 3 silencer, which is carried in a separate pocket. The holster virtually disappears with the proper attire. Photo by Polly Walter.

While I'm not particularly fond of the German-made TPH, it is reliable. Unfortunately, this TPH has only been imported in limited numbers for law-enforcement use thanks to federal legislation, and the workmanship of the American-made TPH seems to be chronically inferior. Both grips of my American TPH split during testing, and after about 650 rounds, the pistol began to produce light primer hits (this seems to be a common problem with the American-made TPH). I returned the TPH to the factory for corrective action, which was effected at no charge. That's the good news. The bad news is that the pistol still delivers light primer hits (misfires) at an alarming rate of approximately 10 to 50 percent, depending on the ammunition being used. The pistol's double-action trigger pull is now a grizzly 13.8 pounds (6.3 kg), while the single-action trigger pull remains a reasonably crisp 25 ounces (0.7 kg). If one does not have access to a German-made TPH, my personal bias is to use a Beretta Model 21. It is interesting that Mossad (Israeli version of the CIA) operatives use .22 caliber Berettas in preference to Walthers.

One correctable cause of light primer hits relates to the special-length barrels (unfortunately, the problem on my TPH is different). It appears that the first batch of barrels were threaded for the German-made TPH, which apparently has a slightly shorter slide than the American-made version. When fitted to an American TPH, the barrel is threaded too far back. Therefore, the suppressor can be screwed on so tightly that the rear of the suppressor mount pushes the slide back very slightly. This may cause the slide to trip the disconnector or alter the geometry so that the hammer doesn't hit the firing pin squarely.

There are two alternative cures. The first option is to chuck the receiver in a lathe and turn down the front of the slide about 0.040 inch (1.02 mm). The second option is to Loctite a custom solid plug into the suppressor to shorten the female threads. The plug is then faced to properly align with the front of the barrel. Finally, a boring bar is used to make a bullet passage. This second cure requires considerable time and skill.

If an individual finds that the rear of the suppressor does not touch the front of the slide, and that the Interarms has failed to cure the problem of light primer hits, then the next logical step is to have a competent gunsmith polish all the springs and relevant surfaces inside the pistol.

Problems with the pistol aside, only one question remained after all the aforementioned testing. What is the relative importance of the Warp 3's internal design versus the use of a liquid coolant? I do realize that the can was designed specifically to use a coolant. I tested the sound signature of the can without any coolant (i.e., dry) to at least get a feel for the liquid's importance. The sound data show that the baffles and environment chambers provide only mediocre performance without a coolant. The coolant reduces the can's sound signature by another 14 to 21 dB when replenished every three rounds.

Clearly, the Warp 3 suppressor provides a lot of performance in a small package. But you must do your part. When using a Walther TPH that provides reliable primer hits, keep your grip firm and a bit low. Keep your gun clean. Keep your powder dry. And keep your suppressor wet. Do your part, and the Warp 3ed Walther works well.

Table 9.7. Sound signatures in decibels of tests on Warp 3 suppressor.

GUN	SUPPRESSOR	COOLANT	FEDERAL HV LR	HANSEN SV LR	RWS SS LR	TEMP., °F (°C)
Walther TPH	None	None	10	159	157	82(28)
Walther TPH	Warp 3	Break Free every 10 shots	135	128	125	82(28)
Walther TPH	Warp 3	Break Free every 3 shots	125	124	122	82(28)
Walther TPH	Warp 3	Water every 3 shots	122	120	120	82(28)
Walther TPH	Warp 3	Urine every 3 shots	123	121	122	82(28)
Walther TPH	Warp 3	None (dry)	143[a]	139[a]	138[a]	82(28)

[a] the first round through a dry suppressor is 2-7 dB louder than the second shot

Table 9.8. Net sound reduction in decibels for Warp 3 suppressor.

GUN	SUPPRESSOR	COOLANT	FEDERAL HV LR	HANSEN SV LR	RWS SS LR	TEMP., °F (°C)
Walther TPH	Warp 3	Break Free every 10 shots	24	29	32	82(28)
Walther TPH	Warp 3	Break Free every 3 shots	34	33	35	82(28)
Walther TPH	Warp 3	Water every 3 shots	37	37	37	82(28)
Walther TPH	Warp 3	Urine every 3 shots	36	36	35	82(28)
Walther TPH	Warp 3	None (dry)	16[a]	18[a]	19[a]	82(28)

Table 9.9. Volumes and sound reductions of various .22 caliber muzzle cans.

SUPPRESSOR	VOLUME, in^3 (cm^3)	SOUND REDUCTION, FEDERAL HV	SOUND REDUCTION, HANSEN SV	SOUND REDUCTION, RWS SS	TEMP., °F(°C)
AWC Warp 3 with Break Free every 3 shots Break Free every 3 shots	2.3 (36)	30	33	36	82(28)
AWC Warp 3 dry	2.3 (36)	16	18	19	82(28)
AWC Archangel	5.9 (93)	24	24	25	82(28)
Vaime A8	7.1 (112)	21	20	25	82(28)

Table 9.10. Bullet velocities in feet per second (and meters per second) with and without Warp 3 suppressor mounted on Walther TPH.

GUN	SUPPRESSOR COOLANT	FEDERAL HV LR	HANSEN SV LR	RWS SS LR	TEMP., °F (°C)	SPEED OF SOUND fps (mps)
Walther TPH	None	985(300)	912(278)	773(236)	82(28)	1,141(348)
Walther TPH	AWC Warp 3 with Break Free every 3 shots	992(302)	927(283)	760(232)	82(28)	1,141(348)

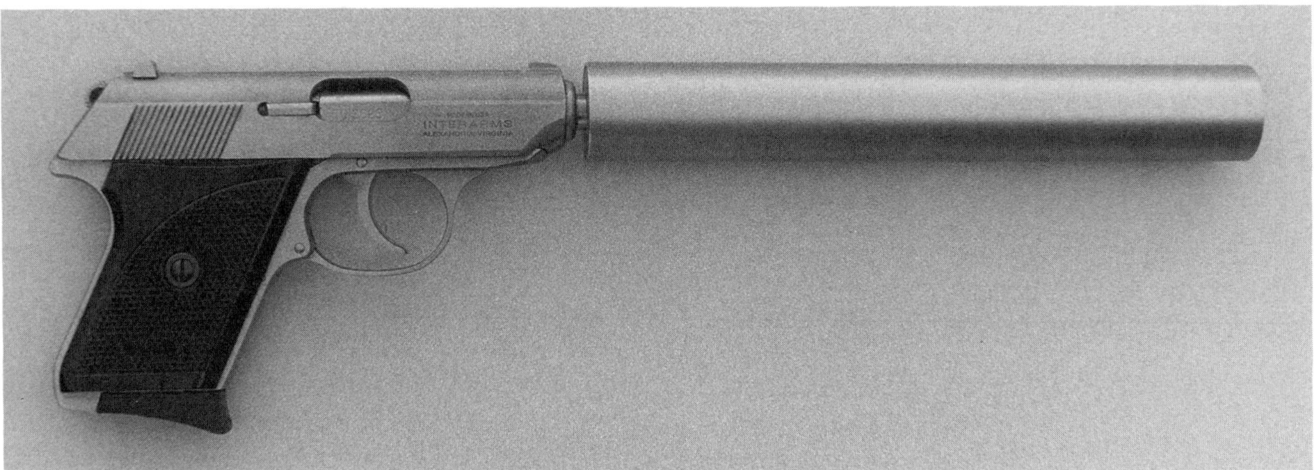

The JR Customs Navy suppressor mounted on a Walther TPH pistol.

The JRC Navy (shown with thread adapter) performs well as a rifle suppressor.

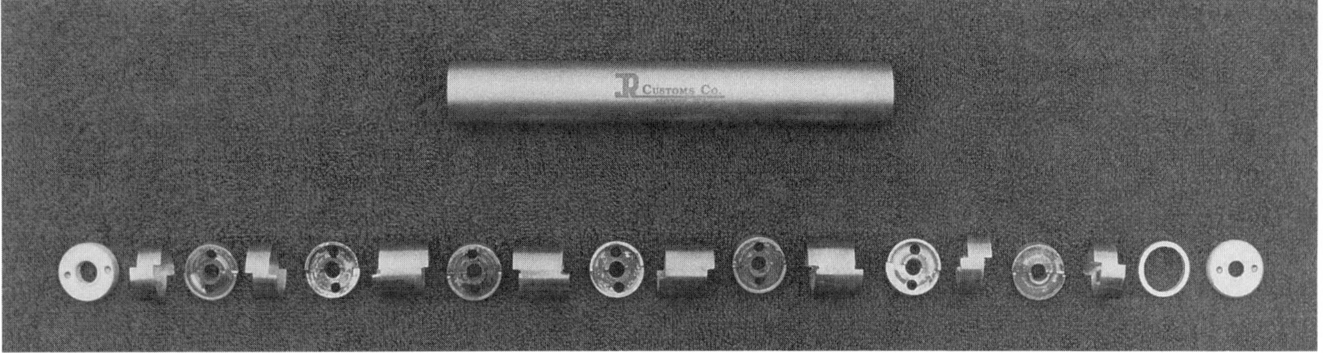

Prototype JRC Navy suppressor disassembled.

Details of Jim Ryan's innovative prototype baffle and spacer design for the JRC Navy suppressor.

JRC NAVY

Jim Ryan of JR Customs initially developed his reputation as a gunsmith, specializing in custom work on the Colt Model 1911 and Browning Hi-Power since 1988. His innovative Bell Collar System replaces the barrel bushing on the Colt 1911 to provide a more durable and accurate pistol. (Brownells marketed the system nationally.) Ryan has also built short-barreled rifles and shotguns, destructive devices, and suppressors. Ryan's three years of experience as a military armorer give his work a practical, no-nonsense edge. This discussion will evaluate the performance of his .22 caliber muzzle can on both a rifle and pistol.

Although the JR Customs Navy suppressor was originally designed as an *artifical environment* pistol can designed to be shot wet, the Navy works well as a rifle suppressor when shot dry. The Navy's sound suppression will be compared to new data on two competing .22 caliber muzzle cans.

The Navy suppressor is constructed entirely out of 304 stainless steel. It is 7.0 inches (17.7 cm) long, 1 inch (2.5 cm) in diameter, and weighs a hefty 12.3 ounces (350 g). The suppressor features seven exotic thick baffles with complex surfaces machined on both sides of each baffle. Two different baffle designs, which are quite different than competing baffles, are employed within each suppressor. Asymmetrical spacers precisely align each baffle and provide variable spacing that is conspicuously different than the appropriate spacing for conventional baffle designs. The sophisticated nature of this suppressor belies Ryan's recent entry into the suppressor field.

In spite of its ample length and weight, the JR Customs Navy suppressor handles surprisingly well on the Walther TPH pistol. Even though the diameter of the can obscures the pistol sights, the Walther's colored inserts allow acceptable shot placement at 15 yards, which is a reasonable effective range for an unsuppressed TPH. Accurate shot placement with the Navy can on the TPH requires that the operator aim with both eyes open, focus on the front sight with the dominant eye, and align the front and rear sights as normal. The bright inserts and stainless suppressor allow the sights to be used in an analogous fashion to an occluded gunsight. This technique will allow consistent shots into the center of mass on a Pepper Popper at 15 yards.

The Navy suppressor handles quite well on a Ruger 77/22 rifle, too. One scarcely notices the extra length or weight.

The performance of the JR Customs Navy suppressor was tested on a Walther TPH pistol and a Ruger 77/22 rifle. Ryan built an adaptor so the 3/8x24 TPI suppressor could be mated to the 1/2x28 TPI rifle barrel. The JRC Navy was also available with 1/2x28 threads for customers who will only use the can on a rifle.

The JRC Navy suppressor tested for this study could be disassembled for cleaning, but subsequently produced cans were sealed units. The complex, asymmetrical baffles and spacers are a very tight fit in the tube, and their complex geometries make reassembly very difficult indeed. Furthermore, the rear end cap on the can tested in this study tended to loosen up after a lot of rounds had heated the tube. Finally, the complex baffles would be very difficult to attack with a bronze brush. Sealing the unit was a reasonable judgment call.

When shot wet with Break Free as designed, maintenance of the sealed suppressor will be simple, since residue tends not to accumulate. Clean the JRC Navy every 2,000 rounds when it is shot wet; clean it every 500 rounds when shot dry. Soak the suppressor in a solvent such as Varsol or Kroil. Hoppe's Number 9 can also be used since the suppressor has no aluminum components. Let soak for two or more days. Drain. Pour some dishwashing detergent and hot water into the central core. Sealing the unit with both hands, shake vigorously for several minutes. Rinse repeatedly with very hot water until no signs of detergent remain. A thin coating of carbon will remain on the inner components, which may function as an acoustic buffer according to one school of thought. Stand the suppressor on its rear end to drain and air dry it, or blow dry with compressed air.

The performance of the JRC Navy suppressor was compared to its primary competitors, the AWC Warp 3 and the AWC Archangel I. The Archangel I was no longer listed in AWC's catalogue at the time of this testing, and the Archangel II had not yet gone into full production.

The Warp 3 was cleaned with Gun Scrubber halogenated solvent and dried for tests in the dry mode. Break Free was added to the rear of the Warp 3 every three shots for tests in the wet mode. The coolant can also be added to the front of the Warp 3 if necessary. The Archangel suppressor was shot dry, as designed.

Prior to testing the JRC Navy suppressor on a rifle and pistol in the dry mode, the suppressor was cleaned thoroughly with Gun Scrubber solvent and dried. Then the can was charged with Break Free for tests in the wet mode. It was charged by inserting the tube from a 16 ounce aerosol can of Break Free into the front of the suppressor and spraying while withdrawing the tube from the suppressor. It was recharged with coolant after every magazine (six rounds).

Three kinds of Long Rifle ammunition were tested: Federal high-velocity, Hansen standard-velocity target, and RWS subsonic. The rifle tests also used Federal CB Longs. More than 1,100 new individual measurements were made while conducting tests on the Navy, Archangel I, and Warp 3 cans.

Initial tests of the JRC Navy suppressor in wet mode demonstrated that results could vary substantially, depending on the consistency of technique when charging the suppressor with Break Free. The learning curve was much longer than with the Warp 3 suppressor, and the tests were repeated using the same kind of ammunition until an optimal and consistent charging technique was developed. These initial data were discarded, and subsequent data are reported here.

The rifle results are summarized in Tables 9.11 through 9.13, and the pistol results are summarized in Tables 9.14 through 9.16 (pages 200-202).

Table 9.11 shows the sound signatures of an unsuppressed Ruger 77/22 and the suppressed signatures using the same rifle with the JRC Navy, AWC Warp 3, and AWC Archangel I suppressors. The Navy and Warp 3 cans provided excellent sound suppression in spite of the fact that they were shot dry (both were designed to be shot wet). The Warp 3 outperformed the outstanding Archangel I with high-velocity and standard-velocity ammo. But the Archangel outperformed the Warp 3 with subsonic LR and CB Longs. Since the Warp 3 was optimized to use the velocity of combustion gases as a suppression tool, these results seem reasonable. The Warp 3 works best with the highest velocity gases.

The JRC Navy suppressor outperformed both AWC suppressors with Long Rifle ammunition. Using CB Longs, the Navy outperformed the Warp 3 and equaled the performance of the Archangel I. The Navy's performance also compares well with an integral suppressor. Ciener's integrally suppressed Marlin 780 bolt-action rifle, for example, produced sound signatures of 124 dB with Federal high-velocity ammo, 121 dB with Hansen standard-velocity, 115 dB with RWS subsonic, and 111 dB with Federal CB Longs at 83 °F. The Marlin's signatures represented net sound reductions of 19, 19, 25, and 23 dB, respectively. Ciener's integrally suppressed Marlin performed well. As Table 9.12 shows, Ryan's Navy muzzle suppressor on the Ruger 77/22 performed even better (except with RWS subsonic ammunition).

Whether comparing the JR Customs Navy with a Ciener integral suppressor or an AWC muzzle can, the JRC Navy suppressor provides excellent performance on a .22 rifle.

Tables 9.14 through 9.16 tell the sound suppression story when the JRC Navy suppressor is mounted on a pistol. The Navy suppressor was quieter than the AWC Warp 3, whether the cans were shot wet or dry. That should not be surprising, since the Navy has much more length and volume. The Warp 3 was specifically engineered to provide the maximum performance in the smallest possible package. In that sense, the Warp 3 had no equal at the time of the testing. Nevertheless, the Navy is noticeably quieter and requires recharging with coolant every six rounds, while the Warp 3 requires recharging with coolant every three rounds for optimal performance.

The Navy suppressor also generated more back pressure than the Warp 3. This increased the pistol's reliability, especially when dirty. The increased back pressure also forced more hot gas and particulates out the ejection port toward the shooter, making eye protection mandatory. When shooting the Navy can wet on the Walther TPH, sooty droplets of Break Free spatter the operator's forearms, torso, and face. Don't wear good clothes. This is the price of outstanding sound suppression on a pocket pistol.

The performance gap between the Navy and Warp 3 widens with lower velocity ammunition. As Table 9.15 shows when both suppressors are shot wet, the net sound reduction of the Navy suppressor is 3 dB better than the Warp 3 with high-velocity ammo, while it is 6 dB better with standard-velocity and subsonic ammo.

The JR Customs Navy suppressor packs powerful performance in a reasonably sized package. As Tables 9.13 and 9.16 show, the Navy suppressor and the other muzzle cans do not adversely affect projectile velocity. This is a conspicuous advantage over integral suppressors with ported barrels. Higher velocity means flatter trajectory, more velocity (better terminal ballistics) for small and medium animals, and a longer effective range.

Another advantage of the JRC Navy is that a single muzzle suppressor may be fitting to a variety of rifles and pistols, which need not be dedicated to suppressed shooting. Thus, for example, one's favorite .22 rifle with trigger job and expensive optics can be used for discreet suppressed shooting, and the suppressor can be removed for hunting. (Again, most states prohibit the use of silencers for the taking of game.)

Table 9.11. Sound signatures in decibels of suppressed and unsuppressed rifles used in JRC Navy tests.

RIFLE	SUPPRESSOR	FEDERAL HV LR	HANSEN SV LR	RWS SS LR	FEDERAL CB LONGS	TEMP., °F (°C)
Ruger 77/22	None	141	139	137	131	64(18)
Ruger 77/22	JRC Navy (dry)	117	114	113	106	64(18)
Ruger 77/22	AWC Warp 3 (dry)	119	117	117	108	64(18)
Ruger 77/22	AWC Archangel I	123	121	115	106	60-64(16-18)

Table 9.12. Net sound reductions of suppressed rifles used in JRC Navy tests, expressed as decibels.

RIFLE	SUPPRESSOR	FEDERAL HV LR	HANSEN SV LR	RWS SS LR	FEDERAL CB LONGS	TEMP., °F (°C)
Ruger 77/22	JRC Navy (dry)	24	25	24	25	64(18)
Ruger 77/22	AWC Warp 3 (dry)	22	22	20	18	64(18)
Ruger 77/22	AWC Archangel I	18	18	22	25	60-64(16-18)

Table 9.13. Muzzle velocities produced by suppressed and unsuppressed rifles used in JRC Navy tests, expressed in feet per second (and meters per second).

RIFLE	SUPPRESSOR	FEDERAL HV LR	HANSEN SV LR	RWS SS LR	FEDERAL CB LONGS	TEMP., °F (°C)	SPEED OF SOUND fps (mps)
Ruger 77/22	None	1,266(386)	1,124(343)	997(304)	647(197)	60(16)	1,118(341)
Ruger 77/22	JRC Navy (dry)	1,237(377)	1,116(340)	986(301)	648(198)	60(16)	1,118(341)
Ruger 77/22	AWC Warp 3 (dry)	1,266(386)	1,128(344)	997(304)	648(198)	60(16)	1,118(341)
Ruger 77/22	AWC Archangel I	1,272(388)	1,133(345)	982(299)	644(196)	64(18)	1,122(342)

Table 9.14. Sound signatures in decibels of suppressed and unsuppressed pistols. Wet suppressors are charged with Break Free.

PISTOL	SUPPRESSOR	FEDERAL HV LR	HANSEN SV LR	RWS SS LR	TEMP., °F (°C)
Walther TPH	None	160	158	157	64(18)
Walther TPH	JRC Navy (wet)	123	119	116	64(18)
Walther TPH	JRC Navy (dry)	137	135	132	64(18)
Walther TPH	None	159	157	157	82(28)
Walther TPH	AWC Warp 3 (wet)	125	124	122	82(28)
Walther TPH	AWC Warp 3 (dry)	143	139	138	82(28)

Table 9.15. Net sound reductions of suppressed pistols used in JRC Navy tests, expressed as decibels.

PISTOL	SUPPRESSOR	FEDERAL HV LR	HANSEN SV LR	RWS SS LR	TEMP., °F (°C)
Walther TPH	JRC Navy (wet)	37	39	41	64(18)
Walther TPH	JRC Navy (dry)	23	23	25	64(18)
Walther TPH	AWC Warp 3 (wet)	34	33	35	82(28)
Walther TPH	AWC Warp 3 (dry)	16	18	19	82(28)

Table 9.16. Muzzle velocities produced by suppressed and unsuppressed pistols used in JRC Navy tests, expressed in feet per second (and meters per second).

PISTOL	SUPPRESSOR	FEDERAL HV LR	HANSEN SV LR	RWS SS LR	TEMP., °F (°C)	SPEED OF SOUND, fps (mps)
Walther TPH	None	948(289)	878(268)	724(221)	64(18)	1,122(342)
Walther TPH	JRC Navy (wet)	967(295)	867(264)	678(207)	64(18)	1,122(342)
Walther TPH	JRC Navy (dry)	966(294)	875(267)	722(220)	64(18)	1,122(342)
Walther TPH	None	985(300)	912(278)	773(236)	82(28)	1,141(348)
Walther TPH	AWC Warp 3 (dry)	992(302)	927(283)	760(232)	82(28)	1,141(348)

About the time that Jim Ryan began developing suppressors of innovative design, another new designer appeared—this time out of Michigan's aerospace industry. Greg Latka brought unprecedented skills to the suppressor industry in the realms of engineering, exotic materials, and fabrication processes. Several problems that had stumped two of the best designers in the business, for example, Latka described in all modesty as "no-brainers" and immediately solved them himself. His suppressor designs are based on a unique and patented approach that he calls the helical free-flow suppressor.

HELICAL FREE-FLOW SUPPRESSOR

Gregory S. Latka, general manager of an aerospace company, is one of the most recent players to enter the arena of suppressor design. In 1989 and 1990, Latka developed a unique and promising

The helical free-flow suppressor mounted on the Intratec TEC-22 pistol, which comes from the factory with a threaded barrel and thread protector.

Latka's suppressor came in a fitted oak case with two extra mounts and a hex wrench for installing the suppressor on the Calico M-100P pistol.

approach to sound suppression, which he calls the helical free-flow suppressor. The first commercial offering based on Latka's Patent Number 5,029,512 was a .22 rimfire suppressor from GSL Technology, Inc. Called the 7/8 Slimline, this muzzle can has a small diameter (7/8 inch), permitting the use of iron sights on a host of rifles and pistols that have not been practical to suppress until now.

Greg Latka is a second-generation engineer. His father worked on the Manhattan Project during World War II and started the family business in 1950. The company began making hose fittings for a wide variety of military and civilian applications, and then began to specialize in high-tech projects for aerospace applications, large weapons systems, and the nuclear navy. Greg joined the company in 1968 as an entry-level laborer at the age of 16 and worked his way up; he now runs the company with his older brother.

The Latka organization has worked on an impressive list of projects. They have produced components for jet fighters and bombers, including the F111, F4, F14, F15, F16, F18, and the B1 bomber. They've worked on such military helicopters as the CH-47 Chinook, AH-64 Apache, Sikorsky Blackhawk, and Cobra gunship. They've also contributed to ground systems, including the M1A1 Abrams tank, Bradley Fighting Vehicle, M60 tank, and M109 howitzer. Other military projects include Sparton electronics sonobuoys, components for the Tomahawk cruise missile, level one components for nuclear submarines, the Patriot missile, and more. They've also contributed to NASA's Gemini and Apollo projects and the Space Shuttle. All Boeing wide-bodied commercial airliners incorporate their products as well. Clearly, the Latka organization has a demonstrated record of producing high-tech products for the most demanding applications. While the Latka name is a new one in suppressor design, it is obvious that he is no shade-tree wannabee.

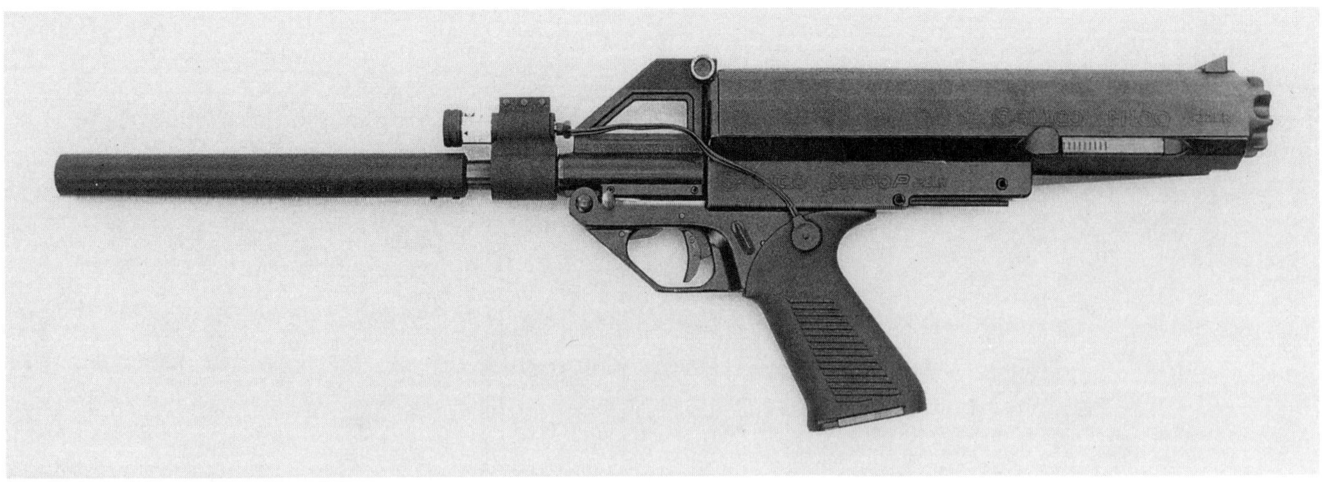

The helical free-flow suppressor mounted on a Calico M-100P pistol.

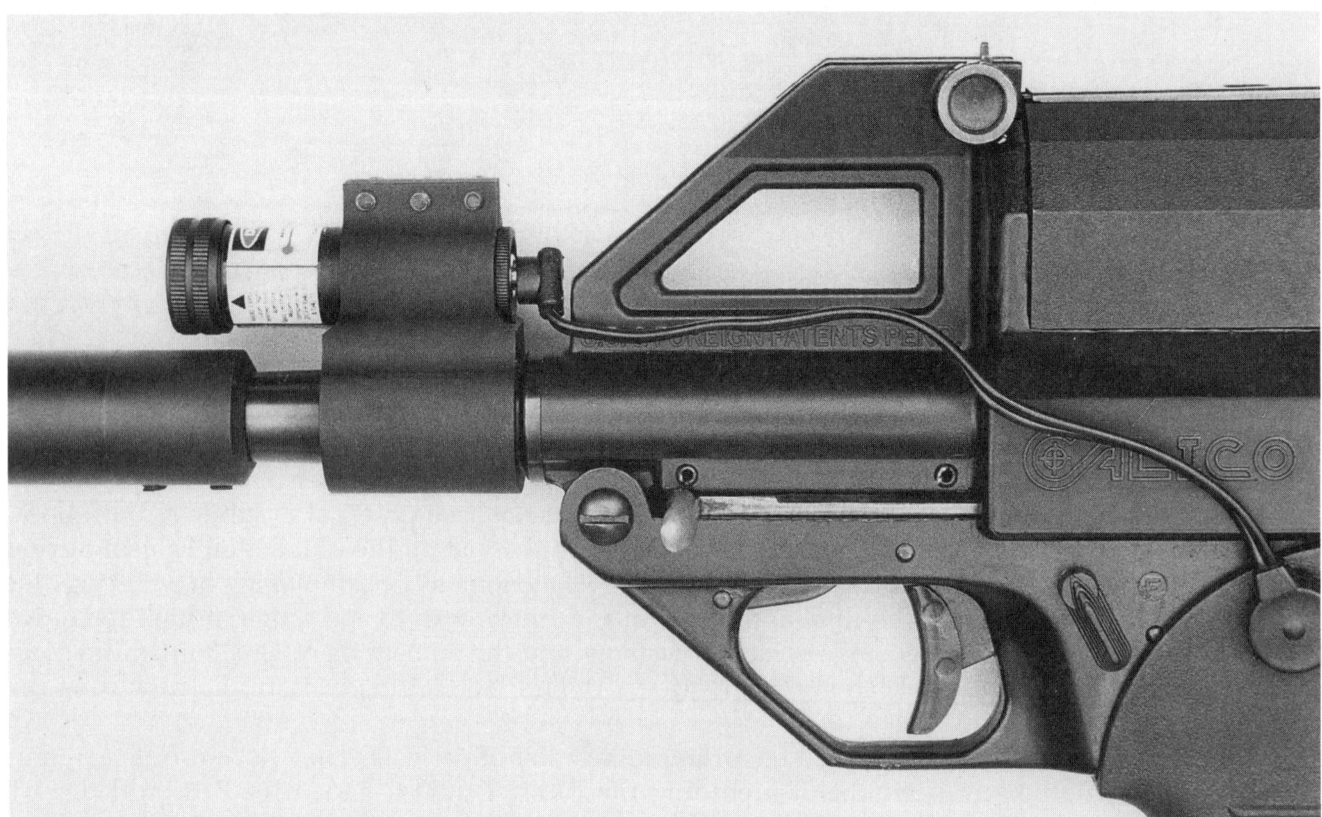

Latka's proprietary laser mount transforms the Calico M-100P pistol from a technical curiosity with almost unusable open sights into an effective system capable of rapid target acquisition and accurate shot placement.

Design

I asked Greg Latka how his helical free-flow suppressor differs from previous designs. "The traditional approach to building a suppressor," Latka said, "has been a baffle design, a mesh design, or a variation of either. The newer designs use a liquid to aid cooling [of the combustion gases]. My suppressors are designed to be used dry.

"All previous concepts use a theme of containment. The gases expand and then contract over and over and over again. The problem with these designs is that if the tube is 8 inches long, then the gases have only an 8-inch distance to travel.

"With my design using the free-flow helical baffle," Latka continued, "a substantial portion of the gases go into a spiraling movement around the outside of the baffles until they have expelled their energy. By stacking the baffles and sheering off the gases as they pass, the gas path becomes about 40 inches in our .22 rimfire suppressor. The suppressor design can be tuned for particular cartridges by carefully calculating groove widths, angles of attack, and baffle length."

Here's how Latka's helical free-flow suppressor works. As the bullet just emerges from the barrel and enters the suppressor, the combustion gases expand into the expansion chamber and start to travel through the diffuser. Meanwhile, a small portion of the gases travel around the bullet and start down the center hole of the suppressor *in front of the bullet*.

Latka's patented conical baffles incorporate a helical groove machined into their outer edge, which forms a spiral passage between the baffles and the inner surface of the suppressor tube. As the bullet enters the helical baffles, the gases deflected by the diffuser start to spiral around the outside of the baffles, while the rest of the gases follow the bullet down the central passage of the suppressor. Each baffle shears off more gas from the main gas stream behind the bullet.

When the bullet reaches the end of the baffle stack, a deflector captures a portion of the main gas jet following the bullet and—at least in theory—redirects these gases back down the outer helix toward the gases spiraling forward between the tube and the baffle stack. This produces pressure fronts traveling in opposite directions in the outer helix. When opposing pressure waves meet head-on, one of two things will happen. If the waves have the same amount of energy, they will cancel each other out. If they have dissimilar energy content, the lesser wave will diminish the amount of energy in the more powerful wave. In practice, I do not believe than this counterflow in the outer spiral improves suppressor performance significantly. The key is how effectively the suppressor diverts a portion of the combustion gases into the outer spiral as soon as the gases enter the suppressor.

As the bullet passes through the deflector, it enters a chamber between the deflector and the front end cap. A machined surface inside the front end cap captures a final portion of the main gas jet and reflects it backward. The bullet exits the suppressor. The gases spiraling through the outer helix do not exit the suppressor until "long after" the bullet has left. This delay is especially noticeable in Latka's suppressor for the 5.56x45mm cartridge. The suppressor produces a slight puff of smoke a second or so after the weapon has fired, when it appears that the gases following the outer helix finally exit the system.

Latka's 7/8 Slimline suppressor is 7.875 inches (200 mm) long, 0.875 inch (22 mm) in diameter, and weighs 4.25 ounces (120 grams). The tube is 2024 aluminum, and the 13 baffles are machined from a proprietary aluminum that stands up to the stress imposed by hot combustion gases. All aluminum components are finished with matte black anodizing. The diffuser at the rear of the suppressor is 303 stainless steel, and 304 stainless steel is used for the rear spacer that both locks the baffle stack in place and reinforces the expansion chamber. Flawless knurling on the shoulder of the rear end cap both facilitates removing the mount and adds an attractive counterpoint to the classy appearance of this suppressor. Knurling on a complex surface also hints at Latka's technical prowess in the machine shop.

Maintenance

The helical free-flow suppressor (HFFS) should be cleaned every 500 to 1,000 rounds. Remove the rear end cap and immerse the unit overnight in any solvent that does not react with aluminum (therefore, avoid Hoppe's No. 9). After soaking, shake the can thoroughly to dislodge any loose particles and drain. Flush with very hot soapy water, shake vigorously, and drain. Rinse with very hot water and then blow the suppressor dry. Apply a high-temperature antiseize compound (colloidal molybdenum or copper compounds work best) to the threads of the rear end cap and screw the mount back into the tube.

Six kinds of Long Rifle ammunition were tested: Federal high-velocity, Hansen standard-velocity target, RWS subsonic, Winchester subsonic, Baikal JUNIOR Steel subsonic, and Eley subsonic. Rifles were also tested with Federal CB Longs. I tested the helical free-flow suppressor on the Ruger 77/22 and the Walther TPH, which I traditionally use as the test firearms for evaluating .22 caliber muzzle cans. I also tested the helical free-flow suppressor on the Intratec TEC-22 pistol and test fired the suppressor on the Calico M-100P pistol.

Performance

Pistol and rifle sound signatures are listed in Tables 9.17 and 9.19, respectively. Net sound reductions are shown in Tables 9.18 and 9.20 (see pages 208-209). Selected projectile velocities are compared in Table 9.21.

Latka's HFFS demonstrated a net sound reduction of 25 dB with high-velocity ammunition in the Walther TPH pistol, while the can produced a 19 dB reduction on the Ruger 77/22 rifle. These data suggest that the suppressor works best with higher velocity gases, so the helical free-flow design should prove to be especially effective when applied to centerfire applications like the 5.56x45, 7.62x51, and .50 caliber BMG.

Performance of Latka's suppressor on the TPH did not match the performance of the AWC Warp 3 or the JR Customs suppressors. But then Latka's can is designed to be shot *dry* rather than wet, so one would not expect the HFFS to perform as well. It is relevant to point out that the HFFS on the TPH was just as quiet as the legendary Dater RST suppressed Ruger Mark II and the silenced OSS HD-MS with high-velocity ammunition, so the HFFS is quiet enough for even tactical applications. It permits completely unobstructed use of the TPH sights, which is a real treat. And, best of all, the shooter doesn't get peppered with particulates and nasty coolants that plague the shooters of special environment suppressors. There is less back pressure and no gunk to be blown back into the shooter's face, arms, and torso. While the HFFS may be too long for covert carry, the suppressor's amazingly light weight and small diameter make the can seem to disappear when shooting. At last there is a way to have good, *clean* fun shooting a suppressed TPH.

In spite of the suppressor's significantly reduced diameter, Latka's HFFS produced a net sound reduction that was within 1 or 2 dB of the AWC Archangel I when mounted on the Ruger 77/22. Frankly, this surprised me. The unusually small diameter of Latka's .22 suppressor gives it only 76 percent of the volume of the same can built with the traditional 1.0 inch tubing. That's a lot less room to make things happen. The HFFS is 0.85 inch (22 mm) longer than the Archangel I, but it still has only 86 percent of the Archangel's gross volume. So performing within a decibel or two of the Archangel can only be described as impressive performance. Furthermore, some adult shooters cannot detect a 1 dB difference in suppressed sound signatures.

The HFFS on the TEC-22 was much louder than the AWC Amphibian with its integral suppressor, but Table 9.21 shows that the suppressed TEC-22 delivers much more velocity (and therefore better penetration) than the Amphibian. For those applications requiring maximum velocity using a suppressed .22 pistol, use of the HFFS should be considered. I would like to see Latka's design applied to a better pistol than the TEC-22 for serious applications, however.

One final point does not show up in the data. The HFFS seems to produce a somewhat lower peak frequency than many muzzle cans, making the sound signature seem slightly quieter to my ear than the meter reading would suggest. Thus it provides world-class performance while providing such a small diameter that the sights are still fully visible on a Walther TPH or a Rossi 62SA takedown pump rifle.

Conclusions

Greg Latka's helical free-flow suppressor is a world-class performer. The 7/8 Slimline produces a sound signature on the Ruger 77/22 that is almost indistinguishable from the AWC Archangel I, which has long been a particular favorite of mine. The HFFS is even more effective as a pistol suppressor since it works best with high-velocity gases. It is not as quiet as an artificial environment can, but its lack of messy coolants makes it much more suitable for sporting applications. The suppressor's unusually small diameter permits mounting on a host of rifles and pistols that have not been practical to suppress until now if one wanted to use the firearm's iron sights. Finally, the workmanship is what one would expect from a successful aerospace company.

The helical free-flow suppressor should hold great promise for reducing the size and weight of suppressors for centerfire rifle cartridges. Latka's design will probably realize its greatest potential when applied to .50 caliber BMG sniper rifles.

Table 9.17. Sound signatures in decibels of suppressed and unsuppressed pistols.

PISTOL	SUPPRESSOR	FEDERAL HV LR	HANSEN SV LR	WINCHESTER SS LR	RWS SS LR	ELEY SS LR	TEMP., °F (°C)
Walther TPH	None	158	156	155	156	155	76(24)
Walther TPH	GSL 7/8 Slimline	132	127	126	125	125	76(24)
Walther TPH	None	157	156	156	—	—	84(29)
Walther TPH	JRC LDES (recharged every 6 rounds)	126	124	123	—	—	84(29)
Walther TPH	None	160	158	—	157	—	64(18)
Walther TPH	JRC Navy (recharged every 6 rounds)	123	119	—	116	—	64(18)
Walther TPH	None	159	157	—	157	—	82(28)
Walther TPH	AWC Warp 3 (recharged every 3 rounds)	125	124	—	122	—	82(28)
TEC-22	None	158	156	—	155	155	75(24)
TEC-22	GSL 7/8 Slimline	133	130	—	128	128	75(24)
Ruger MK II	None	156	154	—	153	—	74(23)
Ruger MK II	AWC Amphibian	123	119	—	114	—	74(23)

Table 9.18. Net sound reductions of suppressed pistols, expressed as decibels.

PISTOL	SUPPRESSOR	FEDERAL HV LR	HANSEN SV LR	WINCHESTER SS LR	RWS SS LR	ELEY SS LR	TEMP., °F (°C)
Walther TPH	GSL 7/8 Slimline	25	26	27	28	27	76(24)
Walther TPH	JRC LDES (recharged every 6 rounds)	31	32	33	—	—	84(29)
Walther TPH	JRC Navy (recharged every 6 rounds)	37	39	—	41	—	64(18)
Walther TPH	AWC Warp 3) (recharged every 3 rounds	34	33	—	35	—	82(28)
TEC-22	GSL 7/8 Slimline	25	26	27	28	27	75(24)
Ruger MK II	AWC Amphibian	33	35	—	39	—	74(23)

Table 9.19. Sound signatures in decibels of suppressed and unsuppressed rifles.

RIFLE	SUPPRESSOR	FEDERAL HV LR	HANSEN SV LR	BAIKAL JS SS LR	ELEY SS LR	RWS SS LR	FEDERAL CB LONGS	TEMP., °F (°C)
Ruger 77/22	None	141	137	138	136	—	131	82(28)
Ruger 77/22	GSL 7/8 Slimline	122	119	115	114	—	109	82(28)
Ruger 77/22	AWC Archangel I	120	120	114	113	—	104	82(28)
Ruger 77/22	None	142	139	—	—	138[a]	131	84(29)
Ruger 77/22	JRC LDES (dry)	128	125	—	—	123[a]	113	84(29)
Ruger 77/22	None	141	139	—	—	137	131	64(18)
Ruger 77/22	JRC Navy (dry)	117	114	—	—	113	106	64(18)
Ruger 77/22	AWC Warp 3 (dry)	119	117	—	—	117	108	64(18)

[a] Winchester Subsonic LR

Table 9.20. Net sound reductions of suppressed rifles, expressed as decibels.

RIFLE	SUPPRESSOR	FEDERAL HV LR	HANSEN SV LR	BAIKAL JS SS LR	ELEY SS LR	RWS SS LR	FEDERAL CB LONGS	TEMP., °F (°C)
Ruger 77/22	GSL 7/8 Slimline	19	19	23	22	—	23	82(28)
Ruger 77/22	AWC Archangel I	21	17	24	23	—	28	82(28)
Ruger 77/22	JRC LDES (dry)	14	14	—	—	15	18[a]	84(29)
Ruger 77/22	JRC Navy (dry)	24	25	—	—	24	25	64(18)
Ruger 77/22	AWC Warp 3 (dry)	22	22	—	—	20	18	64(18)

[a] Winchester Subsonic LR

Table 9.21. Velocities of suppressed and unsuppressed firearms expressed in feet per second (and meters per second), temperature, and speed of sound.

PISTOL	SUPPRESSOR	FEDERAL HV LR	HANSEN SV LR	RWS SS LR	TEMP., °F (°C)	SPEED OF SOUND, fps (mps)
Ruger MK II	None	1,090(332)	1,043(318)	858(262)	74(23)	1,133(345)
Ruger MK II	AWC Amphibian	873(266)	872(266)	680(207)	74(23)	1,133(345)
TEC-22	GSL 7/8 Slimline	1,031(314)	953(290)	927(283)[a]	75(24)	1,134(346)

[a] Winchester Subsonic LR

CALICO M-100P PISTOL

The Calico M-100P pistol certainly has an innovative design. Constructed largely with polymers, the pistol features a barrel length of 6 inches (152 mm) and an overall length of 17.9 inches (455 mm). The M-100P weighs 3.06 pounds (1.39 kg) empty and 3.75 pounds (1.70 kg) with a fully loaded magazine. Its best feature is its detachable helical-feed, 100-round magazine. Although the pistol comes with a black magazine, with two windows in top to crudely monitor the number of remaining rounds, a clear magazine is also available that allows constant monitoring of the magazine contents.

The loading procedure of the Calico magazine is worth mentioning, since this is the heart of the pistol and since the procedure is not entirely intuitive. Begin by depressing the twin latches near the rear of the receiver and lift the magazine from the pistol. Now push the button at the rear center of the magazine to release its spring tension for reloading. Begin to insert rounds into the feed lips under the front of the magazine. Spring tension will gradually increase to the point where inserting rounds becomes difficult. Simply push the button at the rear of the magazine to release this tension as necessary (this procedure will be necessary several times when loading 100 rounds). When the magazine is full, release the spring tension a final time. Now crank the spring 15 revolutions to tension the magazine for proper feeding.

While the pistol's magazine is interesting, the Calico M-100P has two serious flaws: substantial weight and almost worthless sights. For my eyesight, the sights are a fatal flaw, so I never took the M-100P pistol seriously until Latka designed a proprietary mount to mate the Tasco Model LP-2 laser sight to the pistol. Suddenly the Calico became capable of rapid target acquisition and accurate shot placement. Whether firing from a Weaver stance or the more comfortable assault position (due to the Calico's weight), the M-100P could rapidly hit a series of pop cans as long as the laser was not employed in full daylight when the laser dot is not visible. Combined with Latka's helical free-flow suppressor, the laser-sighted Calico proved to be a great tool for eliminating rats and snakes in the barn. The laser also worked well outdoors around dusk, which is a good time to hunt rats at the local dump. Finally, the laser-sighted, suppressed Calico might make a viable home defense weapon for the untrained individual who doesn't tolerate a lot of noise and recoil.

INTRATEC TEC-22 PISTOL

The Intratec TEC-22 is a largely polymer pistol. It features a 4 inch (102 mm) barrel, an overall length of 11.2 inches (284 mm), and a 30-round Ruger-compatible magazine. The TEC-22 weighs 31.2 ounces (885 grams) with an empty magazine. The polymer pistol grip includes a storage compartment, and the pistol handles surprisingly well in spite of the forward weight provided by a loaded magazine.

The worst feature of the TEC-22 is the very stiff ambidextrous safety. The shooter must shift the grip of the firing hand in order to move the safety from S to F. The nonfiring hand must be used to move the safety to the SAFE position. Another idiosyncrasy is that care must be taken to rock the magazine forward after insertion and latching to ensure that its feed lips align properly with the bolt. This motion quickly becomes second nature.

The Intratec's best features are its large-capacity magazine and the fact that the barrel comes threaded from the factory with a knurled thread protector, making the TEC-22 a natural candidate for adding a muzzle can. The suppressed TEC-22 provides substantially more velocity than an integrally suppressed Ruger pistol (since the Ruger barrel is ported), which translates into much more hitting power when shooting reactive targets like falling plates or when using the pistol for animal control. The suppressed TEC-22 is capable of delivering 2 inch groups at 25 yards.

The Classic Ultralight system handles extremely well, in spite of the fact that I was prepared to dislike the little Chinese scope mounted on the rifle tested for this study. Here, Mark White prepares to fire his creation.

SOUND TECHNOLOGY HYBRIDS

The muzzle suppressors currently manufactured by Sound Technology are permanently attached to the barrel. When fitted to a Ruger 10/22 or 77/22, a suppressor/barrel assembly can be swapped with a conventional unsuppressed barrel in less than three minutes, allowing the shooter to discretely target practice and eliminate pests with the suppressed barrel and then use an unsuppressed barrel for hunting or other applications where a suppressor may not be legal or otherwise desirable. Traditionally, Sound Technology has used six ports near the muzzle to vent combustion gases into the rear of the suppressor. Dale Blaylock builds superficially similar systems, which he refers to as "integrated" suppressors. Mark White calls his systems "hybrid" suppressors since they represent a cross-pollination of features found in both the integral suppressor and muzzle can.

This discussion will evaluate the performance of conventional and hybrid suppressors built by Sound Technology for both the Ruger 77/22 and 10/22. As part of his continuing R&D, White produced a smaller, more conventional suppressor without barrel porting and a larger diameter suppressor with barrel porting. These systems were evaluated as well—with some surprising results. During the course of these tests, we also discovered some larger issues relating to both suppression and accuracy.

When mounted on a Ruger 77/22, the Standard Model hybrid suppressor from Sound Technology provides similar sound reduction to the AWC Archangel I muzzle suppressor when using high-velocity and standard-velocity LR ammunition.

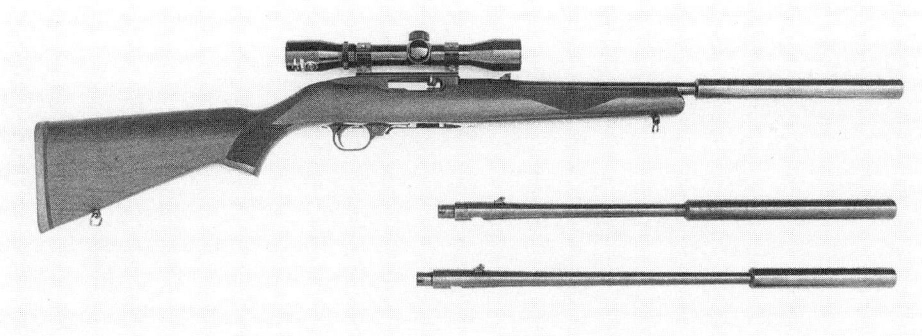

The muzzle cans and hybrid suppressors manufactured by Sound Technology are permanently attached to dedicated barrels, which can be swapped with a factory original barrel in less than three minutes.

Both hybrid and conventional muzzle cans share the aforementioned benefits over integral suppressors. But the hybrid system (with its two-point mount) and the Baikal Classic suppressor/barrel assembly (with its permanently fused suppressor mount) also have some advantages over the muzzle can, especially in terms of alignment, strength, and accuracy.

There is a cost benefit, too. Since White designs his hybrid suppressed barrels so they drop into unmodified rifle stocks, the hybrid suppressor is a tidy and cost-effective alternative to permanently altering a rifle and stock or sending a barrel to a manufacturer for precision threading and refinishing for a conventional muzzle can. Essentially, the owner ends up with two barrels at no extra cost.

A permanently attached suppressor with dedicated barrel avoids potential alignment problems associated with screw-on muzzle cans. Alignment problems have two common origins: 1) poor initial alignment, and 2) degraded alignment as the suppressor unscrews during firing.

Poor initial alignment frequently occurs by simply aligning the suppressor on the barrel threads rather than aligning on matching shoulders on the barrel and suppressor, which are perpendicular to the bore. This is a simple design problem, one that was solved by the Maxim Silent Firearms Company in 1909. Nevertheless, poor initial alignment is commonly encountered in both Europe and the United States, especially when working with inexperienced or lackadaisical manufacturers or machinists. Another cause of initial misalignment is threading that is not concentric with the bore. Since few barrels have a bore that lies in the true center of barrel throughout its length, getting the baffles of a suppressor to align properly with a bore can be a challenge. Ruger barrels are particularly challenging in terms of concentricity.

A colleague in France suggested to me that most muzzle cans align so poorly with their barrel bores that bullets graze baffles more often than not, and this adversely affects accuracy. He test-fired many rimfire and centerfire suppressors (mounted on rifles and pistols) into a swimming pool and recovered the bullets. Striations and gouges on recovered bullets clearly showed that the projectiles did indeed contact the suppressor of most European systems he tested. I have repeated his experiments in the United States and discovered that this is a much more serious problem than I ever would have believed. Bullet contact is most likely to occur if the suppressor unscrews during firing, if the suppressor aligns only on the barrel threads, or if the barrel threading is not concentric with the bore. When White did offer conventional, screw-on muzzle cans, he used tapered pipe threads. "This type of thread has several advantages," White says. "Tapered pipe threads are self-aligning and they automatically compensate for wear, while parallel threads do not. The only problem with using pipe threads is that a special jig is required to provide accurate alignment on a tapered barrel."

Alignment of muzzle suppressors can degrade during use. Muzzle cans commonly loosen during firing because of the torque generated when a bullet travels down a barrel's rifling. Since most rifling is right-handed and suppressors are normally mounted with right-hand threads, the torque caused by each bullet makes the barrel act rather like an impact wrench. The barrel twists slightly, while the inertia of the suppressor causes it to resist twisting too. Thus, the barrel tends to unscrew from the suppressor. Heavier suppressors have more inertia, so they seem to loosen more quickly than lighter suppressors. This problem is worse with centerfire rifle suppressors, centerfire pistol-caliber suppressors, suppressors with coarse threading, and suppressors subjected to full-auto fire. While by no means common with rimfire cartridges since they produce relatively little torque, this problem can be experienced with rimfire suppressors as well.

When a barrel has right-hand rifling, simply using left-hand threads to mount the muzzle suppressor would eliminate this problem, although a sound suppressor may self-tighten beyond the point of easy removal. Another solution, which White now employs with his muzzle cans, is to permanently attach the suppressor to its barrel with low-temperature silver solder.

An additional benefit of permanently attaching the suppressor to the barrel is that the suppressor's tolerances can be a lot tighter, since loosening from the barrel and even thread wear need not be factored into the design. As we'll see, however, tight tolerances in the size of the aperture in the suppressor's front end cap may or may not be a virtue in terms of sound suppression.

Five rather different suppressor systems were tested to determine their performance in terms of velocity and sound suppression.

A Ruger 10/22 fitted with ST Standard Model suppressor, which did not provide better performance than the shorter Baikal Classic can.

Suppressor Systems Tested

One conventional and one hybrid system were tested on the Ruger 10/22, and three different systems were tested on the Ruger 77/22. All were constructed of 4130 steel and blued to match the finish of factory barrels.

Barrel changing is greatly facilitated by using a hex wrench with a ball head on one end. This greatly speeds removing the screws once they've been loosened. Rutland Tool & Supply Company (6630 Roxburgh, Suite 100, Houston, TX 77041-5200) sells a nice set of Allen Ball End L-Keys, Model 2332-0802, for $12.40 plus shipping. White recommends that both hex screws be tightened to exactly the same amount of torque to provide the maximum accuracy potential of the barrel. He typically uses 36 inch-pounds. If one does not have a suitable torque wrench, a field-expedient solution is to pull the end of a 4 inch hex wrench with a trigger gage until it reads 9 pounds. *Overtightening these hex screws can split the steel key that holds the barrel in place!*

The 10/22 Standard Model hybrid system features a 16.1 inch (40.9 cm) barrel. The suppressor (serial number MC467) is 9.7 inches (24.6 cm) long and 1.0 inch (2.5 cm) in diameter. The suppressed barrel is 21.1 inches (53.6 cm) long including the can, has six ports near the muzzle that vent into the rear of the suppressor, and weighs 2.0 pounds (0.9 kg). An unsuppressed factory 10/22 barrel with sights is 18.5 inches (47.0 cm) long and weighs 28.7 ounces (813 grams). When installed on a 10/22 with factory walnut stock, the suppressed rifle is 37.0 inches (94.0 cm) long and weighs 5.6 pounds (2.5 kg) without scope.

A smaller suppressor is used in the other muzzle suppressor/barrel system tested on the Ruger 10/22. Called the Baikal Classic Muzzle Can, this system is designed to provide optimal performance with the inexpensive and very accurate Russian Baikal Junior Brass .22 LR ammo in the 10/22 rifle. The Baikal Classic features a 16.1 inch (41.0 cm) barrel that is not ported. The suppressor is 6.7 inches (17.0 cm) long and 1.0 inch (2.5 cm) in diameter. The suppressor/barrel assembly weighs 2.13 pounds (0.97 kg).

The Baikal Classic tested in this study (serial number MC260) was actually part of a custom rifle system available from Sound Technology as a stock item. Called the Classic Ultralight Match Rifle, the system was actually designed as a field gun. The customized rifle includes both a trigger job and an action job. The trigger on the test specimen produced an incredibly crisp break at 34 ounces (964 grams), and a specially designed trigger stop eliminated overtravel. This was the best trigger job I've yet experienced on a 10/22. The barrel is shortened and crowned, its bore is lapped and polished, and a small Baikal Classic suppressor is permanently attached.

The barreled action is fitted to a black Butler Creek polymer stock that—contrary to advertised specifications—has a shorter length of pull (13.6 inches, 34.6 cm) than the factory stock (13.8 inches, 34.9 cm). The stock's slimmer pistol grip includes dual palm swells and molded diamond checkering. The stock also features a textured nonglare, nonslip finish, as well as a recoil pad and sling swivel studs. The only criticism I have of the stock is that the recoil pads are typically askew.

White removes the pads, drills slightly larger holes, and properly aligns them, holding them in place with both epoxy and screws. The Butler Creek stock weighs 1.4 pounds (630 grams), while a factory birch stock weighs about 1.6 pounds (726 grams), depending on wood density and moisture content. The Classic Ultralight Match Rifle has an overall length of 40.3 inches (102.2 cm) and a weight of 5.9 pounds (2.7 kg) with the scope installed.

White completes the package by installing a black nylon sling, 1 inch (2.5 cm) dovetail base, solid aluminum rings, and a compact Chinese 4x20 scope. He then test fires the system for function and accuracy, making any adjustments that may be necessary until the suppressed rifle is both reliable and accurate.

The design of the Baikal Classic suppressor was developed as part of a tedious empirical testing program. Testing alternative designs using White's technology of interspersed mesh and baffles has proved that the dimensions on the Baikal Classic suppressor are critical. Normally, the design of a muzzle suppressor for a .22 rimfire rifle is the most forgiving of suppressor design problems. Yet changing such seemingly trivial things as the thicknesses of the front and rear end caps by a few percent noticeably degrades performance, not to mention changing the dimensions of the chambers inside the can. Even barrel length affects performance noticeably. A 16.1 inch (40.9 cm) barrel provides the best performance in terms of sound suppression with the Baikal Classic system.

This also seems to be the optimal barrel length in terms of barrel harmonics and vibration nodes when fitted with the Baikal Classic Muzzle Can. Neither factory-original 18.5 inch (47.0 cm) barrels nor barrels shortened to 14.0 inches (35.6 cm) seem to deliver comparable accuracy. White's experimental tenacity has paid some dividends in the performance of the Classic Ultralight Match Rifle, as we'll see in the following discussion on the performance of the various hybrid suppressors now being discussed.

The 77/22 Standard Model hybrid system features a 16.1 inch (40.9 cm) barrel. The suppressor (serial number MC447) is 9.2 inches (23.3 cm) long and 1.0 inch (2.5 cm) in diameter. The suppressor/barrel assembly is 21.0 inches (53.3 cm) long including the can, has six ports near the muzzle that vent into the rear of the suppressor, and weighs 37.4 ounces (1,058 grams). An unsuppressed factory 77/22 barrel without sights is 20.0 inches (50.8 cm) long and weighs 28.2 ounces (799 grams). When installed on a 77/22 with factory American walnut stock, the suppressed rifle is 40.4 inches (102.7 cm) long and weighs 7.7 pounds (3.5 kg) with Shepherd 2.5-7.5 power auto-ranging rimfire scope. An unsuppressed rifle with Shepherd scope is 39.75 inches (101.0 cm) long and weighs 6.8 pounds (3.1 kg).

Another variant (serial number MC453) was tested that was identical in all respects to the 77/22 Standard Model except that the hole in the front end cap was 0.306 inch (7.77 mm) instead of 0.264 inch (6.71 mm) that White normally uses in his .22 caliber suppressors.

Finally, a longer hybrid of larger diameter was also tested on the Ruger 77/22. This Large Experimental Model suppressor (serial number MC454) featured a 16.1 inch (40.9 cm) barrel. The suppressor is 10.0 inches (25.4 cm) long and 1.25 inch (3.2 cm) in diameter. The suppressed barrel is 21.7 inches (55.2 cm) long including the can, has six ports near the muzzle that vent into the rear of the suppressor, and weighs 2.2 pounds (1.0 kg). When installed on a 77/22 with factory polymer stock, the suppressed rifle is 40.3 inches (104.8 cm) long and weighs 7.1 pounds (3.2 kg) with 0.7 pound (0.3 kg) 6x42 Tasco scope.

Suppressed and unsuppressed Ruger 10/22s and 77/22s were tested using Federal Hi-Power high-velocity LR, Hansen standard-velocity target LR, Baikal Junior Brass subsonic LR, and Federal CB Long ammunition.

Performance

Sound signatures are shown in Table 9.22, and the net sound reductions are shown in Table 9.23. Muzzle velocities are shown in Table 9.24 (see pages 217-218).

The Ruger 77/22 with Sound Technology Standard Model hybrid suppressor features six ports in the barrel and a permanently mounted suppressor. This rifle is fitted with a Shepherd 2.5-7.5 power auto-ranging rimfire scope.

The first thing one notices from Table 9.22 is that the 10/22 Standard Model with ported barrel produces virtually the same sound signatures as the smaller and lighter Baikal Classic with unported barrel. The smaller suppressor actually outperformed the larger model with Baikal subsonic LR. These data suggest two obvious questions. Why bother to vent a barrel into the rear of a muzzle can? Why make a bigger suppressor when a smaller one does as well? Mark White's answer to these questions was to discontinue his 10/22 Standard Model in favor of the more conventional Baikal Classic can.

A more striking comparison can be made with the 77/22 Standard Model and the Large Experimental Model. The smaller suppressor is significantly quieter with high-velocity LR ammunition, yet it produces the same sound signature with standard-velocity LR ammo. The larger suppressor is, however, quieter than the smaller can with Baikal subsonic LR and Federal CB Longs.

I was somewhat surprised by the performance of the 77/22 Standard (Large Hole) Model. It was noticeably quieter than the same can with smaller aperture in the front end cap when using high-velocity and standard-velocity LR ammunition, although it was noticeably louder with subsonic LR and CB Longs. Apparently, the cartridges producing higher velocity gases pressurize the front-most chamber of the suppressor, creating an "uncorking" pop analogous to the sound of a champagne cork being pulled. The suppressor with the larger aperture seems to reduce this uncorking sound with high-velocity gases. But the larger aperture allows the premature release of combustion gases produced by lower velocity cartridges, resulting in poorer performance. This suggests that changing the aperture size of a rimfire rifle suppressor is one way to tune the system for the particular ammunition that will be used most often.

Table 9.23 is useful for comparing the performance of these hybrid suppressors to other systems in the marketplace. The 10/22 Baikal Classic provides less net sound reduction than the venerable old AWC R10 suppressed rifle, although Table 9.24 shows that the Baikal suppressor/barrel assembly delivers a lot more velocity. Compared with the AWC Archangel I muzzle can, the 77/22 Standard Model hybrid provides less net sound reduction with high-velocity LR and the same sound reduction with standard-velocity ammo. The Archangel I significantly outperforms the 77/22 Standard Model with subsonic LR and CB Longs, however.

Conclusions

Sound Technology is probably best known for producing the quietest suppressed Marlin Camp Carbines in the business. The company is also well known for employing tensioned, fire-lapped barrels to produce particularly accurate integrally suppressed .22 caliber rifles, often with 22 inch integral suppressors designed to preserve projectile velocity as much as possible while delivering outstanding sound suppression. I've fired several Sound Technology systems that were as accurate as Clark custom guns with match barrels, and one integrally suppressed 10/22 was significantly more accurate than a Clark gun.

The .22 caliber muzzle suppressors from Sound Technology cannot compete with integral suppressors in terms of sound reduction, but they are quiet enough for almost any application as long as the correct ammunition is used. They also provide superior external and terminal ballistics compared to integral systems, so they should be more effective on live targets. Finally, they accumulate less powder residue than integral cans and are much easier to clean.

When mounted on a Ruger 77/22, the Standard Model hybrid suppressor provides similar sound reduction to the AWC Archangel I muzzle suppressor using high-velocity and standard-velocity LR ammunition. Although the Archangel significantly outperforms the hybrid with subsonic LR and CB Longs, the subjective impression is that the hybrid delivers good performance with these rounds.

The Sound Technology practice of permanently attaching the suppressor to a dedicated barrel has additional benefits over integral suppressors besides higher projectile velocity. The suppressor/barrel assembly drops into an unmodified stock. The suppressor/barrel assembly also has some advantages over a conventional screw-on muzzle can, since the permanently mounted can eliminates potential alignment and accuracy problems. And the bore of each barrel used in a suppressed system from Sound Technology is carefully lapped, polished, and vibrationally tuned to provide significantly better accuracy (in most cases) than a barrel fresh from the Ruger factory. A nice spinoff of this solution is that the cost of the required extra barrel is comparable to sending an already-owned barrel off for threading and refinishing for a detachable muzzle can.

White's work to improve the accuracy of barrels is available to anyone with a Ruger 77/22 or 10/22, whether the barrel is already threaded for a muzzle can or is in original factory condition. I sent him the 77/22 barrel I've always used to test muzzle cans. He firelapped and recrowned the barrel, and my groups shrank to about 40 percent of their previous sizes. There is a risk to firelapping, however. If a barrel has been shot out, severely traumatized, or is one of those gravely out-of-spec barrels that sometimes gets past Ruger's quality-control people, then firelapping will seriously degrade accuracy. But if it is among the vast majority of new or moderately used Ruger barrels, then firelapping should help to some degree. I had fired more than 20,000 rounds through my Ruger 77/22 barrel when I sent it to Sound Technology, and the improvement I experienced was dramatic indeed. I suspect the barrel would have been even more accurate if I'd allowed White to shorten it to 16.1 inches in order to change the barrel's harmonics and vibration node—but that would have biased my future sound and velocity data. White charges an affordable fee to firelap and recrown a Ruger rifle barrel, do a trigger job that includes his proprietary trigger stop, and return it all postpaid. He'll even shorten the barrel to 16.1 inches at no extra charge if the customer wishes.

A few words must also be said about the Classic Ultralight Match 10/22 Rifle. Occasionally, myriad variables come together to create a serendipitous system of extraordinary appeal. The Gemtech Quantum-2000 is one such system. The Classic Ultralight Match Rifle is another. The Classic Ultralight system handles extremely well, in spite of the fact that I was prepared to dislike the little Chinese scope. But the rifle fit my body well. Small swinging targets couldn't be missed at 40 yards (37 m) even when the trigger was worked as rapidly as humanly possible. And the Classic Ultralight delivered extraordinary practical accuracy when fired offhand at 100 yards (91 m). When fired with subsonic ammunition and observed from 30 yards (27 m) away, the dominant event when shooting into a distant, soft earthen embankment was the sound of the bullet impact.

No doubt the superb trigger and lapped barrel contributed much of this accuracy, but the performance of this system seemed to exceed the performance one might expect having used each of the components in other systems. The whole seemed to perform better than the sum of the parts, yielding synergistic suppressed excellence.

Some of this synergism is generated by the changed barrel harmonics and vibration node inherent in the precise dimensions used in this system. The standard Ruger 10/22 barrel seems to have an intrinsic problem with harmonics that is eliminated by shortening the barrel to 16.1 inches and adding the weight of a Baikal Classic Muzzle Can. The 77/22 also seems to benefit from being shortened to 16.1 inches.

Surprisingly, some of this synergism relates to the Butler Creek stock. Not only does this stock seem to deliver more accuracy than a factory wood stock, but it dramatically improves the reliability of the rifle. After swapping a Butler Creek stock with the factory stocks of numerous 10/22 barreled actions, it became obvious that the Butler Creek stock had a couple of universal effects: 1) it significantly shortened the cycle time of the 10/22 bolt, and 2) the rifle functioned more reliably and cycled more dependably. Even tired old 10/22s that no longer cycled reliably in their original stocks suddenly became perfectly dependable in the Butler Creek stock. That was an exciting discovery, especially considering the low cost of the stock.

The Classic Ultralight Match Rifle is not the prettiest 10/22 system in the marketplace, or anywhere near the quietest. But the sum total of this 10/22's performance proved to be addictive.

Generally speaking, the Sound Technology muzzle suppressors with their dedicated barrels provide cost-effective and very accurate alternatives both to integral suppressors and screw-on muzzle cans while providing acceptable sound suppression for any application, as long as the operator selects the correct ammunition for a particular task.

Table 9.22. Sound signatures in decibels of suppressor tests.

GUN	SUPPRESSOR	FEDERAL HV LR	HANSEN SV LR	BAIKAL JB LR	FEDERAL CB LONGS	REMINGTON CB LONGS	TEMP., °F (°C)
Ruger 10/22	None	142	139	139	—	—	66(19)
Ruger 10/22	ST Standard Model	122	118	118	—	—	66(19)
Ruger 10/22	ST Baikal Classic	122	118	117	—	—	66(19)
Ruger 10/22	None	141	140	138	—	—	38(3)
Ruger 10/22	AWC R10	117	114	110	—	—	38(3)
Ruger 77/22	None	140	137	137	131	130	58(14)
Ruger 77/22	ST Standard Model	121	120	117	113	—	58(14)
Ruger 77/22	ST Standard (Lg Hole)	120	118	119	—	114	58(14)
Ruger 77/22	ST Lg Experimental	124	120	114	109	—	58(14)
Ruger 77/22	None	141	137	138	132	—	82(29)
Ruger 77/22	AWC Archangel I	120	120	114	104	—	82(29)

Table 9.23. Net sound reductions, expressed in decibels.

GUN	SUPPRESSOR	FEDERAL HV LR	HANSEN SV LR	BAIKAL JB LR	FEDERAL CB LONGS	REMINGTON CB LONGS	TEMP., °F (°C)
Ruger 10/22	ST Standard Model	20	21	11	—	—	66(19)
Ruger 10/22	ST Baikal Classic	20	21	22	—	—	66(19)
Ruger 10/22	AWC R10	24	26	28	—	—	38(3)
Ruger 77/22	ST Standard Model	19	17	20	18	—	58(14)
Ruger 77/22	ST Standard (Lg Hole)	20	19	18	—	17	58(14)
Ruger 77/22	ST Lg Experimental	16	17	23	22	—	58(14)
Ruger 77/22	AWC Archangel I	21	17	24	28	—	82(29)

Table 9.24. Muzzle velocities of suppressed and unsuppressed rifles, expressed in feet per second (and meters per second).

GUN	SUPPRESSOR	FEDERAL HV LR	HANSEN SV LR	BAIKAL JB LR	FEDERAL CB LONGS	REMINGTON CB LONGS	TEMP., °F (°C)	SPEED SOUND, fps (mps)
Ruger 10/22	None	1,221(372)	1,064(324)	1,010(308)	—	—	66(19)	1,124(343)
Ruger 10/22	ST Standard Model	1,200(366)	1,069(326)	995(303)	—	—	66(19)	1,124(343)
Ruger 10/22	ST Baikal Classic	1,163(354)	1,081(329)	1,017(310)	—	—	66(19)	1,124(343)
Ruger 10/22	None	1,228(374)	1,085(331)	961(293)	—	—	38(3)	1,094(333)
Ruger 10/22	AWC R10	972(296)	935(285)	791(241)	—	—	38(3)	1,094(333)
Ruger 77/22	None	1,257(383)	1,136(346)	1,045(319)	649(198)	693(211)	58(14)	1,116(340)
Ruger 77/22	ST Standard Model	1,252(382)	1,140(347)	1,033(315)	655(200)	—	58(14)	1,116(340)
Ruger 77/22	ST Standard (Lg Hole)	1,231(375)	1,222(372)	1,032(315)	—	684(208)	58(14)	1,116(340)
Ruger 77/22	ST Lg Experimental	1,228(374)	1,116(340)	1,031(314)	656(200)	—	58(14)	1,116(340)

GEMTECH VORTEX-2 VERSUS THE AWC ARCHANGEL III

As this book was being completed, two of the leading suppressor manufacturers in the industry introduced new generations of .22 rimfire muzzle cans: the Archangel III from AWC Systems

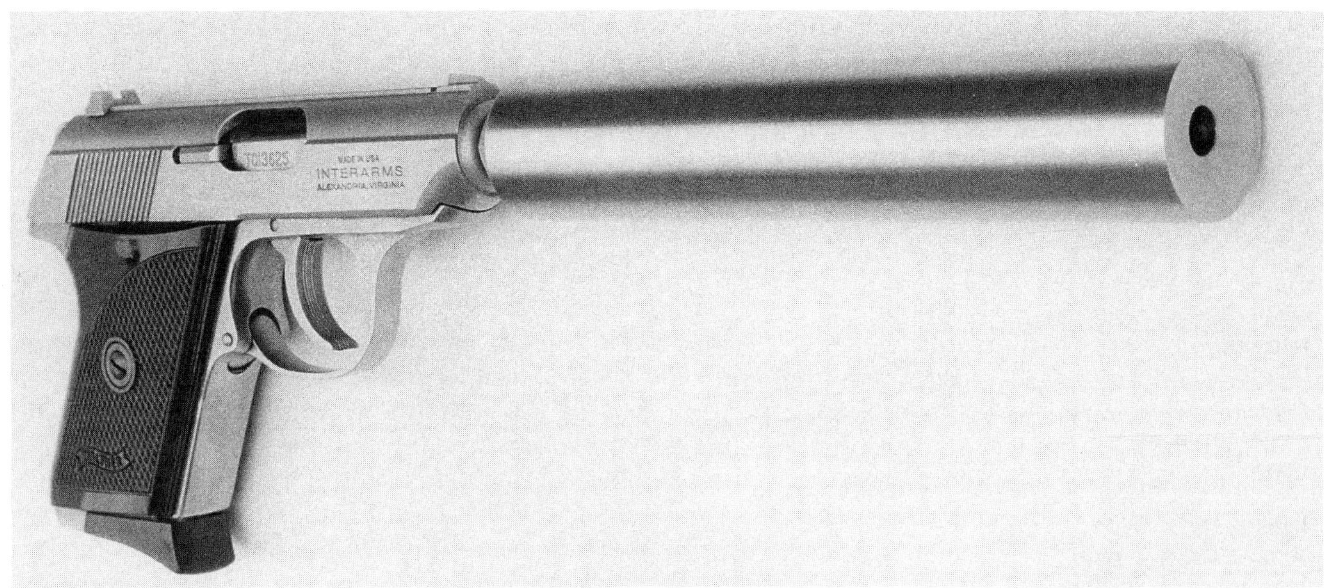

The Vortex-2 produced much better net sound reduction when mounted on a pistol as opposed to a rifle because the suppressor's internal structures—especially the asymmetric surfaces—are more efficient at producing turbulence inside the suppressor with the much higher velocity combustion gases produced by the pistol.

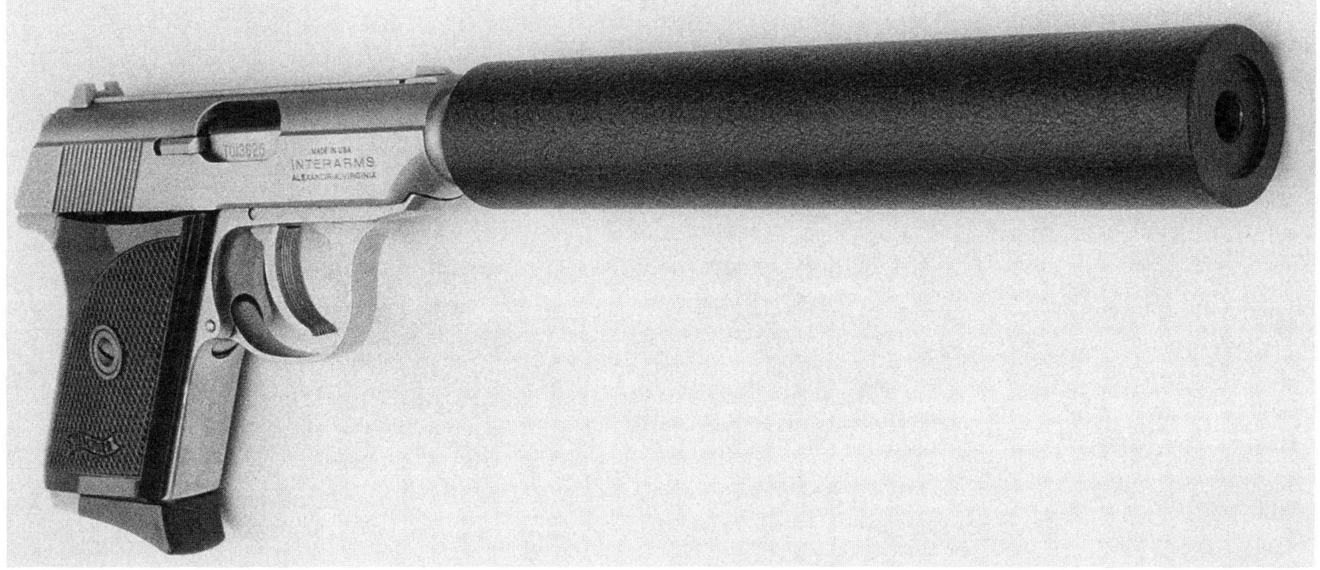

The Archangel III's slanted-sidewall baffles are separated by smooth conical spacers that feature a mouse-hole adjacent to the forward edge of the slanted sidewall, which directs its gas jet into the coaxial expansion chamber formed by the spacer.

Technology and the Vortex-2 from Gemtech. Their performance will be compared to two classic designs from the recent past: the Vaime A8 from Finland and the AWC Archangel (which will henceforth be referred to as the Archangel I). While designed for civilian sport shooters, these suppressors are also relevant to the armed professional.

An increasing number of organizations within the law enforcement community are adding a suppressed .22 rimfire to their tactical arsenals. While the SpecOps and Black Ops communities tend to use suppressed .22 *pistols* in an antipersonnel role, where quiet is more important than terminal ballistics, the law enforcement community tends to use suppressed .22 *rifles* for the selective destruction of objects—such as vehicle tires and yard lights—prior to an entry or tactical operation. The most versatile approach is to employ a muzzle suppressor (as opposed to the more widely seen integral suppressor) on a bolt-action rifle with an auto-ranging scope designed for rimfire cartridges. This combination enables the operator to select from the widest possible variety of ammunition to meet a broad range of tactical problems.

Silencers have long been popular among the civilian shooters of many European countries for reducing noise pollution and making themselves better neighbors. The growth of the environmental movement as well as government interest in the hearing loss experienced by sport shooters has accelerated interested in the use of silencers for improving the both health and environmental quality in northern European countries. Finland has led this movement through an active collaboration among military and academic researchers, the Ministry of Health, the Ministry of Labor, sporting clubs, civilian shooters, and manufacturers to promote the widespread use of silencers to improve the health and well-being of its citizens. A spinoff of this interest has been the development of specialized ammunition designed to maximize velocity while keeping the projectiles subsonic over a wide range of temperatures and common barrel lengths. The ready availability of affordable subsonic ammunition for the civilian marketplace has stimulated a renaissance in the design of muzzle cans relevant to tactical users. And a new subsonic round just developed by Lapua for the civilian marketplace features a heavier bullet that should provide better penetration than any other subsonic round in the marketplace. At the time of this writing, the new Lapua round was not yet available in the United States.

Nevertheless, tactical users can now select from a wide variety of .22 rimfire ammunition for use with muzzle cans. CB Longs, for example, provide reliable feeding in a Ruger 77/22, the quietest sound signature at the muzzle, the least impact noise, and the least danger of ricochet. Within its effective range, the CB Long may be the best bet for taking out a yard or hall light. Employing the now widely available subsonic Long Rifle rounds may provide the optimal (i.e., flattest) trajectory and maximum penetration without generating a ballistic crack from a supersonic projectile. If a ballistic crack will not be a tactical liability, the CCI SGB Long Rifle cartridge may provide the maximum penetration.

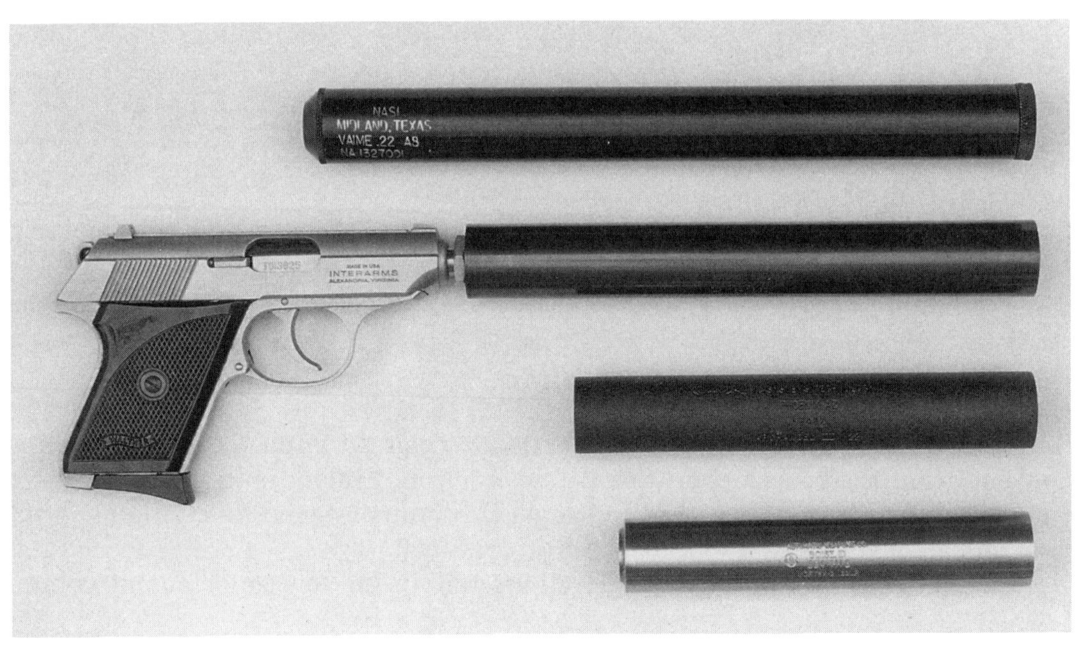

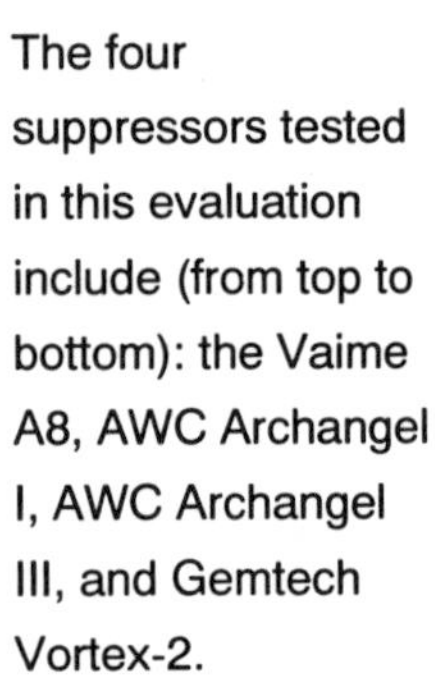
The four suppressors tested in this evaluation include (from top to bottom): the Vaime A8, AWC Archangel I, AWC Archangel III, and Gemtech Vortex-2.

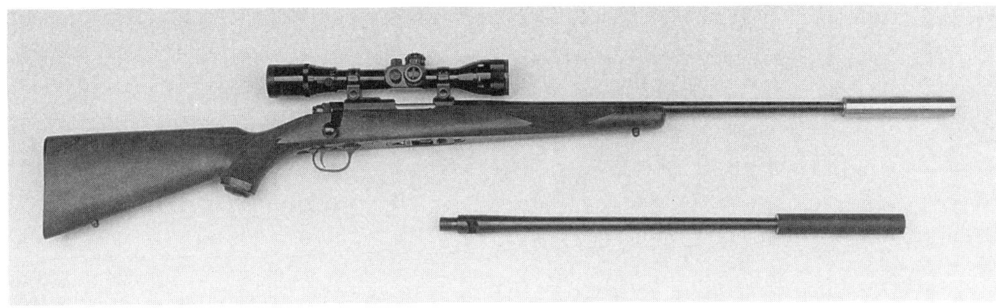

One way to improve the accuracy of a Ruger factory barrel (here shown with a Gemtech Vortex-2 suppressor) is to chop it back to a length of 16.1 inches (40.9 cm) like the separate barrel shown with an AWC Archangel III suppressor. This reduces barrel harmonics dramatically, although the shorter barrel is somewhat louder.

Using an integral suppressor as opposed to a muzzle can will generally produce substantially lower projectile velocities (often 20 to 25 percent lower). Thus the integral suppressor affords a more limited performance range. Using a semiautomatic rifle as opposed to a bolt-action rifle limits the variety of ammunition that can be employed. Therefore, a bolt-action rifle such as the Ruger 77/22 with a good muzzle can provides the best tool for the selective destruction of objects.

But what is the best muzzle can for that rifle? The search for an answer to that question should begin with an examination of the four competing suppressor designs evaluated in this study.

Suppressor Design

Developed by Lynn McWilliams, the Archangel III is actually the fourth generation in the Archangel series, since two different designs were marketed as the Archangel II. The unusually tight bore of the Archangel II delivered disappointing accuracy, a problem not associated with earlier and later designs in the series.

Constructed entirely of 304 stainless steel, the Archangel III evaluated for this book is 6.1 inches (15.4 cm) long and 1.0 inch (2.5 cm) in diameter. Based on the patented work of Charles A. "Mickey" Finn, the suppressor uses eight baffles of the slanted-sidewall type. The slanted sidewall is a diagonal slot of similar radius to the bullet passage, centered on the bullet passage, that creates a diagonal channel going from one side of the rear surface to the opposing side on the front of the baffle. Each slanted sidewall baffle creates a gas jet to push against the stream of combustion gases following the bullet. The gas jet dumps significantly more energy inside the suppressor than the same number of similarly spaced conventional (i.e., conical) baffles. The suppressor's baffles are separated by smooth conical spacers that feature a mouse hole adjacent to the forward edge of the slanted sidewall, which directs its gas jet into the coaxial expansion chamber formed by the spacer. This increases the effectiveness of that chamber. Available in a natural stainless finish or black powder coat, the Archangel III weighs 10.9 ounces (310 grams).

Designed by Dr. Phil Dater and Jim Ryan, the Vortex-2 is substantially lighter than the Archangel III, weighing only 6.7 ounces (189 grams). With a length of 5.4 inches (13.8 cm) and a diameter of 1.0 inch (2.5 cm), the Vortex is also shorter. While the tube and end caps are constructed from 300 series stainless steels, Gemtech uses only five 6061-T6 aluminum baffles, both to improve the rate of heat transfer from combustion gases to the suppressor and to save weight. This design is actually louder with stainless steel baffles, since stainless steel does not rob combustion gases of heat energy as efficiently as aluminum. I would not have thought that there was enough time involved during a suppressed gunshot for heat transfer to be a significant component of the performance equation, but empirical testing suggests otherwise, at least for this particular design.

The Vortex-2 actually incorporates several different baffle designs in its baffle stack. The rearmost two baffles are particularly aggressive at diverting gases from the jet behind the bullet. The key to the performance of these baffles is a series of asymmetric shapes that maximize turbulence. The suppressor is available in a bright polished or nonreflective sand-blasted finish.

The Vaime A8 suppressor represents one of the most attractive designs developed in the 1980s, and the Finnish suppressor makes a suitable European benchmark for evaluating the latest U.S. technology. The design of the Vaime suppressor is discussed earlier in this chapter.

Designed by Lynn McWilliams, the Archangel I has long been one of my favorite .22 rifle suppressors, and its design is also discussed earlier in this chapter.

All four suppressors were tested on the same day on a Ruger 77/22 rifle and a Walther TPH pistol to determine their relative performance.

Performance of a silenced rimfire rifle can be optimized with an auto-ranging rimfire scope, such as this Shepherd 2.5-7.5 power telescopic sight, and a Harris bipod. The Gemtech Vortex-2 suppressor shown here outperforms the Archangel III with every kind of ammunition except CB Longs when employed on a rifle.

Performance

The sound signatures generated during this series of experiments are found in Table 9.25. These data show that the Vortex-2 outperforms the Archangel III with every kind of ammunition except CB Longs when employed on a rifle. When mounted on a Walther TPH pistol, however, the Archangel III outperforms the Vortex-2 with every kind of ammunition.

Remarkably, the out-of-production Archangel I outperformed both the Vortex-2 and Archangel III with high-velocity and subsonic ammunition. The new Gemtech and AWC suppressors are, however, more durable than the Archangel I since they do not employ mesh in their design. The Vaime A8 provided the same performance as the Archangel III with high-velocity and standard-velocity fodder, and the same performance as the Vortex-2 with subsonic ammunition. The out-of-production Finnish suppressor still delivers impressive performance.

The best way to compare suppressed rifle and suppressed pistol tests conducted on the same day—or to compare these tests with other published data—is to look at the difference between the unsuppressed and suppressed sound signatures. These net sound reductions appear in Table 9.26 (see page 224). The data demonstrate an interesting curiosity of exotic baffle design and proprietary spacing: some suppressors work best with combustion gases of a particular velocity. This phenomenon leads to some surprises in the data, such as suppressor performance with standard-velocity ammunition. When fitted to a rifle, none of the suppressors tested in this study produced as much sound reduction with standard-velocity ammunition as they did with high-velocity or subsonic fodder. Yet when fitted to a pistol, the Vortex-2 and Vaime A8 delivered their best net sound reductions with standard-velocity ammo.

Another curiosity is that each suppressor in this study produced much better net sound reduction when mounted on a pistol instead of a rifle. This phenomenon occurs because the internal structures—especially the asymmetric surfaces—are more efficient at producing turbulence inside the suppressor with the much higher velocity combustion gases produced by the pistol. Parenthetically, this phenomenon explains why some suppressor manufacturers provide test data (i.e., net sound reductions) for their .22 rimfire suppressors mounted on a pistol. The data are much more impressive.

Table 9.25. Sound signatures in decibels of .22 LR muzzle suppressor tests.

GUN	SUPPRESSOR	FEDERAL HV LR	HANSEN SV LR	BAIKAL JB LR	REMINGTON CB LONGS	TEMP., °F (°C)
Ruger 77/22	None	141	138	137	132	73(23)
Ruger 77/22	Vaime A8	121	121	114	110	73(23)
Ruger 77/22	AWC Archangel I	118	122	111	110	73(23)
Ruger 77/22	AWC Archangel III	121	121	116	109	73(23)
Ruger 77/22	Gemtech Vortex-2	120	120	114	111	73(23)
Walther TPH	None	157	155	155	—	73(23)
Walther TPH	Vaime A8	125	121	121	—	73(23)
Walther TPH	AWC Archangel I	127	125	125	—	73(23)
Walther TPH	AWC Archangel III	123	120	118	—	73(23)
Walther TPH	Gemtech Vortex-2	127	122	123	—	73(23)

Conclusions

Since each of the suppressors evaluated in this study was produced by some of the best manufacturers in the industry, it should come as no surprise that any of the four muzzle cans will provide enough sound suppression for sporting or tactical applications. Of course, selecting the optimal ammunition for a particular requirement is essential. The Vortex-2 from Gemtech is considerably lighter and somewhat shorter than the Archangel III from AWC Systems Technology. Furthermore, the Vortex-2 outperforms the Archangel III with every kind of ammunition except CB Longs when employed on a rifle. When mounted on a Walther TPH pistol, however, the Archangel III outperforms the Vortex-2 with every kind of ammunition. Whether mounted on a rifle or pistol, both the Vortex-2 and the Archangel III outperform popular integrally suppressed .22s from the 1980s such as Ciener's Marlin 780 rifle and AWC's RST Ruger Mark II pistol. Both the Vortex-2 and the Archangel III are outstanding suppressors.

Table 9.26. Net sound reductions of .22 LR suppressors, expressed in decibels.

GUN	SUPPRESSOR	FEDERAL HV LR	HANSEN SV LR	BAIKAL JB LR	REMINGTON CB LONGS	TEMP., °F (°C)
Ruger 77/22	Vaime A8	20	17	23	22	73(23)
Ruger 77/22	AWC Archangel I	23	16	26	22	73(23)
Ruger 77/22	AWC Archangel III	20	17	21	23	73(23)
Ruger 77/22	Gemtech Vortex-2	21	18	23	21	73(23)
Walther TPH	Vaime A8	32	34	34	—	73(23)
Walther TPH	AWC Archangel I	30	30	30	—	73(23)
Walther TPH	AWC Archangel III	34	35	37	—	73(23)
Walther TPH	Gemtech Vortex-2	30	33	32	—	73(23)

CHAPTER TEN

OPTIMIZING THE PERFORMANCE OF SUPPRESSED .22s

ver the last several decades, Ruger .22 rifles and pistols have become the standard firearms used by the suppressor industry for building silenced rimfire systems. In part, this relates to the method of barrel attachment used for Ruger 10/22 and 77/22 rifles, which provides easy barrel removal and replacement for installing an integral suppressor or threading for a muzzle can. It is interesting to note that sport shooters who own a suppressed .22 rimfire end up shooting much more than they did before they owned a suppressed firearm. It's easier to find a socially acceptable place to shoot, and the shooting experience itself is more fun. A spinoff of this phenomenon is that these shooters become better marksmen. As their skills increase, so does their wish for better performance than they commonly obtain from the typical suppressed or unsuppressed arm. Since the suppressed Ruger 10/22 is by far the most popular silenced arm in the United States, it is appropriate to focus on how to maximize the performance of this rifle.

Although the Ruger 10/22 dominates the suppressed .22 marketplace, it is far from perfect. This chapter begins by comparing the performance of the Ruger 77/22 and 10/22 in terms of velocity and sound signatures as functions of chamber dimensions and barrel length. The chapter then provides details on how to maximize the reliability and accuracy of a suppressed Ruger 10/22. Of course, many of these suggestions will also work with a suppressed Ruger 77/22, a suppressed Ruger pistol, and even unsuppressed firearms. The discussions on maximizing accuracy and reliability are built upon two articles written by Mark White (the president of Sound Technology) that were originally published in *Machine Gun News*. I have expanded these discussions with additional material and imposed my own biases on previously published material with White's approval.

EFFECTS OF CHAMBER DIMENSIONS AND BARREL LENGTH

Chamber dimensions influence the efficiency of powder combustion, which directly affects both the sound signature produced by a firearm and projectile velocity. Barrel length directly affects these variables and indirectly affects accuracy by altering barrel harmonics. It is useful to understand these phenomena when selecting the design specifications for a silenced rifle.

Chamber Dimensions

Back in 1993, Mark White purchased 20 Ruger barrels, half for the 10/22 and half for the 77/22. He then carefully machined a chamber gauge and measured the depth of each chamber.

All of the 77/22 barrels had short enough chambers so the soft nose of a .22 LR bullet would engage the rifling upon closing the bolt. When dropping various brands of .22 LR ammo into 77/22 barrels, the cartridges stopped between 1/16 and 1/8 inch (1.6 to 3.2 mm) before being chambered fully. When firing these barrels in the bolt-action rifle, the typical bullet expands properly and travels the rifling in a symmetrical, uniform manner. Accuracy of the 77/22 is often quite good.

All of the 10/22 barrels White measured had sloppy chambers, which were both larger in diameter and deeper. The chambers commonly ran from 1/4 to 5/16 inch (6.4 to 7.9 mm) deeper than the 77/22. When firing a .22 LR in a 10/22 chamber, it must jump a considerable gap before it hits the rifling. The probability that a given bullet will engage the rifling perfectly square in such a chamber is relatively low. Therefore, the projectile may exit the 10/22 barrel slightly cocked and slightly deformed. With its aerodynamics and center of balance altered by such deformation, it should come as no surprise that the flight characteristics of a deformed bullet are less than ideal. The bullet may even wobble slightly. While some unmodified 10/22s are the proverbial tack-drivers (especially when the rifle was first introduced), most are not. Part of the rifle's pedestrian accuracy relates to the quality of the bore and its concentricity in the barrel, but much of the accuracy loss does relate to the chamber design.

There is a logical explanation, however, why Ruger builds relatively loose chambers into the 10/22 and relatively tight chambers into the 77/22. It relates to the different extraction requirements of the two rifles.

The Ruger 77/22 rifle features two extractors, and the mechanism is externally operated by a hand-turned bolt that can exert considerable leverage. Furthermore, the 77/22's firing pin strikes with greater force, so the chance of a misfire is less. Thus, if a misfire does occur in the bolt-action 77/22, its twin extractors can usually claw out the recalcitrant cartridge with ease.

The self-loading 10/22 has only one extractor, and the rifle must cycle with loads varying from mild target loads to hot hunting loads. If a round misfires or a spent case sticks in the chamber, the design offers no long bolt handle or camming action—just a small operating handle to pull against. Worst of all, the single extractor may not provide a secure enough grip on the cartridge case for extraction.

A chamber designed for maximum accuracy rather than optimal extraction can grip the bullet in the rifling so tightly that the act of unloading a live or misfired round will rip the case from the bullet. Since few shooters go into the field equipped with a cleaning rod to knock out stuck cartridges, cases, or bullets, Ruger designed a long, sloppy chamber for the 10/22 to ensure reliable extraction.

Yet it is possible to have one's cake and eat it too. Volquartsen, as just one example, builds a match barrel with a chamber that is an excellent compromise between the quest for ultimate accuracy and the need to retain reliable extraction. When hunting with such a barrel, however, it is advisable to carry a jeweler's screwdriver or takedown cleaning rod so a misfire or stuck case does not take the gun out of service in the field. It is easier to clear a jam with a screwdriver or pocket knife if one first removes the magazine, and then uses the tool through the magazine well rather than the ejection port. There's a lot more room to work.

By the way, it is not possible to install a 77/22 barrel with its tighter chamber into a 10/22 rifle. That won't work. The stubs are machined differently, and the slice taken out of the bottom is in the wrong place. Besides chamber dimensions, another major variable that is especially relevant to the subject of suppressed .22 rifles is barrel length.

Barrel Length

Legalities and papering aside, optimum accuracy seems to be produced by a barrel of 14 to 16 inches (36 to 41 cm).

If the rifle in question is full auto (such as John Norrell's superb select-fire conversion of the Ruger 10/22), then there are no legal restrictions on barrel length. Any rifle registered as a machine gun may have a barrel of any length. If the arm is not registered as a machine gun and has a barrel shorter than 16 inches, then the arm must be registered as a short-barreled rifle, which entails the same paperwork and transfer tax as a machine gun. This is why most folks do not shorten a rifle barrel to less than 16.1 inches. A shorter barrel is probably more accurate because the barrel is thicker and more rigid throughout its length, which alters the original barrel harmonics and vibration node. But what effect does a shorter barrel have on projectile velocity?

Mark White uses leather gloves to protect his hands from the muzzle blast when firing a Ruger 10/22 action with 2 inch (5.1 cm) barrel.

To answer this question, Mark White fitted a factory new barrel onto a Ruger 10/22 that had been registered as a short-barreled rifle to make the following experiment legal. He then chronographed bullet velocities as he sequentially removed 2 inch (5 cm) sections from the front of the barrel. He used Winchester Wildcat high-velocity LR ammunition for this study at an ambient temperature of 60 °F (16 °C). The results are shown in Table 10.1.

Table 10.1. Bullet velocities produced by Winchester Wildcat high-velocity LR ammunition in Ruger 10/22 barrels of various lengths.

BARREL LENGTH, INCHES (CM)	VELOCITY, FPS (MPS)
18.5 (47.0)	1,229 (375)
16.0 (40.6)	1,226 (374)
14.0 (35.6)	1,212 (369)
12.0 (30.5)	1,197 (365)
10.0 (25.4)	1,175 (358)
8.0 (20.3)	1,152 (351)
6.0 (15.2)	1,088 (332)
4.0 (10.2)	1,004 (303)
2.0 (5.1)	794 (242)

Note that there is very little velocity loss between an 18.5 inch (47.0 cm) and a 12.0 inch (30.5 cm) 10/22 barrel. As with most calibers, much of a projectile's acceleration occurs relatively close to the chamber. The expanding gases have transferred much of their energy to the bullet within the first 10 to 12 inches (25.4 to 30.5 cm) of the 10/22 barrel.

These data illustrate a steady decline in velocity with decreasing barrel length. The only dramatic difference in velocities between adjacent barrel lengths appears between 2.0 and 4.0 inches (5.1 and 10.2 cm).

Readers familiar with .22 LR velocities may note that these data are about 75 fps slower than normal. This is primarily due to the 10/22's long, sloppy chamber, which allows the .22 caliber bullet to completely exit the case before it hits the throat. This arrangement also produces lower pressure, so the powder burns less completely and produces less projectile velocity.

After testing the 10/22 barrel all the way down to 2 inches, White also tested 10.0 and 11.0 inch (25.4 and 27.9 cm) barrels for the Ruger 77/22 bolt-action barrel. The chambers were so tight that the cartridges had to be forced in the last 1/8 inch (3 mm). It was obvious that the lead of each bullet was engraving or engaging the lands of the rifling. The 10 and 11 inch barrels averaged 1,253 and 1,263 fps (382 and 385 mps), respectively.

The short 77/22 barrels produced more projectile velocity than the full-length (18.5 inch) 10/22 barrel. Furthermore, the 10 inch 77/22 barrel produced 78 fps (24 mps) more velocity than the 10/22 barrel of the same length. Therefore, it appears that the Ruger 77/22 produces more projectile velocity than the 10/22 because of its tighter chamber dimensions, not because of its locked breach.

The same ammunition produced an average projectile velocity of 1,246 fps (380 mps) out of a 26.0 inch (66.0 cm) Remington target barrel, contrary to the myth that an extra-long barrel provides an extra measure of velocity.

Finally, White tested a compact Beretta Model 21A pistol with a 2.4 inch (6.0 cm) barrel, which produced an average bullet velocity of 1,116 fps (341 mps). That's roughly equivalent to the velocity that would be produced by a 7 inch (18 cm) Ruger 10/22 barrel. Clearly, altering chamber dimensions and bore diameter can improve the performance of a short barrel dramatically.

To get a better handle on these phenomena, White and I designed a more comprehensive experiment to compare the velocities and sound signatures produced by Ruger 10/22 and 77/22 factory barrels of various lengths. A chop saw was used to shorten the barrels at 2 inch (5.1 cm) intervals from factory length down to 2 inches, and the crown was dressed after each cut. Once the barrel was shortened to within 2 inches of the forestock, the stock was removed and the action was held by hand to avoid any bias that would be created in the sound data by masking from the stock. A wide variety of ammunition was used from hypervelocity to subsonic. All testing was conducted on the same day to minimize environmental effects. The temperature was 70°F (21°C) and the speed of sound was 1,128 fps (344 mps). The overall results are compiled in Tables 10.2 through 10.5 and displayed in Figures 10.1 through 10.4.

Figures 10.5 through 10.7 illustrate the effects of chamber dimensions by directly comparing the velocities produced by the tight-chambered Ruger 77/22 with the loose-chambered 10/22 for a single kind of ammunition commonly used with suppressed rifles. Note that each graph also includes a reference line showing the speed of sound *on that particular day of testing*. Clearly, the tighter chamber of the Ruger 77/22 always delivers more velocity regardless of barrel length and ammunition type, with the trivial exception of standard-velocity ammunition at a barrel length of 2 inches.

These data also support the argument that tighter chambers produce less muzzle blast. The 77/22 generally produces a lower decibel reading than the 10/22 at a given barrel length with high-velocity and standard-velocity fodder. The effect is most pronounced with the fast-burning powder used in subsonic rounds (see Figure 10.8).

I should also note that these experiments complied with BATF regulations concerning short-barreled rifles. *Individuals* who do not own rifle receivers registered as short-barreled rifles (or machine guns) or do not hold a manufacturing license with Special Occupational Tax endorsement (an extra $500 per year) *must not shorten a rifle barrel to less than 16 inches.* BATF has absolutely no sense of humor and could view such an action as a felony. They'd much rather prosecute a harmless tinkerer than an armorer for a drug cartel or the mob; it's safer.

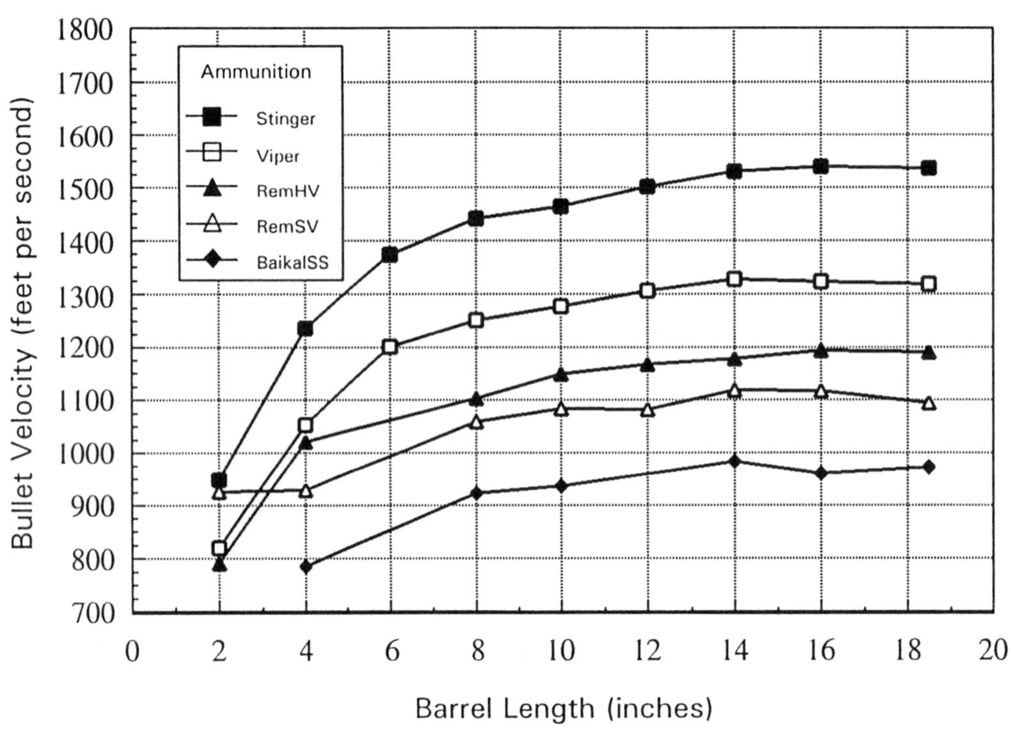

Figure 10.1. Bullet velocity versus barrel length of Ruger 10/22.

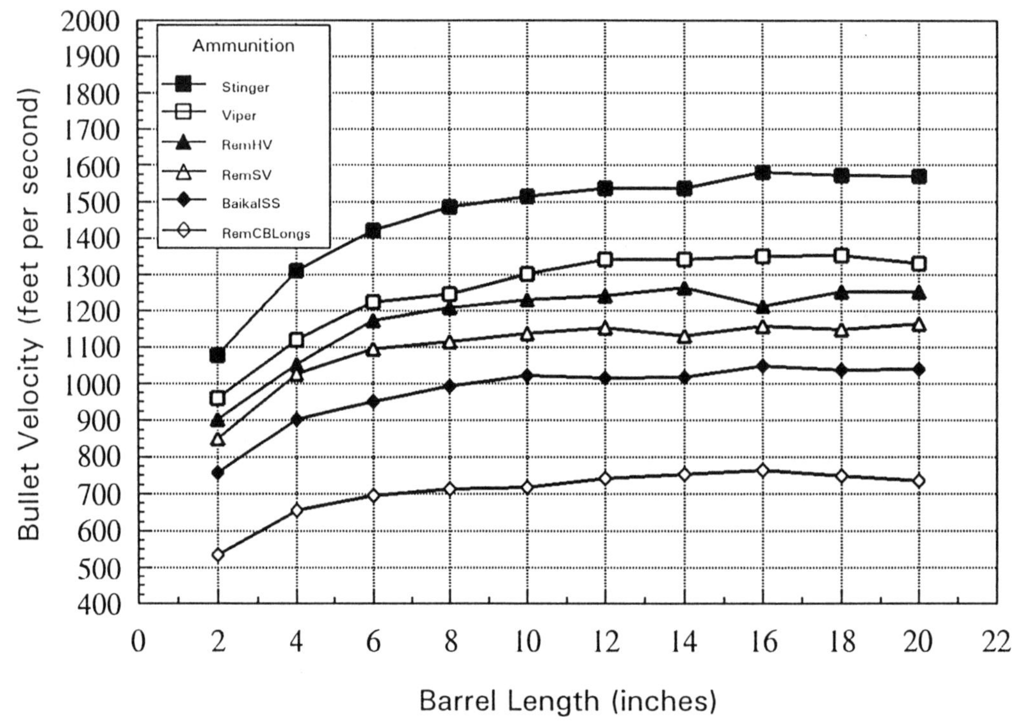

Figure 10.2. Bullet velocity versus barrel length of Ruger 77/22.

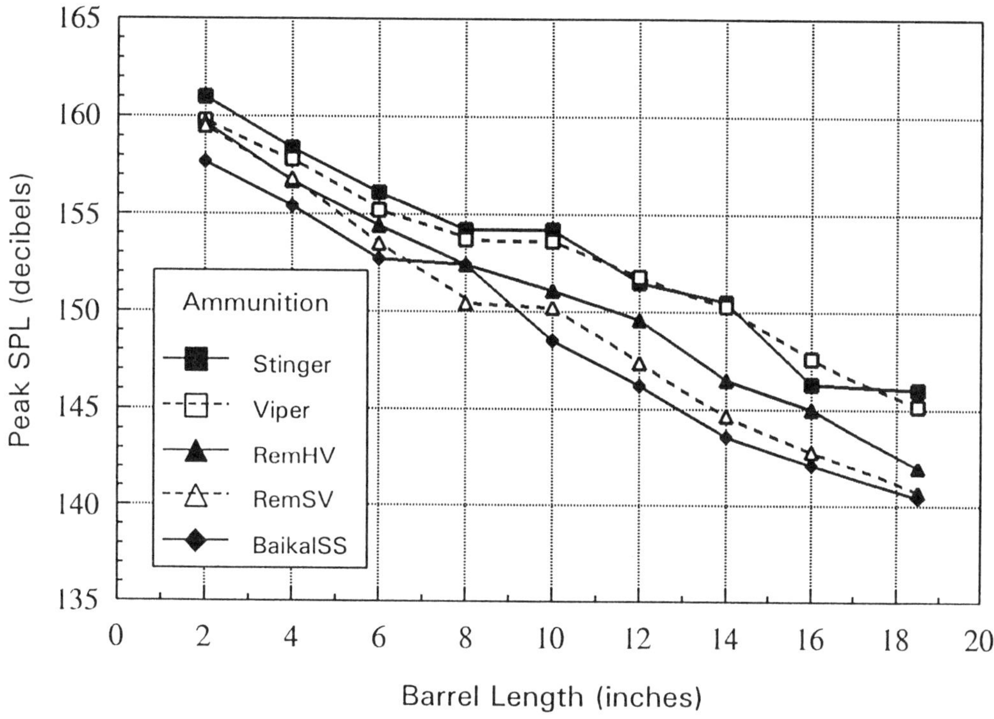

Figure 10.3. Muzzle blast versus barrel length of Ruger 10/22.

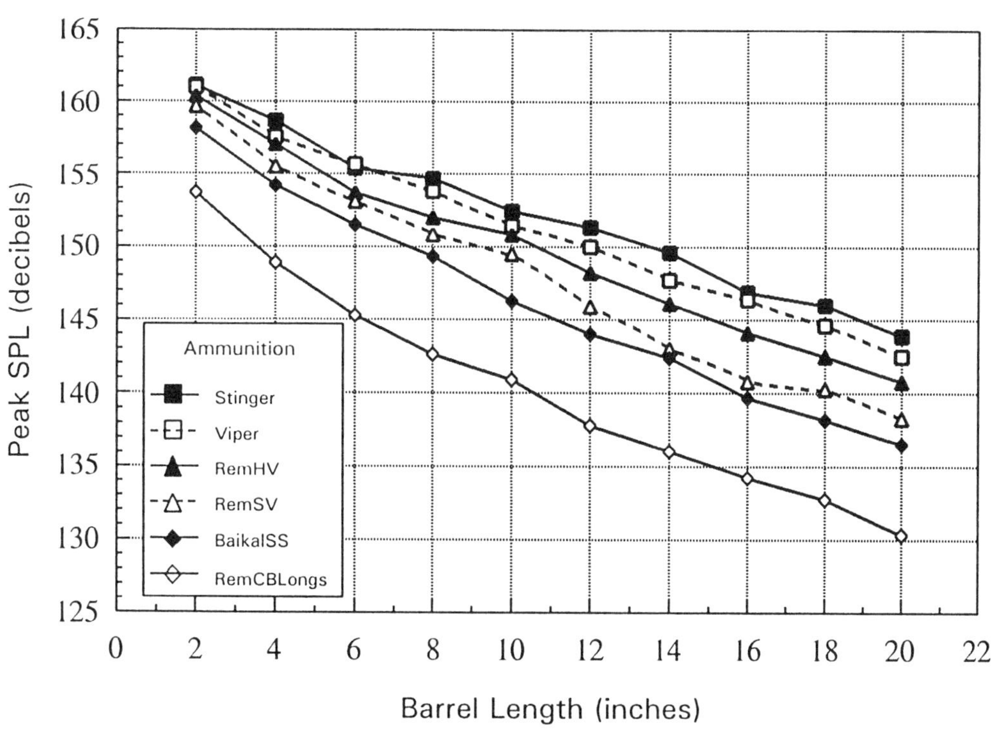

Figure 10.4. Muzzle blast versus barrel length of Ruger 77/22.

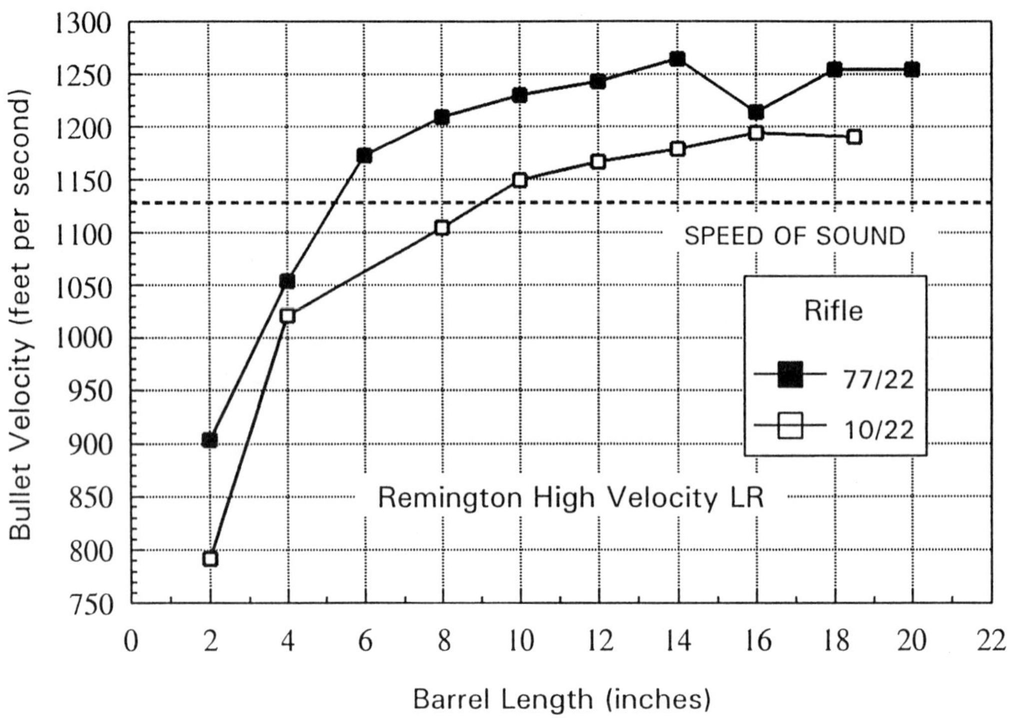

Figure 10.5. Ruger 10/22 and 77/22 velocities with Remington HV.

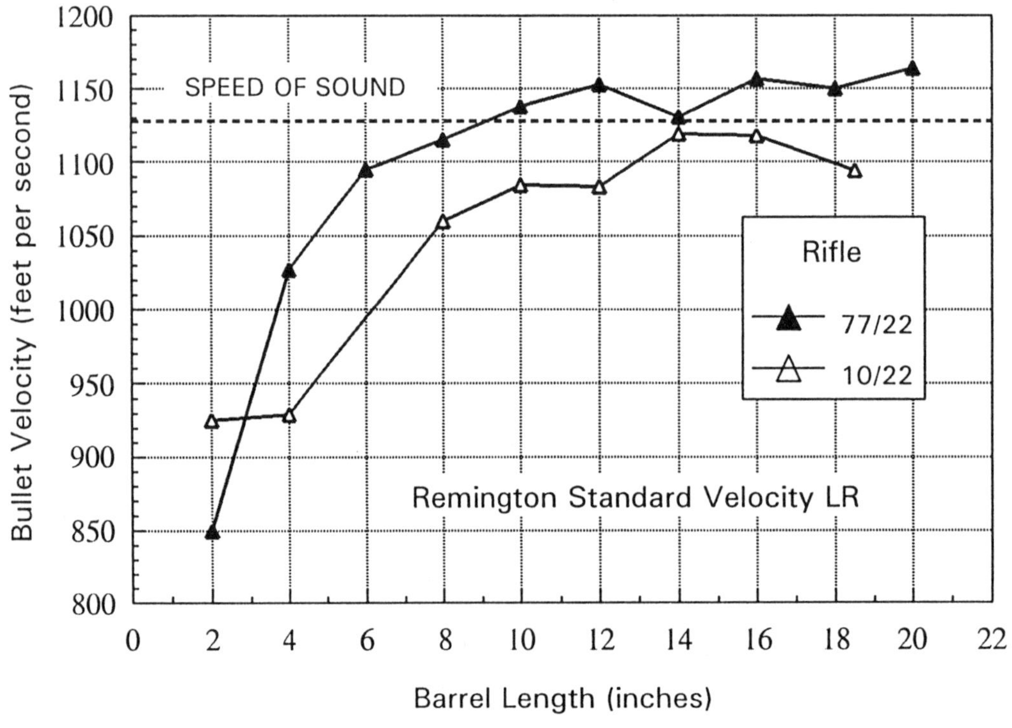

Figure 10.6. Ruger 10/22 and 77/22 velocities with Remington SV.

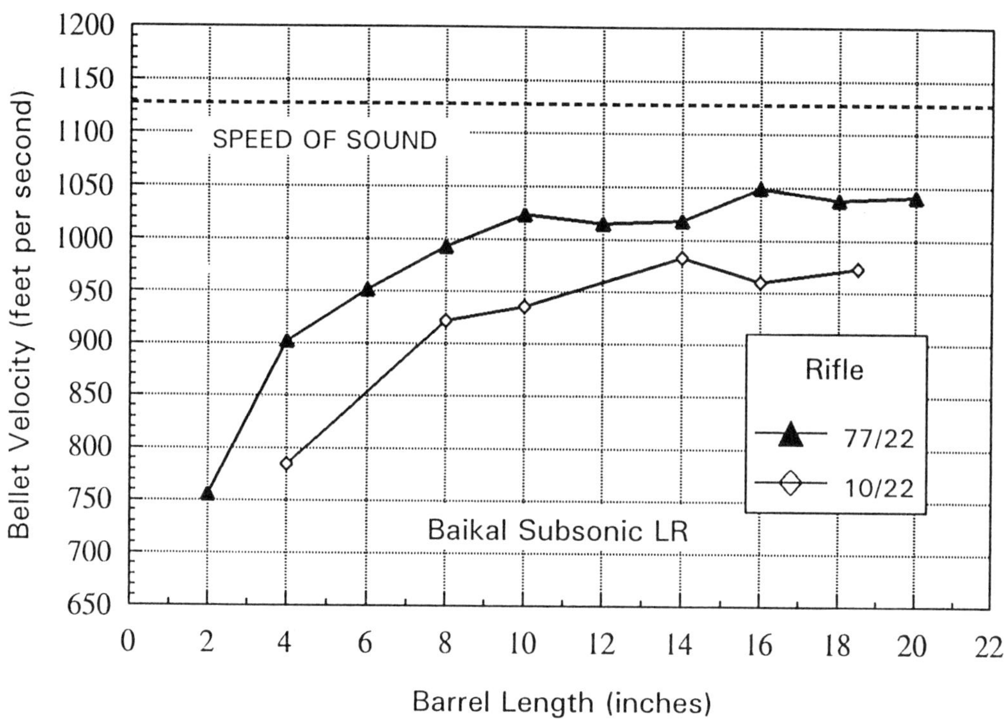

Figure 10.7. Ruger 10/22 and 77/22 velocities with Baikal SS.

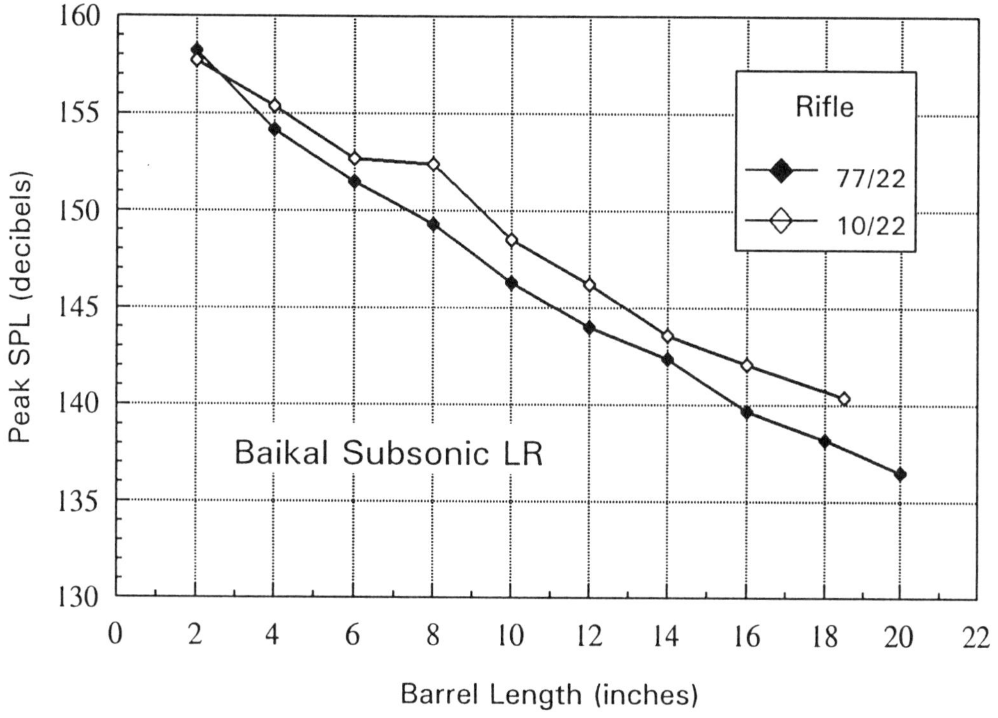

Figure 10.8. Ruger 10/22 and 77/22 muzzle blast with Baikal SS.

Table 10.2. Bullet velocity, expressed in feet per second (and meters per second), versus barrel length for the Ruger 10/22.

BARREL LENGTH, IN (CM)	CCI STINGER LR	REM VIPER LR	REM HV LR	REM SV LR	BAIKAL SS LR
18.50 (47.0)	1,536 (468)	1,318 (402)	1,190 (363)	1,094 (333)	973 (297)
16 (40.6)	1,539 (469)	1,323 (403)	1,194 (354)	1,118 (341)	960 (293)
14 (35.6)	1,531 (467)	1,328 (405)	1,179 (359)	1,119 (341)	983 (300)
12 (30.5)	1,502 (458)	1,307 (398)	1,167 (356)	1,083 (330)	—
10 (25.0)	1,464 (446)	1,278 (390)	1,149 (350)	1,084 (330)	936 (285)
8 (20.3)	1,441 (439)	1,252 (382)	1,104 (336)	1,060 (323)	922 (281)
6 (15.2)	1,374 (419)	1,201 (366)	—	—	—
4 (10.2)	1,236 (377)	1,054 (321)	1,021 (311)	929 (283)	785 (239)
2 (5.1)	948 (289)	820 (250)	792 (241)	925 (282)	—

Table 10.3. Bullet velocity, expressed in feet per second (and meters per second), versus barrel length for the Ruger 77/22.

BARREL LENGTH, IN (CM)	CCI STINGER LR	REM VIPER LR	REM HV LR	REM SV LR	BAIKAL SS LR	REM CB LONGS
20 (50.8)	1,571 (479)	1,331 (406)	1,254 (382)	1,164 (355)	1,041 (317)	735 (224)
18 (45.7)	1,573 (479)	1,353 (412)	1,254 (382)	1,150 (351)	1,038 (316)	747 (228)
16 (40.6)	1,581 (482)	1,351 (412)	1,214 (370)	1,157 (353)	1,049 (320)	763 (233)
14 (35.6)	1,536 (468)	1,342 (409)	1,264 (385)	1,131 (345)	1,018 (310)	752 (229)
12 (30.5)	1,536 (468)	1,342 (409)	1,243 (379)	1,153 (351)	1,015 (309)	742 (226)
10 (25.0)	1,514 (461)	1,303 (397)	1,230 (375)	1,138 (347)	1,023 (312)	717 (219)
8 (20.3)	1,486 (453)	1,247 (380)	1,209 (369)	1,115 (340)	993 (303)	712 (217)
6 (15.2)	1,421 (433)	1,224 (373)	1,173 (358)	1,095 (334)	952 (290)	694 (212)
4 (10.2)	1,310 (399)	1,121 (342)	1,054 (321)	1,027 (313)	902 (275)	655 (200)
2 (5.1)	1,078 (329)	960 (293)	904 (276)	850 (259)	756 (230)	536 (163)

Table 10.4. Muzzle blast, expressed in decibels, versus barrel length for the Ruger 10/22.

BARREL LENGTH, IN (CM)	CCI STINGER LR	REM VIPER LR	REM HV LR	REM SV LR	BAIKAL SS LR
18.5 (47.0)	146.0	145.2	142.0	140.7	140.4
16 (40.6)	146.3	147.6	145.0	142.8	142.1
14 (35.6)	150.5	150.3	146.5	144.7	143.6
12 (30.5)	151.5	151.8	149.6	147.4	146.2
10 (25.0)	154.2	153.6	151.1	150.2	148.5
8 (20.3)	154.2	153.7	152.4	150.4	152.4
6 (15.2)	156.1	155.2	154.4	153.5	152.7
4 (10.2)	158.4	157.8	156.7	156.8	155.4
2 (5.1)	161.0	159.8	159.7	159.5	157.7

Table 10.5. Muzzle blast, expressed in decibels, versus barrel length for the Ruger 77/22.

BARREL LENGTH, IN (CM)	CCI STINGER LR	REM VIPER LR	REM HV LR	REM SV LR	BAIKAL SS LR	REM CB LONGS
20 (50.8)	143.9	142.5	140.8	138.3	136.5	130.3
18 (45.7)	146.0	144.6	142.5	140.3	138.2	132.7
16 (40.6)	146.9	146.4	144.1	140.8	139.7	134.2
14 (35.6)	149.6	147.7	146.1	143.0	142.4	136.0
12 (30.5)	151.3	150.0	148.2	145.9	144.0	137.8
10 (25.0)	152.4	151.4	150.8	149.5	146.3	140.9
8 (20.3)	154.7	153.8	152.0	150.8	149.3	142.6
6 (15.2)	155.4	155.7	153.7	153.1	151.5	145.3
4 (10.2)	158.7	157.6	157.1	155.5	154.2	148.9
2 (5.1)	161.1	161.0	160.4	159.7	158.2	153.7

IMPROVING RELIABILITY OF THE RUGER 10/22

Before suppressing any firearm, it is always useful to test fire the gun first. This is especially true with Ruger firearms, since Sturm, Ruger & Co. seems to have quite erratic quality control when it comes to its .22 rimfire offerings. Barrel quality is particularly variable, and chamber dimensions can be unacceptably out of spec. Suppressing a poor firearm is a wasted effort, although a somewhat disappointing Ruger can frequently be rehabilitated, and an average firearm can be improved to give truly outstanding performance.

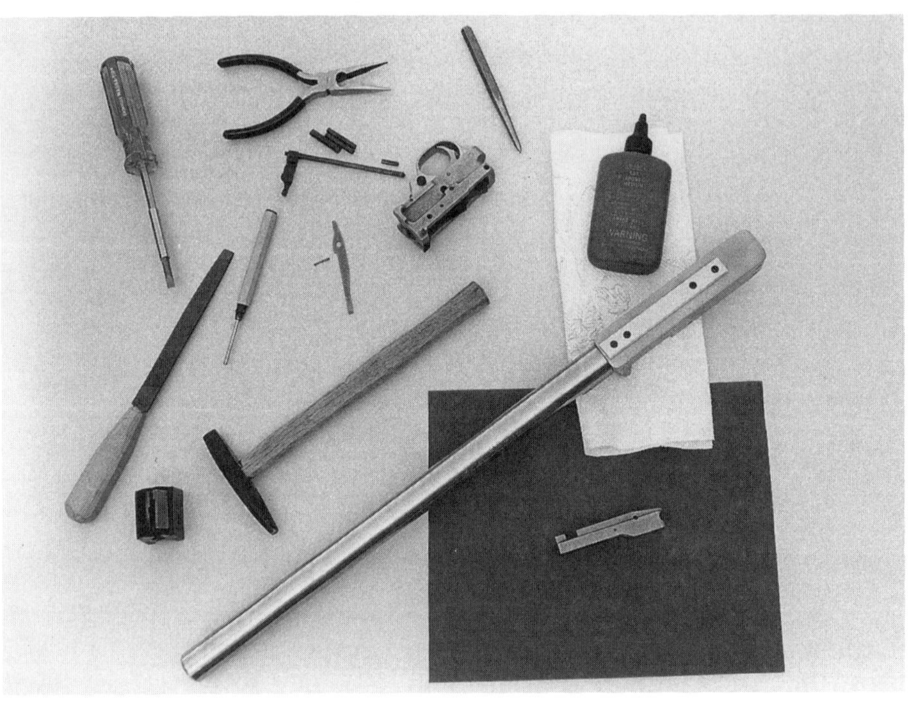

An overview of some of the parts and tools used on the Ruger 10/22.

If test firing a firearm (prior to suppressing it) reveals a catastrophic problem, the best strategy is to return the firearm to the manufacturer. Let the factory take care of obvious problems. For example, Mark White once received a new bolt-action 77/22 that failed to fire. White also received a new stainless Mark II Pistol that shot 48 inch (122 cm) groups at 25 yards (23 m). A small dent in the muzzle crown apparently caused the accuracy problem.

While a skilled individual could have fixed the muzzle crown, what if the problem lay in the chamber or a faulty barrel? Recrowning the barrel would have voided the warranty and necessitated the purchase of a new barrel. White immediately returned both of these guns to the factory, and Ruger replaced the guns with new ones at no cost. The bottom line is: don't waste your time trying to fix a problem that is the responsibility of the manufacturer.

On the other hand, never send a modified firearm back to the factory for repair. If you return a rifle with a spring kit or a trigger job, all the modified parts will automatically be removed and destroyed. That expensive custom work will be replaced with standard factory parts before the firearm is returned, complete with Ruger's heavy, lawyer-inspired trigger pull.

"I don't even want to think," Mark White observed, "about the wrath from BATF that would be visited upon anyone who sent a suppressed arm back to the Ruger factory for repair. If you have a cracked receiver, for instance, have the good sense to put a stock barrel in the action, and put that barreled action into an old factory stock before mailing the unit back to Ruger."

Assuming one has a functioning firearm, there are a number of things the owner can do to enhance the Ruger 10/22's reliability.

Cleaning is an obvious place to start. The 10/22's ejection port is quite small. When the bolt is blown rearward, a substantial amount of gas and spent powder escapes through the chamber into the action. An integrally suppressed carbine will dump considerably more crud into the action because suppressors commonly increase back pressure. Usually, owners will fire their 10/22s until the guns almost cease to function. Then, they'll spray Break Free into the ejection port, cycle the action, and continue to fire. This works several times, after which the rifle simply must be taken apart for cleaning.

Disassembly

Begin disassembly by checking to ensure that the firearm is truly unloaded. Remove the single screw securing the stock to the action (and the barrel band on the economy model), and the barreled action should drop from the stock. Sometimes the safety button needs to be moved a bit so it will clear. If this doesn't do the trick, some tapping with the heel of the hand may be necessary to free the barreled action from the stock.

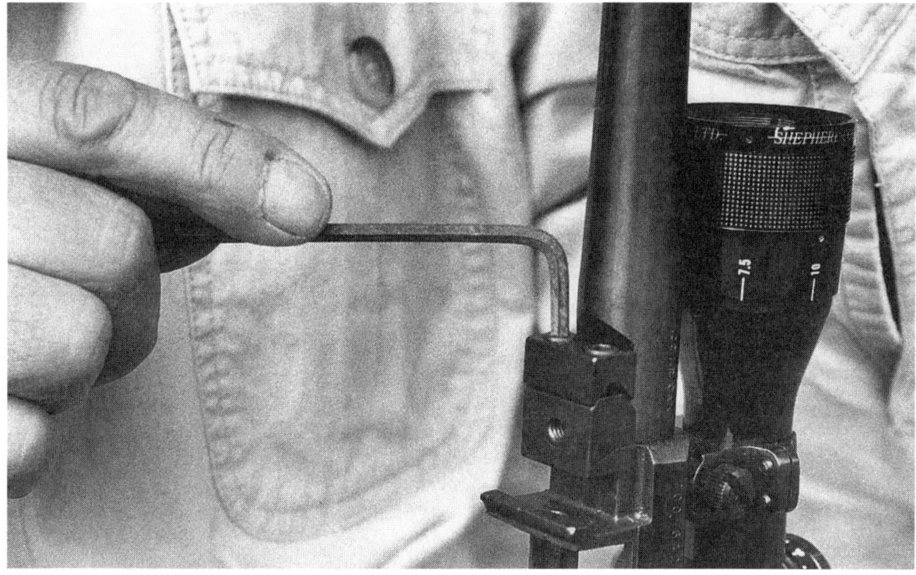

Begin to remove barrel by using the leverage afforded by the long arm of a ball-headed hex (Allen) wrench to loosen two hex screws securing the barrel key.

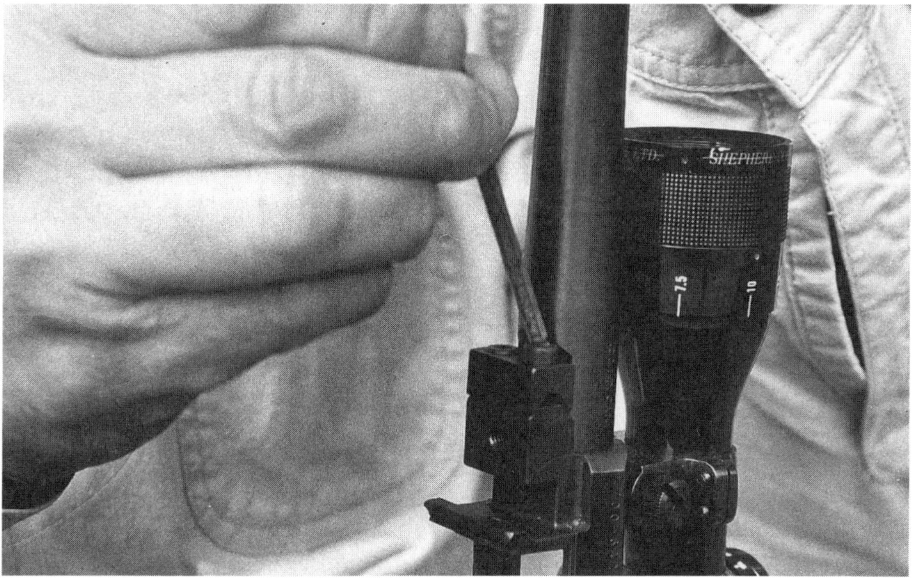

Then use the ball-headed end of the wrench angled appropriately to easily remove the hex screws. The use of a ball-headed wrench greatly facilitates swapping Ruger 10/22 and 77/22 barrels.

As soon as the action is free, three pins commonly fall from the action: the recoil buffer pin is about 1/4 inch (6 mm) in diameter, while the others are 3/16 inch (5 mm). These last two hold the trigger group into the receiver. Push the pins out with a small brass or nylon punch if they haven't already fallen out. These pins are easily lost, so do not try this exercise in the field or on the deck at home.

Place the action on a clean cloth on a table in good light. As one begins further disassembly, take a good look at the pieces and how they go together. White suggests, "I like to take a Polaroid photo of each subassembly when disassembling a gun for the first time. Like inserting 35 mm slides into a Carousel tray, there are eight ways to put it all back together. Seven of them are wrong."

Trigger Group

Fortunately, little of the effluvium escaping rearward from the breach finds its way into the trigger group. Spray liberally with Break Free, and blow out the trigger group with compressed air. Don't forget to shake the Break Free vigorously immediately before use to get the product's Teflon particles properly suspended in the oil. The Teflon settles out very quickly, so repeat the shaking with every use.

Here are some modifications that can be made to improve reliability and trigger pull if you are mechanically gifted. The average shooter should not attempt the following.

The hammer deserves special attention since it provides a significant source of resistance that the bolt must overcome during its rearward travel. Take the hammer out and stone it lightly on both sides to remove any roughness. A sheet of 400 to 600 grit silicon carbide wet-or-dry sandpaper taped to piece of plate glass is ideal for this task. A few strokes on each side are plenty. Then give the forward surface of the hammer about 12 strokes on the paper along its longitudinal axis. This is the surface that bears directly against the bolt, so it should be very smooth.

Mark White made an inexpensive buffing tool out of a surplus 1,725 rpm washing machine motor, a threaded mandrel, and a cloth buffing wheel. He charges the wheel with fine jeweler's rouge and buffs the forward face of the hammer for about a minute. The rouge both slicks and work-hardens the surface, so it slides and wears quite well. It is important to knock down burrs and smooth the surface only. Do not overdo it and change the shape of the metal. Do not remove any metal from the face of the sear.

If the trigger isn't too bad, a very light buffing with a cloth wheel on the sear surfaces will improve its performance. If it needs still more work after buffing, you should send the trigger group to a qualified gunsmith such as Jim Ryan at Gemtech or Mark White at Sound Technology. The average shooter should not attempt to do a trigger job, since this task can be botched easily. Sure signs of a botched trigger job include any of the following problems: 1) the firearm discharges when taken off safe, 2) the gun doubles when the trigger is pressed, or 3) the firearm goes full auto until the magazine is empty. Any of these problems must be corrected immediately by a competent gunsmith to avoid the potential for hurting someone.

Bolt

Take the bolt out by drawing it all the way to the rear and lifting it down and out. This can be a difficult task on some guns. Rinse in solvent and wipe down. Take a drift punch and drive the roll pin holding the firing pin from left to right. Remove the firing pin and its spring. Lightly smooth the top and both sides of the bolt on 600 grit paper taped to a sheet of glass, working only in a lengthwise direction. Then buff the bolt on a wheel like the one White made, and smooth the top and both sides. Also buff the rear surface, where the hammer rubs.

Do nothing to the forward bolt face. Be careful with the extractor: do not polish it or allow it to snag on the cloth wheel. Again, the buffing action (with a slow, circa 1,700 rpm wheel) will smooth and work-harden these surfaces. Neither sanding, stoning, nor grinding is a suitable substitute for buffing with jeweler's rouge. When finished, rinse the bolt with carburetor cleaner (do this outside!) and let dry.

The bolt produces most of the sound classified as action noise, which can be a significant part of a 10/22's overall sound signature. This action noise has two principal components: 1) the bolt slamming forward against the rear of the barrel as a round is chambered, and 2) the slap of the bolt against the rear of the receiver during the action cycle. Strictly speaking, the bolt strikes a 1/4 inch (6 mm) pin set in the rear of the receiver.

I have two proposals for reducing these two sources of action noise. The rear of the Ruger barrel could be machined with an annular groove designed to hold an O-ring, which would buffer the

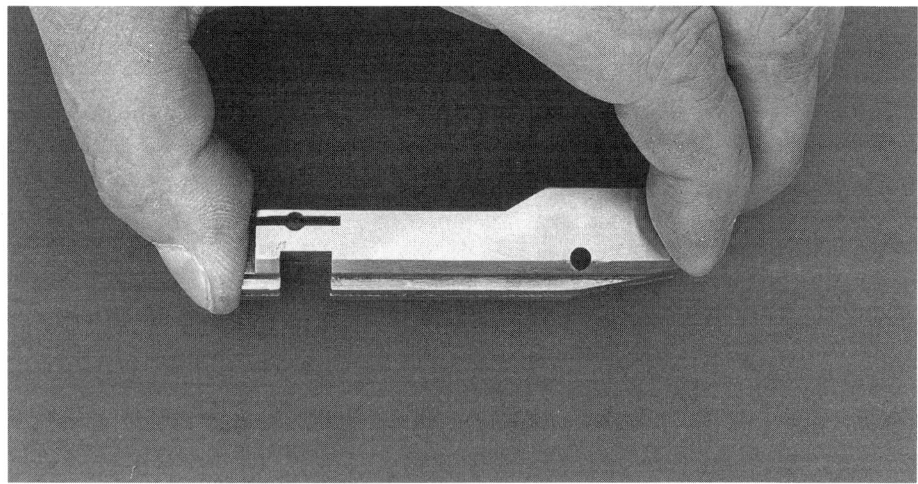

A sheet of 400 to 600 grit wet or dry paper backed by a smooth hard surface can be used to smooth the top and sides of the bolt and firing pin. Do not overdo this. Only a few strokes are necessary. Follow with a light buffing.

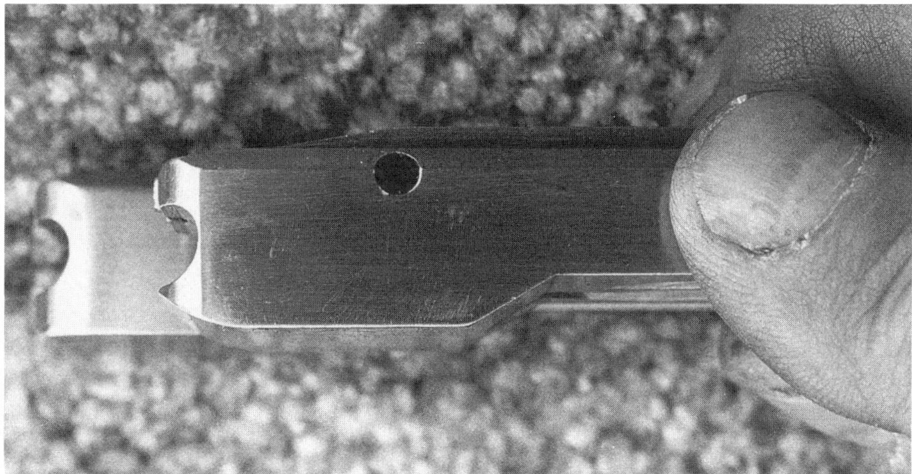

The rear of the Ruger 10/22 bolt in the foreground was chamfered by hand to generally conform with Ralph Seifert's technique for improving reliability.

sound of the bolt striking the barrel. And the steel pin in the rear of the receiver could be replaced with a nylon rod of appropriate dimensions to dampen the sound of the rearward slap of the bolt. I have not yet had the opportunity to test the efficacy of these remedies, but I shall try them at the earliest opportunity. With a bit of luck, and perhaps trying several different materials for the buffers, the sound of the rear of the bolt slamming against the hammer might become the dominant aspect of the 10/22's action noise. I hope to be able to report on a test of these hypotheses in a subsequent volume of this series.

Firing Pin

The most common cause of misfires in the Ruger 10/22 and 77/22 is the firing pin. Both rifles have fairly short firing pins that are designed to avoid damaging the chambers when the rifles are dry fired. This design decision can lead to short stroking of the firing pin, which causes chronic misfires with some kinds of ammunition. Furthermore, some rifles will produce misfires with all types of ammo. Short stroking of the firing pin is especially common with the Ruger 77/22. Ordering a new firing pin will not fix the problem, since it will probably be as short as the old one. The best solution is to modify the 10/22 firing pin or lengthen the 77/22 firing pin.

The 10/22's firing pin is a flat steel stamping made from medium hard, fairly tough steel. The firing pin seems to be responsible for most of the 10/22's misfires. Its fitting is tricky, since a misfire will result if the firing pin won't move far enough forward. If the pin goes too far forward, dry firing will cause it to hit the rear of the barrel, damaging the chamber at the point of impact. This will cause failure to feed or failure to extract. Such damage also degrades accuracy.

If a 10/22 is having problems with misfires, Mark White will take a small, round chain saw file and elongate the rear of the hole where the roll pin goes through, allowing the firing pin to travel farther forward. Typically, this only requires removing about 0.008 inch (0.0003 mm) or so.

It is sometimes necessary to remove some metal from the forward edge of the hook on the bottom of the firing pin. File a little, reassemble, and check with a straight edge held against the forward face of the bolt in good light. In no case should the pin touch that straight edge, since that much forward travel runs the risk of damaging the chamber.

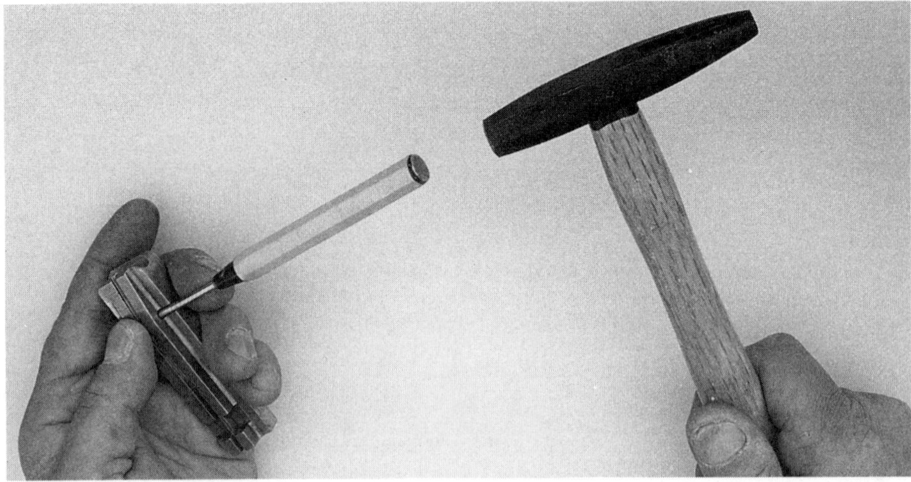

Use a hammer and punch to remove the roll pin from the bolt, which locks the firing pin in place. By tradition, pins are driven from left to right when removing them and from right to left when installing them.

Do not sharpen the striking point of the firing pin. To do so would allow the pin to pierce the rim of the cartridge. If that happens, the bullet could go about halfway down the barrel, and stop. The next shot could bulge the barrel, destroying accuracy. Remember, be careful with the filing. Take only enough out of the rear of the hole to allow sufficient pin travel to ignite the rimmed primer.

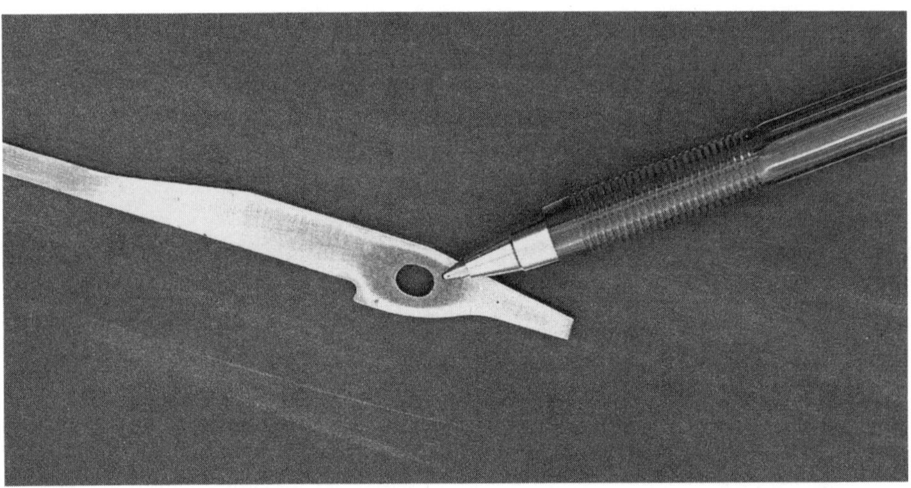

The pen points to the area of the hole in the rear of the Ruger 10/22 firing pin. If, and only if, the firearm suffers failures to fire because the firing pin is too short, this hole needs to be enlarged with a file in very small increments.

Once the 10/22's firing pin is fitted properly, stone both sides lightly and buff smooth. If the firing pin is badly mushroomed at the rear, order a new one.

The 77/22's firing pin is round and requires a different strategy for lengthening. Remove the firing pin and measure with calipers. Place the firing pin on a thick piece of flat metal and hammer repeatedly on the side, rotating the pin 90 degrees or so between blows. Regularly remeasure the length, and stop when the pin is about 0.008 inches (0.02 mm) longer than the initial measurement. Take care not to bend the firing pin during this procedure. This hammering process is an old gunsmithing trick used to restore drillings and other old collectibles with worn and irreplaceable firing pins.

Extractor

Examine the extractor in the bolt face. If it is bent, sticking, worn, or dull, replace it. It takes a weird push, straight to the rear, and then out to remove it. Don't lose the little spring.

Bolt Spring and Follower

The main operating (recoil) spring is a weak point in the design of the Ruger 10/22. The fit between the operating spring and its spring guide is tight, creating friction that wastes some of the energy available to cycle the bolt. The spring is normally a bit stiff. This is usually acceptable in an unmodified 10/22, but the spring can be too stiff for some suppressed systems, depending on such factors as porting, suppressor volume, and baffle design. If you continue to experience feeding problems, removing a coil or two from the operating spring might help. As with the firing pin, do not make any changes if feeding is not a problem.

The best way to remove a few coils is to use a cutting wheel on a Dremel tool. The springs are usually quite soft as springs go and are easy to work. Compress the spring with the bolt handle and buff the exposed portion of the shaft to make it slick. Buff only that portion of the spring guide that rubs against the hole in the bolt handle. A more expensive but interesting alternative is to replace the factory spring-guide-handle assembly with a titanium Power Custom extended bolt handle, which features a lighter (4 ounce; 113 g) spring with polished guide rod and a longer, curved bolt handle that's easier to grasp when charging or clearing the chamber (available as part #713-301-103 from Brownells, 200 S. Front Street, Montezuma, IA 50171-9989). A nice touch with this system is that economical replacement springs can be fitted to the assembly.

Power Custom titanium extended bolt handle, which features a lighter spring than factory specs, plus a polished guide rod and a longer, curved bolt handle that's easier to grasp when charging or clearing the chamber.

Ralph Seifert of RASE has come up with a simple bolt modification that can eliminate the need for using a shortened recoil spring in suppressed Ruger rifles and pistols. The technique also works when using low-recoil-impulse rounds with unsuppressed delayed-blowback arms in general and can even improve the reliability of the Colt Model 1911 .45 pistol and its descendents. Seifert points out that the hammer in delayed-blowback firearms provides a considerable amount of the mechanical resistance to rearward bolt travel as extraction begins. The hammer operates as a lever against the resistive force of the hammer spring. Anything you can do to apply the rearward force of the bolt farther up the lever (i.e., hammer) away from its pivot point will provide more leverage against the hammer spring. This means that the bolt loses less momentum to the hammer spring, so it has more momentum to compress the main operating spring. Applying these principles to the Ruger 10/22 rifle, Seifert chamfers the bottom rear edge of the bolt with a 45-degree bevel across the entire rear of the bolt. When modifying a Ruger Mark II pistol, he chamfers the bottom rear section of the bolt just below the firing pin.

While this may not provide a stand-alone solution to cycling reliability, Seifert's bolt modification can dramatically enhance other strategies such as polishing the bolt. It still may be necessary with some combinations of barrel, ammunition, and suppressor design to shorten the recoil spring.

But if the bolt is chamfered as Seifert suggests, it will not be necessary to remove as many coils from the main operating spring. The resulting spring will be longer and will provide more reliable feeding and chambering. If you are experiencing problems with bolt cycling, I highly recommend trying Ralph Seifert's technique.

Mark White of Sound Technology is so impressed with Seifert's modification that he adds this chamfer to every Ruger 10/22 bolt that goes through his shop. I have gradually added this modification to all of my own 10/22s as well. This chamfer is especially desirable on John Norrell's select-fire 10/22 rifle, although special care must be taken not to destroy the heavily modified bolt. Combined with polishing the bolt and follower, Seifert's bolt modification enables Norrell's select-fire 10/22 to function reliably with a much wider range of ammunition.

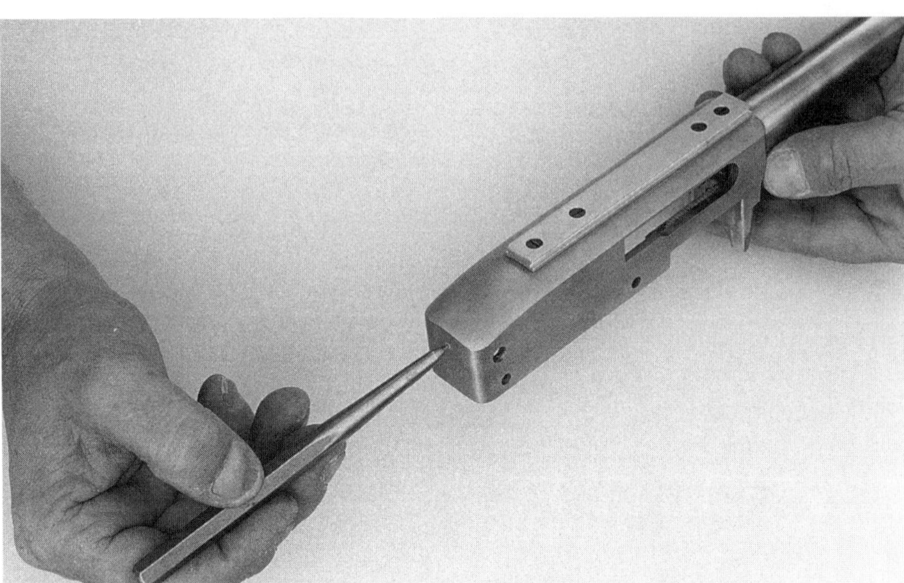

The best way to drill a barrel-cleaning hole in the rear of the Ruger 10/22 receiver is to chuck the barreled action in a lathe and use the tail stock to drill a 15/64 inch hole in the rear. This particular action was merely eyeballed, but the hole was nevertheless located within 0.010 inch of the bore's true center.

Receiver

Clean the inside of the receiver with a suitable solvent. Avoid Hoppe's Number 9; it eats aluminum. Use a small, sharp screwdriver and a bit of rag to get deep into the corners near the barrel, where most of the lube wax and powder residue collects.

Some people like to enlarge the ejection port and even drill a large hole in the left side of the action to encourage the venting of fouling that is ejected from the chamber. Drilling a hole, unfortunately, removes part of the serial number. The act of intentionally destroying a firearm's serial number is a felony in the United States.

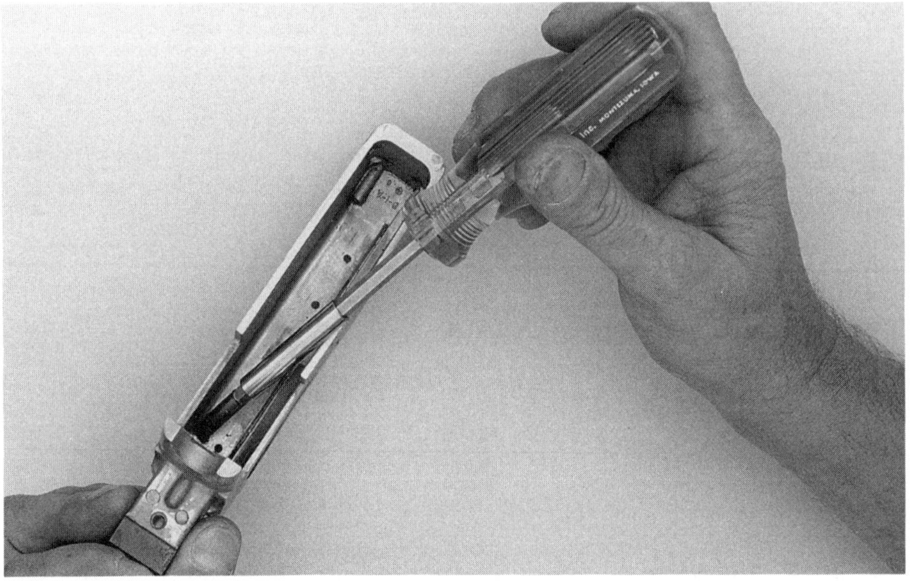

A screwdriver is used to scrape accumulated fouling from the action near the barrel.

Mark White observes, "I do not encourage changing the port or drilling any holes in the receiver to vent the gasses. If Ruger ever changes the design of their receiver, I encourage them to do something about this area, which acts as a trap for crud. One thought which comes to mind is a slanted forward face on the bolt, which would direct the flow of gas to the right and out the port, as seen on the piston and porting of a two-cycle engine. In terms of safety, the covered area of the receiver does prevent gas and brass from a ruptured shell from flying into the face of a right-handed shooter. Unfortunately, a left-handed shooter is not as well protected. Shooting glasses are a must for left-handers using a Ruger 10/22 and are not a bad idea for right-handed shooters as well."

Chamber Dirt and Dings

A dirty chamber is all too common in the 10/22. It should be cleaned from the rear with a bent brass or nylon bore brush and solvent. Once cleaned, it should be examined for a dent from the firing pin. If found, the dent should be reamed out. A very slight chamfer of the edge of the chamber will help cartridges enter the chamber more easily. White keeps a small, dull knife near his lathe for this task. One small twirl with light pressure around the crown of the chamber produces the ideal chamfer. A small twist with a machinist's countersink, by hand, will accomplish the same task. Be careful not to remove too much material.

If the barrel is out of the action, a nylon bore brush can be chucked into an electric drill and used with rouge to polish the chamber. Do not go deeper than 0.75 inch (1.9 cm). Go slow. Don't melt the nylon. Clean with a patch and bore solvent. Keep running patches through until they come out clean. Generally, a .22's bore is kept lubed by the wax on the soft lead bullets, so the bore won't require much cleaning.

All rifles should be cleaned from the breech. Mark White pioneered the boring of a hole in the rear of the Ruger 10/22 receiver so a cleaning rod can be inserted through the rear of the action and the barrel can be cleaned properly from the rear with the action removed from the stock. The barrel need not be removed from the receiver. Upon reassembly of the stock to the barreled action, the stock covers the outside of the hole and the 1/4 inch buffer pin covers the inside of the hole, so this operation is cosmetically benign and relatively gas tight. This feature should be standard on every factory rifle. Since it's not, this is one modification that should be made on every Ruger 10/22, in my opinion. Be forewarned that some aftermarket stocks, such as Butler Creek's fixed stock, will not cover the hole completely. Most, however, will.

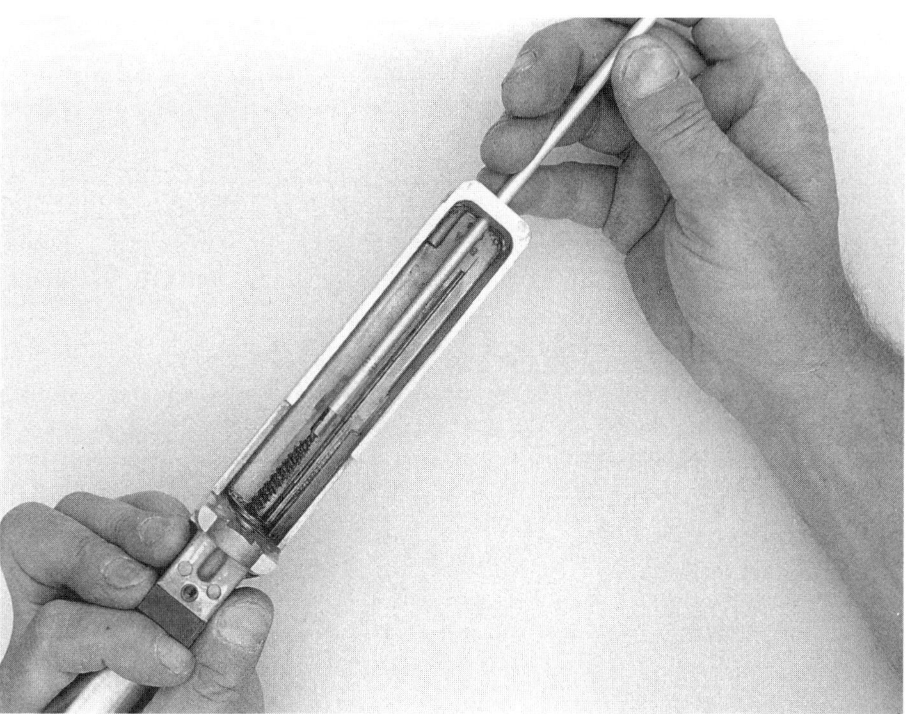

Use a bronze bore brush and solvent to scrub fouling from the chamber and bore. This procedure is much more difficult without an access hole in the rear of the receiver.

White frequently mentions the virtues of a short, tight chamber for a suppressed firearm. A target rifle or pistol produces optimal accuracy when the lands are engraved on the bullet just as the cartridge is fully chambered. This also raises chamber pressure, which produces more complete combustion and, therefore, generates less secondary combustion when the expanding gases reach the suppressor. This produces a lower suppressed sound signature. Extensive sound testing suggests that a tight chamber of custom dimensions can improve a suppressor's efficiency as much as 7 to 9 dB over what might normally have been expected.

Unfortunately, a short, tight chamber can hold the bullet so tightly that it will stick in the rifling when attempting to extract an unfired cartridge. Thus, any shell that is loaded into an extremely short, tight chamber must be fired. A corollary to this law is that misfires must be driven out with a cleaning rod. Such is the price for pushing the edge of the envelope in terms of accuracy and suppression.

A final problem with integrally suppressed firearms is that many small and even some large and well-known suppressor manufacturers don't bother to deburr the ports they've drilled in the barrel. I looked down the barrel of one Ruger 77/22 and discovered that massive burring had reduced the effective bore diameter to about .15 caliber. Burrs not only degrade accuracy, they accelerate the leading shut of the ports and thus dramatically reduce the service life of the suppressed firearm. The easiest way to test for this problem is to run a patch all the way through the bore. If noticeable resistance is encountered, it will be necessary to deburr the ports (a difficult task without the proper tool).

Stainless Barrels

Stainless steel is a wonderful material, but it is very difficult to machine cleanly. Whereas carbon steel cuts freely and takes a crisp edge, stainless tends to gall (ball up) under a cutting tool. Although it's the chrome content of stainless that tends to dull tool edges, the galling action is primarily due to the nickel in the alloy, which tends to smear and cover the steel's surface, thus making it rust resistant. A typical Ruger stainless barrel is often quite soft in some areas and extremely hard (almost crumbly) in others. Most of the major barrel manufacturers dislike stainless because it is difficult to machine cleanly.

I've owned some superb custom stainless match barrels and an extremely accurate stainless Ruger Security Six .357 Magnum revolver, but the quality of Ruger rimfire rifle barrels fabricated from stainless steel has often been disappointing. My experience with dozens of Ruger factory (not custom match) barrels is that the stainless 10/22 and 77/22 barrels produce significantly less accuracy than carbon steel barrels. My recommendation is to avoid *factory* stainless rimfire barrels at all costs. A carbon steel barrel can be fitted inside a stainless steel integral suppressor at the time it is made, thus preserving the aesthetic appearance of the arm without sacrificing accuracy.

Magazines

Magazines are the most common cause of malfunctions when firing automatic weapons, and they affect the reliability of rimfire sporting arms as well. Factory Ruger magazines can be cleaned by spraying with Break Free and blowing them out with compressed air. Disassemble and clean problem magazines. Some factory magazines have a sticking point (typically the second or eighth round), which is caused by a burr on the rotating piece inside the magazine. Simply stone or file off the burr to eliminate the problem.

The most common feeding problem generated by a factory magazine occurs when a 77/22 magazine is inserted into a 10/22 rifle or vice versa. Some basic dimensions differ, and the two magazines present the cartridges differently to the bolt. A person with a practiced eye and time to spare can tell the two magazines apart. The 10/22 magazines are round on the bottom and deeper. The

77/22 magazines are flat on the bottom, tapered in profile, and shallow. Nevertheless, with a score of 77/22 and 10/22 factory magazines mixed up in my kit bag, grabbing the wrong magazine was a continual source of frustration. Dr. Phil Dater (the president of Gemtech) provided an ingenious solution: engrave the bottom of each 77/22 magazine with "77/22" to avoid any confusion. Dater's approach is affordable and foolproof.

I've also had very good luck with Butler Creek magazines, which seem to be more robust than Ramline magazines. Neither should be oiled or sprayed with Break Free, since this would adversely affect the operation of the magazine's ribbon spring.

Reassembly

With all of the major moving parts cleaned and polished, it is time for reassembly. As the parts are assembled, they should be lubricated lightly but thoroughly. Break Free or LSA Weapons Oil Medium (MIL-L-46000B) work well, and both incorporate Teflon. Shake well before using to suspend the Teflon particles properly. Once the rifle is reassembled, cycle the action a few times to make sure everything is working properly.

Do not use WD-40 for anything related to firearms except to cool down a smoking machine gun barrel. WD-40 has little lubricating value, and it has inferior staying power. While on the subject of lubricants, it would be useful to discuss a phenomenon peculiar to blowback actions: high first-round syndrome.

High First-Round Syndrome

A film of almost any lubricant between two smooth surfaces tends to bond those surfaces together loosely. The bolt and receiver of the Ruger 10/22 rifle and Mark II pistol provide suitable surfaces for this phenomenon. This loose bond tends to increase felt recoil early in the operating cycle, which results in slight elevation of the muzzle before the bullet exits.

The result of this loose bond is that the first shot in a string will commonly strike 2 to 3 inches (5 to 8 cm) high at 50 yards (46 m), compared to the center of the group produced by subsequent shots. While this is not a significant problem when plinking, this phenomenon can make a big difference when hunting, competing in a tournament, or working as an animal control officer. The only way to avoid this problem is to use a 77/22 instead of a 10/22 rifle or to install one of Jim Ryan's bolt locks (available from Gemtech) on the Ruger Mark II pistol.

Temperature also affects shot placement. Chemical reactions tend to proceed more rapidly with an increase in temperature. Thus, cartridges tend to produce greater bullet velocity an a hot day than on a cold one. This affects trajectory, which will be flatter on a hot day. Bullet drop will become exaggerated on a cold day.

ACCURIZING THE RUGER 10/22

Much can be done to improve the accuracy of Ruger rifles in spite of the barrel-mounting system used on the 10/22 and 77/22, which does not provide optimal alignment and rigidity. Furthermore, the slice that is taken out of the barrel near the breech for Ruger's barrel retention key certainly does not enhance barrel rigidity.

Factory Ruger barrels are held to their receivers with two hex (Allen) screws and a small steel key. To maximize barrel rigidity in the receiver, these screws should be tightened to an optimal torque, which seems to be about 35 inch-pounds. Tighten both screws to the same tension (the Ruger factory rarely tightens the screws equally). Do not overtighten the screws, since this will split the key. Use a feeler gauge on both sides of the barrel slot to ensure that the slot is not canted in the action. If you don't own an adjustable torque wrench with hex-wrench sockets, a field expedient is to push the end of a 4 inch hex wrench with a kitchen scale until it reads 9 pounds, thus yielding a torque of 36 inch-pounds.

Those with an uncompromising demand for maximizing accuracy remove the Ruger's front mounting bracket from the action, which is then line bored, faced, and threaded to accept a match barrel. Such surgery is not necessary, however, to achieve a considerable improvement in the accuracy of a suppressed or unsuppressed rifle.

Mark White points out that, "Competitions in recent years, like the Chevy Truck Challenge, have tremendously improved the popularity of the 10/22. Its handiness, shootability, and modularity have all combined to push it to the top, where it now stands as the industry standard for competition. In turn, its popularity may have prompted Ruger to increase quality to some degree, as current models appear to be more accurate and reliable than those produced as recently as 1992. The use of this firearm in competition has caused aftermarket 10/22 components to become one of the largest growth areas in the firearms industry." Unfortunately, aftermarket products for the Ruger 77/22 remain woefully lacking.

The following discussion will focus primarily on those factors affecting accuracy of the Ruger 10/22, starting with the barrel, and then moving to action, stock, and sighting equipment.

Barrel

The barrel is the heart of any accurate delivery system. Factors that influence barrel performance include chamber dimensions, bore diameter, rate of twist, smoothness of the bore, uniformity of the bore, and barrel crown. Let's examine these factors starting at the rear and working forward.

The 10/22's chamber should be loose at the rear and tight at the front. As each new cartridge is stripped from its magazine, it needs to be elevated about 5/16 inch (8 mm) from its former position. The feed lips in the magazine hold the cartridge for some time during its forward and upward travel. So there is a time when the rear of the case is restrained from upward travel by those feed lips, while the bullet and the forward portion of the case are trying to enter the chamber. Something has to give, and it won't be either the magazine or the barrel's chamber.

Often the nose of the soft lead bullet will have been somewhat deformed by striking the rear of the barrel as the cartridge finds its way into the chamber. The rear of the bullet can bend in the case as it tries to travel this curved route, deforming the skirt. Granted, some of these deformities will be ironed out when the bullet takes to the rifling. But not all of them.

To analyze this feeding process on a particular 10/22, cycle the action slowly by hand and tap the bolt forward slowly with a small mallet to get an idea of just what takes place. Eject the chambered shell and examine it. Usually the side of the lead bullet will have been scraped by the bolt when its mate above was being chambered. The tip will also have been mashed a bit, and the shell will be a bit crooked from traveling that curved path. While proper magazine selection and forward guidance is part of the story, a chamber with the optimal dimensions for both feeding and accuracy is responsible for most of the reliability/accuracy equation.

A factory Ruger barrel may have the proper chamber dimensions, but it may not. Since the 10/22 has become so popular for competition shooting, much effort has been directed at developing the optimal chamber for it. Several tooling manufacturers have developed chamber reamers that combine easy feeding with a gentle but tighter throat. Brownells sells a Bentz .22 LR match reamer with a 1.5 degree throat angle specifically designed for match ammo in semiauto guns. Using the proper reamer with plenty of cutting oil is the first step toward achieving an optimal chamber. Such a chamber should be cut on a new barrel blank, since Ruger's barrel-mounting system makes cutting back and rechambering a factory barrel more trouble than it's worth.

Once the chamber has been reamed, a little lapping and polishing will remove tool marks and blemishes in the chamber and throat so lead accumulation is less likely to occur. A barrel that is already chambered can be opened up a bit at the rear and polished. J.B. Bore Cleaner works well for the initial polishing, and fine rouge works for the final stage. White recommends that the bullet portion of 30 to 50 rounds be dipped in a mixture of oil and rouge for fire-lapping. Place each round by hand into the chamber to avoid contaminating magazines with abrasive. Flush the bore with carburetor cleaner when done, and run a lightly oiled patch down the bore. *White has found that, once a barrel has been properly fire-lapped, using a bore brush is neither necessary nor desirable.* Two or three patches are all that is necessary to clean the bore. Furthermore, scouring a fire-lapped bore with even a mild brush seems to eventually degrade accuracy in his experience.

Moving down the barrel, the rifling should have the optimal bore dimension and twist. The .22 rimfire arm is commonly encountered with a groove diameter of about 0.223 inch (5.56 mm), with a twist of from 1 turn in 13 inches (33 cm) to 1 in 18 inches (46 mm). A 1 in 16 inch twist tends to be most common. Ruger's bores tend to be a little bigger than other manufacturers. As production reamers and rifling buttons wear, the bores get smaller, decreasing both bore and groove size. Reamers jam and break when they get dull and are often tossed out before they get greatly undersized. Rifling buttons, however, can still be used in a smaller state. The bottom line is that bores (i.e., groove diameter) can range from 0.218 inch (5.54 mm) to 0.227 inch (5.77 mm). A groove diameter of 0.223 inch is considered optimal.

The reason that serious shooters test-fire a variety of different ammunition in search of the most accurate round is that different brands (and even different lots) of ammunition may or may not provide the ideal match of bullet hardness and diameter with a particular barrel's bore size and rifling style.

As a rule, the well-lubricated soft lead .22 bullets do not cause significant bore wear. Throat wear and erosion may be a factor after 50,000 rounds, but bore wear should not be a factor. Heavily used bolt-action target rifles are often cut back a mere 1/8 inch (3.2 mm) and rechambered to restore accuracy lost through throat erosion. Shooting bursts of full-auto fire from a .22 rimfire machine gun will, however, heat a barrel more rapidly, and shooting through a hot barrel will generate more rapid throat erosion.

Bore straightness and barrel concentricity are very important to accuracy, especially during rapid fire. A crooked bore is often capable of one or two moderately accurate shots. But as the barrel heats up from subsequent shots, the thinner side of a barrel's wall will expand more rapidly, walking the shots away from the thinner section. Mark White has chopped quite a number of Ruger barrels in half, and he observed that well over 70 percent of them did not have the bore concentric with the outer diameter of the barrel. Whereas some of these barrels were fairly true about 9 inches (23 cm) from the breech, most were from 1/8 to 3/16 inch (3.2 to 4.8 mm) out. A way to correct this problem is to shorten the barrel, say to 16.1 inches (40.9 cm) to avoid paying a $200 registration fee for a short-barreled rifle if more were removed, and then lathe-turn and recontour the barrel between centers to obtain the greatest degree of concentricity.

With regard to accuracy in factory Ruger rifle barrels, some are excellent, some are fair, and some are poor. "In my experience," Mark White observes, "it is possible to make a fair barrel shoot a little better, but I have never been able to do anything with a poor one. Often, poor barrels have poor chambers, out-of-spec bores, crooked bores, or scrubbed bores [which have been ruined by the use of a Tornado brush or a steel brush that is harder than the barrel]. On occasion, I have spent considerable time with these sows' ears, all to no avail. Before I suppress or chop a barrel these days, I put it into a good action and fire five shots on paper. If something is wrong, it shows up right away and I discard that barrel."

Over the last decade, a number of innovative manufacturers have begun to supply aftermarket match-grade barrels for the 10/22. They start with air-gauged premium barrels that have been carefully bored, reamed, rifled, and straightened. These blanks have been properly turned between centers using multiple light cuts to avoid deforming the metal. The match barrels are then carefully chambered with a short, tapered reamer of optimal dimensions, cut to length, and carefully crowned. There is no magic to the operation—just patience, knowledge, and careful craftsmanship.

Clark makes one such barrel (blued or stainless) profiled to a standard contour that will drop into an unmodified factory stock and action. Clark and others also make a straight match barrel with no taper (about 0.920 inch or 23.4 mm in diameter) that fits a standard action but requires either routing out a larger channel in the factory stock or the purchase of an aftermarket stock designed expressly for these barrels. Clark, Shilen, D&J Custom, and Volquartsen all make high-quality barrels. Their short chambers also generate higher pressures that produce an extra 75 fps or so over 10/22 barrels from the Ruger factory.

"Unless you really want the shiny look of stainless steel," White suggests, "stick with regular blued steel for gun barrels. It cuts more crisply and thus tends to be more accurate than stainless. I have heard of a few instances where blued or stainless match blanks were purchased for use in suppressed 10/22s. Typically, they were not worth the extra expense. In my experience, an accurate blued factory barrel that has been intelligently ported [i.e., deburred], fire-lapped, and tensioned will make a very accurate suppressed rifle."

The last thing that a bullet touches on the way out is the muzzle crown, which must be perfect for maximum accuracy. Cleaning the rifle from the muzzle will damage that crown. White pioneered the installation of a 0.24 inch (5 mm) hole in the rear of the receiver in line with the bore, which allows cleaning from the rear. A bronze brush (never stainless steel) or cleaning patch makes a *one-way* trip from breech to muzzle. Push the brush or patch out the muzzle, remove the brush or patch, and carefully withdraw the rod. Even though White developed this cleaning port at the rear of the 10/22's receiver for Sound Technology, he encourages other suppressor manufacturers and gunsmiths to use the technique with his blessing. At the time of this writing, Gemtech is the only other company that incorporates this feature into its suppressed 10/22s. Everyone should.

A lubricated .22 rimfire bullet carries enough wax or grease for a short 16 or 18 inch (41 or 46 cm) barrel. When fired in longer barrels, the bullets begin to run dry and coat the lands with lead. Because of this phenomenon, target shooters with 24 inch (61 cm) barrels often have to clean the lead out of the last 6 to 8 inches (15 to 20 cm) of their barrels.

The so-called "muzzle star" occurs because combustion gases blow past the bullet on the non-driving side of each land as the bullet starts down the bore and is forced to spin. As the bullet reaches the muzzle, these gas jets (usually six or one for each land) blow a mixture of lube and lead across the face of the muzzle. Remove this deposit with a hard cloth, and the star will soon reappear. If the crown is not perfect, the gas jets will be uneven, and parts of the star may be thicker than others when examined under a strong hand lens. This can be a useful tool when trying to determine whether the crown is adversely affecting accuracy. A poor crown may have an indentation or bump that strikes each bullet on the way out, causing it to wobble.

Sometimes the face of the barrel was not cut square with the bore, which releases more gas on one side than on the other as the bullet exits. This also causes the projectiles to tip and wobble at the critical instant of departure.

Barrels whip and vibrate to one degree or another when they are fired, and this can degrade accuracy. The traditional way to minimize harmonic vibration is to use a heavy barrel. White has used a different system for several decades to improve the accuracy of rifles that is based on tensioning a barrel inside a tube. In essence, the system uses a steel tube that slips over a barrel with a groove carefully machined near the breech to receive the tube. The barrel's muzzle end is threaded and a machined nut is used to draw the barrel in tension, leaving the tube in compression. White typically uses about 800 pounds (364 kg) of tension for a .22 rimfire rifle barrel. While the heavy barrel system may be described as passive, the White's tensioned barrel is more akin to a live or active system.

His system has both advantages and liabilities over the use of a heavy barrel. The advantages of the tensioning include lighter weight, increased rigidity, a tendency not to walk shots as the system heats up, and a light "choke" where the 60° threads of the tensioning nut squeeze the muzzle of the barrel inward. The advantage of the passive system is that its greater weight dampens shooter-induced oscillations to a greater degree. The tensioned barrel has been used with great success by Smith & Wesson in its 422 series pistols and by Dan Wesson Arms in its revolvers.

Few suppressor manufacturers incorporate tensioned barrels into any of their designs. Those systems that do incorporate tensioned barrels deliver better accuracy than comparable systems that don't. Gemtech and Sound Technology, for example, use tensioned barrels; Jonathan Arthur Ciener does not.

Action

The Ruger 10/22 usually suffers from a heavy, lawyer-inspired trigger that can require a pull of up to 17 pounds (7.7 kg). The accuracy produced by almost any Ruger rifle or pistol can be improved significantly with a trigger job. One must be careful when reducing the pull, however, since making it too light may allow the hammer to follow the bolt forward, resulting in full-auto fire that will not stop until the magazine is empty. One must be particularly careful to ensure that the safety still functions after a trigger job. Some improperly light triggers allow the gun to fire as soon as the safety is released or when the gun is bumped. Trigger work should be performed by a competent gunsmith. A Volquartsen drop-in hammer provides one of the easiest and safest ways to improve the trigger.

Safety

The safest way to carry a Ruger 10/22 rifle is with the bolt locked open. Take the time to learn how to manipulate the bolt-locking device. Engage the excellent cross-bolt safety whenever appropriate. A less obvious but very real safety problem arises with suppressed .22s simply because they are so quiet. Some people become lulled by the lack of a painful muzzle blast into a lack of respect for the firearm. *It is imperative to remember that a suppressed firearm can be just as deadly as a conventional firearm.* Remember to always keep the muzzle pointed in a safe direction. And keep the finger off the trigger until the sights are aligned on the target.

Sighting Systems

Ruger's leaf sights may work for young eyes, but they become increasingly unsatisfactory with age. For those who must have iron sights, replace the rear sight with the Williams receiver sight WGRS-RU-22 fitted with either a large peep or the WGRS Ghost Ring Aperture. Either fold down the original rear sight and leave it or drift it out with a punch and fill the slot with a blank filler from Brownells. The ghost ring is very fast for snap shooting, yet it is surprisingly accurate in skilled hands. It is my rear sight of choice.

A fixed 4- or 6-power scope with duplex reticle seems to be the standard for most casual shooters and small-game hunters. (For caribou, however, I prefer the out-of-production 7.5x Leupold. For spring ptarmigan hunts on steep, snow-covered mountain slopes, I used to prefer a 10-power scope.) Decades of hunting in the Alaskan bush have given me a strong bias in favor of fixed-power scopes over variables. A fixed-power scope is generally more robust, brighter, lighter, and cheaper than a variable.

Nevertheless, the auto-ranging 2.5-7.5x Shepherd rimfire scope has become my favorite scope for the 10/22 and 77/22 in recent years. The auto-ranging feature corrects for bullet drop of high-velocity ammunition out to 250 yards and permits the skilled shooter to make shots at unprecedented distances. The Shepherd also features a mechanism for sighting in the scope with a single shot.

The Shepherd scope is particularly useful for rifles equipped with muzzle cans. This is because every time the suppressor is screwed onto the barrel, it will index differently and will probably be tightened with a different torque. Both of these variables can affect the point of bullet impact, and any rifle will probably need to be resighted every time the suppressor is installed. Being able to rezero with a single round makes this telescopic sight particularly friendly.

The 2.5-7.5x Shepherd rimfire scope that appears throughout this volume has now been superseded by the Model 310-P.22 scope, which varies from 3x to 10x and features a ranging reticle that corrects for the drop of high-velocity LR ammunition out to 500 yards in 50-yard increments. The new scope is 14 inches (36 cm) long, and its objective bell is 2 inches (5 cm) in diameter on a 1 inch (2.5 cm) tube. The 310-P.22 scope weighs 21 ounces (595 grams).

Like its predecessor, the 310-P.22 features a three-leg fixed reticle with a fourth leg formed by a moveable reticle with ranging circles that subtend about 9 inches at the range indicated to the right of the circle. Each circle is about the size of a crow or standing prairie dog. (Centerfire Shepherd scopes use an 18 inch circle, which corresponds to the distance between the top of a deer's shoulder and the bottom of its chest.) The sight picture also includes a scale indicating 1 MOA increments. While this scale might be expected to make for a very cluttered sight picture, the reality is that the marks are so fine that they are barely noticeable during normal shooting activities. In fact, with my aging eyes, these scales are so fine that they are unusable. The circles on the ranging reticle, however, work well even with my tired eyes.

The sighting procedure is simplicity itself (see Figure 10.9). Use a solid rest to fire a trial shot at the bull on a paper target at a distance of 50 yards. Hold the cross hair on the target and use the large knobs on the scope to move the smallest circle on top of the ranging reticle so that it centers

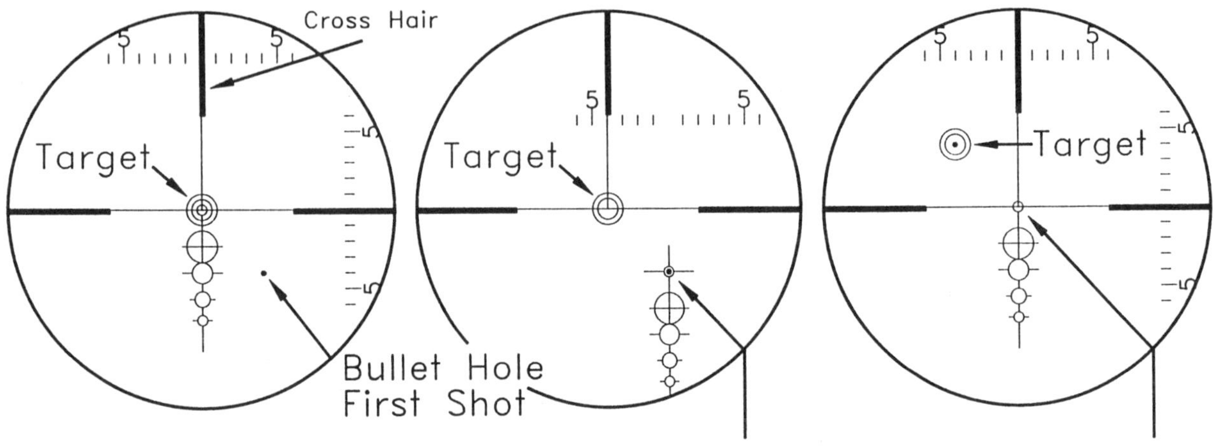

Figure 10.9. One-round zeroing procedure for the Shepherd auto-ranging .22 rimfire scope. Step 1: use a solid rest to fire a trial shot at the bull on a paper target at a distance of 50 yards. Step 2: hold the cross hair on the target and use the large knobs on the scope to move the smallest circle on top of the ranging reticle so that it centers around the bullet hole. Step 3: use the small knobs to move the smallest circle so it is centered around the junction of the cross hairs. Drawing by Mike Smith.

around the bullet hole. Now use the small knobs to move the smallest circle so it is centered around the junction of the crosshairs. That's it.

With a 50-yard zero, the ranging reticle corrects for a drop of 5.4 inches at 100 yards, 46.3 inches at 200 yards, and 488 inches at 500 yards. Using a chronograph and a computer program such as Ballistic Explorer Version 4.02a (Oehler Research, P.O. Box 9135, Austin, TX 78766) will enable an individual to determine the precise distances where the auto-ranging reticle will be true when using different ammunition or nonstandard barrels.

The bottom line is that if the Shepherd scope wasn't so expensive, I'd have one on nearly every .22 rimfire rifle I own (Shepherd Scope Ltd., P.O. Box 189, Waterloo, NE 68069).

Every Ruger 10/22 comes with an aluminum scope base that has a 3/8 inch dovetail, which does not provide a strong enough mount in my experience. A good 1 inch Weaver-type scope base is mandatory. While any good scope rings will do, I particularly like Burris Weaver-style "Zee" scope rings. The scope base should be both screwed and glued to the receiver with Acraglas Gel. Some competition shooters dislike the flexibility of the joint between the Ruger's barrel and action. The Weigand Combat 10/22 cantilever scope mount provides an excellent solution for these folks.

Aftermarket Stocks

More vendors manufacture aftermarket stocks for the Ruger 10/22 than any other component for that rifle. Unfortunately, there is a real dearth of stocking options for the Ruger 77/22. Even worse, the so-called Crime Bill passed by Congress in 1994 outlawed folding stocks, which eliminated many useful options, especially for those of us who routinely travel in very remote places by kayak, canoe, and bush plane.

Aftermarket 10/22 stocks range from cheap plastic to sophisticated polymer, traditional wood, and laminated wood stocks in plain, fancy, and exotic configurations. Many are available for both the standard contour barrel or the 0.920 inch (23.4 mm diameter) untapered match barrels that have become popular. Since most .22 rimfire suppressors come with a full 1.0 inch (25.4 mm) diameter tube, an extra 0.080 to 0.100 inch must be removed from the barrel channel before the tube will fit.

Most stocks have a length of pull (the distance from butt to trigger) of about 14.0 inches (35.6 cm). Jeff Cooper, who ran rifle classes at his prestigious Gunsite shooting school for many years, found that his clients generally performed better with rifles cut to a shorter 12.5 inch (31.8 cm) length of pull. Most (but not all) people feel more comfortable with a shorter pull.

Colonel Cooper strongly asserts that an individual should develop the ability to bring an arm to bear with great speed. In his rifle course, he directed considerable emphasis on delivering a single aimed shot in a very rapid fashion. The moment of decision having been reached, the rifle is quickly brought to the shoulder, the sights are aligned, and the trigger is pressed, all in one smooth, swift motion. With practice, this sequence of events can be completed in less than a second—and with surprising accuracy. Rifles with short length of pull work much better for this exercise, since they tend not to catch on clothing, backpack straps, and other impedimenta. The snap shot is an invaluable technique for the sport shooter and hunter as well as for the armed professional.

The factory 10/22 stock has a low comb or cheek rest designed for open sights. When used with a scope, that comb is too low for a proper cheek weld. An aftermarket stock with raised comb or roll-over cheekpiece will enable the shooter to achieve a much more rapid and repeatable cheek weld, and this will significantly improve the practical accuracy of the rifle as well as the speed of target acquisition.

Proper Bedding for Wood Stocks

All wood stocks are subject to warping due to changing moisture content. For best accuracy, rifles stocked in wood should have their actions and about 1 inch of the breech end of the barrel bedded in plastic. Here's how to bed a rifle properly.

Fill all holes and relief cuts in the 10/22's action with oil-based modeling clay. If this is not done properly, the barreled action will become permanently bonded to the stock. Use another bit of modeling clay to dam up the area about an inch ahead of the barrel retention block. The barrel and action must be coated with a release agent. While axle grease or lard works, Brownells sells a release agent that probably works better. Spread thoroughly with your fingers and ensure that all holes, threads, and other surfaces are thoroughly covered with a thin layer.

Mark White has used several products for rifle bedding. Brownells Acraglas Gel is designed expressly for this application. Acraglas is expensive, reliable, fairly strong, slow setting, stable, and quite permanent. Marinetex is designed for maritime applications rather than gunsmithing. It is a steel-filled epoxy that is medium priced, fast setting, very strong, stable, and adequate for high-stress areas. Marinetex will not run in most situations. Both compounds are moisture and temperature stable. White says that he tends to use Acraglas Gel, except for magnum rifles, where he uses Marinetex.

Make a dry run with the stocked action, snugging up the single screw to ensure that the release agent and modeling clay will keep out all the unwanted bedding compound. Don't forget to wrap the treated barrel with Saran Wrap before fitting the barreled action into the stock. You don't want to contaminate the wood with release agent.

Mix the Acraglas Gel and smear it into the forward part of the action area and under the rear inch (or 3 cm) of barrel in the stock. A small amount of bedding material under the rear of the action will also be helpful, but don't overdo it here. Insert the action into the stock and tighten the single stock screw into the action. Be careful not to get it too tight. Overtightening can spring the barrel upward, so the scope may not have sufficient range of reticle adjustment to zero on the target. Remove any excess that squeezes out with paper towels.

Wait a few hours until the epoxy has set. Try to remove the action from the stock before the epoxy reaches full strength. Once the stock and barrel are separated from each other, it is time to free-float the barrel. The barrel channel should be opened up so that no part of the barrel touches wood. It would be nice to have a gap of at least 1/16 inch (2 mm) around the barrel. Coarse, aggressive sandpaper wrapped around a wooden dowel of the appropriate size works well for this operation. Wrapping sandpaper around a deep socket wrench of proper diameter also works. A dollar bill or sheet of typing paper should move easily between the barrel and the wood stock. Once the barrel is free floated properly, clean all the grease and clay from the stock and barreled action. Seal the raw wood with varnish or more Acraglas. Reassemble when dry.

Selecting the Best Ammunition

Selecting the best ammunition for a suppressed firearm is a bit more complicated than selecting ammunition for an unsuppressed firearm. When a given round fired through a suppressed arm produces a projectile velocity that exceeds the speed of sound, the resultant ballistic crack will seem nearly as loud as an unsuppressed firearm. A subsonic projectile produces a barely noticeable hissing or whizzing.

Furthermore, transonic velocities are less accurate than either subsonic or supersonic velocities. Legendary test pilot Chuck Yeager, who became the first person to fly faster than the speed of sound, noted a considerable amount of buffeting and instability as he pushed his aircraft through the sound barrier. To a lesser extent, this instability also affects rifle bullets as they cross the sound barrier. Furthermore, even a bullet's ballistic coefficient is different at supersonic and subsonic velocities.

Subsonic cartridges avoid this buffeting and have the same ballistic coefficient throughout their flight, so they tend to provide the best accuracy. Plus, subsonic rounds do not produce a ballistic crack (except with some firearms used in extreme environmental conditions).

Finding the optimal ammunition for a particular firearm is an important factor in the accuracy equation. Usually, one will buy just one box of a number of different lots and brands of .22 ammo. Some stocking dealers will occasionally offer a deal on sampler assortments of ammunition to help their customers find the best ammo for their particular firearm. Many shooting enthusiasts will try a sampling of 20 or more variations at one sitting.

The sampling exercise is often conducted as follows. Each box of ammo is labeled with a number using a felt-tip marker, and a series of targets is labeled with matching numbers. Some people use small targets in clusters of five. Others use white poster board with self-adhesive bull's-eyes. The target is stapled to a stand 50 yards downrange from a sturdy bench rest. Five shots from each numbered box of ammunition are carefully discharged at the corresponding target.

Some groups will be noticeably larger than others, and this ammunition can be eliminated from further consideration. Fire a second set of five shots from each of the remaining samples to verify which is best. Note which produces a ballistic crack from the suppressed firearm and which does not, since stealth is an important factor in the overall performance equation.

When you find a particular variety and lot of ammunition that works well in terms of accuracy and sound suppression, purchase that ammunition in quantity. Since the resources of a freelance writer are limited, I can rarely afford to purchase more than 30,000 rounds of a particular rimfire ammunition at a time. It seems to go quickly, so I'd buy more if I could. Still, 30,000 rounds was enough to raise the eyebrows and hackles of the fellow who manages the local freight company the week after the fiery conclusion to the Branch Davidian fiasco in Waco, Texas. In these paranoid times, it might be useful to have a disarming explanation for quantity ammunition purchases for nosy locals.

Special subsonic LR ammunition has become readily available in recent years, which is a boon to suppressor enthusiasts, especially those who like to use muzzle cans. Eley and RWS make outstanding but very expensive .22 LR hollowpoint subsonic cartridges. The RWS hollowpoint is a particular favorite of mine for the taking of small game. Winchester introduced an appealing truncated cone hollowpoint subsonic LR made in Australia, but the ammunition was quickly withdrawn from the market because of quality-control problems. One lot of Winchester subsonic had dangerously high powder charges. Remington has subsequently introduced an excellent and affordable subsonic hollowpoint, which has the added virtue that the cartridges are not heavily smeared with greasy wax like RWS subsonic fodder. Lapua Oy has just developed a subsonic Long Rifle cartridge that features a 48 grain projectile. This subsonic rimfire has wonderful possibilities for sporting, military, and clandestine use. But at the time of this writing, no one is importing this round into the United States from Finland. One of the most interesting subsonic additions to the American marketplace is Russian Baikal .22 LR ammunition.

Baikal subsonic is really a family of solid-point .22 LR ammunition that comes in a number of variants (based on accuracy), from expensive Olympic and Sniper grades to the remarkably affordable Junior Steel and Junior Brass. Baikal Junior Steel has a steel case and is the least expensive. It works fine in firearms with strong strikers and powerful extractors, but the tougher steel cases suffer from ignition and extraction difficulties in Ruger rifles. Baikal Junior Brass costs slightly more than Junior Steel (but only a fourth as much as RWS subsonic) while delivering comparable accuracy to RWS. Baikal Junior Brass also produces a similar sound signature to RWS in a suppressed firearm.

Recent tests with a highly refined target rifle suggested that Baikal Junior Brass can produce 1.2 inch (3.0 cm) 10-shot groups at 100 yards (91 m). Baikal JB does have two liabilities, however: 1) the cartridges are heavily coated with lubricant like RWS subsonic, which tends to accumulate in magazines, and 2) the Russian ammunition produces more powder residue than the other subsonic rounds. Thus, the cleaner and nearly as affordable Remington subsonic LR would provide a longer service life for integrally suppressed firearms that cannot be disassembled for cleaning.

The most accurate .22 rifle of any kind that I've tested to date was a single-shot suppressed rifle from Sound Technology based on the Thompson Contender action. Using Baikal Sniper subsonic LR ammunition, the suppressed rifle delivered 1/4 to 3/8 inch (6 to 10 mm) groups at 100 yards (91 meters). Group size opened up to 7/16 inch (11 mm) using the intrinsically less accurate but much less expensive Baikal Junior Brass subsonic. CCI Green Tag and Eley standard-velocity match ammunition also produced 1/4 to 3/8 inch groups. It is interesting to note that the domestically produced CCI Green Tag habitually delivers equal performance to the imported Eley at about one-fourth of the price.

CHAPTER ELEVEN

SUPPRESSED .22 MACHINE GUNS

hose who love the recreational shooting of machine guns face two considerable constraints: the cost of ammunition and finding a discreet place to shoot. A robust and reliable .22 rimfire machine gun would help solve the first problem. And a suppressor capable of handling a large volume of rather dirty ammo would help solve the latter problem.

Only two .22 rimfire machine guns are worthy of consideration, in my opinion. The first is the American 180, which features large drum magazines and a seductively high rate of fire. For discreet shooting that is also easy on one's long-term hearing, a high-quality muzzle can such as Dr. Philip Dater's MK-22 suppressor makes a valuable addition to the AM 180. A vastly more durable full-auto option (in terms of firearm rather than suppressor lifespan) featuring a more traditional rate of fire was developed by John Norrell. He designed a select-fire conversion for the Ruger 10/22 rifle that is far, far superior to other conversions. When combined with Norrell's integral suppressor specifically designed to meet the demands of full-auto fire with relatively dirty rimfire ammunition, the Norrell 10/22 is the best solution to both problems in my opinion.

NORRELL SUPPRESSED SELECT-FIRE 10/22

I first became aware of John Norrell back before

The Norrell select-fire suppressed Ruger 10/22 fires at a rate of 750 to 800 rounds per minute. Photo by Polly Walter.

1986, when it was still legal to remanufacture demilled machine gun receivers for private ownership. His specialty as a Class 2 manufacturer was difficult or odd receiver rewelding, with particular attention to cosmetic appearance. A friend sent Norrell two torch-cut halves from M14 receivers for remanufacturing. Norrell welded the halves together and machined them back to spec. His work looked flawless. Furthermore, he went above and beyond the call of duty by Magnafluxing the receiver to check for invisible flaws as well.

That same "give the customer 110 percent" attitude is particularly evident in his select-fire and suppressed Rugers. Combine that attitude with an inspired ability for both design and problem-solving, and you have an invaluable resource for the Class 3 community. Norrell has tackled such diverse problems as repairing a Larand suppressor that had never worked properly and solving the chronic problem of splitting first-generation plastic M11/9 magazines. But I believe his crowning achievement is the select-fire, suppressed Ruger 10/22 rifle.

Select-Fire Conversion

Norrell's select-fire conversion consists of a modified bolt and trigger pack that can be installed in any Ruger 10/22 carbine. This was the first closed-bolt 10/22 conversion in the marketplace, and it is still the best. It consists of a modified bolt and trigger pack that can be installed in any Ruger 10/22 carbine. Norrell invested 1-1/2 years to develop the conversion. It shows. He offered both full-length and shorty versions with either factory wood or aftermarket folding stocks. A special shortened law enforcement model with laser sight is still available.

The standard select-fire mechanism features a small button located on the trigger itself. Pull the

The trigger housing is the registered item in Norrell's conversion (top) of the factory Ruger trigger pack (bottom). Note the adjustable, spring-loaded plunger Norrell installs in the left front of the trigger housing to slow down the action and lock the bolt shut.

upper part of the trigger where the button is installed for fully automatic fire. There is no selector lever in this design, so the operator can decide instantly whether to shoot in semi- or full-auto mode without taking time to employ a selector switch. This makes the system especially useful to law enforcement personnel, animal-control officers, and ranchers protecting valuable livestock.

Unfortunately, this ingenious button selector proved awkward to use with folding stocks because their pistol grips lowered the position of the hand. So Norrell developed a variant of his trigger pack with a conventional selector lever alongside the trigger. Push the selector forward for semiautomatic fire and pull it rearward for fully automatic.

The system fires from a closed bolt at an advertised cyclic rate of 900 to 1,000 rounds per minute. When Norrell's integral suppressor is added to the system, the ported barrel reduces the back pressure available to cycle the bolt, so the advertised cyclic rate drops to 750 to 800 rounds per minute. Capt. Monty Mendenhall measured considerably different cyclic rates with a 16 inch (40.6 cm) integrally suppressed Norrell system: 1,171 rpm with CCI Blazer, 1,114 rpm with CCI Mini Mag, 1,061 rpm with Federal Eagle high-velocity, and 914 rpm with CCI standard-velocity ammunition.

Norrell's conversion parts are precision machined from quality tool steel and are properly heat treated. Tolerances are so precise that conversion parts are made by a tool and die maker rather than by a machinist. Once the precision sears are made, Norrell spends an additional 22 hours of work himself to complete the conversion.

Firing from a closed bolt means Norrell's conversions are safer and more accurate than competing designs that fire from an open bolt. Norrell's bolt closes on the cartridge in the chamber before the auto sear releases the hammer. Furthermore, Norrell adds an antibounce weight to the rear of the bolt to eliminate the light primer hits common to some other closed-bolt conversions. His system also incorporates an adjustable, spring-loaded plunger in the trigger housing to slow down the action and lock the bolt shut. The plunger can also be used to adjust the select-fire system when swapping the conversion between suppressed and unsuppressed rifles. A quarter turn is the most that's normally needed.

Some competing closed-bolt conversions use delicate parts. The TEK conversion, for example, is subject to wear. After enough wear, you can't pull the bolt back. Norrell's plunger and antibounce weight are not subject to wear, for all practical purposes.

Some competing conversions disable such desirable features as the ability to lock the bolt back for cleaning or to comply with a particular range's safety procedures. Norrell's select-fire design retains all the 10/22's basic features. His conversion is robust and durable, like the rifle it fits. I know of one of his 10/22 conversions with more than 110,000 rounds through it. The system exhibits no appreciable wear. Norrell's prototypes have fired more than 300,000 rounds and are still going strong. The American 180, on the other hand, must have the loading block replaced after about 30,000 rounds. This is, however, an easy job that does not require tools.

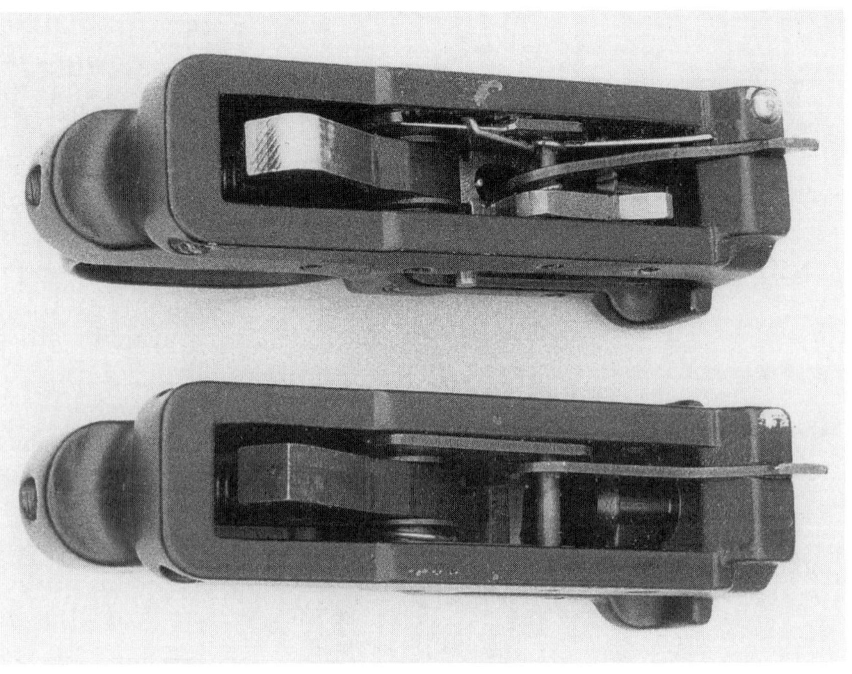

Norrell's conversion (top) of the factory Ruger trigger housing (bottom). Note the plunger protruding from the front of the modified housing.

The trigger housing is the registered item in Norrell's 10/22 conversion. With passage of the infamous 1986 legislation, Norrell and several subcontractors (including S&H Arms) manufactured and registered a quantity of fully transferable trigger housings before the May 1986 deadline. These transferable conversions remained available into the 1990s and can still be located occasionally through Class 3 dealers.

Norrell also offers economical post-1986 dealer sample select-fire conversions to law enforcement agencies and to dealers with a police letter. Some SWAT and Special Reaction Teams (SRTs) are beginning to issue a full-auto .22 to the lead man in an entry team. Subsequent members usually carry H&K MP5s or .223 caliber (5.56 mm) carbines. The reduced penetration of the .22 rimfire reduces the risk of what the military calls "collateral damage" due to rounds penetrating thin walls and doors common to modern homes and apartment complexes. This is a significant consideration with the increased tempo of raids on drug dealers and crack houses in residential neighborhoods.

Furthermore, the .22's minimal recoil increases hit probability over weapons like the MP5 (especially when employed in Norrell's law enforcement version with laser sight) out to 25 yards. The rapid .22 hits are the equivalent of buckshot, so the system provides plenty of terminal performance. And a big tactical plus is that a number of instantaneous .22 hits in a confined area will shred Kevlar body armor that would stop a .357 magnum. Clearly, this system has interesting possibilities for home defense as well.

Suppressor Design

Norrell's family of suppressed .22s is based on a ported barrel surrounded by brass eyelets encased in a stainless steel tube. Other internal components are made from aluminum and stainless steel. Tubes and receivers are beadblasted and finished with a molybdenum resin, which looks similar to the finish on a Colt M16 and adds a definite milspec ambiance.

The full-length 10/22 suppressor features a barrel ported with 1/8 inch (3.3 mm) holes and shortened to 16.5 inches (41.9 cm), surrounded with 3 ounces (85 g) of brass eyelets, encased in a 1x18 inch (2.5x45.7 cm) suppressor tube. The shorty model features a ported barrel shortened to 9 inches (22.9 cm), surrounded with 2 ounces (57 g) of brass eyelets, encased in a 1x11 inch (2.5x27.9 cm) tube. Both models have the original iron sights installed on the tubes. This design might sound familiar to some-

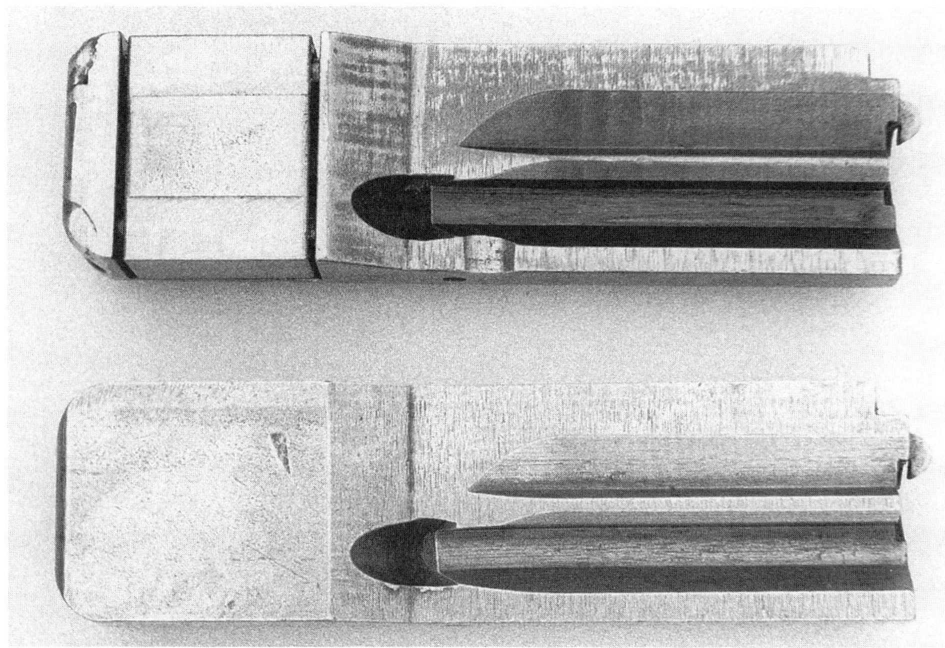

Norrell modifies the factory bolt (bottom) by installing an antibounce weight and notching the bolt to capture a spring-loaded plunger in the modified trigger housing.

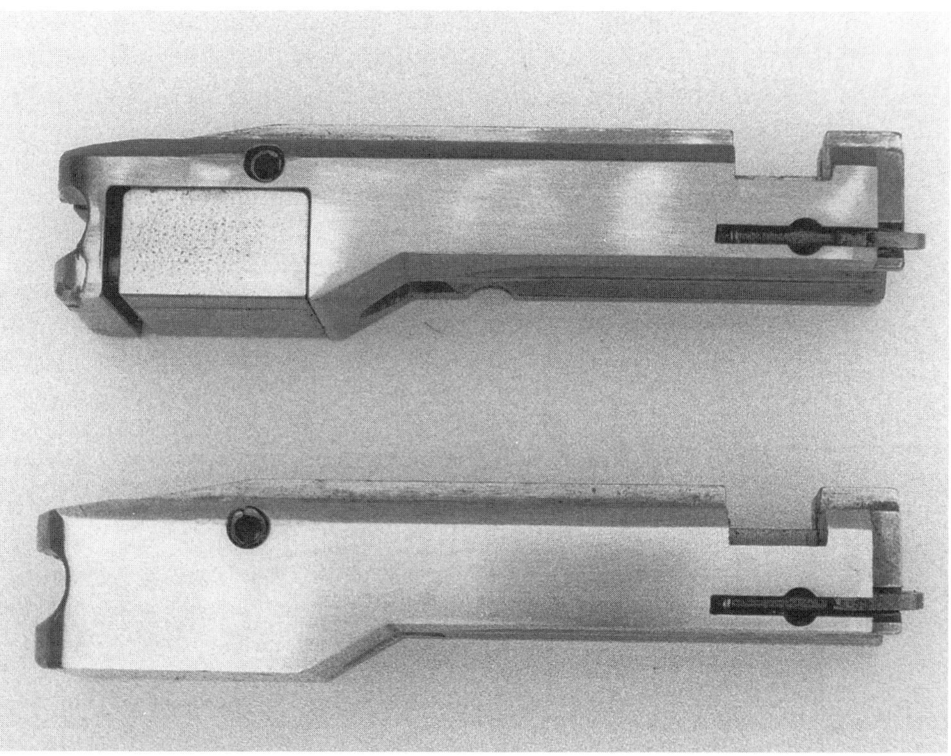

Side view comparing factory bolt (top) with Norrell's modified bolt and its antibounce weight.

one who has peeked inside a Ciener .22 rimfire suppressor. But Norrell's design is more robust, the ports are deburred, and the barrel is hand lapped. Furthermore, the Norrell system is specifically engineered for periodic cleaning and maintenance required by the double whammy of dirty ammo and a large volume of full-auto fire. All my Ciener suppressed .22s came with written warnings that disassembly voided their warranties.

The shorty model is usually a two-stamp gun: one for the select-fire trigger pack and one for the suppressor. I know one individual who had Norrell register his as a three-stamp gun so he could install a semiauto trigger pack and use it as a short-barreled rifle. Now he can swap out components with a half dozen different rifles to perfectly match his specific needs at the moment and not worry about legalities.

One particularly valuable feature of the Norrell integral rifle suppressor is that the outer (registered) tube is lined with 1.5 inch (3.8 cm) lengths of thin (0.02 inch, 0.5 mm) tubing, which collect carbon residue and keep the outer tube relatively clean. This greatly facilitates disassembly and makes cleaning far easier. Yet this extra tubing and the overall robust design are still contained in a suppressor that measures only 1 inch (2.5 cm) in diameter and adds only 6 ounces (170 g) net weight over a standard Ruger 10/22 carbine.

Maintenance

The receiver should be cleaned every 500 rounds. The 18 inch suppressor should be disassembled and cleaned every 1,500 rounds to ensure easy disassembly. The 11 inch suppressor should be cleaned every 1,000 rounds. The select-fire conversion and the suppressor come with detailed instructions for disassembly, maintenance, operation, and troubleshooting.

It is worth spending an extra $80 on Norrell's ingenious disassembly tool and $15 for a spanner (which I highly recommend). If these tools are used for disassembly, cleaning, and repacking, the 18 inch suppressor can be delayed to every 8,000 rounds, and the 11 inch suppressor then only requires maintenance every 4,000 rounds. If one delays cleaning much beyond these recommendations, disassembly of the suppressor may prove to be impossible, even with the special disassembly tool. If that happens, return the system with an approved Form 5 (remove the registered trigger housing if you have a select-fire conversion), and Norrell will clean and repack the suppressor for $50 plus postage.

About $11 worth of brass eyelets are needed to repack the suppressor. Even if you completely disregard the tremendous convenience of the disassembly tool and the fact that it largely eliminates any potential danger of dinging the registered tube during disassembly, the savings in brass eyelets because of longer maintenance intervals will quickly pay for the tool.

Reliability

The Norrell select-fire conversion is extremely sensitive to different ammunition and magazines. But it is highly reliable with the proper combination of ammo and magazines.

Norrell's .22 systems were designed for Remington high-velocity Long Rifle ammunition. The use of Remington high-velocity fodder proved to be especially important when the Norrell conversion was fitted with an integral suppressor. The ported barrel of an integral suppressor reduces the amount of back pressure available to cycle the bolt. Subsonic, standard-velocity, and hypervelocity ammunition tend not to cycle the action, or they generate failures to feed properly. Other brands of conventional high-velocity Long Rifle ammo are not generally reliable either.

After I had Mark White of Sound Technology perform a trigger and action job (including Ralph Seifert's idea of chamfering the bottom rear of the bolt), the Norrell system performed well with a fairly wide array of high- and standard-velocity ammunition. The select-fire rifle even cycled with Baikal Junior Brass subsonic ammunition when fitted with a 14 inch (35.6 cm) unported barrel. The select-fire conversion was made on a trigger group with the worst trigger pull I'd ever experienced on a Ruger 10/22. After White's ministrations, the Norrell conversion now has one of the cleanest trigger breaks I've ever experienced on a 10/22, vastly improving the system's practical accuracy, especially at long distances. Everything White did is discussed in Chapter 10, "Optimizing the Performance of Suppressed .22s."

I had White install a muzzle brake on the 14 inch plain barrel, which did an excellent job of keeping the weapon on target during full-auto bursts of any length. The results were dramatic, indeed, when shooting at floating targets in a pond at a range of 200 to 250 yards (180 to 230 m). White builds muzzle brakes for the Ruger 10/22 for both right-handers like myself and left-handers too.

While not intended to function as flash hiders, White's muzzle brakes worked fairly well in this regard. When firing a Norrell system fitted with a plain barrel and White's muzzle brake, an observer standing 15 yards (14 m) to the right of the operator observes a mild glow inside the slots of the muzzle brake and from the ejection port of the rifle. No flame emerges from the front of the muzzle brake.

Besides ammunition, magazines constitute the other wild card in the performance of the Norrell select-fire conversion. I've found four magazines that function flawlessly: the 10-round rotary magazine that Ruger supplies with the rifle, the Eagle 30-round magazine, the older design *single*-column Ram-Line magazine (except for the variant with two black sides), and the Butler Creek 25-round magazine.

I found that the double-column Ram-Line magazines do not function reliably. The teardrop-shaped Mitchell 50-round magazine and the impressive-looking Sanford 50-round drum proved to be most disappointing. The Eaton 25-round magazine also failed to function reliably.

I should note, however, that a friend has been able to use the most recently made double-column, 30-round Ram-Line magazines with his Norrell conversion by slowly and meticulously loading them so all cartridges line up perfectly. Few people have that level of patience when they're in the mood to rock and roll. Most folks preferred to purchase a bunch of the single-column Ram-Line magazines from Norrell, since he had purchased a huge quantity of them when they went out of production.

Suppressor Performance

To get a handle on suppressor performance, I measured sound signatures of the both the 18 inch and 11 inch Norrell suppressors. Ciener and AWC R10 suppressors were also tested for comparison. The sound signatures appear in Table 11.1. Net sound reductions are shown as decibels in Table 11.2 and average velocities appear in Table 11.3.

Neither the Norrell shorty nor Ciener guns would cycle with Hansen standard-velocity ammunition, but they functioned flawlessly with CCI standard-velocity. Ironically, the CCI produced consistently lower velocities. Data for Hansen ammo are reported to facilitate comparisons with previously published suppressor evaluations.

The unmodified long Norrell gun functioned only with high-velocity rounds, digesting a wider variety of ammunition than an evaluation of the gun published in the June 1991 issue of *Machine Gun News*. The Norrell 18 inch gun also demonstrated much better sound reduction in the present evaluation. Clearly, a 90 degree temperature difference affects performance.

The Norrell 18 inch suppressor is a solid performer. Where handiness is more important than quiet, Norrell's 11 inch suppressor provides about the minimally acceptable performance in terms of sound suppression. It is certainly a handy and fun package. One observer compared the muzzle signature of the 18 inch Norrell suppressor to a pellet rifle and the signature of the 11 inch Norrell suppressor to a pellet pistol.

Norrell's suppressors are quiet enough for discreet target practice, plinking, and animal control. They are more robust and easily cleaned than a Ciener suppressor. And the 18 inch suppressor can tolerate a longer maintenance interval than the AWC R10. Perhaps most important, these Norrell suppressors will gracefully tolerate a large volume of automatic fire.

The Norrell select-fire Ruger 10/22 is without peer. And Norrell's integral suppressors allow the gun to reach its full potential. It's an outstanding system, which is what one expects from a master craftsman like John Norrell.

Table 11.1. Sound signatures in decibels of Norrell 18 inch and 11 inch integral suppressors tests.

GUN	SUPPRESSOR	FEDERAL HV LR	CCI MINI MAG LR	HANSEN SV LR	CCI SV LR	TEMP., °F (°C)
Ruger 10/22	None	141	141	139	139	70-72(21-22)
Ruger 10/22	Norrell 18 inch	119	119	119	119	78(26)
Ruger 10/22	Norrell 11 inch	129	—	126	125	72-74(22-23)
Ruger 10/22	Ciener	120	—	120	120	75-76(24)
Ruger 10/22	AWC R10	118	—	—	—	65(18)
American 180	None	—	—	151[a]	—	53(12)
American 180	AWC MK-22	—	—	124[a]	—	53(12)

[a] Remington standard velocity target LR

Table 11.2. Net sound reductions of Norrell 18 inch and 11 inch integral suppressors tests, expressed as decibels.

GUN	SUPPRESSOR	FEDERAL HV LR	CCI MINI MAG LR	HANSEN SV LR	CCI SV LR	TEMP., °F (°C)
Ruger 10/22	Norrell 18 inch	22	22	20	20	78(26)
Ruger 10/22	Norrell 11 inch	12	—	13	14	72-74(22-23)
Ruger 10/22	Ciener 21	—	19	19		75-76(24)
Ruger 10/22	AWC R10	23	—	—	—	65(18)
American 180	AWC MK-22	—	—	27[a]	—	53(12)

[a] Remington standard velocity target LR

Table 11.3. Velocities in feet per second (and meters per second) produced during tests of Norrell 18 inch and 11 inch integral suppressors .

GUN	SUPPRESSOR	FEDERAL HV LR	CCI MINI MAG LR	HANSEN SV LR	CCI SV LR	TEMP., °F (°C)	SPEED OF SOUND, fps (mps)
Ruger 10/22	Norrell 18 inch	975(297)	—	957(292)	929(283)	78(26)	1,137(347)
Ruger 10/22	Norrell 11 inch	1,004(306)	959(292)	971(296)	924(282)	72-74(22-23)	1,131-1,133(345)
Ruger 10/22	Ciener	1,038(316)	—	932(284)	945(288)	75-76(24)	1,134-1,135(346)
Ruger 10/22	AWC R10	981(299)	—	—	—	65(18)	1,123(342)

AWC MK-22 SUPPRESSOR

Phil Dater developed my favorite muzzle can for the American 180 in May of 1987. Marketed by his original Automatic Weapons Company (a Division of Antares Technologies, Inc.) when the company was based in Albuquerque, New Mexico, the suppressor was essentially a scaled-down version of his very successful MK-9 9mm submachine gun suppressor. Like its 9mm predecessor, the MK-22 is a coaxial design built from 6061-T6 aluminum with 18-8 stainless steel baffles and is finished in a black hard-coat anodizing. The MK-22 is 8.1 inches (20.6 cm) long and 1-5/8 inches (4.1 cm) in diameter. It weighs 17.8 ounces (508 g). When mounted on an AM 180 with 14.0 inch (35.6 cm) barrel, the MK-22 lowered the muzzle signature from 151 to 124 dB, for a net sound reduction of 27 dB. Even though this suppressor is long since out of production, it can still be obtained as a special-order item from Dater by contacting him at Gemtech in Boise, Idaho.

Firing an American 180 with AWC MK-22 suppressor. Photo by Polly Walter.

Dr. Dater's AWC MK-22 suppressor mounted on American 180 submachine gun.

Close-up view of AWC MK-22 suppressor.

This AM8 was the first suppressor that Dr. Dater designed for the American 180 submachine gun. Photo by Dr. Philip H. Dater.

CHAPTER TWELVE

THE EVOLUTION OF SUBMACHINE GUN SUPPRESSORS

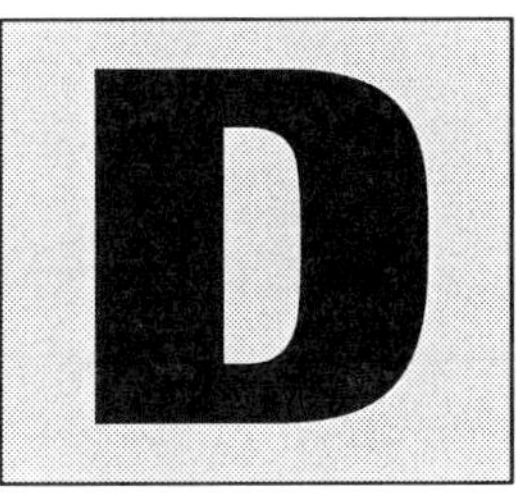

uring the dark early days of World War II, the U.S. military establishment returned to its abandoned yet distinguished heritage of unconventional warfare, which dates back 150 years before Mao Tse-tung developed his primer on the subject.

American colonials began this tradition during the French and Indian War (1754-1763). Maj. Robert Rogers, who was commissioned in 1756 as a captain in command of a company of Rangers, developed unconventional warfare to a high art during his campaigns against both Indian warriors and French regulars in the Great Lakes region. In fact, every modern graduate of the U.S. Army Ranger School still learns *The Rules of Rogers' Rangers*.

Several decades after Rogers fought with the English against the French, Americans fought against the English during their bid for independence from the Crown. The Americans used the tactics Rogers had developed, since unconventional warfare provided the only realistic hope of successfully waging war against the British, who had professional officers, better training, and better resources. Perhaps the most spectacular unconventional warfare seen during the War of Independence was waged by Maj. Francis Marion, the Swamp Fox, who led partisans and guerrillas in fierce campaigns against British troops in the southern colonies.

The tradition of unconventional warfare continued during the Civil War. The Confederacy faced a similar

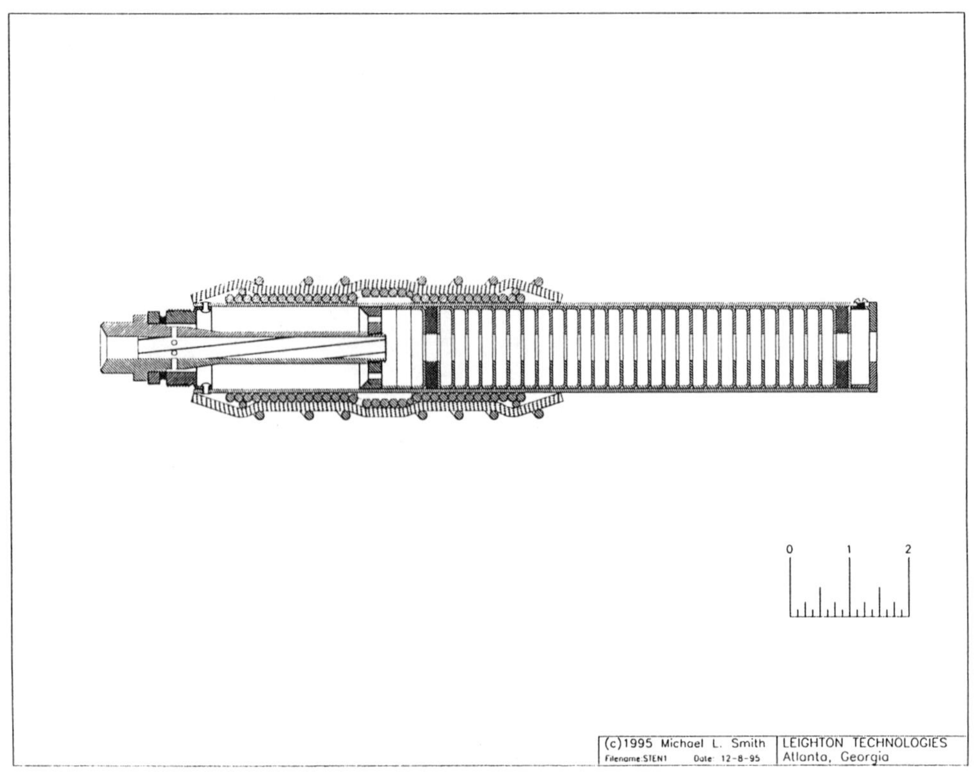

Figure 12.1. Type I variant of the British WWII-vintage Sten silencer. Drawing by Mike Smith.

tactical problem that the American Colonials had faced eight decades earlier. The Confederates had to prosecute a war against an established military with more men and materiel, backed by more resources and manufacturing might, to sustain a long and vigorous war. As Union forces began to invade their soil, Confederate forces supplemented conventional tactics with spirited unconventional warfare. Col. John Mosby, the Gray Ghost, became one of the most successful unconventional warriors of the day. His battalion of fighters killed, wounded, or captured 1,200 Union soldiers from 1863 through 1864 at a cost of only 20 men.

As the ninteenth century closed with the so-called pacification of the American Indian, and the United States earned a new level of respect as one of the major world powers, the professional military saw little need for the Indian-like tactics of unconventional warfare. Such tactics had become both unnecessary and embarrassing for a world power. The United States, after all, was no longer an underdog. Yet underdog Pancho Villa would use unconventional tactics to successfully protest U.S. recognition of a Mexican regime he hated. Villa's raids against U.S. border towns that began in 1914 prompted President Woodrow Wilson to send a punitive expedition under the command of Gen. John J. Pershing into Mexico to nab Villa in 1916. Thanks to Villa's skill in unconventional warfare, Pershing only succeeded in earning the outrage of the Mexican government for his flagrant violation of Mexico's sovereign borders.

Not until the United States found itself at war with the formidable Axis powers of Germany, Japan, and Italy did the American military again see itself as the underdog. Initially faced with few options to resist Axis expansion, the United States and Britain both turned to unconventional warfare. The learning process was quick and brutal. One of the earliest lessons was the potential value of replacing the knife and crossbow with more efficient and effective weapons like silenced firearms. The British developed one of the earliest, most effective, and most popular silenced weapons introduced for clandestine and commando operations: the silenced Sten Mark IIS. The United States briefly considered the offer of a small company to reintroduce the production of Maxim silencers for weapons like the Springfield rifle and the Reising submachine gun. The Office of Strategic Services (OSS) eventually opted for a silencer for the M3 "Greasegun," which was patterned after the silencer developed by Bell Labs and produced by High Standard for the HD-MS .22 rimfire pistol. Thus, the Allies initiated the first widespread use of silenced submachine guns to meet the operational requirements of unconventional warfare and clandestine operations.

MAXIM-SILENCED REISING

As far as I know, Hiram P. Maxim never met Eugene Reising, the inventor of the Reising Model 50 and Model 55 submachine guns. That's too bad. The marriage of their inventions might have rewritten a chapter or two in the history of World War II. Maxim would have realized his dream of providing a valuable tool to the military, and Reising might have been able to overcome the disastrous performance of his inventions by finding a role where they excelled.

As it turns out, however, the Reising submachine guns probably represent the most spectacular small-arms failure of the Second World War. In fairness to Eugene Reising, much of the blame should

From top to bottom are a Reising Model 60 semiautomatic carbine, a Reising Model 50 submachine gun with Cutts Compensator, and a Reising Model 50 with Maxim Model 1910 silencer.

go to the manufacturer (Harrington and Richardson) and the armorers of the United States Marine Corps. Although the original bid specifications stipulated fully interchangeable parts, each gun required hand fitting at the factory. Somehow this information never made it to the Marine armorers who participated in the invasion of Guadalcanal, where the Reising received its combat debut. It would not be an overstatement to say that the Reising was a complete failure. Marines "lost" or destroyed their Reisings as soon as a substitute—any substitute—came to hand during the fighting.

Admittedly, the Reising was an unusually complex gun with small springs and no cutouts for self-cleaning. And the 20-round magazines managed to combine the worst features of both single-feed and double-feed magazines into a single design. But it was how the armorers cleaned weapons that guaranteed the Reising's failure. They would disassemble a number of guns and dump all the parts into a solvent tank, virtually guaranteeing that not one hand-fitted gun got back many of its original parts. No wonder the guns failed so miserably on Guadalcanal.

The Reising Model 50 has, however, provided long and admirable service to many U.S. police departments, where its susceptibility to dirt has not been a liability, and its handiness and closed-bolt accuracy have been an asset. Of the approximately 100,000 Reisings manufactured from 1941 to 1945, some were made with feeble folding stocks (the Model 55), but they were not successful in either the civilian or military environment. A semiautomatic version of the Model 50, called the

While the Maxim silencer isn't much bigger than the Cutts Compensator, it reduces the Reising's sound signature by 22 decibels.

Model 60, was sold commercially with an 18 inch barrel. They were popular with civilian railroad employees who guarded important railroad bridges during the World War II. A .22 rimfire variant of the Model 60 was called the Model 65.

While historians scoff at the Reising submachine guns, they seem to universally admire Maxim silencers. Maxim silencers have a reputation for working very well indeed. Unfortunately, not many Maxim silencers have survived for the modern collector, even though they were once relatively common, especially in the northeastern United States.

The success of the Maxim silencer with sport shooters contrasts with their failure in the military marketplace. This is ironic, since Hiram Maxim initially believed that his only significant market would be the military.

Blackjack Pershing's men carried several Springfields equipped with Maxim Model 15 silencers on his ill-fated attempt to capture Pancho Villa, but they did not prove effective during an attempt to quietly neutralize several lookouts, probably due to the ballistic crack produced by the Springfield's supersonic round. The American Expeditionary Force took some sniper rifles with Maxim silencers to Europe during World War I, but the static nature of trench warfare did not provide a significant advantage to the sniper with a silenced weapon. The tactical environment of World War II, however, provided many opportunities to successfully use silencers for commando raids, resistance fighting, and clandestine operations.

The accompanying photos show a Reising Model 50 submachine gun that apparently was equipped long ago with a Maxim Model 1910 silencer in .44 caliber (11.2 mm) by state police. It is

The Reising submachine gun with Maxim silencer is lighter, quieter, and handier than the Ingram M10 .45 caliber submachine gun with SIONICS suppressor, and it has four times the effective range.

a remarkably similar arrangement to what U.S. forces considered adopting for commando and clandestine operations early in World War II. The silencer tube measures 7-1/8 by 1-1/4 inches (18.1 by 3.2 cm), and the complete unit weighs 0.94 pound (426 g). This silenced Reising would have made an interesting weapon for special operations during World War II. The Reising is light and fires from a closed bolt, which enables the system to provide both rapid target acquisition and excellent shot placement. Even though the Reising was issued with a Cutts Compensator, the light weapon is somewhat of a handful on full auto. The Maxim silencer, which isn't much bigger than the Cutts Compensator, not only makes the gun quiet, it also makes the weapon easy to control, even with long bursts.

This is especially remarkable when one considers that the silencer was made years before the advent of submachine guns. This silencer was never intended to cope with the tremendous volume of gas produced by automatic fire. In fact, the only reason this .44 caliber suppressor can be used on the .45 caliber Reising is that the holes in the baffles were designed to be 1/16 inch (1.5 mm) larger than their nominal caliber. It is quite a tribute to Hiram Maxim that his silencer is noticeably quieter than a Vietnam-era SIONICS suppressor. Even more remarkable is that the Maxim performs better with a third of the volume and three-quarters of the weight. The Maxim reduces the weapon's sound signature by 22 dB, while a new, Vietnam-era SIONICS .45 caliber suppressor with virgin wipes on an Ingram M10 submachine gun reduces the sound by 19 dB.

This unlikely marriage of the Maxim Model 1910 silencer and the Reising Model 50 submachine gun makes a weapons system that performs well even by modern standards. The system is lighter, quieter, and handier than the Ingram M10 .45 caliber submachine gun with SIONICS suppressor, and it has four times the effective range in my hands. While U.S. Army Special Forces still used the silenced M10 (in 9mm) for special operations until relatively recently, I can't help wondering what might have been if Eugene Reising had tried his invention with a silencer designed by Hiram Maxim.

The Maxim exceeds the performance of a SIONICS-type suppressor, whether using WerBell's original spiral diffusers or an AWC rebuild with Dater-designed stainless steel baffles and no wipe, but the best can for the .45 ACP Ingram in my experience is the RASE Model SMG-45 suppressor.

A former research engineer at Grendel, Ralph Seifert is the owner of RASE, an innovative Class 2 manufacturer specializing in suppressors as well as .45 ACP conversions for the AR-15 and M16.

RASE MODEL SMG-45

RASE submachine gun suppressors are a coaxial design superficially similar to Dater's classic MK-9 suppressor, which is discussed in detail later in this chapter.

Above: The RASE SMG-45 suppressor dramatically outperforms other .45 ACP suppressors tested in this study.

Left: An oblique view of the RASE SMG-9 suppressor on the Uzi submachine gun shows numerous sets of holes in the front end cap, which provide redundant attachment points for a takedown tool should one or more sets of holes eventually wear after repeated disassembly.

Drawing on earlier work by Dater and adding his own experience as a design engineer with Grendel, RASE designer Ralph Seifert developed coaxial suppressors that do not generate the distinctive ringing sound sometimes experienced with competing coaxial designs. This ringing is caused when combustion gases vent from the primary expansion chamber into the outer coaxial tube, causing an additional component to the weapon's sound signature that sounds like a "clank" to the shooter. The inner tube of Seifert's design contains a primary expansion chamber just in front of the muzzle terminated by a structure he calls a gas reverser and then a baffle stack, all of which is surrounded by a secondary expansion chamber.

A particularly innovative feature of Seifert's design is a spiral structure in the outer tube called a centrifugal gas separator, which partitions gas based on velocity so the gas cannot escape from the outer coaxial tube until a considerable amount of energy is lost. When combined with other design features, this gives RASE muzzle cans a softer sound signature than competing designs.

The inner and outer suppressor tubes and the front end caps are constructed of 6061-T6 aluminum that has been bead blasted and finished in black anodizing. The baffles are 18-8 stainless steel and the mount is blued 4140 tool steel. These robust suppressors have a comparable length but slightly larger diameter than Dater's MK-9 suppressor, which is a 9mm design. All RASE 9mm submachine gun suppressors have from 12 to 15 baffles, an outer diameter of 2.2 inches (5.6 cm), range in length from 12.12 to 12.5 inches (30.8 to 31.8 cm) depending on the mount, and weigh from 30 to 35 ounces (851 to 992 g) also depending on the mount. The variant with a mount designed to replace the barrel-retaining nut on the Uzi submachine gun is 12-7/16 inches (31.6 cm) long, weighs 30.3 ounces (859 g), and features 14 baffles plus the gas reverser. The RASE .45 caliber suppressor is also 12-7/16 inches long, but it weighs 35.6 ounces (1,009 g), employs 13 baffles plus the gas reverser, and features case-hardened threads for mounting on the coarse threads of the Ingram submachine gun. Sound signatures and net sound reductions are shown in Tables 12.1 and 12.2.

Even though the RASE is one of the largest and heaviest submachine gun suppressors in the marketplace, it handles very well on Ingram-type submachine guns and acceptably well on the Uzi, which are the only submachine guns I've personally used with RASE muzzle cans. The RASE Model SMG-45 suppressor is my favorite suppressor for the Ingram M10 .45 caliber submachine gun.

It is interesting, however, that the Maxim Model 1910 silencer is so much smaller and lighter than the RASE suppressor and only delivers 5 dB less performance (in terms of net sound reduction). It's too bad that production of the Maxim did not resume in World War II.

Table 12.1. Sound signatures in decibels of .45 caliber submachine gun suppressors.

GUN	SUPPRESSOR	WINCHESTER USA 230 GR FMJ	TEMPERATURE, °F (°C)
Reising Model 50	None	159	62(17)
Reising Model 50	Maxim Model 1910	137	62(17)
Ingram M10	None	162	62(17)
Ingram M10	Cobray M10 .45	143	62(17)
Ingram M10	None	161	76(24)
Ingram M10	Cobray M10 .45[a]	140	76(24)
Ingram M10	None	161	71(22)
Ingram M10	Cobray M10 .45[a]	141	71(22)
Ingram M10	None	161	80(27)
Ingram M10	RASE	134	80(27)

[a] rebuilt by AWC with Dater baffle stack replacing WerBell-style spirals

Table 12.2. Net sound reductions in decibels produced by .45 caliber submachine gun suppressors.

GUN	SUPPRESSOR	WINCHESTER USA 230 GR FMJ	TEMPERATURE, °F (°C)
Reising Model 50	Maxim Model 1910	22	62(17)
Ingram M10	Cobray M10 .45	19	62(17)
Ingram M10	Cobray M10 .45[a]	21	76(24)
Ingram M10	Cobray M10 .45[a]	20	71(22)
Ingram M10	RASE	27	80(27)

[a] rebuilt by AWC with Dater baffle stack replacing WerBell-style spirals

In any event, it was World War II that stimulated the first use of submachine guns on a widespread scale. Ironically, the cheapest and ugliest submachine gun of the period, the British Sten, provided an ideal platform for silencing to meet the mission requirements of Allied commandos and partisans.

Although British commandos almost mutinied when their Thompson submachine guns were replaced with Stens, the little weapon that looked like something cobbled together by a plumber had a number of virtues. The Sten Mark II was available in quantity; its barrel was easily accessible for porting and the installation of an integral suppressor; the front sight was located on the receiver (not the barrel), which greatly facilitated the addition of an integral silencer; and the Sten's smooth action was unusually quiet, making it an ideal weapon for silencing. Best of all for operators working behind the lines, the Sten Mark II and its silenced variant, the Mark IIS, could be quickly broken down into the stock, receiver, and barrel (or integrally suppressed barrel) assemblies for ready concealment in handbags, packages, vehicles, or other hiding places.

Not only does the Sten Mark IIS represent the first outstanding suppressed submachine gun, but the development of the Sten itself is one of the most underrated stories of small-arms development in the twentieth century. To really understand and appreciate the silenced Sten, one needs to understand and appreciate the development of the Sten itself.

DEVELOPMENT OF THE STEN

It's hard to convey, much less overstate, the desperate situation facing Britain in the summer of 1940. Even though 1,200 naval vessels, trawlers, and pleasure boats somehow managed to rescue about 340,000 troops from Dunkirk between May 26 and June 4, their weaponry, ammunition and equipment were largely left behind. The *Luftwaffe* began pounding Britain in what would come to be known as the Battle of Britain. And German U-boats were so incredibly successful at sinking supplies from the United States and Canada that German submariners called this the Happy Time. An invasion of Britain loomed on the horizon.

The remnants of the British Expeditionary Force and local defense volunteers (called the Home Guard) desperately needed huge numbers of guns immediately. British forces were virtually unarmed. Only 70,000 military rifles remained to protect the British Isles. A few Lend Lease guns were trickling in (including Thompsons, which were highly prized), but many never made it past the U-boats. New military units being formed throughout the country could only be issued one or two rifles per company.

A call went out to the civilian population to donate any shotguns or other firearms they owned. These 20,000 miscellaneous family heirlooms helped but fell far short of needs. Soldiers marching on drill fields carried wooden facsimiles of rifles and Thompsons to fool German spies into thinking they were fully armed. Vast quantities of glass bottles were collected to make gasoline and "sticky" bombs. Churchill vowed to defend Britain from the landing beaches to the village green. Yet everyone realized the invasion would be a sticky wicket indeed. The situation was further complicated by the urgent demand for weapons and supplies by British and colonial troops fighting the Italians in northern and eastern Africa.

It was during this darkest hour that a British major and a young civil service worker decided to develop a submachine gun that could be made cheaply and rapidly. Maj. (later Col.) Reginald V. Shepperd was, at the time, the director of the Birmingham Small Arms Company (BSA). Harold J. Turpin worked as a designer at the Royal Small Arms Factory (also called the Enfield Lock Arsenal and the Enfield Lock Small Arms Factory) in Enfield. They fired their first prototype within 30 days of deciding to attempt the project.

The prototype was crude compared to the old-world craftsmanship of the Lanchester submachine gun (which was about to enter production) and the finely finished Thompson. The new gun looked like a piece of scrap iron used by some apprentice for welding practice, for great blobs of unfiled welding dominated its appearance. Considering that the British traditionally prided themselves on the fit and finish of their weapons almost as much as their effectivess, it's somewhat surprising that the new gun was embraced so warmly and immediately. Only essential parts were closely machined on the new design.

Yet the new gun, which the inventors called the Sten, performed well and impressed Britain's War Office. Most modern accounts report that the first two letters of "Sten" come from the first letter of each inventor's last name, while the last two letters stand for Enfield, where most authors report the gun was first produced. But a magazine account of the gun's development, which was published during the war, reported that the "en" stood for England. I don't know which is correct.

The Sten Mark I was hailed as the simplest automatic weapon in the world. It only had 45 parts. It was light and easy to carry, fired at 550 rounds per minute, and would be issued with eight 32-round magazines, giving the individual British infantryman unprecedented firepower. Best of all, considering Britain's time-critical need and limited resources, the gun could be brought into production cheaply and quickly. In fact, the Sten went from concept to production within three months at an initial cost of about $12 apiece. The American Thompson and German MP38 each cost about $120 apiece.

The young civil service worker organized production. Unfortunately, conventional production facilities were already committed to other projects, so he improvised. He found an unused hen house awash in old feathers. The building was cleaned and outfitted with an old vertical drill, capstan lathe, and a couple of benches. He hired a foreman with extensive engineering experience and an 18-year-old apprentice. The local employment exchange found a dozen and a half married women willing to work part time. Soon they had been trained to perform rough drilling and turning and even some light fitting.

This scene was repeated in an ever-growing number of improvised, decentralized workshops. This decentralization helped insulate production from the intense German bombing. Eventually, each small part was made by a number of improvised factories. Few looked like workshops from the outside, so they made unlikely targets. Furthermore, if several operations were necessary to finish a particular part, each operation would be performed in a different workshop. And they were widely dispersed, so a large bombing raid could not critically impact production.

Turpin cut through mountains of red tape to secure buildings and to requisition worn, decrepit, and antique machines that could be used for making rough parts. He enlisted the help of little factories that had produced hardware, bicycles, jewelry, lawn mowers, and toys. He also managed to find some quality machine tools necessary to finish critical parts. Parts were sent from the decentralized workshops to a temporary BSA factory at Shirley for final assembly. He returned to London three weeks after he had begun to report that production already exceeded expectations by three times. Headquarters had the good sense to give him a free hand to continue boosting production as rapidly as possible.

About 200 Stens were produced in August of 1941. Then BSA established a major factory at Tyseley in September. Production rose to 1,000 in October and then to 2,000 in November. By July 1942, BSA's production had reached 20,000 per month, and several other factories were assembling Stens at a similar rate. More than 100,000 Mark I Stens were produced before a simplified and improved Mark II was introduced in 1942. On August 19, 1942, the Sten saw its combat debut in a large-scale commando raid on the German-held fortified city of Dieppe, on the coast of France.

Improvisation remained the key to the explosive growth of Sten production. It didn't matter how a part was made as long as it worked. One shop, for example, didn't have the equipment to machine a particular piece, so it made the part from two strips of flat steel that were bent and welded together. In one tiny workshop, a retired gentleman (who worked by himself) produced 540 bolt pins per hour. Then inspiration struck, and he invented a machine that boosted production to 5,000 pins per hour. By 1943, such scenes were being repeated in more than 300 shops. Production of the Mark II peaked at 47,000 in a single week! And production cost dropped to $5.20 per gun. By the end of the war, Britain had manufactured about 5.5 million firearms of all types, if memory serves me correctly. Some 68 percent—that's 3,750,000—were Stens.

Not all improvisations at boosting production worked, however. In an attempt to reduce the use of steel and machine tools, bronze bolts were cast for the Sten in large numbers. They seemed to work fine, and they were easy to machine down from their normal 1.5 pounds (680 g) to a 1.0 pound (454 g) version for the silenced version of the Sten, the Mark IIS.

Unfortunately, the fixed firing pins didn't hold up in firefights, leaving the soldier in question at a serious social disadvantage at the worst possible moment. So armorers immediately began a campaign of throwing away every bronze bolt they encountered and replacing it with a steel bolt. As a result, bronze bolts are apparently rarer in American collections than Petersen Devices and FG42s. In fact, I am only aware of three bronze bolts in private American collections.

The Mark II was also manufactured in Canada and New Zealand. The Canadian Stens made at the famous Long Branch Arsenal generally show the best workmanship. They were also the most expensive Sten Mark II made by the Allies, at a cost of $13.55 apiece. But the most expensive Stens of the war were made by the Germans.

In 1944, the Germans developed a scheme to supply their guerrilla units fighting behind Allied lines with an exact copy of the British Mark II. Two original Stens were given to the Mauser plant at Oberndorf, where plans were drawn up to copy the Sten to the smallest detail. Even the markings were copied to hide the origin of the guns. Production of the *"Gerät Potsdam"* ("Potsdam tool," as the clone was called) was begun within six weeks of the first conversations. Mauser delivered the complete order (25,000 to 28,000 guns) only six weeks after production had started up. Aside from the welding of seams, only very minute details differed from the original version. Most of the guns were used in France toward the end of the war.

Since Mauser had to tool up and produce these clones in such a short time, they were paid the unprecedented price of $450 per gun. After delivery, the company produced a modified Sten more to German tastes based on work that began in November of the previous year. The new version was called the MP3008 and was intended to equip *Volksstürm* units. It used standard MP38 magazines feeding in German fashion from below the receiver. Mauser initially built 150 prototypes, which were provided to six firms early in 1945. At least five of these companies actually produced the gun, but only about 10,000 were delivered.

While Canadian versions of the Sten generally displayed the best workmanship, the German versions were the crudest. Yet the firm Walter Steiner, Eisenkonstruktionen (located in Suhl) took the trouble to knurl the bolt-retracting handle. Go figure.

British commandos had bitterly resisted initial attempts to replace their Thompsons with Stens, but they soon developed a grudging affection for the weapon, especially the silenced Mark IIS. The Mark II also became the weapon of choice for resistance fighters on the Continent, since it could be disassembled into easily concealable pieces that could be hidden in a coat or large purse. More than half a million Stens were supplied to resistance groups by the end of the war.

STEN MARK IIS

It is safe to say that the Sten Mark IIS was one of the most successful tools for quiet killing to come out of World War II. Britain fielded at least three variants of the silenced Sten during the war: the Type I, the Type II, and the Type SOE.

The silenced Stens shared the need for a lightened bronze or steel bolt weighing 1.0 pound (454 g) and a main operating (recoil) spring with two spirals removed. The bronze bolt does not create the ringing characteristic of a steel bolt slamming forward during the action cycle, so the action noise is softer. The tradeoff is that the fixed firing pin machined into the face of the bronze bolt is fragile and prone to breaking at inopportune moments when reliability is more important than a slight reduction in action noise.

The most commonly cited source of information on the Type I and Type II silenced Stens is Frankford Arsenal Report R-1896. Some of the information in that report is excellent, but some must be viewed as questionable. For example, the report asserts that the lightened bolt and shortened operating spring were necessary to keep the cyclic rate at 450 rounds per minute. That view is flawed.

The ported barrels in the Sten Mark IIS (a number of different barrel designs were used) vented enough gas from the barrel so that considerably less energy was available to push the fired case against the face of the standard 1.5 pound (680 g) bolt. With less energy pushing the bolt back against the recoil spring, the bolt could not travel backward far enough to engage the sear. Thus the weapon would fire a long continuous burst, whether the selector was set on "R" for repetition or "A" for automatic. Sometimes the bolt might catch the sear after five or ten rounds. Sometimes the bolt would continue to short stroke until the entire magazine contents had been fired.

This was more than an inconvenience, even during training, because the Mark IIS silencer was not particularly robust. More than one British armorer has reported on the fact that even firing a single magazine on full auto could compress the silencer's baffle stack into the forward end of the silencer, destroying its effectiveness to the point that it sounded like an unsilenced weapon (see, for example, Laidler and Howroyd, 1995). Contrary to Frankford Arsenal Report R-1896, the Sten Mark IIS was intended for semiautomatic fire only.

Type I

The Type I silencer is illustrated in Figure 12.1. The suppressor and barrel assembly is 13 inches (33 cm) long, 1.56 inches (3.96 cm) in diameter, and weighs 2.25 pounds (1.02 kg). The approximately 4.75 inch (12.1 cm) barrel features six 0.11 inch (2.8 mm) holes located 0.72 inch (1.8 cm) forward of where the cartridge base would sit when a round is chambered. These ports vent into a primary expansion chamber with a volume of 4.4 cubic inches (72 cc). This porting not only enhances suppressor efficiency per se, it also lowers gas pressure in the barrel enough to keep the velocity of standard-issue ammunition below the speed of sound, so the weapon does not produce a ballistic crack. Forward of the barrel and primary expansion chamber, the suppressor contains 30 flat, equally spaced baffles. The bullet passage through each baffle measures 0.44 inch (1.12 cm) in diameter. The space between the first two baffles is filled with nine mesh disks, as is the space between the last two baffles.

Frankford Arsenal Report R-1896 asserts that dropping a bolt on an empty chamber in the Sten Mark II produces a 100 dB sound signature. The report also claims that firing the Type I silencer from a closed-breech test jig produced a peak SPL of 112 dB at a distance of 5 meters from the system. Applying the inverse square law to these data to simulate a microphone distance of 1 meter from the weapon provides mixed results. The bolt-closing decibel value is almost within the range of believable numbers. But the suppressed sound signature isn't anywhere near the ballpark. It is clear that these data are irretrievably flawed by equipment that was not up to the task.

It is not clear whether the problem was the tape recorder used to capture microphone output for later analysis using an oscilloscope or, possibly, the pre-amp or some other component within the system. The fact that the SPL of a relatively long impulse event (bolt closing) is almost believable while the SPL of a very brief event (the suppressed gunshot) isn't even close to a meaningful number suggests that the system's effective rise time is not fast enough. The net result is that there is simply no way to apply a statistical procedure to these data to transform them into meaningful numbers. All of the sound data in the Frankford Arsenal report must be dismissed. The subjective reporting, however, remains interesting.

The report says that, although the Type I silencer was "somewhat bulky, in general it compensates for this by very good acoustical performance and long service life. To a subjective listener, the system sounded as an abrupt initiation and gradual cessation of a relatively mild hiss. Compared to other silencers and silenced barrels with respectable energy outputs, the Sten was one of the quieter systems tested at Frankford Arsenal."

Type II

From the outside, the Type II suppressor is very similar to the Type I. The Type II is 13.5 inches (34.3 cm) long, 1.56 inches (3.96 cm) in diameter, and weighs 2.5 pounds (1.14 kg). The inside of the suppressor is quite different, however (see Figure 12.2). The barrel is shortened to about 3.55 inches (9.0 cm) and features two sets of ports, which vent into a smaller primary expansion chamber that contains 2.7 cubic inches (44 cc) of free volume. In front of the barrel and primary expansion chamber, the suppressor contains 18 conical baffles with the same-size bullet passage as used for the Type I baffle. The Frankford Arsenal Report says that the Type II suppressor tested in its study has half the cone in the front-most six baffles machined away "presumably for experimental purposes."

Yet an original British assembly drawing in my collection (which is dated February 2, 1944) shows the same modification as part of the standard Type II design. The cutouts in each of the front six baffles are oriented 180 degrees from the adjacent modified baffles, probably with the intent of creating a diagonal flow of combustion gases between each baffle. A flat washer holds three felt wipes against the front end cap of the suppressor in the Frankford Arsenal Type II suppressor, whereas the washer holds four felt wipes in the original British drawing.

A number of variations of the basic Type II design can be encountered. A common variant, for example, was tested to obtain the sound data reported in Tables 12.3 and 12.4 (see pages 288-289). This variant of the Type II features nested tubes rather than a single one-piece tube for the outer suppressor casing.

While the Frankford Arsenal sound data are seriously flawed, the subjective description of the Type II's sound signature compared to the Type I remains interesting. Tables 12.3 and 12.4 show sound data I collected using a Sten Mark IIS Type II suppressor. Subjectively, the sound produced by the system is a combination of bolt slap and an uncorking sound from the suppressor. "To a subjective listener," the report states, "the Type II Sten sounded like a clap-initiated, gradually diminishing hiss. In general, it seemed somewhat louder than the Type I Sten." Regarding the Type I Sten, the report says, "To a subjective listener, the system sounded as an abrupt initiation and a gradual cessation of a relatively mild hiss. Compared to other silencers and silenced barrels with respectable energy outputs, the Sten [Type II] was one of the quieter systems tested at Frankford Arsenal." My own experience shooting the Type II Sten Mark IIS revealed an altogether satisfying sound quite unlike a gunshot, but the noise is nevertheless noticeably louder than suppressors created for the Sten several decades later by Jonathan Arthur Ciener and Dr. Philip H. Dater.

Type SOE

Information about the Sten silencer used by the Special Operations Executive (SOE) remains somewhat elusive. The initial variant of the Type SOE silencer is readily distinguished from the Types I and II by its greater length (24 inches, 61 cm), larger diameter (2 inches, 5 cm), and domed front end cap. The design uses a tube within a tube. The inner tube is approximately 1.6 inches (4.1 cm) in diameter and contains about 22 baffles in front of what appears to be about a 6.7 inch

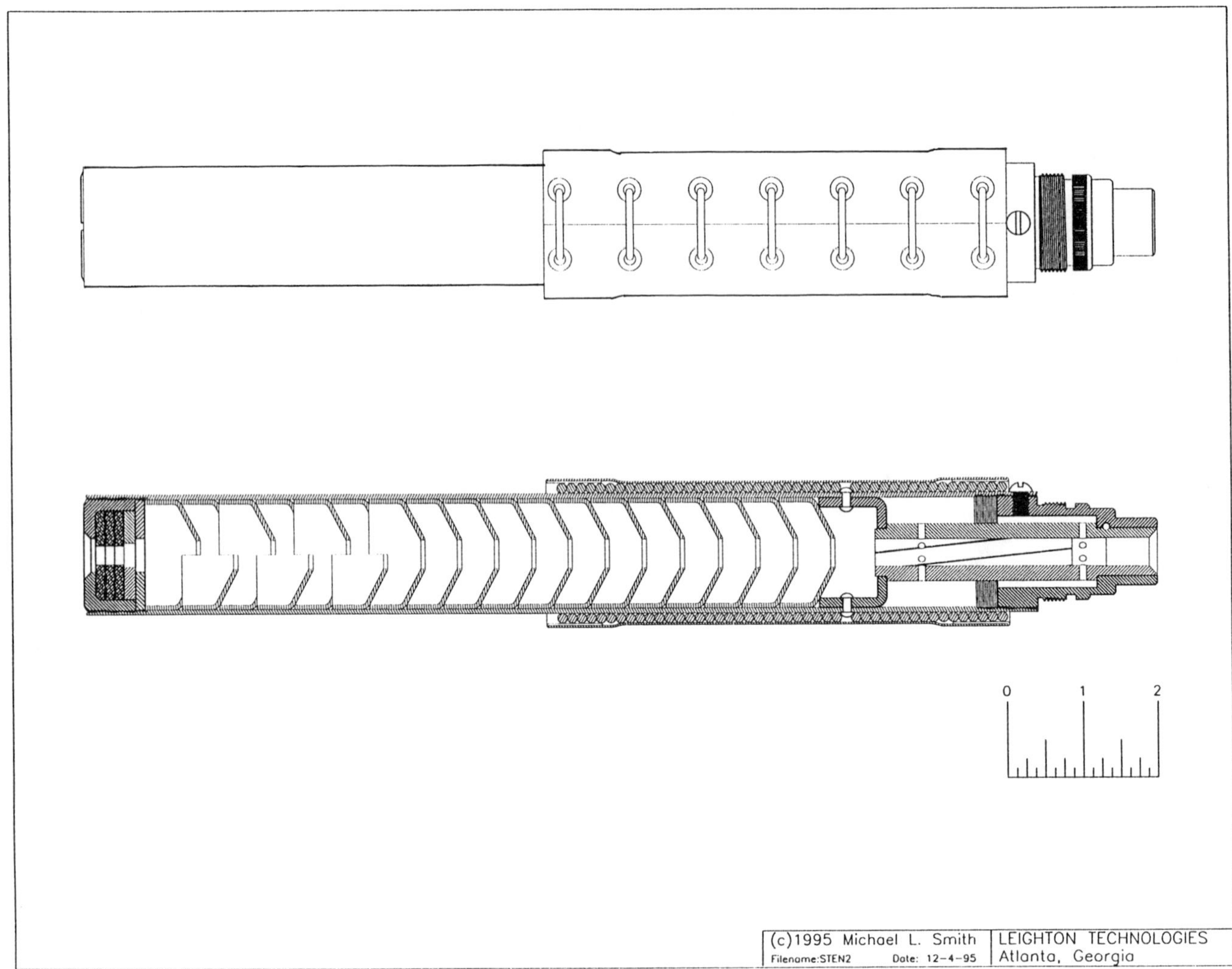

Figure 12.2. Type II variant of the British WWII-vintage Sten silencer. Drawing by Mike Smith.

(17.0 cm) ported barrel (see Figure 12.3). Several felt wipes separate the baffle stack from the front end cap. This inner tube is surrounded by eight asbestos spacers that both deaden the ringing of the inner casing and keep the outer tube cooler to the touch.

This initial design of the Type SOE silencer should have been the quietest of the Mark IIS variants. This first SOE variant is more awkward to use than the Type I and Type II because of the suppressor's considerable length. The first system is also more difficult to conceal than other suppressed variants when broken down, because the suppressor is much longer than the receiver or stock. But the initial SOE suppressor never went into production because maintaining proper alignment to avoid bullet contact with baffles proved to be a serious problem with this very long design. A shorter coaxial suppressor with a 12 inch (30.5 cm) overall length became the production variant. The production silencer is noteworthy for its 2.0 inch (5 cm) outer tube with short (0.5 inch, 1.3 cm) extensions of 1.6 inch tubing at the front and rear of the suppressor. The SOE Mark IIS was issued with one of several stocks, including the standard "T" stock, Canadian-pattern skeletonized stock, and a skeletonized pistol grip instead of a stock. The Type SOE silencer was also used for special operations by Australian personnel, who mounted them on Austen sub-

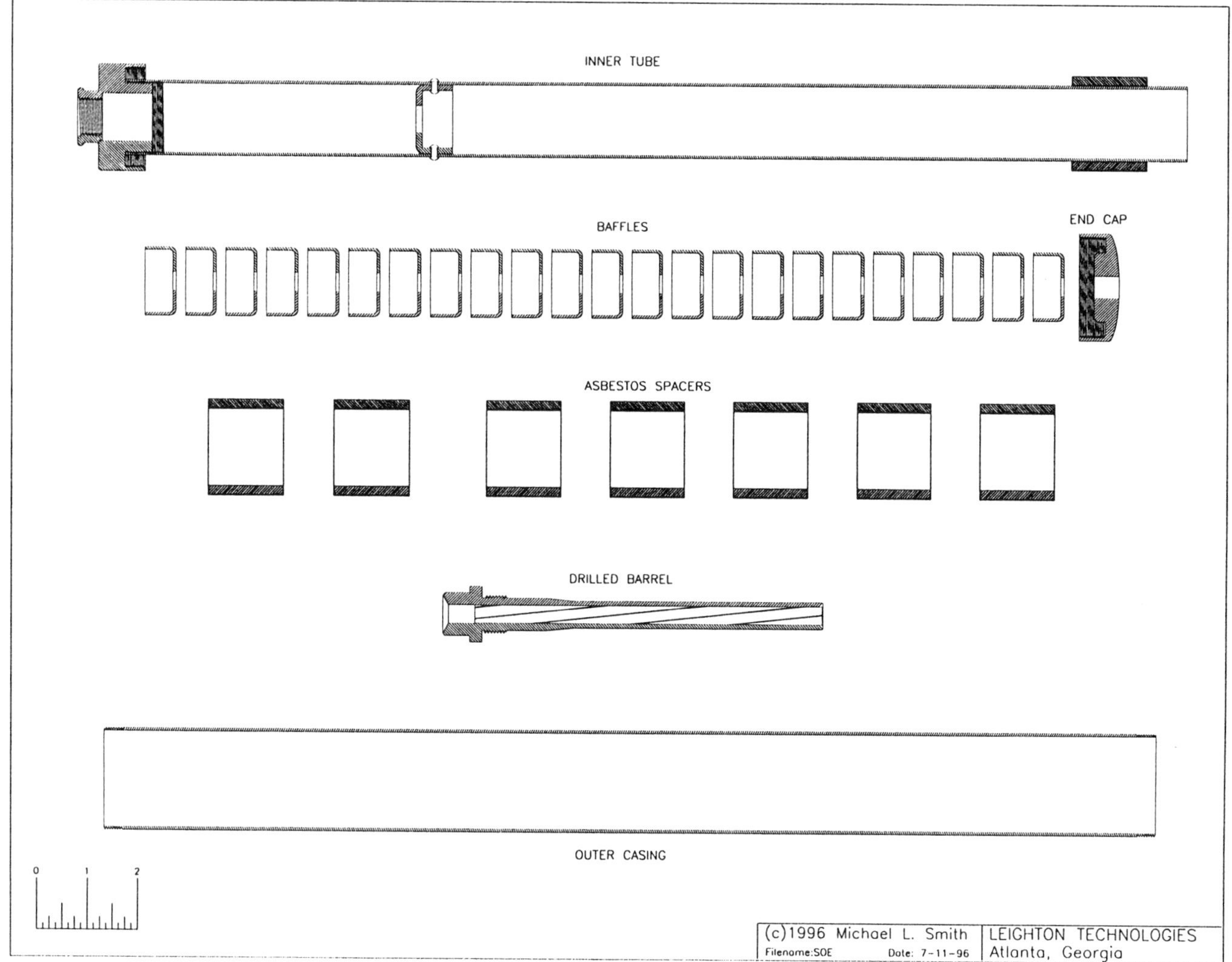

Figure 12.3. Sketch of an unusual prototype of the SOE variant of the British WWII vintage Sten silencer. A slightly different design was shortened to provide the production variant of the Type SOE silencer. Drawing by Mike Smith.

machine guns.

From World War II through the Vietnam era and even today, the silenced Sten Mark IIS and its descendants remain the yardstick by which every other silenced pistol-caliber weapon is measured. The U.S. civilian marketplace stimulated the development of new suppressors for the Sten in the late 1970s, when remanufactured Sten Mark II machine guns became popular with beginning machine gun collectors because of their affordability and good performance.

SILENCING THE STEN

Private collectors who own a Sten really owe it to themselves to add a quality suppressor. There is something quite addictive about making things happen downrange with scarcely a sound except the bullets striking the target, especially when you use your "sow's ear" to outperform someone with a glamor gun that cost three to ten times as much as the humble old Sten. While few World War II vintage Sten suppressors are on the BATF registry in the United States, a number of modern suppressors can equal and even outperform the original designs.

Silencing Options

Silencing options for the Sten Mark II fall into two broad categories: 1) adapting muzzle cans to the Sten using a specially threaded barrel, and 2) installing an integral suppressor and ported barrel assembly made specifically for the Sten. The following discussion will evaluate two examples in each category.

If you already own a 9mm SIONICS (or a clone such as a MAC, RPB, or Cobray) suppressor for an Ingram M10 or Cobray M11/9 submachine gun, the simplest solution would be to purchase a special barrel for the Sten that is threaded for a SIONICS-type suppressor. This is also a cheap option if you own an AWC MK-9 suppressor, which features interchangeable barrel mounts. The SIONICS-type suppressor weighs 1.2 pounds (544 g), while the AWC MK-9 can weighs 1.8 pounds (816 g).

An advantage of this option besides economy is that it requires no modification of the recoil spring. The liabilities of this approach are threefold: 1) the Cobray suppressor is inefficient and hard to maintain, even if one could still buy wipes thanks to the McClure-Volkmer Bill in 1986, which essentially outlawed the possession wipes outside of a registered suppressor tube; 2) the suppressor obscures the lower half of the front sight; and 3) the use of muzzle cans has no effect on projectile velocity, so the suppressed weapon will still generate a very loud ballistic crack when used with supersonic ammunition. There also remains the matter of aesthetics. Both the Cobray and AWC MK-9 suppressors mounted on a special barrel look like an afterthought on the Sten rather than part of an integrated system.

Sten Mark II with an SG-9 integral suppressor with special ported barrel marketed by the Automatic Weapons Company. The seven-cell magazine pouch was issued to British paratroopers and commandos during World War II.

Perhaps the most common special Sten barrel with SIONICS-type threads was originally marketed by the Parts Division of Numrich Arms (now called The Gun Parts Corporation) in West Hurley, New York. There is a potential problem with this barrel. Three different measurements on the barrel obtained from Numrich were so out of spec that they had to be turned down on a lathe for the barrel to headspace properly and to accept suppressors with SIONICS-type threads. Even so, it is probably cheaper to buy the Numrich barrel and clean it up rather than to start from scratch with a 9mm barrel blank.

Another silencing option is to purchase a suppressor/barrel assembly made specifically for the Sten. Such systems were developed by Jonathan Arthur Ciener and the Automatic Weapons Company, among others.

AWC's SG-9 integral suppressor was originally marketed in 1981 for both the Sten Mark II and the Smith & Wesson Model 76 submachine guns. The basic design of this suppressor dates back to 1979, when Dr. Philip H. Dater began building suppressors with aluminum tubes for the S&W submachine gun. He called this suppressor the Model M76.

The SG-9 featured interchangeable barrel/barrel nut assemblies that allowed mounting it on either weapon (see Figure 12.4). Dater's original design was 11.0 inches (27.9 cm) long, while the

Left: Sten Mark II with Cobray suppressor and special Numrich barrel.

Below Left: The top Sten bolt is a 1.0 pound steel bolt for suppressed Stens, the second and fourth from the top are standard 1.5 pound steel bolts, and the third from the top is a 1.5 pound bronze bolt.

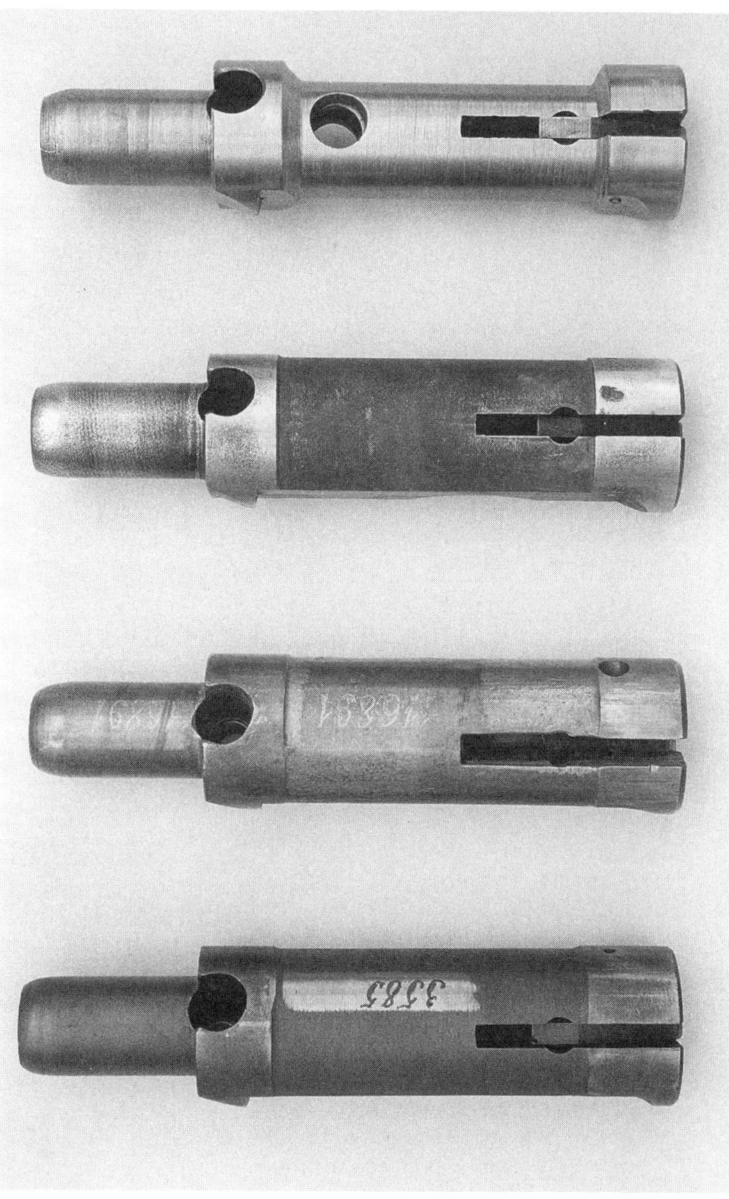

second-generation cans were 12.0 inches (30.5 cm) long and 1.75 inches (4.4 cm) in diameter with an aluminum tube or 1.62 inches (4.2 cm) in diameter with a steel tube. The aluminum suppressor weighed 2.3 pounds (1.0 kg); the steel version weighed 3.0 pounds (1.4 kg). Dater reported a sound reduction of 18 dB. He also reported that the muzzle signature of the suppressed S&W Model 76 was only 6 dB louder than the bolt falling on an empty chamber.

After Dater, Lynn Mcwilliams, Tim Bixler, and others founded the AWC Division of Armament Systems and Technology in mid-1983, Dater's SG-9 was offered only in the steel-tube version for the Sten Mark II and the S&W Model 76 and its clones (Global Weapons 76A1 and M&K Arms MK-760). This updated design was 14.0 inches (35.6 cm) long and 1.63 inches (4.1 cm) in diameter. It weighed 3.0 pounds (1.4 kg). The improved SG-9 was an excellent and popular design, but interest in the Sten and the Model 76 and its clones declined as more glamorous remanufactured automatic weapons became available to the U.S. collector. The SG-9 suppressor was finally dropped from the AWC line at the end of 1985.

Paradoxically, the McClure-Volkmer Bill of 1986 that outlawed the future

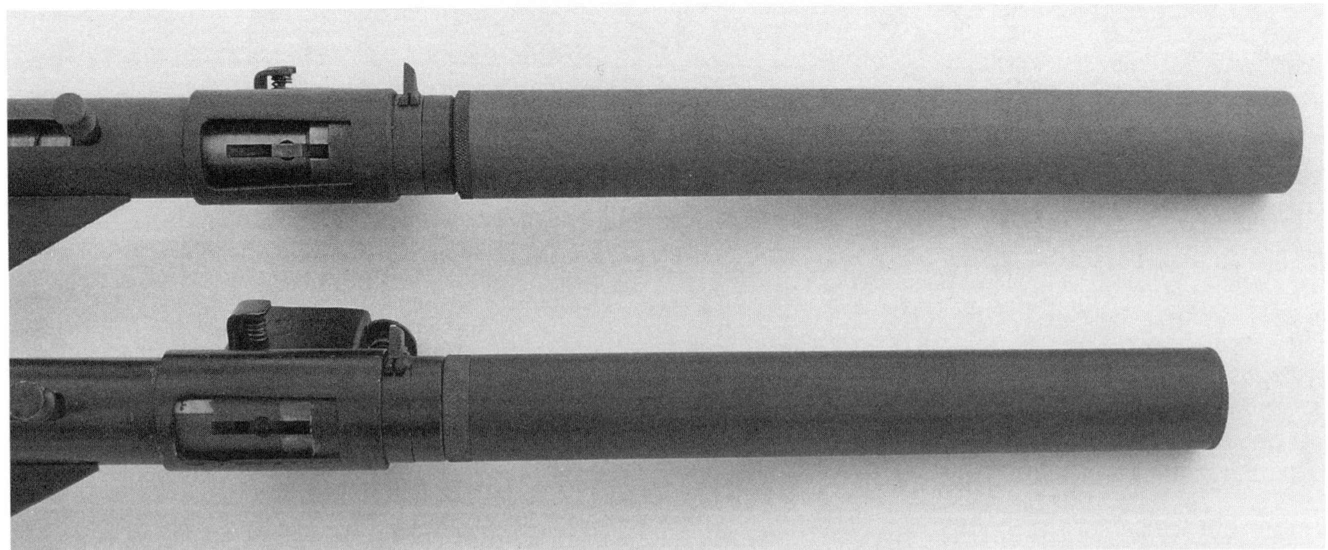

Above: The top Sten has an AWC SG-9 suppressor and a lightened 1.0 pound steel bolt, while the bottom Sten has a Ciener suppressor and a standard 1.5 pound steel bolt.

Right: A close-up view showing a lightened 1.0 pound steel bolt in the top Sten with AWC SG-9 suppressor and a standard 1.5 pound steel bolt in the bottom Sten with Ciener suppressor.

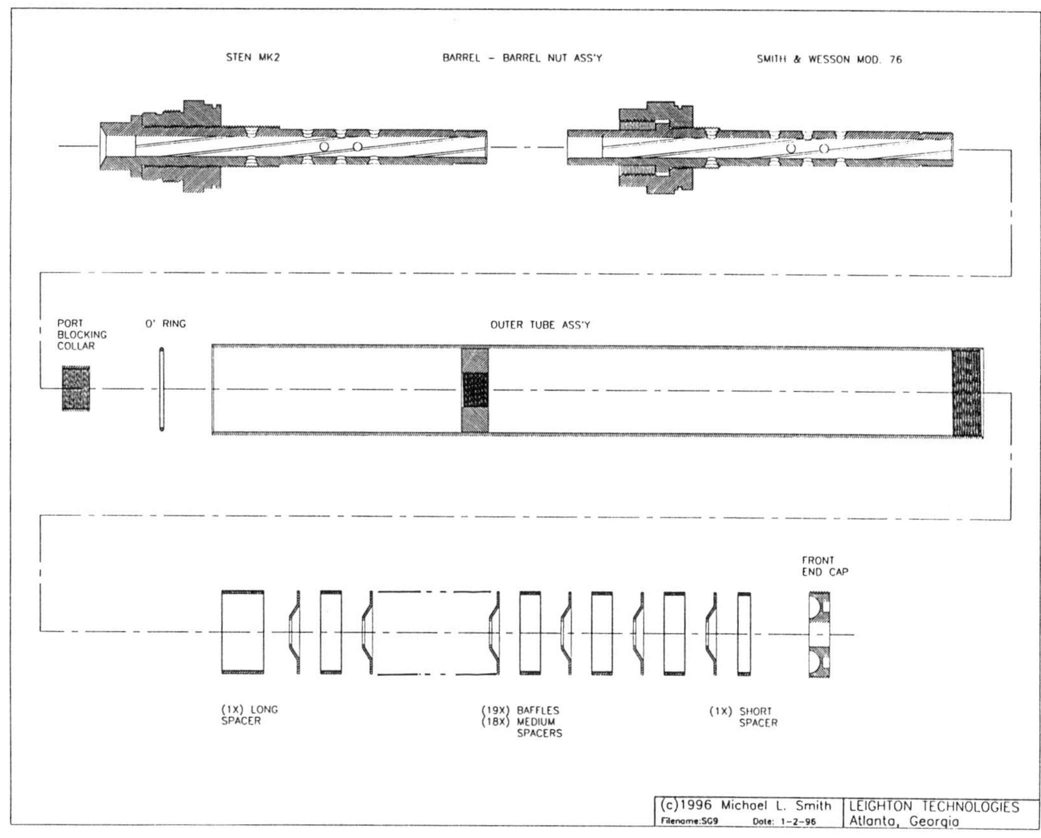

Figure 12.4. Dater's SG-9 design featured interchangeable barrel/barrel nut assemblies that allowed mounting the suppressor on either the Sten Mark II or S&W Model 76, as well as a port blocking collar for adjusting projectile velocity. Drawing by Mike Smith.

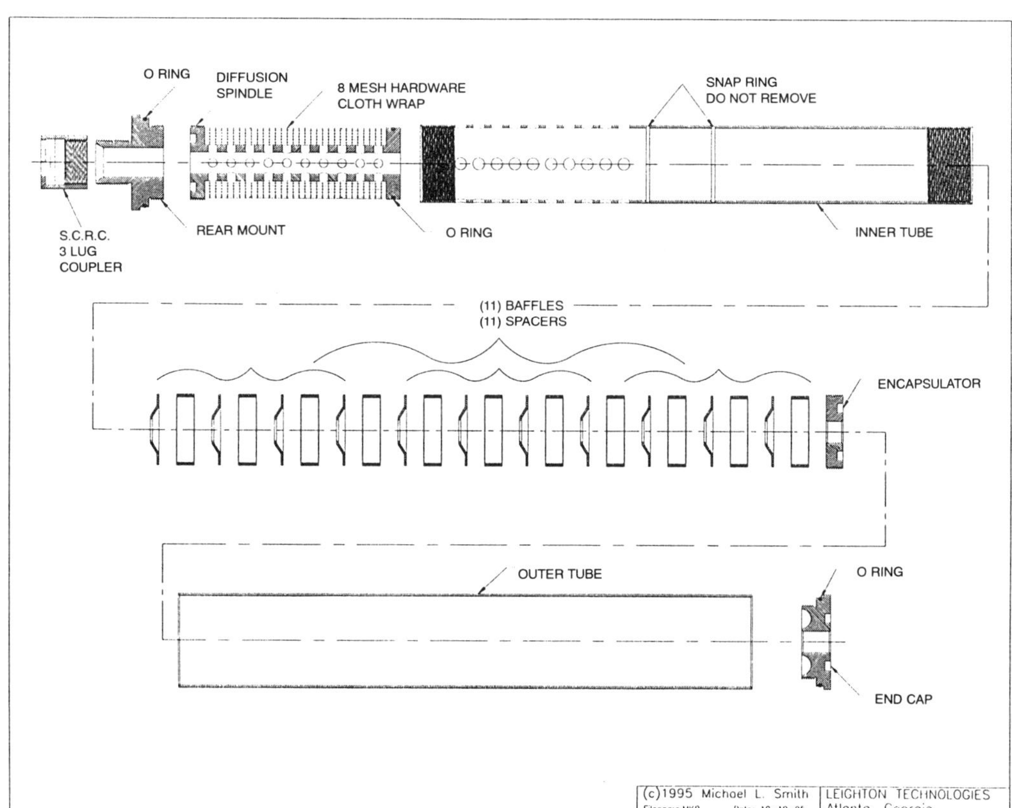

Figure 12.5. AWC MK-9 suppressor with Bixler three-lug mount for the MP5. Drawing by Mike Smith.

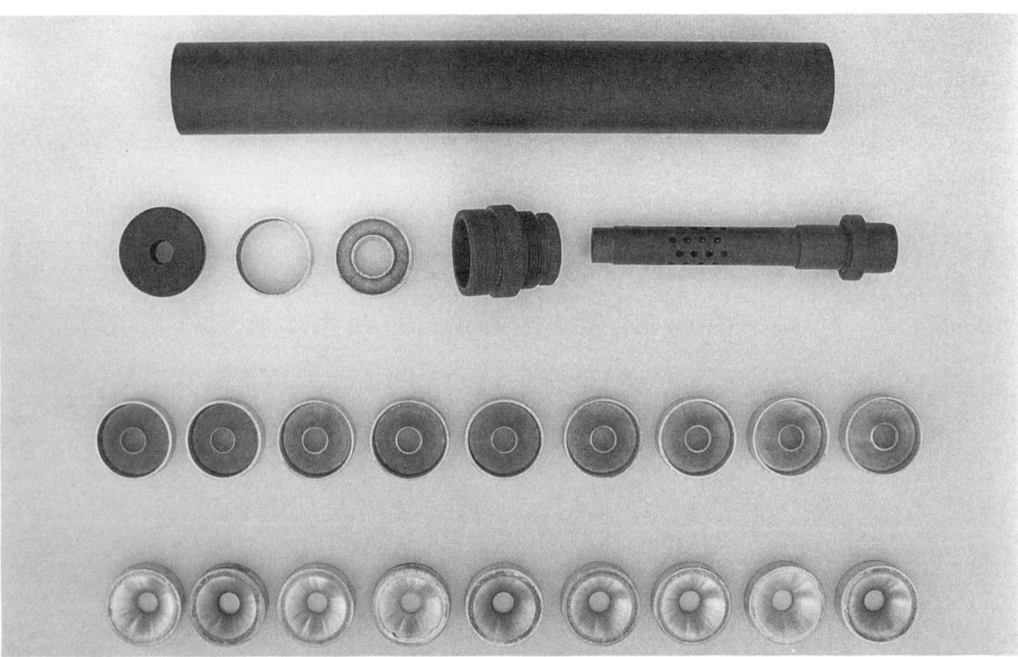

The Ciener integral suppressor for the Sten Mark II features a 4.38 inch ported barrel and a 3.13 inch primary expansion chamber. The 18 baffles are identical to those Ciener uses in his other 9mm submachine gun suppressors.

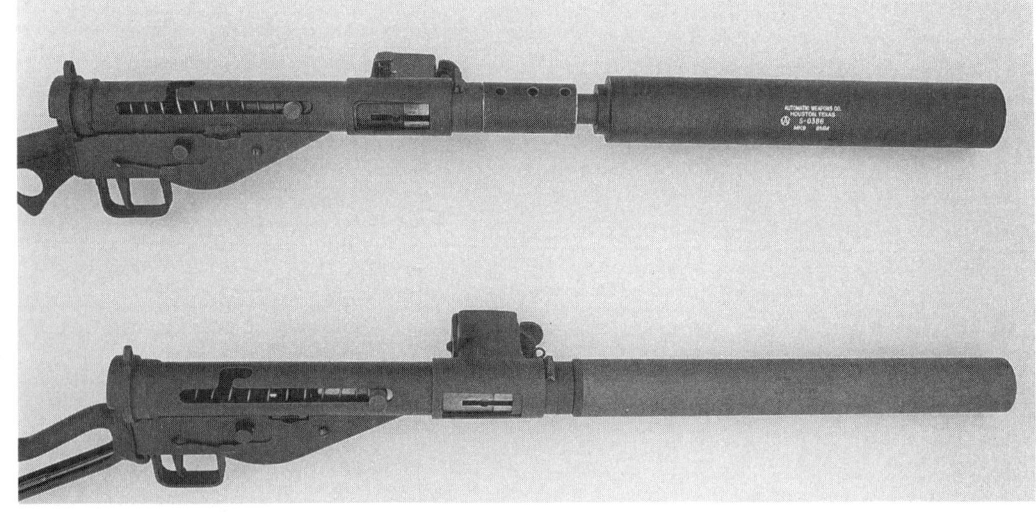

The top Sten Mark II has an AWC MK-9 suppressor mounted on a special Numrich barrel; the bottom Sten has the AWC SG-9 integral suppressor with ported barrel.

manufacture of machine guns for civilian ownership in the United States stimulated renewed interest in the suppressor, since a large number of Stens suddenly flooded the market. The SG-9 went back into production. The latest version featured a gray, Parkerized steel finish and a Shilen match barrel. The suppressor evaluated in this study was made in 1985. The tube, front end cap and barrel retaining nut are made from 4130 steel, the 18 baffles are 18-8 stainless steel, and the 18 spacers are made from 6061-T6 aluminum. The spacers separate the baffles by 3/8 inch (10 mm). The primary expansion chamber at the rear of the suppressor is 4.2 inches (10.6 cm) long and is filled with eight mesh hardware cloth to diffuse the rapidly expanding combustion gases.

The barrel has 24 ports 5/32 inch (4.1 mm) in diameter arranged in four rows of six holes per row. A port blocking collar is provided to screw over the rearmost hole in each row when using subsonic ammunition or when maximum velocity is required of supersonic ammunition. Removal of the port blocking collar should lower the velocity of normally supersonic loads to subsonic velocities.

The Ciener suppressor is 12.0 inches (30.5 cm) long and weighs 1.01 pounds (458 grams) with-

This Numrich barrel is designed to mount any 9mm suppressor with SIONICS-type threads to the Sten Mark II submachine gun.

out the barrel. The barrel porting is designed to reduce suppressor ammo to subsonic velocity. The special barrel is 4.38 inches (11.1 cm) long and weighs 0.41 pounds (186 g). The barrel has 32 ports 1/8 inch (3.3 mm) in diameter arranged in eight rows of four holes per hole. The primary expansion chamber is 3.13 inches (8.0 cm) long and does not contain mesh for diffusing the combustion gases. The 18 baffles with integral spacers are identical to the baffles Ciener uses in his other 9mm submachine gun suppressors.

How much do these different systems add to the weight of a Sten? A Sten Mark II weighs 6.62 pounds (3.0 kg). Of that total, the barrel weighs 0.77 pound (349 g) and the barrel sleeve weighs 0.35 pound (159 g). The Numrich special barrel with SIONICS threads weighs 0.86 pound (390 g), and suppressor weights have already been mentioned. Thus the long and the short of it is that a Sten equipped with a SIONICS-type suppressor weighs 7.91 pounds (3.6 kg), the Sten with the AWC MK-9 weighs 8.51 pounds (3.9 kg), the Sten with the AWC SG-9 weighs 8.50 pounds (3.9 kg), and the Sten with Ciener suppressor weighs 6.92 pounds (3.1 kg). The SG-9 system feels substantially heavier than the Ciener system, but both handle very well. I personally prefer the feel of the SG-9 system, and the extra weight improves my hit probability. My preference might change if I had to carry the weapon a lot, since a Mark II with Ciener suppressor seems virtually as light as an unsuppressed weapon.

Installing any of these suppressors is as easy as replacing the barrel. But the installation process does not end there, since silenced Stens are quite sensitive to suppressor design, ammunition, bolt weight, and length of recoil spring.

I have found that both the AWC SG-9 and WWII suppressors require shortened recoil springs to function in Stens with the standard 1.5 pound (680 g) steel bolts. Unmodified Stens worked reliably with the Ciener and AWC MK-9 suppressors and the SIONICS clones. Your experience with your Sten may be different.

A particular combination of suppressor, firearm, and ammunition may yield some surprises, so one should always approach a new combination with caution. A common problem is the runaway. Many years ago, when I first mated an SG-9 suppressor to a Sten, I loaded a magazine with Winchester ammunition, moved the selector to semiautomatic, and squeezed the trigger. Instead of one round zipping down range, a 32-round burst chewed up my target. The suppressor reduced the back pressure to the point that the bolt wasn't kicked back far enough to engage the sear. So the recoil spring pushed the bolt forward, stripping another round into the chamber and so on until the magazine was empty.

Now I never load more than three rounds into a magazine when I test a new combination of suppressor, weapon, and ammunition. The runaway was easy enough to control safely, but the experience offended both my dignity and my pocketbook.

I solved the problem by removing 1/4 spiral from the spring at a time, and then trying again. On that *particular* Sten with a standard 1.5 pound steel bolt, I ultimately removed 3-3/4 coils of the recoil spring. This is the limit for most recoil springs; removing any more may prevent the weapon from chambering and firing a round. Temperature can also be a factor. I use a spring with 3-1/4 coils removed at temperatures below 20 °F (-7 °C). The British Special Operations Executive approached this problem during World War II by using a lightened (1.0 pound; 454 g) bronze or steel bolt, by removing two spirals of the recoil spring, and by never loading the magazines with more than 25 rounds. The Sten that I modified worked reliably with 32 rounds in the magazine. Be sure to replace any modified parts (like the recoil spring and bolt) if you remove the silencer. Failure to do so could damage your Sten.

Maintenance

Any suppressor should be completely disassembled and cleaned immediately after every time it is shot with corrosive ammo, even with the cheap, barely corrosive Egyptian ammo that has been widely sold throughout the United States in 36-round boxes. The following guidelines apply when shooting noncorrosive ammo.

The SIONICS and its clones should be disassembled and cleaned (and its wipe should be replaced) every 500 rounds. The Ciener suppressor and AWC's SG-9 should be disassembled and cleaned every 2,000 rounds. (I should note, however, that Ciener's Sten suppressor comes with a warning that disassembling the can will void its warranty, so consider the implications before you take it apart.) AWC's MK-9 requires partial disassembly and cleaning every 2,000 rounds, and complete disassembly and cleaning every 5,000 to 10,000 rounds.

Before a suppressor is used the first time, and after every cleaning, all threaded surfaces should be coated with an antiseize compound. Colloidal molybdenum or copper compounds designed for high-temperature applications work the best. A look at one such problem should be instructive.

After shooting about 700 noncorrosive rounds through a new SG-9 suppressor, bonding of the threaded components in the suppressor prevented disassembly. I finally used a 50-cent plastic tool designed for removing champagne corks to unscrew the barrel retaining nut from the rear of the suppressor. But I needed a couple of college jocks (one to hold the tube and another to apply torque to the spanner) to break the seal between the suppressor tube and the front end cap. But there was one bond that we couldn't break.

The problem involved an interesting feature unique to the SG-9: the port blocking collar, which is a knurled aluminum ring (current production uses a steel ring) screwed onto the barrel just forward of the barrel retaining nut. The collar covers the rearmost set of holes in the barrel when using subsonic ammunition or when the ballistic crack of supersonic ammunition is not a liability. Removing the collar vents propellant gases into the rear expansion chamber more quickly, which keeps the bullets of otherwise supersonic cartridges below the speed of sound. But I couldn't remove the collar when I wanted to shoot supersonic ammo.

I tried soaking the assembly in sol-

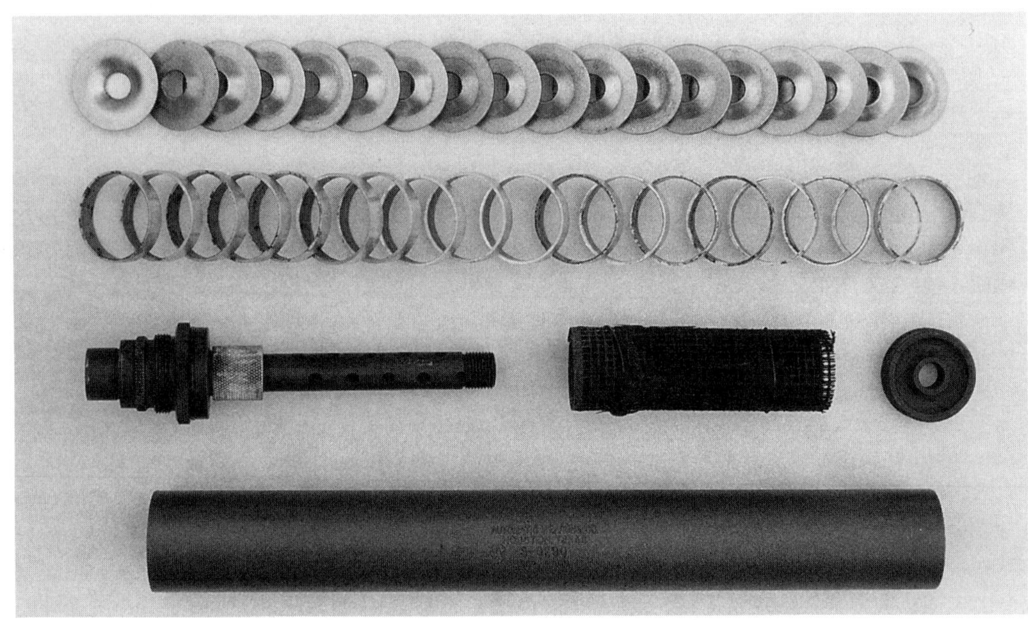

The AWC SG-9 suppressor disassembled.

vent for weeks, and still I could not remove the collar. I finally took the barrel assembly to a machinist. We put the barrel in the six-jawed precision chuck of a lathe, and still we could not unscrew the port blocking collar with Vise Grips or a pipe wrench with a long cheater bar. The only way to remove that collar is to turn it down to nothingness on a lathe.

None of these problems with threaded components would have occurred if I had coated all threaded surfaces with antiseize compound.

Performance

The sound signatures of the Sten with four suppressors and an unsuppressed Sten were recorded for both Winchester USA 115 grain supersonic and Samson 158 grain subsonic ammo. Ambient temperature ranged from 65-67 °F (18-19 °C) for the first set of tests, and subsequent tests were conducted at 11 °F (-12 °C). Since the Ciener system was unavailable during the warmer testing, I duplicated two of the earlier tests to see if temperature might affect the results. Table 12.3 shows the actual sound signatures, and Table 12.4 (see page 289) simplifies the data into net sound reduction for a particular combination of ammo and suppressor. The port blocking collar was installed in the SG-9 suppressor.

Using supersonic ammo, the best performer was the AWC MK-9, followed by the AWC SG-9, the Cobray, and the Ciener. The SG-9 integral suppressor was the winner with subsonic ammo, however, followed by the AWC MK-9, the Cobray (with virgin wipe), and the Ciener. These results are a bit surprising, since conventional wisdom suggests that an integral suppressor should be quieter than a muzzle can. Another surprise was that Winchester USA ammo produced a ballistic crack 80 percent of the time with the Ciener system at 11 °F (-12 °C).

That unexpected ballistic crack stimulated me to measure the muzzle velocities produced by the integral suppressors. The temperature during velocity testing remained 8 °F (-13 °C). At least 10 rounds were fired to obtain an average muzzle velocity. The results are shown in Table 12.5. Note that the velocities reported for the unsuppressed Sten were not statistically different from velocities produced by using the muzzle cans with the threaded Numrich barrel, so the latter data were not incorporated into the table.

Since most writers state that the speed of sound is about 1,100 fps (335 mps), the chronograph data seem to suggest that neither the Ciener nor the AWC SG-9 system should produce a ballistic crack. The speed of sound, however, varies with temperature. In fact, according to the commonly used formula habitually published in engineering books, the only variable affecting the speed of sound is temperature.

According to the aforementioned engineering formula, the actual speed of sound is 1,087 fps (331 mps) at 32 °F (0 °C), and 1,060 fps (323 mps) at 8 °F (-13 °C). Every Winchester USA round shot in both systems produced a ballistic crack at 8 °F, while several rounds through the Ciener system did not produce a ballistic crack at 11 °F. Remarkably, the slowest Winchester velocity recorded at 8 °F was 1,029 fps (314 mps), and it still produced a ballistic crack. These observations can be explained by the inherent variability of the data, which are not statistically different than the calculated speed of sound.

Conclusions

I prefer the appearance and handling characteristics of the integral suppressors (Ciener and AWC SG-9) over the muzzle cans. Both integral systems are well made, but the tube and baffles of the SG-9 are more robust. Both effectively reduce the weapon's sound signature while improving hit probability, although the SG-9 outperforms the Ciener system on both counts. But the Ciener system is both easier to carry and faster to bring on target because it is shorter and much lighter. A big plus for the Ciener system is that it does not require a modified recoil spring for reliable functioning.

The MK-9 muzzle can also performed well. In fact, once while shooting subsonic ammunition through a Sten fitted with an MK-9 at -20 °F (-29 °C), the suppressor reduced the Sten's sound signature so much that I actually heard the "twang!" of the recoil spring as it pushed the bolt forward! That was a heady experience. Nevertheless, I still prefer to use the integral Ciener or SG-9 systems. The integral systems provide plenty of sound suppression and are safer, since an integral suppressor cannot unscrew from the barrel during use (as is possible with a muzzle can mated to a barrel with course threads). While AWC Systems Technology no longer manufactures SG-9, Dr. Philip Dater (who designed this system) will still manufacture the unit as a special-order item. Contact him in care of Gemtech.

Table 12.3. Sound signatures in decibels of Sten and Ingram submachine gun suppressors.

GUN	SUPPRESSOR	WINCHESTER 115 GR SUPERSONIC	SAMSON 158 GR SUBSONIC	TEMP., °F (°C)
Sten Mk II	None	159	157	36(2)
Sten Mk II	Original IIS Type II	137	134	36(2)
Sten Mk II	None	160	157	65(18)
Sten Mk II	AWC SG-9	134	123	65(18)
Sten Mk II	Cobray	134	130	66(19)
Sten Mk II	AWC MK-9	128	126	67(19)
Sten Mk II	None	161	157	11(-12)
Sten Mk II	AWC SG-9	131	123	11(-12)
Sten Mk II	Ciener	136	131	11(-12)
Ingram M10 9mm	None	162	159	66(19)
Ingram M10 9mm	Cobray M10 9mm	136	132	66(19)
Ingram M11 .380	None	158[b]	—	66(19)
Ingram M11 .380	Cobray M11 .380	137[b]	—	66(19)
Ingram M10 9mm	None	161	159	71(22)
Ingram M10 9mm	Cobray M10 9mm[a]	133	131	71(22)
Ingram M11 .380	None	158[b]	—	71(22)
Ingram M11 .380	Cobray M11 .380[a]	136[b]	—	71(22)

[a] rebuilt by AWC with Dater baffle stack replacing WerBell-style spirals
[b] Winchester USA .380 ACP, 95 grain FMJ

Table 12.4. Net sound reductions in decibels produced by Sten and Ingram submachine gun suppressors.

GUN	SUPPRESSOR	WINCHESTER 115 GR SUPERSONIC	SAMSON 158 GR SUBSONIC	TEMP., °F (°C)
Sten Mk II	Original IIS Type II	22	23	36(2)
Sten Mk II	AWC SG-9	26	34	65(8)
Sten Mk II	Cobray	26	27	66(19)
Sten Mk II	AWC MK-9	32	31	67(19)
Sten Mk II	AWC SG-9	30	34	11(-12)
Sten Mk II	Ciener	25	26	11(-12)
Ingram M10 9mm	Cobray M10 9mm	26	27	66(19)
Ingram M11 .380	Cobray M11 .380	22[b]	—	66(19)
Ingram M10 9mm	Cobray M10 9mm[a]	28[b]	28	71(22)
Ingram M11 .380	Cobray M11 .380[a]	22[b]	—	71(22)

[a] rebuilt by AWC with Dater baffle stack replacing WerBell-style spirals
[b] Winchester USA .380 ACP, 95 grain FMJ

Table 12.5. Projectile velocities expressed as feet per second (and meters per second) produced by Sten and Ingram submachine guns.

GUN	SUPPRESSOR	WINCHESTER 115 GR SUPERSONIC, fps (mps)	SAMSON 158 GR SUBSONIC, fps (mps)	TEMP., F (°C)	SPEED OF SOUND, fps (mps)
Sten Mk II	None	1,253(382)	988(301)	8(-13)	1,060(323)
Sten Mk II	AWC SG-9[a]	1,090(332)	914(279)	8(-13)	1,060(323)
Sten Mk II	Ciener	1,058(322)	905(276)	8(-13)	1,060(323)
Sten Mk II	None	1,259(384)	995(303)	76(24)	1,135(346)
Sten Mk II	Original IIS Type II	886(270)	751(229)	76(24)	1,135(346)
Ingram M10	.45 ACP	833(254)[b]	—	76(24)	1,135(346)
Ingram M10	9x19mm	1,131(345)	925(282)	76(24)	1,135(346)
Ingram M11	.380 ACP	975(297)[c]	—	76(24)	1,135(346)

[a] port blocking collar installed
[b] Winchester USA .45 ACP, 230 grain FMJ
[c] Winchester USA .380 ACP, 95 grain FMJ

TROUBLESHOOTING THE SILENCED STEN

The Sten Mark II had an expected lifespan of one to two years of combat, but the gun could require some tinkering along the way.

An account published in 1943 described several problems with the Sten. A Canadian commando who had run out of ammunition complained that his Sten's skeleton stock caved in when he hit a German with the gun. The Sten did not make a durable club. But that should not give any American collector heartburn. The other common complaint, however, would.

This 1943 article reported that new Stens commonly produced runaways during the first 100 rounds fired from the gun. After 100 rounds, the problem generally cured itself. Runaways remain one of the most common afflictions facing the American collector.

As Philip Dater points out in his excellent manual for the SG-9 suppressor, when firing a Sten for the first time with a particular kind of ammunition or with a new suppressor, the magazine should only be loaded with five rounds. The selector should be set to "R" for repetition (semiauto), and then the gun should be fired into a safe backstop. If the ammo doesn't deliver enough recoil impulse to the bolt, or if something is retarding the free travel of the bolt (like grit from beadblasting, a bent tube, or an improperly installed extractor), the bolt will not recoil far enough to engage the sear adequately. So the gun goes full auto as long as cartridges remain in the magazine.

Sometimes cleaning or better lubrication is all that's needed. Sometimes a weak trigger spring can cause this problem. Hotter ammunition may work. Or the recoil spring can be shortened a quarter turn at a time until the bolt reliably engages the sear with the selector on "R." In the case of one well-known producer of remanufactured Stens prior to May of 1986, the internal diameter of his tube was too small. The only solution is to turn down the diameter of the hardened bolt with a carbide cutter on a lathe. The process will trash the cutter, but at least your Sten will work.

Magazines, however, cause most malfunctions. Most of these feeding problems are caused by bent or burred feed lips on the magazine. The first trick is to separate reliable from unreliable magazines. One person I know numbers her magazines so she can track (log) specific problems. Burrs along the inside of the feed lips are easily removed with a file. Spread feed lips can often be bent back into place. Since 34 million magazines were made for the Sten during World War II, simply replacing recalcitrant magazines is an affordable final solution. Even after Congress banned the importation and manufacturing of large-capacity magazines in 1994, Sten magazines remained quite affordable in the States.

Sometimes magazines don't fit properly in the magazine housing. Usually the retainer screw for the magazine catch is too long, and a shorter screw solves the problem. A few magazines may actually prove to be too large for some magazine housings, however. The easiest solution is to find magazines that do fit.

Extraction problems may simply suggest it's time to clean the gun—or it may be time to replace a tired extractor spring. Extraction problems may also be caused by a rough chamber in the barrel. This can easily be buffed with a Dremel tool or even emery cloth wrapped around a cleaning jag mounted in an electric drill.

Some guns will only produce single shots when the selector is set on "A" for full-auto fire. Look at the trip lever. It should sit against the side of the trigger housing when set on "A". If not, remove the lever and bend it enough so that it will assume the proper position. Sometimes a weak trigger spring can cause this problem, too.

Misfires and light primer hits suggest a problem with the depth of the barrel shoulder. The barrel should fit exactly flush with the rear of the bushing welded to the front of the receiver tube. The barrel may not be made to spec, or sometimes a burr or dirt can prevent the barrel from seating properly. The correct shoulder depth on the barrel is 0.540 inch (13.7 mm).

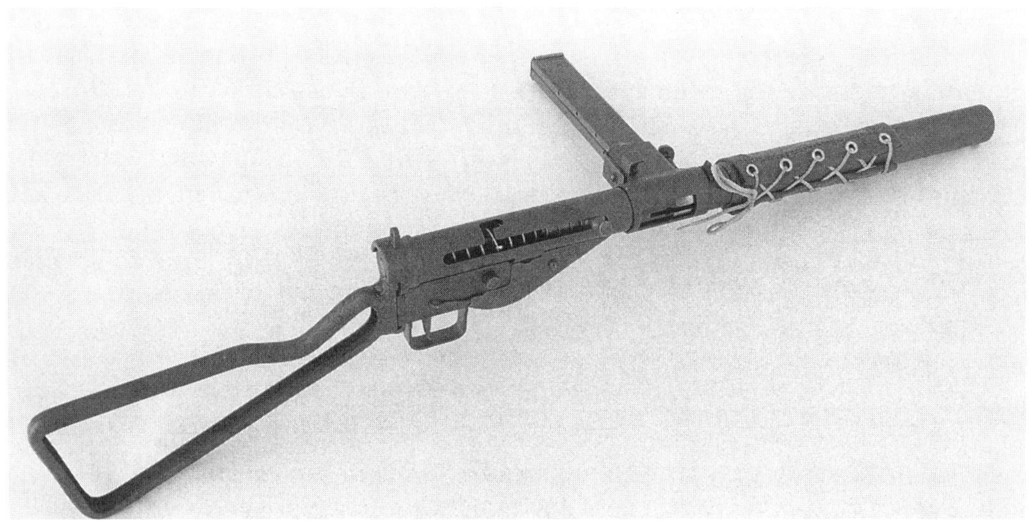

Sten Mark IIS with a variant of the Type II silencer.

Since Stens have been manufactured in Britain, Canada, New Zealand, Argentina, Israel, Indonesia, Germany, China, and Belgium, it should not come as a surprise that all parts do not interchange freely. Even different parts kits from Britain, for example, may have incompatible plungers and cocking handles. A plunger may be too long and block the insertion of a barrel. A cocking handle may be too long and rub on the receiver. Fortunately, it's easy to grind down these two particular pieces to fit. In other cases, a trial-and-error search for compatible parts may provide the only convenient solution.

More serious problems can be seen on home-built Stens on the BATF registry that are not constructed to proper dimensions or geometry. This happens if the builder followed any of several pamphlets and adhesive-backed templates, which I discovered had substantial errors. Since so much published information on Sten design and construction contains errors, and since even some prolific NFA manufacturers screwed up royally, if none of these procedures has solved your problems, find someone with a Sten that works flawlessly and meticulously compare the guns and magazines side by side.

Stens and Sten magazines together constitute the greatest bargain available to the American collector and sport shooter of automatic weapons. Many serious collectors put more rounds though their Stens than through all their glamor guns put together. The Stens may be ugly and cheaply made, but they perform at a bargain price, they are relatively easy to troubleshoot, and they conjure up a rich history. Especially when silenced, the Sten Mark II is a worthy addition to any serious collection.

Even though the silenced Sten saw use as late as the Vietnam War, a quest had already developed not long after World War II to meet the growing need for submachine guns that provided reduced size and weight for the burgeoning realms of special operations, counterterrorism, executive protection, and drug enforcement. The rapid evolution of submachine guns after World War II provided both challenges and opportunities for suppressor design.

THE QUEST FOR BETTER SUBMACHINE GUNS

The first submachine guns that appeared during and soon after World War I were built like the rifles of the day, using machined parts and wooden stocks. These first-generation submachine guns (such as the Thompson Model 1921 and the MP28,II) featured careful craftsmanship, robust construction, fine finishes, and substantial weight. They were also slow and expensive to produce, which made them impractical to manufacture in large quantities for military applications.

In the late 1930s, Germany pioneered the use of metal stampings and folding stocks, synthetic components such as phenolic resins, simplified design, and a more utilitarian finish in an effort to more rapidly and economically produce lighter and more user-friendly submachine guns. The MP38 was the first second-generation submachine gun, and the MP40 (which was basically the same design with an extruded rather than machined receiver) solidified the design principles generally associated with second-generation submachine guns. The British Sten and American M3 "Greasegun" are additional examples of second-generation submachine guns.

The open and accessible barrel designs, plus the placement of their front sights on their receivers, made the Sten Mark II and M3 Greasegun well-suited to the design of integral suppressors. Silenced versions of both weapons were fielded that used ported barrels to vent combustion gases into an integral suppressor. Whereas the Sten's ported barrel dropped the projectiles of 9mm military ammunition to subsonic velocities, the .45 ACP ammunition used in the M3 was already subsonic, so the porting provided increased efficiency and a shorter overall length than would have been possible with a muzzle can. The design of the MP38 and MP40 were not compatible with this approach, stimulating the Germans to pioneer the use of special subsonic rounds with muzzle cans.

Israel Military Industries (IMI) introduced one of the first successful third-generation submachine guns in 1951: the Uzi. The key characteristic of third-generation submachine guns is the use of a bolt that has a hollowed front portion that telescopes over the barrel to reduce overall length. While the Uzi was generally thought to be incompatible with the use of a silencer, Gordon Ingram developed his M10 and M11 submachine guns in the late 1960s expressly for use with sound suppressors developed by Mitchell WerBell III. Their inventions were widely marketed by the Military Armament Corporation (and later by RPB and SWD), which stimulated a considerable reassessment of tactical doctrine in the military and law enforcement communities and ultimately spawned the Golden Age of suppressor design in the 1980s and 1990s.

While Ingram's submachine guns and WerBell's broad spectrum of suppressors (designed for everything from .22 rimfire pistols to sniper rifles) stimulated tactical doctrine in the fields of special and black operations, the Uzi captured the public's imagination. Probably no submachine gun has become as recognizable to the public at large since the Thompson. Stunning Israeli military successes have conjured up a mystique that exceeds the weapon's ability to deliver. Don't get me wrong; it's an excellent weapon capable of sterling performance. Yet by the early 1980s, when working professionals selected a submachine gun, there was a good chance another weapon would be adopted for a particular application. This trend became quite apparent to IMI as well as to Action Arms, which imported the Uzi into the United States from 1980 until the early 1990s.

IMI responded to this need in 1982 with the Mini Uzi, which featured significantly reduced size and weight, a vastly improved folding stock, a higher rate of fire, and a muzzle brake machined into the end of the counterbored barrel. But the Mini Uzi never really achieved commercial success.

As suppressor design and tactical doctrine matured in the early 1980s, fourth-generation submachine guns, the Heckler & Koch MP5 and the integrally suppressed MP5 SD, began to dominate the law-enforcement and special operations markets in the Western world. Unlike most other submachine guns, the MP5 fires from the closed bolt, which provides superior accuracy when its selector is set on semiautomatic. By the 1990s, the MP5 series had largely driven its competitors from the marketplace.

The MP5 is not always the best choice for a given tactical requirement, however. The Beretta 12S submachine gun, for example, may be a superior tactical tool for a particular mission. The Beretta particularly excels at placing accurate and rapid double taps on multiple and rapidly moving targets. Furthermore, the Beretta 12S is much less sensitive to dirt and different types of ammunition than the MP5. Although noted submachine gun instructor Ken Hackathorn prefers the MP5, he concedes that the Beretta performs virtually as well as the MP5 in the hands of a skilled operator at close quarters. I find that the Beretta 12S gives me a 5 to 10 percent speed advantage over the MP5 in the CQB (Close Quarter Battle) environment. At least some of the people responsible for the security of U.S. embassies agree, for the State Department has purchased large numbers of the Beretta 12S over the years. The Beretta is particularly popular with U.S. embassies in the Middle East, Asia, and Southern Europe. The U.S. Navy also uses the Beretta 12S in small numbers, and it decided to add another 200 Beretta submachine guns to its inventory in the mid-1990s.

While the Beretta 12S performs well in the CQB environment whether suppressed or unsuppressed, it has not received the wide acceptance of the H&K MP5 or the IMI UZI. This phenomenon relates more to public relations than engineering excellence.

I suspect the major reason for such disparate acceptance relates to the tremendous successes of the British Special Air Service (SAS) with the MP5 and Israeli military with the UZI, as reported by the media. People always seem to equate military success with the weapons themselves rather than with training and individual initiative—which are the real bottom line.

The commercial success of the MP5 was assured on May 6, 1980, when a counterterrorist team from the 22nd SAS Regiment at Hereford stormed the Iranian embassy in London that had been seized by Iraqi terrorists. The SAS team neutralized the terrorists and rescued 19 hostages in just 11 minutes.

Unfortunately for Beretta, no spectacularly successful counterterrorist operation employed the Model 12 or 12S. Acceptance of the Beretta was also harmed in certain circles because the international terrorist Illich Ramírez Sánchez preferred the Beretta Model 12 over other weapons. (The 44-year-old Venezuelan terrorist emeritus, commonly known as Carlos the Jackal, was finally captured as this was being written.) Finally, as CQB tactical doctrine evolved, many organizations began to employ the submachine gun in a semiautomatic (rather than full-auto) mode, which gave a decided advantage to a closed-bolt weapon like the MP5.

Politics and media hype aside, the Beretta 12S has still achieved widespread sales worldwide, even though the Beretta is clearly an also-ran in the United States. Nevertheless, it continues to be adopted by agencies that recognize the merits of a simple and robust submachine gun. CQB cognoscenti agree that the Beretta 12S is one of the finest open-bolt submachine guns ever made. Many skilled and open-minded professional operators have discovered that the Beretta provides faster full-auto acquisition of multiple and rapidly moving targets within the CQB envelope than the ubiquitous and highly regarded MP5.

I personally prefer the Beretta 12S or H&K MP5 for *unsuppressed* work in close quarters, since I can engage multiple targets more quickly. My assessment changes, however, for *suppressed* work in the CQB envelope. Then my choice becomes a toss-up between the MP5 and the Mini Uzi, each with a short muzzle can. The suppressed MP5 and Mini Uzi display different advantages and liabilities that more or less cancel out in terms of their practical effectiveness in my hands. Both weapons enable me to rapidly place multiple hits on multiple targets at close quarters.

So why hasn't the Mini Uzi done better in the marketplace? One factor may be that the market was slow to recognize the value of a quality compact submachine gun. Consider, for example, that H&K did not introduce the Personal Defense Weapon (PDW) until a decade after the creation of the Mini Uzi.

But perhaps the principal reason for the Mini Uzi's lack of commercial success was that it was introduced too late to capture a large market share. Things would have been different if it had been introduced in 1975. Ironically, the Israeli success that may have contributed more to Uzi sales worldwide than any other enterprise—the Entebbe Raid in 1976—relied on suppressed Ingram M10 submachine guns rather than Uzis! The Israeli 259 Commandos concluded that the Ingram was a superior weapon for the needs of Operation Thunderball since it handled better in confined spaces and could be more easily suppressed at that time. The Mini Uzi would have been a much better weapon had it been available, and the success of Operation Thunderball would have provided an exceptional marketing tool.

But that was not to be. The Mini Uzi has never captured a significant market share, in spite its virtues. Because of its shorter barrel, suppressors designed specifically for it can be shorter or quieter than suppressors designed for the full-sized Uzi. Due to its short overall length and balance, a suppressed Mini handles much better than many other suppressed submachine guns, especially for CQB requirements.

The standard Mini Uzi has two principal liabilities: its rate of fire is twice the desirable rate, and it is significantly less accurate than a closed-bolt submachine gun for semiautomatic fire.

Most operators obtain three- to four-round bursts with the Mini during training exercises, but I am able to attain two-round bursts 86 percent of the time, with the remaining bursts running three rounds. So is criticizing the high cyclic rate just so much bull? Not really. The high rate precludes squeezing off a single round to engage a distant target. Furthermore, it is important to note that even skilled operators tend to shoot significantly longer bursts under the stress of combat. Burst length may double, and the last rounds in a very long burst may not hit the target. While long bursts gobble up more ammo and necessitate more frequent tactical reloads, the most serious implication is that long bursts slow down the acquisition of multiple targets. And engaging multiple targets at close quarters is the primary mission of the submachine gun. There is only one way to mitigate the problem of long bursts when the operator is under extreme stress: learn to deliver the shortest possible bursts during training exercises.

The main liability of open-bolt operation is inferior semiautomatic accuracy to that of a closed-bolt weapon. Although shooting from the prone or a supported weak-hand position can significantly improve the accuracy of semiautomatic fire from the open-bolt Mini Uzi, neither technique is really suitable for work at close quarters. Some agencies require that submachine guns only be employed in semiautomatic mode. I strongly disagree with such restrictions because they are motivated by public relations rather than tactical considerations, but it is clear that any group operating under such constraints would be better served by an H&K or Colt submachine gun.

It is important to note that open-bolt operation does not significantly degrade the accuracy of full-auto fire in the hands of a skilled operator. Unskilled operators, however, will perform better with a closed-bolt weapon for full-auto fire.

Top instructors Chuck Taylor and Ken Hackathorn like the Mini Uzi. Taylor says that the Mini Uzi provides excellent human engineering along with small size and better tactical performance than the full-sized Uzi. Hackathorn says the Mini is a fine submachine gun when used for full-auto applications by a skilled operator at close quarters.

In Hackathorn's experience, skilled operators can consistently place three to four hits on a target from a single burst from a Mini Uzi, and they can engage multiple targets very quickly. This requires both good trigger control and an appropriate grip with the nonfiring hand. When an inexperienced operator grasps the weapon just in front of the trigger guard, he places his grip close to the weapon's pivot point, which exaggerates muzzle climb and shot dispersion. Optimal control of the Mini Uzi is provided by grasping the barrel nut with the thumb and forefinger of the weak hand. Grasping the weapon this far forward maximizes the leverage exerted by the nonfiring arm against the weapon's tendency to rise during full-auto fire. The nonfiring hand is used to pull the weapon back into the shoulder; the operator should not try to pull down against the muzzle climb. It is important to note that this grip places the hand dangerously close to the muzzle of an unsuppressed weapon, so the technique should be limited to advanced operators who will take the time to develop the muscle memory needed to employ the technique safely with the Mini Uzi.

Although the Mini Uzi is commonly seen south of the border in places like Guatemala, El Salvador, Colombia, and Venezuela, it is a relative rarity in the States. The H&K MP5 dominates the

U.S. law enforcement market. A number of departments have adopted the full-sized Uzi, but relatively few have adopted the Mini Uzi.

The Mini Uzi will remain a rarity in the States. As this book was being prepared, Action Arms broke off negotiations to continue importing Uzi products. This rift between Action Arms and Israel Military Industries had been brewing for some time. Very large minimum orders that required cash in advance, delays of a year or more before some orders were filled, substantial inflation in Israel, and the uncertainty of possible legislation under the Clinton administration made the economics of importing IMI products increasingly unattractive.

Furthermore, Action Arms has experienced a lot of frustration over IMI ammunition. After Action Arms had invested a lot of energy introducing the American market to IMI's Samson ammunition, the Israelis gave the line to another importer that markets the ammunition as its own brand. On top of that, Action Arms had to order a half-million rounds at a time, with no guarantee when or if a particular order would be filled. For example, Action Arms only got half the black-tipped 9x19mm carbine ammo it had ordered—and six weeks after placing the most recent order for ammunition, IMI had not even acknowledged the order.

IMI apparently could not care less. An independent source says that the company is now more interested in brokering arms deals rather than producing products themselves. So it appears that the Uzi family of weapons will disappear from the American marketplace. As an aside, an Israeli gunpowder plant blew up in 1992, and it is not clear what impact that will have on the continued availability of IMI subsonic 9x19mm ammunition. Action Ammo Ltd. (P.O. Box 19630, Philadelphia, PA 19124) would like to continue offering Samson black-tipped 9x19mm ammunition and a few other popular Samson calibers, but it remains to be seen whether the Israelis will cooperate. Neither Action Ammo nor the new ammunition importer is marketing the outstanding 158-grain subsonic blue-tipped 9x19mm ammunition formerly available from Action Arms. It is the end of an era.

So what's the bottom line on the Mini Uzi? It was the right idea at the wrong time. As Gene Stoner has told me on more than one occasion, "Timing is everything."

It is tempting to observe that the Uzi provided seemingly insurmountable challenges to suppressor design, while the Mini Uzi provided considerable opportunities. This would be an oversimplification of a vastly more complicated story. Nevertheless, looking at the evolution of suppressors for the Uzi and Mini Uzi provides an excellent framework for discussing the evolution of suppressors since World War II.

SILENCING THE UZI AND MINI UZI

The Uzi family of weapons is among the more difficult to suppress. When the U.S. government funded research to develop an effective Uzi suppressor several decades ago, scientists on the project concluded that it was not practical to silence the weapon. Suppressor technology has matured considerably since then, and now a diverse array of technologies provide a wealth of silencing options. But before examining the evolution of Uzi and Mini Uzi suppressors, it is important to ask the question: "*What performance criteria are relevant to the armed professional when selecting a suppressor for a submachine gun?*"

Assuming that a submachine gun suppressor is a robust and durable design that does not degrade accuracy, the amount of sound suppression has traditionally been the most important criterion. As suppressor technology and tactical doctrine have matured, many operators now prefer a suppressor of minimum size or weight rather than maximum sound suppression. This trade-off is particularly relevant for entry teams. A short suppressor facilitates rapid target acquisition in close quarters and would be relevant for aircraft crews who have limited space in their kits, if suppressed submachine guns were issued for E&E (escape and evasion), but they're not. Clearly, some missions will require maximum sound suppression, while others will benefit from the shortest or lightest suppressed weapon.

Choice of ammunition is also relevant. If the goal is to hide the fact that a shot has been fired, then subsonic ammunition is essential to avoid the ballistic crack of a supersonic projectile. If one suppressed weapon with supersonic ammunition produces the same sound meter reading as another suppressed weapon with subsonic ammunition, the subsonic sound signature will sound *much* quieter to the ear of an observer because there is no ballistic crack. If suppressed weapons are employed to preserve the operator's hearing or to enhance command and control during an operation, then either supersonic or subsonic ammunition can be used, although subsonic ammo will work best for these applications. The hottest possible supersonic ammunition may be the best choice if opponents are likely to be wearing body armor, although a suppressed carbine of rifle caliber—such as the M4 variant of the M16A2—would be a better choice for this application.

If the purpose of using a suppressed weapon is to hide the fact that a shot has been fired, an obvious question remains: how much suppression is enough?

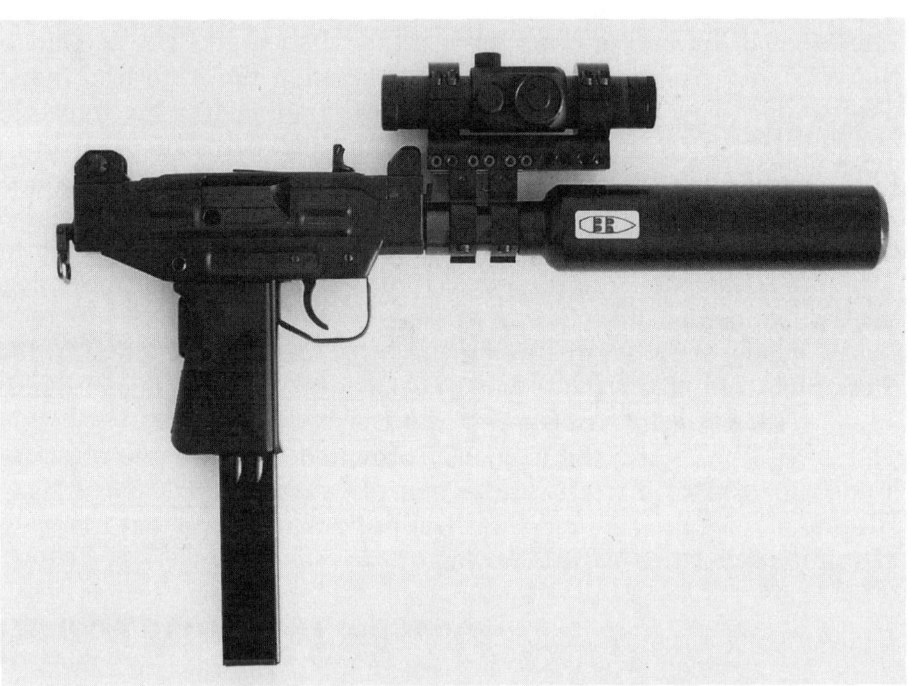
Uzi pistol with BR-Tuote adapter for electronic dot sight and BR-Tuote R12U suppressor. Photo by Juha Hartikka.

To answer this question, it is important to realize that the muzzle signature of a suppressed weapon—as sensed by the sound meter and the shooter—is less important than the subjective sound of the suppressed weapon to the target downrange. This experiment employed an Uzi with S&H suppressor, since it was one of the louder suppressors tested in this study. With my eyes closed to minimize extraneous information and my body turned 90 degrees from the weapon, I had a trusted and competent operator (Capt. Monty Mendenhall) shoot Samson 158-grain subsonic rounds past my nose and behind my head from about 30 yards (27 m) away. I also faced directly toward and away from the shooter. The dominant sounds were the rather high-frequency "clink" of the bolt closing and the low-frequency "thump" of the bullet striking soft dirt 30 yards beyond where I stood. From the target's perspective, the S&H suppressor lowered the apparent muzzle signature to less than the action noise. For the Uzi employed within the CQB envelope, a sound signature of 131 dB appears to be the point of diminishing returns for tactical applications with subsonic ammunition. A weapon with less action noise would benefit from a quieter suppressor.

The contention that 131 dB is enough for many tactical applications is supported by observations on five occasions, when I noticed that residents engaged in normal activities in conventional

When equipped with a short suppressor (like this SCRC Mark 25A) and subsonic ammunition, the Mini Uzi would provide aircrews with an outstanding weapon for E&E. Any opposing pair of the six radial holes in the SCRC suppressor can be used for disassembly with a takedown tool.

frame houses and a small apartment building did not notice when a suppressed firearm with a muzzle signature of 130 to 131 dB was fired with subsonic ammunition within 13 to 23 feet (4 to 7 meters) of the structure.

Keeping the preceding observations in mind, we're ready to examine the evolution of Uzi suppressors, which began several decades ago when the U.S. government contracted with the American Machine & Foundry Company to develop effective suppressors for a variety of weapons, including the Uzi.

American Machine and Foundry

American Machine and Foundry (AMF) research on submachine gun suppressors focused on porting barrels to lower the velocity of standard supersonic rounds to subsonic velocity. This widely accepted approach had the advantage of using standard ammunition, but the subsonic projectiles of standard weight provided much-reduced stopping power. The establishment had not yet accepted the concept of using a heavier bullet at subsonic velocity to eliminate the ballistic crack while maximizing the amount of power delivered to the target.

Since the Uzi's bolt telescopes over a substantial portion of the barrel inside the receiver, AMF was not able to port the barrel into a primary expansion chamber as it had done with its other submachine gun suppressors to achieve subsonic velocity. So AMF cut out part of the receiver, drilled two rows of holes in the barrel, and welded a manifold to the barrel. The manifold fed ignition gases to a stainless steel tube that extended along the outside of the receiver to the primary expansion chamber in the silencer. But AMF couldn't use a conventional concentric expansion chamber; it had to be eccentric. This sounds complicated. Yet this is only a brief overview, because a number of parts on the Uzi and the standard AMF silencer were modified or replaced.

The system was costly and unwieldy, but it did lower the muzzle signature from 155 to 126 dB. Unfortunately, the process of welding the manifold to the barrel ruined the Uzi's accuracy. AMF concluded that the Uzi was not a suitable weapon for silencing. Jonathan Arthur Ciener thought otherwise.

Jonathan Arthur Ciener

The oldest continuously active suppressor manufacturer in the United States, Ciener began manufacturing suppressors in 1976 when a few post-auction MAC suppressors were kicking around, and that was it. He succeeded where AMF had failed by engineering a suppressor around a longer barrel, which is ported in four rows of five holes per row alternating with four rows of six holes per row. The diameter of the holes is 3/32 inch (2.4 mm). A standard Uzi barrel is 10.2 inches (26.0 cm), while Ciener's barrel is 11.7 inches (29.7 cm). The suppressor is 1.5 inches (3.8 cm) in diameter and 12.0 inches (30.5 cm) long. The suppressor itself weighs 1.01 pounds (459 g), while the 0.71 pound (322 g) special barrel is only 0.10 pound (45 g) heavier than the normal barrel. Thus, Ciener's suppressor system adds 1.11 pounds (503 g) to the Uzi, which weighs 7.7 pounds (3.5 kg) unloaded with a folding stock. So the suppressed Uzi weighs 8.8 pounds (4.0 kg) unloaded.

The front end cap and tube of Ciener's Uzi suppressor are aluminum, anodized in a dark gray finish. The front end cap is knurled, so no special tools are required for disassembly. Behind this cap are 16 aluminum baffles with integral spacers 0.35 inch (9 mm) wide that are not finished. Ciener machines these baffles from solid bar stock on a computerized lathe that spits one out every 45 seconds. The rear expansion chamber is formed by an aluminum spacer 0.53 inch (13.5 mm) wide. Behind this spacer lies a solid aluminum bushing 0.35 inch (9 mm) wide that fits on the turned-down tip of the special barrel provided with the suppressor. The rear end cap, which is blued steel, is knurled for easy disassembly. The cap has teeth that approximate the teeth on the Uzi's barrel nut, so the suppressor can be screwed onto the receiver in place of the barrel nut.

I tested the sound signature of the Uzi with Ciener suppressor using Winchester USA 115 grain FMJ supersonic and Samson 158 grain FMJ subsonic ammunition. The sound signatures appear in Table 12.6 (see page 308), and the net sound reductions are found in Table 12.7 (see page 309). The ambient temperature was 55 °F (13 °C).

Using supersonic ball, the Ciener suppressor dropped the sound signature 27 dB. The ported barrel did not lower the Winchester ammo to subsonic velocity, so there was a noticeable ballistic crack that sounded something like a .22 rimfire rifle with standard-velocity ammunition. Ciener's ported barrel actually increased bullet velocity from 1,250 fps (381 mps) to 1,283 fps (391 mps) with Winchester ammo, a gain of 33 fps (10 mps). Using subsonic ammo, the Ciener suppressor reduced the Uzi's sound signature 25 dB, while the special barrel increased bullet velocity from 971 fps (296 mps) to 1,014 fps (309 mps), a gain of 43 fps (13 mps).

Although Ciener's Uzi suppressor can no longer be regarded as state of the art, it performs well enough for tactical use. The system's principal liabilities are the use of aluminum baffles (which are not anodized) and the dependence on a special barrel, making it not practical to install the suppressor during an operation. This system is only available for the full-sized Uzi, although the suppressor works fine with the Mini Uzi's factory barrel.

Ciener developed the first commercially successful suppressor for the Uzi submachine gun.

AWC Systems Technology

AWC Systems Technology was born, in a sense, because of an article Peter Kokalis wrote about the now legendary suppressor designer Dr. Phil Dater in the November 1981 issue of *Soldier of Fortune*. Dater's business (called the Automatic Weapons Company, or AWC) had prospered before the article, but he still had to work as a diagnostic radiologist. Thanks in large measure to the Kokalis article, however, the demands of the suppressor business grew to the point where Dater had to choose between the suppressor business and his medical career. So in early 1983, Dater talked the problem over with several friends and customers, and soon Lynn McWilliams had created Armament Systems and Technology, Inc., to produce and market Dater's suppressors. Phil Dater was vice-president in charge of R&D. Tim Bixler was McWilliams' vice-president in charge of manufacturing and actually performed much of the machine work himself. One of the most impressive suppressors developed during this period was the MK-9.

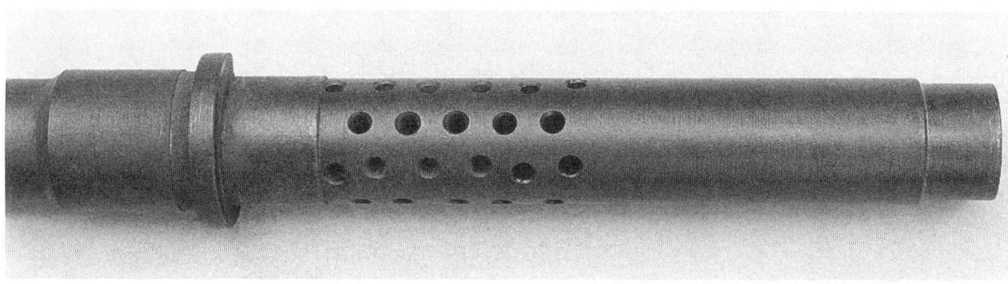

The Ciener system requires a longer, special ported barrel to dump combustion gases into the rear chamber of the suppressor.

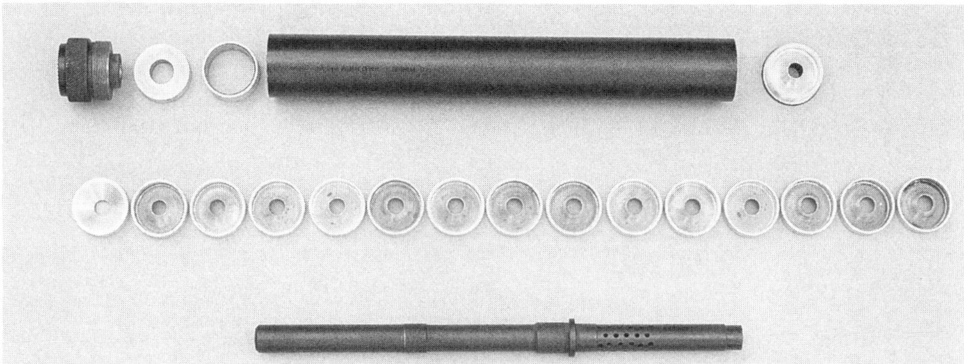

The Ciener Uzi suppressor disassembled for cleaning.

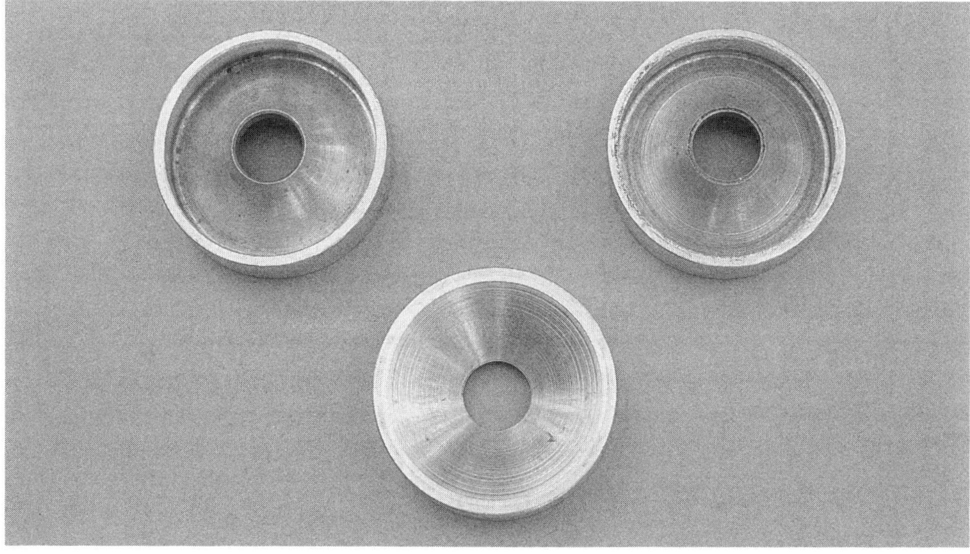

Details of Ciener's baffle design.

The AWC MK-9 represented a departure from traditional suppressor designs. The central core of the MK-9 generally resembles AWC's older SG-9 suppressor (designed for the Sten and S&W 76) with a rear expansion chamber (which AWC calls a "thermal diffuser") and a series of stainless-steel baffles separated by aluminum spacers. Unlike previous designs, the rear expansion chamber of the MK-9 vents to an outer coaxial chamber that encapsulates the inner core over the entire length of the can. The MK-9 terminates with a front cap that breaks up escaping pressure waves.

The evolution of the MK-9 began when Dater designed an ultralight suppressor for the Jati submachine gun at the request of the importer. The can featured two coaxial tubes, a thermal diffuser (a perforated diffusion spindle wrapped in 8-mesh hardware cloth) in the rear quarter of the inner tube, and a vacant forward inner tube. Dater simultaneously developed an improved model that incorporated baffles in the front three-quarters of the inner tube. That became the prototype for AWC's MK-9 suppressor. Unlike the production version, the prototype featured a one-piece thermal diffuser and rear mount.

Dater told me that Tim Bixler suggested that they separate the diffusion spindle and rear mount so that they could simply change the mount to mate the can to a variety of weapons. Only rarely would it be necessary to change the thermal diffuser as well. Bixler designed the interchangeable mounting and diffuser assemblies that transformed the best muzzle can of the day into a truly classic design. Now slightly dated, the MK-9 still remains the standard against which all other submachine gun suppressors are measured.

The tube of the MK-9 is made from aircraft-grade aluminum alloy. The suppressor's inner tube has a hard anodized finish and a grayish black color, while the outer tube is black. The MK-9 attaches to the barrels of many different weapons by exchanging the suppressor's rear end cap and thermal diffuser.

The same mount is used for the Uzi and Mini Uzi. A smaller mount of similar design is used for the Micro Uzi. Once the mount is installed on the rear of the can, the suppressor is installed on the weapon by simply removing the existing barrel nut and then dropping the suppressor directly over the existing barrel. The can is then screwed onto the receiver until it locks up against the little trip latch that secures the normal barrel nut.

The MK-9 suppressor has a length of 12.0 inches (30.5 cm). The specimen used for testing had a weight of 29.4 ounces (836 g). A 10 inch (25.4 cm) version, called the MK-9A, was specifically designed for a major law enforcement agency that uses the Mini Uzi for counterterrorist work. The shorter version is only 4 dB louder than the full-size model, but it is no longer listed in the AWC Systems Technology catalog. Both versions have a diameter of 2.0 inches (5.1 cm), which is less than the rear chamber of the older SIONICS suppressor.

I tested the MK-9 suppressor with threaded mount on an Uzi fitted with a threaded FBI-length barrel from SCRC at an ambient temperature of 56 °F (13 °C). The data appear in Tables 12.6 and 12.7. Using Winchester supersonic ammunition, the MK-9 lowered the Uzi's sound signature by 31 dB. Using Samson subsonic ammunition, it provided a net reduction of 34 dB.

I then tested the MK-9 with a barrel-nut adapter on an Uzi with a factory barrel. The ambient temperature was 80 °F (27 °C). Using Winchester supersonic ammunition, the MK-9 produced a net reduction of 31 dB. Using Samson subsonic ammunition, the suppressor lowered the sound signature by 30 dB.

It is interesting that the style of mount used to attach the MK-9 to the Uzi has a significant effect on the suppressor's performance with subsonic ammunition. In either case, the MK-9 provides outstanding sound suppression, but the can is bit long for use on an entry weapon. For this reason, Lynn McWilliams wanted to develop a more compact suppressor for use at close quarters.

The result was the TAC NINE suppressor, which uses technology quite different from that of the MK-9. Built upon earlier work by Charles A. "Mickey" Finn and Doug Olsen, the TAC NINE uses a complex array of geometric surfaces that are welded precisely together. Then the welded internal array is inserted into the stainless tube and the tube is welded shut. Constructed entirely of stainless steel, the TAC NINE measures 9.0 inches (22.8 cm) long with three-lug mount for the H&K MP5 and 8.75 inches (22.2 cm) long with a threaded mount, which is commonly available in 1/2x28 and

1/2x32 TPI. The suppressor measures 1.375 inches (3.5 cm) in diameter. The variant with three-lug adapter weighs 23 ounces (649 g); the threaded variant weighs 20.5 ounces (580 grams). The suppressor comes in either of two finishes: a matte black polymer coating or a natural matte stainless finish.

A threaded FBI barrel (from SCRC) was used for testing the TAC NINE suppressor on the Uzi. The temperature was 56 °F (13 °C). Using Winchester supersonic ammunition, the TAC NINE lowered the muzzle signature by 26 dB. Using Samson subsonic ammunition, the TAC NINE produced a net sound reduction of 28 dB. That's good performance from such a small package.

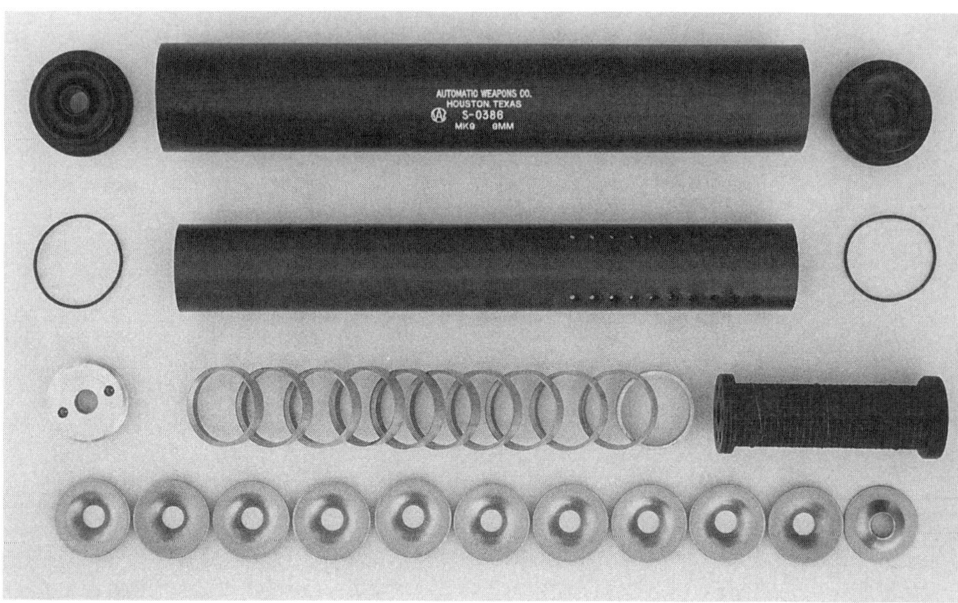

The AWC MK-9 suppressor is a coaxial design that features interchangeable rear mounts.

TAC NINE suppressor from AWC Systems Technology mounted on an Uzi submachine gun equipped with threaded FBI match barrel from SCRC.

SCRC

Although Tim Bixler and his company, SCRC, may not be as well known to the public as Phil Dater or the late Mitchell WerBell III, Bixler has been working in the Class 3 realm since the late 1970s. He first came to my attention in 1980, when one of his inventions was illustrated in Nelson and Musgrave's book, *The World's Machine Pistols and Submachine Guns*, volume II. Since then, Bixler has earned the reputation among professional operators and discriminating private collectors as a versatile master craftsman with uncompromising attention to detail.

Bixler's varied background has prepared him well for developing and producing Title 2 technology suitable for the most demanding applications. After mustering out of the U.S. Navy, he worked as a machinist, Chicago cop, and commercial diver. When a case of the bends cut short Bixler's diving career, he began work as a machinist building commercial diving gear from scratch. By the time Dater was designing the MK-9 suppressor for AWC, Bixler was responsible for actually producing most of the AWC product line. When Armament Systems and Technology was allowed to die for various reasons in 1986, Bixler turned his full attention to SCRC.

Among Bixler's diverse projects was an attempt to improve upon Dater's MK-9 can and its shorter variant, the MK-9A. Bixler developed a more strongly sloping stainless-steel baffle using a different process. This lowered the can's sound signature by about 2 dB when mounted on the H&K MP5. Bixler called his standard 12.0 inch (30.5 cm) can the Mark 25 and his compact 10 inch (25.4 cm) can the Mark 25A. Both have a diameter of 2.0 inches (5.1 cm). These variants will henceforth be referred to as "old-model" suppressors. The old-model Mark 25 weighs 32.1 ounces (910 g), while the old model Mark 25A weighs 30.0 ounces (850 g). Aside from the baffle design, the old-model SCRC Mark 25 series cans were the same as AWC's MK-9 cans.

SCRC suppressors can be provided with a variety of mounting options, including Bixler's patented mount for the three-lug barrel of an MP5, a mount for any barrel threaded 1/2x28 TPI, and mounts for the Ingram M10 and M11. Easily the most popular mount in the business for the three-lug barrel, Bixler's MP5 mount has been adopted by many of his competitors. Other meticulously engineered SCRC mounts replace the barrel-retaining nuts on the Uzi and Walther families of weapons. SCRC suppressors can also be provided with special ported barrels for the Sten and S&W M-76. Bixler also builds three-lug match barrels for the Uzi and Mini Uzi so his clients can use their MP5 suppressors and flash hiders on a variety of weapons. Since these barrels are difficult to build and he doesn't really make any money on them, Bixler only sells the three-lug Uzi barrels to clients who purchase or already own an SCRC MP5 suppressor.

The tremendous care in the design and manufacture of Bixler's mounts is legendary among suppressor cognoscenti. His investment in tooling and meticulous craftsmanship exceed what is necessary to make a quality functional mount. Bixler's Uzi mount, for example, seems more like fine art than milspec engineering.

The simplicity of the design belies the work that went into it. While other manufacturers commonly use simplified serrations on their Uzi suppressors to engage the trip latch, Bixler's rear mount absolutely duplicates the barrel nut issued with the Uzi. Bixler's mount has 82 teeth cut at the same leading and trailing angles as the Uzi nut, which required developing special tooling at substantial expense. The mount is properly heat treated and coated with black Teflon S.

The same mount is used for the Uzi and Mini Uzi. A smaller mount is used for the Micro Uzi. The suppressor mounts on the weapon by simply removing the existing barrel nut and then dropping the suppressor directly over the existing barrel. The can then screws onto the receiver until it locks up against the trip latch that secures the normal barrel nut.

The old-model Mark 25 and 25A suppressors were good performers, especially when the Uzi was fitted with an FBI-length barrel. The Mark 25A, for example, lowered the weapon's sound signature by 28 dB at 52 °F (11 °C). Using Samson subsonic, the Mark 25A produced a net reduction of 27 dB.

But Bixler believed he could build an even better can for subsonic ammunition. He redesigned the thermal diffuser, shortened its spindle to make room for two more baffles, and eliminated the wire mesh wrap around the diffuser spindle. He used different spacing between baffles in the front instead of the rear of the central core. Bixler then permanently sealed the components within the inner coaxial tube to idiot-proof the suppressor. These variants will henceforth be referred to as "new-model" suppressors. While a new-model Mark 25A mounted on a Mini Uzi (tested on the same day as the old model) was 4 dB louder with supersonic ammunition, the new model was 2 dB quieter with subsonic ammunition. Unpublished data using the H&K MP5 show that the long variant is noticeably quieter than the short variant.

The decision to seal the components into the central core was sort of an epiphany for Bixler, since he and Dater had been staunch early proponents of suppressors that could be completely disassembled by the user for cleaning and maintenance. Others, however, had long maintained that a sealed unit could not be screwed up by users who either failed to read or failed to understand a manual's instructions for disassembly/maintenance/reassembly. Bixler's current submachine gun cans reflect an interesting compromise between the two philosophical views.

All the SCRC suppressors tested in this study provided excellent sound suppression. All were handy and well engineered. While both the long and short models handled well on both guns, the shorter version was significantly handier on the Mini Uzi. With an Uzi mount, the SCRC suppressors work best on a full-sized Uzi when the weapon is fitted with a shorter FBI barrel (available from SCRC). Otherwise, the issue barrel extends far enough into the suppressor to degrade its efficiency significantly.

Another option with the full-sized Uzi is installing an SCRC match three-lug barrel and purchasing the suppressor with the three-lug MP5 mount. This setup was tested at 67 °F (19 °C); see Table 12.6 for the sound signatures and Table 12.7 for the net sound reductions. The new-model MK-25A with three-lug mount and Winchester supersonic ammunition lowered an Uzi's sound signature by 24 dB. Using Samson subsonic, the new-model Mark 25A produced a net reduction of 29 dB.

Either the three-lug or the Uzi mounting system will deliver the same performance when mounted on the on the Mini Uzi.

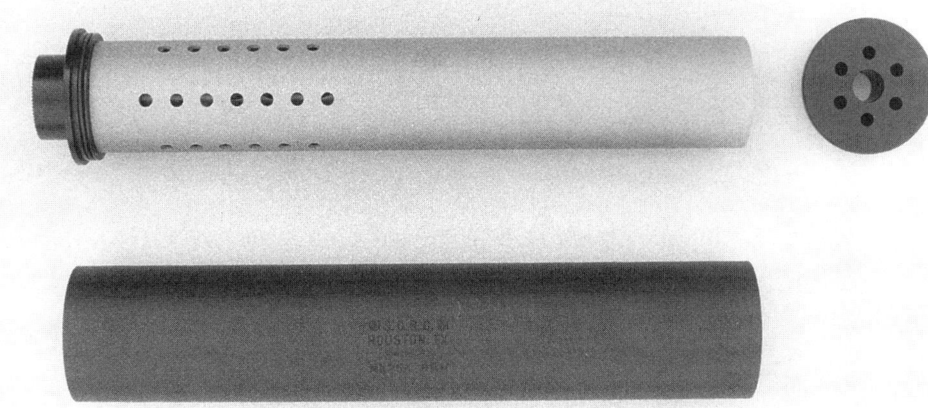

SCRC Mark 25A suppressor disassembled for cleaning. The central baffle stack is permanently sealed, and it is cleaned by immersing in a solvent for several days. The six radial holes do not penetrate the front end cap and are used for disassembly.

The SCRC Mark 25A suppressor with Uzi mount replaces the barrel nut on the Mini Uzi (the longer Mark 25 should be used on the full-sized Uzi because of the longer barrel).

Automatic Weapons Company

The Automatic Weapons Company (a division of Antares Technologies, Inc. in Boise, Idaho) was Phil Dater's original suppressor company. The MK-9 series of muzzle cans, already covered in the section of this chapter on AWC Systems Technology, uses a universal diffusion spindle in the primary expansion chamber so that only the rear mount needs to be changed to adapt the can to different weapons. Dater's original MK-9 and MK-9A cans featured different diffusion spindles for each type of weapon.

The MK-9A suppressor used for these tests is actually Dater's prototype with Bixler mount and a diffusion spindle optimized for the Mini Uzi. This is identical to the earliest AWC production variant with interchangeable mount. The suppressor tube is 10.0 inches (25.4 cm) long and 2.0 inches (5.1 cm) in diameter. Total length with front end cap and mount is 10.7 inches (27.1 cm). The suppressor weighs 27.0 ounces (766 g).

Using a universal diffusion spindle was popular with both dealers and end users since the simplified mounting systems were cheaper. But Dater's original concept of using an optimally designed diffusion spindle for each mount produced about a 2 dB advantage with subsonic ammunition when mounted on most weapons.

The AWC (ATI) MK-9A suppressor lowered the Mini Uzi's sound signature from 159 to 133 dB with Winchester USA supersonic ammunition, for a net sound reduction of 26 dB at 94 °F (34 °C). Using Samson subsonic ammo, the MK-9A lowered the Mini's sound signature from 155 to 127 dB, for a net reduction of 28 dB. This is respectable performance.

Nevertheless, Dater has recently redesigned this suppressor into a shorter and more effective variant, called the MK9-K. The suppressor features an entirely different primary expansion chamber that eliminates the diffusion spindle and uses innovative geometry to more aggressively divert combustion gases into the outer coaxial tube. The MK9-K comes with either a three-lug mount for the H&K MP5 or a 1/2x28 TPI mount for a threaded barrel (such as SCRC's FBI barrel for the Uzi). The MK9-K was not available for testing in time for this T&E, but it was later evaluated on the MP5 and is discussed toward the end of this chapter.

S&H Arms

While Tom Seslar of S&H Arms was in business, he was probably best known for his conversions of semiautomatic Heckler & Koch weapons into museum-grade, select-fire reproductions of the MP5 and its variants like the PDW. Seslar's Uzi suppressor is actually based on a design he has long used for the MP5 SD. He points out that his suppressor design was inspired in the early 1980s by Phil Dater's SG-9 suppressor. In fact, Seslar purchased his baffles from Dater until 1986, when BATF temporarily interpreted new legislation to mean that manufacturers could not purchase suppressor components from one another.

Seslar's Uzi suppressor is 12.4 inches (31.5 cm) in overall length. The tube is 11.9 inches (30.2 cm) long, 1.5 inches (3.8 cm) in diameter, and finished in a black hard-coat anodizing. The tube features a large knurled surface to facilitate mounting and dismounting the suppressor on the weapon. Few manufacturers bother with this additional expense, but such attention to detail was typical of Seslar. The tube, primary expansion chamber, front end cap, and spacers are constructed of 6061-T6 aluminum, and the 15 baffles are 304 stainless steel. A 3.5 inch (8.9 cm) primary expansion chamber separates the rear mount of the S&H suppressor from the baffle stack. The rear mount is made from 4140 steel and is finished in manganese phosphate. The suppressor weighs 20.1 ounces (572 g).

Prototype AWC MK-9A built by Dr. Dr. Philip H. Dater when the Automatic Weapons Company (a division of Antares Technologies) was located in Taos, New Mexico. The rear suppressor mount simply screws onto the receiver in place of the muzzle nut.

Using Winchester supersonic ammunition at 80 °F (27°C), the S&H Uzi suppressor reduced the weapon's sound signature from 159 to 133 dB, for a net reduction of 23 dB. Using Samson subsonic ammunition, the signature dropped from 157 to 131 dB, for a net reduction of 26 dB. The S&H Uzi suppressor provides a similar muzzle signature to the new-model SCRC MK-25A suppressor with supersonic 9mm ammunition, while the S&H can is noticeably louder with subsonic 9mm ammunition. Unpublished data suggest that the suppressor would be about 4 dB more efficient on the MP5. Such differences between the Uzi and MP5 relate both to how far the barrel extends into the suppressor and to the substantial noise generated by combustion gases leaving the ejection port of the Uzi (this latter noise is absent with a closed-bolt gun). Even though this is a dated design, the S&H suppressor is also quite effective with .22 rimfire ammunition, which makes it attractive if much training is conducted with a .22 conversion kit installed in the full-sized Uzi. The suppressor is longer than optimum for the Mini Uzi.

Subsequent to this testing, Seslar redesigned the primary expansion chamber of the Uzi suppressor, enabling him to add several more baffles and improve the amount of sound suppression produced by the Uzi can. S&H Arms Manufacturing Company of Berryville, Arkansas, is no longer in business.

Precision Arms International

John Leasure of Precision Arms International, Inc. (PAI), entered the suppressor field in the early 1990s and was subsequently granted a patent in 1992 for his baffle and spacer design. Leasure pushed the envelope of the complex thick baffle approach pioneered by Mickey Finn and his associates. Leasure developed a new generation of suppressors that feature novel internal design and all-titanium construction.

Even though titanium has the tensile strength of steel but only half the weight, suppressor manufacturers have shied away from this material for several reasons. Titanium is quite expensive, it's a bitch to machine without special ceramic cutters since the metal is rather gummy, it galls badly when two titanium surfaces move against each other, and it can ignite like a magnesium flare if it overheats when being machined. The *coup de grace* was titanium's reputation for not holding up to the erosive power of hot combustion gases.

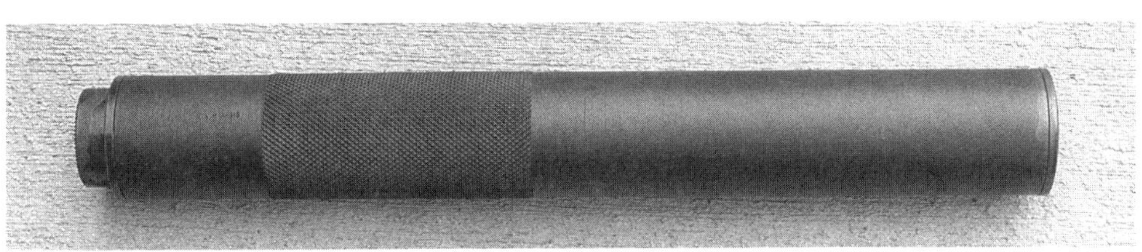

The S&H Arms Uzi suppressor was built by Tom Seslar. Photo by Polly Walter.

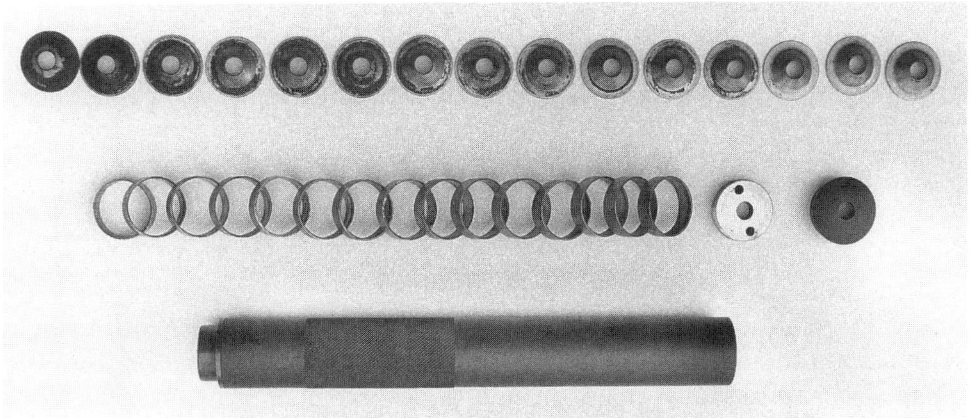

S&H Arms Uzi suppressor disassembled for cleaning. Photo by Polly Walter.

Leasure commissioned the United Titanium Association

to conduct a study on the effects of gunpowder ignition gases on titanium. It turns out that titanium is indeed subject to erosion from friction when two surfaces rub against each other at high velocity. Thus an experimental titanium barrel did experience severe erosion. But components not subjected to rubbing, such as a suppressor, did not experience erosion. Leasure concluded from this research that titanium is the optimal material for building suppressors.

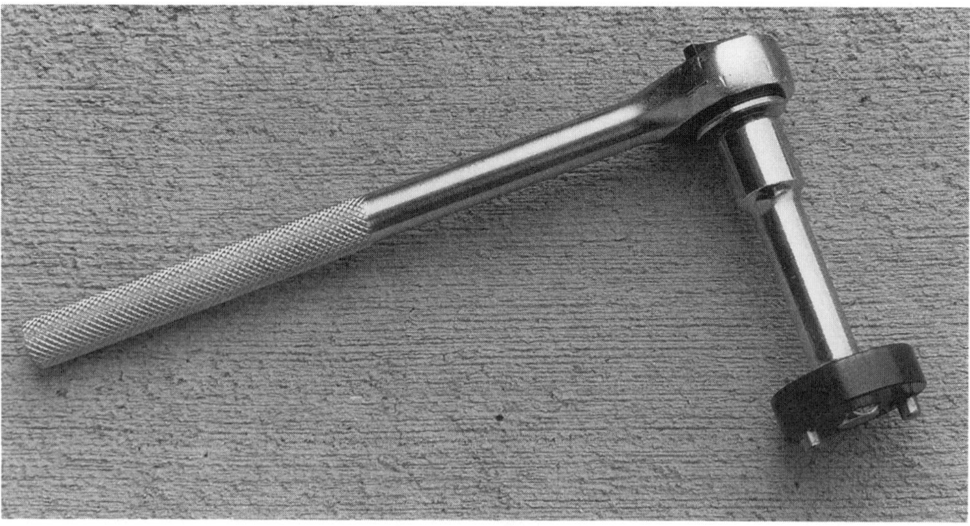

The S&H disassembly tool mounts on a standard 3/8 inch ratchet and is the handiest in the business.

Besides the use of novel materials, the prototype PAI Uzi and Mini Uzi suppressors evaluated for this book introduced another interesting new technology.

The most visible aspect of this technology is a series of six radial holes perforating the domed front end cap around the bore. This feature is covered by a disclosure patent. The holes help break up both the precursor wave (the gases that precede the bullet out of the barrel) and the pressure wave of the gas stream following the bullet. The function of these radial holes can be demonstrated by using an air hose to inject an air stream into the rear of the suppressor. Very little gas exits the large center hole in the front end cap; most exits from the small radial holes.

A baffle of traditional design shears off and slows a small portion of the gas stream following the bullet. Each baffle shears a little bit more from the stream. Complex thick baffles, such as the ones used in this design, actually shear off gas and create a gas jet that pushes against the gas stream following the bullet so that more gas is removed from the stream, thus reducing the remaining energy in the gas stream that would be perceived as sound.

The PAI baffles themselves include channels called "beveled diversion passage pairs" adjacent to and leading between ports in the spacers. The spacers actually form a separate coaxial chamber between each baffle. The spacer dimensions are tuned for each chamber. There is no spacer between the front baffle (which also functions as an encapsulator for the baffle stack) and the front end cap to enable maximum function of the six radial vents in the front end cap. Diversion passage pairs are machined into both the front and rear surfaces of the baffles. All internal components are bead blasted to increase surface area, although any benefit will quickly disappear with the buildup of carbon.

The inside of the 0.065 inch (1.65 mm) thick suppressor tube is threaded for its entire length to both facilitate assembly and increase surface area. The rear of the Uzi suppressor contains a long expansion chamber designed to accommodate the factory Uzi barrel. The Mini Uzi suppressor is basically the same design with a shorter expansion chamber. Ports vent combustion gases from the inner chamber to an outer coaxial chamber that runs the length of the expansion chamber. In front of the expansion chamber are only four baffles. The baffles are designed and spaced differently from preceding complex thick-baffle suppressors, including PAI's MP5 suppressor.

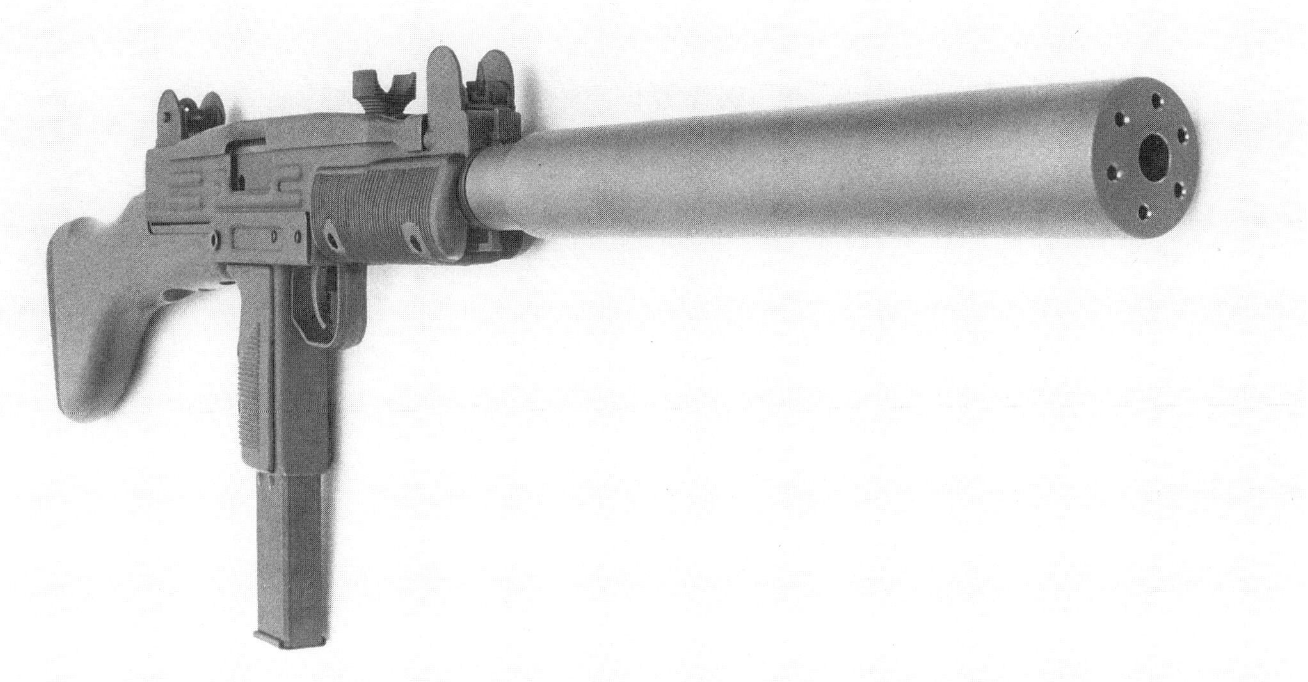

The Precision Arms SOS Uzi suppressor is constructed entirely out of titanium. Six radial holes perforate the domed front end cap and function to break up both the precursor wave (the gases that precede the bullet out of the barrel) and the pressure wave of the gas stream following the bullet.

The titanium tube of the SOS Uzi suppressor designed for the full-sized Uzi is 10.7 inches (27.2 cm) long and 1.5 inches (3.8 cm) in diameter. A domed front cap and the rear Uzi barrel-nut mount increase the total length to 12.0 inches (30.6 cm). The suppressor weighs 20.7 ounces (585 g).

The shorter SOS Mini Uzi suppressor is 8.2 inches (20.8 cm) long and 1.5 inches (3.8 cm) in diameter. A domed front cap and the rear mount increase the total length of the suppressor to 9.6 inches (24.5 cm). The suppressor weighs 17.0 ounces (484 g).

When using Winchester supersonic ammunition at an ambient temperature of 94 °F (34 °C), the long PAI Uzi suppressor lowers the Uzi's muzzle signature from 157 to 132 dB, for a net sound reduction of 25 dB. Using Samson subsonic ammunition, the PAI Uzi suppressor lower's the weapon's signature from 154 to 126 dB, for a net reduction of 28 dB.

The short PAI Mini Uzi suppressor lowers the Mini's muzzle signature from 159 to 140 dB, for a net sound reduction of 19 dB. Using Samson subsonic ammunition, the PAI Mini Uzi suppressor lower's the weapon's signature from 155 to 128 dB, for a net reduction of 27 dB. While this shorter suppressor provides excellent suppression with subsonic ammunition, its performance is disappointing with supersonic ammunition. The supersonic signature is below the pain threshold by the narrowest of margins, so the PAI Mini Uzi suppressor could still be used with supersonic ammo indoors to maintain command and control. But this can clearly performs best with subsonic fodder.

I have two criticisms of these prototype PAI suppressors that are cosmetic rather than functional. Although the titanium tubing is classified "seamless," a small seam is visible over the length of the suppressor. And the data required by BATF is hand stamped (albeit neatly) rather than engraved. Neither quality will affect performance adversely; these observations are simply made for completeness. About the time Precision Arms reorganized as Silent Options, the company began to engrave the tubes with the required data after turning down 0.085 inch thick tubing to the proper outside diameter to remove the visible seam. That improved the cosmetics of the titanium suppressors up to virtually the same level as the best aluminum and stainless steel suppressors in the industry.

The Precision Arms SOS Mini Uzi suppressor performs well with subsonic ammunition. Constructed entirely of titanium, the suppressor is 9.6 inches long and weighs 17 ounces.

Table 12.6. Sound signatures in decibels of Uzi submachine gun suppressors.

GUN	SUPPRESSOR	WINCHESTER 115 GR SUPERSONIC	SAMSON 158 GR SUBSONIC	TEMP., °F (°C)
Uzi	None	158	154	55(13)
Uzi	Ciener	131	129	55(13)
Uzi	None[a]	159	157	56(13)
Uzi	AWC MK-9[b]	128	123	56(13)
Uzi	None	159	157	80(27)
Uzi	AWC MK-9[c]	128	127	80(27)
Uzi	None[a]	159	156	56(13)
Uzi	AWC TAC NINE[b]	133	128	56(13)
Uzi	None[a]	159	157	52(11)
Uzi	SCRC MK-25A, old Model[d]	131	130	52(11)
Uzi	None[e]	158	156	67(19)
Uzi	SCRC MK-25A, new model[f]	134	127	67(19)
Uzi	None	159	157	80(27)
Uzi	S&H	133	131	80(27)
Uzi	None	157	154	94(34)
Uzi	Silent Options SOS Uzi	132	126	94(34)
Mini Uzi	None	159	155	94(34)
Mini Uzi	AWC (ATI)	133	127	94(34)
Mini Uzi	None	159	155	94(34)
Mini Uzi	Silent Options SOS Mini Uzi	140	128	94(34)

[a] FBI-length barrel
[b] suppressor fitted via screw-on mount to threaded FBI-length barrel
[c] suppressor fitted via barrel-nut adapter over factory barrel
[d] suppressor fitted via barrel-nut adapter over FBI-length barrel
[e] SCRC three-lug barrel
[f] suppressor fitted to SCRC three-lug barrel

Table 12.7. Net sound reductions in decibels produced by Uzi submachine gun suppressors.

GUN	SUPPRESSOR	WINCHESTER 115 GR SUPERSONIC	SAMSON 158 GR SUBSONIC	TEMP., °F (°C)
Uzi	Ciener	27	25	55(13)
Uzi	AWC MK-9[a]	31	34	56(13)
Uzi	AWC MK-9[b]	31	30	80(27)
Uzi	AWC TAC NINE[a]	26	28	56(13)
Uzi	SCRC MK-25A, old Model[c]	28	27	52(11)
Uzi	SCRC MK-25A, new model[d]	24	29	67(19)
Uzi	S&H	26	26	80(27)
Uzi	Silent Options SOS Uzi	25	28	94(34)
Mini Uzi	AWC (ATI)	26	28	94(34)
Mini Uzi	Silent Options SOS Mini Uzi	19	27	94(34)

[a] suppressor fitted via screw-on mount to threaded FBI-length barrel
[b] suppressor fitted via barrel-nut adapter over factory barrel
[c] suppressor fitted via barrel-nut adapter over FBI-length barrel
[d] suppressor fitted to SCRC three-lug barrel

SILENCING THE MP5

The three lugs near the end of the MP5's barrel were incorporated as a means of attaching a blank-firing device and a flash hider. Heckler & Koch developed a relatively quick-to-employ system for mounting one of these muzzle devices to the three-lug barrel, but the H&K mount was neither robust enough nor provided sufficiently precise alignment to use for attaching a relatively long and heavy suppressor. Therefore, the U.S. Navy stipulated that weapons delivered to them include 1/2x32 TPI threads in front of the lugs for attaching a suppressor. Then, at about the same time in the 1980s, Tim Bixler of SCRC and Tim LaFrance of LaFrance Specialties invented and patented robust and reliable three-lug mounts suitable for their proprietary flash hiders and suppressors. Both Bixler and LaFrance produced outstanding products. Their flash hiders, for example, are vastly superior to the H&K product.

Bixler made his patented mount available to other suppressor manufacturers, who quickly appreciated the virtues of a three-lug mount: 1) the suppressor will not loosen during firing, which is a potential problem when a suppressor is screwed onto a threaded barrel; 2) the system requires no barrel modification; and 3) mounting and dismounting a suppressor is much faster than using a mount for a threaded barrel.

When I first tried Bixler's mounting system soon after its introduction in the 1980s, I immediately came to two conclusions: the design was brilliant, and the mounting procedure was foolproof. My first assessment stands, but my second conclusion was wrong.

The mount is not *fool*proof. There are some remarkably resourceful fools out there, who have managed to fasten the three-lug mount to the barrel improperly and then proceed to shoot the suppressor off the weapon. Some of these folks were experienced law enforcement officers who were members of special tactical teams. Others were advanced civilian shooters. Did they fail to read the instructions? Or did they simply have a catastrophic lapse of common sense? The mounting procedure is simplicity itself and takes less time than reading the following instructions. This procedure is much faster than using a conventional threaded mount or a mount that replaces the barrel nut on weapons like the IMI Uzi or the Beretta 12S.

Mounting instructions

1. Loosen the rear coupling nut (on the mounting assembly) 2+ turns.
2. Align the suppressor to the firearm so the barrel lugs line up with the cutouts inside the rear coupling nut.
3. Push the suppressor past the three lugs on the barrel.
4. Turn the suppressor body clockwise until tight. IMPORTANT: the rear coupling nut must rotate approximately 1/10 turn clockwise in order to engage the three lugs. Watch for this movement.
5. *Verify that the suppressor is mounted properly by pulling the suppressor body forward.* The suppressor should pull off the barrel if it is not mounted properly.

Follow this five-step kata and mounting the suppressor will be both rapid and secure. Always try to pull the suppressor off the barrel to ensure that the can was mounted properly. This last procedure should protect the operator from disaster.

Bixler's patented mount is superior to the H&K three-lug mount and became the dominant MP5 mount in the marketplace. His mount has been used by JR Customs, the Automatic Weapons Company (Antares Technologies, Inc.), AWC Systems Technology, Precision Arms, Silent Options, SIOPTS, Knight's Armament, RASE, and SCRC.

I should point out, however, that not all three-lug barrels are created equal. Some aftermarket three-lug barrels and some three-lug adapters that are screwed onto original threaded barrels do not conform closely enough to original H&K specs. Ryan and Dater, for example, only guarantee proper alignment with original German H&K barrels and three-lug barrels converted by S&H Arms. Needless to say, I've had no problems with Bixler's mount on SCRC three-lug barrels built by Bixler for the Uzi and Mini Uzi. I've also had no problem with British Aerospace barrels for the MP5. Ironically, although Vollmer made some of the most beautiful MP5 conversions in the marketplace, its three-lug conversion does not fit Bixler's mount precisely enough for adequate suppressor alignment.

To dismount a suppressor with Bixler's three-lug mount, simply turn the suppressor body counterclockwise until the rear coupling nut rotates about 1/10 turn. This frees the lugs from the recesses inside the nut. Now simply pull the silencer forward off the barrel.

Bixler sold his patent in the mid-1990s, and the new manufacturer raised prices to the point that several companies began to develop alternative quick mounts. Tony Marfione designed a clever spring-loaded mount for a titanium suppressor he developed for the Spec Op's Shop in Madisonville, Tennessee. Both suppressor and mount were impressive. The spring-loaded mount provided much quicker attachment than previous designs. His innovative suppressor also provided solid sound reduction.

Unfortunately, the spring-loaded coupler tends to accumulate fouling. If not cleaned at regular intervals, it can become quite difficult to remove the suppressor from a three-lug barrel. The mount has several other liabilities as well. The spring is too stiff, requiring a great deal of force to compress. Furthermore, the mount does not feature a positive stop to engage the barrel lugs, so the mount can be twisted too far and fail to grasp the lugs. The mounting procedure must be tried again. The Marfione mount was a step in the right direction, but it was not the final answer.

Then aerospace engineer and suppressor designer Greg Latka joined forces with Gemtech in 1995. Using superior design and metallurgy, Latka developed a patent-pending spring-loaded quick mount that appears to be the proverbial better mousetrap. The TRI-LOCK mount eliminates the potential problem of incorrect installation, and the spring is effectively shielded from fouling by the by-products of powder combustion. Alignment is outstanding, and the system appears to be both robust and foolproof. First issued on Gemtech's outstanding flash hider for the MP5, which works better than the H&K flash hider and costs half the price, the TRI-LOCK is now available on all of its MP5 suppressors instead of Gemtech's standard MP5 suppressor mount for an additional $75 at the time of purchase. The Gemtech story begins with the convergent evolution of suppressors designed by two competitors: Dr. Philip H. Dater and James Ryan.

JR CUSTOMS S9-K VERSUS AWC MK9-K

I wasn't surprised when it happened. We've all seen countless westerns and martial arts films based on the theme. Some young buck wants to prove himself, so he takes on the old master. So it was inevitable that young Jim Ryan (of JR Customs) would square off with Phil Dater (of the original Automatic Weapons Company) in the demanding realm of submachine gun suppressors.

Nevertheless, it was rather fearless of Ryan, since one of the top foreign suppressor designers privately refers to Doc Dater as "the grand old man of suppressor design." (Dater disavows such a moniker; only Hiram P. Maxim warrants that level of respect as far as Dater is concerned.)

Ryan picked a difficult time to challenge Dater in the marketplace, for Dater had recently introduced a new generation of suppressor called the MK9-K, which had begun to take the law enforcement community by storm. Their duel in the marketplace was particularly interesting because both of their suppressors for the H&K MP5 were almost identical in design.

Usually when two almost identical products appear in the marketplace, it is safe to assume that one is a rip-off of the other. Yet another possibility exists: convergent evolution. Nature is filled with examples. Both the mako shark and the bluefin tuna have almost identical designs. They are warm-blooded, high-speed, open-water predators. Their bodies have almost identical ballistic coefficients, and their tails have the same asymmetric shape to produce lift as well as thrust. Most impressive of all, they both have an incredibly complex net of blood vessels that serve as a countercurrent heat exchange mechanism to enable the maintenance of a core temperature that is precisely 18 °F (10 °C) warmer than the surrounding water. Yet the tuna has a skeleton of bones, while the shark has a skeleton of cartilage. In fact, the two fish evolved these strikingly similar structures independently and 100 million years apart. One might argue that they are as closely related to each other as we are to iguanas. The bottom line is that, given enough time, the same solution may appear to solve a similar problem. That's what has happened with these designs from Dater and Ryan.

Both trace their heritage back to a very simple chambered suppressor developed by Don Walsh (which did not employ baffles in the design) and a coaxial suppressor designed by Reed Knight. Dater essentially married those concepts with his SG-9 suppressor to create the MK-9. His suppressor featured a central core of stainless-steel baffles in front of a rear primary expansion chamber with a perforated diffusion spindle wrapped in 8-mesh hardware cloth. The spindle assembly served as a thermal diffuser between the central axis of the suppressor and an outer coaxial chamber. The primary expansion chamber vented into an outer coaxial chamber that encapsulated the entire length of the inner core. This design provided outstanding suppression and an unusually cool surface.

Soon after the introduction of the MK-9, suppressor design, subsonic ammunition, and tactical doctrine began to mature rapidly. Many operators began to prefer a suppressor of minimal size or weight rather than maximum sound suppression. This trade-off became especially relevant for entry teams, since a short suppressor facilitates rapid target acquisition in this up-close-and-personal environment. Lynn McWilliams responded to this need with the TAC NINE suppressor, which used complex thick baffles. The TAC NINE design built upon the earlier work of Charles A. Finn and Doug Olsen.

Soon after the introduction of the TAC NINE, Ryan and Dater came to several conclusions more or less simultaneously. The coaxial design concept suffered from two faults. The gas entering the primary expansion chamber needed to be diverted more aggressively into the outer coaxial chamber. And the suppressor needed to be shorter than previous coaxial submachine gun suppressors to meet the tactical requirements of entry teams. Both men promptly addressed these problems in a remarkably similar manner. Ryan called his new suppressor the S9-K; Dater called his the MK9-K.

Both cans feature a coaxial design with a sealed central core that contains strongly sloping baffles of 18-8 stainless steel. All other components are made from aircraft-grade aluminum alloys, with the exception of the three-lug mounts, which are steel. Both suppressors employ similar technology in the primary expansion chamber to aggressively direct combustion gases into the outer coaxial tube. Both suppressors can be partially disassembled for cleaning, although the inner tube with its baffle stack and primary expansion chamber is permanently sealed. Finally, both suppressors could be ordered with a mount for a threaded barrel (1/2x28 or 1/2x32 TPI).

There are some differences, however. The front and rear caps on Dater's MK9-K screw into the central tube, while the caps on Ryan's S9-K screw into the outer tube. At least in theory, Dater's approach should provide more precise alignment of the baffles with the bore. It's hard to say whether this advantage is real or imagined. Dater also uses a more aggressive technique for diverting combustion gases into the outer coaxial tube from the primary expansion chamber, which should translate into slightly better performance. And finally, all of Dater's aluminum components are hard-coat anodized. Ryan's aluminum components are coated with a baked-on molybdenum finish, which is not as durable as anodizing.

Otherwise, the two suppressors are very similar indeed. The tube of Dater's MK9-K is 7.0 inches (17.8 cm) long and 2.0 inches (5.1 cm) in diameter. The knurled front and rear caps and three-lug mount increase the overall length to 8.5 inches (21.6 cm). It

Doc Dater's new MK9-K suppressor on H&K MP5.

Jim Ryan's new S9-K suppressor on H&K MP5.

weighs 20.4 ounces (577 g). The tube of Ryan's S9-K suppressor is 7.0 inches (17.9 cm) long and 2.0 inches (5.1 cm) in diameter. The thinner knurled end caps and the three-lug mount increase the suppressor's overall length of 8.4 inches (21.4 cm). Ryan's suppressor weighs 20.5 ounces (581 g). Talk about convergent evolution! Both Ryan's and Dater's suppressors intended for the MP5 use Tim Bixler's three-lug mount.

Since Ryan's and Dater's MP5 suppressors appear to be nearly identical twins, the maintenance requirements of the S9-K and the MK9-K are the same. Disassembly is nearly the same as well.

Disassembly and Maintenance

Jim Ryan's S9-K suppressor breaks down into two subassemblies by unscrewing the knurled front end cap, which is threaded into the outer suppressor tube and remains permanently attached to the inner coaxial tube. The end cap does not accept a takedown tool, which is a minor oversight. This oversight is complicated by two facts: the end cap is too thin to provide optimal gripping surface, and the cap is harder to unscrew than Dater's. If the front cap won't budge, fire several rounds through the suppressor to heat up and expand the outer tube and try again immediately. If that doesn't work, heat the can for 20 minutes in a 200°F (93 °C) oven, then run cold water on the outer tube. The cap should unscrew easily. The rear end cap and three-lug mount remain permanently attached to the outer tube. The inner coaxial tube contains the permanently sealed components of the baffle stack and rear expansion chamber.

Phil Dater's MK9-K suppressor can be disassembled into three components by unscrewing the thick, knurled front end cap by hand. The first MK9-Ks Dater produced (like the one evaluated for this T&E) featured a front end cap that was drilled to accept a two-pronged takedown tool. Dater subsequently redesigned the cap to eliminate the need for a takedown tool. The front end cap threads into the inner coaxial tube, which contains the permanently sealed components of the baffle stack and rear expansion chamber. The rear end cap and three-lug mount are permanently attached to the inner coaxial tube. When completely disassembled, the MK9-K assemblies consist of the outer tube, the front end cap, and the inner coaxial tube (with rear mount, primary expansion chamber, and baffle stack).

The external and internal designs of Dater's MK9-K suppressor (top) and Ryan's S9-K suppressor are virtually identical.

Dater's front end cap unscrews by hand more easily than Ryan's. And Dater's components are hard-coat anodized while Ryan's are not, so Dater's threads will be less subject to galling than Ryan's. My personal bias is that I'd be willing to pay a bit more for either the S9-K or the MK9-K and have the manufacturer provide a takedown tool with compatible front end cap. In fact, I especially like Tim Bixler's approach of drilling three sets of holes in a radial pattern in the front end cap in case one set of holes eventually gets worn out. I realize that's overengineering, but I learned two things from flying skydivers over the years: 1) always anticipate potential problems, and 2) anything worth doing is worth overdoing.

The ideal system, to my way of thinking, would be to use Dater's current front end cap drilled in Bixler's six-hole pattern to accept the takedown tool designed by Tom Seslar of S&H Arms, which snaps onto a 3/8 inch socket drive. Seslar's tool is quick and inexpensive to make, and yet it's the most effective and practical takedown tool that I've ever used.

Both suppressors should have the threaded components coated with a high-temperature antiseize compound (colloidal molybdenum or copper compounds work best) before using the suppressor for the first time. Now that Dater has eliminated the takedown tool from his system, he treats threaded components with antiseize compound before shipping the suppressor. As far as I know, he is the only suppressor manufacturer to do so. The suppressors should be disassembled and cleaned every 2,000 rounds.

Soak the components in a solvent such as Varsol, Kroil, or lacquer thinner. Avoid Hoppe's Number 9, since it will attack aluminum components. Let soak for two or more days. Drain. Pour some dishwashing detergent and hot water into the central core. Sealing the unit with both hands, shake vigorously for several minutes. Rinse repeatedly with very hot water until no signs of detergent remain. Stand the core on its rear end to drain and air dry, or blow dry with compressed air. Treat threaded surfaces with a colloidal molybdenum or copper high-temperature antiseize compound and reassemble.

Performance

Ryan's S9-K and Dater's MK9-K were tested with two commercial and two custom loads. Winchester USA 115 grain supersonic and Winchester Silvertip hollowpoint 147 grain subsonic loads are commercially available. Two custom loads featuring Winchester 147 grain bullets were developed by Dr. Dater specifically for the H&K MP5. One load uses 5.1 grains of AA#5 and one uses 3.7 grains of WW231. Dater's subsonic loads remain subsonic in an MP5 under a wide range of atmospheric conditions, whereas the Winchester subsonic round (which was designed for pistols) can go supersonic under the right conditions. Some earlier tests were conducted with Samson 158 grain subsonic (bluetip) ammunition. I learned the hard way that this IMI round should be avoided in the MP5. The bolt unlocks prematurely when firing the Samson subsonic round, with disastrous consequences for the bolt carrier and other components.

Suppressed and unsuppressed sound signatures are listed in Table 12.8 (see page 317) and net sound reductions are listed in Table 12.9 (see page 317). Selected projectile velocities are compared in Table 12.10 (see page 318).

The accompanying graphs compare the ballistic performance of an MP5 using supersonic and three kinds of subsonic ammunition to a factory original MP5 SD using supersonic and subsonic ammunition. The MP5 data are valid whether or not a muzzle suppressor is mounted on the weapon. Figure 12.7 compares bullet paths, which are fairly similar (except for Samson subsonic in the MP5 SD) out to 120 yards. It should be no surprise, however, that the MP5 provides flatter trajectories with all loads compared to the MP5 SD. Figure 12.6 compares projectile velocities downrange, and again the MP5 provides better performance than the MP5 SD.

Both suppressors perform very well for such short suppressors. Each worked best with a different load. And—with the proper load—each suppressor was as quiet as an MP5 SD using supersonic ammunition (which leaves the SD at subsonic velocity due to the ported barrel). That is a remarkable achievement in such a short suppressor.

Although the designs of both cans are virtually the same, Dater's MK9-K does outperform Ryan's S9-K. This performance advantage can be traced to Dater's superior method of diverting combustion gases from the primary expansion chamber into the outer coaxial tube.

Conclusions

Both Jim Ryan's S9-K and Phil Dater's MK9-K suppressors provided the next logical step in the evolution of submachine gun suppressors. They are substantially shorter than the venerable MK-9 suppressor, while producing very good sound suppression with subsonic ammunition. The trend toward suppressors of minimal length and weight will continue, since evolving tactical doctrine shows that speed of target acquisition in the CQB tactical envelope is more important than maximum sound suppression. Dater's MK9-K suppressor with 147 grain subsonic rounds is as quiet as the MP5 SD with 115 grain supersonic loads that were dropped to subsonic velocity by the SD's ported barrel. As the accompanying graphs show, the MP5's subsonic rounds provide slightly flatter trajectories and significantly superior velocity (i.e., penetration) downrange to any rounds fired in the MP5 SD. There is no tactical reason to use an MP5 SD if the operator has access to an MP5 with short suppressor like the MK9-K or S9-K and a suitable 147 grain cartridge. The MP5 SD is a bit more compact and a bit more robust than an MP5 with a muzzle can, but these considerations are trivial compared to the velocity issue.

Since these suppressors are virtually twins, I was intrigued by the reactions of the two designers when they learned of this fact. Both men reacted with admiration for each other rather than hostility. This reaction deepened as they got to know each other and examined each other's work. Each had produced unique designs that were superior to suppressors for comparable applications in the other's inventory. Only the MP5 suppressors were virtually the same. Other muzzle suppressors and integral suppressors were quite different. Ryan had developed a superior integrally suppressed Ruger pistol. Dater was about to market a superior .223 caliber (5.56 mm) suppressor, and so on.

It didn't take Ryan and Dater long to conclude that their design approaches, products, and personalities complemented each other's. It became obvious that pooling their resources and selecting the best products from each line would give them a very strong position in the marketplace if they formed a unified company. So they did. Instead of dueling in the marketplace, they have joined forces.

Ryan and Dater formed a new corporation called Gemini Technologies in the summer of 1993. Doing business as Gemtech, Dater and Ryan began to push the edge of the envelope with their new offerings. One of their first projects was a very small and light suppressor specifically tailored for the law-enforcement market. They called it the MINITAC.

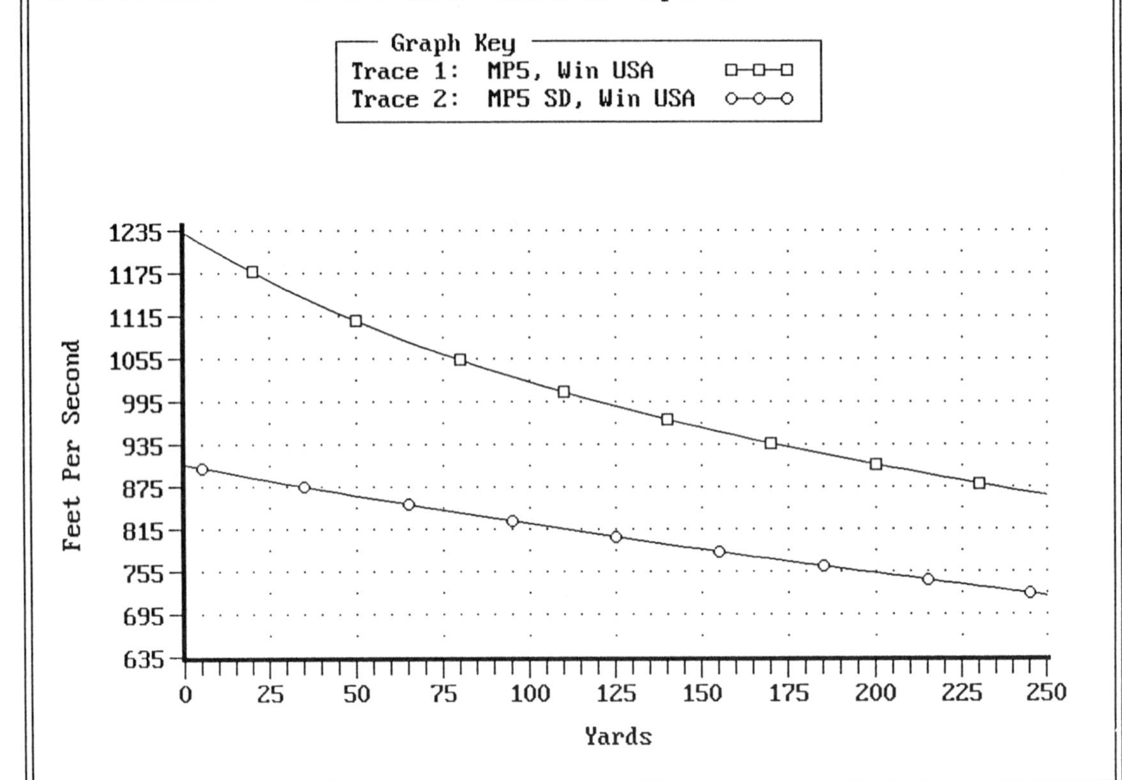

Figure 12.6. Bullet velocities produced by H&K MP5 and MP5 SD with Winchester USA 115 grain FMJ ammunition.

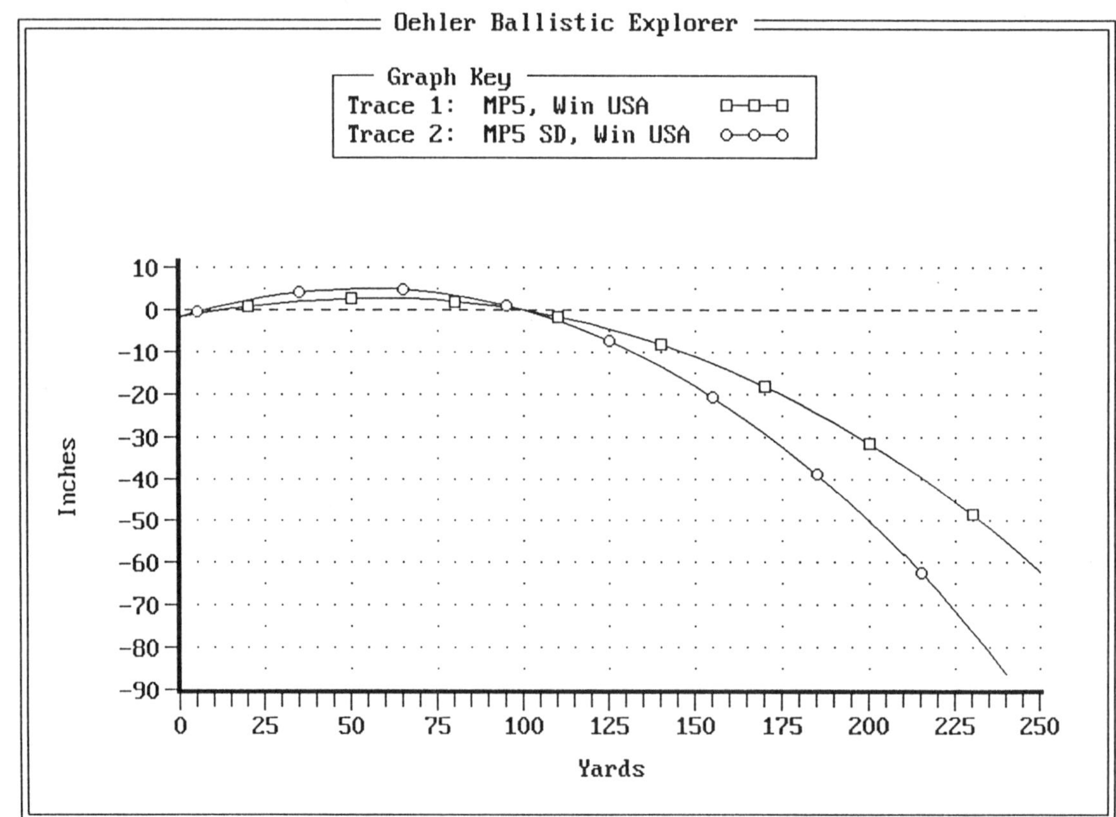

Figure 12.7. Bullet trajectories produced by H&K MP5 and MP5 SD with Winchester USA 115 grain FMJ ammunition.

Table 12.8. Sound signatures in decibels of MP5 suppressor tests.

GUN	SUPPRESSOR	WINCHESTER USA SUPERSONIC	DATER AA#5 SUBSONIC	DATER WW231 SUBSONIC	WINCHESTER SILVERTIP HP SUBSONIC	SAMSON SUBSONIC	TEMP., °F (°C)
H&K MP5	None	157	156	155	156	—	96(36)
H&K MP5	AWC (ATI) MK9-K	129	124	125	126	—	96(36)
H&K MP5	JRC S9-K	130	127	126	129	—	96(36)
H&K MP5	None	159	—	—	—	156	56(13)
H&K MP5	AWC MK-9	125	—	—	—	125	56(13)
H&K MP5	None	159	—	—	—	156	52(11)
H&K MP5	SCRC MK-25 (new model)	125	—	—	—	123	52(11)
H&K MP5	SCRC MK-25A (new model)	127	—	—	—	123	52(11)
H&K MP5	None	157	—	—	—	155	71(22)
H&K MP5 SD	Factory integral	127[a]	—	—	—	126	71(22)

[a] Subsonic projectile velocity due to ported barrel

Table 12.9. Net sound reductions in decibels provided by MP5 suppressors.

GUN	SUPPRESSOR	WINCHESTER USA SUPERSONIC	DATER AA#5 SUBSONIC	DATER WW231 SUBSONIC	WINCHESTER SILVERTIP HP SUBSONIC	SAMSON SUBSONIC	TEMP., °F (°C)
H&K MP5	AWC (ATI) MK9-K	28	32	30	30	—	96(36)
H&K MP5	JRC S9-K	27	29	29	27	—	96(36)
H&K MP5	AWC MK-9	34	—	—	—	31	56(13)
H&K MP5	SCRC MK-25 (new model)	34	—	—	—	33	52(11)
H&K MP5	SCRC MK-25A (new model)	32	—	—	—	33	52(11)
H&K MP5 SD	Factory integral	30[a]	—	—	—	29	71(22)

[a] Subsonic projectile velocity due to ported barrel

Table 12.10. Projectile velocities and speed of sound for a given temperature, expressed in feet per second (and meters per second).

GUN	WINCHESTER USA SUPERSONIC	DATER AA#5 SUBSONIC	DATER WW231 SUBSONIC	WINCHESTER SILVERTIP HP SUBSONIC	SAMSON SUBSONIC	TEMP., °F (°C)	SPEED OF SOUND, fps (mps)
H&K MP5	1,242(379)	1,013(309)	950(290)	987(301)	—	96(36)	1,156(352)
H&K MP5	1,233(376)	—	—	—	957(292)	71(22)	1,129(344)
H&K MP5 SD	907(276)	—	—	—	765(233)	71(22)	1,129(344)

GEMTECH'S MINITAC

As suppressor technology and tactical doctrine have matured in recent years, the quest for the quietest possible suppressor has given way to finding the optimal mix of design and performance characteristics for a given mission. When the task of a suppressor is to protect an operator's hearing and to enhance command and control in the CQB environment, professional users have begun to demand the shortest and lightest possible suppressors. In this role, the speed of target acquisition in a confined space is more important than the sound signature per se, as long as the suppressed gunshots do not degrade operator hearing. Hiding the fact that a shot has been fired is frequently irrelevant for such applications.

That leaves the question: what is the maximum acceptable sound signature when downsizing a suppressor for CQB applications, if there is no need to hide the fact that a shot has been fired? Many professional users prefer a suppressed CQB or entry weapon that at least drops the sound signature below the pain threshold, which is about 141 dB. Some manufacturers who have designed muzzle devices to meet these requirements prefer to call their cans "sound moderators" rather than sound suppressors to minimize confusion in the marketplace. Navy veteran Tom Seslar of S&H Arms and former Chicago cop Tim Bixler of SCRC, for example, have produced outstanding moderators for the MP5 and 9x19mm Steyr AUG, respectively.

Designers Phil Dater and Jim Ryan of Gemtech produced a muzzle can that blurs the distinction between moderators and suppressors. Gemtech's MINITAC suppressor has the length and weight characteristics similar to a moderator with performance similar to several commercially successful full-sized suppressors.

The MINITAC's tube is 7.5 inches (19.1 cm) long, the overall length with mount is 8.9 inches (22.3 cm), and the diameter is 1.4 inches (3.5 cm). The suppressor weighs a mere 11.1 ounces (316 g). The tube and baffle spacers are aircraft-grade aluminum alloys, the 13 strongly sloping baffles are 18-8 stainless steel, and the three-lug mount is a proprietary steel. The front of the MINITAC's primary expansion chamber terminates in a novel asymmetric device that dumps more energy from the expanding combustion gases than more conventional designs. The MINITAC was introduced using the quick-detach MP5 mount that was designed and patented by Tim Bixler.

All of the MINITAC's aluminum components receive nonreflective, black hard-coat anodizing, the internal stainless steel components are left unfinished, and the steel mounting collar has a dark gray phosphate finish.

When it was introduced, the MINITAC represented the latest example of a downsizing trend that began in the 1980s. A suitable baseline is provided by the aging yet outstanding MK-9 suppressor, which was designed by Phil Dater and marketed by AWC Systems Technology.

The Evolution of Smaller Suppressors

I've regarded the AWC MK-9 as the standard against which all other subgun suppressors have been measured since its introduction in the mid-1980s, so it makes a suitable baseline for understanding the MINITAC's place in the evolution of submachine gun suppressors. The MK-9 is approximately 12.0 inches (30.5 cm) long and weighs about 32 ounces (910 g), depending on the mount. AWC Systems Technology then marketed a shorter variant called the MK-9A, which was developed for a federal agency. The MK-9A is 2 inches shorter, 2.5 ounces (70 g) lighter, and 4 dB louder than the MK-9.

AWC eventually replaced the MK-9A with the innovative and dramatically smaller TAC NINE suppressor, which was designed by Doug Olsen. Its tube is 8.3 inches (21.1 cm) long, the overall length with MP5 mount is 9.0 inches (22.8 cm), the diameter is 1.4 inches (3.5 cm), and it weighs 23.0 ounces (649 g). Whereas the TAC NINE has similar dimensions to the MINITAC, it weighs twice as much and has a thoroughly different internal design.

AWC recently replaced the TAC NINE with the CQB 9mm suppressor designed by Mickey Finn. Several generations of CQB suppressors have appeared, and all will be evaluated in the second volume of *Silencer History and Performance.*

About the time the TAC NINE appeared in the marketplace, Dater designed a compact coaxial suppressor designed to supplant the MK-9 and the MK-9A. Ryan independently designed an almost identical suppressor for his company, JR Customs, which soon stimulated Dater and Ryan to join forces as Gemini Technologies, Inc. The new MK9-K is 8.5 inches (21.6 cm) long, and it weighs 20.4 ounces (577 g). Ryan thought they could make a much lighter can for CQB applications to improve handling in confined spaces and increase the speed of target acquisition. Subsequent R&D produced the Gemtech MINITAC.

Note that the two MINITAC suppressors used to research and illustrate this chapter were manufactured before Dater officially merged his original Automatic Weapons Company (not to be confused with AWC Systems Technology) with the company owned by Jim Ryan and Mark Weiss (JR Customs) to form Gemini Technologies. While these specimens carry the AWC logo, the R&D that produced the MINITAC was a joint effort between Dater and Ryan, and subsequent production was through Gemtech. While all other Gemtech suppressors are available to any quali-

Suppressor designer Phil Dater test-fires the Gemtech MK9-K suppressor. Photo by Polly Walter.

fied purchaser, Gemtech restricted the sale of the MINITAC to the military and law-enforcement communities.

Clearly, the MINITAC is compellingly small and light for CQB applications. But how well does it actually perform?

Dater prepares to test fire the Gemtech MINITAC suppressor. Photo by Polly Walter.

Performance of the MINITAC

I first analyzed the sound signatures of an MP5 with and without a MINITAC suppressor at 84 °F (29 °C). Using a custom 147 grain subsonic load developed by Dr. Dater for the MP5, the MINITAC lowered the weapon's signature from 157 to 135 dB, for a net reduction of 22 dB. The suppressor did, however, exhibit a considerable first-round pop with a wide variety of supersonic and subsonic loads that I also fired through the MINITAC.

This specimen of the MINITAC was manufactured before Phil Dater officially merged his original Automatic Weapons Company (not to be confused with AWC Systems Technology) with Jim Ryan's company to form Gemini Technologies, although the R&D that produced the MINITAC was a joint effort between Dater and Ryan.

I should note that Dater's load used for this study features a 147 grain Winchester FMJ bullet and 5.1 grains of AA#5 powder. Dater has also used the same bullet with 3.7 grains of WW231 powder. The former gives a muzzle velocity of 950 fps (290 mps), while the latter gives a muzzle velocity of about 850 fps (259 mps) from an MP5. About a year after I conducted this particular study, Dater developed a superior load using 3.7 grains of N-320 VihtaVuori Oy powder and the same bullets. The VV320 load gives a muzzle velocity of about 960 fps (293 mps) and is unusually quiet whether suppressed or unsuppressed.

It would be useful to point out some interesting information about bullet velocities produced by the loads used for testing. A potential problem exists because so-called subsonic rounds for the

The MINITAC (mounted on the MP5) is a recent example of a downsizing trend that began in the 1980s. Shown for comparison are the relatively large AWC MK-9 and the subsequently designed, intermediate-size AWC MK-9A.

9x19mm cartridge are generally designed for pistols, not longer-barreled submachine guns. Therefore, these 147 grain subsonic rounds are typically transonic in the MP5, meaning that the projectile may or may not exceed the speed of sound at a particular temperature and other atmospheric conditions. The Winchester subsonic round frequently produces a ballistic crack—which sounds similar to an unsuppressed .22 rifle—when fired in the MP5; this can be disastrous if a mission requires hiding the fact that a shot has been fired. Dater's subsonic loads never go supersonic in an MP5. Yet no major manufacturer, not even Black Hills Shooters Supplies, produces ammunition tailored to remain subsonic in the MP5. As far as I know, only G&L Arms (6064 Mooretown Road, Williamsburg, VA 23188) stocks subsonic ball and hollowpoint ammunition designed to remain subsonic in the MP5 over a wide range of atmospheric conditions, although these are reloads.

Detailed data on subsequent testing of MINITAC sound signatures appear in Table 12.11 (see page 322), net sound reductions appear in Table 12.12 (see page 322), and first-round pop is reported in Table 12.13 (see page 323).

The sound data suggest that the MINITAC's performance is similar to some full-sized suppressors produced in the 1980s. Clearly, the MINITAC lowers the MP5's sound signature below the pain threshold. But these data also suggest that the MINITAC's performance falls far short of the best full-sized suppressors. That should not be surprising, since there is no free lunch in suppressor design. The surprise is that the MINITAC is so quiet when it only has 31 percent of the volume and 34 percent of the weight of the MK-9 suppressor and 90 percent of the volume and 48 percent of the weight of the TAC NINE. Professional operators who tested this little suppressor were impressed with its sound signature and light weight.

Therefore, if the role of a suppressor is to preserve operator hearing and to enhance command and control, then the design and performance of the little MINITAC makes it a logical choice for entry teams and CQB applications. If the mission may require hiding the fact that a shot has been fired, then a better choice remains a quieter medium-size suppressor such as Gemtech's MK9-K, which is still small enough to readily employ in confined spaces. When the quietest possible sound signature is required, a full-size suppressor like AWC's MK-9 may be the best choice, although it is rather bulky for CQB applications and it normally produces about the same sound signature as the much smaller MK9-K with subsonic ammunition.

Soon after Gemtech introduced the MINITAC, a widely experienced aerospace engineer joined the company and quickly developed a much better suppressor and a vastly improved quick-mount. Gemtech called the new suppressor the Raptor and the new snap-on mount the TRI-LOCK.

Table 12.11. Sound signatures in decibels of TRI-LOCK suppressor tests.

GUN	SUPPRESSOR	WINCHESTER USA SUPERSONIC	G&L SUBSONIC	DATER VV320 SUBSONIC	WINCHESTER SILVERTIP HP SUBSONIC	TEMP., °F (°C)
H&K MP5	None	158	157	154[d]	156	36(2)
H&K MP5	Gemtech Raptor[a]	137	130	128[d]	131	36(2)
H&K MP5	AWC MK-9[a]	127	124	122[d]	123	36(2)
H&K MP5	None	157	—	155[c]	156	96(36)
H&K MP5	Gemtech MK9-K[b]	129	—	125[c]	126	96(36)
H&K MP5	None	157	156	154[d]	156	71(22)
H&K MP5	Gemtech MINITAC[b]	139	136	130[d]	135	71(22)
H&K MP5	Gemtech Raptor[a]	137	131	126[d]	129	71(22)

[a] TRI-LOCK mount
[b] Bixler mount
[c] uses 3.7 grains of WW231 powder
[d] uses 3.7 grains of N-320 VihtaVuori Oy powder

Table 12.12. Net sound reductions in decibels provided by TRI-LOCK suppressors.

GUN	SUPPRESSOR	WINCHESTER USA SUPERSONIC	G&L SUBSONIC	DATER VV320 SUBSONIC	WINCHESTER SILVERTIP HP SUBSONIC	TEMP., °F (°C)
H&K MP5	Gemtech Raptor[a]	21	27	26[d]	25	36(2)
H&K MP5	AWC MK-9[a]	31	33	32[d]	33	36(2)
H&K MP5	Gemtech MK9-K[b]	28	—	30[c]	30	96(36)
H&K MP5	Gemtech MINITAC[b]	18	20	24[d]	19	71(22)
H&K MP5	Gemtech Raptor[a]	20	25	28[d]	27	71(22)

[a] TRI-LOCK mount
[b] Bixler mount
[c] uses 3.7 grains of WW231 powder
[d] uses 3.7 grains of N-320 VihtaVuori Oy powder

Table 12.13. First-round pop, expressed in decibels.

WEAPON	SUPPRESSOR	WINCHESTER USA	G&L SUBSONIC	DATER SUBSONIC	WINCHESTER SUBSONIC	TEMP., °F (°C)
H&K MP5	Gemtech Raptor[a]	+5	+1	+1[d]	0	36(2)
H&K MP5	AWC MK-9[a]	-5	-3	+2[d]	+2	36(2)
H&K MP5	Gemtech MK9-K[b]	-1	—	+1[c]	0	96(36)
H&K MP5	Gemtech MINITAC[b]	+7	+8	+7[d]	+9	71(22)
H&K MP5	Gemtech Raptor[a]	-1	+3	+2[d]	1	71(22)

[a] TRI-LOCK mount
[b] Bixler mount
[c] uses 3.7 grains of WW231 powder
[d] uses 3.7 grains of N-320 VihtaVuori Oy powder

THE RAPTOR

The most frustrating aspect of selecting and using a silencer is not finding a unit that is quiet; it's finding a good suppressor that mounts securely on the weapon and always provides proper alignment with the bore. The suppressor must stay put without loosening and going out of alignment during prolonged firing. Maintaining proper alignment during use has profound implications on the accuracy provided by a suppressed weapon. In extreme cases, poor alignment can even endanger the operator. But even a secure mounting system may not be enough. One popular and quite secure mounting system, for example, can sometimes impair accuracy (more about that later). Besides these security and alignment issues, the next most common complaint is that many suppressors may be quiet, but they may be too long or too heavy when operating in the CQB environment. The new Gemtech Raptor sound suppressor addresses all of these common complaints and introduces a revolutionary snap-on mounting system that is superior to anything else in the marketplace.

A new asymmetrical five-prong flash hider from Gemtech also uses the new patent-pending mount, which inventor Gregory Latka calls the TRI-LOCK. Latka also designed the Raptor, based on his own work, and an asymmetric .22 caliber baffle developed by Phil Dater and Jim Ryan the previous year. Latka's design of the Raptor suppressor and TRI-LOCK mount may represent the most important event thus far in the development of muzzle cans for the H&K MP5, MP5K, and PDW submachine guns.

Although Dater and Ryan are well known to suppressor cognoscenti, Latka is a relative newcomer to the field. When Latka, who is an aerospace engineer, first turned his attention to suppressor design, he quickly received Patent Number 5,029,512 for his innovative helical free-flow suppressor in 1991. After marketing suppressors of his own design, he joined Gemtech in 1995. His exceptional experience with exotic materials and advanced manufacturing techniques for the military and aerospace industries has significantly upgraded Gemtech's R&D and manufacturing capabilities. The team's learning curve is now much shorter. Development of the Raptor is a prime example. The new suppressor went from initial concept to full production in just three weeks. It is my experience that projects which come together smoothly and quickly tend to be more satisfactory over the long haul than projects that require a lot of tweaking throughout their development.

The introduction of the Raptor suppressor with TRI-LOCK mount was timely, to say the least. Increasingly sophisticated users had come to demand smaller and lighter suppressors. Furthermore, I'd begun receiving an increasing number of complaints that some muzzle cans were affecting accuracy adversely. This is not an intrinsic problem with suppressors but rather relates to how the suppressors are mounted on a weapon.

MP5 Suppressors and Accuracy

Many muzzle cans out there in the real world align so poorly with the bores of their firearms that bullets graze the baffles. It also appears that some (but not all) baffle designs that force jets of gas across the bullet path may increase bullet yaw inside the suppressor. That can lead to bullets grazing the baffle, according to prevailing theory. A careful examination of the gas velocities and distances involved seems to undermine this theory, however. Some other factor must be causing bullets to graze baffles in these cases.

A more plausible explanation is that bore diameter or alignment with the barrel may be the real underlying problems. Some suppressors unquestionably have such tight bores through their baffles that bullet grazing is likely, but this is a relatively rare phenomenon in the mid-1990s. Alignment remains the most prevalent problem today.

The two most common causes of alignment problems relate to threaded mounts: 1) the barrel threads are not concentric with the bore, and 2) the threaded barrel lacks a shoulder perpendicular to the bore that acts as a stop to force the suppressor into proper alignment. The very coarse Ingram/SIONICS threads, for example, feature such a shoulder that provides good alignment of the suppressor as long as the can remains screwed tightly against the barrel shoulder. If the suppressor loosens and backs off the threads several degrees, however, the shoulder no longer has any effect, and the suppressor can become dangerously misaligned. This has caused more than one operator to shoot through the side of the suppressor.

The three lugs near the end of the MP5's barrel were originally incorporated as a means of attaching a blank-firing device and a flash hider, not sound suppressors. Since the H&K mount was neither robust enough nor provided sufficiently precise alignment for attaching a relatively long and heavy suppressor, the U.S. Navy stipulated that weapons delivered to them include 1/2x32 TPI threads in front of the lugs for attaching a suppressor.

The fine Navy threads help but do not cure the problem of muzzle suppressors becoming loose during firing. Suppressors loosen from a combination of factors. The suppressor heats quickly from rapid or full-auto fire. The heated suppressor expands, which loosens its grip on the barrel threads. Also, the suppressor tends to come unscrewed from the barrel because the torque generated when a bullet travels down a barrel's rifling causes the weapon to twist about the axis of the bore during recoil. Since most rifling is right-handed, and suppressors are normally mounted with right-hand threads, the torque caused by each bullet makes the barrel act rather like an impact wrench. The barrel twists slightly, while the inertia of the suppressor causes it to resist twisting too. Thus, the barrel tends to unscrew from the suppressor. Heavier suppressors have more inertia, so they seem to come loose more quickly than lighter suppressors. This problem is worse with suppressors subjected to full-auto fire. When a barrel has right-hand rifling, simply using left-hand threads to mount the muzzle suppressor would eliminate this problem, although a sound suppressor may self-tighten beyond the point of easy removal.

While the U.S. Navy opted for mounting suppressors to the MP5 and MP5K with fine right-hand threads, Tim Bixler of SCRC and Tim LaFrance of LaFrance Specialties developed alternative mounting systems for the MP5 at about the same time in the 1980s. Bixler's quick couple

Greg Latka designed the Gemtech Raptor based on his own work and an asymmetric .22 caliber baffle developed by Phil Dater and Jim Ryan the previous year.

quickly became the dominant MP5 mount in the marketplace.

While I've used suppressors with the Bixler quick coupler more than any other MP5 mount, the design had a subtle eccentricity that I discovered in the mid-1990s. Some people began to notice that shot placement with some suppressors is most reproducible if the same part of the suppressor always points to 12 o'clock, as an arbitrary standard.

If the silencer has an unusually tight bullet passage, like the Knight's Armament SOCOM .45 pistol suppressor, and the can is not aligned precisely, bullets may graze baffles, which will either shift the group, degrade accuracy, or both. Knight's suppressor can be indexed at 10 different radial positions "around the clock" until the suppressed pistol aligns properly and delivers acceptable accuracy.

Remarkably, this phenomenon is also seen with some high-tech MP5 suppressors that do not have unusually tight bores. It turns out that they all use Bixler's otherwise outstanding quick mount for the three-lug barrel. Experienced operators place a temporary mark on the tube of their MP5 suppressors using the Bixler mount and check for this phenomenon. If present, the operator then determines the optimal orientation and places a dab of paint or a small scratch as an index mark to ensure repeatable alignment with a particular barrel lug.

The reason some suppressors exhibit a sweet spot in terms of orientation with the weapon is that the main component of the Bixler mount is a casting. Small variations from one casting to another (which probably relate to uneven cooling after the parts are cast) can sometimes cause subtle variations in alignment. This is not a design flaw per se, since a mount that is machined (not cast) to the same specs will not exhibit a sweet spot. This occasional problem with the Bixler mount is the design's only liability in my experience.

Gemtech now offers the spring-loaded quick mount developed by Greg Latka, which appears to provide improved convenience and consistent shot placement regardless of orientation. The TRI-LOCK mount eliminates the potential problem of incorrect installation, since it includes a positive stop that prevents rotating its locking recesses past the barrel's lugs. The mount's spring is effectively shielded from fouling by the by-products of powder combustion. Alignment is outstanding. Installation is a snap, both figuratively and literally. And the system appears to be both robust and foolproof. Mounting a suppressor with the TRI-LOCK takes a similar amount of time to locking the bolt of an MP5 in the open position. Before mounting the suppressor, however, the operator should place the weapon on safe, remove the magazine, lock the bolt in the open position, and verify that the chamber is empty. The four-step mounting procedure takes about two seconds:

1. Align the grooves in the suppressor mount with the lugs on the barrel.

2. While holding the weapon in the firing position, pull the suppressor onto the barrel against spring tension until the suppressor can be rotated counter-clockwise.
3. Rotate the suppressor 60 degrees until it stops. Release backward pressure, allowing the spring in the TRI-LOCK to push the suppressor forward.
4. Try to rock the suppressor to ensure that the pocket recesses in the mount have engaged the barrel lugs. While the TRI-LOCK has never failed to index properly in my experience, always rocking the suppressor should become an instinctual behavior (like actually looking into a chamber to ensure that a weapon is truly unloaded), no matter what three-lug adapter is used on the MP5.

The classic AWC MK-9 suppressor used as a benchmark during this T&E was retrofitted with Gemtech's TRI-LOCK mount.

To remove a suppressor with the TRI-LOCK, pull the suppressor rearward, rotate it 60 degrees clockwise, and slide it off the barrel.

First issued on Gemtech's Raptor suppressor and new flash hider for the MP5 (which works better than the H&K flash hider and costs half the price), the TRI-LOCK is now available as an option on all Gemtech MP5 suppressors instead of a threaded mount or the company's standard MP5 quick mount. The TRI-LOCK costs an additional $75 at the time of purchase. Once someone has the opportunity to try the TRI-LOCK, I can't imagine he would consider the cheaper manual mount on the Raptor or the larger suppressors made by Gemtech for the MP5 family of weapons.

Named after the birds of prey, the Raptor suppressor continues Gemtech's tradition of developing the smallest and lightest possible suppressors for the armed professional.

Design

Gemtech's Raptor sound suppressor is constructed from 6061-T6 and 2024 aircraft-grade aluminum, and the TRI-LOCK is made from 2024 aluminum and 303 stainless steel. The Raptor with TRI-LOCK measures 9.1 inches (23.1 cm) in length and 1.4 inches (3.5 cm) in diameter. It weighs 9.8 ounces (277 g). The front end cap is screwed into place using a special tool from the rear of the suppressor. The Raptor's seven aluminum baffles feature an asymmetric design to enhance performance, and the first several baffles incorporate an additional structure designed by Dr. Dater to enhance turbulence. The baffles, which do not require spacers between them, feature a tongue and groove system that aligns the baffles so that the asymmetric surfaces align properly during assembly and prolonged use. The new blast baffle at the front of the primary expansion chamber and the unusual internal structure of the domed front end cap particularly enhance the performance of this suppressor. The suppressor tube, front end cap, and outer shell of the TRI-LOCK are finished in a black hard-coat anodizing.

The Raptor replaces the similarly sized MINITAC suppressor, which has the same diameter but

Although designed for the three-lug barrel on the H&K MP5, Gemtech's quick-mount flash hider can also be mated to the Colt 9mm submachine gun with Gemtech's three-lug adapter for the Colt weapon.

is 8.9 inches (22.6 cm) long, weighs 11.1 ounces (316 g), and features 11 stainless steel baffles of much simpler design. The MINITAC makes an interesting benchmark for comparing the Raptor's performance. Another useful benchmark is Dater's classic MK-9 suppressor, which he designed in the mid-1980s. Even though the MK-9 is no longer in production, Gemtech retrofitted this vintage suppressor with a TRI-LOCK quick mount, yielding a package that measures 13.3 inches (33.8 cm) long and 2.0 inches (5.1 cm) in diameter. It weighs 30.1 ounces (853 g). The currently produced Gemtech MK-9K is a shortened, product-improved descendent of the MK-9. The MK-9K has the same diameter, but overall length is reduced to 8.5 inches (21.6 cm) with the Bixler quick mount. The suppressor weighs 20.4 ounces (577 grams).

Performance

The mean (average) sound signatures measured during this testing appear in Table 12.11, net sound reductions appear in Table 12.12, and Table 12.13 provides the first-round pop produced by each suppressor in the study. Note that the Raptor and MK-9 were tested side by side on one day, whereas the Raptor and MINITAC were tested side by side on a much warmer day. The first thing you notice from the net sound reduction data is that the Raptor performs better with Winchester supersonic and G&L subsonic ammunition at a cold temperature, while the Raptor performs better with the Dater and Winchester subsonic fodder at a moderate temperature.

Considering the more sophisticated design of the Raptor, it should come as no surprise that it outperforms the MINITAC by every measure with every kind of ammunition. The Raptor is significantly quieter than the MINITAC with all types of ammunition, and it has almost eliminated first-round pop. It should also come as no surprise that a well-designed suppressor with a larger volume, like the MK-9K, still manages to outperform the low-volume Raptor. The big surprise is that the MK-9 with TRI-LOCK mount provides significantly better performance than it ever had before using alternative mounts on the MP5. I double-checked the calibration of the sound meter after obtaining these data to ensure that there was no equipment problem. It appears that the MK-9 suppressor provides more sound suppression with the TRI-LOCK than with other mounts because of the conical geometry inside the mount, which seems to encourage combustion gases to move away from the bore toward the porting at the rear of the inner coaxial tube. In fact, the MK-9 with TRI-LOCK provides better net sound reduction than an MP5 SD, whether using supersonic or subsonic ammuni-

AWC MK-9 suppressor retrofitted with Gemtech's TRI-LOCK mount (top), Gemtech MINITAC suppressor with Bixler mount (center), and Gemtech Raptor suppressor with TRI-LOCK mount (on MP5).

Gemtech's Raptor suppressor provides significantly better sound reduction than the now discontinued MINITAC and much faster mounting and dismounting thanks to the new TRI-LOCK mount.

tion. It would be interesting to see whether the TRI-LOCK enhances the performance of the MK-9K suppressor, as well. Unfortunately, a MK-9K with TRI-LOCK was not available for testing during this study. Nevertheless, a number of conclusions can be drawn from this evaluation.

Conclusions

The Raptor suppressor provides better sound reduction than its predecessor, the MINITAC. Furthermore, the Raptor is 12 percent lighter in spite of its larger and vastly superior TRI-LOCK mount. Since the Raptor only uses seven baffles instead of the MINITAC's eleven, the longer TRI-LOCK mount only adds 0.2 inch (0.5 cm) to the Raptor's overall length. The Raptor provides plenty of performance for entry teams, CQB applications, and most other operations in the real world. If, however, the mission requires the maximum possible sound reduction, I'd opt for the Gemtech MK9-K.

THE BOTTOM LINE

How much suppression is enough? Consider that the Sten Mk IIS produced a sound signature of about 137 dB and was highly successful during combat and clandestine operations from World War II through the Vietnam era. In the modern tactical environment, however, the 131 dB level seems to be an acceptable sound signature when using subsonic ammunition in a suppressed submachine gun for most applications. Some of the suppressors evaluated in this study are much quieter than 131 dB. Other suppressors are especially short or lightweight. Some missions will require maximum sound suppression, while others will benefit from the shortest or lightest suppressor. The current marketplace offers a sufficient diversity of suppressors to satisfy any realistic mission requirement. Nevertheless, some interesting and rather revolutionary technologies should appear in the marketplace in the next few years. Suppressors will continue to become quieter, smaller, and lighter.

Two related questions important to the armed professional remain unanswered. Will the quietest suppressor provide the least chance of ignition when operating in an explosive atmosphere? And will using a suppressor that delivers the maximum amount of sound suppression also maximize the concentration and aggressiveness of the operator? These questions are beyond the scope of this study.

CHAPTER THIRTEEN

THE EVOLUTION OF CENTERFIRE PISTOL SUPPRESSORS

he typical semiautomatic pistol of centerfire caliber is hard to silence because the weight of the suppressor retards the rearward movement of the barrel, which provides energy to cycle the slide. Thus the Beretta 92F, the Colt 1911 and its descendents, the Browning Hi-Power, or any other pistol that depends on the rearward movement of its barrel is more likely to malfunction with a suppressor than pistols like the H&K P9S that do not require barrel movement. Glock pistols are particularly difficult to suppress because of this phenomenon.

It is difficult to engineer around this problem, although Maxim and others did develop some relevant designs early in this century. The advent of World War II stimulated the first really intense effort at suppressing centerfire handguns.

One solution was to use a manually operated action, such as the .32 ACP Welrod developed by the British during World War II for clandestine operations. Since the cartridge does not operate the pistol's action, the weight of the suppressor and the back pressure generated by the ammunition are irrelevant. The designer can concentrate on the development of an effective suppressor relatively unburdened by silencer size and weight.

The Russians used the 7.62mm Model 1895 Nagant revolver, which is the only wheel gun that is practical to silence, due to the unusual design of both the seven-shot revolver and its cartridge. Cocking the hammer causes the cylinder to move forward so that the front of the chamber extends over the rear of the barrel. The bullet is seated below the mouth of the long tapered cartridge case, making the round look like a blank. The forward part of the case forms a seal so that combustion gases are not vented between the cylinder and barrel. Since the standard load of the day was subsonic, the silenced Nagant produced no ballistic crack and was effective when fielded.

AWC HP-9 suppressor on Beretta 92F with custom sights. Photo by Polly Walter.

The Germans experimented with a lightweight but virtually empty suppressor tube that depended on its sheer volume and two rubber wipes at the front of the suppressor to moderate the Luger's sound signature. The Luger required manual cycling of the action. A smaller suppressor developed for the P38 pistol was more practical.

The P38 suppressor featured four baffles that were separated by springs in front of each baffle. At least in theory, these springs would also absorb some of the energy from the combustion gases, thus improving the performance of the suppressor. While the barrel of the P38 does recoil rearward, it does so in a straight line much like the Beretta 92F. This requires less of a recoil impulse than a Browning-type design, where the rear of the barrel drops as part of the unlocking process. Therefore, the P38 is much more forgiving when the weight of a suppressor is added to the barrel, so the P38 functioned reliably with this four-baffle design. The P38 suppressor was also used on MP38 and MP40 submachine guns in very limited numbers.

Concurrent with suppressor development in wartime Germany was the creation of special subsonic rifle and pistol rounds designed to keep projectile velocity just low enough to prevent a ballistic crack over a wide range of temperatures. The 9x19mm German subsonic round, which was marked with a green tip, pioneered the use of a heavier bullet to provide better terminal ballistics (i.e., more penetration) as well as more back pressure for operating a semiautomatic action. The subsonic round featured a 10 gram (154 grain) projectile and reduced charge of faster-burning powder compared to the standard 9x19 round, which featured a bullet weight of 8 grams (approximately 124 grains).

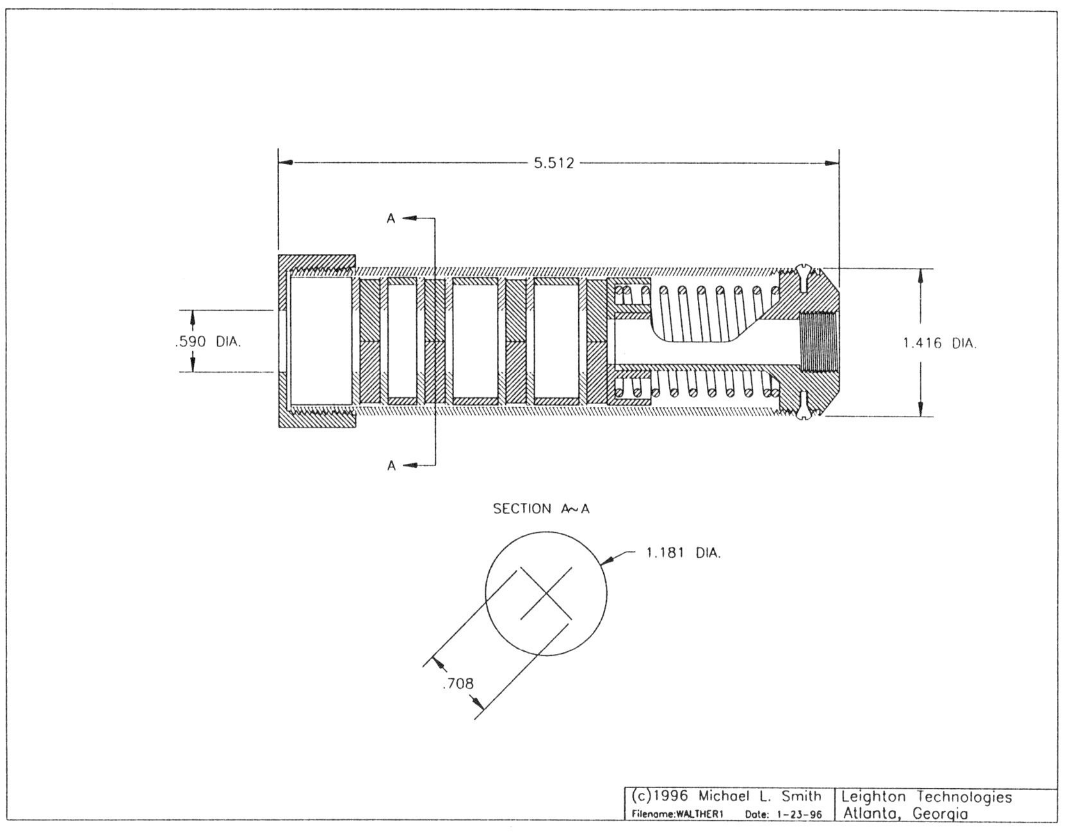

Figure 13.1. This Walther Model SD9b suppressor was one of the very first practical muzzle cans for a pistol of major caliber. It was this suppressor that stimulated the design of the U.S. Navy Hush Puppy. Redrawn by Mike Smith from a rough sketch by Siegfried Huebner dated November 15, 1964.

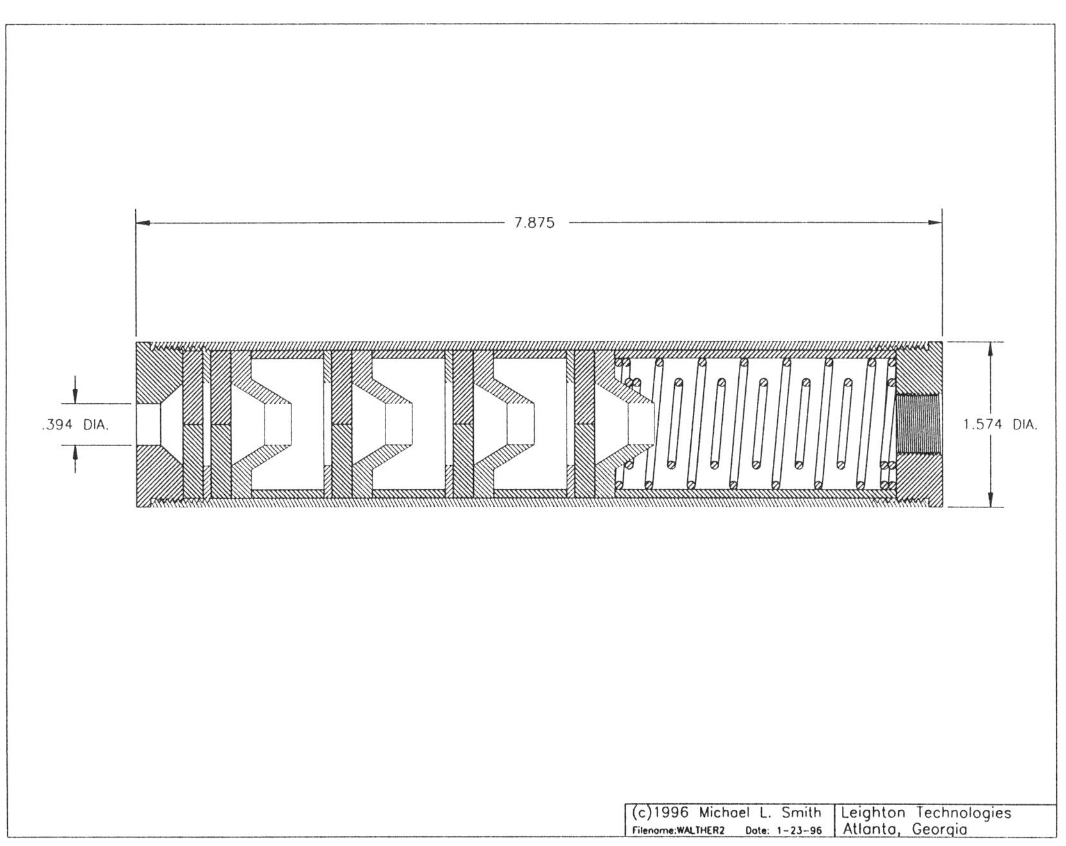

Figure 13.2. An improved Walther design using baffles and thinner wipes, redrawn by Mike Smith from a rough sketch by Siegfried Huebner dated November 3, 1970.

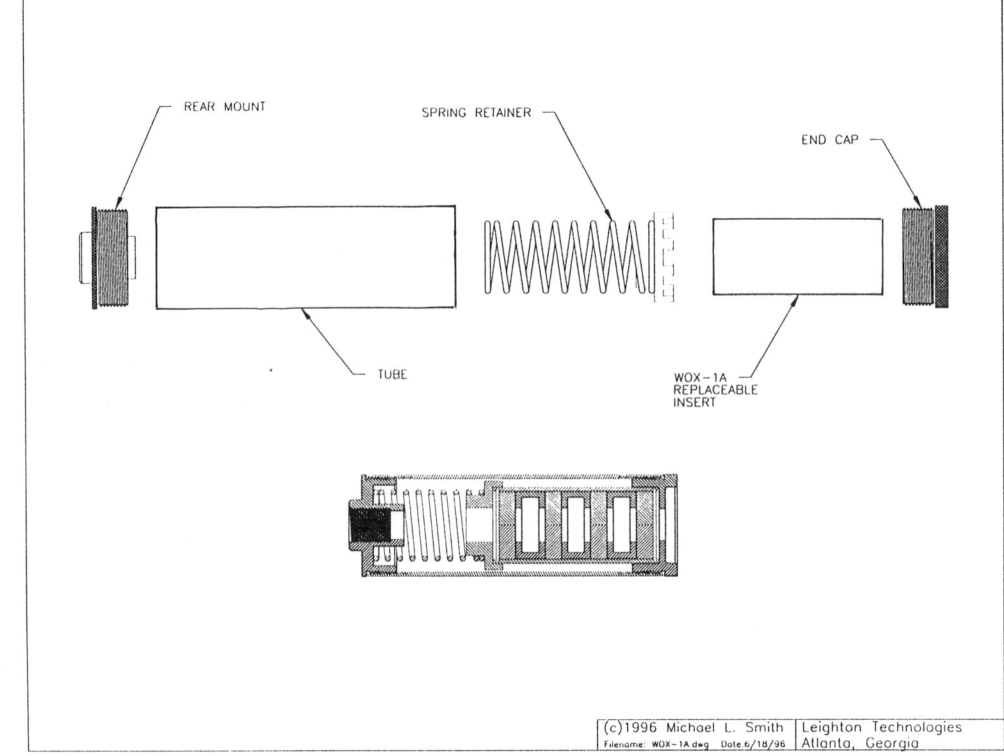

Figure 13.3. The WOX-1A suppressor, which quickly became known as the Hush Puppy because it was frequently used to silence Viet Cong watch dogs. Drawing by Mike Smith.

While it is important to recognize the technological contributions of German designers during World War II, it is also important to note that Germany fielded few suppressors during the war because German authorities somehow found the very notion of using silencers rather unseemly. Allied authorities had no such compunctions.

After the war, Walther developed silencers for its pistols that included several compact designs for the P38 that used wipes. Figure 13.1 is redrawn from the original sketch made by Siegfried Huebner on November 15, 1964. Figure 13.2 shows an improved design using baffles and thinner wipes originally sketched by Siegfried Huebner on November 3, 1970. The U.S. Navy purchased a small number of the Walther Model SD9b can shown in Figure 13.1 for testing and evaluation about the time Southeast Asia began heating up. The Navy developed a product-improved version of this suppressor (see Figure 13.3), which was used with great effectiveness by Navy SEALs in Vietnam, where the suppressor quickly became known as the Hush Puppy because it was frequently used to silence Viet Cong watch dogs.

Suppressors like the Hush Puppy that use wipes to achieve light weight and reliable function do exhibit some disadvantages compared to wipeless designs:

1. Wipes degrade accuracy since they touch the bullet as it travels through the can.
2. Wipes create more back pressure, so gas and powder residue are forced back out the rear of the barrel into the shooter's face. This is unpleasant and dangerous without eye protection.
3. Wipes can no longer be purchased directly from the manufacturer in the United States thanks to the McClure-Volkmer legislation of 1986. Now an individual must transfer the suppressor back to the manufacturer for "repair" on a Form 5 (a Form 3 may be quicker if you're a dealer). That's a lot of bother and expense every 20 to 40 rounds!

Clearly, wipeless designs that began to appear in the mid to late 1980s, like the Vaime A2 (made in the United States by North American Sales International) and the AWC Invicta, became much more practical in the civilian and law enforcement marketplace. As we shall see later in this treatise, however, there is still a role for a suppressor using wipes in the military and clandestine environments.

THE HUSH PUPPY

Back during the Vietnam era, U.S. Navy SEAL Teams discovered the need for a silenced pistol of major caliber for the removal of enemy guard dogs and sentries and for other special operations. This led to the development of the WOX-1A suppressor by the Naval Ordnance Laboratory in the late 1960s. It is not widely known that Smith & Wesson also conducted R&D during this period on a small suppressor using wipes, but knowledge about this work seems to have been purged from the S&W corporate culture. The WOX-1A became the first widely fielded suppressor for a major caliber semiautomatic pistol.

The Hush Puppy was issued with a modified, steel-framed Smith & Wesson Model 39 Pistol. The Navy named the experimental eight-shot weapon the WOX-13A Pistol. It featured elevated sights to see over the suppressor, a threaded 5 inch barrel, and a detachable tubular shoulder stock. Perhaps the pistol's most unusual feature was a slide lock on the left side of the frame that could be employed to keep the action closed and quiet when firing. If less than maximum quiet was acceptable, the pistol could be fired in its normal semiautomatic mode. According to one (unconfirmed) source, about 120 of these pistols were produced.

Lee Juras of the Super Vel Cartridge Corporation developed a special subsonic cartridge using a 159 grain FMJ bullet for this system. It was an unusually hot round that generated very high pressure and a lot of stopping power. Unfortunately, employment of the slide lock combined with the hot ammo led to structural failures. By the end of 1968, Smith & Wesson had developed an improved pistol with double-column, 13-round magazine to solve these problems. (A remarkably similar pistol was later marketed by Smith & Wesson as the Model 59.) The Hush Puppy was adopted as the Mark 3, Mod. O Silencer and the improved S&W pistol was adopted as the Mark 22, Mod. O Pistol. I have not yet discovered how many of these systems were produced.

The Hush Puppy was really a suppressor within a suppressor. The can was 5 inches long and weighed 8 ounces. A bullet entering the rear cap (which threaded onto the barrel) entered a large primary expansion chamber, where the ignition gases quickly expanded and cooled. A large snap

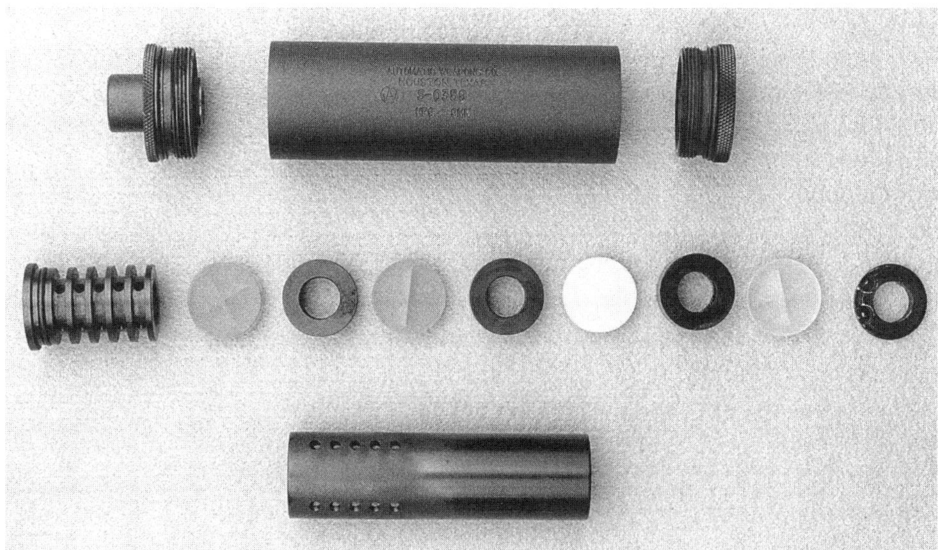

The Hush Puppy is really a suppressor within a suppressor.

ring in this expansion chamber forced a "silencer insert" against the can's front cap. This insert, which had a much smaller diameter than the can, contained alternating synthetic wipes and spacers. The open space between the insert and the outer tube formed an extension of the primary expansion chamber.

Since the wipes only had a life span of about 25 rounds with subsonic ammo and a life span of only several rounds with supersonic ammo, the SEALs issued the Mark 26, Mod. O Accessory Kit, which contained 22 subsonic rounds and a new silencer insert. Underwater carry was facilitated by an O-ring-sealed chamber plug and muzzle cap for the pistol and water-tight plugs for the suppressor as well. The Navy received a patent for the modifications that sealed the suppressor and pistol for underwater carry but not for the suppressor itself.

The Navy was quite happy with the Hush Puppy suppressor, but it continued to have extraction problems with the hot Super Vel ammo and the Smith & Wesson pistol. The cases tended to stick in the chambers. The Navy turned to Reed Knight of Knight's Armament Company for a solution to the problem in the late 1970s.

Reed Knight is not well-known to the civilian shooting community, but the suppressors he designs are at the cutting edge of technology and are highly regarded in the military marketplace.

Knight solved the Navy's problems with the Mark 22, Mod. O Pistol by going to a stronger Beretta pistol with beefier extractor and by designing a more robust slide lock that did not stress the frame or slide (see Figure 13.4,). Although one unconfirmed source said that several S&W pistols experienced structural failures after less than 200 rounds, Knight's second-generation slide lock for the Beretta pistol, which was marketed with his final variant of the Hush Puppy (called the Snap-On), has a demonstrated life span in excess of 11,000 rounds (see Figure 13.5). Knight also produced a new subsonic round for the Navy in the early 1980s, which featured a 170 grain FMJ bullet exiting the barrel at 975 fps. This round produced 40,000 psi, which was right at the edge of the envelope for the Beretta. This is too hot for many other pistols, including the Navy's old Smith & Wessons.

The round warrants further discussion. The following information comes from two usually reliable sources. Knight's U.S. Navy round used a Sierra 170 grain .357 FMJ bullet designed for handgun silhouette shooting. The bullet was resized to 0.354 inch. A die was used to form a 0.010 inch boattail of 4 to 5 degrees. A normally reliable source claims the charge was 5.0 grains of Unique. (*Do not try to duplicate this load; it is too hot for civilian use.* The information is presented for historical purposes only. The author, Paladin Press, and the author's informants can accept no liability for the use or misuse of this or the following information.)

If you are an experienced handloader and wish to develop a more reasonable 170 grain subsonic load with this resized and boat-tailed bullet, carefully work up to no more than 4.7 grains of Unique (do not use any other powder). This load should only be used in a Beretta 92 series pistol in sound condition. No warranties expressed or implied. (Isn't this Age of Litigation wonderful?) Tim Bixler of SCRC prefers a more moderate load using 4.5 grains of Unique, which produces a muzzle velocity of about 780 fps and a computed muzzle energy of 227 foot-pounds out of an H&K MP5. Use only virgin brass with either load.

When the U.S. Navy exhausted the subsonic ammo made by Knight, it adopted a special 147 grain FMJ subsonic round made for it by Winchester. The commercially available 147 grain subsonic hollowpoint *must not be used* in any suppressor using wipes, including the variant of Knight's Hush Puppy, which was manufactured under license and marketed to civilians by AWC Systems Technology.

The design of AWC's HP-9 Hush Puppy (see Figure 13.6) differs from both the Navy's early Mark 3, Mod. O Silencer and the Snap-On suppressor subsequently manufactured by Knight's Armament for the military. The HP-9 measures 4.75 inches (12.0 cm) long and 1.5 inches (3.8 cm) in diameter. The can weighs 8.0 ounces (230 g). It also is a suppressor within a suppressor.

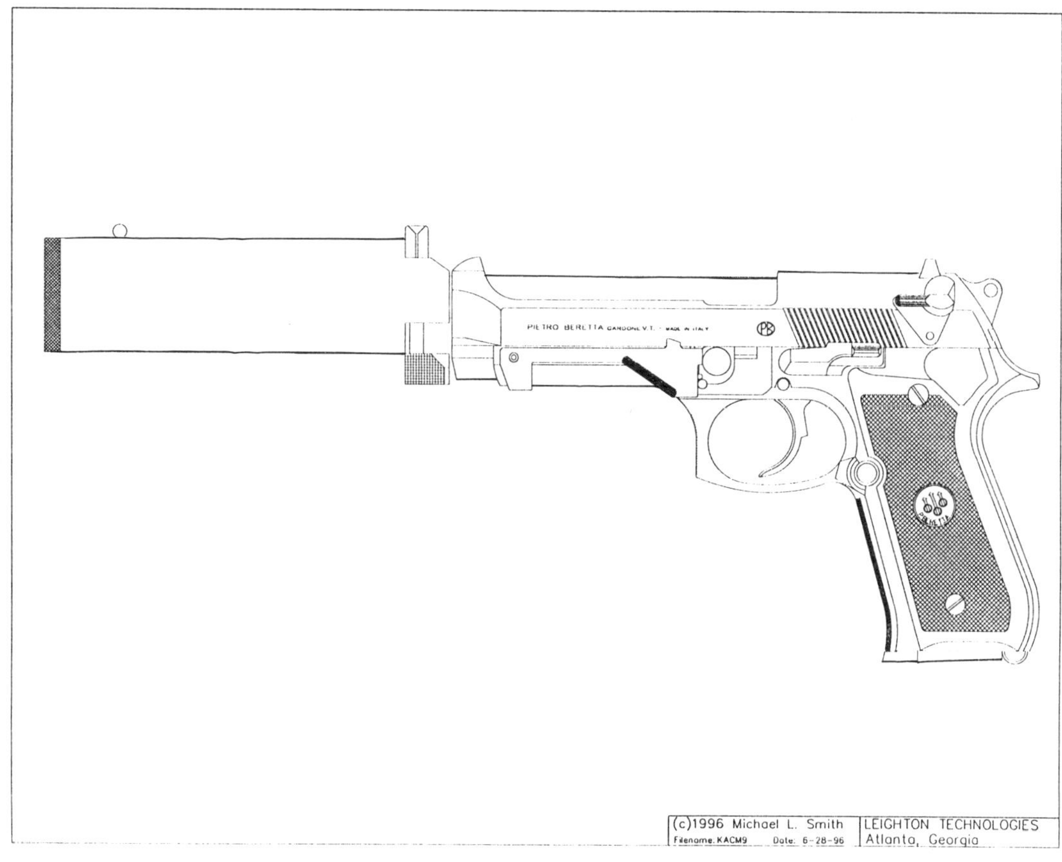

Figure 13.4. Reed Knight solved the Navy's problems with the Mark 22, Mod. O Pistol by going to a stronger Beretta pistol with beefier extractor and by designing a much more robust slide lock that did not stress the frame or slide. Drawing by Mike Smith.

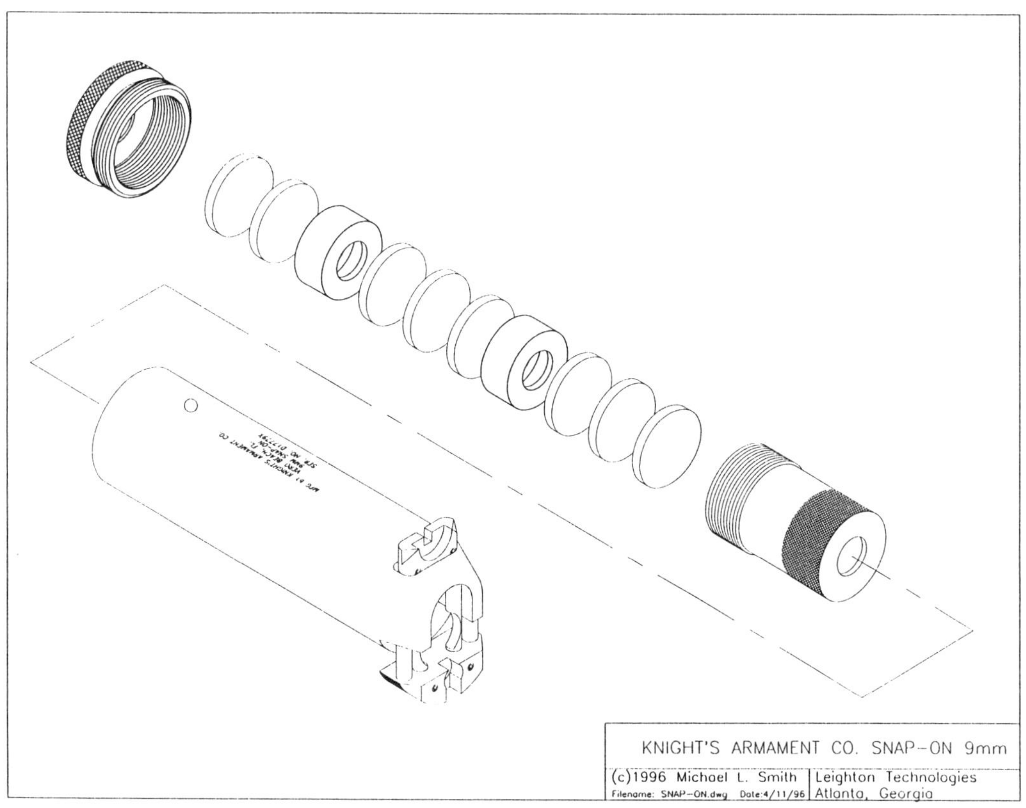

Figure 13.5. The Snap-On from Knight's Armament is the successor to Knight's Hush Puppy suppressor. The Snap-On is currently in use by U.S. Army and Air Force personnel.

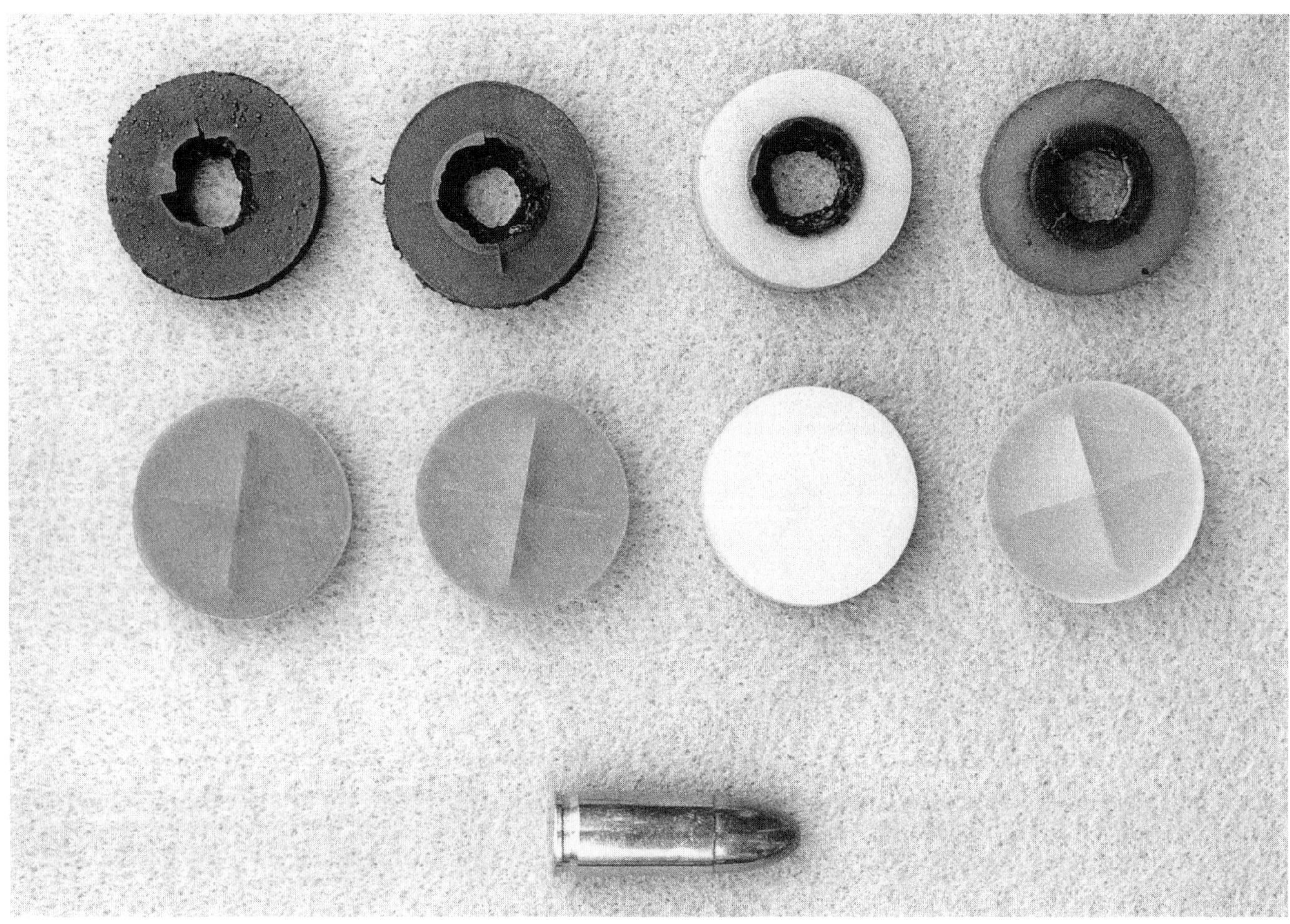

The wipes on top have had 90 rounds of Samson 158 grain subsonic ammo pass through them, yet they still reduce the Beretta's sound signature to about 141 dB.

An inner coaxial chamber (reminiscent of the one found in AWC's MK-9 submachine gun suppressor) of 1.00 inch (2.5 cm) inner diameter extends from the rear to the front cap. The rear 1.5 inches (3.8 cm) of the inner tube is perforated with four rows of 1/8 inch (3.3 mm) holes, with five holes per row. An O-ring-sealed spindle is inserted into the rear of this tube to form a primary and five secondary expansion chambers. The spindle is perforated with four 1/8 inch holes per secondary expansion chamber. Each secondary chamber communicates via four holes in the inner coaxial tube into the outer coaxial expansion chamber. The spindle is inserted into the inner coaxial tube so the two sets of holes are offset by 45 degrees. In front of the spindle are four polyurethane wipes separated 3/8 inch (9.7 mm) from each other by three aluminum spacers with 7/32 inch (5.6 mm) shoulders to provide support for the wipes. An aluminum cap separates the front wipe from the snap ring, which remains permanently in the front of the inner tube.

The polyurethane wipes, which have a durometer reading of 80A and almost seem like a polyester, measure 1.00 inch (25.4 mm) in diameter and 0.25 inch (6.4 mm) in thickness. AWC marketed wipes made from a variety of materials over the years. The most recent version supplied by SCRC uses different materials for each of the four wipes in the stack. Each wipe has an X-shaped cut in the center, with each cut measuring 23/32 inch (18.3 mm) across.

To disassemble this central core, begin by soaking the assembly in powder solvent. Drain. Place

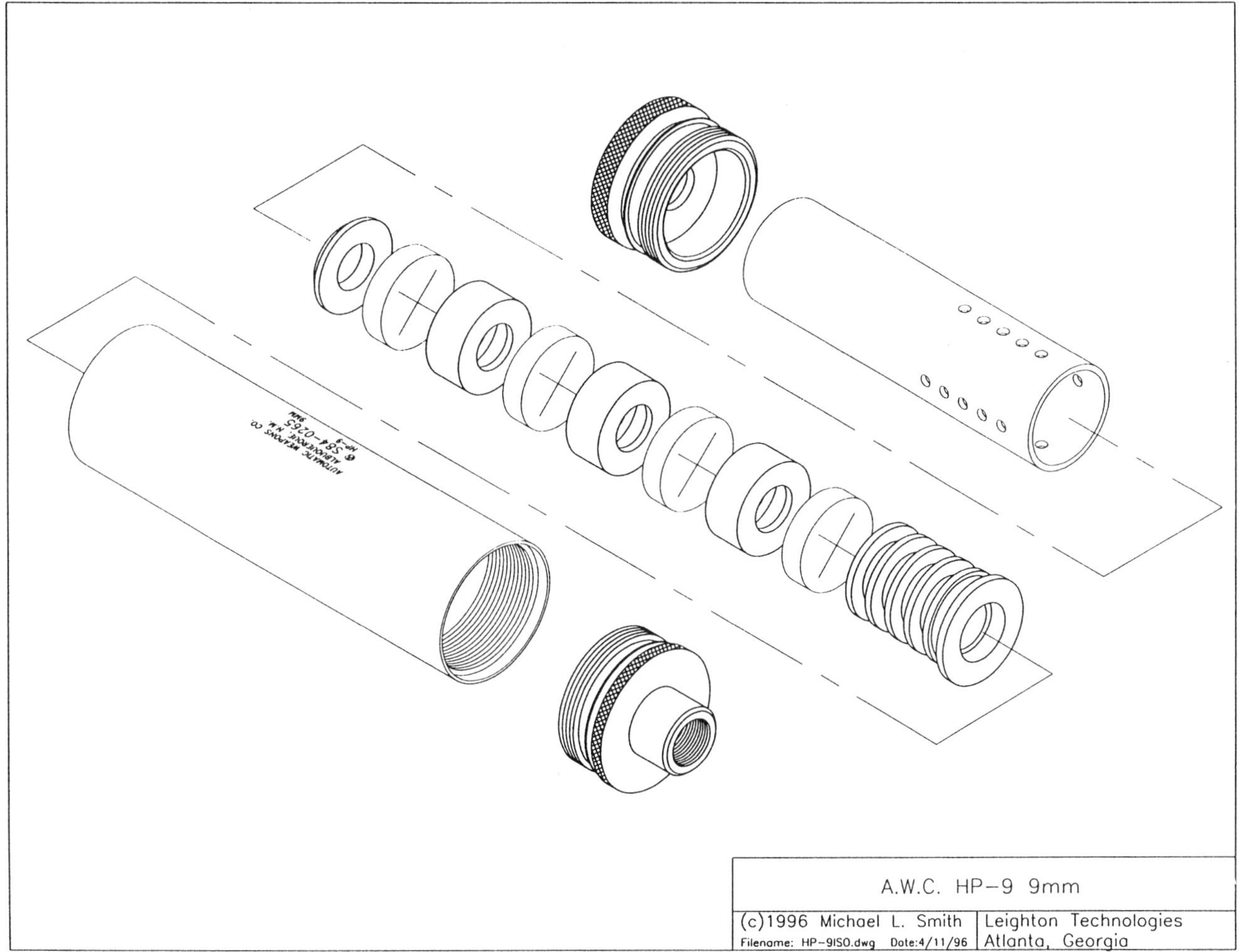

Figure 13.6. Internally, this Hush Puppy suppressor made by AWC Systems Technology is a clone of the second-generation Hush Puppy made by Knight's Armament for the U.S. Navy. The main differences relate to the threading design of the mount and color of the rear end cap. Knight Hush Puppies feature a chrome-plated rear end cap so the operator can see the pistol sights well enough to obtain proper sight alignment. Drawing by Mike Smith.

a 3/4 inch (circa 19 mm) hardwood dowel against the front cap, taking care not to damage the snap ring, and gently drive the stack out the rear of the tube. Clean with almost any solvent, but avoid Hoppes No. 9, which attacks aluminum.

Now to the bottom line. How effectively does the HP-9 reduce a pistol's sound signature? To answer this question, I mounted the suppressor on a Beretta 92F pistol and used Samson 158 grain subsonic ammunition. Supersonic ammunition was not tested for two reasons: 1) supersonic ammo quickly destroys the wipes, and 2) the loud ballistic crack produced by a supersonic projectile destroys the ability to hide the fact that a shot has been fired under most circumstances. Ten rounds were fired to obtain an average sound signature of the unsuppressed pistol, and 90 rounds were fired through virgin wipes to examine their performance with use.

Performance

The unsuppressed Beretta had a muzzle signature of 160 dB. A complete listing of data for all 90 rounds fired through the HP-9 is provided in Table 13.1 (see page 341). Assuming a wipe life of 25 rounds, the HP-9 Hush Puppy had a mean signature of 132 dB, while the mean sound signature only increased to 134 dB for 50 rounds. This represents a reduction of 28 dB for 25 rounds and 26 dB for 50 rounds. Such performance compares favorably with the Vaime A2 suppressor at a reduction of 27 dB and the AWC Invicta at a reduction of 23 decibels. If one measures wipe life using the performance of the AWC Invicta as the yardstick, the wipes will last 35 to 40 rounds with Samson subsonic ammo before the wipes should be replaced.

AWC HP-9 suppressor disassembled.

Not shown by these data is the fact that the Hush Puppy produces a lower frequency sound signature than the other suppressors, making the sound less recognizable as a gunshot. When shooting at paper targets, the dominant sound produced by the Hush Puppy was the sound of the bullets striking the wipes inside the can. When shooting at flesh (in this case a feral dog attacking a valuable horse), the dominant sound was the bullet striking the target.

Until Reed Knight developed a new generation of suppressor (called the Snap-On) based on similar technology and Vaime developed a lightweight design that did not use wipes, the Hush Puppy was my favorite 9mm pistol suppressor. It is light, compact, and highly effective. The wipes generate more back pressure than wipeless designs. Combined with its light weight, this enables the Hush Puppy to allow reliable cycling on a much broader array of pistols than competing designs.

Unfortunately, this increased back pressure also forces hot gases and powder residue out the rear of the barrel into the shooter's face. This is unpleasant and dangerous without eye protection, but this is a small price to pay for its sweet sound and high reliability. Another major liability is that the thick wipes degrade accuracy and limit the weapon's effectiveness to several armspans. Another liability of this design is that wipes are expensive. A more serious problem for civilian and law-enforcement users is that wipes became difficult to obtain since legislation in 1986 decreed that individual suppressor parts were restricted items. The legislation required that an individual would have to return the Hush Puppy on a Form 5 to the manufacturer every time he needed new wipes. Clearly, that was not practical.

Table 13.1. Change in sound signature (measured in decibels) of AWC HP-9 Hush Puppy suppressor (starting with virgin wipes) using Samson 158 grain subsonic ammunition.

SHOT NUMBER	dB	SHOT NUMBER	dB	SHOT NUMBER	dB
1	134	31	135	61	141
2	133	62	134	62	141
3	132	33	135	63	143
4	134	34	137	64	139
5	133	35	135	65	141
6	132	36	135	66	140
7	134	36	138	67	140
8	132	38	137	68	141
9	133	39	138	69	140
10	132	40	136	70	141
11	130	41	137	71	141
12	131	42	136	72	141
13	135	43	138	73	141
14	134	44	138	74	140
15	135	45	138	75	140
16	133	46	138	76	139
17	131	47	139	77	139
18	130	48	139	78	140
19	134	49	139	79	140
20	134	50	138	80	142
21	132	51	137	81	140
22	133	52	138	82	142
23	131	53	141	83	141
24	133	54	142	84	141
25	131	55	140	85	142
26	134	56	139	86	141
27	134	57	140	87	141
28	130	58	141	88	143
29	132	59	141	89	140
30	132	60	142	90	141

Tim Bixler of SCRC developed an ingenious solution to this problem that complies fully with the 1986 legislation. He designed a cheap, voluminous suppressor called the Mark 100 that contains 100 randomly packed urethane wipes that fit the HP-9. A qualified individual or law enforcement agency can purchase the Mark 100 for not much more than the value of the wipes alone and then repack the Hush Puppy 25 times. When more wipes are needed, the Mark 100 can is simply transfered back to Bixler on a Form 5 (one does not need to be a dealer or pay a transfer tax), and he refills the can at the bargain price of $150. That's substantially less per wipe than the retail price before the 1986 legislation, so the refills are an exceptionally good deal. (Owners of Reed Knight's latest Snap-On Suppressor should note that they can obtain 200 of the new 1/8 inch/3.3 mm wipes for the same price as 100 of the 1/4 inch wipes.) This process is still a substantial inconvenience, however, since the BATF paperwork commonly takes 60 to 90 days in each direction. Thus, the 1986 legislation has effectively killed this technology for the civilian and law-enforcement markets.

While the Hush Puppy remained the smallest effective 9mm silencer and continued to fill an important tactical niche two decades after its introduction, the search continued for a light and effective 9mm suppressor that provided better accuracy and did not require rebuilding after one or two magazines of ammunition.

The Vaime A2 suppressor mounted on a Beretta 92F pistol (called the "Pistol, Semi-automatic, 9mm, M9" in milspeak) may be long, but the weight does not seriously affect this operator's speed of target acquisition.

VAIME A2

Researchers at Oy Vaimennin Metalli Ab (Vaime) in Finland developed an interesting solution. No longer in business, Vaime was for a time one of the world's most experienced manufacturers dedicated to the design and production of suppressors. The factory produced suppressors marketed under the Vaime name and made integral suppressors for manufacturers of weapons that marketed the suppressed weapons under their own brand name. Vaime seemed to specialize in light suppressors that were idiot-proof when maintenance (i.e., cleaning) was eventually required. They also produced what was in its heyday the most effective sniper rifle with an integral suppressor that was accurate with 7.62x51 NATO subsonic ammunition.

North American Sales International in Midland, Texas, became the authorized agent for

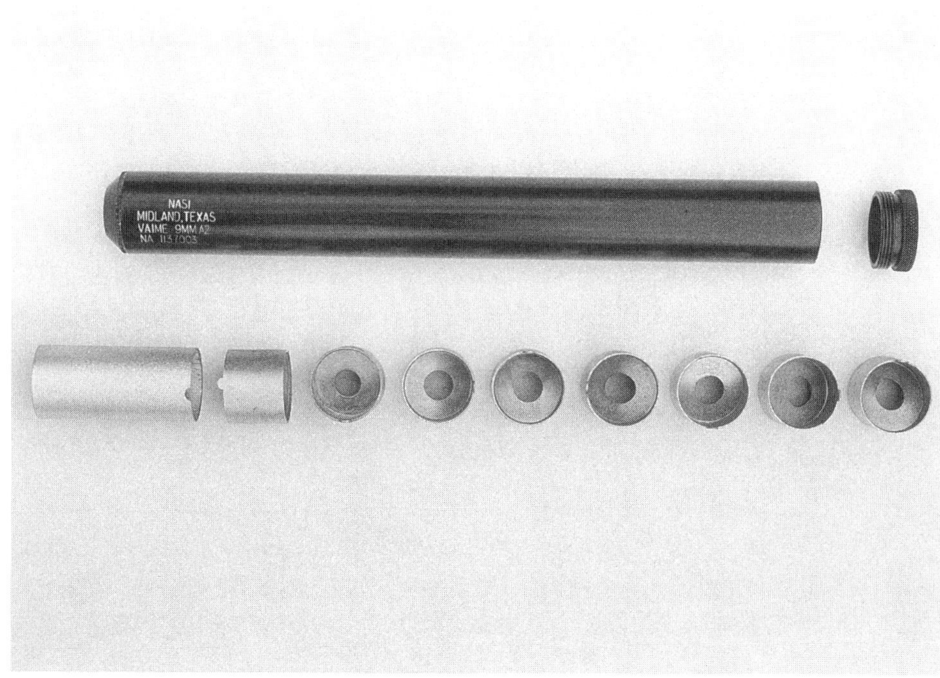

The aluminum tube of the Vaime A2 suppressor contains a baffled primary expansion chamber plus eight slanted baffles with integral spacers that incorporate a unique tongue and groove arrangement that automatically indexes each slanted baffle 90 degrees from the preceding one.

Vaime suppressors in the Western Hemisphere in the mid-1980s until management problems precipitated the company's demise several years later. North American Sales manufactured a full line of Vaime suppressors at its Texas facilities that were transferable to government agencies and qualified U.S. citizens.

Design

The Vaime A2 suppressor consists of an aluminum tube, two end caps, and a series of nine cast-aluminum slanted baffles. The baffles incorporate an ingenious built-in spacer with a tongue and groove system that automatically offsets each baffle from the preceding one by 90 degrees. These baffles seem to be the same baffles used in the Vaime submachine gun suppressor, only they have been turned down to minimal wall thickness to reduce the can's diameter and weight.

The suppressor works by rerouting hot gases produced by a fired cartridge so that the gases can be slowed and cooled before they exit the suppressor. When the bullet exits the barrel and enters the suppressor, the expanding gases are vented into a large expansion chamber that incorporates the rearmost baffle. As the bullet continues through the suppressor, it passes through eight more baffles equally spaced in the suppressor tube and then exits through the front end cap. This cap screws into the suppressor tube, and the rear cap (which is threaded to screw onto the barrel) is glued permanently to the tube. Although gluing on the rear cap lowers the cost of manufacturing the unit, the suppressor would be easier to clean if the rear cap could be removed from the tube (i.e., unscrewed) for cleaning, which would make the removal of encrusted internal components much easier.

Pistol suppressors generally obscure pistol sights, so I sent my Beretta to Ray Ketcham, who was best known for his work on combat-style Government Model .45s and combat shotguns. Ketcham designed high sights that are mounted on top of the old sights much like he mounted Burris scopes on the barrels of scout rifles, using a unique tongue and groove approach. Threading the barrel for the suppressor (5/8 x 18 TPI) and making a screw-on thread protector completed the job. Ketcham's company, called the Gunworks, is no longer in operation.

Performance

The Vaime A2 suppressor was tested on a Beretta 92F pistol, which is the commercial variant

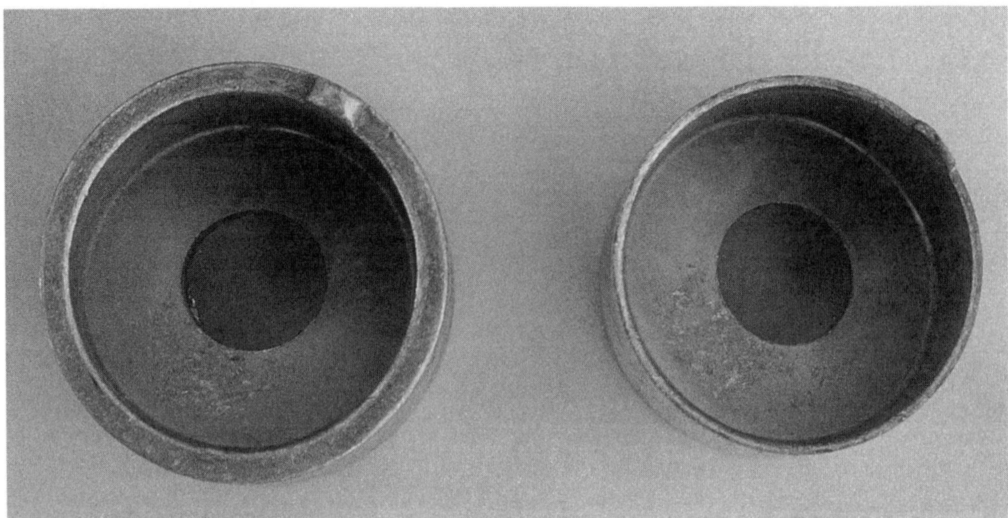

The baffles in the pistol suppressor appear to be turned-down versions of the baffles in the Vaime submachine gun suppressor, which have a thicker wall on the spacer.

The overall cosmetic quality of the Vaime suppressor is poor, but suppressor performance is excellent. The tube has numerous scars and tool marks, and the lettering is of variable quality. Note that the suppressor was originally stamped A3 and then restamped A2.

of the U.S. service pistol ("Pistol, Semiautomatic, 9mm, M9" in milspeak). The Beretta is relatively difficult to suppress because of how it operates. Upon firing, the pressure developed by the combustion gases pushes the slide-barrel assembly backward. After a short run, the locking block stops the rearward movement of the barrel. At this point, the block releases the slide, which continues its rearward movement. The slide then extracts and ejects the fired cartridge case, cocks the hammer, and compresses the recoil spring. The slide then moves forward, strips the next cartridge from the magazine, and feeds the cartridge into the chamber. The Beretta is hard to silence because the weight of the suppressor retards the rearward movement of the barrel.

The Beretta's barrel recoils in a straight line like the P38, so it is much more forgiving than pistols based on Browning's designs. A good example of this phenomenon is AWC's Warp 6 suppressor, which functions reliably on the Beretta 92F but requires a recoil booster in the form of a Nielsen device to cycle reliably on a Browning-type pistol.

It turns out that if a suppressor does not use wipes, then the maximum suppressor weight that will enable the Beretta 92F to function reliably is 7 to 8 ounces (198 to 227 g) using 147 grain bullets. A Glock or other Browning-based design will only tolerate a suppressor weight of 3 to 5 ounces, depending on the length of the suppressor. A longer can's center of gravity is farther forward, which increases the rotational moment of inertia. Therefore, longer cans must be lighter for the pistol to cycle.

At first, the Beretta functioned reliably with the Vaime suppressor and Samson 158 grain subsonic ammunition, but the pistol would not cycle using 115 grain Winchester USA supersonic loads. Samson subsonic ammunition generates a lot of unburned powder residue, and the Beretta began to experience stoppages after about 20 rounds. Much of this problem was traced to an unusually rough mechanism that smoothed out after about 400 rounds. Most Berettas will work fresh out of the box with this suppressor. Once broken in, the test gun and suppressor functioned reliably with all ammunition.

I tested the sound signature of the Vaime A2 suppressor using both the Samson subsonic and Winchester supersonic ammunition at a temperature of 65 °F (18 °C) and compared it to the signature of an unsuppressed Beretta using the same ammunition and barrel length. The sound signatures are listed in Table 13.2 and the net sound reductions appear in Table 13.3 (both tables appear on page 347).

Using subsonic ammunition, the Vaime A2 suppressor lowered the Beretta's sound signature from 159 to 132 dB, a net sound reduction of 27 dB. Using supersonic ammunition, the suppressor lowered the sound signature from 161 to 135 dB, a reduction of 26 dB.

While the Vaime A2 suppressor provided similar performance to the Hush Puppy with subsonic ammunition, it exhibited two problems common with large-bore rifle and pistol suppressors. These problems both occur with the first shot: a much louder first shot and "first round flash," which is a particular liability during night operations. Both phenomena occur whether using subsonic or supersonic ammunition. The first round using subsonic ammo is about 7 dB louder than subsequent shots. The first round using supersonic ammunition is about 8 dB louder than subsequent shots.

This lowers the suppressor's efficiency (for the first round only) to a 20 dB drop for subsonic and an 18 dB reduction for supersonic ammunition. To put these numbers in perspective, a Vietnam-era SIONICS silencer for the 9mm Ingram M10 submachine gun probably reduced a weapon's sound signature by 26 dB. The additional noise from the first shot might jeopardize some missions, so it is useful to understand why this phenomenon occurs and what can be done about it.

The loud first shot is caused by secondary combustion of unburned powder residue and ignitable gases from the first shot. The first shot consumes most of the oxygen in the suppressor, so subsequent shots aren't as loud. The effect of the first shot lasts for several minutes. This knowledge led to a common solution by American snipers in Vietnam, which was to fire a round into the ground before entering the operational area, and then immediately tape the opening of their rifle suppressor to seal out fresh air. Another common strategy was to spray aerosol bug repellent into the suppressor. This replaced the oxygen in the suppressor with inert gas. Yet another approach is to add a small amount of water, grease, or oil to eliminate this problem. These materials evaporate with the first shot, cooling the combustion gases and largely eliminating both first-round pop and first-round flash with the Vaime 9mm pistol suppressor.

What about size, weight, and ease of handling? The suppressor measures 9.5 inches (24.1 cm) long and has a diameter of 1.25 inches (3.2 cm), yet it only weighs 12.3 ounces (349 g). The suppressor is too long for practical holster carry when mounted on the pistol, but its weight does not inhibit the speed of target acquisition.

Finally, some observations on maintenance of the Vaime suppressor would be useful. Before using the Vaime A2 suppressor for the first time, it should be completely disassembled. If the front end cap will not unscrew, shoot one round through the completely assembled suppressor and then immediately try to unscrew the front end cap again.

Unfortunately, the threads of the front end cap are not anodized in the American-made variant of this suppressor, so they are especially vulnerable to galling and corrosion. But even if the threads were anodized, it would still be essential to treat them with an antiseize compound. Colloidal molybdenum or copper compounds designed for high-temperature applications seem to

Vaime A2 suppressor on Beretta 92F with custom elevated sights by Ray Ketcham of the Gunworks.

work the best. Without such treatment, I have seen threaded suppressor components bond—sometimes permanently—after as few as 500 noncorrosive rounds.

Conclusions

The Vaime A2 is a light and effective 9mm suppressor that will function reliably with the Beretta 92F pistol. One of the first commercially successful dry, wipeless pistol suppressors and a significant achievement in its day, the Vaime can be considered both loud and long by standards of today. About the time of the Vaime's introduction, several designers began to develop wet technologies that used coolant media inside a suppressor. This strategy enabled the development of shorter and quieter designs. One of the first commercial entries using wet technology was the Invicta from AWC Systems Technology.

Table 13.2. Sound signatures in decibels of 9mm pistol suppressors.

GUN	SUPPRESSOR	WINCHESTER 115 GR SUPERSONIC	SAMSON 158 GR SUBSONIC	TEMP., °F (°C)
Beretta 92F	None	—	160	65(18)
Beretta 92F	AWC HP-9	—	132[a]	65(18)
Beretta 92F	None	161	159	65(18)
Beretta 92F	Vaime A2	135	132	65(18)
Beretta 92F	None	160	160	65-68(18-20)
Beretta 92F	AWC Invicta	140	137	65-68(18-20)
Inglis Hi-Power	None	163	160	12(-11)
Inglis Hi-Power	Larand	132	131	12(-11)
Beretta 92F	None	162	161	82(28)
Beretta 92F	Warp 6[b]	132	129	82(28)
Beretta 92F	Warp 6[c]	135	133	82(28)

[a] based on 25 rather than 10 rounds
[b] without recoil regulator installed
[c] with recoil regulator installed

Table 13.3. Net sound reductions in decibels of 9mm pistol suppressors.

GUN	SUPPRESSOR	WINCHESTER 115 GR SUPERSONIC	SAMSON 158 GR SUBSONIC	TEMP., °F (°C)
Beretta 92F	AWC HP	--	28[a]	65(18)
Beretta 92F	Vaime A2	26	27	65(18)
Beretta 92F	AWC Invicta	20	23	65-68(18-20)
Inglis Hi-Power	Larand	31	29	12(-11)
Beretta 92F	Warp 6[b]	30	32	82(28)
Beretta 92F	Warp 6[c]	27	28	82(28)

[a] based on 25 rather than 10 rounds
[b] without recoil regulator installed
[c] with recoil regulator installed

AWC INVICTA

The Invicta was part of a new generation of pistol suppressors developed by Lynn McWilliams that used coolant media rather than wipes to achieve good sound reduction in a small, light package. The Invicta was specifically designed for the Beretta 92F and its Taurus clone. Its sibling, the Abraxas, was engineered for the 9mm H&K P9S (this early Abraxas was a very different design than the suppressor of the same name introduced in the mid-1990s by AWC Systems Technology). And the Exeter was designed for semiautomatic and fully automatic weapons chambered in .22 rimfire.

Cooled Suppressors

Suppressor cognoscenti have used liquids or greases to improve suppressor performance by cooling combustion gases since the 1950s, although the first actual use of liquid coolant in a suppressor dates back at least as far as an Italian company in the late 1920s. In the mid-1960s, the U.S. Army's Human Engineering Laboratory suggested adding fluid such as water or bug spray into its 5.56x45mm M2 and M4 suppressors to eliminate the first-round pop, which is a phenomenon common to muzzle cans and many integral suppressors. The U.S. Army's Springfield Armory tested a captured Chinese Type 37 silenced submachine gun in 1964 that used mesh and felt soaked in oil to improve performance. This 9x19mm imitation of the silenced OSS M3 "Greasegun" was apparently influential. Four years later, the U.S. Army's Frankford Arsenal issued a study (Report R-1896) that analyzed silencer principles, designs, and performance. The report suggested introducing "a highly volatile solid or liquid into the propellant gas just prior to propellant exit from the silencer" to improve performance.

Charles A. "Mickey" Finn raised the use of coolants to high art in the early 1980s by designing suppressors specifically to hold and dispense coolants as needed. I believe Lynn McWilliams of AWC Systems Technology subsequently coined the phrase "artificial environment" cells to describe the relevant internal structures designed to use coolant liquids and greases. Finn's use of coolants was patented in Europe, South Africa, and Australia. Although Finn's U.S. patent mentions his use of coolants, no claim is made on this aspect of his design in the States. Inert gases have also been studied as coolant media, and Lynn McWilliams has conducted some particularly interesting research in this area. Suppressors that use liquid or grease coolants are commonly referred to as "wet" cans, while suppressors that do not use a liquid or grease are called "dry" cans.

The use of coolants has both advantages and disadvantages. The advantages include: 1) the elimination of first-round pop, 2) a substantial reduction in the weapon's sound signature compared to a comparably sized dry can, and 3) the ability to design a much smaller wet can than would be possible with a dry design. The principal tactical liability is that a wet can liberates a small cloud of mist with every shot, which can disclose the operator's position. The other liability is that the suppressor must be refilled with coolant every 3 to 30 rounds, depending on the design of the suppressor and the particular weapon used with the can. The last major liability is that full-auto fire purges coolant too rapidly to make wet suppressors practical for this application.

Wet technology has proved to be irresistible when designing small, light suppressors for semiautomatic pistols in recent years. So it should come as no surprise that the AWC Invicta suppressor uses a grease coolant to achieve its substantial performance in such a small package. The high latent heat of evaporation of lithium grease makes it particularly suitable for this application.

Invicta Design

The Invicta is 8.0 inches (20.3 cm) long and 1.38 inches (3.5 cm) in diameter. The suppressor weighs 7.0 ounces (201 g). The end caps and tube are made of black anodized aluminum. The end

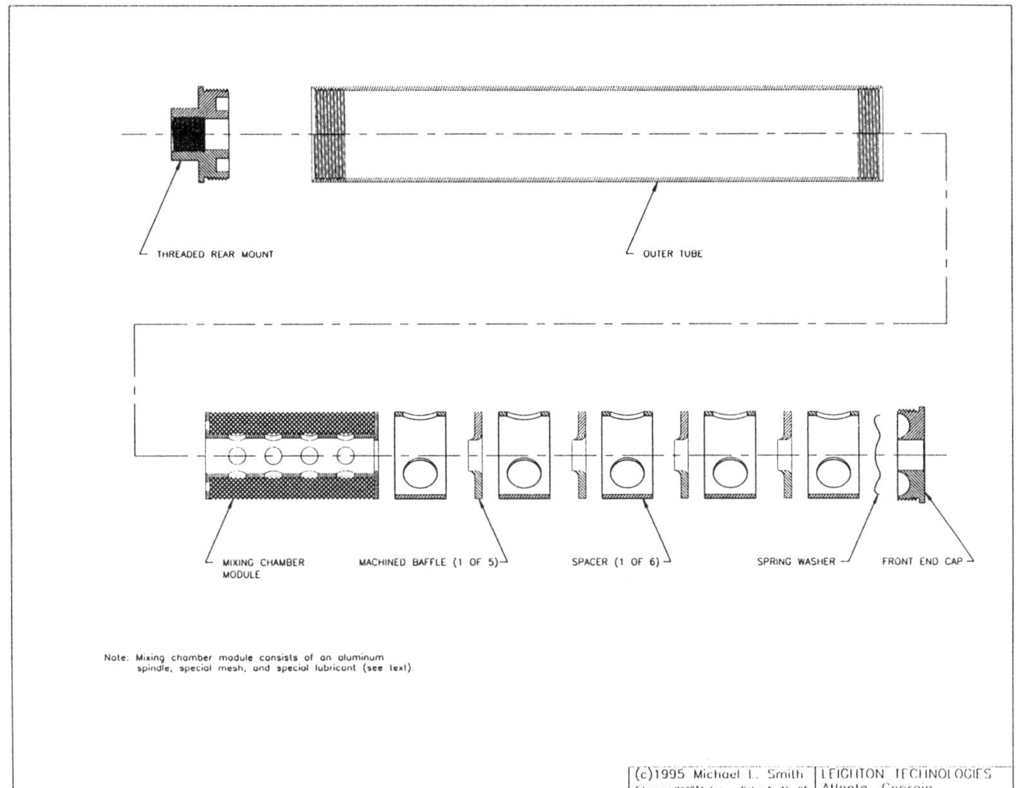

Figure 13.7. The Invicta suppressor from AWC Systems Technology was part of a new generation of pistol suppressors developed by Lynn McWilliams that used coolant media rather than wipes to achieve good sound reduction in a small, light package. The Invicta was designed specifically for the Beretta 92F and its Taurus clone.

caps are knurled, so the suppressor can be disassembled without tools. Behind the front end cap is a spring washer that keeps the stack of five baffles and six spacers aligned snugly against the mixing chamber module at the rear of the suppressor (see Figure 13.7).

This mixing chamber module and its special lubricant are the key to the suppressor's performance. The module is wrapped in mesh that is saturated with Mobil Premium Lubricating Grease, Mobilith SHO 460. Some grease vaporizes with each shot, which cools the suppressor, combines with any resident oxygen, and flushes out powder residue. This system eliminates the problems of first-round pop and first-round flash that commonly plague large-caliber suppressors. Furthermore, the grease lowers the sound signature relative to the same design without the lubricant. Wheel bearing grease can be used in a pinch, but it will smoke excessively.

This vaporizing lubricant may also eliminate the need to coat all threads with a high-temperature antiseize compound, as long as the suppressor is cleaned and the mixing chamber module is lubricated carefully and correctly every 100 rounds. Nevertheless, I always used a molybdenum antiseize compound on the threads rather than risk permanent bonding of the end caps to the tube.

Disassembly and cleaning of the Invicta are straightforward. But lubrication and reassembly require careful attention to detail or the suppressor could be damaged.

To begin disassembly, remove the two end caps by unscrewing them counterclockwise. Use a large dowel or a similar object to push the guts of the suppressor out the back of the suppressor tube. This will leave the forward-most spacer and spring washer in the front of the tube. These are easily removed with your fingers.

Cleaning this wet can proved to be much easier than its contemporary dry cans. The front end cap, spacers, and baffles can simply be wiped clean. No soaking in solvent overnight. No elbow grease with a bronze brush. Just wipe clean. Then wipe the inside of the tube clean with a rag and the dowel used to push out the suppressor's guts. Use Q-Tips to remove all the grease that has

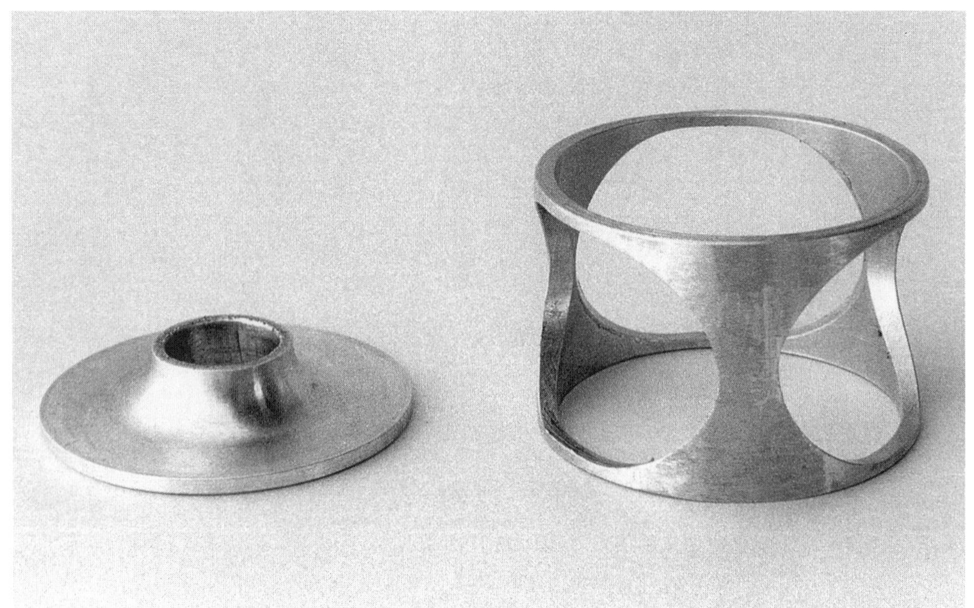

Baffle and skeletonized spacer from AWC Invicta.

The AWC Invicta mounted on the Beretta 92F.

accumulated in the collection recesses of the rear end cap. Remove any remaining grease with a paper towel. Finally, lubricate the mesh on the mixing chamber module.

Proper lubrication is critical to ensure that the suppressor can be disassembled after another 100 rounds, to maintain maximum sound reduction, and to eliminate first-round pop and first-round flash. Use a heaping tablespoon of the grease supplied with the suppressor. Completely cover the mesh of the mixing chamber module. Force the grease down into the mesh by slapping the grease with your fingers. Continue this process until some grease becomes visible in the central bore. *Do not* allow any grease to enter the grease collection recess in the rear suppressor cap.

Reassembly of the Invicta shares a potential problem with the M60 general-purpose machine gun. A critical part can be installed backward. To reassemble the Invicta, first push the mixing chamber module into the rear of the tube. The front of the module goes in first. This is critical. The front features threads and a small hole, while the rear of the module features a relief cut and a large hole. It is imperative that the bullet enter the large hole first. Now screw on the rear end cap hand tight.

Place the suppressor upright on a flat work surface with the rear end cap on the surface. Insert a spacer followed by a baffle. Repeat this process, alternating baffles and spacers until the last spacer is used. Install the spring washer, and screw on the front end cap. If the front end cap does not seat fully, then a baffle is misaligned, and it becomes essential to correct this problem before using the suppressor.

Performance

Now that we've seen how the Invicta works, let's examine how well it works. I tested the sound signature of the Invicta suppressor using both the Samson 158 grain FMJ subsonic and Winchester USA 115 grain supersonic ammunition. The temperature varied from 65 to 68 °F (18 to 20 °C) during these tests.

Even though the AWC catalogue claimed that the Invicta lowers a pistol's sound signature by 33 dB, I was unable to duplicate that performance. Using subsonic ammunition, the AWC Invicta lowered the Beretta's sound signature by 23 dB (from 160 to 137 dB). Using subsonic ammo on a colder day, the Vaime A2 suppressor lowered the sound signature 27 dB (from 159 to 132). Using supersonic ammunition, the Invicta lowered the sound signature 20 dB (from 160 to 140). Using supersonic ammo on a colder day, the Vaime A2 suppressor lowered it 26 dB (from 161 to 135). The Beretta/Invicta system did not cycle reliably with the 115 grain supersonic load. This should not be surprising, since the Invicta was designed to use 158 to 170 grain subsonic rounds, which deliver a greater recoil impulse to the slide.

Thus, based on 10-shot averages, the Vaime A2 suppressor is quieter than the AWC Invicta regardless of whether subsonic or supersonic ammo is used. Those data are relevant for sport shooters interested in discreet target practice. But that's not the whole story for tactical users of suppressed pistols.

The tactical use of suppressed pistols demands that the system hide the fact that a shot has been fired. That usually means a single subsonic round to the head of the target. If a second shot is required, the mission has probably been blown. Therefore, first-round performance is crucial in the tactical environment.

The AWC Invicta below the longer but thinner Vaime A2 suppressor.

The first round through the Invicta was no louder than subsequent shots. But the first subsonic round through a Vaime A2 suppressor was about 7 dB louder than subsequent shots. This lowered the Vaime's efficiency (for the first round only) to a 20 dB drop for subsonic ammunition. Recall that the Invicta's suppression of the first subsonic round was 23 dB. This gives a tactical edge to the Invicta.

What about size, weight, and ease of handling? The Invicta is 1.5 inches shorter than the Vaime A2. Even though it's 0.13 inch larger in diameter, this in no way interferes with Ray Ketcham's (The Gunworks) custom sights for the Beretta. And the Invicta weighs about 5 ounces less. Yet, in spite of these differences, they both handled well.

The AWC Invicta has a much better finish than the Vaime A2. The Vaime tube still shows the scratches and dings common on aluminum tubing when it arrives from the supplier, and the anodizing itself appears inferior to the Invicta. The Invicta is much easier to clean. The Vaime is foolproof to reassemble, whereas it is easy to install the mixing chamber module backward in the Invicta. Both are quiet enough for sporting use, and both are suitable for animal control and tactical use with subsonic ammo. The Invicta is quieter on the first shot, but the Vaime A2 is quieter on subsequent shots.

The critical difference is durability. The Invicta features a thin tube with thin skeletonized spacers that do not reinforce the tube. As a result, several Invictas have experienced structural failures of the tube. The bottom line is that all Invictas should be retired from active service and relegated to display as an interesting and important design in the evolution of centerfire pistol suppressors. The Vaime suppressor tested for this study, on the other hand, continues to provide acceptable service after nearly a decade of use.

About the same time that AWC began to market the Invicta, the unusual and patented suppressor designs of Don Walsh (which have been intermittently available over the last decade under the Larand brand name) reappeared in the marketplace. Perhaps the most interesting feature of the Larand patent was that the design enabled Walsh to produce eccentric suppressors that allowed the use of iron sights on pistols and rifles.

LARAND

Don Walsh began by rebuilding other people's WWII vintage suppressors and marketing suppressors of his own design in the late 1970s. Early on, he concluded that mesh technology held more potential than baffle technology, and his designs reflected that strategy. A book published in 1983 showed a photo of wire mesh donuts as the prime internal components of Larand suppressors, but Walsh told me in May of 1989 that the secrets he revealed in that interview were a disinformation campaign meant to throw off the competition. He cited the design of a particular company's .22 and .25 caliber pistol suppressors as one example of the success of his disinformation.

His interests largely turned from the civilian to the law enforcement and military markets in 1981. His 1982 Interrand Corporation catalog listed suppressors for 9mm pistols, 5.56mm assault rifles, 7.62mm battle rifles, belt-fed machine guns to .50 caliber, and sniper rifles. Prices ranged from $250 for submachine gun cans to $750 for suppressing the .50 BMG Ma Deuce.

Then Walsh dropped out of sight for quite some time, apparently pursuing other projects overseas. Larand suppressors reappeared in the marketplace in 1989 through Arlington Armament Services (AAS) in Arlington, Virginia. Owned by Francis and Jerome Headley, AAS marketed Larand suppressors fabricated on premises by Don Walsh himself. During a number of long conversations with the Headleys, I developed a real fondness for these guys, and I really wanted to see them succeed.

But it was not auspicious timing for starting up a suppressor business. With the post-Stockton hysteria and the ban on importing semiautomatic rifles, folks seemed to pour their discretionary

Larand suppressor was designed for use with the Inglis Hi-Power pistol with shoulder stock.

funds into the purchase of semiautomatic firearms. Suppressor sales plummeted across the country. It seemed like a good time to send off my prized Inglis Hi-Power and a .45 ACP Heckler & Koch P9S pistol to have custom suppressors installed. I figured I'd get speedy service with the reduced competition for Don's time. In fact, I was told a 30-day turnaround. Perfect.

It didn't work out that way. I sent off my pistols and waited. And waited. Finally, I began to hear rumors that Don Walsh had dropped out of sight again. Then a friend of mine claimed that Walsh was trying to open a bar in Bangkok. It looked like the close of another colorful chapter in the continuing saga of silencer design.

Francis Headley finally sent me the suppressor for my Inglis Hi-Power along with an apology for the very long delay. And he sent a refund for the other suppressor which was "99 percent done" but required a slight boring out of the tube through which the bullet travels. Since only Walsh could perform that operation (his suppressor designs depend on an unusually tight bullet-to-passage fit), Headley felt he could not deliver the can, which was producing large groups from bullet contact with the suppressor's inner tube.

The 9mm can built for my Inglis pistol measures 9-13/16 inches (25.0 cm) long and 1-3/4 inches (4.4 cm) in diameter. The suppressor tube and end caps are made of steel. The can weighs 16.0 ounces (453 g). Competing contemporary designs weighed 7 to 12 ounces. The Larand suppressor was mounted on an Inglis Hi-Power with extra-length barrel. One must use a Bar-Sto barrel made expressly for the *Canadian* version of the pistol, since barrels made for the more common European Hi-Powers are not interchangeable.

Testing was conducted at an ambient temperature of 12 °F (-11 °C). Neither Winchester USA 115 grain supersonic nor Samson 158 grain subsonic ammunition would cycle the action, which had to be worked by hand after each shot.

The eccentric design of the Larand suppressor permits use of the Hi-Power's sights.

Performance

Using Winchester supersonic ball, the Larand suppressor lowered the pistol's report from 163 to 132 dB, a net sound reduction of 31 dB. The first round through a cold can was 1 dB louder. This compares well with contemporary competition. The AWC Invicta, for example, lowered a Beretta 92F's sound signature 20 dB, and the Vaime A2 reduced the Beretta's report by 26 dB.

Using Samson subsonic ammunition, the Larand suppressor lowered the pistol's report from 160 to 131 dB, a net sound reduction of 29 dB. This also compares well with contemporary designs cited in Tables 13.2 and 13.3. The AWC Invicta lowered a Beretta 92F's sound signature 23 dB, and the Vaime A2 reduced the Beretta's report by 27 dB.

The Larand suppressor may achieve its performance in part through its large size and substantial weight. This particular suppressor exceeds upper limits of size and weight that can be tolerated on a handgun without a shoulder stock, since its considerable mass significantly retards the speed of target acquisition using a modified Weaver stance. The Larand does, however, balance nicely when employed with the stock.

The sights on the pistol were somewhat obscured by the can but were still usable. The minor irritation of having to cycle the action by hand was offset by the absence of mechanical noise, which can be a real asset in some circumstances.

Another minor irritation was the inferior blueing, which included areas that were apparently too dirty to accept blueing and others where the blueing had been worn off during the assembly process at the factory. The can arrived looking well used, like a seasoned veteran rather than a new, factory-fresh suppressor.

The weight of the can was more disconcerting than I anticipated when I gave Walsh the go-ahead to use the largest diameter available for his pistol suppressors. I've also heard a complaint about the weight of a .45 caliber pistol can from the owner of one made during this same period. Apparently, 1989 production never reached a level to permit the economic anodizing of aluminum tubes, so production may have been limited to suppressors with steel tubes. This is ironic, since Larand suppressors were originally known for their light weight.

What is the future of Larand suppressors? As soon as my suppressor was shipped, no one would either return my phone calls to the AAS answering machine or answer my letters, which included SASEs. AAS went the way of the passenger pigeon. Don Walsh returned to his old stomping grounds in Bangkok, where he still lives at the time of this writing. Even though an individual in Arizona purchased the Larand patent from Walsh sometime around 1990, the Larand suppressors have not reappeared in the marketplace. Technology has evolved well beyond the Larand design, and it is unlikely that these suppressors will reappear on the world stage.

The quest continued for a truly reliable and effective centerfire pistol suppressor that did not employ wipes. One author finally suggested that it was impossible to design an effective wipeless, major-caliber pistol suppressor that would still allow pistol actions to cycle. Then AWC Systems Technology revolutionized the field with the introduction of the Warp 6.

AWC WARP 6

AWC married two very different technologies to produce an effective solution to the problem of achieving substantial sound reduction and reliable functioning of semiautomatic centerfire pistols: the Warp 6 suppressor with Recoil Regulator Device.

The recoil regulator, which suppressor cognoscenti usually call a Nielsen device, was first developed by Qualatec in Oceanside, California. The Nielsen device ensures that the pistol cycles by using combustion gas to briefly counter the inertial effect of the suppressor's weight on the barrel. As previously mentioned, negating the suppressor's inertia is crucial for most pistols (like the Glock, SIG, Ruger P85, Browning Hi-Power, and Beretta) since the weight of the suppressor retards the rearward movement of the barrel, which provides energy to cycle the slide.

The device actually drives the main cylinder body and suppressor away from the barrel, which gives the barrel a momentary relief from the suppressor's burden. Then a spring load on the piston pushes the mass of the suppressor system back toward the barrel, which applies a little more recoil to the barrel assembly.

AWC's Recoil Regulator Device permits the suppression and reliable function of most 9mm pis-

Warp 6 suppressor with Recoil Regulator Device mounted on a Beretta 92F with custom sights by the Gunworks.

tols. Fixed-barrel designs like the H&K P9S do not require the regulator and should not have it installed. The recoil regulator is designed specifically for the Warp 6 suppressor, and AWC only sold the regulator to verifiable owners of the Warp 6.

AWC's catalog says the recoil regulator is made from 304 stainless steel, but it is actually a product of superior metallurgy. AWC uses 17-4-PH heat-treatable stainless with very precise heat treating. I like it when a company actually delivers *more* than it claims.

Although the design looks deceptively simple in theory, it is really difficult to produce in practice. The device requires tolerances that are too demanding to be produced on conventional machine tools. An aerospace precision grinder is required to achieve tolerances of half a thousandth of an inch with meticulous surfaces. Then the components require exacting heat treatment. The recoil regulator device is a remarkable achievement.

The regulator measures 1.5 inches (44.5 mm) long and 1.075 inches (26.9 mm) in diameter. It weighs 4.7 ounces (135 g). It was available in a bead-blasted, optically flat finish or in a black chrome sulfide (which was available at no extra charge when the device was purchased with the Warp 6 suppressor).

The device came with a spanner for disassembly and maintenance every 100 rounds or so. Complete maintenance instructions were also provided. Since the regulator by itself does not lower a pistol's sound signature, the regulator does not require registration with BATF.

The Warp 6 is based on the patented slanted-sidewall designs of Charles A. "Mickey" Finn, a name not heard much among civilian shooters and law enforcement, but highly respected in the Black Ops and SpecOps communities. The Warp 6 suppressor itself is constructed of 304 stainless steel. Like the Warp 3 .22 rimfire suppressor, the Warp 6 is sealed to prevent disassembly. The tube measures 6.75 inches (171.5 mm) long and 0.98 inches (24.5 mm) in diameter. The suppressor weighs 6.7 ounces (190 g). It was bead blasted to provide a nonreflective surface and was also available in a black chrome sulfide finish at a small extra cost ($25 retail).

This was a remarkably small design when it was introduced, especially for a wipeless 9mm suppressor (see Table 13.4, page 358). In fact, the Warp 6 has a smaller volume than most .22 caliber muzzle cans of today. The Warp 6 is even smaller than the Vaime A8 and AWC Archangel, which represented the state of the art in .22 muzzle cans when the Warp 6 was introduced.

One reason the Warp 6 achieves big performance in a small package is because of Finn's proprietary (patented) system of baffles and environment chambers. The Warp 6 also packs in the performance because it employs several lubricants to cool the combustion gases. Internal components are coated with Break Free by spraying the Teflon-based lubricant in each end (most operators soon skip this step). Then about a teaspoon of lithium grease is smeared in the rearmost section of the can. A common lead pencil with hexagonal cross-section or a disposable chopstick makes an excellent tool for applying grease inside the can. With each shot, these lubricants vaporize, cooling the gases. The internal components of the suppressor also slow and cool the gases, robbing them of energy that would be perceived as sound.

A secondary benefit from the lubricants is that they coat the internal components of the can, reducing the rate of carbon buildup. The lubricants greatly facilitate cleaning the can of fouling by unburned powder residue by immersion in a solvent. This is important because the Warp 6 cannot be disassembled for cleaning.

This suppressor was designed for tactical users. When mounted on a Heckler & Koch P9S, the Warp 6 made an interesting choice for amphibious operations. The P9S is desirable for this application because it features both a fixed barrel and a single-column magazine. A swimmer, for example, can lock out of a submarine with the suppressor mounted and the single-column magazine loaded in the gun. The swimmer then rotates the gun until all the air bubbles disappear and chambers a round. The operator could then shoot the gun underwater or poke the end cap of the suppressor out of the water if, for example, he needed to take a target off a boat, platform, or beach. The single-column magazine design and barrel design of the P9S are crucial for this application. The P9S will cycle reliably in semiautomatic when immersed. It is critical, however, that the barrel be completely full of water. A lot of air in the barrel must be avoided.

One informant tells me that the P9S with Warp 6 is "so gosh dang quiet in that environment that it is just unbelievable if you've got the gun below the surface and all you've got sticking out of the water is the front end cap, and the bullet is pushing a column of water ahead of it as it exits the gun."

As far as I know, the P9S is the only 9mm pistol suitable for amphibious operations, such as when a swimmer wears the gun in a holster through the surf, where wet sand can work its way into the magazine. According to one (unconfirmed) source, the double-column, single-position feed magazines of pistols like the Beretta, SIG, and Glock jam, so the swimmer only gets to use the round that was manually racked into the chamber. A second magazine may be inserted, but it will also cease to function after the first round is manually racked into the chamber. While the H&K's magazine design provides much of its reliability in this environment, the gun itself is also toleranced very nicely.

Glock has reportedly delivered special firing pins to the U.S. Navy so the (unsuppressed) Glock can be fired more reliably underwater, but I have not been able to learn whether any progress has been made on magazine reliability.

The lubricants in the Warp 6 must be replaced periodically. Tactical users will want to add grease every time they reload (every 15 to 20 rounds). For most realistic tactical scenarios, more than one shot should not be required, and more than three shots means the shooter is in deep *merde*. Nevertheless, extra lithium grease can easily be carried in small bottles marketed to backpackers. Light oils like WD40 can also be used in place of Break Free, but flammable fluids with low flash points must be avoided.

Performance

AWC's experience suggests that the Beretta 92F does not require the Recoil Regulator Device for reliable functioning with the Warp 6 suppressor. That was not my experience. My own 92F did not function reliably with either Winchester USA 115 grain supersonic or Samson 158 grain subsonic ammo unless the device was installed since the action on this early pistol is particularly rough. This is an unusual problem. A much more likely explanation if a similar problem occurs is that shooters are not gripping the pistol firmly enough or keeping their forearms too loose when shooting. A modified Weaver two-handed stance with stiff wrist and firm isometric tension pulling back with the weak hand will probably cure this problem with any suppressor of reasonable length and weight.

While a firm grip and good stance did not allow my Beretta to function with just the Warp 6 suppressor, the pistol functioned flawlessly when the Recoil Regulator Device was added to the system. The only downside to using the recoil regulator on the Beretta 92F is that it obscures noticeably more of the factory sights than the Warp 6 suppressor, since it has a slightly larger diameter.

The Beretta's factory sights are still theoretically usable with the Warp 6 system, but the sight picture is mediocre and it takes me too long to engage a target. For this reason, I prefer a good set of elevated sights.

To test the performance of the Warp 6 suppressor, I measured sound signatures using Winchester USA 115 grain supersonic and Samson 158 grain subsonic FMJ ammunition. The sound signatures are shown in Table 13.2, and the net sound reductions appear in Table 13.3. Ambient temperature during the testing was 82 °F (28 °C).

One of the design criteria for the Warp 6 was to produce a wipeless suppressor that was as quiet as the Hush Puppy. AWC exceeded this requirement. The Warp 6 without recoil regulator reduced the sound signature of Samson subsonic ammo by 32 dB, while Table 13.3 shows that the Hush Puppy reduced the muzzle signature of this ammo by 28 dB.

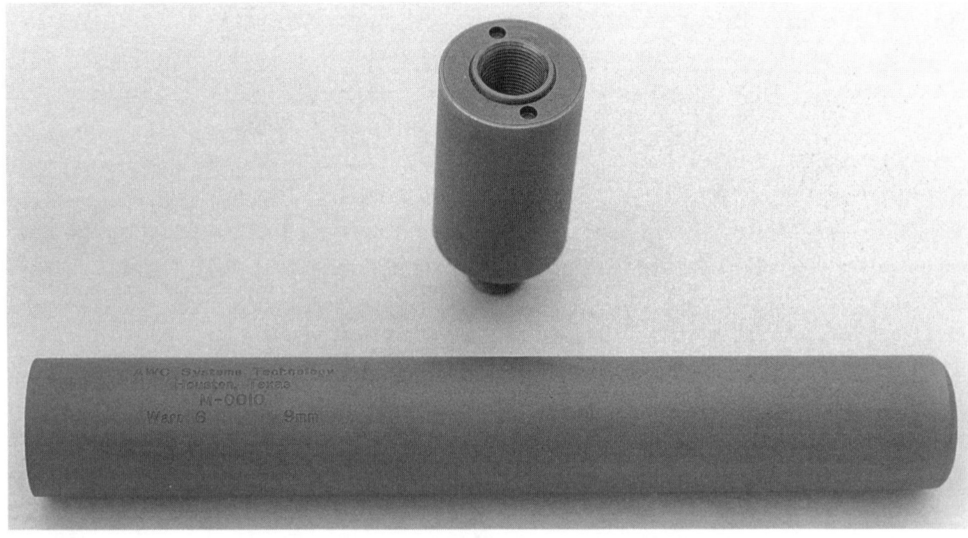

AWC Warp 6 suppressor and dismounted Recoil Regulator Device, which permits reliable semiautomatic functioning on an unprecedented variety of 9mm pistols.

Adding the recoil regulator reduced the suppressor's performance to equal that of the Hush Puppy. That is still excellent performance. But it was a surprise. I expected that the recoil regulator would improve, rather than degrade, the amount of sound reduction achieved by the Warp 6, since it performed work with the combustion gases. I also expected this work to lower the energy level of the gases and thus lower the resultant sound signature. I repeated the experiment several times, taking care to add the same amount of grease and Break Free before every string of 11 rounds. I continued to observe the same results.

While this was a surprise, it is in no way an indictment of the Warp 6 suppressor with Recoil Regulator Device. Quite the contrary. The system demonstrated a level of sound reduction that has proven sufficient on numerous tactical and clandestine operations. It eliminates the logistical hassle of replacing wipes. The system provided a robust design that permits a totally unprecedented variety of handguns to cycle reliably with a suppressor, enabling individuals and agencies to suppress their own 9mm handgun of choice.

The Warp 6 suppressor with Recoil Regulator Device was a formidable achievement in the quest for the ultimate major-caliber pistol suppressor. The system represented a whole new state of the art. The Warp 6 was eventually replaced with a shorter and lighter variant called the Abraxas.

Table 13.4. Volumes of 9mm pistol suppressors compared.

SUPPRESSOR	CUBIC INCHES	CUBIC CENTIMETERS
AWC Warp 6	5	82
AWC HP-9 Hush Puppy	8	123
Vaime A2	11	183
AWC Invicta	11	184
Larand	23	380

AWC NEXUS

The U.S. Joint Special Operations Command (JSOC) recently issued contracts to Colt and Heckler & Koch to develop a new, suppressed .45 caliber offensive pistol. (JSOC includes such special operations forces as the Navy SEALs; the Army's Delta Force, Special Forces, and 75th Ranger Regiment; and the Air Force Special Operations Wing.) The new pistol will be used as the primary weapon for engaging hostiles, whether conventional military or terrorists, at extremely close range. The entire offensive handgun project will be covered in the second volume of *Silencer History and Performance.*

This concept has practical applications within the civilian and law enforcement communities as well. SRT and SWAT teams could use such a suppressed pistol as an entry weapon as well as for hostage rescue and other scenarios. Animal control personnel would find this system much more effective on feral dogs than the traditional .22 rifle. Homeowners could use the system as a home-defense weapon that wouldn't produce both short- and long-term hearing degradation when fired indoors. And sport shooters could exploit additional safe places to shoot if they could eliminate the socially offensive noise pollution of an unsuppressed .45 pistol.

Until recently, the concept of suppressing a .45 pistol in anything remotely resembling a practical package remained pure fantasy land. The problem was twofold. It seemed disproportionately more difficult to design an effective suppressor with a .45 caliber hole in the front than with a .38 caliber (9 millimeter) hole. And any suppressor big enough to do the job was too big and heavy to be practical.

An early attempt to suppress a .45 pistol used a modified barrel bushing that was designed to mate the Military Armament Corporation M10 submachine gun suppressor to the Colt Model 1911 and its clones. But the can obscured the pistol's sights and was far too heavy to allow the normal semiautomatic functioning of the pistol. Furthermore, the adapter was badly designed and tended to kill pistol slides after a surprisingly small number of rounds had been fired.

Then Don Walsh designed an eccentric suppressor for the .45 caliber Model 1911 and H&K P9S pistols that allowed the use of the pistols' iron sights. The Model 1911 would not cycle with these Larand suppressors, but the fixed-barrel P9S would. The Larand suppressor was still too bulky for practical employment as a tactical tool, however. Vaime in Finland developed a smaller, lighter .45 pistol suppressor that functioned on the P9S. The Vaime can was suitable for tactical employment. But by this time, Heckler & Koch had discontinued the P9S pistol.

Until relatively recently, the venerable old Colt and its clones remained the only practical .45 caliber pistol for the tactical environment. But no one could design a suppressor for the Model 1911 that would permit the gun to cycle reliably, since the weight of the suppressor would retard the rearward movement of the barrel, which provides energy to cycle the slide. Eventually, suppressor and arms designer Tim LaFrance developed an ingenious suppressor with modified Colt pistol that did function reliably in semiautomatic mode. A remarkable technological achievement, the LaFrance system nonetheless was too heavy and expensive to achieve widespread popularity.

Then AWC applied two very different technologies to the problem. A new can was developed that used a small number of slanted-sidewall baffles plus a lithium grease to create artificial environment cells that could cool and slow combustion gases in a much smaller, lighter package than traditional baffle technology. And a Nielsen device was added to briefly counter the inertial effect of the suppressor's weight on the barrel when the gun was fired.

Upon firing, combustion gases leaving the barrel drive the main suppressor body and the recoil regulator's outer collar away from the barrel, giving the barrel a momentary relief from the suppressor's burden. Meanwhile, the same pressure drives the barrel and the recoil regulator's piston in the opposite direction, which applies enough energy to the barrel assembly to initiate proper slide movement for reliable semiautomatic cycling. The rearward piston travel compresses the regulator's spring, which then returns the piston for firing the next round. Unlike the Warp 6 suppressor, the recoil regulator forms an integral part of the suppressor at the rear of the can. Furthermore, an interesting feature of the Nexus regulator is that the device can be turned on and off at will. Turning the regulator on or off takes less than four seconds.

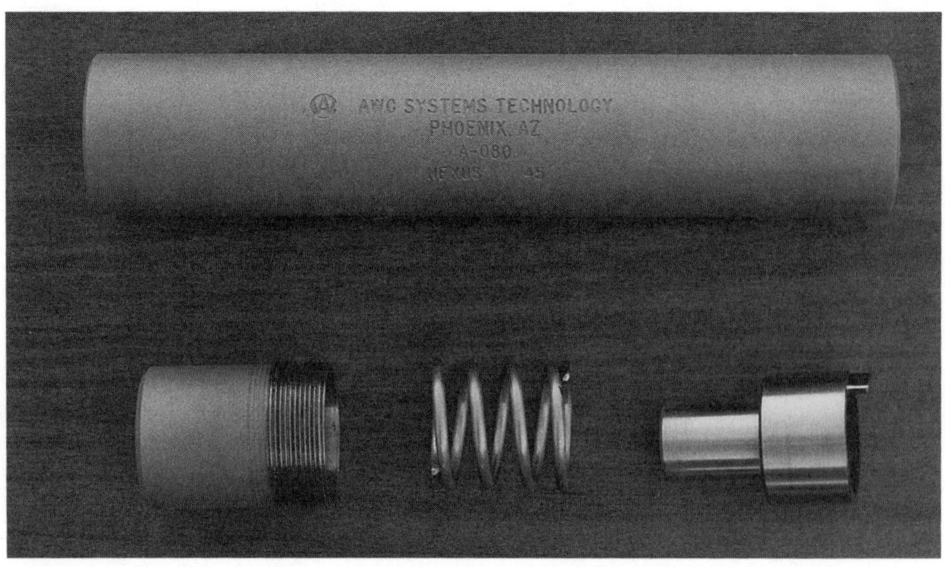

Nexus suppressor with recoil regulator disassembled into its components: outer collar, spring, and piston. The regulator can be turned off in seconds to act as a de facto slide lock.

This gives the operator two interesting tactical choices. The recoil regulator can be turned on to allow multiple hits in semiautomatic mode, where body armor or multiple targets may be encountered. Or the regulator can be turned off to eliminate action noise or to facilitate the recovery of spent brass on those covert missions when shell casings must not be left behind in the operational area.

Using the regulator in the off position as a de facto slide lock warrants further discussion. Using a slide lock on a 9mm pistol with one of Reed Knight's Hush Puppy or Snap-On suppressors lowers the weapon's sound signature dramatically. A slide lock has the same effect on any suppressor using wipes, for this setup significantly increases the residence time of combustion gases in the suppressor, which decreases the amount of energy (sound) escaping from the system per unit time. Turning the Nexus regulator off when using the Colt Model 1911 does not lower the sound signature significantly. While this procedure does eliminate the Colt's modest action noise, turning the regulator off actually increases the muzzle signature by slightly more than 1 dB (see Table 13.5, page 365). Worse, pulling the slide back to eject the spent case is very difficult (much more difficult than a 9mm pistol with a slide lock), and the case tends to jam in the action unless the pistol is held upside down as the slide is pulled back. This was quite frustrating during the sound testing. It would be entirely unacceptable in the tactical environment. I strongly believe that the recoil regulator should be left on by tactical users when firing the Nexus on the Colt Model 1911 unless the recovery of spent cases is absolutely mandatory.

The regulator must be turned off, however, when using the Nexus on fixed-barreled pistols like the H&K P9S to avoid damaging the pistol.

Circumstantial evidence suggests that a 9mm predecessor to the Nexus may have been available to the covert and SpecOps world for some time before AWC brought out the Nexus. An author of best-selling technothriller novels—who is known to have access to a lot of relatively inaccessible information about the military and clandestine worlds—described a remarkably similar can in .22 rimfire in a recent novel, but the suppressed system in his book could not function as described because the suppressor was mounted on a small pistol of necessarily fixed-barrel design. Thus the Navy SEAL in the novel could not have turned off the can's recoil regulator to eliminate the pistol's action noise. A fixed-barrel pistol would have cycled whether the regulator was turned on or off.

I suspect the inspiration for this passage was a 9mm pistol suppressed with a system very similar to the Nexus. Independent hints of hints and rumors of rumors tend to support the view that a 9mm Nexus-like suppressor has been in the U.S. inventory for some time now, at least in limited numbers.

The Nexus suppressor is constructed of 304 stainless steel, and it's available in a matt stainless or black chrome sulfide finish. It is 8.0 inches (20.3 cm) long, 1.4 inches (3.5 cm) in diameter, and weighs 16.0 ounces (450 g).

The Nexus comes with a threaded 5.5 inch (14.0 cm) barrel, which should be fitted to the gun by a competent gunsmith. I'd also recommend that the gunsmith throat the barrel for improved feeding. The barrel includes a thread protector.

Before firing the suppressor, the rear of the can needs to be charged with a lithium-based grease. A large tube of lithium grease is supplied with the suppressor, and it is readily available locally from any Mobil outlet, or more can be purchased from AWC. The Nexus manual suggests that more grease should be added after firing three magazines. The only potential tactical liability of this particular grease is that it produces smoke when a round is fired through the Nexus. A nonsmoking lubricant of some sort would be desirable for those applications where disclosure of the operator's location could be disastrous. Jim Ballou reports that the shaving cream Barbasol works well.

To add grease, grasp the main suppressor tube with the weak hand and unscrew the collar of the recoil regulator (at the rear of the suppressor) in a counterclockwise direction. Separate the recoil regulator from the main suppressor assembly. Use a wooden pencil, disposable chopstick, or similar implement to coat the inner surfaces of the suppressor with about a tablespoon of lithium grease. Do not block the bullet passage itself, as this might increase back pressure.

Now disassemble the recoil regulator, which consists of the outer collar plus a piston and spring. Wipe the parts clean with a cloth or paper towel. Then smear the piston and the inside of the collar with grease. Insert the protruding tang from the piston into one of the two slots cut into the baffle-retention ring, which is the rearmost fitting inside the suppressor tube. Place the spring

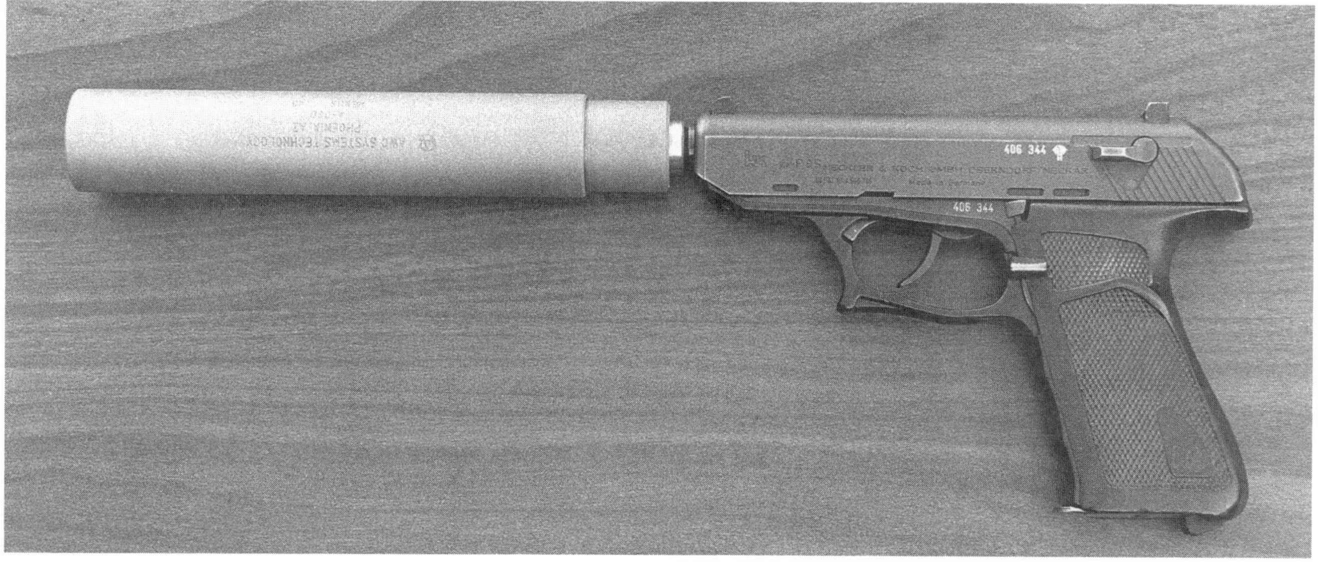

The Nexus recoil regulator must be turned off when the suppressor is mounted on the H&K P9S.

over the piston shaft. Then place the regulator collar over the spring. Push down on the collar until it touches the threads inside the suppressor and turn it clockwise until fully seated. It is quite important to make sure the piston remains centered in the collar (it should be flush or extend slightly from the rear of the collar) or the recoil regulator could be damaged when the gun is fired. Now the suppressor can be screwed onto the special barrel as tightly as possible using hand pressure only.

From time to time, the user will want to clean the Nexus thoroughly. Disassemble the Nexus into its four main components as just described. Wipe off as much grease as possible and soak for several days in a solvent such as Varsol, Kroil, or other suitable solvent. Since there are no aluminum components, Hoppe's No. 9 can also be used. After draining, the components can then be washed in hot soapy water. Flush with very hot water and allow to drain or blow it dry with compressed air. Lubricate and reassemble as already described.

The Nexus, configured as it is after reassembly, will allow the Colt Model 1911 pistol to function reliably in semiautomatic mode. The regulator may be turned off, as previously mentioned, to simulate a slide lock on the Colt or to safely use the can on a fixed-barrel design like the H&K P9S. Before attempting to turn the regulator off, be sure to remove the magazine and clear the weapon first. Close the Colt's slide and lower the hammer on the empty chamber. Check to see whether the suppressor is cool enough to handle.

Hold the pistol in the strong hand and use the weak hand to pull the suppressor away from the gun about 3/16 inch (5 mm) while twisting the can clockwise as if trying to tighten the suppressor on the barrel. Pulling the can away from the gun will take a lot of effort. Twist the can about a quarter turn. The recoil regulator is now in the off position. Twisting the can another quarter turn will return the regulator to its normal on position (semiauto operation on the Colt). It is not necessary to pull the can away from the pistol to select the on position; merely twist the can clockwise until a click is heard.

Some slanted-sidewall suppressors provide excellent sound suppression but disappointing accuracy because the bullet passage is too tight and the bullet can graze one or more baffles as it traverses the suppressor. Therefore, I was interested in testing the accuracy potential as well as the sound signature of the Nexus.

Performance

The ambient temperature during the tests was 45 °F (7 °C). While I normally test pistol-caliber suppressors with Winchester USA ammunition, none was available at the time of the testing. So I used Fiocchi 230 grain FMJ ammunition. Each mean (average) value represents a minimum of 10 rounds, except as noted. Some tests used seven rounds (a full magazine) to get a handle on how many magazine reloads could be fired before the suppressor needed to be repacked with lithium grease.

The test results can be found in Tables 13.5 to 13.8 (see page 365). In a break with tradition, the data are reported to the nearest tenth of a decibel. I normally report data to the nearest whole decibel for several reasons. The nominal accuracy of the B&K meter is 1 dB (even though the meter's scale can be easily interpolated to the nearest tenth of a decibel). Day-to-day variation due to temperature, altitude, humidity, and other imponderables can exceed 1 dB. And shot-to-shot variation in suppressed sound signatures far exceeds 0.1 dB. So comparing data from different days to the nearest 0.1 dB would not be meaningful.

But I always record data to the nearest 0.1 dB since I believe that the tenths are meaningful on the same day under the same conditions. I use the tenths as a sort of quality control on the testing of unsuppressed sound signatures, especially when someone is helping me with the testing. If the unsuppressed signatures vary over a small range, then the quality of the testing is going to be as good as possible when testing the suppressed signatures as well. I'm reporting the Nexus data to the nearest 0.1 dB since I think this extra detail suggests some trends that may be both real and interesting.

The first thing I learned is that Fiocchi ball ammo may be louder than Winchester USA ball. While I was unable to compare their sound signatures under the same test conditions, a variety of prior tests suggest that Winchester ammo may be about 2 dB quieter than Fiocchi.

The sound signatures listed in Table 13.5 show some things one would expect, as well as some surprises. The Nexus performed well. And the Colt pistol with Colt 5 inch (12.7 cm) barrel was a bit louder (0.6 dB) than the Colt pistol with 5.5 inch (14.0 cm) AWC barrel. No surprises here.

But here are some things that surprised me. The Colt pistol with AWC 5.5 inch barrel was 0.5 dB louder than the H&K pistol with AWC 5.5 inch barrel. The Nexus was 1.4 dB quieter on the P9S with both pistols firing in semiautomatic mode. And perhaps the biggest surprise was that the sound signature of the Nexus on the Colt was actually 1.3 dB louder with the recoil regulator turned off. This contrasts with AWC's Warp 6 suppressor, which was 3 to 4 dB quieter without its recoil regulator.

Perhaps the following may explain these surprises. It appears that the "delayed blowback" P9S (H&K doesn't like this term) may absorb more gas energy during the action cycle than the "short recoil" Colt. Less remaining energy means the gas produces less sound as it leaves the pistol barrel. So the P9S is quieter than the Colt. If the Nexus suppressor is slightly more efficient with lower velocity gas, then the suppressed P9S would be quieter than the Colt in semiautomatic mode.

The Colt may be quieter with the regulator turned on (semiautomatic mode) because the work performed in cycling the action absorbs a significant amount of energy from the combustion gases. But the more likely explanation is that operating in semiautomatic mode allows some gas to escape from the ejection port, so less gas escapes from the muzzle of the suppressor as sound.

The net sound reductions shown in Table 13.6 show excellent performance for a small .45 caliber suppressor. A .45 caliber Cobray M10 suppressor with virgin wipe provides a 17 dB reduction. A Maxim Model 1910 silencer gives a 22 dB reduction, and a Precision Arms SO45 suppressor provides a 26 dB reduction.

There remains the question of how frequently the suppressor should be repacked with lithium grease. In a sense, this is a purely academic question for the professional operator, since all surprise on a mission would have been lost before the first magazine was emptied. If action continued after seven or eight rounds, the professional would want to remove the suppressor at the earliest possible moment to improve the speed of target acquisition. Furthermore, there are valid psychological reasons (relevant to both the operator and his opponents) for wanting to make a lot of noise during a firefight.

An early attempt to suppress a .45 caliber pistol used a modified barrel bushing that was designed to mate the Military Armament Corporation M10 submachine gun suppressor to the Colt Model 1911 and its clones.

This question of how frequently the suppressor should be repacked is relevant, however, for training and sporting applications. Table 13.8 shows the sound signatures of 35 rounds fired consecutively (without repacking a freshly packed can), with one minute of rest between each seven-round magazine. These data show that AWC's recommended repacking after three magazines is probably conservative at that rate of fire (about one round every 45 seconds).

Adult shooters standing a meter from the suppressor could barely tell the difference between 140.9 dB (the mean sound signature of the third magazine) and 141.7 dB (the mean signature of the fifth magazine). So adding grease after five magazines instead of three is probably acceptable from a suppression point of view.

But this is not a reasonable maintenance interval if the Nielsen device is used with the suppressor, since no grease remained in the rearmost chamber of the can or on the piston after 35 rounds. *Adequate lubrication of the piston is absolutely critical to the life span of the regulator.*

Furthermore, the slide did not cycle as positively during the fourth and fifth magazines. Even though there were no failures to feed, the slide barely cycled on several occasions during the course of firing the last two magazines. So AWC's recommendation of repacking the Nexus with grease after three magazines is probably good advice. The Nexus would function flawlessly for the first three magazines and continued to perform reliably and quietly for another two magazines without repacking. Following the guidelines in the suppressor's excellent manual should maximize the performance and life span of the system.

The final question to be resolved is accuracy. Frank Smith of Bob's Tactical and Jim Ballou conducted the accuracy testing. They used a Series 70 Colt with King Tappen sights that had tritium inserts. The sights were tall enough to clear the suppressor's profile. Smith was able to consistently obtain 1-inch five-shot groups at 25 yards. Clearly the exotic baffle design of the Nexus does not degrade accuracy.

The accuracy exhibited by the Nexus with its AWC barrel exceeds the JSOC requirement that the new offensive pistol must deliver groups no larger than 2.5 inches at 25 yards. The Colt Model 1911 with Nexus suppressor could provide the law-enforcement community and qualified civilians with a system that could function well in the tactical environment envisioned by JSOC. An accessory "active aiming module" (a flashlight for target identification and illumination for iron sights, or a laser) could be added to the receiver in front of the trigger guard. Tritium iron sights and an optical sight could be added. And magazine capacity could be increased to 13 rounds by replacing the Colt frame with one from Para-Ordnance, at least until the so-called Crime Bill passed by Congress in 1994 outlawed large-capacity magazines. Thus, when the Nexus was first introduced, one could build a pistol with capabilities similar to the JSOC offensive pistol with off-the-shelf components. The key ingredient is the outstanding Nexus suppressor.

Whether suppressing an old government veteran Model 1911, a tuned carry gun, or a customized clone of the JSOC concept, the AWC Nexus provides excellent sound suppression in a reliable package.

SILENT OPTIONS TITANIUM PISTOL/SMG SUPPRESSOR

Imagine a quick-mount suppressor small and light enough to employ on the Beretta 92F or 92SB pistol that will also attach quickly to an H&K MP5 submachine gun's three-lug barrel without modification. Surely such a suppressor must be too big for practical employment on a pistol, too heavy for reliable functioning of the Beretta, or too flimsy to hold up to the demands of full-auto fire when mounted on a submachine gun. A new titanium suppressor called the Silent Option suggests that such ambitious design goals may actually be attainable. Yet any scientist will admit that not every experiment is a success, and any engineer will admit that some new technologies never

Table 13.5. Sound signatures in decibels of suppressor tests.

GUN	SUPPRESSOR	SOUND SIGNATURE (dB)
Colt Model 1911 w/Colt barrel	None	164.5
Colt Model 1911 w/AWC barrel	None	163.9
Colt Model 1911	AWC Nexus, first 7 rounds, regulator on	135.1
Colt Model 1911	AWC Nexus, first 7 rounds, regulator off	136.4
H&K P9S w/AWC barrel	None	164.4
H&K P9S	AWC Nexus, first 7 rounds, regulator off	133.7

Table 13.6. Net sound reductions in decibels.

GUN	SUPPRESSOR	SOUND SIGNATURE (dB)
Colt Model 1911	AWC Nexus, first 7 rounds, regulator on	28.8
Colt Model 1911	AWC Nexus, first 7 rounds, regulator off	27.5
H&K P9S	AWC Nexus, first 7 rounds, regulator off	30.7

Table 13.7. Net sound reductions expressed as fractions of original (unsuppressed) sound pressure (SP).

GUN	SUPPRESSOR	FRACTION OF UNSUPPRESSED SP
Colt Model 1911	AWC Nexus, first 7 rounds, regulator on	1/800
Colt Model 1911	AWC Nexus, first 7 rounds, regulator off	1/550
H&K P9S	AWC Nexus, first 7 rounds, regulator off	1/1,200

Table 13.8. Sound signatures in decibels of five magazines fired through Nexus (regulator on) on Colt Model 1911 without repacking suppressor.

	1ST MAG	2ND MAG	3RD MAG	4TH MAG	5TH MAG
	135.5	138.6	140.5	139.2	143.1
	132.2	135.9	141.1	141.6	142.5
	133.4	134.4	139.2	141.1	141.8
	136.4	137.1	140.1	140.0	140.7
	135.3	137.7	140.4	141.9	141.5
	136.5	134.9	142.1	144.1	140.8
	136.1	138.9	143.1	141.6	141.8
MEAN	**135.1**	**136.8**	**140.9**	**141.4**	**141.7**

live up to their promise. Therefore, it is always prudent to critically evaluate the design and performance of promising new technologies like this compact titanium suppressor. Simply fondling the little Silent Option suppressor suggests that it should hold great promise for CQB applications.

The Silent Option suppressor was manufactured by Silent Options, Inc., of Saluda, Virginia. The original variant of this suppressor features a simple screw-on mount employing 1/2x28 TPI threads. The variant tested in this study features a titanium quick-mount system for H&K-type three-lug barrel. Mounting on a Beretta pistol requires that the pistol barrel be threaded to accept a three-lug barrel extension. Although the adapter can simply be torqued onto the barrel, the adapter will eventually loosen with use. Thus, installing the extension with low-temperature Loctite is preferable to checking the tightness of the extension on the barrel every 10 rounds or so. Loctite ensures proper suppressor alignment but precludes readily disassembling the pistol in the field for cleaning or maintenance.

The suppressor tube is 6.22 inches (15.8 cm) long and 1.0 inch (2.5 cm) in diameter. The rear mount and domed front end cap bring the overall length of the suppressor to 7.24 inches (18.4 cm). The suppressor weighs a mere 6.0 ounces (167 g) because every component is made from titanium, which has the tensile strength of steel but only half the weight. The outer surface of the titanium suppressor is simply bead blasted to give a nonreflective gray finish. Due to its three-lug mount, the Silent Option is about 0.5 inch (1.3 cm) longer than the outstanding Warp 6 pistol suppressor made by AWC Systems Technology. Yet, even with its three-lug mount, the Silent Option is still 0.7 ounce (23 g) lighter than the Warp 6. The three-lug pistol barrel extension does, however, add 0.8 ounce (25 g) to system weight.

The internal design of this suppressor is a simplified distillation of a patent issued in 1992 plus improvements to the design. The only aspect of this technology visible from the outside of the can is a series of six radial holes perforating the domed front end cap around the bore. The radial holes help break up both the precursor wave (the gases that precede the bullet out of the barrel) and the pressure wave of the gas stream following the bullet. Much of the combustion gas exits from the small radial holes rather than the large center hole.

Since the Silent Option is a wet can designed originally for use on the Beretta 92F, it produces a cloud of vaporized coolant with every shot no matter what gun is fitted with the suppressor.

The variant of the Silent Option suppressor shown here features a titanium quick-mount system for H&K-type three-lug barrel. Tests were conducted with this Beretta 92SB pistol, which was fitted with a Knight's Armament slide lock. The pistol barrel was also threaded to accept a three-lug barrel extension.

The little titanium suppressor is only 7.24 inches (18.4 cm) long, and it weighs a mere 6.0 ounces (167 g). The titanium quick mount attaches rapidly and securely to the MP5's three-lug barrel.

The inside of the suppressor tube is threaded for its entire length. The increased surface area creates more turbulence and accelerates heat transfer, thus theoretically improving suppressor performance. The threading also saves weight since the complex, thick baffles are screwed into position, thus eliminating the need for separate spacers. Saving weight is critical for the Beretta pistol to function reliably with the suppressor attached, and the simplified assembly helps mitigate the high cost of titanium.

The design of the Silent Option features a large primary expansion chamber and five complex, thick baffles that function quite differently than do traditional conical baffles. A traditional baffle shears off and slows a small portion of the gas stream following the bullet. Each baffle symmetrically shears a little more gas from the stream. A complex thick baffle, such as the ones used in this design, asymmetrically shear off gas much more aggressively and create one or more gas jets that push against the gas stream following the bullet. The jets remove more gas from the stream, increasing turbulence and reducing the remaining energy in the combustion gases that would be perceived as sound.

The Silent Option baffles use channels called "beveled diversion passage pairs" to generate gas jets from the main gas stream following the projectile. Diversion passage pairs must be machined into both the front and rear surfaces of the baffles to create this effect. The baffles are bead blasted to increase surface area.

Operators using wet cans commonly carry a supply of grease in a small plastic jar taped to their load-bearing equipment. To charge the Silent Option, use a wooden pencil, chopstick, or similar implement to insert about a teaspoon of grease into the rear of the suppressor. Mobil Premium Lubricating Grease is an affordable and readily available lithium grease that works well and was used for testing the performance of the Silent Option and other wet cans. Push some grease into the chamber in front of the rearmost baffle and distribute the grease evenly around the inner surface of the chambers. Do not block the bullet passage itself, since this can increase back pressure.

Performance

To objectively test the performance of the Silent Option suppressor, the can was test-fired on a Beretta 92SB pistol fitted with a Knight's Armament slide lock as well as an H&K MP5 submachine gun using Winchester USA 115 grain supersonic ball, Winchester 147 grain subsonic hollowpoints,

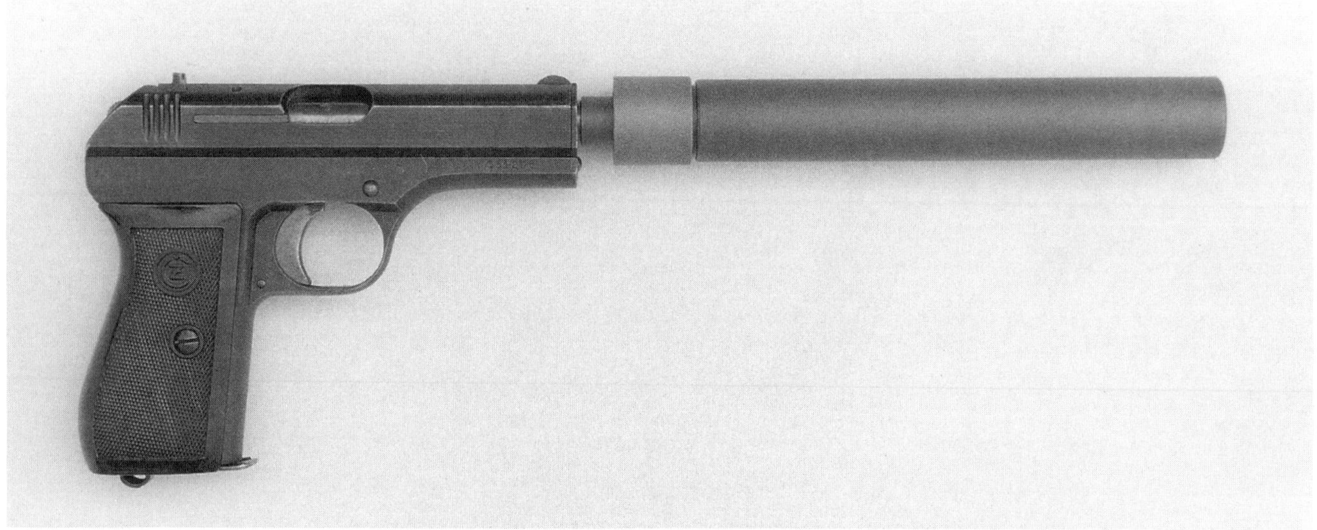

The 9mm Silent Option suppressor works surprisingly well on a .32 caliber pistol like this CZ 27.

and G&L 147 grain subsonic ball ammunition. The MP5 tests were also conducted with the 147 grain FMJ round developed specifically for the MP5 by Philip Dater (details of this load are discused in the previous chapter). Sound signatures appear in Table 13.9 (see page 372), while net sound reductions are listed in Table 13.10 (see page 372).

Suppressor cognoscenti may question the incorporation of a slide lock in the testing of this particular suppressor. A slide lock does improve a weapon's sound signature dramatically when the suppressor uses wipes. When employed with a suppressor like the Silent Option that does not use wipes, however, using a slide lock generally creates little or no improvement to the sound signature. Many suppressed systems will actually be louder when a slide lock is employed. This study tested the performance of the Silent Option suppressor with and without slide lock engaged because some operational requirements still favor the use of a slide lock: 1) when the mechanical noise of a cycling firearm is objectionable, 2) when the noise or bright flash of combustion gases escaping from the ejection port is objectionable, or 3) when fired brass must be recovered.

The unsuppressed Beretta 92SB pistol usually produced the same mean (average) sound signatures whether or not the slide was locked: 160 dB with Winchester USA supersonic ammunition, and 158 dB with Winchester subsonic. G&L subsonic ammunition, however, produced a 159 dB signature with the slide unlocked and 158 dB with the slide locked. Suppressed sound signatures might differ depending on whether or not the slide lock was engaged: 135 dB (unlocked) and 135 dB (locked) with Winchester USA; 130 dB (unlocked) and 132 dB (locked) with Winchester 147 grain subsonic hollowpoints; and 125 dB (unlocked) and 126 dB (locked) with G&L subsonic. Thus, the net sound reductions are: 27 dB (unlocked) and 27 dB (locked) with Winchester USA supersonic; 28 dB (unlocked) and 26 dB (locked) with Winchester subsonic; and 34 dB (unlocked) and 32 dB (locked) with G&L subsonic. This solid performance becomes particularly interesting with the G&L ammunition.

The sound signatures of the suppressed Beretta 92SB started getting noticeably louder after about 10 rounds, so the suppressor should be recharged with grease every time the magazine is changed. It became apparent during the course of testing that hollowpoints purged grease from the

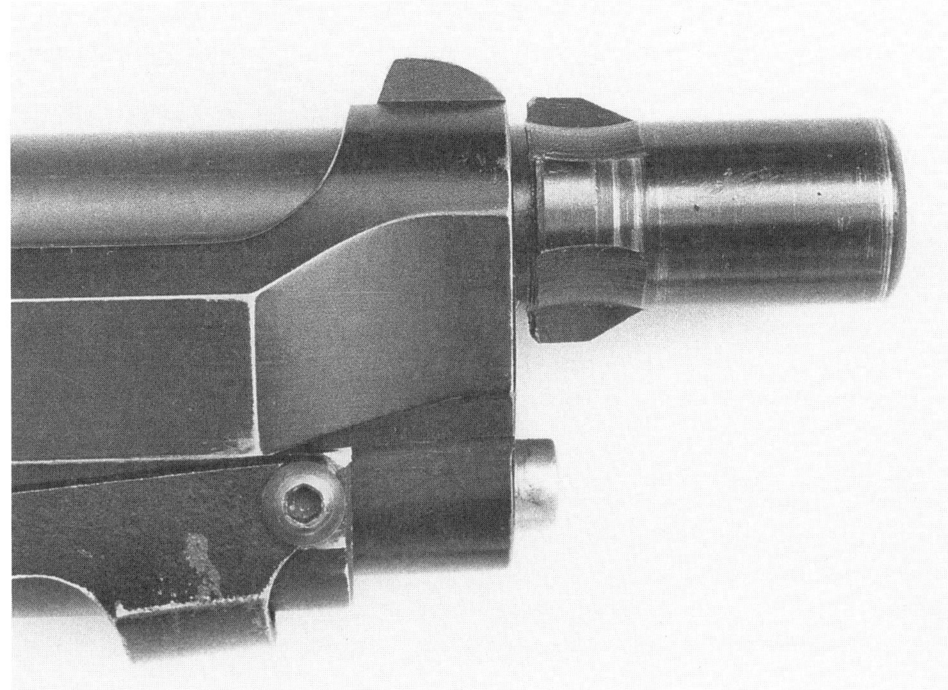

Adding a three-lug adapter to the Beretta pistol adds 0.8 ounce (25 grams) to system weight, which is not enough weight to adversely affect reliability when employed with the titanium Silent Option suppressor.

suppressor more rapidly than FMJ ammunition. If operational constraints permit, optimal performance will be attained by adding grease after every 10 rounds.

The grease lasts longer when the Silent Option is employed on the MP5 since combustion gases have a lower velocity and temperature when they reach the suppressor. The mean (average) unsuppressed sound signatures of the MP5 were 158 dB with Winchester USA supersonic ammunition, 156 dB with Winchester subsonic, 157 dB with Dater subsonic, and 157 dB with G&L subsonic. The MP5 produced the following suppressed signatures: 125 dB with Winchester USA ammunition, 129 dB with Winchester subsonic, 127 dB with Dater subsonic, and 127 dB with G&L subsonic. This is impressive performance. All of the aforementioned means were calculated based on a sample size of 10 rounds.

Testing continued with G&L ammunition until a full magazine of 30 rounds was fired to determine whether the coolant grease would be exhausted. Based on a sample size of 30 rounds through the MP5, the Silent Option's mean signature was 132 dB. The last round was 135 dB. That's much better performance than one might expect from a wet suppressor. The net sound reductions are, therefore, 33 dB with Winchester USA, 27 dB with Winchester subsonic, 30 dB with Dater subsonic, and 30 dB with G&L ammunition based on a sample size of 10 rounds. The sound reduction was 25 dB based on 30 rounds of G&L subsonic. When employed on the MP5, the Silent Option should be repacked with grease after 30 rounds of semiautomatic fire to maintain good performance.

The temperature was 86 °F (30 °C) while testing the Silent Option, and the speed of sound was 1,145 fps (349 mps). Projectile velocities did not differ significantly whether or not a suppressor was attached to the weapon, or whether the slide on the Beretta 92SB was locked or unlocked. Space constraints preclude discussion of the velocity data and exterior ballistics.

How do these data compare to other pistol suppressors in the marketplace? All of the following were tested on a Beretta 92F. The AWC Warp 6 (also a wet can) produced a net sound reduction of 30 dB with supersonic ammunition and 32 dB with subsonic fodder at 82 °F (28 °F), the AWC Hush Puppy (which uses wipes) produced a net sound reduction of 28 dB with subsonic ammunition at 65 °F (18 °C), and the Finnish Vaime A2 suppressor (a dry can) produced a net sound reduction of 18 dB with supersonic and 20 dB with subsonic ammo at -1 °F (-18 °C).

It's also useful to compare the Silent Option's performance to some classic submachine gun suppressors mounted on the MP5. The outstanding but large AWC MK-9, which is approximately 12.0 inches (30.5 cm) long and weighs about 32 ounces (910 g), produced a net sound reduction of 32 dB with supersonic and 31 dB with subsonic fodder at 52 °F (11 °C). The smaller and lighter AWC TAC NINE suppressor, which is 9.0 inches (22.8 cm) long and weighs 23.0 ounces (649 g), produced a net sound reduction of 30 dB with supersonic and 27 dB with subsonic ammo at 56 °F (13°C). And the diminutive Gemtech MINITAC, which is 8.9 inches (22.3 cm) long and weighs a mere 11.1 ounces (316 g), reduced the MP5's sound signature by 23 dB with Winchester USA supersonic and 24 dB with G&L subsonic fodder.

Clearly, the Silent Option suppressor performs well compared to some classic competitors among both pistol and submachine gun suppressors. Since the Silent Option employs wet technology, the operator must realize that the can will only perform well for no more than one magazine's worth of semiautomatic shooting before it will need to be repacked with grease. If operational requirements demand a longer maintenance interval, then other options in the marketplace should be explored. These options will be larger and/or heavier, so the Silent Option suppressor with three-lug mount is really in a class by itself.

The Silent Option mounted securely and aligned properly on the MP5 with original barrel and a Beretta 92SB fitted with a one piece three-lug barrel extension. When an experimental two-piece, three-lug extension was fitted to a .32 caliber CZ 27 pistol, alignment was not satisfactory. The first round struck two baffles, broke the barrel extension in two, and hurled the suppressor 20 feet to the

The evolution of technology over the last decade has enabled the steady downsizing of suppressors. This trend is illustrated by the AWC MK-9 (on bottom) followed by the SCRC Mark 25A, the Silent Options SOS, the Gemtech MINITAC, and the Silent Options pistol/SMG can evaluated in this chapter.

left of the operator. Stick with Silent Option's one-piece barrel extension to avoid this problem. Remarkably, bullet impact merely gouged two baffles, and the suppressor continues to function well. I've seen similar events destroy other suppressors; this design appears to be bulletproof.

While the concept of a quick-detach mount for a pistol suppressor is an extremely good idea, only two systems available at the time of this writing are worthy of consideration in my opinion: 1) the Snap-On system from Knight's Armament, and 2) the QUIK-SNAP system from Gemtech.

Silent Option's practice of adding an H&K-type three-lug adapter and attaching it with Loctite is just not practical. I'd prefer to save the weight and simply screw the little titanium suppressor directly onto a threaded pistol barrel.

I did have several complaints during the course of this research that were not related to design of the Silent Option suppressor or its performance. Both phone numbers for Silent Options were voice mail. Messages were returned. But I was hard to reach myself, so games of telephone tag lasted a week or more before I was able to actually talk to someone. My other complaint was that deliveries and subsequent service were among the slowest in the industry. Only one other shop was sometimes as slow in my experience. A much more serious problem eventually became evident.

Customers began to complain to me that Silent Options failed to provide warranty service. I even have letters on file from people who wrote that they paid for suppressors that were never delivered. Whether these problems were generated by undercapitalization, mismanagement, infighting among investors, or a combination of these factors is irrelevant to the population of disgruntled clients. It appears that Silent Options and its predecessor, Precision Arms, managed to alienate a substantial number of customers. It is a shame that customer service never improved to a level worthy of the technology.

Table 13.9. Sound signatures in decibels of Silent Option pistol suppressors.

GUN	SUPPRESSOR	WINCHESTER 115 GR SUPERSONIC	WINCHESTER 147 GR SUBSONIC	G&L 147 GR SUBSONIC	DATER 147 GR SUBSONIC	TEMP., °F (°C)
Beretta 92SB[a]	None	160	158	159	—	86(30)
Beretta 92SB[b]	None	160	158	158	—	86(30)
Beretta 92SB[a]	Silent Option	135	130	125	—	86(30)
Beretta 92SB[b]	Silent Option	135	132	126	—	86(30)
H&K MP5	None	158	156	157	157	84(29)
H&K MP5	Silent Option	125	129	127[c]	127	84(29)
H&K MP5	Silent Option	—	—	132[d]	—	84(29)

[a] slide unlocked
[b] slide locked
[c] mean (average) of 10 rounds
[d] mean (average) of 30 rounds

Table 13.10. Net sound reductions in decibels of Silent Option pistol suppressor.

GUN	SUPPRESSOR	WINCHESTER 115 GR SUPERSONIC	WINCHESTER 147 GR SUBSONIC	G&L 147 GR SUBSONIC	DATER 147 GR SUBSONIC	TEMP., °F (°C)
Beretta 92SB[a]	Silent Option	27	28	34	—	86(30)
Beretta 92SB[b]	Silent Option	27	26	32	—	86(30)
H&K MP5	Silent Option	33	27	30[c]	30	84(29)
H&K MP5	Silent Option	—	—	25[d]	—	84(29)

[a] slide unlocked
[b] slide locked
[c] mean (average) of 10 rounds
[d] mean (average) of 30 rounds

Silent Options is no longer in business. After considerable legal machinations, the patented designs are now being manufactured under license by a company called SIOPTS that is apparently under completely different ownership.

A key part of the story on the overall development of tactical suppressors for 9x19mm pistols and submachine guns over the last several decades has been the quest for effective subsonic ammunition. Once suppressor technology turned from the use of wipes, then the stage was set for the development of jacketed hollowpoint ammunition tailored to optimize terminal ballistics at subsonic velocities. That story remained untold until 1994, when the folks at Woodin Laboratory published the results of their historical research in the *International Ammunition Association Journal.* Since relatively few people in the sporting and tactical communities have access to that journal, it is worth providing a more broadly accessible forum for this important story. Therefore, the following discussion is based almost verbatim on that article with the kind permission of Bill Woodin.

DEVELOPMENT OF 9MM SUBSONIC JHP AMMUNITION

In the spring of 1985, the U.S. Navy approached the Ordnance Products Division of Olin Corporation's Winchester Group with a request to purchase a large number of Silvertip hollowpoint bullets as components for use in assembling special subsonic 9x19mm cartridges. The bullets of interest were the type used in the .357 Magnum 145 grain Silvertip HP cartridge. This unusual request was based on a need for ammunition with improved lethality for use in suppressor-equipped pistols and submachine guns used by certain U.S. Navy SpecOps units having specific antiterrorist responsibilities.

Prior to that time, the Navy's only officially adopted 9mm subsonic ammunition was the MK 144 Mod O ball cartridge. This round, which is loaded with a 158 grain (10.3 g) FMJ bullet, was developed and approved for service use during the Vietnam War in the Mk 22 suppressed pistol. This weapon, used by Navy swimmers, was a modified version of the Smith & Wesson Model 39 and was known informally as the Hush Puppy. No effort was made to use jacketed hollowpoint (JHP) ammunition in the MK 22 pistols, since the projectiles would begin to expand upon contact with the wipes, with disastrous consequences in terms of accuracy, suppressor life, and even safety of the operator. Furthermore, the MK 144 didn't function well in the closed-bolt H&K submachine guns that were becoming increasingly popular with SpecOps units. Since military units involved in hostage rescue missions were authorized to use JHP ammunition, it became clear that a more effective cartridge was needed.

Certain Navy units had experience using 9mm 115 grain (7.5 g) JHPs in 1983 during combat operations in Grenada. While this ammunition provided adequate terminal ballistics when fired in standard pistols and submachine guns, it delivered inadequate performance when fired from integrally suppressed submachine guns like the H&K MP5 SD, which use a ported barrel to reduce projectiles to subsonic velocity.

A particular senior enlisted ordnance specialist from the Norfolk Naval District, who had a great deal of operational and technical experience, came up with the idea of loading heavier bullets to deliver modest, near-sonic velocities. The visionary chief theorized that the heaviest possible JHP expanding bullet traveling at the maximum subsonic velocity would be highly lethal. Events over the next several years would prove him right. The chief conducted experiments with handloads using bullets pulled from .357 Magnum 145 grain (9.4 g) Silvertip cartridges. Early test results of his special loads looked promising enough to warrant further research.

The R&D staff at East Alton looked into the Navy's problem. Although the 145 grain Silvertip bullet was excellent for its intended purpose, it was somewhat oversized for 9mm barrels. Furthermore, it was designed for controlled expansion at velocities above those possible from standard, much less subsonic 9x19mm cartridges. These researchers developed a proposal to fabricate some special heavy-bullet 9mm cartridges under an experimental order. After a technical meeting between government and Olin engineers, the Navy placed a purchase order for 100,000 rounds of 9mm subsonic ammunition to be tested in Navy pistols and submachine guns. The proposed cartridges were to have 140 grain (9.1 g) JHP bullets of the proven Silvertip design but without nickel-plated jackets. The specified velocity was to be 975 fps (297 mps) from a 4 inch (10 cm) barrel. The order was to consist of two groups of 50,000 rounds; each group would use a different 140 grain bullet. The two bullet configurations differed slightly in nose shape. The Type A bullet was more blunt, similar to the .357 145 grain Silvertip, while the Type B was more slender, similar to the 9mm 115 grain Silvertip. These cartridges were identified at East Alton by product codes Q4192-A and Q4192-B.

By fall 1985, the initial run of subsonic ammo was delivered to the government for testing and evaluation. The Navy insisted on very stringent waterproof testing standards and crimped-in primers. All cartridges of this initial order were packed in 50-round white paper cartons and used the commercial headstamp "WIN 9mm LUGER."

The Navy specified that function and casualty testing would be conducted in a series of particular submachine guns and pistols including, but not limited to, the H&K MP5, H&K P9S, H&K P9, H&K P7, and Beretta 92S. These weapons were known to have chambers cut in accordance with NATO specifications as opposed to chambers of commercial firearms, which are cut to SAAMI specifications. As a consequence of the blunt profile of Type A bullets, the carton labels were marked to indicate that the ammunition was intended only for use in certain weapons. Cartons containing Type B rounds lacked this restrictive wording.

Very thorough testing of the Q4192 ammunition was done at locations in Illinois, Virginia, and California. The testing regimen included routine ballistic performance tests conducted in accordance with industrial standard, function, and casualty testing per military specifications and testing of wound ballistics and lethality. The terminal effects of the subsonic JHP proved to be as good or better than anticipated, giving deep penetration in 20 percent ordnance gelatin and showing good controlled expansion that produced a large permanent wound channel. Bullets typically expanded to a final diameter that was 50 to 70 percent larger than the original diameter. Tests conducted in both simulated and actual animal tissue indicated that this was indeed a very deadly load. Although the Navy selected Type B bullets for follow-up testing, both types proved effective and overall results were positive. All the technical and operational people involved with the project wanted to conduct further research to optimize the subsonic JHP.

By the end of 1985, the Weapons Department at the Naval Weapons Support Center (NWSC) at Crane, Indiana, became involved in the new 9mm subsonic JHP project. The Navy granted a new contract with East Alton for a production run of 200,000 rounds to be used for extensive technical testing, all with the Type B 140 grain bullet. These cartridges received a military-style headstamp and were packed in 50-round paper cartons. The initial cartridges were headstamped "9MM WCC 85," while final production was headstamped "WCC 86 9mm." Primers were the unplated brass type and were secured by an annular ring crimp.

Testing and evaluation suggested that bullet weight could be increased by about 5 percent to provide a greater recoil impulse to operate the weapon (and provide better penetration as well) while still maintaining an initial velocity of 975 fps (297 mps). Design engineers at East Alton decided to lengthen the bullet to arrive at an optimal weight of 147 grains (9.6 g). This has subsequently become the standard weight for 9x19mm subsonic cartridges.

Researchers paid a great deal of attention to the selection of propellants to minimize muzzle flash. Prior to this time, military cartridge specifications generally did not address the visible flash signature of pistol ammunition. The Navy was, however, very interested in reducing the amount of

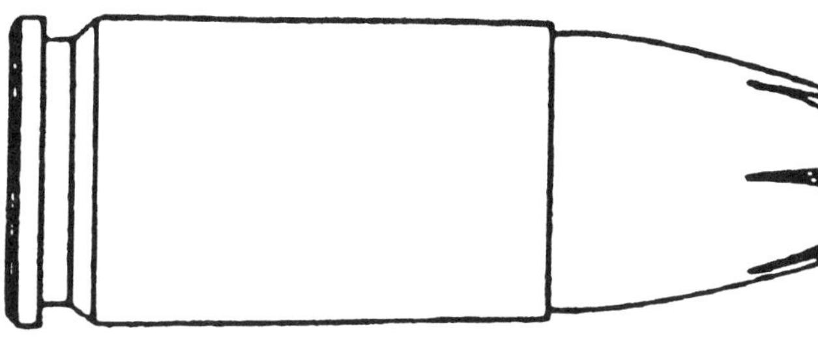

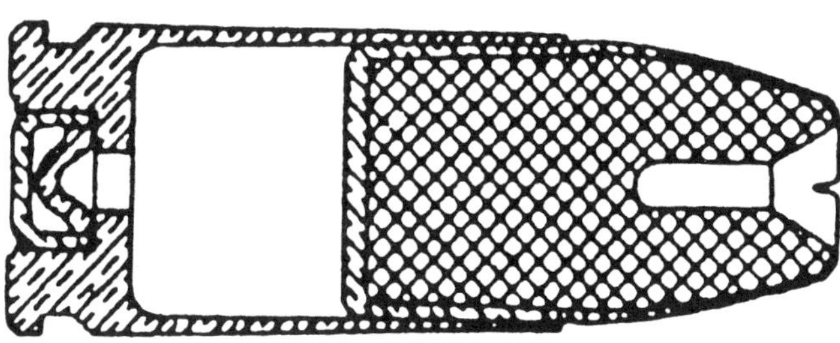

Figure 13.8. The 9x19mm subsonic JHP cartridge is loaded with a long 147 grain bullet. The bullet jacket has varying thickness and is designed for controlled expansion upon impact. Drawing by E.L. Scranton.

visible flash at the muzzle, particularly when fired from pistols. Specifically modified ball powders were developed successfully that produced little or no muzzle flash in subsonic JHP ammunition. This characteristic has since become a standard part of the cartridge specification. It is also significant to note that the desired velocity level was achieved without the need to maximize chamber pressure in the +P range.

In 1986, the Navy placed another order of 500,000 rounds for the 147 grain JHP cartridge. Some stoppages were noted with this round because of extraction problems caused by cases sticking in the fluted chamber of the MP5 submachine gun and its variants. Analysis of this problem showed that case hardness, which was caused by work-hardening and annealing, was a critical factor that needed to be closely controlled. The case-sticking problem was eliminated in successive production lots by carefully controlling this characteristic.

In the following year, the Navy began buying this ammunition in large quantities for operational use by certain military organizations. Packaging was changed to typical military brown boxes with the wording "9MM L (SUBSONIC)." The letter "L" indicates low-velocity loading. Similarly, the cartridge was headstamped "9MM L WCC 87." Use of the new subsonic JHP ammunition quickly spread to other government agencies and eventually spread throughout the law-enforcement community. Shortly thereafter, this type ammunition was also released for commercial distribution.

In 1986, the Federal Bureau of Investigation experienced a tragic shootout in Miami, Florida,

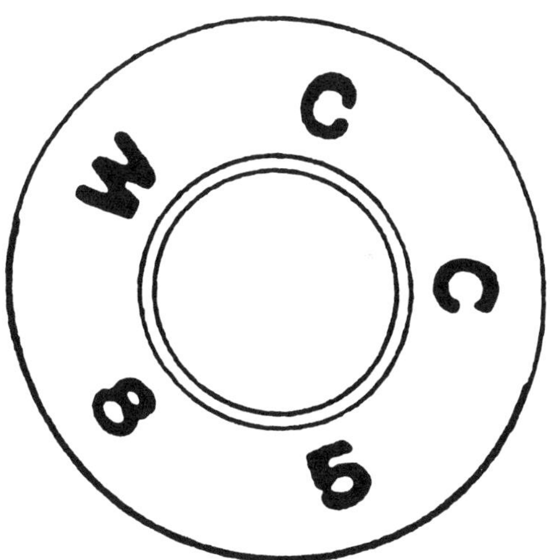

Figure 13.9. These headstamps appeared during the early development of a 9x19mm subsonic round by Olin at East Alton. Primers were secured by an annular ring crimp, which suggests the military nature of these cartridges. Drawing by E.L. Scranton.

Figure 13.10. These dated headstamps were used on qualification and limited production lots of subsonic rounds. The 85 date had 140 grain bullets, while the 86 date had 147 grain bullets. Drawing by E.L. Scranton.

which left two special agents dead and five others wounded. Much of the shooting occurred after the armed criminal, who was firing a semiautomatic 5.56mm rifle, sustained a well-placed hit from a 9mm 115 grain JHP bullet. This bullet did enough damage to eventually become fatal, but the desperado was still able to kill the agent who fired the shot. The villain then continued to fire for several more minutes, causing additional casualties. This fiasco stimulated the FBI Firearms Training Unit at Quantico, Virginia, to take a long, hard look at its effectiveness criteria and performance standards for handgun ammunition.

I feel compelled to point out, before continuing this discussion, that the criminal use of a semiautomatic rifle is rare in the extreme. For example, a compilation of violent crimes by weapon category in Illinois revealed that claw hammers were used to kill more than twice as many people as semiautomatic rifles during the period of record. Media hysteria over this issue is not supported by the facts.

As an immediate response to improve lethality after the Miami shootout, the FBI adopted the Navy's subsonic 147 grain JHP ammunition as standard issue for use in 9mm pistols. A large number of federal, state, and local law enforcement agencies have subsequently followed the FBI's lead.

As a long-term solution, the FBI decided to buy more powerful 10mm pistols and ammunition. The 10mm program, however, has proved only partially successful. It is significant to note that the Bureau has subsequently acquired many new 9mm pistols. After a great many law enforcement shootings, the "street results" suggest that subsonic 147 grain JHP ammunition can provide good terminal ballistics. Furthermore, after extensive ballistic testing under a variety of conditions using all other available 9mm loadings, the FBI continues to issue the 147 grain subsonic load.

In 1988, NSWC in Crane gave some thought to having cartridges loaded to a velocity that was somewhat lower than standard for use in submachine guns. This notion was based on a low but troublesome incident rate of stoppages observed with the Olin cartridges in the MP5 series of weapons. To evaluate this idea, the Navy issued a contract for 3 million reduced-velocity rounds to the Federal Cartridge Company. These cartridges were loaded to a velocity of 865 fps (264 mps) and were headstamped "FC 89 9MM S." The letter "S" was used to indicate that this load was specifically intended for submachine guns. Although this load is about 110 fps (34 mps) slower than the standard subsonic round, tests of this new Type S round demonstrated its adequate reliability in submachine guns. With pistols, however, the round provided somewhat diminished reliability due to its lower recoil impulse. Furthermore, these cartridges produced less bullet expansion when fired into ordnance gelatin.

Figure 13.11. Headstamps of 9x19mm subsonic rounds representing later production. The letter "L" signifies a subsonic load, while the letter "S" indicates a special loading for submachine guns. Drawing by E.L. Scranton.

50 CARTRIDGES
CAL 9MM L (SUBSONIC)
WCC87J030-004
NOO164-87-C-0202
OLIN CORPORATION

50 CARTRIDGES
CAL 9MM (SUBSONIC)
N00164-88-C-0265
LOT FC- 89G001-006

Figure 13.12. These box labels reflect traditional military packaging. The top label shows the first use of the letter "L," which also appears on the headstamps, while the lower label was on a package of cartridges headstamped "9MM S," indicating a special loading for submachine guns.

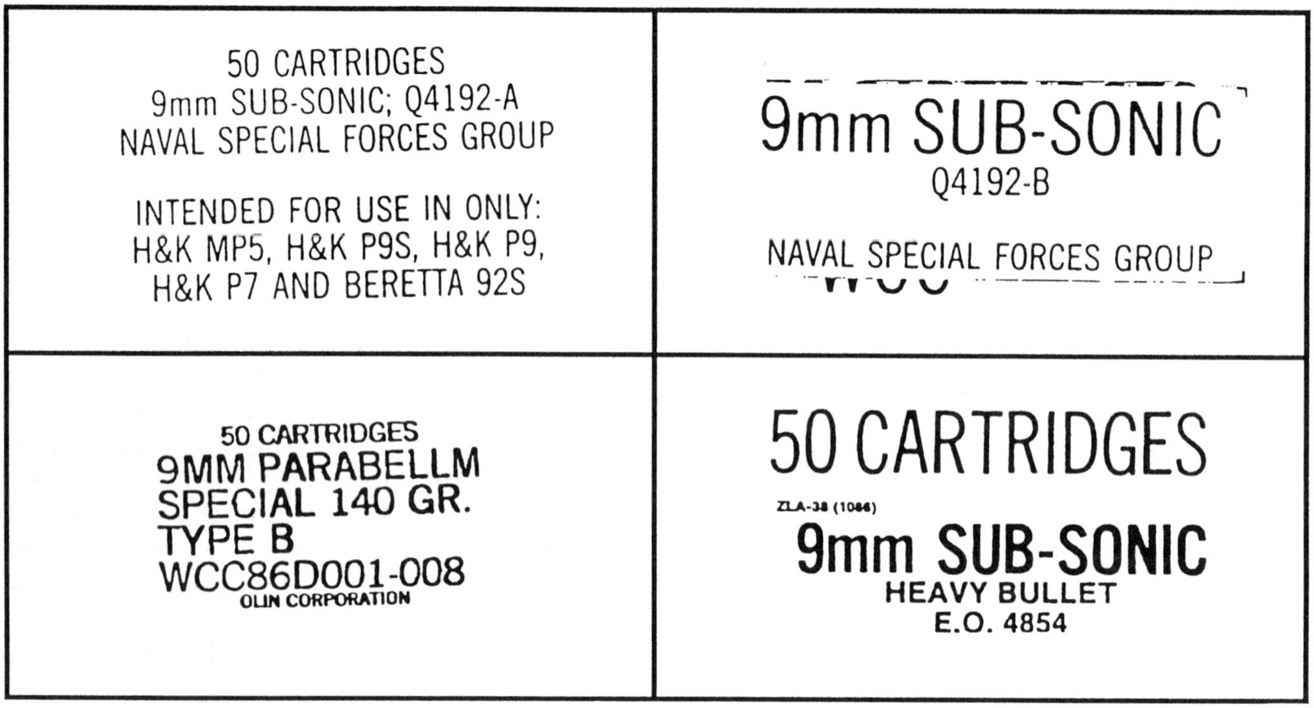

50 CARTRIDGES 9mm SUB-SONIC; Q4192-A NAVAL SPECIAL FORCES GROUP INTENDED FOR USE IN ONLY: H&K MP5, H&K P9S, H&K P9, H&K P7 AND BERETTA 92S	9mm SUB-SONIC Q4192-B NAVAL SPECIAL FORCES GROUP
50 CARTRIDGES 9MM PARABELLM SPECIAL 140 GR. TYPE B WCC86D001-008 OLIN CORPORATION	50 CARTRIDGES ZLA-38 (1086) 9mm SUB-SONIC HEAVY BULLET E.O. 4854

Figure 13.13. These early carton labels, circa 1985 and 1986, were used for the first loadings of 9x19mm subsonic ammunition in the United States. The last label indicates the change of bullet weight from 140 to 147 grains.

After this experience with the reduced-velocity Type S load and successful improvement of the original load, the Navy concluded that it was practical to use only a single round for both pistols and submachine guns. All subsequent procurements have been made at the 975 fps velocity (out of a 4 inch barrel) and feature the "9MM L" box label and headstamp.

For logistic management and inventory control purposes, the 9mm JHP subsonic round received the U.S. Department of Defense Identification Code (DODIC) of A260. More recently, the round received the formal Navy-style nomenclature of MK 234 Mod 0, thereby indicating that the 9mm subsonic cartridge has been fully and officially approved for service use.

Fairly early on during development of this ammunition, it became apparent that the subsonic round was inherently very accurate. Dispersion testing at East Alton was conducted in rigid accuracy barrels mounted in a mechanical fixture. Ten-shot groups were fired for dispersion measurement at 50 yards (46 m). Some test groups fired with the subsonic 147 grain JHP load showed extreme spreads of 1.6 inches (4.1 cm) measured center to center. Typical production lots delivered groups of 2.0 inches (5.1 cm). This level of accuracy compares favorably with the best match-grade ammunition used for competitive pistol shooting. As a result, the Olin marketing staff created and distributed literature identifying this ammunition as "OSM" for Olin Super Match. Olin strongly implied the suitability of this round for target shooting with pistols. Color brochures on the OSM were widely disseminated at trade shows for several years, and a great deal was written in various gun magazines and trade journals about this "9mm OSM" ammunition. While the name OSM became widely recognized in certain military circles, it is curious that it never appeared on any carton labels used for packaging or shipping this ammunition.

As a spinoff of OSM's accuracy, it is noteworthy that when Winchester introduced its first commercial 9mm loading specifically intended for match purposes in 1990, it was a 147 grain subsonic load. Called the Super Match brand, it was catalogued as product number X9MMTCM. The Super Match round, however, uses a truncated-cone FMJ bullet with a flat nose instead of a hollowpoint. It is important to note that the FMJ subsonic round delivers vastly inferior terminal ballistics to the JHP subsonic round. And its blunt nose makes the truncated-cone FMJ round unsuitable for use with suppressors containing wipes.

To say that 147 grain JHP subsonic ammunition has caught on well in the marketplace would be an understatement of considerable magnitude. Many millions of rounds are produced every year by at least eight major ammunition companies. And the development of a good tactical round has also stimulated interest in the development of better sound suppressors for pistols and submachine guns.

Winchester first introduced its JHP subsonic round to law enforcement customers using product code Q4217. This was superseded by a Ranger brand designated RA9147HP. More recently, the subsonic round has evolved into the commercially offered Winchester Subsonic load with the product number XSUB9MM. A Silvertip loading, which features a nickel-plated bullet jacket and thus sports a traditional silvery appearance, is catalogued as product number X9MMST147. Finally, a 9mm 147 grain hollowpoint was marketed in Winchester's Black Talon line of ammunition as product number S9MM. Still available to government and law enforcement agencies as of 1994, the Black Talon has been withdrawn from civilian sales. It has been replaced by a similar premium load called Supreme SXT, which carries the brief designation S9.

The success of the 147 grain JHP subsonic round is demonstrated by the fact that every major U.S. manufacturer, as well as many foreign companies, now produce similar loadings. Even though other bullet weights and types are still purchased by law enforcement agencies, primarily for economical training purposes, the subsonic 147 grain JHP has become the preferred law-enforcement load for 9mm duty weapons. High-performance descendents of the Navy JHP include Remington's Golden Saber, Federal's Hydra-Shok, Speer's Gold Dot, Hornady's XTP, and the Eldorado Starfire. These rounds tend to perform well in pistols, but not all of them provide good terminal performance in the H&K MP5 SD submachine gun. As will be discussed in the second volume of *Silencer History and Performance*, selecting the appropriate 147 grain JHP for use in the MP5 SD is absolutely critical to achieve adequate terminal ballistics.

Perhaps the bottom line to this discussion is that the U.S. Navy is seldom seen as the originator of innovative concepts or advancements in small-arms ammunition. In the case of the 9x19mm JHP subsonic round, however, it is clear that the Navy has made a significant contribution to not only the military community but to the civilian and law-enforcement communities as well. It is reasonable to expect that 147 grain JHP subsonic ammunition will play a major role wherever 9mm weapons are used for decades to come.

CHAPTER FOURTEEN

SAFETY AND THE USE OF SUPPRESSORS

he use of suppressors does entail two categories of potential safety problems: misalignment of the suppressor with the bore and unsafe gun-handling practices.

Dangerous misalignment is most likely to occur when screw-on muzzle cans loosen from the barrel during use, as previously described. When employing any screw-on muzzle can, verify that the suppressor is still tightly in place before shooting and at every magazine change. Be aware that suppressors can get very hot very quickly, so use a glove, hat, or other insulation as necessary to avoid burns.

A more serious danger is that a few individuals with IQ waivers have become lulled away from the maintenance of safe gun-handling procedures simply because a suppressed firearm is quiet. One must never equate the lack of noise with a lack of danger downrange. *Safe gun handling must become a permanent part of a shooter's character*, whether one is shooting suppressed or unsuppressed arms. The four basic rules cover every conceivable situation, whether one is engaged in sporting or tactical activities.

THE RULES OF SAFE GUN HANDLING

RULE 1. All guns are always loaded.

There are no exceptions. Don't *pretend* this is true; be deadly serious about it. Follow this simple rule and you'll never utter those unforgivable words, "But I didn't know it was loaded!"

RULE 2. Never let the muzzle cover anything you are not willing to destroy.

This is the most frequently violated rule, especially with handguns. Frequently the violator will provide the lame excuse, "It's not loaded." Bull! See Rule 1.

RULE 3. Keep your finger off the trigger until your sights are on the target.

There is no delay in the speed of target acquisition by following this rule. Furthermore, there is no need to discharge a firearm before target acquisition, so there is absolutely no excuse for violating this rule.

RULE 4. Be sure of your target.

Know what your target is. Know what is in line with your target and what is behind it. Never shoot at anything you have not positively identified.

Make these rules a permanent part of your personality. Insist that everyone you encounter honors these rules as well.

LIST OF SUPPRESSOR MANUFACTURERS

Note: Only government agencies and specially licensed importers can import suppressors into the United States from foreign countries. Qualified individuals cannot legally own imported suppressors. Private citizens should refrain from contacting manufacturers who restrict their sales to the military and law enforcement communities.

Arms Tech Inc., 5121 North Central Avenue, Phoenix, AZ 85012. *Military and law enforcement sales only.*

Asesepänliike BR-Tuote Ky, Sahamyllynkatu 33, 80170 Joensuu, Finland.

AWC Systems Technology, P.O. Box 41938, Phoenix, AZ 85080-1938.

Blaylock Gun Works, Rt. 3, Box 103-A, Lot 25, Victoria, TX 77901.

Brügger and Thomet Mfg. Co., Overlandstrasse 10, 3700 Spiez, Switzerland.

Gemtech, P.O. Box 3538, Boise, ID 83703.

GSL Technology, Inc., P.O. Box 6288, Jackson, MI 49204.

John Norrell Arms, 2608 Grist Mill Road, Little Rock, AR 72207.

Jonathan Arthur Ciener, Inc., 8700 Commerce Street, Cape Canaveral, FL 32920.

Knight's Armament Company, 7750 9th Street SW, Vero Beach, FL 32968. *Military and law enforcement sales only.*

LaFrance Specialties, P.O. Box 178211, San Diego, CA 92177.

Linneo Oy Ltd., P.O. Box 44, SF-62101 Lapua, Finland.

Ops Inc., P.O. Box 377, Shingletown, CA 96088. *Military sales only.*

Parker Hale Limited, Golden Hillock Road, Birmingham B11 2PZ, England.

R.A.S.E., P.O. Box 866, Cocoa, FL 32926.

S.C.R.C., P.O. Box 660, Katy, TX 77492-0660.

SAPL, B.P. 04, 61550 Gauville, France.

SIOPTS, 570A Industrial Park Drive, Newport News, VA 23608.

Sound Technology. Winter Information (September–April): P.O. Box 391, Pelham, AL 35124. Summer Information (May–August): P.O. Box 1132, Kodiak, AK 99615. *Mark White's actual manufacturing facilities are in Alabama, so it's hard to get orders filled during the warm months in Alaska.*

Special Op's Shop, P.O. Box 978, Madisonville, TN 37354.

Stopson Creations, La Ferme Saint Benoit, 78121 Crespieres, France.

Summers Machine Enterprises, Route 7 Box 672, Thomasville, NC 27360.

S.W.I.S.S., P.O. Box 18835, San Antonio, TX 78218.

Ward Machine, 5620 Lexington Road, Corpus Christi, TX 78412.

REFERENCES

Albert, D.G., and J.A. Orcutt. 1990. Acoustic pulse propagation above grassland and snow: comparison of theoretical and experimental waveforms. *Journal of the Acoustic Society of America*. 87:93-100.

American Machine & Foundry Company. No date. *Silencers: Principles and Patterns*. Volume 2. Reprint by Paladin Press, Boulder, CO. 78 pp.

Anttonen, H., J. Hassi, P. Riihikangas, and M. Sorri. 1980. Impulse noise exposure during military service. *Scand. Audiol. Suppl.* 12:17-21.

Anttonen, H., M. Sorri, and P. Riihikangas. 1983. The impulse noise exposure and the effect of protectors in army. Pages 313-316 in G. Rossi, editor. *Noise as a Health Problem: Proceedings of the Fourth International Congress. Volume 1.*

Berger, E.H. 1993a. The naked truth about NRRs. Cabot Safety Corporation, Indianapolis, IN. EARLog 20. 4 pp.

Berger, E.H. 1993b. Overview and index to the EARLog series, numbers 1 - 20. Cabot Safety Corporation, Indianapolis, IN. 4 pp.

Brüel, P.V. 1975. Noise: do we measure it correctly? Brüel and Kjaer A/S, Naerum, Denmark. 40 pp.

Brüel and Kjaer. 1974. B&K instructions and applications: Impulse Precision Sound Level Meter 2209. Naerum, Denmark. 87 pp.

Bullen, R.B., and A.J. Hede. 1982. Assessment of community noise exposure from rifle shooting. *Journal of Sound and Vibration.* 82:29-37.

Chatterton, P.F., and R.M. Taylor. 1980. Attenuation of low frequency noise using reactive silencer techniques. Pages 241-248 in H. Moller and P. Rubak, editors. *Proceedings of Conference on Low Frequency Noise and Hearing,* May 7-9.

Crum, R.A., and E.M. Owen. 1987. Silencer testing. *Crime Laboratory Digest.* 14(2):74-75.

Cumings, R.J. 1990. Fireworks-related injuries of the ear. *The Hearing Journal.* 43:19-24.

Dancer, A., P. Grateau, A. Cabanis, T. Vaillant, and D. LaFont. 1991. Delayed temporary threshold shift induced by impulse noises (weapon noises) in men. *Audiology.* 30(6): 345-356.

Dancer, A., P. Grateau, A. Cabanis, G. Barnabè, G. Cagnin, T. Vaillant, and D. Lafont, 1992. Effectiveness of earplugs in high-intensity impulse noise. *Journal of the Acoustical Society of America.* 91(3):1677-1689.

Finland Ministry of Labor. No date. Suppressors and shooting range structures: summary. Publication 73. 9 pp.

Fuchs, G.L., C.C. Herran, and A. Bonet. 1977. Silencing of the CSR-105 cannon. International Congress on Acoustics, Madrid, Spain. p. 232.

Garinther, G.R. 1985. Proposed aural nondetectability limits for Army materiel. U.S. Army Human Engineering Laboratory, Aberdeen Proving Ground, MD. *Technical Memorandum 3-85.* 56 pp.

Garinther, G.R., and J.T. Kalb. 1983. An acoustical assessment of the impulse noise of grenade simulators exploding in enclosures. U.S. Army Human Engineering Laboratory, Aberdeen Proving Ground, MD. *Technical Memorandum 9-83.* 51 pp.

Gilbert, K.E., and M.J. White. 1989. Application of the parabolic equation to sound propagation in a refracting atmosphere. *Journal of the Acoustic Society of America.* 85:630-637.

Hede, A.J., and R.B. Bullen. 1982. Community reaction to noise from a suburban rifle range. *Journal of Sound and Vibration.* 82:39-49.

Henderson, D., and R.P. Hamernik. 1986. Impulse noise: a critical review. *Journal of the Acoustic Society of America.* 80:569-584.

Hodge, D.C., and G.R. Price. 1978. Hearing damage risk criteria. U.S. Army Human Engineering Laboratory, Aberdeen Proving Ground, MD. *Technical Memorandum 25-78.* 191 pp.

Huebner, S.F. 1976. *Silencers for Hand Firearms.* Haessner Publications, Newfoundland, NJ. 97 pp.

Huebner, S.P. 1986. Der Mündungsknall, vom Blätterrauschen bis zum Kanonendonner. *Waffenjournal.* 1986:69-75.

International Organization for Standardization. 1994. Acoustics–testing of silencers in situ. Draft international standard. Geneva, Switzerland. ISO/DIS 11820, PREN 31820. 33 pp.

Kjellberg, A., M. Goldstein, and F. Gamberale. 1984. An assessment of dB(A) for predicting loudness and annoyance of noise containing low frequency components. *Journal of Low Frequency Sound and Vibration*. 3(3):10-16.

Kokinakis, W., and R.R. Rudolph. 1982. As assessment of the current state of the art of incapacitation by air blast. *Acta Chir. Scand.* Suppl. 508:135-151.

Kryter, K., and G.R. Garinther. 1965. Auditory effects of acoustic impulses from firearms. *Acta Oto-Laryngol.* Suppl. 211. 22 pp.

Kryter, K.D. 1991. Hearing loss from gun and railroad noise: relations with ISO Standards 1999. *Journal of the Acoustic Society of America*. 90.

Kukkola, A. 1994. Ampumaratamelun yhteiskunnalliset kustannukset. Diplomityö. Lappeenrannan teknillinen korkeakoulu. Tuotantotalouden osasto, Lappeenranta, Finland.

Kyttälä, I. 1994. Vaimentimet ja ampumaratarakenteet, yhteenveto. Sisäisen lausuntokierroksen -94 yhteenveto. Moniste. Työministeriö, Tampere, Finland.

Kyttälä, I., and R. Pääkkönen. 1996. Aseiden vaimentimet ja ampuumaratarakenteet. Työterveyslaitos, Helsinki, Finland. 16 pp.

Kyttälä, I., R. Pääkkönen, and K. Pesonen. 1993. Vaimentimien mittaukset 1992. Tiivistelmä. Selvityksiä 1/93. Työsuojeluhallitus. Tampere University of Technology, Tampere, Finland. 64 pp.

Laidler, P., and D. Howroyd. 1995. *The Guns of Dagenham: Lanchester, Patchett, Sterling*. Collector Grade Publications. Cobourg, Ontario, Canada. 310 pp.

Marino. J. 1981. Le grand livre des silencieux et des armes silencieuses. Editions De Vecchi S.A., Paris, France. 150 pp.

McLean, D.B. 1968. *Firearm Silencers. Volume I, US.* Normount Armament Company, Forest Grove, OR. 123 pp.

Minnery, J.A., and J. Ramos. 1980. *American Tools of Intrigue*. Desert Publications, Cornville, AZ. 128 pp.

NATO. 1987. Final report on the effects of impulse noise. Defense Research Group, North Atlantic Treaty Organization, Brussels, Belgium. Document AC/243 (Panel 8/RSG.6)D/9. 94 pp.

Nixon, C.W., R.L. McKinley, J.W. Steuver, and A.R. McCavitt. 1992. What can active noise reduction headsets do for you? Pages 107-110 in 1992 Industrial Hearing and Conservation Conference, University of Kentucky, Lexington. April 1-4.

Odess, J.S. 1972. Acoustic trauma of sportsman hunter due to gun firing. *The Laryngoscope.* 72(11):1971-1989.

Opetusministeriö. 1993a. Ampumaratojen melu - ja turvarakenteiden kehittäminen. Liikuntapaikkajulkaisu 39, Suomen Ampujainliitto ry, MV-konsultit/Maa ja Vesi Oy, Insinööritoimisto Kari Pesonen Oy. SVUL-paino, Helsinki, Finland. 79 pp.

Opetusministeriö. 1993b. Sisäampumaratojen suunnittelu - ja käyttöopas. Liikuntapaikkajulkaisu 38, Suomen Ampujainliitto ry, Projekti-insinöörit Oy. SVUL-paino, Helsinki, Finland. 43 pp.

Pääkkönen, R. 1988. Low-frequency high level noise impulses near weapons and explosions. *Journal of Low Frequency Noise and Vibration.* 7(2):42-49.

Pääkkönen, R. 1991a. Low-frequency noise impulses from explosions. Pages 44-48 in Proceedings of 6th International Congress on Low-frequency Noise and Vibration, Leiden, The Netherlands.

Pääkkönen, R. 1991b. Low frequency noise impulses from explosions. *Journal of Low Frequency Noise and Vibration.* 10(3):78-82.

Pääkkönen, R. 1992a. Sound approach to ear protection. Pages 30-31 in Work Health Safety 1992, Institute of Occupational Health, Tampere, Finland.

Pääkkönen, R. 1992b. Effects of cup, cushion, band force, foam lining and various design parameters on the attenuation of earmuffs. *Noise Control Engineering Journal.* 38(2):59-65.

Pääkkönen, R. 1993. Low-frequency impulse noise and its attenuation by hearing protectors and other technical means. Tampere University of Technology, Tampere, Finland. Publication 117. 135 pp.

Pääkkönen, R. 1995. Noise control of heavy weapons and explosions. *Applied Acoustics.* 45:263-278.

Pääkkönen, R., and I. Kyttälä. 1993. Kiväärien ja pistoolien äänenvaimentimet. Loppuraportti 1. Ministry of the Environment, and National Board of Labor Protection, Tampere, Finland. Työhallikkon julkaisu 29. 96 pp.

Pääkkönen, R., and I. Kyttälä. 1994a. Attenuation of rifle and pistol noise with the use of suppressors and subsonic bullets. *Acta Acoustica.* 2(1994):29-36.

Pääkkonen, R., and I. Kyttälä. 1994b. Effects of rifle-calibre muzzle brakes and suppressors on noise exposure, recoil, and accuracy. *Acta Acoustica.* 2(1994):143-148.

Pääkkönen, R. & Kyttälä, I. 1995. Attenuation of rifle noise with the use of suppressors and subsonic bullets and the effect of muzzle brakes to noise. Pages 393-397 in Proceedings of the 10th International Conference on Noise Control. Noise Control '95. 20-22 June 1995, Central Institute for Labor Protection, Warsaw, Poland.

Pääkkönen, R., and M. Lehkonen. 1990. Comparison of the accuracy of noise and air blast systems. Pages 57-72 in U. Sundbäck, editor. Proceedings of the Nordic acoustical meeting 90, Luleå, Sweden, June 11-13. Tekniska högskolan i Luleå. NAM 90.

Pääkkönen, R., J. Pekkarinen, J. Starck, J. Ylikoski, and E. Toppila, 1995. Military noise and its reduction. Pages 20-23 in From Research to Prevention, Institute of Occupational Health, Tampere, Finland.

Pääkkönen, R., and J. Tikkanen. 1990. A low-volume, low-frequency noise chamber. *Applied Acoustics*. 29:151-165.

Pääkkönen, R., and J. Tikkanen. 1991. Attenuation of low-frequency noise by hearing protectors. *Annals of Occupational Hygiene*. 35(2):189-199.

Pääkkönen, R., H. Anttonen, and J. Niskanen. 1991. Noise control on military shooting ranges for rifles. *Applied Acoustics*. 32:49-60.

Pääkkönen, R., T. Vienamo, J. Järvinen, and E. Hämäläinen. 1991. Development of a new noise helmet. Am. Ind. Hyg. Assoc. J. 52(10):438-444.

Paulson, A.C. 1987a. A new standard in suppressor design: the AWC MK-9. Part 1. Firepower. 4(5):cover,40-43,90-91.

Paulson, A.C. 1987b. A new standard in suppressor design: the AWC MK-9. Part 2. Firepower. 4(6):54-57.

Paulson, A.C. 1989a. A new Vaime pistol suppressor. *Machine Gun News*. 3(4):cover,16-19.

Paulson, A.C. 1989b. Dr. Shush and Eugene Reising. *Machine Gun News*. 3(5):3,6-9.

Paulson, A.C. 1989c. OSS silenced pistol. *Machine Gun News*. 3(6):28-30.

Paulson, A.C. 1989d. Ciener Uzi suppressor. *Machine Gun News*. 3(7):18-20.

Paulson, A.C. 1989e. Vaime silenced sniper rifle. *Machine Gun News*. 3(8):3,12-14.

Paulson, A.C. 1989f. A maintenance-free silencer for the Beretta 92F pistol? *Machine Gun News*. 3(9):24-26.

Paulson, A.C. 1990a. The AWC MK-9 suppressor. *Machine Gun News*. 3(10):28-31.

Paulson, A.C. 1990b. An affordable silenced .308 sniper/hunting rifle. *Machine Gun News*. 3(11):12-13.

Paulson, A.C. 1990c. Duel of the .22 cal muzzle cans. *Machine Gun News*. 3(12):24-26.

Paulson, A.C. 1990d. Silencing options for the Sten. Part 2. *Machine Gun News*. 4(2):3,6-9.

Paulson, A.C. 1990e. Hush Puppy pistol suppressor. *Machine Gun News*. 4(7):cover,14-16.

Paulson, A.C. 1991a. Larand suppressor for the Inglis Hi-Power. *Machine Gun News*. 4(11):cover,8-9.

Paulson, A.C. 1991b. Norrell select-fire suppressed Ruger 10/22. *Machine Gun News.* 5(1):28-31.

Paulson, A.C. 1991c. A suppressed Kalashnikov. *Machine Gun News.* 5(2):34-36.

Paulson, A.C. 1991d. Precision Arms Spectre. *Machine Gun News.* 5(3):32-35.

Paulson, A.C. 1991e. The AWC Warp 6 suppressor. *Machine Gun News.* 5(4):16-20.

Paulson, A.C. 1991f. The AWC Warp 3 suppressor. *Machine Gun News.* 5(5):26-29.

Paulson, A.C. 1991g. Marlin 780 rifle with Ciener suppressor. *Machine Gun News.* 5(7):18-21.

Paulson, A.C. 1992a. G2 compact rifle system. *Machine Gun News.* 5(8):14-17.

Paulson, A.C. 1992b. The McMillan M89 silenced sniper rifle. *SWAT.* 11(1):41-48.

Paulson, A.C. 1992c. SCRC Mark 25 and Mark 25A suppressors. *Machine Gun News.* 5(9):26-29.

Paulson, A.C. 1992d. The Centurion suppressed carbine. *Machine Gun News.* 5(10):12-16.

Paulson, A.C. 1992e. AWC's Nexus .45 ACP suppressor. *Machine Gun News.* 5(12):cover,28-32.

Paulson, A.C. 1992f. Red Ryder stealth rifle. *Machine Gun News.* 5(12):3,40-42.

Paulson, A.C. 1992g. JR Customs Navy suppressor. *Machine Gun News.* 6(1):3,21-24.

Paulson, A.C. 1992h. Mark White and his suppressed .45 caliber carbine. *Machine Gun News.* 6(2):cover,26-29.

Paulson, A.C. 1992i. S&H Uzi suppressor — it even works with .22 ammo! *Machine Gun News.* 6(4):34-37.

Paulson, A.C. 1992j. The suppressed .22 rifles of Dale Summers. *Machine Gun News.* 6(5):38-41.

Paulson, A.C. 1992k. Performance of the .22 Larand suppressor that never existed. *Machine Gun News.* 6(6):34-35.

Paulson, A.C. 1992l. Precision Arms suppressed Ram-Line pistol. *Machine Gun News.* 6(7):26-31.

Paulson, A.C. 1993a. Modern silenced 22s . . . legally possible for most of us. Pages 46-55 in *Gun Digest.* Volume 47.

Paulson, A.C. 1993b. JR Customs LDES. *Machine Gun News.* 6(9):32-34.

Paulson, A.C. 1993c. Norrell's ultimate integral 9mm suppressor. *Machine Gun News.* 7(1):44-46.

Paulson, A.C. 1993d The helical free flow suppressor; a new approach from the aerospace industry. *Machine Gun News.* 7(4):cover,22-25,27.

Paulson, A.C. 1993e. Duel of Doc Dater's and Jim Ryan's MP5 suppressors. *Machine Gun News.* 7(5):22-27.

Paulson, A.C. 1993f. Sound Technology. The suppressed Ruger 15/22 and other rimfire rifles. *Machine Gun News.* 7(7):40-44.

Paulson, A.C. 1994a. The .45 caliber Mini Uzi. *Machine Gun News.* 7(9):34-37.

Paulson, A.C. 1994b. An interview with Dr. Philip H. Dater. *Machine Gun News.* 7(10):26-29.

Paulson, A.C. 1994c. Silencing the Uzi. State of the art SMG sound suppression. *Fighting Firearms.* 2(1):48-59.

Paulson, A.C. 1994d. The Operator. *Fighting Firearms.* 2(2):26-29,78.

Paulson, A.C. 1994e. Performance of AWC's CQB M16 suppressor. *Machine Gun News.* 8(3):26-28.

Paulson, A.C. 1994f. Design and performance of the French *Silencieux Unique.* Machine Gun News. 8(6):36-39.

Paulson, A.C. 1995a. Gemtech's MINITAC MP5 suppressor. *Fighting Firearms.* 3(1):24-26,80.

Paulson, A.C. 1995b. Gemtech's Quantum-2000 suppressed rifles. *Machine Gun News.* 8(10):24-29.

Paulson, A.C. 1995c. High tech and all wet. *Fighting Firearms.* 3(2):22-27.

Paulson, A.C. 1995d. The .22 caliber Maxim Model 1910 silencer. *Machine Gun News.* 8(12):18-24.

Paulson, A.C. 1995e. AWC Amphibian II: SpecOps suppressor excels wet or dry. *Fighting Firearms.* 3(3):68-70,75-77.

Paulson, A.C. 1995f. Up close and quiet: new cans meet CQB demands. *Fighting Firearms.* 3(3):32-37,79-81.

Paulson, A.C. 1995g. Sound Technology's hybrid .22 suppressors. *Machine Gun News.* 9(1):24-31.

Paulson, A.C. 1995h. Top performance in a tiny package: compact cans for concealed carry. *Fighting Firearms.* 4(4):62-66,68-71,81-82.

Paulson, A.C. 1996a. Silent Operator: Gemtech's suppressed .22 gets even quieter. *Fighting Firearms.* 4(1):50-56,75-76.

Paulson, A.C. 1996b. Mystique, mystery and misinformation: suppressed Sterling Patchett Mark 5. *Fighting Firearms.* 4(1):50-56,75-76.

Paulson, A.C. 1996c. An evaluation of the Parker Hale .22 rimfire silencer. *Machine Gun News.* 9(8):40-43.

Pesonen, K. 1994a. Äänenvaimentimien vaikutus luotiaseiden laukausääniin ja ympäristömeluun. Ympäristönsuojelutekniikan julkaisuja 3/1994. Teknillinen korkeakoulu, ympäristötekniikan laboratorio, Espoo, Finland. 60 pp.

Pesonen, K. 1994b. Äänenvaimentimien vaikutus haulikkojen laukausääniin ja ympäristömeluun. Ympäristönsuojelutekniikan julkaisuja 2/1994. Teknillinen korkeakoulu, ympäristötekniikan laboratorio, Espoo, Finland. 87 pp.

Phillips, Y., and J. Jaeger. 1981. Risk assessment for human exposure to blast overpressure in gunner position of M198 155 mm howitzer firing the M203 charge. WRAIR Report. 15 pp.

Phillips, Y.Y., A. Dancer, and D.R. Richmond. 1985. Nonauditory effects of repeated exposures to intense impulse noise. Presented at NATO Advanced Study Workshop, Noise-Induced Hearing Loss: Basic and Applied Aspects, Il Ciocco, Italy. 11 pp.

Plomp, R. 1967. Hearing losses induced by small arms. *Int. Audiol.*, Soesterberg, Holland. 6:31-36.

Price, G.C. 1982. Rating the hazard from intense sounds: putting theory into practice. Pages 111-122 in H.M. Borchgrevink, editor. Hearing and hearing prophylaxis. *Scand. Audiol.* Suppl. 16.

Price, G.C. 1983a. Mechanisms of loss for intense sound exposures. Pages 335 to 346 in R.R. Fay and G. Gourevitch, editors. *Hearing and Other Senses: Presentations in Honor of E.G. Weaver.* The Amphora Press.

Price, G.C. 1984. Practical applications of basic research on impulse noise hazard. Pages 821 to 826 in *Inter-Noise 84*, Honolulu, HI. December 3-5, 1984.

Price, G.R. 1979. Implications of basic research in hearing for the design of safer weapons. U.S. Army Human Engineering Laboratory, Aberdeen Proving Ground, MD. *Technical Memorandum 20-79.* 17 pp.

Price, G.R. 1983b. Relative hazard of weapons impulses. *Journal of the Acoustic Society of America.* 73:556-566.

Price, G.R. 1983c. A damage-risk criterion for impulse noise based on a spectrally dependent criterion level. Pages 261-264 in Proceedings of the 11th ICA Conference, Paris, France.

Price, G.R. 1986. Hazard from intense low-frequency acoustic impulses. *Journal of the Acoustic Society of America.* 80:1076-1086.

Price, G.R. 1989. Hazard from weapons impulses: histological and electrophysical evidence. *Journal of the Acoustic Society of America.* 85:1245-1254.

Price, G.R. 1992. Modeling the ear's response to intense impulses and the development of improved damage risk criteria. Pages 93-96 in 1992 Industrial Hearing Conference, University of Kentucky, Lexington. April 1-4.

Price, G.R., and S. Wansack. 1989. Hazard from an intense midrange impulse. *Journal of the Acoustic Society of America.* 86:2185-2191.

Puutio, M., and R. Pääkkönen. 1992. Sound attenuation of military masks. Pages 91-94 in K. Nieminen and R. Pääkkönen, editors. Chemical Protection '92. Symposium Proceedings. Publication A1. Research Centre of Defence Forces, Lakiala, Finland.

Rice, C.G., and A.M. Martin. 1973. Impulse noise damage risk criteria. *J. Sound Vib.* 28(3): 359-367.

Rössle, R. 1950. Pathology of blast effects. Pages 1260-1273 in German Aviation Medicine in World War II. Volume 2. U.S. Government Printing Office, Washington, DC.

Ruedi, L., and W. Fürrer. 1947. *Das akustische Trauma.* Verlag von S. Karger, Basel, Germany. 196 pp.

Sanow, Ed. 1994. Muzzle blast and your hearing. *Handguns.* May:55-59,80-81.

Sneck, H.J., and D.A. Driscoll. 1981. Cannon muzzle noise suppression facility analysis and tests. *Noise Control Engineering Journal.* 16(2):81-89.

Sörensen, S., and J. Magnusson. 1979. Annoyance caused by noise from shooting ranges. *Journal of Sound and Vibration.* 62:437-442.

Stochko, L.W., and H.A. Greveris. 1968. *Silencers: Patterns and Principles.* Frankford Arsenal Report R-1896. Reprinted by Paladin Press, Boulder, CO. 205 pp.

Thomas, D.G. 1973. *U.S. Silencer Patents 1888-1972. Volume I, 1888-1935.* Paladin Press, Boulder, CO. 329 pp.

Thomas, D.G. 1973. *U.S. Silencer Patents 1888-1972. Volume II, 1936-1972.* Paladin Press, Boulder, CO. 328 pp.

Thomas, D.G. 1978. *Silencer Patents. Volume III, European Patents 1901-1978.* Paladin Press, Boulder, CO. 253 pp.

Thomas, D.G. 1979. *Nazi Silencer Patents 1938-1945.* Paladin Press, Boulder, CO. 34 pp.

Thomas, R.K. 1987. Problems and tactical use of low signature weapons. *Military Technology.* 87(4):95,97-98,101-103,105-109.

Tikkanen, J., and R. Pääkkönen. 1990. Impulse propagation around a weapon. Department of Electrical Engineering, Physics, Tampere University of Technology, Finland. Report 11-90. 37 pp.

Truby, J.D. 1972. *Silencers, Snipers & Assassins.* Paladin Press, Boulder, CO. 209 pp.

Truby, J.D. 1972. *Quiet Killers I.* Paladin Press, Boulder, CO. 79 pp.

Truby, J.D. 1979. *Quiet Killers II.* Paladin Press, Boulder, CO. 80 pp.

Truby, J.D. 1983. *Silencers in the 1980s.* Paladin Press, Boulder, CO. 107 pp.

Työsuojeluhallitus. 1993. Vaimentimien mittaukset 1992, Tiivistelmä. Selvityksiä 1/93, Tampere, Finland. 47 pp.

U.S. Army Human Engineering Laboratory. 1966. Acoustical considerations for a silent weapons system: a feasibility study. Aberdeen Proving Ground, MD. HEL Technical Memo 10-66. 74 pp.

U.S. Army Missile Command. 1993. Military standard noise limits for military materiel (metric). Redstone Arsenal, AL. MIL-STD-1474C. 56 pp.

Vos, J., and F.W.M. Geurtsen. 1987. Leq as a measure of annoyance caused by gunfire consisting of impulses with various proportions of higher and lower sound levels. *Journal of the Acoustical Society of America.* 84(2):1201-1206.

Walton, D.W. 1984. International weapon blast overpressure experiment. Aberdeen Proving Ground, U.S. Army, Aberdeen, MD. ADA Report SDS148614, USACSTA-6109. 35 pp.

Ward, D.W. 1980. Effects of impulse noise on hearing: summary and overview. *Scandinavian Audiology Supplement.* 12:359-367.

Ylikoski, J., J. Pekkarinen, and J. Starck. 1987. The efficiency of earmuffs against impulse noise from firearms. *Scandinavian Audiology.* 16:85-88.

Ylikoski, M.E., J.O. Pekkarinen, J.P. Starck, R.J. Pääkkönen, and J.S. Ylikoski. 1995. Physical characteristics of gunfire noise and its attenuation by hearing protectors. *Scandinavian Audiology.* 24:3-11.

Zwislocki, J.J. 1966. Loudness as a function of sound intensity and duration: an analysis. Laboratory of Sensory Communication, Syracuse University, Syracuse, NY.

PRESSURE (psi) VERSUS SOUND PRESSURE LEVEL (dB)

PRESSURE PSI	SPL DECIBELS	PRESSURE PSI	SPL DECIBELS	PRESSURE PSI	SPL DECIBELS
0.000001	50.8	0.02	136.8	900	229.8
0.000002	56.8	0.03	140.3	910	229.9
0.000003	60.3	0.04	142.8	920	230.0
0.000004	62.8	0.05	144.7	930	230.1
0.000005	64.7	0.06	146.3	940	230.2
0.000006	66.3	0.07	147.7	950	230.3
0.000007	67.7	0.08	148.8	960	230.4
0.000008	68.8	0.09	149.8	970	230.5
0.000009	69.8	0.1	150.8	980	230.6
0.00001	70.8	0.2	156.8	990	230.7
0.00002	76.8	0.3	160.3	1000	230.8
0.00003	80.3	0.4	162.8	1100	231.6
0.00004	82.8	0.5	164.7	1200	232.3
0.00005	84.7	0.6	166.3	1300	233.0
0.00006	86.3	0.7	167.7	1400	233.7
0.00007	87.7	0.8	168.8	1500	234.3
0.00008	88.8	0.9	169.8	1600	234.8
0.00009	89.8	1	170.8	1700	235.4
0.0001	90.8	2	176.8	1800	235.9
0.0002	96.8	3	180.3	1900	236.3

PRESSURE PSI	SPL DECIBELS	PRESSURE PSI	SPL DECIBELS	PRESSURE PSI	SPL DECIBELS
0.0003	100.3	4	182.8	2000	236.8
0.0004	102.8	5	184.7	2100	237.2
0.0005	104.7	6	186.3	2200	237.6
0.0006	106.3	7	187.7	2300	238.0
0.0007	107.7	8	188.8	2400	238.4
0.0008	108.8	9	189.8	2500	238.7
0.0009	109.8	10	190.8	2600	239.1
0.0010	110.8	20	196.8	2700	239.4
0.0020	116.8	30	200.3	2800	239.7
0.0030	120.3	40	202.8	2900	240.0
0.0040	122.8	50	204.7	3000	240.3
0.0050	124.7	60	206.3	3100	240.6
0.0060	126.3	70	207.7	3200	240.9
0.0070	127.7	80	208.8	3300	241.1
0.0080	128.8	90	209.8	3400	241.4
0.0090	129.8	100	210.8	3500	241.6
0.0100	130.8	200	216.8	3600	241.9

APPENDIX TWO

SPEED OF SOUND VERSUS TEMPERATURE

Temp., °F	Temp., °C	Speed of Sound, fps	Speed of Sound, mps
-90	-68	942	287
-89	-67	944	288
-88	-67	945	288
-87	-66	946	288
-86	-66	948	289
-85	-65	949	289
-84	-64	950	290
-83	-64	951	290
-82	-63	953	290
-81	-63	954	291
-80	-62	955	291
-79	-62	956	291
-78	-61	958	292
-77	-61	959	292
-76	-60	960	293
-75	-59	961	293
-74	-59	963	293

Temp., °F	Temp., °C	Speed of Sound, fps	Speed of Sound, mps
-73	-58	964	294
-72	-58	965	294
-71	-57	966	295
-70	-57	968	295
-69	-56	969	295
-68	-56	970	296
-67	-55	971	296
-66	-54	973	296
-65	-54	974	297
-64	-53	975	297
-63	-53	976	298
-62	-52	978	298
-61	-52	979	298
-60	-51	980	299
-59	-51	981	299
-58	-50	982	299
-57	-49	984	300

Temp., °F	Temp., °C	Speed of Sound, fps	Speed of Sound, mps
-56	-49	985	300
-55	-48	986	301
-54	-48	987	301
-53	-47	989	301
-52	-47	990	302
-51	-46	991	302
-50	-46	992	302
-49	-45	993	303
-48	-44	995	303
-47	-44	996	304
-46	-43	997	304
-45	-43	998	304
-44	-42	999	305
-43	-42	1001	305
-42	-41	1002	305
-41	-41	1003	306
-40	-40	1004	306
-39	-39	1005	306
-38	-39	1007	307
-37	-38	1008	307
-36	-38	1009	308
-35	-37	1010	308
-34	-37	1011	308
-33	-36	1013	309
-32	-36	1014	309
-31	-35	1015	309
-30	-34	1016	310
-29	-34	1017	310
-28	-33	1019	310
-27	-33	1020	311
-26	-32	1021	311
-25	-32	1022	312
-24	-31	1023	312
-23	-31	1024	312
-22	-30	1026	313
-21	-29	1027	313
-20	-29	1028	313
-19	-28	1029	314
-18	-28	1030	314
-17	-27	1031	314
-16	-27	1033	315
-15	-26	1034	315
-14	-26	1035	315
-13	-25	1036	316
-12	-24	1037	316
-11	-24	1038	317
-10	-23	1040	317
-9	-23	1041	317
-8	-22	1042	318
-7	-22	1043	318
-6	-21	1044	318
-5	-21	1045	319
-4	-20	1046	319
-3	-19	1048	319
-2	-19	1049	320
-1	-18	1050	320
0	-18	1051	320
1	-17	1052	321
2	-17	1053	321
3	-16	1055	321
4	-16	1056	322
5	-15	1057	322
6	-14	1058	322
7	-14	1059	323
8	-13	1060	323
9	-13	1061	323
10	-12	1062	324
11	-12	1064	324
12	-11	1065	325

Temp., °F	Temp., °C	Speed of Sound, fps	Speed of Sound, mps
13	-11	1066	325
14	-10	1067	325
15	-9	1068	326
16	-9	1069	326
17	-8	1070	326
18	-8	1071	327
19	-7	1073	327
20	-7	1074	327
21	-6	1075	328
22	-6	1076	328
23	-5	1077	328
24	-4	1078	329
25	-4	1079	329
26	-3	1080	329
27	-3	1082	330
28	-2	1083	330
29	-2	1084	330
30	-1	1085	331
31	-1	1086	331
32	0	1087	331
33	1	1088	332
34	1	1089	332
35	2	1090	332
36	2	1092	333
37	3	1093	333
38	3	1094	333
39	4	1095	334
40	4	1096	334
41	5	1097	334
42	6	1098	335
43	6	1099	335
44	7	1100	335
45	7	1101	336
46	8	1102	336

Temp., °F	Temp., °C	Speed of Sound, fps	Speed of Sound, mps
47	8	1104	336
48	9	1105	337
49	9	1106	337
50	10	1107	337
51	11	1108	338
52	11	1109	338
53	12	1110	338
54	12	1111	339
55	13	1112	339
56	13	1113	339
57	14	1114	340
58	14	1116	340
59	15	1117	340
60	16	1118	341
61	16	1119	341
62	17	1120	341
63	17	1121	342
64	18	1122	342
65	18	1123	342
66	19	1124	343
67	19	1125	343
68	20	1126	343
69	21	1127	344
70	21	1128	344
71	22	1129	344
72	22	1131	345
73	23	1132	345
74	23	1133	345
75	24	1134	346
76	24	1135	346
77	25	1136	346
78	26	1137	347
79	26	1138	347
80	27	1139	347

Temp., °F	Temp., °C	Speed of Sound, fps	Speed of Sound, mps
81	27	1140	347
82	28	1141	348
83	28	1142	348
84	29	1143	348
85	29	1144	349
86	30	1145	349
87	31	1146	349
88	31	1147	350
89	32	1148	350
90	32	1150	350
91	33	1151	351
92	33	1152	351
93	34	1153	351
94	34	1154	352
95	35	1155	352
96	36	1156	352
97	36	1157	353
98	37	1158	353
99	37	1159	353
100	38	1160	354
101	38	1161	354
102	39	1162	354
103	39	1163	354
104	40	1164	355
105	41	1165	355
106	41	1166	355
107	42	1167	356
108	42	1168	356
109	43	1169	356
110	43	1170	357
111	44	1171	357

Temp., °F	Temp., °C	Speed of Sound, fps	Speed of Sound, mps
112	44	1172	357
113	45	1173	358
114	46	1174	358
115	46	1175	358
116	47	1176	359
117	47	1177	359
118	48	1178	359
119	48	1179	360
120	49	1181	360
121	49	1182	360
122	50	1183	360
123	51	1184	361
124	51	1185	361
125	52	1186	361
126	52	1187	362
127	53	1188	362
128	53	1189	362
129	54	1190	363
130	54	1191	363
131	55	1192	363
132	56	1193	364
133	56	1194	364
134	57	1195	364
135	57	1196	364
136	58	1197	365
137	58	1198	365
138	59	1199	365
139	59	1200	366
140	60	1201	366
141	61	1202	366

ABOUT THE AUTHOR

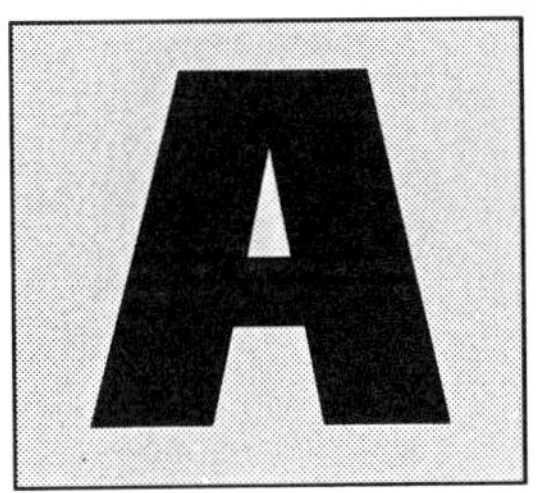

research scientist who has worked from tropical jungles and reefs to the Arctic's polar ice, Alan C. Paulson has published the results of his research in major refereed science journals in the United States, Canada, and Europe. Currently a contributing editor to *Fighting Firearms* magazine and the suppressor technology editor for *Machine Gun News*, Paulson has also worked as a college teacher, pilot, and biologist with the Alaska Department of Fish & Game. A freelance writer for several decades, he has published numerous articles in the realms of science and technology as well as the first in a series of books on regional history. He has also written scores of articles on the technology of automatic weapons and suppressors for such publications as *Fighting Firearms*, *International Combat Arms*, *SWAT*, *Firepower*, *Gun Digest*, and *Machine Gun News*. Paulson is a member of the Institute for Research on Small Arms in International Security, the International Wound Ballistics Association, and numerous other professional societies.

INDEX

A

D

E

F

G

H

I

J

K

L

M

N

O

P

R

S

T

U

V

W

Book design by Robert Mitchell

OFFGUARD: A PAPARAZZO LOOK AT THE BEAUTIFUL PEOPLE

123456789RABP79876

Library of Congress Cataloging in Publication Data

Galella, Ron.
Offguard: a paparazzo look at the beautiful people.

1. Photography—Portraits. 2. Photography, Journalistic. I. Title.
TR681.F3G34 779'.2'0924 75-46628
ISBN 0-07-022729-2
ISBN 0-07-022733-0 pbk.

Photo of Galella and Brando on page 92 by Peter L. Gould.
Photo of Galella in boat on page 80 by Tom Wargacki
Photo of Galella in helmet on page 94 by Paul Schmulbach
Photo of Galella with Angeleen on page 142 by Gene Spatz